Web Content Managen
Documentum

Set up, Design, Develop, and Deploy
Documentum Applications

Concise, practical information on Documentum Web
Content Management to get the most from this system

Gaurav Kathuria

PUBLISHING

BIRMINGHAM - MUMBAI

Web Content Management with Documentum

Set up, Design, Develop, and Deploy Documentum Applications

Copyright © 2006 Packt Publishing

First published: June 2006

Production Reference: 1130606

Published by Packt Publishing Ltd.
32 Lincoln Road
Olton
Birmingham, B27 6PA, UK.

ISBN 1-904811-09-4

www.packtpub.com

Cover Image by www.visionwt.com

Credits

Author
Gaurav Kathuria

Development Editor
Douglas Paterson

Assistant Development Editor
Nikhil Bangera

Technical Editor
Ashutosh Pande

Editorial Manager
Dipali Chittar

Indexer
Niranjan Jahagirdar

Proofreader
Chris Smith

Production Coordinator
Manjiri Nadkarni

Layouts and Illustrations
Shantanu Zagade

Cover Designer
Shantanu Zagade

About the Author

Gaurav Kathuria completed his B. Tech. (Hons.) in Chemical Engineering from I.I.T. Kharagpur in the year 2000 and has since been a prominent performer in diverse software fields, from IT services through product development to software consultancy.

He has a rich experience of designing, developing, and managing software systems using object-oriented languages and technologies like Java/J2EE and Documentum.

He started working with Documentum 4i in the year 2001 and has ever since had an extensive experience architecting/designing complex Documentum 4i and 5x projects.

He has also given in-house training on Documentum system architecture, fundamentals, and Web Publisher in many of the organizations he has worked in.

This book is dedicated to

God: Who has always showered his choicest blessings on me and given me much more than I ever wanted in my life. I thank Him for all that he has done for me.

My family: My father (Mr. P.N. Kathuria) has always been a guiding star in my life, mentoring and steering me through thick and thin. Extremely diligent and sincere in all his endeavors; I have learnt and am still learning a lot from him.

My mother (Mrs. Sarita Kathuria) has selflessly devoted her entire life for the well-being of our sweet little family. She has always been the shoulder I cried on when I was in distress and she has been the one who praised me most when others disapproved me.

My sister (Ms. Gunjan Kathuria) is the sweet little sister I always wanted in my life. Her affection and care has given a new meaning to my life.

My wife (Mrs. Gunjan Grover) has blossomed our house with love and respect for everyone. Her mere presence fills up and completes the missing bit in my life…

My friends: Neeraj Jain, Nisha, Hima, Nishant Anchal, and Abhishek Singh, who have always been by my side, making this world a better place to live in.

Documentum team mates: Mansoor Sheikh, Arnab Ghosh, Amit Kapur, Prashant Shukla, Gajendra Sahu, Gurmeet Singh, Prasun Misra, Tanveer Haider, Arpana Bansal, Preeti Dua, Kapil Bharati, Akash Narang, Kesavan, Usha Parolkar, Anjali Nanda, and other software professionals with whom I have worked on various Documentum projects. They all have been a source of inspiration for me in some way or the other.

I thank you all for your love and support!

Acknowledgements

Dr. Louay Fatoohi, Dr. Douglas Paterson, and the entire crew at Packt Publishing Ltd. for honoring me by publishing this book in the most stringent of timeframes.

Johnson Stephen: My pal, colleague, and a software testing maestro. He 'unknowingly' guided me to write a book as a precursor to establishing myself and starting up my own consultancy in future.

M. Scott Roth: Author of '*A Beginner's Guide to Developing Documentum Desktop Applications*'.

Scott applauded my decision to write this book on Documentum technology and constantly provided the much needed support and zeal.

Anil Baid: The owner and head of 'Solutions Infosystems'. He has been an extremely helping hand for me, without whom this book would have never seen the light of day.

Rakesh Dahiya: The Facilities manager at 'Solutions Infosystems' who guided me often regarding the various publishing avenues available and the tips and tricks of the trade.

Ashwin Razdan: Media Manager, whatistesting.com; an extremely versatile personality who assisted me in getting the book shaped up to the right standards by providing the much needed direction and support.

Sachin Jain: The Accounts and legal head at 'Solutions Infosystems' whose valuable advice steered me clear of several difficult situations during the book authoring process.

Pankaj Jain and Pradeep Gautam ('Econsultants India').

My sincere apologies to those whose names might have inadvertently been missed out from this list. You all are very important to me.

Table of Contents

Preface   1

Chapter 1: Content and Documentum   5

  1.1 Need for an Effective CMS   7
  1.2 Qualities of a Good CMS   8
  1.3 Why Documentum?   10
  1.4 Documentum Features   11
  1.5 Summary   12

Chapter 2: Documentum Essentials   13

  2.1 Documentum Cornerstone   13
  2.2 Docbase   13
  2.3 DocBroker   15
  2.4 DocApp   16
  2.5 Object Types   16
  2.6 Attributes   18
    2.6.1 Object ID (Object Identifier: r_object_id Attribute)   19
    2.6.2 Attribute Types   19
  2.7 DQL   21
  2.8 API   22
  2.9 Cabinets and Folders   23
  2.10 Versioning   24
  2.11 Lifecycles   25
  2.12 Workflows   26
  2.13 Summary   28

Chapter 3: Documentum Advanced Concepts   29

  3.1 DMCL   29
  3.2 DFC   29
  3.3 BOF   30
  3.4 WDK   31
  3.5 Web Publisher   32
  3.6 ACL   33

3.7 Alias Set   **34**

3.8 Users and Groups   **36**

3.8.1 Users   36

3.8.2 Groups   36

3.9 Renditions   **37**

3.10 Registered Tables   **38**

3.11 Data Dictionary   **38**

3.12 Methods and Jobs   **39**

3.12.1 Methods   39

3.12.2 Jobs   40

3.13 Summary   **42**

Chapter 4: Web Content Management System   **43**

4.1 When Should you Use a WCM System?   **43**

4.2 When Should you Not Use a WCM System?   **44**

4.3 Documentum WCM Architecture   **45**

4.4 How do you Enter Content in the System?   **46**

4.4.1 Web Publisher   46

4.5 Where and How is the Content Stored?   **47**

4.5.1 Content Server   47

4.6 How do you Perform System Administration?   **48**

4.6.1 Documentum Administrator   48

4.7 How do you Create Multiple Renditions of the Content?   **50**

4.7.1 Content Rendition Services   50

4.8 How do you Publish Content to a Website?   **52**

4.8.1 Site Caching Services   52

4.8.2 SCS Architecture   53

4.9 How do you Query the Published Content for Displaying on Websites?   **54**

4.9.1 Documentum JDBC Services   54

4.10 How do you Deploy Website Content to a Server Farm?   **55**

4.10.1 Site Deployment Services   55

4.11 Summary   **56**

Chapter 5: Setting Up the Documentum Suite   **57**

5.1 Installing Content Server   **58**

5.1.2 Prerequisites   59

5.2 Installing Content Server 5.2.5   **60**

5.3 Installing Content Server 5.2.5 SP2   **64**

5.4 Summary   **66**

Chapter 6: Creating Our First Docbase   67

6.1 Creating a Docbase   **67**

6.2 Installing Web Publisher Server Files and DocApp   **75**

6.2.1 What does Web Publisher Server Files Contain?   76

6.2.2 What does WebPublisher DocApp Contain?   76

6.3 Beginning Installation   **76**

6.4 Stopping and Starting Docbase and DocBroker   **80**

6.5 dmcl.ini   **81**

6.6 server.ini   **81**

6.7 Summary   **82**

Chapter 7: Setting Up Publishing   83

7.1 SCS Source 5.2.5   **83**

7.1.1 Prerequisites   84

7.1.2 Installing SCS Source 5.2.5   84

7.1.3 Installing SCS Source 5.2.5 SP2   88

7.2 SCS Target 5.2.5   **89**

7.2.1 Prerequisites   89

7.2.2 Installing SCS Target 5.2.5   89

7.2.3 Installing SCS Target 5.2.5 SP2   97

7.3 Summary   **98**

Chapter 8: Setting Up Documentum Application Builder   99

8.1 Documentum Application Builder   **100**

8.1.1 Prerequisites   101

8.2 Installing DAB 5.2.5 SP2   **101**

8.3 Summary   **105**

Chapter 9: Setting Up Documentum Administrator and Web Publisher   107

9.1 Documentum Administrator   **107**

9.1.1 Prerequisites   108

9.1.2 Installing Documentum Administrator 5.2.5 SP2   108

9.2 Web Publisher   **113**
9.2.1 Prerequisites   113
9.2.2 Installing Web Publisher 5.2.5 SP2   113
9.3 Summary   **118**

Chapter 10: Designing Documentum Applications   **119**

10.1 Case Study—Simple Newspaper Website   **119**
10.2 Beginning Documentum Design   **121**
10.3 Using Documentum Application Builder (DAB)   **122**
10.4 Creating Custom Objects in DocApp   **123**
10.5 Summary   **124**

Chapter 11: Designing and Creating Custom Object Types   **125**

11.1 Creating Object Types   **126**
11.1.1 Type Names   127
11.1.2 Limitations of Object Type Names   127
11.1.3 Supertype   128
11.2 Designing and Creating Custom Attributes of Object Type(s)   **137**
11.3 Adding Attributes to an Object Type   **138**
11.3.1 Attribute Names   139
11.3.2 Limitations of Object Type Attribute Names   139
11.3.2.1 Label   140
11.3.2.2 Data Type   140
11.3.2.3 Length   140
11.3.2.4 Repeating   140
11.3.2.5 Default Search Value   140
11.3.2.6 Allowable Search Operators   140
11.3.2.7 Input Mask   141
11.3.2.8 Conditional Value Assistance   145
11.4 Querying Registered Tables using DQL for Value Assistance   **149**
11.5 $value() Keyword   **153**
11.6 Summary   **155**

Chapter 12: Creating Lifecycles, Alias Sets, and Permission Sets   **157**

12.1 Alias Sets in a Lifecycle   **157**
12.2 Creating an Alias Set   **158**
12.3 Creating Permission Sets   **161**
12.4 Creating a Custom Lifecycle   **163**
12.5 Promoting and Demoting Content through a Lifecycle   **178**

12.5 Expiring Content — **183**

12.6 Summary — **185**

Chapter 13: Working with Web Publisher Template Files — **187**

13.1 Creating a Template File — **190**

13.2 Summary — **194**

Chapter 14: Creating Rules Files — **195**

14.1 Creating a Rules File — **195**

14.1.1 IMGALTTEXT Element — 205

14.1.2 DATE Element — 205

14.1.3 BODYTEXT Element — 206

14.1.4 REPEATBLOCK Element — 206

14.1.5 NEXTLINKNAME Element — 207

14.1.6 NEXTLINKURL Element — 208

14.2 Final Template in Web Publisher Editor — **208**

14.3 Miscellaneous Rules File Widgets — **210**

14.3.1 Choice Widget — 210

14.3.2 Checkbox Widget — 210

14.3.3 Textselector Widget — 210

14.3.4 Xselector Widget — 211

14.4 Summary — **212**

Chapter 15: Creating Presentation Files — **213**

15.1 Creating a Presentation File — **214**

15.2 Viewing Content Renditions — **220**

15.3 Reapplying Presentation Files — **221**

15.4 Using XDQL in Stylesheets — **222**

15.5 XDQL Example in XSL Stylesheet — **223**

15.6 Create_Dynamic_Content Job — **227**

15.7 Summary — **229**

Chapter 16: Folder Mapping — **231**

16.1 Anatomy of the FolderMap.xml File — **234**

16.2 Limitations of Folder Map — **234**

16.3 Folder Mapping Examples — **235**

16.3.1 Property Matching: Using Wildcard (*) — 235

16.3.2 Property Matching: Using Multiple Properties in <attr_list> — 237

16.3.3 Placing a Content File in Multiple Locations with <path_list> — 239

16.3.4 Property Matching: Simple Repeating Attribute — 241

16.3.5 Property Matching: Repeating Attribute Index   244
16.3.6 Dynamic Folder Mapping   246
16.3.7 Dynamic Folder Mapping with Repeating Attribute   248
16.4 Summary   **250**

Chapter 17: Using Instruction Files   251

17.1 Limitations of Instruction Files   **252**
17.2 Instruction File Examples   **253**
17.2.1 Deleting an XML Element from an XML File with \<delete-element>   253
17.2.2 Adding an XML Element to an XML File with \<insert-element>   262
17.2.3 Updating the Value of an XML Element in an XML File with
\<update-element-value>   265
17.3 Summary   **267**

Chapter 18: Automatic Property Extraction (APE)   269

18.1 How Automatic Property Extraction Works   **270**
18.2 Simple Example for Automatic Property Extraction   **271**
18.3 Testing our First XML Application   **277**
18.4 Populating Repeating Attributes using Automatic Property Extraction   **280**
18.5 Testing the Second XML Application   **282**
18.6 Using Two-Way Attribute Extraction   **285**
18.7 Testing the Two-Way Attribute Extraction XML Application: **287**
18.8 Summary   **290**

Chapter 19: Working with Workflows   291

19.1 Designing Custom Workflows   **292**
19.2 Setting Up a Custom Workflow Template   **293**
19.3 Creating a Custom Workflow Template   **300**
19.3.1 Performer Tab for Activities   312
19.3.2 Trigger Tab for Activities   312
19.3.3 Notification Tab for Activities   313
19.3.4 Transition Tab for Activities   313
19.4 Adding a Package to Connection Flows   **314**
19.5 Summary   **315**

Chapter 20: Testing Custom Workflows   317

20.1 Creating Users for Workflow in Documentum   318
20.2 Submitting Content to the Custom Workflow   319
20.3 Summary   326

Chapter 21: Publishing from Docbase Using SCS   327

21.1 Limitations of SCS   328
21.2 Publishing Types   328
21.3 Steps for Setting Up a Site Publishing Configuration   328
21.4 Testing and Publishing Using Site Publishing Configuration   339
21.5 Published Data   341
21.6 Unlocking Locked Publishing Operations   342
21.7 Monitoring the SCS Source Status   343
21.8 Summary   344

Chapter 22: Web Viewing Content Files   345

22.1 Prerequisites   346
22.2 Setting Up and Using Web View   347
22.3 Testing Web View   352
22.4 Summary   354

Chapter 23: Using DFC   355

23.1 Introduction to DFC   356
23.2 Environment Readiness   357
23.3 Simple Example Demonstrating DFC Usage   358
23.4 Creating and Linking a File in a Docbase Cabinet   359
23.5 Running Docbase Methods via DFC   362
23.6 Creating Users in Docbase with DFC   366
23.7 Summary   368

Chapter 24: Configurations and Customizations Using WDK   369

24.1 WDK Directory Structure   370
24.2 WDK Application Elements   372
24.3 A Simple WDK Configuration Example   373
24.3.1 New Content Screen before Configuration Changes   373
24.3.2 Modified New Content Screen after Configuration Changes   375

24.4 A Simple WDK Customization Example   **379**
24.5 Summary   **395**

Chapter 25: Documentum Deployment   397

25.1 DocApp Migration   **399**
25.2 Configuring DocApp Objects and Creating/Installing a DocApp Archive   **399**
25.3 Deployment of Web Publisher Code and Custom Scripts   **410**
25.4 Summary   **414**

Chapter 26: Using DQL and API Commands   415

26.1 DQL   **416**
26.1.1 Uses of DQL   416
26.1.2 Command Tools   416
26.1.3 DQL Examples   417
    26.1.3.1 Creating a Document Object   417
    26.1.3.2 Updating Attributes of a Document Object   418
    26.1.3.3 Appending a Value in a Repeating Attribute   419
    26.1.3.4 Inserting a Value into a Repeating Attribute   419
    26.1.3.5 Associating a Document Object with a Cabinet   419
    26.1.3.6 Retrieving a Document Object from the Docbase   421
    26.1.3.7 Deleting a Document Object from the Docbase   423
26.2 API   **423**
26.2.1 Command Tools   423
26.2.2 API Commands   425
26.2.3 Categorizing API Methods   426
26.2.4 API Method Examples   427
    26.2.4.1 Creating a Document Object   427
    26.2.4.2 Setting the Attributes of the Object   428
    26.2.4.3 Associating a Content File with the Document Object   429
    26.2.4.4 Associating a Document Object with a Cabinet   429
    26.2.4.5 Saving the Document Object in the Docbase   430
    26.2.4.6 Obtaining a Reference to the Document Object in Docbase   431
    26.2.4.7 Setting Specific Attribute Information   432
    26.2.4.8 Viewing all Attributes and Values for an Object   432
    26.2.4.9 Deleting an Object from the Docbase   434
26.3 Summary   **434**

Appendix A: Frequently Asked Questions and Answers   435

Appendix B: New Features and Enhancements in Release 5.3   449

B.1 Content Server Changes   449

B.2 Object Types Changes   452

B.3 API and DQL Changes   452

B.4 DFC Changes   452

B.5 BOF Changes   453

B.6 Application Builder and Application Installer Changes   453

B.7 WDK Changes   454

B.8 Documentum Administrator Changes   454

B.9 Web Publisher Changes   455

Index   457

Preface

One of the world leaders in Enterprise Content Management, the EMC Documentum family of applications helps you manage all types of content within a single repository. With the Web Content Management suite of applications, you can efficiently manage content and underlying processes for your websites, and ensures that they are responsive to business needs.

To fully realize the power of this system can seem daunting, but this book will help you achieve that. With easy-to-follow examples, this book will take you along the simplest and most straightforward route to success. Along the way, you will learn insights that only a seasoned professional would know.

Packed with practical examples, this book will get you hands-on with the powerful features of Documentum to grow your skills and confidence. You will see tips and tricks to handle complexities of the system, and avoid the common errors that waste your time.

What This Book Covers

Chapter 1: This chapter discusses the need for content management systems and provides an introduction to Documentum.

Chapter 2: This chapter introduces the Content Server and discusses the essential concepts related to Documentum, such as Docbases, DocApps, DocBrokers, and objects. This chapter also touches on the versioning capabilities of Content Server and introduces lifecycles and workflows.

Chapter 3: This chapter covers the advanced concepts in Documentum, such as DMCL, DFC, BOF, WDK, ACL, renditions, registered tables, the data dictionary, methods, and jobs.

Chapter 4: This chapter introduces the Documentum product suite.

Chapter 5: This chapter discusses the installation of Content Server 5.2.5 and service pack 2.

Chapter 6: This chapter discusses the detailed steps for creating a Docbase and installing Web Publisher files on the newly created Docbase. It also discusses how to start and stop Docbases and DocBrokers and finally discuss some important keys in the dmcl.ini and server.ini files.

Chapter 7: This chapter covers setting up Site Caching Services (SCS) components for publishing documents created in a new Docbase.

Chapter 8: This chapter briefly introduces Documentum Application Builder as a client tool for creating and managing Documentum DocApps, and then covers the detailed steps for its installation.

Chapter 9: This chapter discusses the installation of Documentum Administrator and Web Publisher.

Chapter 10: This chapter provides an introduction to designing Documentum applications and then touches on Web Publisher templates, Rules files, and Presentation files architecture.

Chapter 11: This chapter discusses Documentum object types and their attributes. It also discusses Value Assistance and creating and querying registered tables in Documentum.

Chapter 12: This chapter covers Documentum Alias Sets, Permission Sets (ACL), and Lifecycles in detail.

Chapter 13: This chapter provides detailed instructions on how to create a sample template in Web Publisher.

Chapter 14: This chapter introduces Rules files and looks at creating Rules files in Web Publisher and setting preferences for invoking the Rules Editor, and discusses available Rules-file widgets.

Chapter 15: This chapter introduces Presentation files and discusses the detailed steps to create them and associate them with template files in Web Publisher. The chapter also discusses firing DQL queries through XDQL and how to automatically reapply presentation files on active content files to creating updated renditions in the Docbase.

Chapter 16: This chapter discusses Folder Maps in Web Publisher and their limitations, and provides multiple examples of configuring Folder Maps by using various property-matching mechanisms, single and repeating attributes, and dynamic folder mapping at run time.

Chapter 17: With the help of detailed examples, this chapter discusses how to use Instruction Files to delete an XML element from a content XML file, add a new XML element to it, and update the existing value of an XML element.

Chapter 18: This chapter discusses Automatic Property Extraction (APE) and also discusses using APE to populate repeating attributes and for two-way attribute extraction.

Chapter 19: This chapter contains a detailed discussion on Workflows and Workflow templates, and also contains an example of creating a custom Workflow.

Chapter 20: This chapter provides detailed steps on how to test the custom Workflow created above.

Chapter 21: This chapter discusses Site Caching Services (SCS) in detail and explains how to create a Site Publishing Configuration in Documentum Administrator for defining source and target host parameters for publishing using SCS. It also discusses a simple browser-based mechanism for viewing the status of SCS Source publishing operations.

Chapter 22: Through detailed steps, this chapter discusses how to set up WebView in Documentum using a Site Publishing Configuration in Documentum Administrator.

Chapter 23: This chapter discusses Documentum Foundation Classes (DFC) and contains detailed examples on how DFC can be used to programmatically create Docbase sessions, create and link files in Docbase cabinets, and create users in Documentum

Chapter 24: This chapter discusses the Web Development Kit (WDK) framework, along with examples on its configuration and customization.

Chapter 25: This chapter discusses deploying Documentum applications on different test and production environments.

Chapter 26: This chapter explains the use of DQL queries and Server API commands as handy tools for inspecting the Documentum Docbase.

Appendix A: This contains answers to frequently asked questions (FAQs) based on the content covered in this book.

Appendix B: This contains a list of features and enhancements that have been added in Documentum version 5.3.

What You Need for This Book

To get the most from this book, you will need access to a working installation of the Documentum product suite.

This book has been written for Documentum product suite version 5.2.5 SP2 running on a Windows environment including the SQL Server 2000 database server. You will also need the Apache Tomcat 4.1.30 platform, and Apache Ant 1.6.5 installed.

Conventions

In this book, you will find a number of styles of text that distinguish between different kinds of information. Here are some examples of these styles, and an explanation of their meaning.

There are three styles for code. Code words in text are shown as follows: "External presentation files provide standard frames and wrappers to the content embedded within the <body></body> elements of HTML content files."

A block of code will be set as follows:

```
<?xml version="1.0" encoding="UTF-8"?>
<ROOTTAG>
  <TITLEOFPAGE/>
  <SHORTDESC/>
</ROOTTAG>
```

When we wish to draw your attention to a particular part of a code block, the relevant lines or items will be made bold:

```
<?xml version="1.0" encoding="UTF-8"?>
<ROOTTAG>
  <TITLEOFPAGE/>
  <SHORTDESC/>
</ROOTTAG>
```

Any command-line input and output is written as follows:

```
DQL> create dm_document object set object_name = TestDocumentCreated_via_DQL',setfile
    'c:\Test\testing_dql.xml' with content_format = 'xml'
```

New terms and **important words** are introduced in a bold-type font. Words that you see on the screen, in menus or dialog boxes for example, appear in our text like this: "clicking the Next button moves you to the next screen".

Warnings or important notes appear in a box like this.

Tips and tricks appear like this.

Updates made to the Documentum suite in release 5.3 are marked out with a heading as follows:

Documentum 5.3 Update

Updates made to Documentum in release 5.3 will appear here.

Reader Feedback

Feedback from our readers is always welcome. Let us know what you think about this book, what you liked or may have disliked. Reader feedback is important for us to develop titles that you really get the most out of.

To send us general feedback, simply drop an email to feedback@packtpub.com, making sure to mention the book title in the subject of your message.

If there is a book that you need and would like to see us publish, please send us a note in the SUGGEST A TITLE form on www.packtpub.com or email suggest@packtpub.com.

If there is a topic that you have expertise in and you are interested in either writing or contributing to a book, see our author guide on www.packtpub.com/authors.

Customer Support

Now that you are the proud owner of a Packt book, we have a number of things to help you to get the most from your purchase.

Errata

Although we have taken every care to ensure the accuracy of our contents, mistakes do happen. If you find a mistake in one of our books—maybe a mistake in text or code—we would be grateful if you would report this to us. By doing this you can save other readers from frustration, and help to improve subsequent versions of this book. If you find any errata, report them by visiting http://www.packtpub.com/support, selecting your book, clicking on the Submit Errata link, and entering the details of your errata. Once your errata have been verified, your submission will be accepted and the errata added to the list of existing errata. The existing errata can be viewed by selecting your title from http://www.packtpub.com/support.

Questions

You can contact us at questions@packtpub.com if you are having a problem with some aspect of the book, and we will do our best to address it.

Content and Documentum

Every single bit of information seen on a website can be classified as content be it text, graphics, rich media, video, engineering drawings, XML, images, scanned files—just about anything and everything!

Content can be of various kinds, from pure textual pages to training material, online reference manuals, graphical screenshots and even complex data graphs.

One of the simplest ways to describe content management would be through the example of a daily newspaper website. Most of us start off our day browsing through our favorite newspaper edition (be it the conventional hard copy or the online version). Have you noticed something in particular about most newspapers? The structure or layout of most of the sections in the newspaper remains constant everyday. What typically changes is the actual *content* within the same sections on a daily basis.

The layout of the headlines remains constant—though the actual headlines change everyday. Sections like cartoons, the editorial corner, and weather report maintain the same look-and-feel everyday but their content changes everyday with the latest edition of the newspaper.

The online version of the newspaper needs to be updated every day with the new HTML, graphics, and text depending on the news. Imagine the time it would take to update the website's HTML/JSP pages manually every day to reflect the latest news. This would cause an increased dependence on the technical web developers to update the content. Updating several hundreds of HTML pages every day would also cause a time and resource problem.

Additionally it would mean technical web developers dealing with content they don't even understand and yet had to safely upload within the security boundaries of the organization. The editorial staff and content contributors/authors would have to rely on the IT staff every day so that their content could make its way to the actual website.

The problems multiply since the IT staff turnover is extremely high in most organizations—imagine having to recruit new web developers on a periodic basis to maintain live websites. Moreover, what if the page updates take a substantially long time—so much so that by the time the updated content shows up on the website, it's too late and practically stale!

The current business circumstances require immediate and correct data to be up 24/7 on the organization's websites. A lackadaisical attitude can literally throw a business out of the current market space. The problems of managing content on websites will keep on growing with time because of the increased visibility of websites today.

It is easy to understand now the need for an effective content management methodology that can result in:

- Decreased dependence on IT staff to run and maintain the core business
- Reduction in cost and better ROI to maintain the core business
- Non-technical contributors maintaining their business website all by themselves
- Not having the non-IT staff learn Internet web technologies like HTML, JavaScript, JSP, etc. to run the core business
- Always having the most up-to-date information available on the business website without unnecessary delays
- Security mechanisms restricting the editing of information by unrelated business divisions, for example, restricting the editing of sensitive financial information to the administrative department
- Automation of content creation/approval/publishing through a workflow mechanism
- Reduced expenses in maintaining hardcopy versions of documents/manuals/content
- Rollback mechanisms in case the updated content needs to be pulled off the website
- Effective capture and use of content metadata for indexing and searching

This list is not complete—the virtues of having a good content management methodology are many and varied. The above list simply gives us an idea about the criticality of content management in today's demanding business space.

In a nutshell, what exactly is content management? One of the numerous available websites on content management describes content management as follows:

> Content management is the organizing, categorizing, and structuring of information resources (text, images, documents, etc.) so that they can be stored, published, and edited with ease and flexibility. A **content management system** (CMS) is used to collect, manage, and publish content, storing the content either as components or whole documents, while maintaining dynamic links between components.

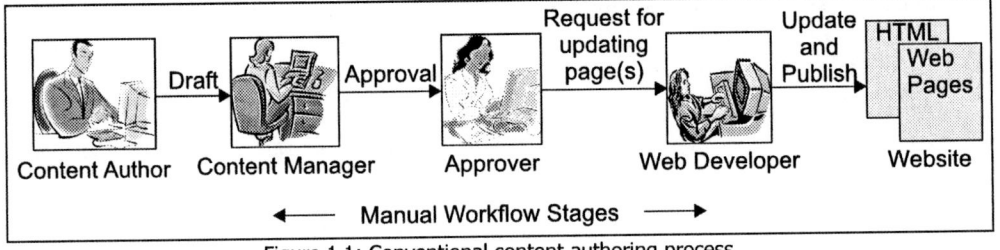

Figure 1.1: Conventional content authoring process

Figure 1.1 represents the conventional process of creating content for a website, getting it approved by a sequence of business users and finally having the web developer (IT staff) update the HTML pages to reflect this approved content.

However, this method is not without its drawbacks. It is a time consuming process to author content and get it manually reviewed and approved by a string of business users and then a heavy dependency on the IT staff to make the changes manually in website pages. By the time the sequence of steps gets completed, the content is probably stale and is no longer appropriate to show up on the organization's website!

1.1 Need for an Effective CMS

Most of the above mentioned problems with content management can be solved by using a content management system (CMS). A good CMS allows the content authors to create content in the form of articles through some pre-defined **templates**. The content author simply needs to provide content (plain text, pictures, etc.) in the template fields. The content management system then uses some pre-defined rules to style the article, thus separating the actual content from its display/layout structure. The author needs to be concerned only about the core content and not about its look-and-feel and formatting, thus saving loads of time and pain. Some content management systems also optionally require the author to enter metadata for content, for example creator name, keywords, etc. so that these can be associated with the content and be used for indexing and searching the website.

Unlike the traditional content management approach of an author manually getting the content/ articles approved by editors and senior members from business content approval divisions, a good CMS has an automated workflow mechanism. The author simply specifies the sequence of approvers to get the article approved and the automatic workflow does the rest of the work. It ensures that the content does not get published to the website until and unless the sequence of editors and approvers approve it via the automated workflow.

This requires the IT staff (web developers) to prepare the templates and associated rules as a one-time activity, along with stylesheets that format the entered content articles and are responsible for the look-and-feel of the website.

The IT staff additionally needs to configure and establish the CMS software once and from then onwards the content authors simply use the system and templates, getting rid of future dependency on web developers.

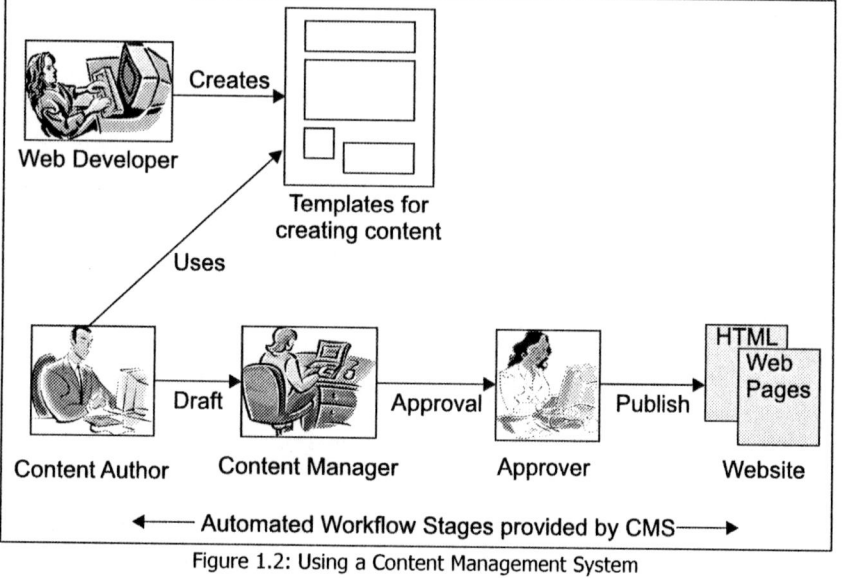

Figure 1.2: Using a Content Management System

Figure 1.2 simply gives a graphical perspective to the benefits of using a CMS.

The one-time effort that a web developer puts in creating templates/rules so that later content creators can use it going forward is a good money-saving approach.

The automated workflow available in a CMS routes the content through its different lifecycle stages finally getting it approved and publishing it to the business website.

1.2 Qualities of a Good CMS

Owing to the high demand, tons of companies have come into play today offering content management services. Fortunately or unfortunately we have numerous content management systems available today in the market each with its own positives and negatives but with the same end goal—ease of managing content.

A good CMS should be meticulously chosen because most are quite costly and involve training overhead so that the end users (mostly business content contributors/editors/approvers) can effectively use them.

Following are some (but not all) of the points that should be considered while evaluating a CMS for one's organization. Always remember one thing—there is no "one size fits all" solution available! One should analyze one's business needs first and then choose from the range of CMS available in market.

A good CMS:

- Allows the non-technical core business personnel to author/publish content without the assistance of IT staff(web developers)
- Separates the actual content from the structure(look-and-feel) by allowing an easy way to create templates and associated rules/presentation files
- Ensures that the content contributors adhere to the organization's website standards and also maintain security and navigational elements
- Ensures a mechanism to publish content in a timely manner so that the website information is always up to date
- Consolidates business data and content in a single storage repository for faster retrieval and also reduces the cost of maintaining hardcopy versions of content
- Allows authoring content via standard web browsers thus reducing training needs
- Creates an audit trail of activities performed on the content/articles for security reasons
- Restricts content editing on the basis of the role/group/division of the user in the business
- Provides a process mechanism to control content authoring, reviewing, and publishing through an automated workflow
- Provides support on multiple OS platforms and web browsers and can be easily integrated with web application servers and third-party software or existing business systems
- Provides a version control/history mechanism to allow rollback of specific content/pages to their older versions
- Provides document control through a simple check-in/check-out user interface
- Schedules automatic publishing/removal of content at specified release/expiry dates
- Allows easy creation/management of CMS users, groups, and roles
- Provides a built-in rich text editing interface to allow content authoring with extensive features like formatting, hyperlinks support, image/file upload, and copy-paste from other authoring applications
- Rules out the need to install any software on the end user machines
- Supports multiple simultaneous users
- Supports indexing/searching on the basis of metadata for the content
- Provides an extensive reporting system for both end users and system administrators

1.3 Why Documentum?

There are numerous content management systems existing in the market today, each offering its own specialized features. Documentum, Broadvision, Ektron products, Vignette Content products, and Interwoven product suite are some of the available content management systems in the market today. This book is not intended to highlight the benefits of using Documentum as a web content management solution vis-à-vis other available products.

Documentum provides Enterprise Content Management (ECM) solutions enabling diversified organizations to integrate their distributed content and related business processes on a single platform, thus uniting teams to collaboratively create, manage, process, and deliver their unstructured content. Documentum's clientele includes several big organizations that are successfully utilizing its widespread capabilities in expanding their core business by reducing their operating costs, deriving better ROIs, and achieving increased customer satisfaction by delivering just in time.

Documentum should primarily be construed as a platform that consists of a wide variety of products that collaboratively work together to provide enterprise-level content management facilities. Documentum not only provides large number of out-of-the-box (OOTB) features available in the product suite but also a customizable/configurable platform that can individually suit the specific needs of different enterprises.

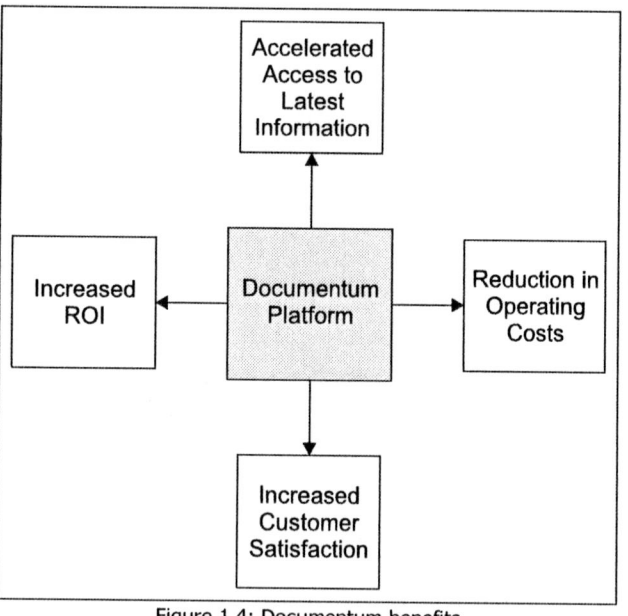

Figure 1.4: Documentum benefits

1.4 Documentum Features

Choosing the right CMS has always been an intriguing question for all and sundry. However, while evaluating Documentum, there are a lot of features that can catch your attention. Some of these are very basic functionality that any good CMS should offer and some are very specific only to Documentum.

Listing all the available features from Documentum would not be possible and this might qualify as not doing enough justice to it.

However, following list should serve as a quick reference for people who are using Documentum for their projects/businesses:

- Allows creating, managing, and archiving content through "lifecycles" (or Business Policies in Documentum's lingo)
- Supports integration with several industry-standard authoring applications like Microsoft Office products, Adobe publishing products, CAD applications, and XML authoring tools
- Provides a web-based collaborative environment (Documentum 'eRoom') that exposes content management services
- Encrypts content in Documentum repository and beyond via Records Management, SSL, and LDAP
- Provides automatic versioning of documents/content and history tracking
- Allows creation of multiple renditions of the content in varied formats, such as HTML and PDF
- Supports virtual document management for assembling information from various sources
- Supports the ability to parse, validate, and transform XML documents with XSLT support
- Supports clustering, load balancing and back-up/recovery features
- Provides content authoring/managing capability through Documentum Web Publisher and publishing capability through Site Caching Services (SCS)
- Deployment of website content to multiple servers through Site Deployment Services (SDS)
- Deployment of content from source to subscribers based on business rules via Content Distribution Services(CDS)
- Supports numerous archival/storage techniques, for example, RAID, optical laser disks, CD, and DVD jukeboxes
- Supports automated workflows to route a content item in the various phases of its lifecycle (creation, review, and approval)

- Provides workflow process extension to external participants and organizations via Inter-Enterprise Workflow Services for better collaboration

- Provides an exhaustive data dictionary (containing information in the repository and its objects) for the applications to use in order to enforce business rules or provide value assistance to users

- Supports business objects to encapsulate business rules that can be further exposed as web services to third-party applications

- Supports indexing/searching on the basis of metadata for the content

- Supports multiple simultaneous users

- Provides a wide range of library services for content management

- Allows automatic intelligent extraction of a list of properties for a Documentum document via Content Intelligence Services (CIS)

- Provides content aggregation services to collect content from multiple sources for storage in a centralized location

- Offers products like Content Services that allow interaction with Documentum CMS from various enterprise applications like SAP, Siebel, and Lotus Notes

- Supports high-availability by having multiple Content Servers serve a single repository and repository replication for backup purposes

- Complies with UTF-8 Unicode—single-byte and double-byte character languages

1.5 Summary

In this chapter we discussed what content management systems (CMS) are, along with their benefits and drawbacks. We saw how content management systems can serve as a boon to the organization by reducing dependence on IT staff for maintaining business websites and by providing a secured, streamlined, and automated mechanism for entering and publishing data to the websites. On the other hand, content management systems do entail training overheads to get the business users familiar with using the automated systems.

Documentum is an enterprise content management system that helps organizations integrate their unstructured content on a single platform. We discussed some qualities of a good content management system and how the Documentum product suite addresses most (if not all) of these.

Finally, we touched upon some striking features of the Documentum platform and how it helps organizations in collaboratively creating, managing, processing, and delivering their vast unstructured content.

2

Documentum Essentials

The Documentum product suite is an immensely vast sea and describing the complete set of offerings from Documentum within a single book would be unreasonable. However, for those who have just begun exploring Documentum, there are some salient features that one should at least be familiar with in order to conceive/design and develop Documentum applications better.

Those readers who have already worked with Documentum and/or are aware of the fundamentals surrounding Documentum may want to skip this chapter and jump over to subsequent chapters.

While going through the next few chapters, you can always come back to this chapter for a quick reference.

2.1 Documentum Cornerstone

The Content Server forms the heart of Documentum, providing essential services to create, version, manage, and archive content and objects in the Documentum system.

Content Server (earlier known as 'eContent Server') houses a repository, which Documentum terms a 'Docbase', to store the various content and its associated properties (metadata).

Documentum 5.3 Update

Note that Documentum release 5.3 adds some new and improved features in the Content Server, such as support for dynamic groups, i.e. groups whose list of members is to be treated as a list of potential members, and enhanced object-level permission assignments via ACLs (Access Control Lists).

2.2 Docbase

Docbase should be thought of as a huge centralized repository that stores content and metadata in the form of 'objects' and their properties.

Metadata for the content is nothing but the different attributes that describe the content; for example its owner, creation date, version number, etc.

Some attributes can be 'single-valued' having just one value, for example the name of the content, while others can be 'multi-valued' having multiple values, for example the keywords describing the content.

Documentum relies on the underlying RDBMS to store the metadata for various objects in various tables. On the other hand, the content files for the numerous objects are stored in any of these storage types:

- The host server's OS file system
- In an RDBMS as BLOBs (Binary Large Objects)
- A content storage device (for example: EMC Centera)
- An external system outside Documentum's boundaries

Additionally, Content Server has an embedded full-text search engine, Verity, and so the Docbase repository contains a number of full-text indexes, allowing users to perform a full content-based search on the Docbase.

Content attributes as well as the data within content files can be searched using this feature.

Documentum 5.3 Update

Note that in release 5.3, Documentum has replaced Verity with Fast Search & Transfer™ (FAST™) as its new search infrastructure.

If one installs Documentum Media Services apart from the Content Server, the Documentum system can then manage digital content such as video and audio files.

Note that each Documentum Content Server installation is not limited to a single Docbase. It can host multiple Docbases. However, each of these multiple Docbases must be identified by a unique identifier termed a **Docbase ID**.

Documentum ships numerous valid Docbase IDs along with its software for use within one's organization. A valid Docbase ID cannot start with a zero (0).

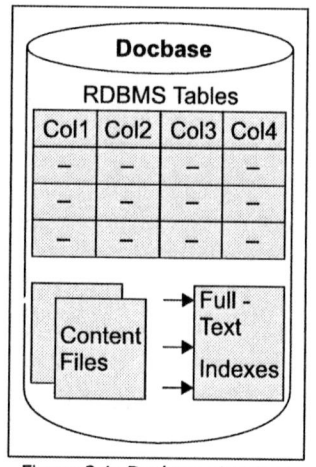

Figure 2.1: Docbase structure

Figure 2.1 depicts the Docbase as a logical unit comprising of content files, RDBMS (database) tables and full-text indexes.

Documentum 5.3 Update

It is worth pointing out that the Documentum 5.3 release calls Docbases **repositories**.

2.3 DocBroker

Whenever a client wants to make a connection with the server, DocBroker acts as a bridge or an intermediary. (Please refer to figure 2.2)

Instead of DocBrokers requesting information from the servers, it works the other way round—Content Servers broadcast their connection information at regular intervals to multiple DocBrokers and the same information is sent back to the requesting clients.

The client can choose which server to use from the returned information.

Clients such as Web Publisher and Documentum Application Builder can communicate with multiple DocBrokers by defining a primary and backup DocBroker in the client's dmcl.ini file.

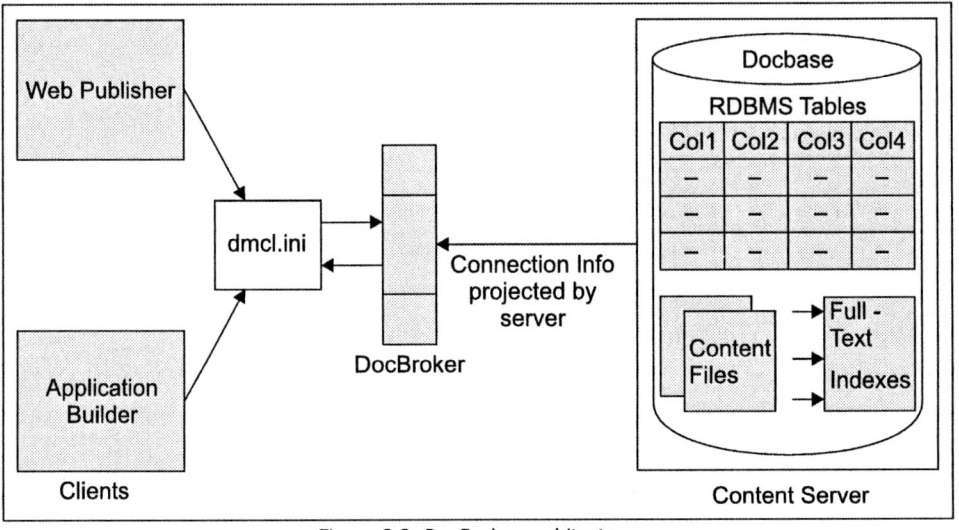

Figure 2.2: DocBroker architecture

Documentum 5.3 Update

DocBrokers are termed **connection brokers** in Documentum release 5.3.

2.4 DocApp

A DocApp is nothing but a packaging unit for Documentum objects.

Typically all development work in Documentum projects happens on a development Docbase and the developed objects are released on a test Docbase for system testing before getting finally released over to the production Docbase.

A DocApp works as a deployable packaging unit to move objects across Docbases.

Within a DocApp one can include multiple Docbase objects like lifecycles, workflows, folders, etc. and create a DocApp **archive** from it. An archive is a file representation of a DocApp on the file system.

This archive is then installed over to another Docbase through a Documentum DocApp installer. We shall look further into this in Chapter 25.

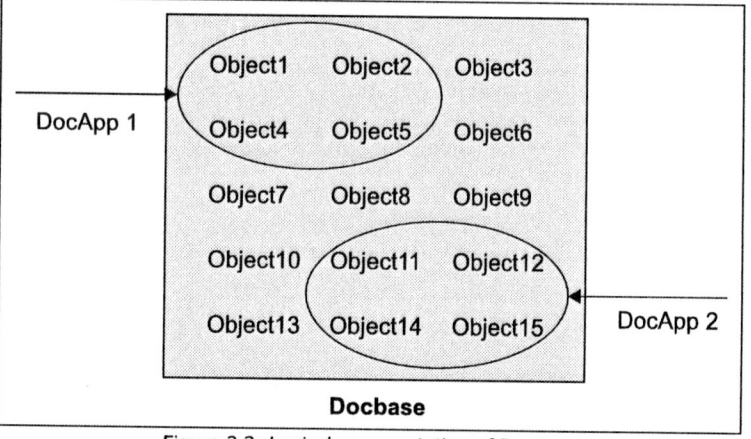

Figure 2.3: Logical representation of DocApps

2.5 Object Types

If you have just started using Documentum, remember an important rule of thumb—start thinking of everything in the Documentum system as an object. Folders within which documents are stored are objects, documents created are themselves objects, workflows used to get the documents reviewed are objects, and in fact the users creating the documents are also objects!

Too many objects around? It might take a little while to get used to this philosophy, but very soon you will start realizing its importance.

Documentum is an object-oriented system and every object in Documentum belongs to an object type. Internally, the Content Server uses the object type as a template to create various instances of objects. An object type is composed of several attributes that describe the various objects created from it. We shall cover object types and attributes via detailed examples in Chapter 11.

Too much jargon for now? Let us take an example to simplify things:

A user creates an article that he or she wants to get published over to the organization's website. The article could be of document type (dm_document in Documentum lingo).

The user fills in the attributes of the article, for example its title and subject.

- Object type: document (dm_document to be specific)
- Attributes of object type: title and subject
- Created document: of object type dm_document with values specified for attributes title and subject

Documentum object types follow a hierarchy as shown in figure 2.4. The subtype extends from a supertype and inherits all the attributes (properties) of its supertype. Note that a subtype can further be a supertype for another object type. All object types individually have their own specific attributes and inherited attributes of their supertype.

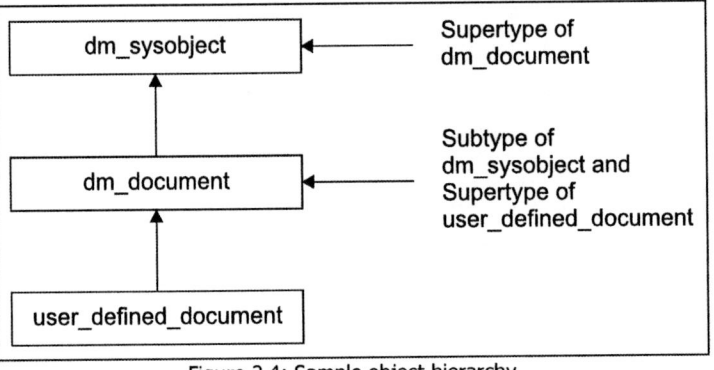

Figure 2.4: Sample object hierarchy

Note that it is not mandatory for object types to extend from another object type. Documentum allows the existence of object types with no supertype.

The table shown in figure 2.5 lists a few Documentum objects and their respective object types.

Entity	Documentum object type
Access Control List (ACL)	dm_acl
Workflow activity	dm_activity
Alias Set	dm_alias_set
Audit Trail	dm_audittrail
Cabinet	dm_cabinet
Category	dm_category
Content object	dmr_content
Document	dm_document
Folder	dm_folder
Format	dm_format
Group	dm_group
Job	dm_job
Method	dm_method
Lifecycle definition (Policy)	dm_policy
Procedure	dm_procedure
Workflow process definition	dm_process
Registered table	dm_registered
Relation	dm_relation
SysObject	dm_sysobject
User	dm_user
XML Application	dm_xml_application
XML Config	dm_xml_config

Figure 2.5: Sample Documentum object types list

2.6 Attributes

Attributes are the properties that describe objects in Documentum. For example, for a news article, the name of its author and its creation date can be considered its attributes.

It should be noted that all persistent objects stored in the Docbase are eventually subtypes of the internal persistent object type.

The persistent object type has three attributes that all subtypes inherit. r_object_id is specifically what everyone working with Documentum should understand:

- r_object_id is a unique identifier generated by the Content Server and assigned to all objects at the time of their creation. It should be noted that within the Docbase, no two objects can share the same r_object_id.

- i_is_replica and i_vstamp are internal server-generated attributes normally not required in typical applications.

2.6.1 Object ID (Object Identifier: r_object_id Attribute)

Object IDs are generated by the Content Server whenever a new object is created in a Docbase. These are represented as 16-character strings, used to uniquely identify objects within a Docbase. The first two characters in the object ID of an object are called **type identifiers** and represent the object type of the object in question.

For example, consider a dm_document object having the r_object_id 090015558000c629. The first two characters (09) in this object ID represent the type of the object: dm_document in this example. The table shown in figure 2.6 shows some common Documentum object types and their type identifiers.

Object type	Type identifier
ACL (dm_acl)	45
Alias Set (dm_alias_set)	66
Cabinet (dm_cabinet)	0c
Content (dmr_content)	06
Document (dm_document)	09
Folder (dm_folder)	0b
Group (dm_group)	12
Job (dm_job)	08
Lifecycle policy (dm_policy)	46
Method (dm_method)	10
User (dm_user)	11
Workflow process (dm_process)	4b
SysObject (dm_sysobject)	08

Figure 2.6: A few object types and their type identifiers

2.6.2 Attribute Types

Attributes can be divided into various categories.

- **Single valued and Repeating attributes**: Single valued attributes, as the name suggests, can have just one value. An example of this would be the title or the subject of a document. Repeating attributes can hold multiple values. An example of this would be the keywords for a document. A document for example can have many keywords to describe it, unlike its title which can be just one.

- **Read-write and Read-only attributes**: Read-write attributes can be modified by applications as well as users. Examples: title, object_name, a_content_type, etc.

It should be noted that attributes starting with a_ would typically be used by application developers and not by users.

Read-only attributes are managed by the server and it is advisable not to tamper with these. These can, however, be read by applications.
Examples: r_object_id, r_creation_date, i_contents_id, etc.

- **Computed attributes**: Apart from the attributes of persistent objects, which are stored in the Docbase, Content Server computes certain attributes for the objects. These attributes are called computed attributes and are not persistently stored in the Docbase but generated by the server at run time. Examples: _alias_set, _policy_name, etc.

Figure 2.7 depicts a few Documentum object types and some sample attributes that belong to them.

Object Type	Attribute names
Persistent Object	r_object_id
	i_is_replica
	i_vstamp
SysObject (dm_sysobject)	r_object_type
	r_modify_date
	r_creation_date
	r_version_label
	i_chronicle_id
	object_name
	a_effective_date
	a_expiration_date
	title
	subject
	authors
	keywords
Folder (dm_folder)	r_folder_path
Cabinet (dm_cabinet)	is_private
User (dm_user)	user_name
	user_os_name
	user_group_name
Group (dm_group)	group_name
	users_names

Figure 2.7: Sample object types and some of their attributes

2.7 DQL

DQL is short for Document Query Language and uses syntax that is a superset of ANSI-standard SQL (Structured Query Language). For those familiar with SQL, DQL can be simply thought of as a Documentum wrapper over SQL.

DQL is used to perform the following operations in a Docbase:

- Query, update, and delete objects in Docbase
- Create new objects in Docbase
- Search content in Docbase
- Query Registered tables

Example of a simple DQL query:

```
select r_object_id from dm_document where object_name = 'SampleDocument.xml'
```

The above query selects the unique Object ID of an object of type dm_document whose name is SampleDocument.xml

DQL queries can be fired from within:

- Documentum Administrator (a Documentum web client)
- DFC (Documentum Foundation Classes)
- IDQL utility

IDQL is an interactive utility/tool installed along with the Content Server and allows us to execute DQL queries against a Docbase. Figure 2.8 shows how a sample DQL query is fired using the IDQL utility.

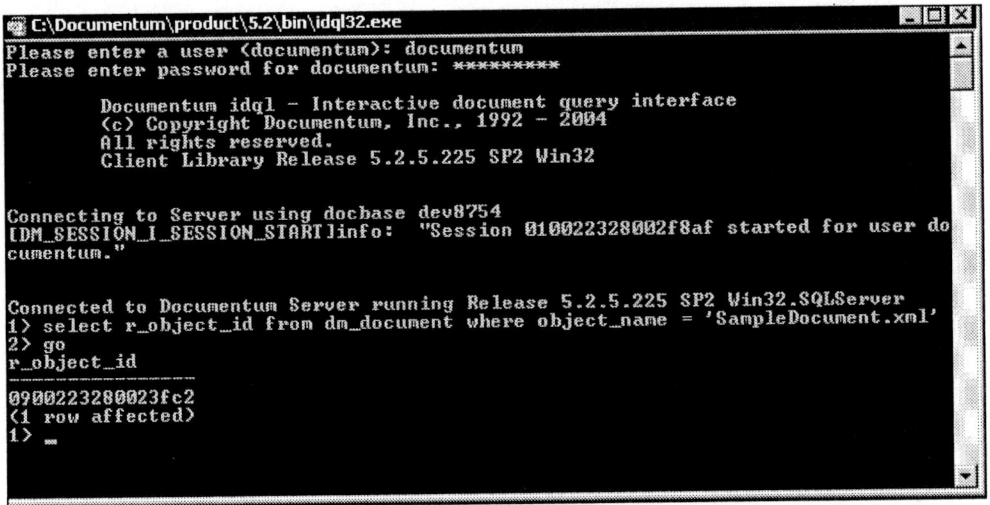

Figure 2.8: IDQL tool

Documentum 5.3 Update

Documentum release 5.3 has introduced a new querying approach called an FTDQL query which is similar to a SELECT statement, with the difference that the query is run against the full-text index rather than the Docbase (repository) for performance gains.

In order to learn more about DQL queries, please go through Chapter 26.

2.8 API

API commands (also referred to as Server API) are instructions sent to the Content Server by clients via DMCL (Documentum Client Library). Similar to DQL, API commands are used to:

- Query, update, and delete objects in Docbase
- Create new objects in Docbase

Unlike DQL queries, which can manipulate multiple objects at a time, API commands are meant to be executed on one object at a time.

Example:

```
get,c,0900223280023fc2,object_name
...
```

Result: SampleDocument.xml

Let us break down the API command to explain the example:

- get: A Server API method used to retrieve information about a particular attribute value
- c: Signifies the current Docbase session
- 0900223280023fc2: r_object_id of the object in question
- object_name: Name of attribute whose value needs to be retrieved

Note that the arguments to Server API methods are positional and should not include any white spaces.

IAPI is an interactive utility/tool installed along with the Content Server, which allows one to execute Server API methods against a Docbase. Figure 2.9 shows how a sample API command is fired using the IAPI utility.

```
C:\Documentum\product\5.2\bin\iapi32.exe                              _ □ X
Please enter a user (documentum): documentum
Please enter password for documentum: **********

        Documentum iapi - Interactive API interface
        (c) Copyright Documentum, Inc., 1992 - 2004
        All rights reserved.
        Client Library Release 5.2.5.225 SP2 Win32

Connecting to Server using docbase dev8754
[DM_SESSION_I_SESSION_START]info:  "Session 0100223280002f8b1 started for user do
cumentum."

Connected to Documentum Server running Release 5.2.5.225 SP2 Win32.SQLServer
Session id is s0
API> get,c,09002232800023fc2,object_name
...
SampleDocument.xml
API> _
```

Figure 2.9: IAPI tool

In order to know more about API commands, please go through Chapter 26.

2.9 Cabinets and Folders

Objects in the Docbase are organized by placing them within cabinets and folders. **Cabinets** form the highest level of organization and contain **folders**, documents and other objects. Objects can reside within cabinets or within folders. Folders are present within cabinets or within other folders.

Organizing objects within cabinets and folders can help us categorize the content better and enables faster searching for critical information.

Cabinet object type in Documentum is dm_cabinet and folder object type is dm_folder. It should be noted that dm_folder is a supertype of dm_cabinet object type.

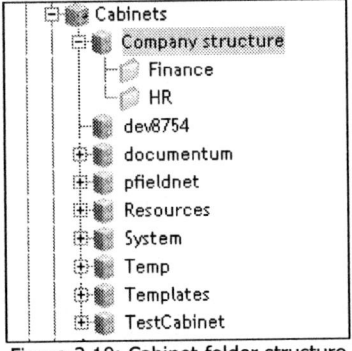

Figure 2.10: Cabinet-folder structure

Figure 2.10 shows a sample cabinet-folder structure in a Docbase as seen in 'Web Publisher' client.

2.10 Versioning

Like any good CMS, Documentum internally manages multiple versions of the same document and maintains a history of all updates that have gone in since the initial creation of the document. **Versioning** is an automatic feature provided by the Content Server through **version labels**.

All SysObjects are versioned by Content Server except folders, cabinets and their subtypes. The various versions for a document are stored within a **version tree**. Version labels are stored in the r_version_label repeating attribute of SysObjects or their subtypes.

There are two kinds of version labels:

- **Numeric (or implicit) labels**: These are server-generated numeric labels and are stored in the first position of the r_version_label attribute.

  Example : r_version_label[0]=1.0

- **Symbolic labels**: These are either system-defined or user-defined descriptive labels. Unlike numeric labels, these convey meaningful information and hence are useful for one's applications. They are stored in the second position onwards in the r_version_label attribute and are case-sensitive.

  Example : r_version_label[1]=WIP

It should be noted that CURRENT is the only symbolic label that the Content Server assigns automatically to the last checked-in version of a document.

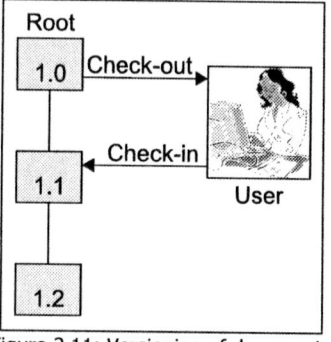

Figure 2.11: Versioning of documents

Since we are discussing versioning, this is a good place to discuss the r_object_id and i_chronicle_id attributes of SysObjects in Documentum. A version tree in Documentum contains the original object and all its modified versions. How does Content Server deduce which version tree a particular object belongs to? The answer is: through the i_chronicle_id attribute.

Note that the i_chronicle_id attribute stores the object ID (r_object_id) of the original (root) version of the object. Every time a new version is created, Content Server copies the i_chronicle_id value to the new object created. Let us take a small example.

Create a new document. The Content Server assigns an object ID and chronicle ID to the document. Check it out and check it back in. The server now assigns a new object ID but retains the original chronicle ID. Again check it out and check it back in. The server again assigns a new object ID but retains the original chronicle ID.

Refer to Figure 2.12 to understand how Content Server manages different versions of the original document. For the original (root) version of the document, the value of object ID and chronicle ID is same.

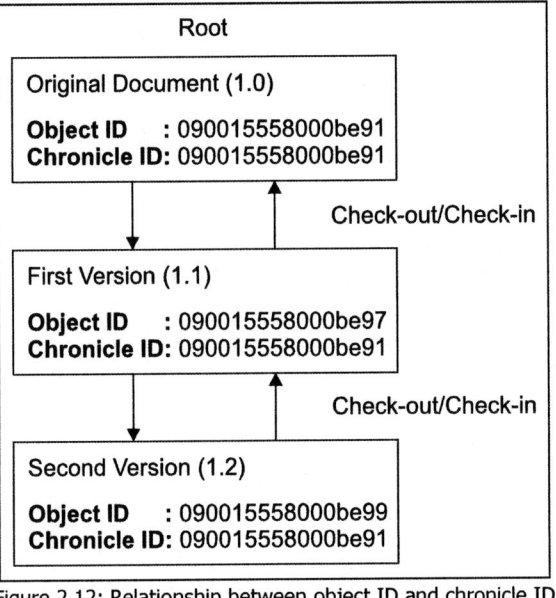

Figure 2.12: Relationship between object ID and chronicle ID

2.11 Lifecycles

Documents in an enterprise progress through a well-defined authoring-review process.

Let us take an example of such a process:

1. A document is created by an author. At this initial stage of creation, the document is in the draft state.
2. The document is being worked upon by the author and hence falls under the 'Work in progress' state.
3. When it is sent out for the first round of review, it might be under the 'In Review' state
4. And when the document is finally approved, it falls under the 'Approved' state (say).

Content Server provides lifecycles to automate these various stages in the life of a document.

Simply speaking, a lifecycle is a sequence of states that describe the various stages in the life of an object. Documentum stores lifecycles in the form of a policy object (dm_policy) in the Docbase.

Figure 2.13 shows a sample lifecycle as it is seen in Documentum Application Builder.

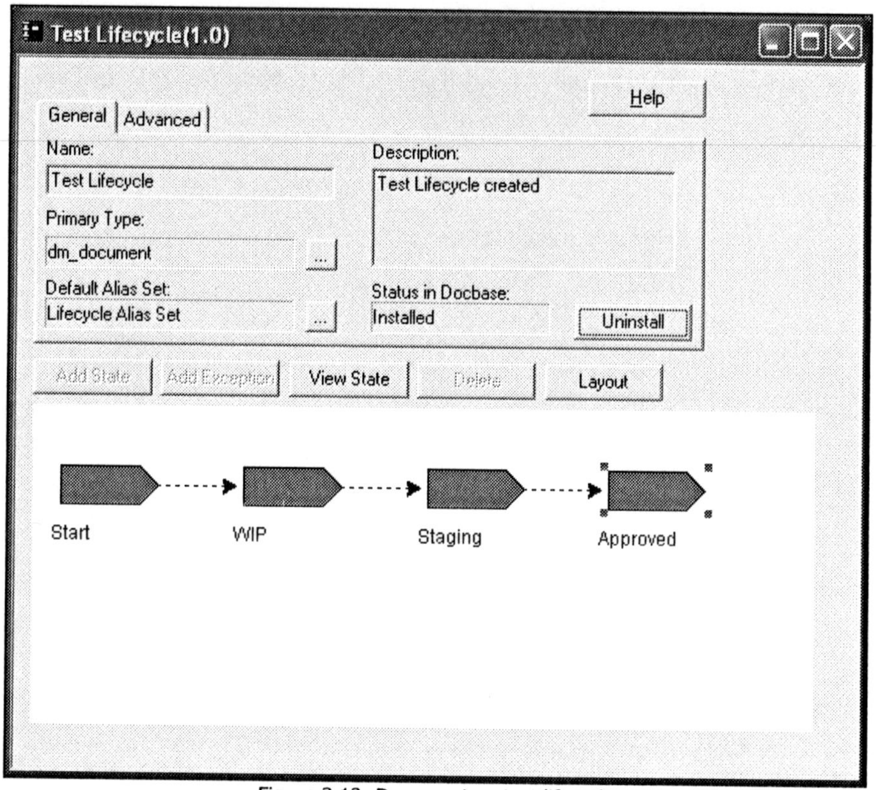

Figure 2.13: Documentum test lifecycle

We will delve deeper into lifecycles in Chapter 12.

2.12 Workflows

In plain terms, a workflow models a business process. The following example can explain this better:

An online newspaper publishing firm requires various approvals of the created content, before publishing over to its live newspaper website. Instead of manually transferring hard copies of content to various groups of reviewers, a workflow can formalize, standardize, and automate the whole process.

Workflows consist of numerous activities, each comprising various tasks to be performed. Users or designated automated scripts carry out the tasks and pass over the document in question to the subsequent activity. What a workflow does, in essence, is routing the content through the various stages of its lifecycle via different users. Each user receives the designated task in one's Inbox and may also receive an email notification for the same. Documentum stores workflow definitions in the form of business process objects ('dm_process') in the Docbase.

Figure 2.14 shows a sample Documentum workflow template as seen in Workflow Manager tool.

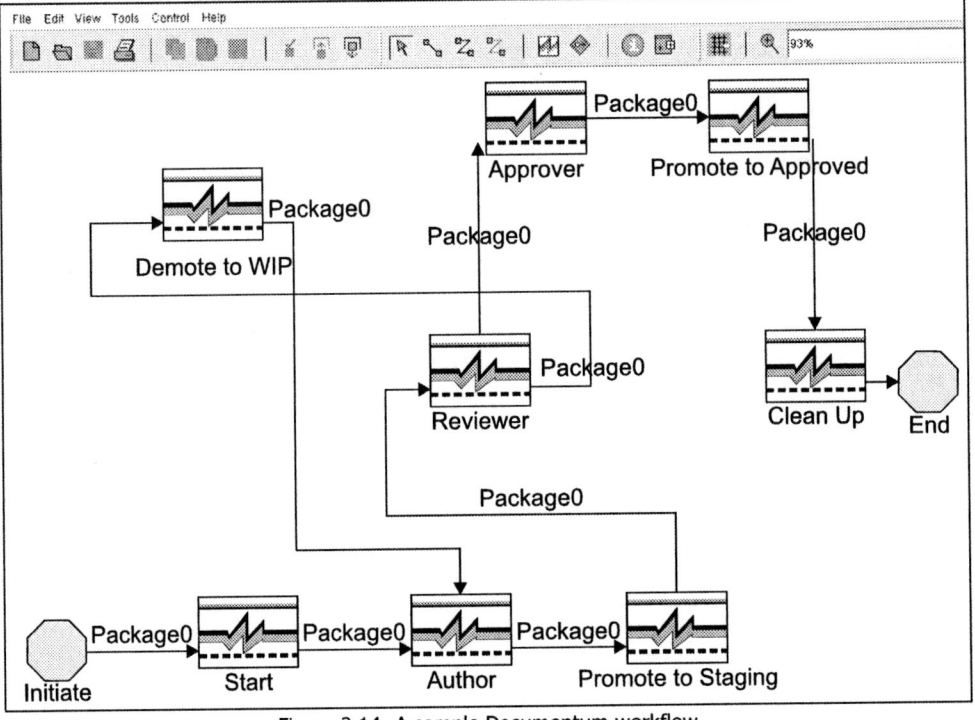

Figure 2.14: A sample Documentum workflow

We shall cover workflows in details later in Chapter 19.

This concludes our discussion of Documentum basics. Please do not be bogged down if you still do not understand much of the topics covered in this chapter. As and when you start putting your hands into the Documentum system, you will understand these concepts better and appreciate them more. If you feel that you have a basic understanding of Documentum now, you may please proceed to the next chapter to cover some of the advanced features in Documentum.

2.13 Summary

In this chapter we talked about Content Server, the backbone of Documentum architecture, hosting Docbases. A Docbase can be thought of a logical repository, consisting of content files and their associated metadata. A DocApp, on the other hand is a packaging unit of a Docbase, consisting of objects from the Docbase.

We went on to discuss DocBrokers, which act as an intermediary allowing clients to make connections with Content Servers.

We saw how the Documentum system treats all entities in the form of objects. Objects can be treated as run-time instances of templates called object types in Documentum. Objects in Documentum have their own metadata, which is termed properties or attributes.

We saw an example of using DQL (Document Query Language) and Server API commands to query and manipulate objects in the Docbase.

We also touched upon the versioning capabilities of Content Server and had a brief introduction to lifecycles and workflows. While lifecycles represent the logical stages in the life of an object, workflows model a business process and define how the objects move into different lifecycle states, under what conditions, and who the participating entities are.

3

Documentum
Advanced Concepts

We can now proceed further with the assumption that you have brushed up your basic concepts about the Documentum system. In this chapter, we will discuss some more vital aspects of Documentum architecture. Needless to say, you may skip this chapter and move on if you already understand the concepts listed below.

Let us not forget that the Documentum system is extremely vast and is not just limited to the basic/ advanced concepts we discuss.

> For an exhaustive understanding of the system, going through Documentum's product manuals is strongly recommended.

3.1 DMCL

DMCL stands for Documentum Client Library which provides a communication layer (RPC) between end clients and the Content Server.

Client requests reach the Content Server via the DMCL layer, which consists of a C++ library of APIs that get executed on the Content Server.

It is recommended not to execute direct DMCL API calls from the client. Instead, what should be used is a set of Documentum Java classes or a DFC, described below.

3.2 DFC

DFC stands for Documentum Foundation Classes and is an Object-Oriented (OO) Framework consisting of APIs for accessing and extending Content Server functionality. Simply speaking, it is a set of Java interfaces and classes written as a wrapper over DMCL. Apart from the regular DMCL capabilities, DFC also provides features such as data validation, virtual document management, etc.

Additionally, DFC also provides a Documentum Java-COM Bridge (DJCB) so that the Java interfaces can be used from within a Microsoft COM environment as well as by programs in Visual Basic, for example. DFC also includes a Business Objects Framework (BOF) that enables developers to model application business rules in the form of reusable modular components/elements.

Figure 3.1 shows how the request-response paradigm works between clients and Content Server via the DMCL and DFC layer.

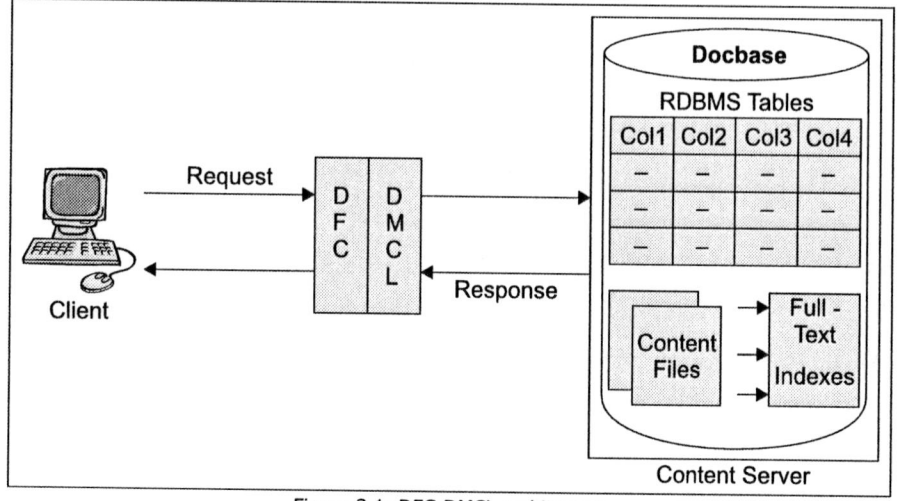

Figure 3.1: DFC-DMCL architecture

We will learn more about DFC through numerous examples in Chapter 23.

Documentum 5.3 Update

Documentum release 5.3 includes some enhancements made to the DFC. Some of the new features introduced in DFC as part of release 5.3 are:

- Support for Unified Client Facilities (UCF) to assist content-related services such as check-out, check-in, import, and export as the content transfer mechanism for WDK-based applications
- Deeper integration with .NET

3.3 BOF

The **Business Objects Framework** (BOF) is built into DFC and helps developers create reusable business logic components called **Business Objects**. Applications using DFC can access BOF easily and can use BOF as pluggable components/entities in middle-tier or client applications. Let's take a simple example to understand this.

Assume that you require a specific business functionality of performing some particular validation whenever a particular document of some particular object type is checked-in into the Docbase. This can be achieved by using BOF and overriding the check-in functionality for the particular object type. Once written, the same business object is called irrespective of the client application used—be it Webtop, Web Publisher, some Desktop application, or some custom DFC class for that matter. In short, what we achieve is a reusable component/functionality.

There are two types of Business Objects:

- **Type-based (TBO)**: This is useful in extending a particular Content Server object type and including new custom methods or overriding existing methods. This type of Business Object works on all objects in the Docbase of a particular object type only.

  Example: Some custom behavior added for an object type `my_custom_document` (where `my_custom_document` object type extends Documentum `dm_document` object type)

- **Service-based (SBO)**: Unlike type-based Business Objects, this type of Business Object is not limited to a particular Docbase object type. Instead this works as a generic service provided to all object types in the Docbase and not just one particular object type.

  Examples: Check-in method overridden globally in the Docbase irrespective of the object types, Documentum Inbox object, etc.

Note: For those coming from an EJB (Enterprise Java Beans) background, consider TBOs analogous to Entity Beans and SBOs analogous to Session Beans.

Documentum 5.3 Update

In Documentum release 5.3, TBOs are associated not just with object types but also with a Docbase (repository). Additionally, Documentum has added support for accessing Business Objects via Web Services in this release.

3.4 WDK

Web Development Kit (WDK in short) is a framework provided by Documentum, on which one can build a web application for talking to the Content Server.

The WDK programming model is completely based on J2EE and XML and WDK applications can be deployed on any application server that confirms to J2EE standards. WDK applications interact and fetch data from the Content Server via DFC calls.

Following are some features of the WDK framework:

- Consists of reusable and configurable components that generate HTML controls/widgets, providing access to the Content Server Docbase
- Provides a tag library of configurable UI controls
- Provides framework services like branding, history, error handling, messaging, internationalization, and content transfer

In short, WDK is a set of server-side reusable components supported by Documentum that allow one to rapidly develop and deploy web-based applications.

WDK architecture consists of:

- **Presentation model**: Incorporates JSP tag libraries to separate the UI from business logic.
- **Component model**: Incorporates server-side components that extend the Content Server functionality.

Figure 3.2 represents a simplified version of the WDK architecture, showing how the various Documentum entities fit in the various layers.

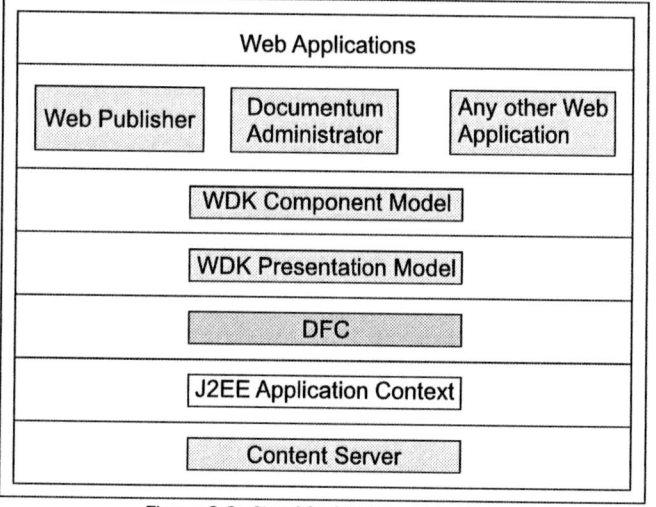

Figure 3.2: Simplified WDK architecture

Webtop is a Documentum reference implementation with WDK components. Web Publisher tool is built over Webtop and is used mostly for content authoring and publishing.

WDK and its usage are discussed in detail in Chapter 24.

3.5 Web Publisher

Web Publisher is a browser-based web application provided by Documentum for content creation, review, and finally publishing to websites.

In the Documentum architecture, Web Publisher utilizes the content management services from Content Server, publishing services from **SCS** (Site Caching Services), and rendition (see section 3.9) management from **CRS** (Content Rendition Services).

Apart from these, Web Publisher also works with a host of other Documentum products.

Web Publisher defines its own specific groups in order to divide the responsibilities of the participating entities. For example, a content author can use Web Publisher to use predefined templates and create content for the website without requiring any knowledge of web design/construction.

A web developer on the other hand, understands web design and uses Web Publisher to create content templates, automates the review process through workflows, and maintains the website categories and structures.

An administrator has the highest privileges and maintains the Web Publisher system, administering and monitoring it and running reports for various objects and events.

Throughout this book, we shall explore Web Publisher in great detail and utilize it for various operations such as content authoring, categorizing, and publishing.

3.6 ACL

ACL (Access Control List) forms a part of Documentum's security mechanism to restrict certain groups/users from accessing a particular object. Documentum stores restricted objects as dm_acl objects. Note that all SysObjects in Docbase have an ACL assigned to them.

An ACL, also called a **permission set**, stores information regarding the groups/users that have access to a particular object as well as their access levels (or privilege levels).

Keep in mind that the permission levels are hierarchical, which means a permission level of 'READ' for example would grant permission levels above it as well—'NONE' and 'BROWSE'.

Go through the table shown in figure 3.3 to understand the basic access levels available in Documentum:

Permit level (r_accessor_ permit attribute)	Permission	Short Description
1	NONE	No access to the object.
2	BROWSE	User can view the object's attributes but not its associated content.
3	READ	User can view the content as well but not modify it.
4	RELATE	User can attach an annotation (i.e. comment) to the object.
5	VERSION	User can create a new version of the object but not update the existing version.
6	WRITE	User can write and update the existing version of the object.
7	DELETE	User can delete the object.

Figure 3.3: Basic permissions in Documentum

Apart from providing the above basic permission levels, Documentum provides some extended permission levels as well.

The table in figure 3.4 shows the extended permissions available in Documentum pre version 5.3:

Permission	Short Description
Change State	User can change the object's lifecycle state.
Change Permission	User can change the object's permission.
Change Ownership	User can change the object's owner.
Execute Procedure	User can execute an external procedure associated with the object.
Change Location	User can change the object's location, from one folder to another say.

Figure 3.4: Extended permissions in Documentum (pre 5.3)

It is worth mentioning here that Documentum uses two reserved aliases in ACLs:

- dm_owner: Symbolizes the current owner of the object
- dm_world: This is an alias for all the users present in the Docbase

Let us take an example of a sample ACL attached to a folder in the Docbase:

ACL name: OrganizationHR_ACL

The permissions are as follows:

- dm_owner: DELETE
- Hr_group: WRITE
- Finance_group: READ
- dm_world: NONE

This means that the owner of the ACL (i.e. the one who created this ACL) has the highest rights—DELETE. The Human Resources (HR) group in the organization has WRITE access to the folder. The Finance group in the organization has just READ access to the folder. All other groups can not even see the folder since they have NONE access to the folder.

3.7 Alias Set

An Alias Set, as the name suggests is a list of Aliases. Now what exactly is an Alias? An Alias in plain terms should be considered to be a placeholder for value. An Alias resolves to a particular value called the Alias value. Alias sets are stored as dm_alias_set objects in Docbase.

Let us take an example here, in order to clear up all confusions.

An organization's workflow needs to go through a sequence of reviewers before it can be finally approved and published over to the website. A content author creates the content and needs to send it to his or her content manager for review. After the initial review, it needs to be finally approved by an approver.

Now, for each individual content author, his or her manager and approver would be different. Should a separate workflow be created individually for each content author? Or should it be hard-coded with the actual names of all the content authors in the organization and their content managers and approvers? What would happen if a new author or manager joins the organization in the future?

An alias set comes to our rescue! An alias set can be created for the workflow with placeholders for content authors, content managers, and approvers, etc. At run time, when the workflow is executed, the alias names can be substituted with their actual values.

In Documentum, an Alias Set can have placeholders for the following entities:

- Unknown (this is for the case when no existing entity fits)
- User
- Group
- User or Group
- Cabinet Path
- Folder Path
- Permission Set

Figure 3.5 shows a sample Alias S set in the Docbase as seen in Documentum Application Builder.

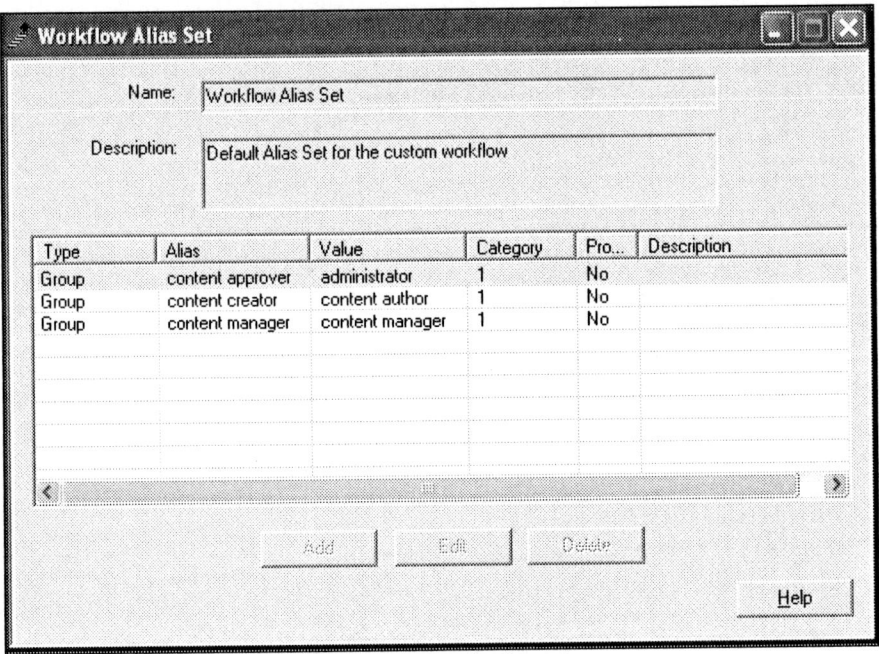

Figure 3.5: Sample alias set

We shall create custom Alias Sets in Chapter 12.

3.8 Users and Groups

It might sound bizarre, but Documentum stores users and groups in the form of objects!

3.8.1 Users

Users are stored as `dm_user` objects in the Docbase. We will now discuss some important attributes of the `dm_user` object:

- **user_name**: This is the actual name of the user and can contain spaces, for example 'Gaurav Kathuria'. Internally Content Server assigns this value to the `owner_name` attribute for the objects created by this particular user.

- **user_os_name**: This is what Documentum uses to validate the user's credentials for authentication purposes, for example 'gauravk'.

- **user_address**: This stores the user's email address and is used by Content Server to send notifications.

These three attributes are mandatory for a user object and should always be filled in when creating a Documentum user.

Each user has certain user privileges assigned to him or her:

- None (no special privileges)
- Create Type (can create object types)
- Create Cabinet (can create cabinets)
- Create Group (can create groups)
- Sysadmin (system administration privileges)
- Superuser (highest-level privileges)

Users in Documentum can be created through numerous mechanisms:

- DQL queries
- API commands
- LDIF file (import users)
- Documentum Administrator user interface
- DFC classes

3.8.2 Groups

Documentum groups are nothing but sets of Documentum users and groups. Documentum stores groups as `dm_group` objects. Let us take an example to understand the importance of groups in Docbase.

Imagine there is a permission set (ACL) assigned to an object and specific users have access to it. For example, all the users in the HR department have WRITE access to it and users in the Finance department have READ rights.

If we were to design the ACL giving specific rights individually to each of the users in HR and Finance departments, we would end up in a mess. We would have to revisit the ACL whenever a new user joins the HR or Finance department

Groups save us this pain. Instead of individually assigning rights to users, we club all HR users as an HR group and all Finance users as a Finance group and then assign rights at the group level and not to specific users. Groups can be of two types:

- **Public**: If a sysadmin or a superuser creates a group, the group is marked as public.
- **Private**: If a user with 'Create group' privilege creates a group, the group is marked as private.

Internally Documentum does not treat these two types of groups differently. It is up to the individual applications to interpret it as per the business needs.

Groups can be created via the following means:

- DQL queries
- API commands
- Documentum Administrator user interface
- DFC classes

3.9 Renditions

Rendition of a document is pretty much the representation of the original document with differences only in its format. Content Server internally has converters to support numerous renditions. Additionally, integrating Media Services with Content Server can provide support for rich media formats as well.

An example of rendition is as follows:

A web developer creates a content template, say `create_article.xml`, and attaches presentation XSL files to it in order to transform it to an HTML file and a WML file. The content created from this template is rendered in the form of an HTML file as well as a WML file for display on a website and a wireless application respectively.

The HTML and WML files differ from the original content file only in format and not in their content.

Figure 3.6 explains this in a simplified fashion.

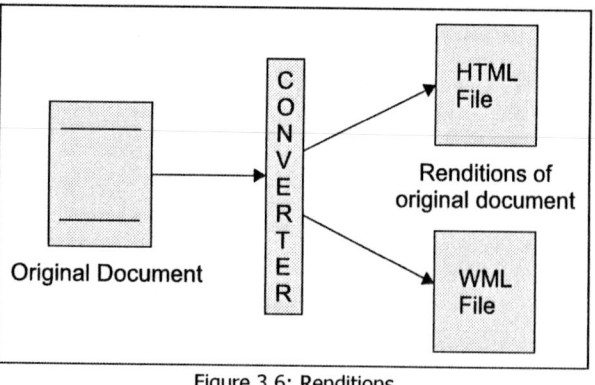

Figure 3.6: Renditions

3.10 Registered Tables

Most applications maintain some application tables in order to store data specific to the application. These application tables may contain records that Documentum clients need access to. For example, a dropdown in a Documentum client application might need to display a list of all the countries in the world from an external database table, so that the content author can choose one while creating content.

The external database table is not known to the Content Server until you register it. In short, **registered tables** are the normal RDBMS tables that the Content Server is aware of, in spite of them not being part of the Docbase.

Documentum creates a `dm_registered` object for the 'Registered' table, allowing developers to use DQL queries to fetch the information from the table.

The `dm_registered` object contains information about the name of the table, table owner, table columns, and access rights defining who has access to query the table and perform operations like insert/update/delete rows.

We shall be dealing with registered tables in greater detail in Chapter 11.

3.11 Data Dictionary

The Data Dictionary (DD) in the Docbase stores information about Documentum object types and their attributes. The Data Dictionary is very useful in the following scenarios:

- **Value assistance shown to the users**
  Example: A dropdown showing the possible set of values for the attribute

- **Application of some business-specific rules**
  Example: Constraints like 'not null' and 'unique key' on the values of an attribute

DD can support multiple locales and hence one can localize the stored information as per the default locale of various end users. Also, DD information is managed internally by Content Server and can be made available to end users once we publish the data it contains.

At the time of writing this book, the DD information for the following locales is provided by Documentum when the Content Server is installed:

- English
- French
- German
- Italian
- Japanese
- Korean
- Spanish

3.12 Methods and Jobs

Methods are executable programs and scripts in Docbase that can be scheduled to run automatically by jobs, which are Documentum objects (dm_job) that are used to automatically execute method objects. The following sections discuss methods and jobs in detail.

3.12.1 Methods

Method scripts can be written either in Java, Docbasic (Documentum's proprietary language), or some other languages. In Documentum, a method is treated as a method object (dm_method) and its attributes define various method parameters such as execution agent, method type, timeout period, and method arguments. Methods can be executed by the following server execution agents:

- **Content Server**: This is the default execution agent for methods unless a specific execution agent is specified. Content Server is used to execute method objects associated with Docbasic scripts or scripts in other programming languages.
- **Method Server**: This is a daemon process always running while the Docbase is up and is managed by the Content Server. Note that the Method Server is installed by default along with the Content Server. Method Server can be used to execute method objects associated with Docbasic scripts.
- **Java method server**: During Content Server installation, Documentum installs Apache Tomcat application server as a Java method server on the Content Server host. The Java method server can be used to execute method objects that call Java methods in turn.

Documentum methods can be created, modified, and viewed from within Documentum Administrator at the following location: Administration | Job Management | Methods.

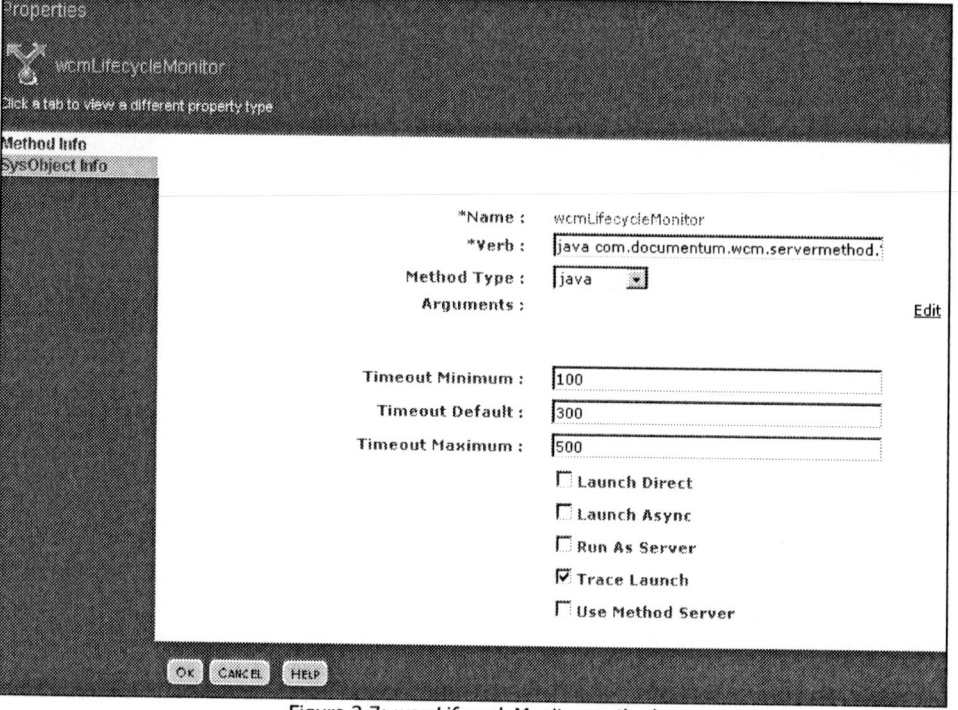

Figure 3.7: wcmLifecycleMonitor method

Figure 3.7 shows a sample method wcmLifecycleMonitor as seen in Documentum Administrator.

3.12.2 Jobs

Instead of invoking methods manually or via scripts, jobs can be used to periodically schedule their execution. dm_job object attributes define job parameters like associated method, execution schedule, method arguments, etc.

A job is executed by the Documentum agent exec process, which is installed with the Content Server. Figure 3.8 shows how jobs and methods work together in Documentum architecture.

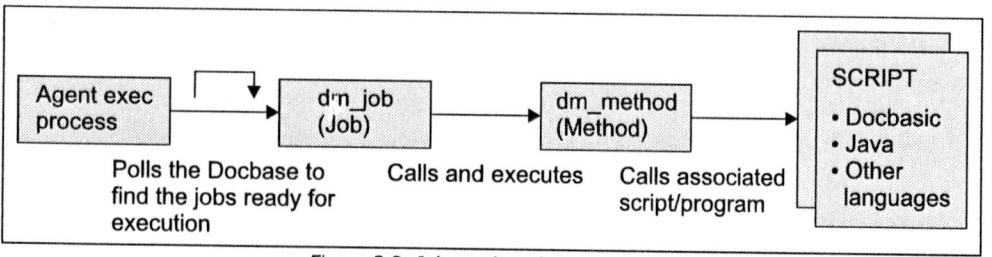

Figure 3.8: Jobs and methods execution

Documentum jobs can be created, modified, and viewed from within Documentum Administrator at the following location: Administration | Job Management | Jobs.

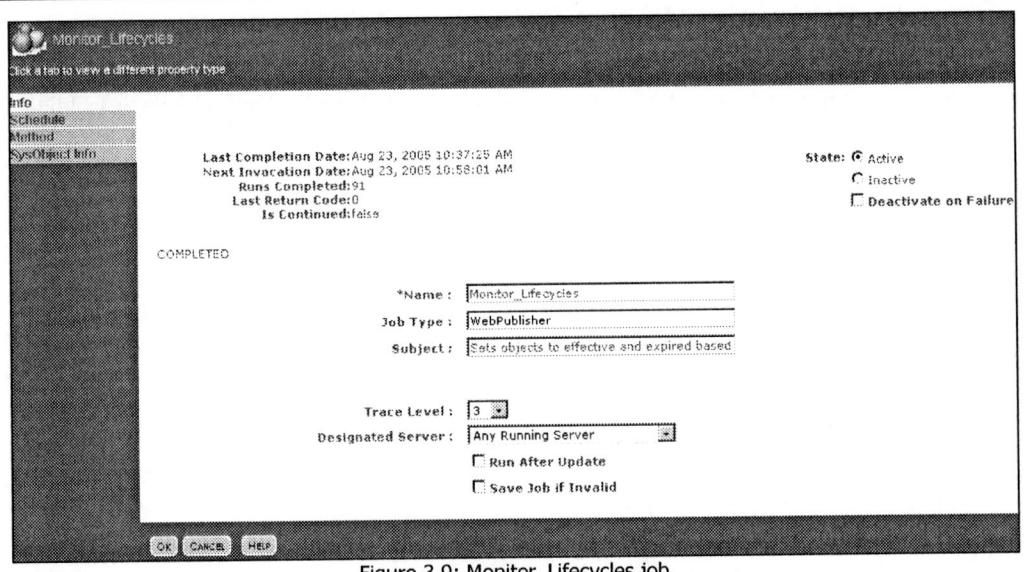

Figure 3.9: Monitor_Lifecycles job

Figure 3.9 shows a sample job (Monitor_Lifecycles) as seen in Documentum Administrator. This job in turn calls the method wcmLifecycleMonitor as seen in figure 3.10.

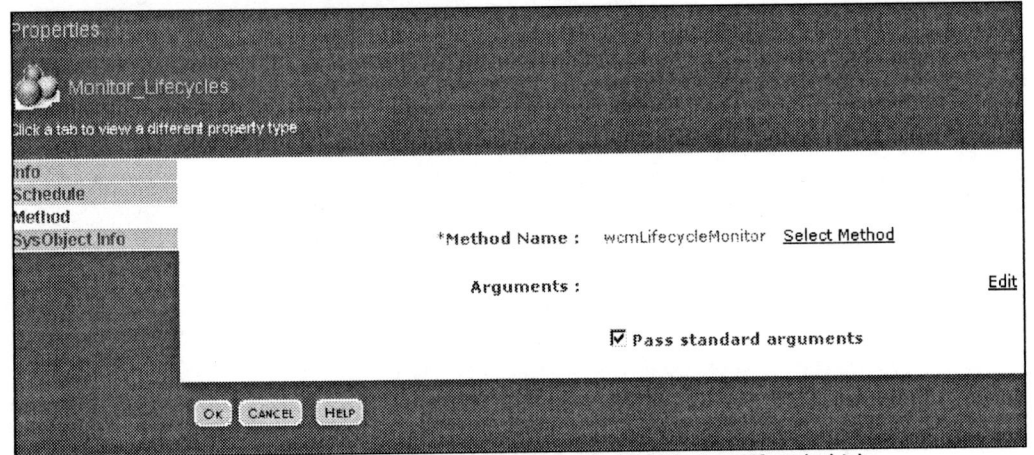

Figure 3.10: 'wcmLifecycleMonitor' method called by 'Monitor_Lifecycles' job

Documentum 5.3 Update

Documentum release 5.3 introduces a new feature called **Job Sequences**. This allows you to configure multiple jobs to run in a sequence (in a specified order) at the specified times.

This is all we wanted to cover in the Documentum advanced concepts section for now. You will understand these concepts better as you read through the following chapters.

Treat this as a ready-to-refer chapter in case you are confused about the terminologies or feel like refreshing your concepts again. Feel free to jump back to this chapter any time you need.

3.13 Summary

In this chapter, we touched upon some of the advanced concepts in Documentum.

We discussed the DMCL (Documentum Client Library) as a client library serving as an RPC layer between clients and Content Server. DFC (Documentum Foundation Classes) on the other hand act as a wrapper over DMCL exposing APIs to perform basic content management functions. DFC consists of a set of Java interfaces and classes and has a built-in Business Objects Framework (BOF) that helps you create reusable business components by extending and customizing content management capabilities.

We went on to discuss the Documentum WDK (Web Development Kit), which serves as a framework consisting of several server-side reusable components, allowing us to rapidly develop and deploy web-based applications that need to talk to Content Server.

Webtop is a reference web-client implementation provided by Documentum built over WDK. Web Publisher is an extension to Webtop. It is a web browser-based application that provides a rich user interface for content creation, review, and publishing to websites.

We also talked about Access Control Lists (ACLs) that help in imposing security restrictions on Documentum objects by allowing only certain rights to specific groups or users in the Docbase.

Alias Sets are an integral part of the Documentum system, defining placeholders for various entities in the Documentum architecture so that the same objects can be reused in multiple contexts.

We saw how groups and users in Documentum are treated as objects. Users are a part of one of more groups in the Documentum system. Renditions in Documentum are documents differing from the original version only in their formats. Registered tables are RDBMS tables registered with the Docbase so that the data from these can be used within the context of a Docbase. The Data Dictionary in Documentum is a repository that stores information about all Documentum object types and their properties (attributes). Finally, we discussed methods, which are executable programs in Documentum Docbases that can be scheduled to run automatically via Documentum jobs.

4

Web Content Management System

Having discussed some of the key Documentum features in the preceding chapters, let us commence our journey into the world of Documentum by helping an actual enterprise deal with the age-old problem of managing large volumes of content in the website.

It is a safe assumption that whoever is reading this book is either genuinely interested in knowing more about Documentum or perhaps needs to evaluate if it could be a good content management option to meet his or her specific business requirements.

Either way, we should first find out if there really is a need for web content management (WCM in short) in the project at hand. All WCM systems have their own share of merits and demerits. We should meticulously analyze the business requirements to verify that the business needs can be fulfilled by a good content management system.

Documentum is an enterprise content management system and offers a multitude of rich tools to cater to the needs of ever-growing businesses. However, let's not forget that there is a caveat. Good CMS systems are costly and entail training overheads for the end users who eventually use them. Additionally, we need to have a development/system team to set up and configure the CMS system and a system administrator to monitor the CMS system as well to ensure smooth operation.

4.1 When Should you Use a WCM System?

Documentum as a WCM system is fruitful when the business requires frequent updates to the content on the website/portal. What this means is, a business that needs to keep on updating its business information displayed on its websites to ensure that the website users can view the most up-to-date information available at a given point of time is a good candidate for a WCM.

This can be better explained through a few examples:

- **An online shopping website**: An online shopping website uploads its product information such as product descriptions, product images, price, and stock availability details etc. At any given point of time, this information needs to be up to date, lest the customer purchases something at a stale cost rate. The stock information, if not updated on the site, would result in purchase orders for a product that is not available in the shop!

Instead of updating the website's HTML/JSP pages manually on a daily/weekly basis, the online shopping website firm can manage it effectively through a WCM system. Latest content information can be updated through the WCM content authoring tool and new product information can be easily entered without requiring any knowledge of web scripting tools.

- **An online newspaper website**: A newspaper website's structure/layout remains more or less constant but its actual content changes everyday. In fact the old news expires everyday from the site and is archived in some cases as well. Moreover, the news articles surfacing on the site have to pass through a group of reviewers via a workflow mechanism before they get finally approved. With a WCM system installed, content creators and editors need not learn web technologies/scripting languages in order to upload/edit content on the site. Once trained, they can author content via the authoring tool(s) provided by the content management system itself. So, a newspaper site can be considered a good candidate for a WCM system.

4.2 When Should you Not Use a WCM System?

This is a very debatable area and can vary as per the type and nature of one's business and customer needs.

However, the following may be considered as some handy tips based on past experiences with projects involving 'content-heavy' websites. It should be noted that these are personal view points and should not be deemed to be universal industry-standard or globally accepted rules.

Stop and think twice before starting off with a WCM system if:

- Most of the data on the website is fairly static and less prone to updates.

  If you do not require making frequent content updates on the site, try and come up with an alternative mechanism for managing the content. Using an automated content management system in such scenarios might turn out to be overkill and result in extra and unwanted costs.

- You have neither the time nor the money for training the employees.

  For smaller firms running on low revenue margins, purchasing a CMS system, getting it installed/set-up by a bunch of software developers/experts, and later on getting the business users trained on using the system can turn out too costly an affair. Such organizations should analyze and plan their expenses and/or time and work out the resource requirements in detail before taking the plunge.

- There isn't much content to be displayed on the site.

  There are a few transaction-heavy sites such as banking sites, online flight booking websites, etc. that do not require a lot of data to be fed manually by the site content contributors.

Only websites that require managing a wide array of unstructured data should be considered right candidates for a content management system.

4.3 Documentum WCM Architecture

If you have done your homework well and are convinced of your business requirement for an effective Web Content Management system like Documentum, then welcome aboard!

Let us discuss a typical Web Content Management architecture using the Documentum product suite.

What we shall discuss going forward is not the 'best possible' WCM architecture, but a reasonably standard one that meets most of the common web-based content needs for many enterprises.

An advanced WCM architecture is not just limited to the products/components depicted in figure 4.1. Depending on one's business requirements, there could be variations in the design and architecture and some more components could be added or existing ones removed from the figure 4.1.

Do not worry if you are unable to understand all the components depicted in the architecture. As you continue reading the rest of the book, all of these will get clearer and more comprehensible.

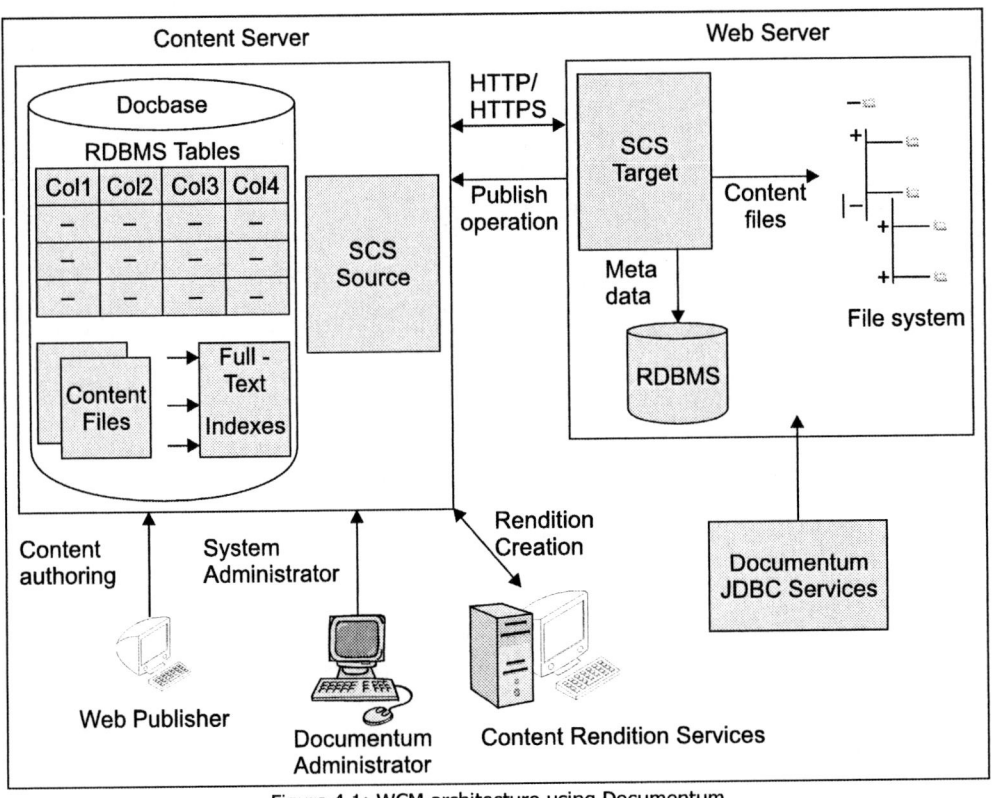

Figure 4.1: WCM architecture using Documentum

4.4 How do you Enter Content in the System?

Web Publisher is one of the simplest tools to enter content in the Documentum system and forms the entry point into a WCM system. It is a web-based client tool that connects to the Content Server Docbase and assists content authors, managers, and administrators in creating, managing, and administering content for a business site.

4.4.1 Web Publisher

The good part about using Web Publisher is that it simply requires a one-time setup of the Web Publisher system and the business-specific customized files on an application server. The Web Publisher end users (or clients) need not perform any installation on their laptops/desktops and can simply access the Web Publisher URL via a range of supported browsers.

The dmcl.ini file on the application server host where Web Publisher has been installed points to the correct DocBroker and port. It is through this that the connection to the Docbase is made.

Sample dmcl.ini file:

```
[DOCBROKER_PRIMARY]
host =<<Your DocBroker host Name>>
port =1489 # default port
```

The wide range of operations available in Web Publisher is not just limited to creating or managing content for the website. Web Publisher is an integral part of the Documentum WCM architecture and has an intuitive GUI that allows:

- Setting up groups, users, and roles for the end users of Web Publisher

- Creation of intuitive categories or taxonomies, using which business users can create classified content for their organization.

- Creation of delivery (web) cabinets from where the created content can be published out of the Documentum system.

- Setting up security for Docbase objects by attaching Permission sets (ACLs) to the objects in question.

- Promoting and demoting objects in Lifecycle states. Using Web Publisher's 'Promote', 'Demote' and 'Power promote' features, one can push a document to the next state(s) in its lifecycle or demote it to its previous state(s).

- Creation of content templates and associated rules and presentation files, so that users can simply use the templates to create content without learning any web scripting technologies.

- Getting the content items reviewed and approved by other users by pushing them to workflows. It is worth mentioning that Documentum Web Publisher provides some out-of-the-box workflows available for use.
  Examples: Request new content, submit to website workflow, etc.

- Integration with utility services and tools like automatic property extraction, Content Intelligence services, Inter-Enterprise workflow services, In-Context editing, eWebEditPro Rich Text Editor, etc.

- Running numerous reports to administer system objects, for example the available lifecycles, workflows, active content, etc.

Depending upon the 'role' of the logged in Web Publisher user, Web Publisher GUI appears differently to different users, sometimes offering restricted functionality. For example, a content author would not be shown the delivery web cabinets, while a web developer or an administrator can view these. Moreover, not all content management features are available to all Web Publisher users.

For example, a content author is not allowed to import files, while a content manager can do so; a content manager cannot 'power promote' objects, while a web developer has these rights; and so on and so forth.

These settings can be tweaked by changing some context-sensitive role configuration files and reloading the updated files in the Web Publisher system.

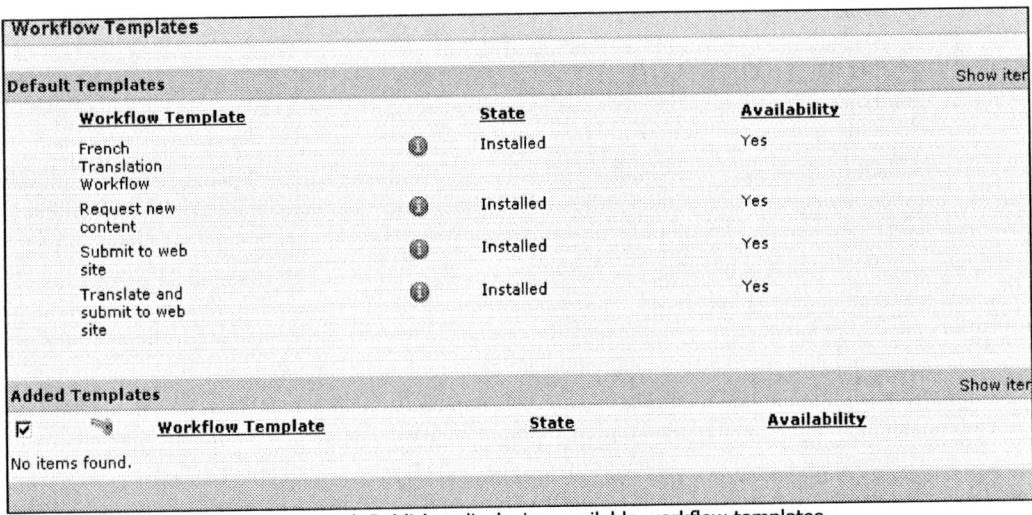

Figure 4.2: Web Publisher displaying available workflow templates

Figure 4.2 shows a list of installed and available workflows in the Docbase as seen in 'Web Publisher'. If you wish to learn about workflows in detail, you may jump over to Chapter 19.

4.5 Where and How is the Content Stored?

As discussed earlier, Content Server serves as the lifeline in the Documentum system by providing a wide variety of content management services

4.5.1 Content Server

The Content Server should be considered as a back-end server that hosts the business-specific Docbases. Remember that a Docbase is nothing but a logical set of content files (stored in the host server OS's file system), metadata for content (stored in the underlying RDBMS), and the full-text indexes for objects. No matter which tool one may use to create content, it is stored within a Docbase, which is managed by the Content Server.

There are numerous configurations possible in Documentum distributed architecture that provide a failover mechanism. One could set up multiple servers for a single Docbase or provide object replication from one Docbase to another Docbase, etc.

Documentum's security mechanism obfuscates the actual names of the content files on the underlying host server's OS. So, if you create a content item using Web Publisher for example, the content file that is stored on the OS will not be easily recognizable.

4.6 How do you Perform System Administration?

Documentum content management system, like any other existing CMS in the market, requires system administration and monitoring to ensure the smooth running of the system.

4.6.1 Documentum Administrator

While Web Publisher serves as a simple-to-use content authoring tool in the WCM architecture, **Documentum Administrator**, which is another web-based tool, is primarily used for Documentum system administration. Similar to Web Publisher, Documentum Administrator can be accessed via the supported web browsers. Like Web Publisher, Documentum Administrator requires an application server host where it can be installed.

Once installed, Documentum Administrator serves as an excellent tool to perform and manage a wide range of operations on Documentum Docbases, for example:

- Configure and maintain Documentum servers and Docbases
- Create and maintain Documentum users, groups, and roles
- Create and maintain object types and their attributes
- Create and maintain Documentum jobs and methods
- Create and maintain formats and permission sets(ACLs)
- Create and maintain Docbase federations
- Create and maintain storage areas
- Create and maintain site publishing configurations
- Execute DQL queries and API commands
- Monitor resource usage
- Audit management

The various system administration tasks that can be performed via Documentum Administrator require appropriate user privileges.

For example, audit configuration and purging requires the user to have the 'config audit' and 'purge audit' privileges respectively.

In the absence of the necessary privileges, Documentum Administrator cannot be used for system administration purposes.

Figure 4.3 shows a simple DQL query that has been fired using the DQL Editor in Documentum Administrator.

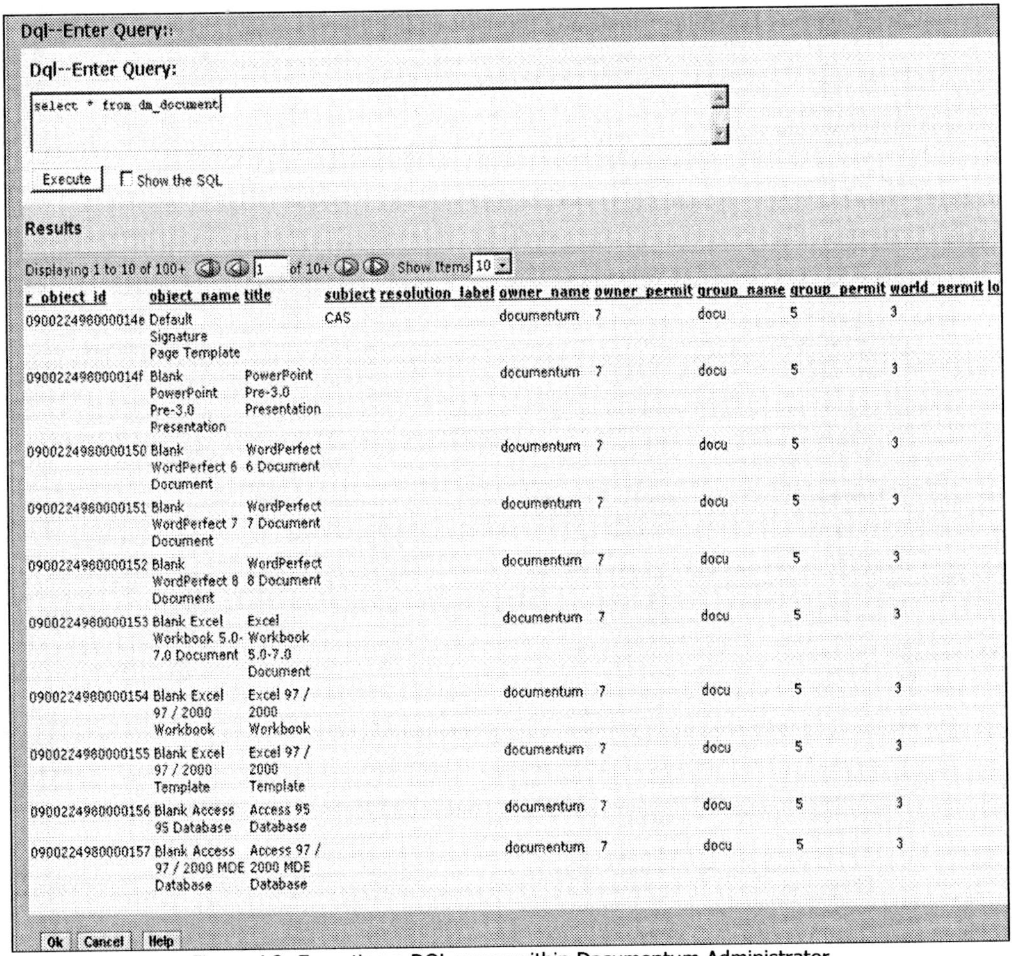

Figure 4.3: Executing a DQL query within Documentum Administrator

4.7 How do you Create Multiple Renditions of the Content?

Content Rendition Services (CRS), formerly known as AutoRender Pro, is a Documentum tool that generates renditions or alternative formats of the original document in a Docbase.

4.7.1 Content Rendition Services

CRS deals with requests from client applications (say Web Publisher) for rendition (for example PDF, Text, HTML) of original documents. CRS, however, does not produce renditions for documents that are in the checked-out state in the Docbase.

CRS should be run on a separate dedicated networked work station and should be the only software executed on the particular work station.

Figure 4.4 indicates some source formats in Documentum Docbase and whether their PDF and HTML renditions are possible via CRS.

Source Formats	HTML rendition possible?	PDF rendition possible?
Microsoft Word	Yes	Yes
Microsoft Excel	Yes	Yes
Microsoft PowerPoint	Yes	Yes
WordPerfect	No	Yes
Lotus WordPro	No	Yes
PostScript	No	Yes
PDF	No	Yes

Figure 4.4: CRS renditions for some Documentum formats

Figure 4.5 shows how the content rendition services serve rendition requests from Docbases.

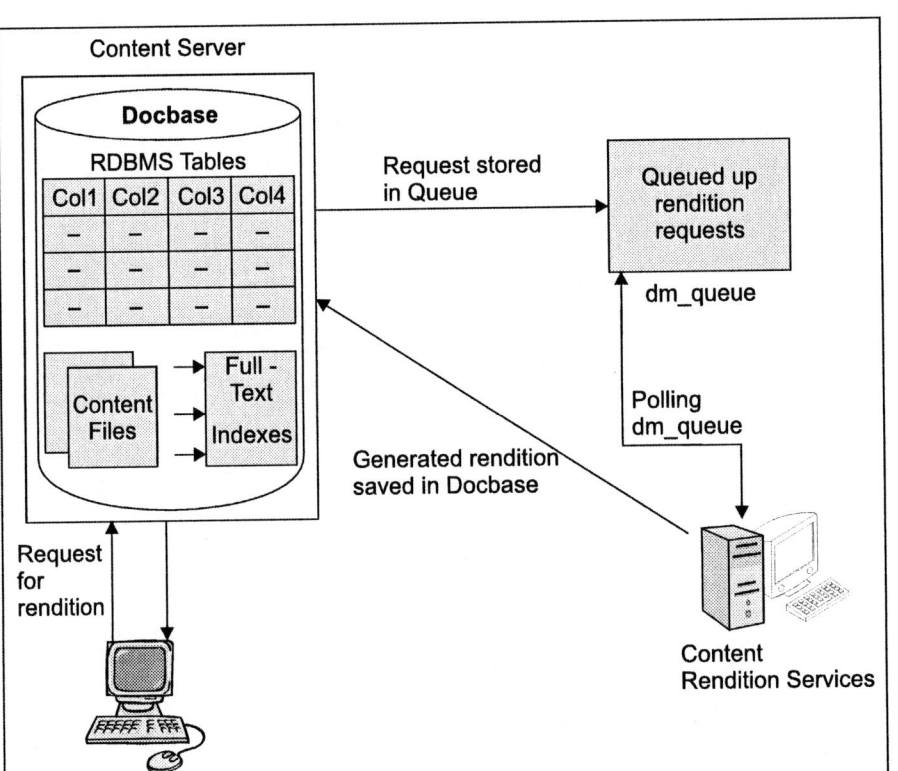

Figure 4.5: Generating renditions via CRS

The process of generating renditions via CRS is as follows:

1. The client sends a rendition request to the Content Server.
2. The Content Server stores the rendition request from the client in a dm_queue.
3. CRS polls the dm_queue at pre-configured intervals to find out if there are any pending rendition requests to be served.
4. CRS creates renditions as per the rendition requests in dm_queue, and sends them across to Content Server, which saves the renditions in the Docbase.

We can configure the frequency with which CRS polls the Docbases for rendition requests. Also, note that one CRS workstation can serve the rendition requests for a maximum of eight Docbases.

Documentum 5.3 Update

Content Rendition Services has been split into two products: Document Transformation Services (DTS) and Advanced Document Transformation Services (ADTS).

4.8 How do you Publish Content to a Website?

We have seen how the content can be entered in a Docbase using the Web Publisher tool and how system administration can be performed by using Documentum Administrator.

The content and its properties (metadata) in the Documentum system now need to be published out to the website so that it can be displayed on the site. It is the Documentum **Site Caching Services** (SCS), formerly known as WebCache, that helps us publish content and its metadata (document attributes) from Documentum Web Publisher system to a website, ensuring that the content seen on the website is accurate.

4.8.1 Site Caching Services

SCS does not create, manage, or store content in Documentum; this is done by Content Server. SCS simply exports the documents (whose object type is a sub type of dm_sysobject object type) and their associated attributes from Docbase to a pre-configured website.

The integration of SCS with Web Publisher happens via a 'Site Publishing Configuration', which is created using Documentum Administrator. It is through the Site Publishing Configuration that one can specify which types of documents need to be published, from which folders in Web Publisher they need to be published, and other details.

We shall cover Site Publishing Configurations in detail in Chapter 21.

The following configuration parameters need to be filled in when creating a Site Publishing Configuration for a Docbase from where content needs to be published via SCS:

- Name of the configuration
- Web Publisher delivery cabinet from where the documents need to be published
- Version label of the documents to be published, for example. 'Staging', 'WIP', etc.
- Host name and port number of the target where documents have to be published
- Connection type: whether secure or non-secure
- Target root directory where documents are published
- Whether metadata for documents (i.e. object attributes like title, subject, keywords, etc.) needs to be published to a target database
- If metadata has to be published, then the name of the table that will store the published attributes and the specific attributes to be published.
- Formats of documents to be published, for example HTML, PDF, XML, Excel, etc.
- Export directory on Content Server host's file system
- Whether online synchronization is required
- Any custom scripts to be executed on the target before and/or after publishing operation
- Target server authentication details like transfer user name, password, and domain

4.8.2 SCS Architecture

Site Caching Services comprises two major components:

- **SCS Source**: Installed on the server where Docbase exists
- **SCS Target(s)**: Installed on the machine(s) where the documents need to be published

Figure 4.6 depicts the Documentum SCS architecture in a simplified manner.

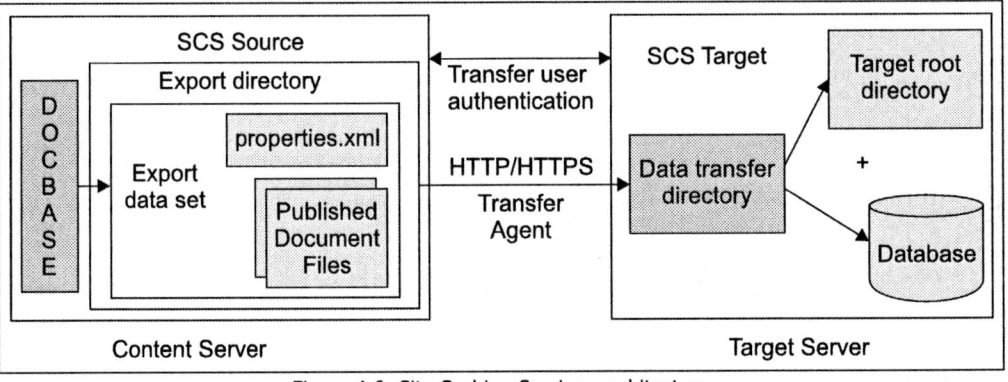

Figure 4.6: Site Caching Services architecture

The following steps explain in brief how the SCS publishing process works in Documentum:

1. A Site Publishing Configuration is made in Documentum Administrator, specifying the export directory on the Content Server host's file system and the target server where data needs to be published.

2. When publishing commences, documents and optionally attributes (if specified in Site Publishing Configuration) from Docbase are placed in the 'export directory' on the Content Server machine. This is called an **export data set** consisting of the actual published document files and a properties.xml file containing a list of published attributes for documents.

3. SCS connects to the target server (web server host) as the **transfer user** specified in the Site Publishing Configuration

4. After transfer user authentication, if connection to the web server host has been established, SCS transfers the export data set to the **data transfer directory** on the web server host. It should be noted that the data transfer directory is specified while installing SCS Target on the web server host.

5. SCS then moves the target repository (documents + attributes data set) from the data transfer directory to the **target root directory** on the web server host. The target root directory is specified while creating the Site Publishing Configuration. It is the webroot of the website and corresponds to the publishing folder in Docbase

6. The documents along with their containing folders are copied over to the target root directory, while the attributes are inserted into the database by reading values from

the properties.xml file. It should be noted that the database host and connection parameters are specified while installing SCS Target on the web server host.

SCS Publishing can happen in numerous ways:

- Invoking it manually through Web Publisher (Tools | Publish option)
- Invoking through Site Publishing Configuration directly in Documentum Administrator
- Running a scheduled publishing job at pre-defined intervals
- Invoking publishing via DQL, API, or a custom written DFC script

No wonder SCS plays a vital role in web content management by publishing content and its attributes over to a target file system and database, thus saving the website applications the overhead of reading data from Documentum system directly.

Through scheduled jobs, updated incremental data can be published on the target servers, maintaining the integrity of the site and ensuring that data is displayed on the site in a timely and accurate manner.

4.9 How do you Query the Published Content for Displaying on Websites?

Once the data has been published over to the target server, the applications need to query the published data (content files and their associated properties and attributes) for display on the website.

This is where Documentum JDBC Services, formerly known as eConnector for JDBC, comes into the picture. JDBC is a standard interface to access a database from Java-based applications.

4.9.1 Documentum JDBC Services

Documentum JDBC Services is a Documentum utility tool that supports most of the standard JDBC APIs and helps applications perform the following functions:

- Making connections to either Docbase or SCS repository.
- Issuing DQL queries in Docbase or SQL queries in SCS repository.
- Retrieving content files and associated metadata (attributes) from Docbase or SCS repository.
- Connecting to databases using logical names rather than their actual names through its support for JNDI (Java Naming and Directory Interface).
- Reusing existing connections in a pool, saving the overhead of opening and closing new database connections through its support for creation of database connection pools.

Both Docbase JDBC Drivers and SCS JDBC Drivers are available from Documentum JDBC Services. The Docbase JDBC Driver implements JDBC APIs using Documentum's proprietary DQL (Document Query Language). On the other hand, the SCS JDBC Driver serves as a 'wrapper driver' that supports database connections with standard JDBC drivers for common database servers like Oracle, Sybase, etc.

Figure 4.7 should give you a brief idea about the Documentum JDBC Services architecture.

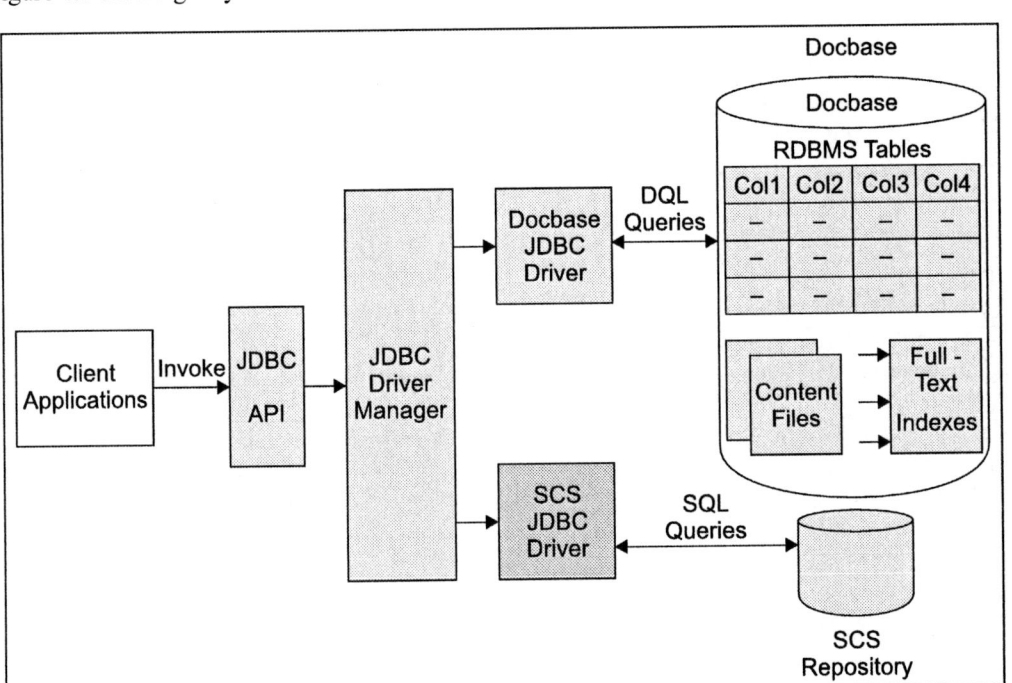

Figure 4.7: Documentum JDBC Services architecture

4.10 How do you Deploy Website Content to a Server Farm?

SDS or Site Deployment Services, formerly known as ContentCaster, is a configurable Java-based application that helps in deploying website content from an SCS Target server to directories on multiple local or remote servers.

4.10.1 Site Deployment Services

SDS is useful when one needs to synchronize and replicate the website content across multiple site locations.

Following are some of the key features of SDS:

- Supports integration with third-party load balancers
- Can recover from system failures even if the deployment operation halts mid-way
- Performs byte-level differencing, ensuring that only the changed bytes are updated during deployment
- Provides centralized monitoring of content updates

- Supports multi-stage deployment as well as multi-version rollback
- Supports automatic rollback of updates or installations
- Highly scalable as far as handling large volume and large size of files is concerned

Now that you understand a standard Documentum WCM system, you should analyze your specific business needs in order to evaluate which WCM tools cater to your requirements best.

Having said that, let us move on with our journey and get started with the basic Documentum infrastructure and installing/configuring the Documentum product suite for WCM architecture.

4.11 Summary

We started off this chapter describing scenarios where a web content management (WCM) system should be used in a business application and where it should be avoided. WCM systems add value to organizations that have content-heavy websites that need to be updated with business-critical data at any given point of time, without the dependence on IT staff. On the other hand, organizations that require infrequent updates to their websites and do not have the capacity or the budget for training and CMS infrastructure costs should not use WCM systems.

We went ahead to discuss a sample WCM architecture using the Documentum product suite consisting of entities and tools such as Web Publisher, Content Server, Documentum Administrator, Content Rendition Services, Site Caching Services, Documentum JDBC Services, and Site Deployment Services.

Content Server, discussed in the earlier chapters, is the foundation of Documentum architecture, providing the basic content management services required for a content management system.

Web Publisher (WP) is a content authoring tool providing a rich user interface for creating and managing content for a business website.

Documentum Administrator (DA) is a web-based tool used for performing several system administration tasks in the Documentum system.

Content Rendition Services (CRS) is a tool used for generating multiple renditions/formats of documents in a Documentum Docbase.

Site Caching Services (SCS) helps in publishing documents and their associated attributes from Docbase to a pre-configured website.

Documentum JDBC Services is a Documentum tool that supports most of the standard JDBC APIs and helps applications make connections to either Docbase or SCS repository and manipulate data contained in these.

Lastly we saw that Site Deployment Services (SDS) is a Java-based application that helps in deploying business website content from an SCS Target server to directories on multiple local or remote servers.

5

Setting Up the Documentum Suite

Enough of theory, right? Let us now get geared up for a plunge into the Documentum ocean!

The assumption here is that you have understood the need for a WCM system, have analyzed your business needs well, and are enthusiastic to haul out the most from the Documentum WCM product suite.

Make sure that you have procured the adequate licenses from Documentum before we begin our journey. Download the correct versions of the various Documentum products from Documentum's download site:

`https://documentum.subscribenet.com`

Remember that you will need to enter a valid login and password before you get access to the software installables.

Once you have downloaded the executables from the Documentum site, the most important question you face is where to start from. The other critical aspects that come to mind are: what is the correct installation sequence, any pre-requisites, things to be aware of, and so on and so forth.

Sit back and relax—quite a bit of homework has been done for you. Figure 5.1 is a chart you can follow for installation sequence. This should not be treated as the best possible Documentum installation sequence, but in most projects it will work out well.

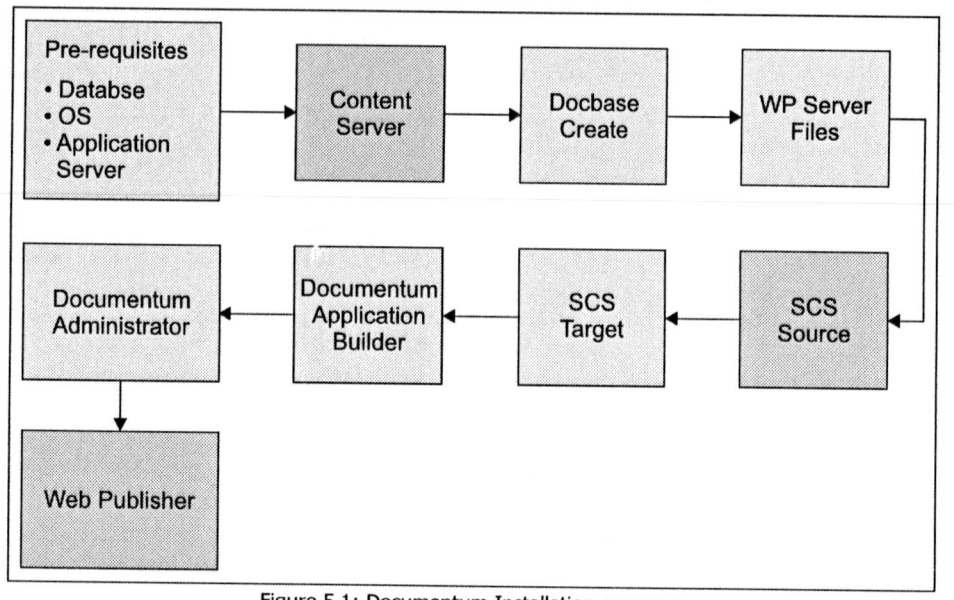

Figure 5.1: Documentum Installation sequence

5.1 Installing Content Server

We will be installing Content Server 5.2.5 SQL Server for Windows (base install) and then updating it with the SP2 (service pack 2) patch.

It is strongly recommended that you go through the complete Release Notes and Installation manuals for the Documentum software in question. What has been mentioned in the book is just the checklist that one should follow and what one needs to be specifically cognizant of.

To begin, download the following Content Server software installers from the Documentum site:

- `Content_Server_5.2.5_windows_sql.exe`
- `Content_Server_5.2.5_SP2_windows_sql.exe`

Please note that throughout the book we will be referring to the Documentum product versions 5.2.5 SP2 on a Windows environment with SQL Server DB, IIS Web server, and Tomcat application server. The installation steps and configurations will pertain to the specific product version 5.2.5 SP2 only. For an upgrade path or for knowing more about the latest Documentum suite versions, please get in touch with your local support for Documentum.

There can be only one Content Server installation on a Windows host. Do not attempt to install two content servers on the same Windows machine. However, this is possible in the case of a UNIX or Linux environment. Moreover, on UNIX and Linux systems, multiple installations can be created on a single host, including installations of different versions of the Server. For example, both 5.2 and 5.3 installations can exist on a single UNIX host!

Once Content Server has been installed, multiple Docbases can be created for the Content Server in question.

5.1.2 Prerequisites

Figure 5.2 mentions some of the prerequisites for starting the installation of Content Server:

Entity	Comments
Database	Should be available either locally or remotely and should be setup correctly.
	Code page should be set in accordance with Content Server's UTF-8 code page. For SQL Server you can use any collation (i.e. code page)
	Case-sensitive SQL Server should be installed with row-level locking.
	SQL Server client should be installed on the Content Server machine irrespective of whether DB is local or remote.
	Docbase owner (i.e. the Database user) is the account used to connect to underlying RDBMS. This should be available.
SMTP Server	SMTP server should be available on the network or be present on the Windows 2000 machine.
Network	Properly set up TCP/IP network should be available.
Environment Variables	Set the PATH system variable to point to 'Java'
Installation Owner	The user who installs Content Server software should have a valid OS account.
	Limitations for installation owner's user name: Consists of numbers, letters, hyphens (-) and underscores (_). The first character should be a letter. All characters must be ASCII.
	If SQL Server DB is installed in a different domain from Content Server, the installation owner should be a valid user in the remote domain.
Hardware	700 MB hard disk space, 512 MB RAM, and minimum 400 MHz CPU.
Java Runtime Environment	Sun JRE 1.3.1, 1.4.1 (and IBM J2RE 1.3.1 for AIX OS)
Others	For supported combinations of Windows OS, RDBMS versions and JRE, please refer to Release Notes from Documentum.

Figure 5.2: Prerequisites for installation of Content Server

> Do not use spaces in the name of the installation directory for Documentum. For example, do not install under `c:\Documentum Installation\`.

No further delays! Let us kick-off the installation of Content Server 5.2.5 and then subsequently install the SP2 patch over it.

5.2 Installing Content Server 5.2.5

Follow these instructions to get Content Server installed:

1. Log in as the installation owner and extract `Content_Server_5.2.5_windows_sql.exe` on the Content Server machine and run `ContentServer.exe`.

2. Click the Next button.

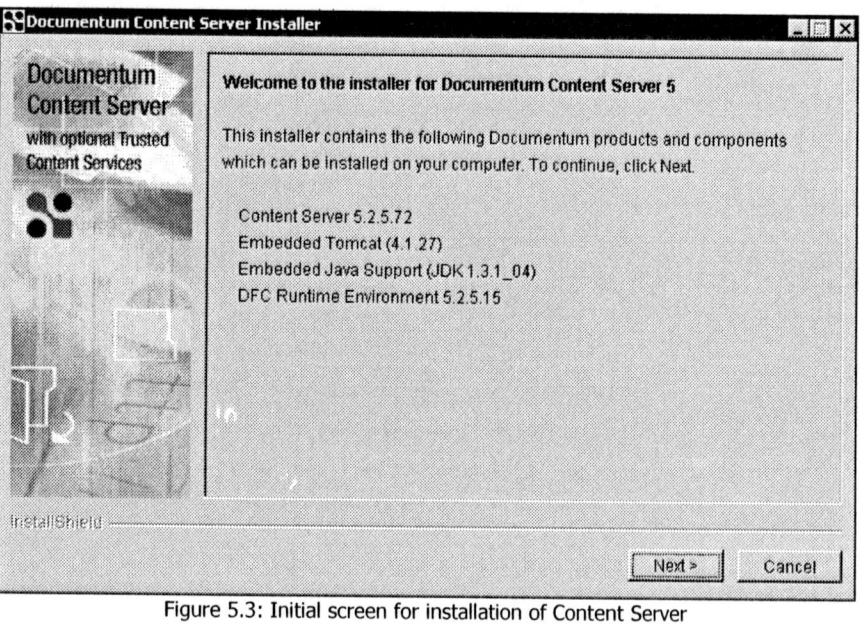

Figure 5.3: Initial screen for installation of Content Server

3. Choose the installation directory or continue with the default shown.

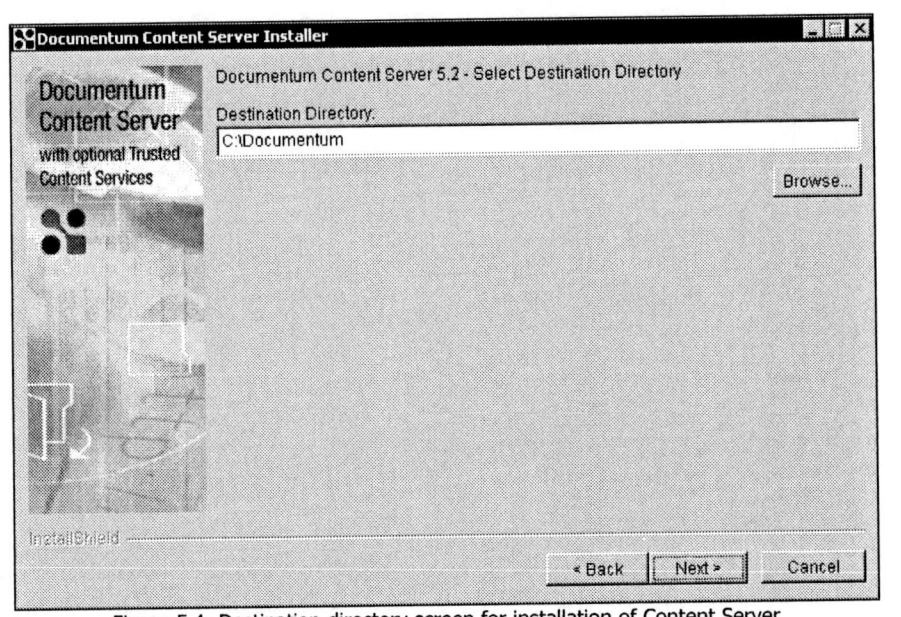

Figure 5.4: Destination directory screen for installation of Content Server

4. Choose the DFC destination directory or continue with the default shown.

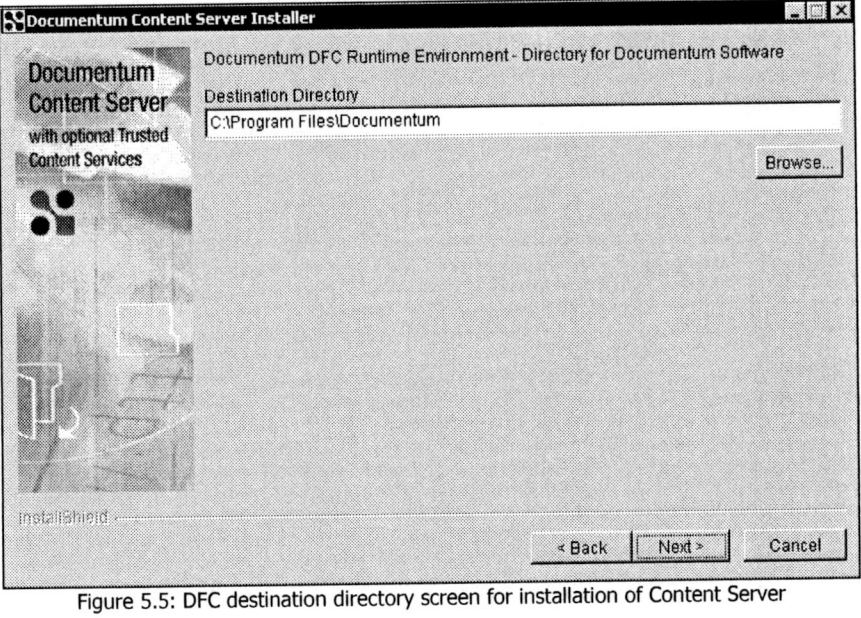

Figure 5.5: DFC destination directory screen for installation of Content Server

5. Choose the user directory or continue with the default shown.

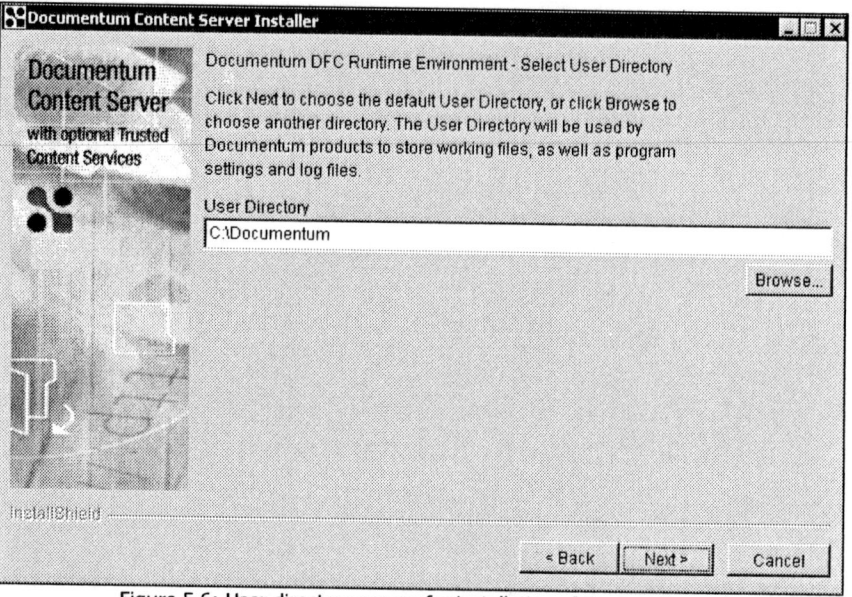

Figure 5.6: User directory screen for installation of Content Server

6. Provide the name of the DocBroker host and port number or choose the default. Documentum defaults the current Content Server machine as DocBroker host.

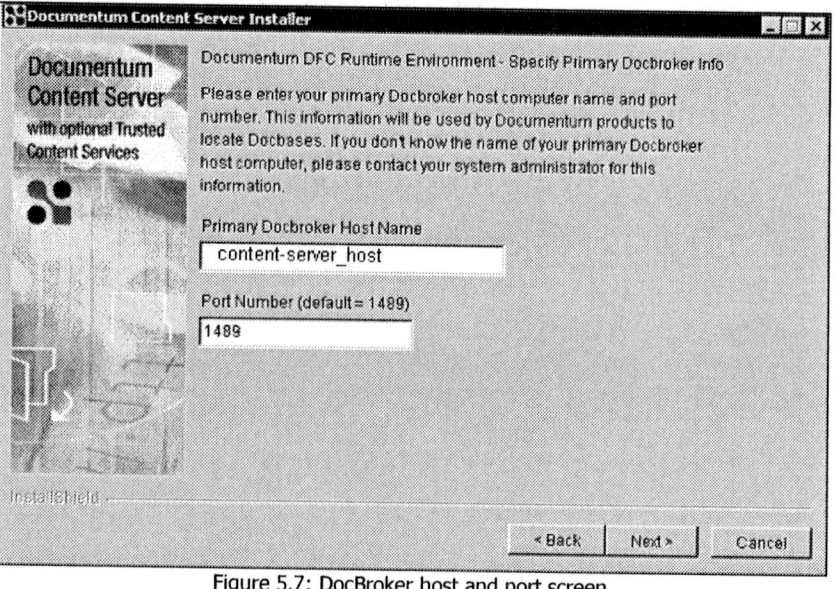

Figure 5.7: DocBroker host and port screen

7. If required, optionally choose to install the DFC developer documentation and click the Next button.

8. If required, optionally enable Trusted Content Services (TCS) and provide the license key. Then click the Next button.

9. If required, optionally enable Content Services for EMC Centera and provide the license key. Then click the Next button.

10. Optionally provide alternativee port numbers for starting and shutting Apache Tomcat server (available with Content Server installation) or choose the defaults. Then click the Next button.

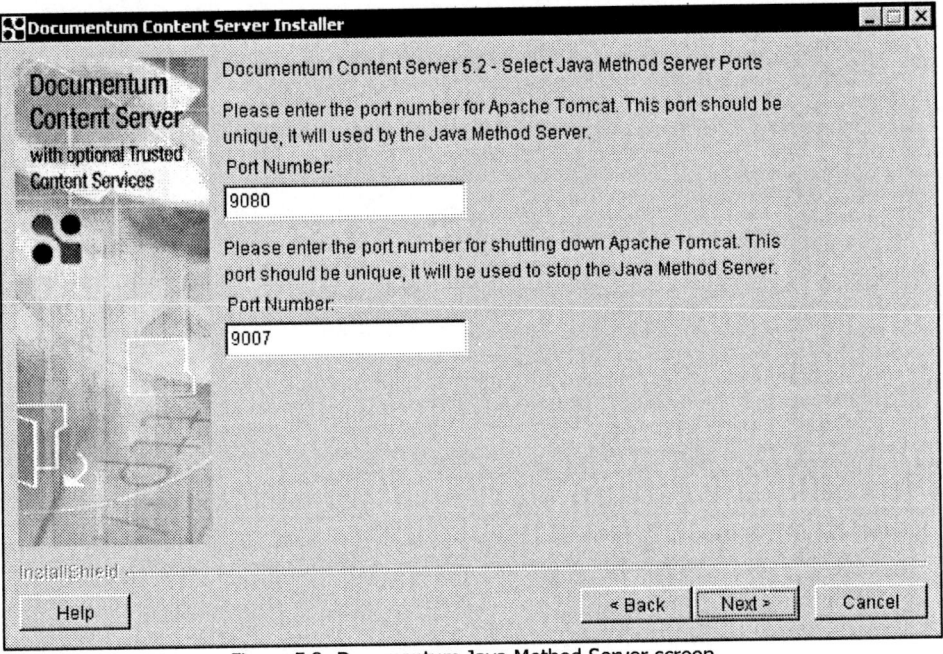

Figure 5.8: Documentum Java Method Server screen

11. Choose the Configure server now option if you need to continue creating the Docbase. We will first complete the Content Server installation and then upgrade to 5.2.5 SP2. Later we will create the Docbase.

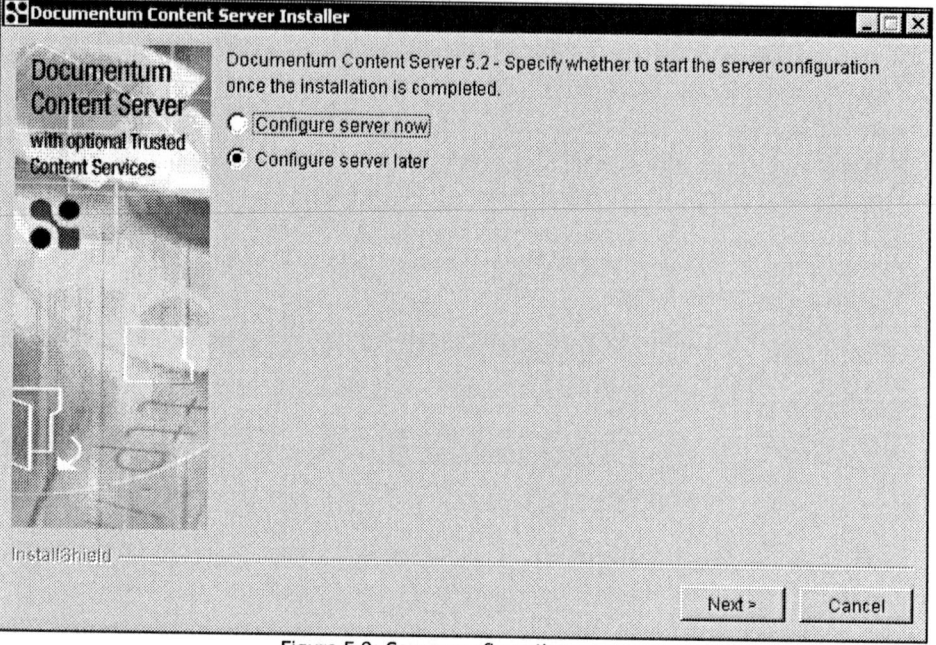

Figure 5.9: Server configuration screen

12. The system needs to be restarted after the installation is done. We will first install the Content Server 5.2.5 SP2 patch and then restart the machine.

5.3 Installing Content Server 5.2.5 SP2

1. Log in as the installation owner and extract
    `Content_Server_5.2.5_SP2_windows_sql.exe` on the Content Server machine and
    run `ContentServerSP.exe`.

2. Click the Next button.

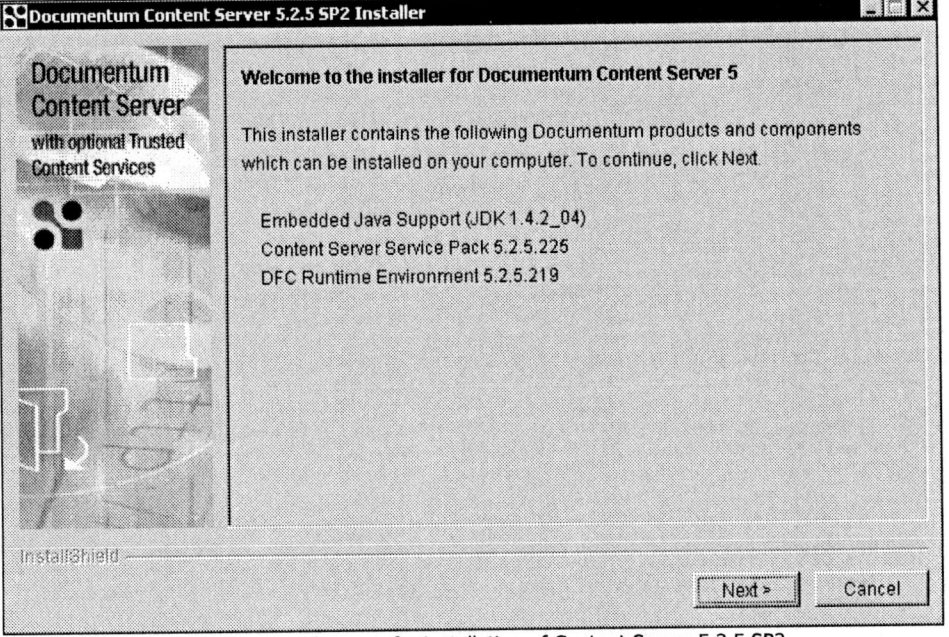

Figure 5.10: Initial screen for installation of Content Server 5.2.5 SP2

3. If required, optionally choose to install the DFC developer documentation and click the Next button.

4. Stop the following services on the Content Server machine:

   o Any existing Docbases
   o Any existing DocBrokers
   o Documentum Java Method Server

5. We will finish off the installation and later configure the server (i.e. create Docbases)

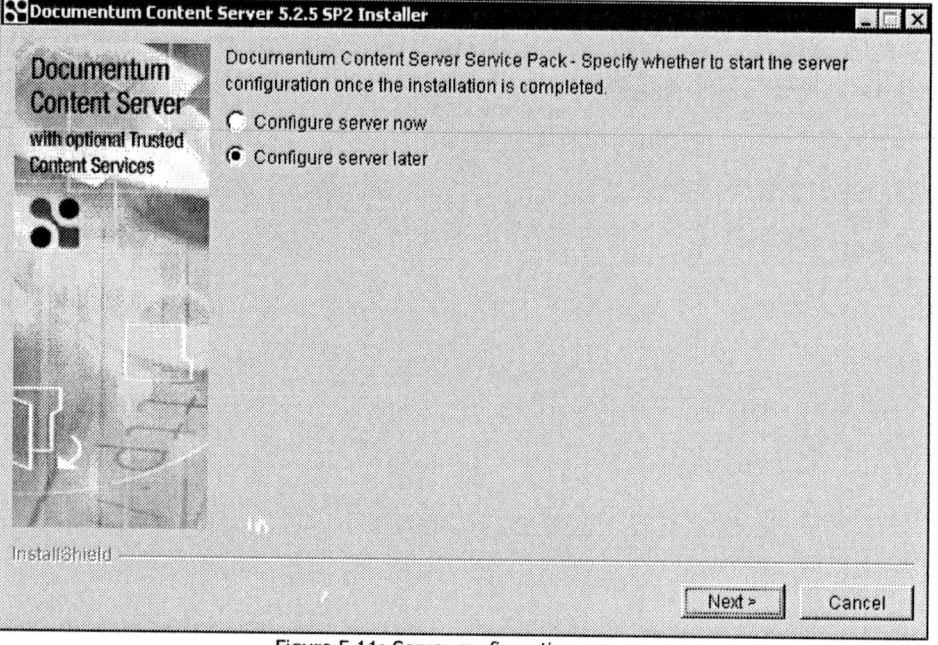

Figure 5.11: Server configuration screen

6. Restart the Content Server host machine.

That's it! We are done with installing Content Server 5.2.5 SP2. In the subsequent chapter we will create and configure a Docbase so that we can start developing our custom objects in the newly created Docbase.

5.4 Summary

We began this chapter by discussing the product installation sequence for a simple WCM system involving the following tools:

- Content Server
- Site Caching Services
- Documentum Application Builder
- Documentum Administrator
- Web Publisher

We discussed the prerequisites for installing Documentum Content Server and then discussed the steps involved in installing Content Server 5.2.5 SP2 on a Windows platform.

6

Creating Our First Docbase

We have set up Content Server in the previous chapter and are all set to create our first Docbase. Once the Docbase is ready, we can create our custom DocApps in the Docbase and play around with our custom-defined objects.

First things first—let's come up with a good (and of course rational) name for your Docbase before we jump ahead. In this book, dev_doc is the name we have chosen. Our custom Docbase will be referred to by this name throughout this book.

6.1 Creating a Docbase

As with almost all commercial software, there are a handful of prerequisites for setting up a Docbase. There is no harm repeating that one should always consult the concerned Release Notes in their entirety to avoid any unforeseen hiccups during the installation process.

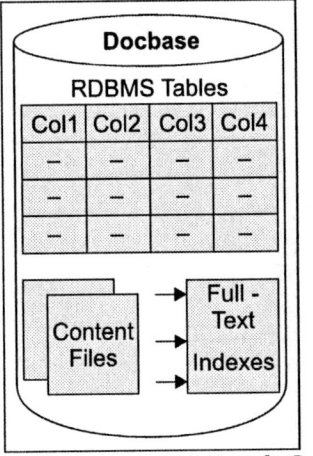

Figure 6.1: Logical representation of a Docbase

Figure 6.2 lists some points to be borne in mind before commencing with Docbase creation:

Entity	Comments
Content Server	Should be setup correctly before creating a Docbase.
Windows Regional Settings	Need to be set to specify a four-digit date format.
Docbase Name	Limitations: Maximum length is 32 characters. Can consist of letters, numbers, and underscores. The first character should be a letter. Should not contain white spaces or non-alphanumeric characters. Cannot have the name "docu". Must be unique in the case of multiple Docbases on the same Content Server.
Docbase ID	Limitations: Must be a number in the range 1 to 16777215. Should not start with zero (0). Must be unique in the case of multiple Docbases on the same Content Server.
Docbase Owner	Limitations for installation owner's user name: Consists of numbers, letters, hyphens, and underscores. The first character should be a letter. All characters must be ASCII. Password should consist of numbers, letters, periods, hyphens, and underscores. Must be unique in case of multiple Docbases on the same Content Server.
ODBC Data Source	Should be correctly configured in case of SQL Server.

Figure 6.2: Prerequisites for setting up a Docbase

1. Set up a DSN (Data Source Name) on the Content Server machine, so that the Docbase can connect and talk to the underlying SQL Server RDBMS. On your Windows machine, go to Programs | Administrative Tools | Data Sources (ODBC). Choose System DSN and click the Add button.

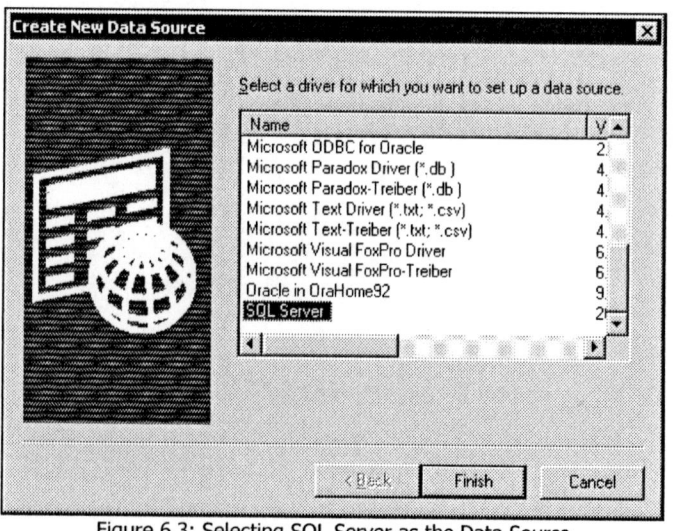

Figure 6.3: Selecting SQL Server as the Data Source

After choosing SQL Server, click the Finish button.

2. Specify the DSN name and a short description. Also provide the host name of the SQL Server DB. In this example, SQL Server was installed locally on the same machine as the Content Server.

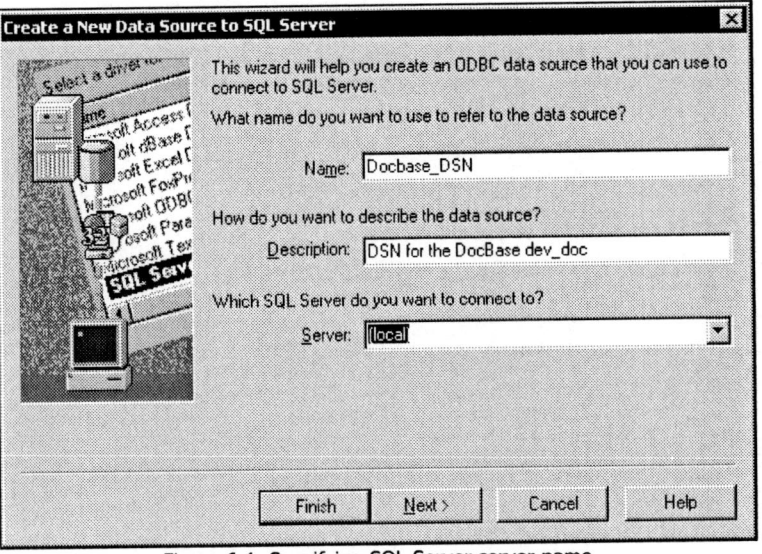

Figure 6.4: Specifying SQL Server server name

3. In the case of SQL Server authentication, provide a valid login ID and password.

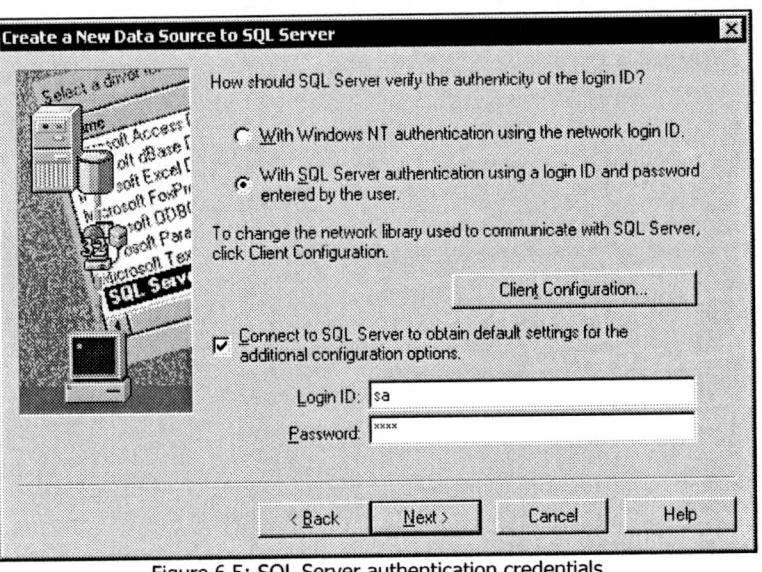

Figure 6.5: SQL Server authentication credentials

4. Do not change the default database or the language of SQL Server system messages unless required. Click the Next button till you reach the Finish button.

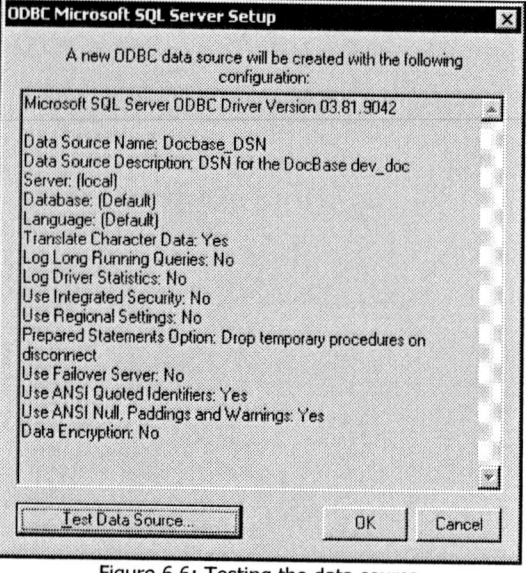

Figure 6.6: Testing the data source

5. Click on Test Data Source to check whether the database connection can be established correctly. If this works fine, click OK.

The created DSN now shows up along with other DSNs in the System DSN tab. Finally click on OK. We have successfully created a DSN for connecting to a SQL Server database.

6. Log in as the installation owner on the Content Server machine and go to Programs | Documentum | Documentum Server Manager. From the Documentum Server Manager panel, select the Utilities tab and click on Server Configuration.

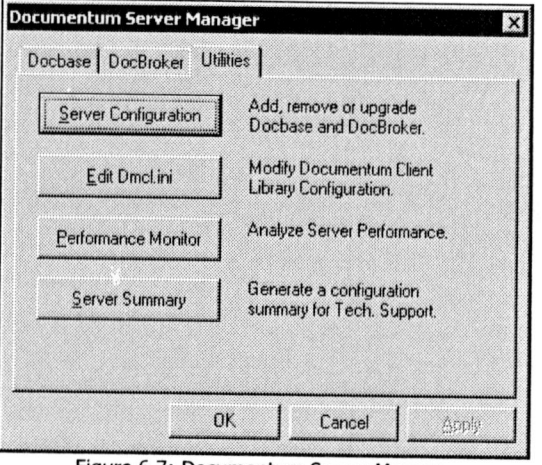

Figure 6.7: Documentum Server Manager

The following error message might be seen if the domain is unavailable due to connectivity issues or if some changes have been made to the domain the user is a member of:

"Unable to initialize admin dll (OSEnv)"

7. Enter the installation owner's password and click Next.

8. If required, optionally enable the Trusted Content Services (TCS) and provide the license key. Then click the Next button.

9. If required, optionally enable Content Services for EMC Centera and provide the license key. Then click the Next button.

10. Select the configuration type:

- **Express Configuration**
    - Quick. Less information needs to be provided during the installation procedure. Default parameters provided by Documentum during setup.
    - Limits the amount of customization we can do to the Docbase and Content Server.

- **Custom Configuration**
    - Lengthier mechanism requiring more inputs from user during installation.
    - Allows customization of Docbase configuration scripts, data files, etc.

This example uses the Express Configuration type to create the Docbase.

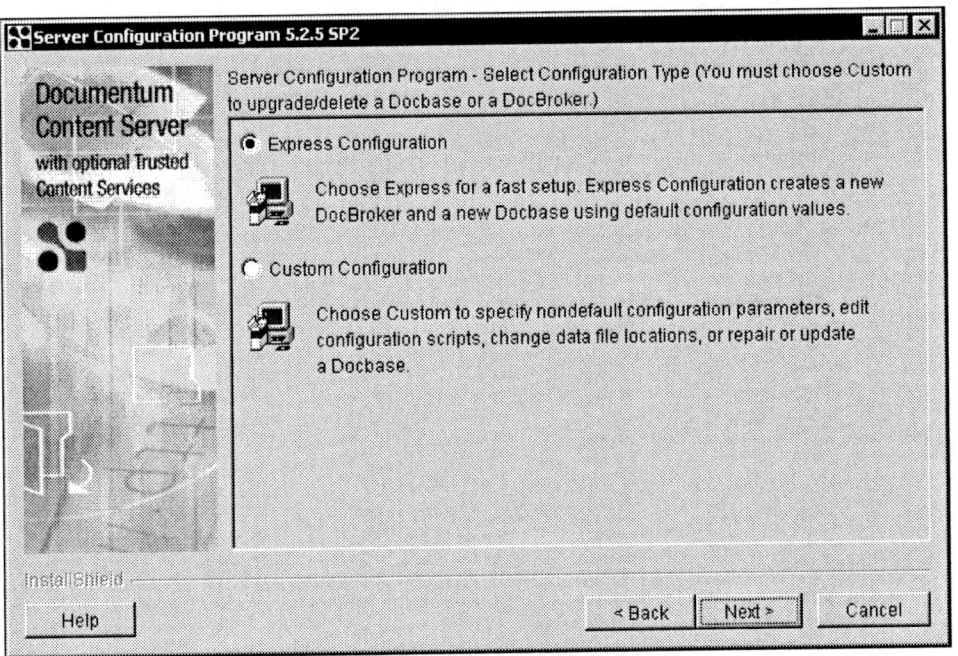

Figure 6.8: Choosing configuration type

11. If required, optionally choose Content Storage Services. Then click the Next button.

12. Provide a valid Docbase Name and Docbase ID (as per the limitations specified in the beginning of the chapter). Choose Docbase Size, Windows Authentication Domain, and specify whether the Windows Service Startup Type for managing the Docbase should be automatic or manual.

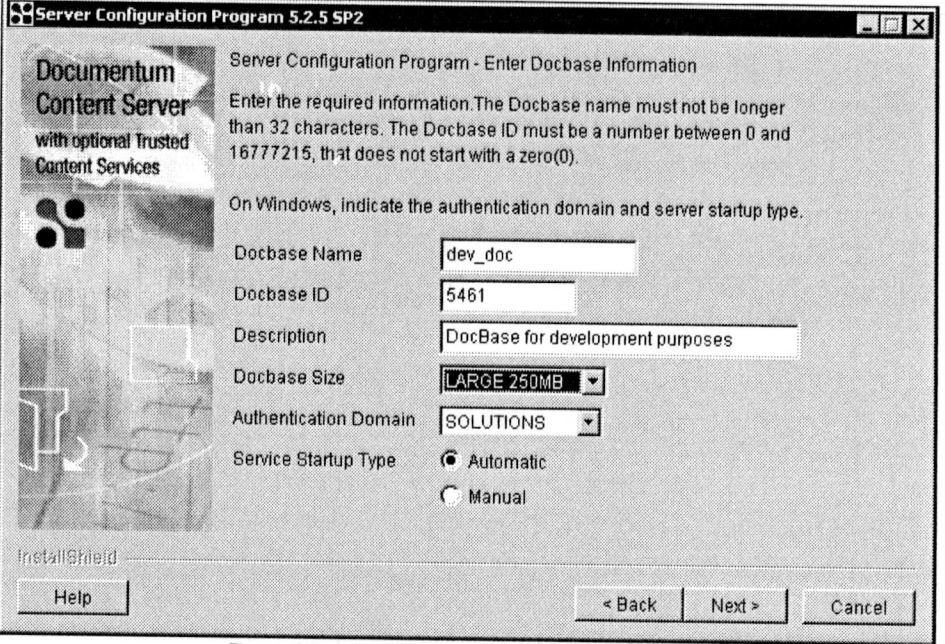

Figure 6.9: Specifying Docbase parameters for setup

13. Either allow Documentum to create/configure a Docbase owner (database user) for you or choose an existing SQL server database account if you have already made one.

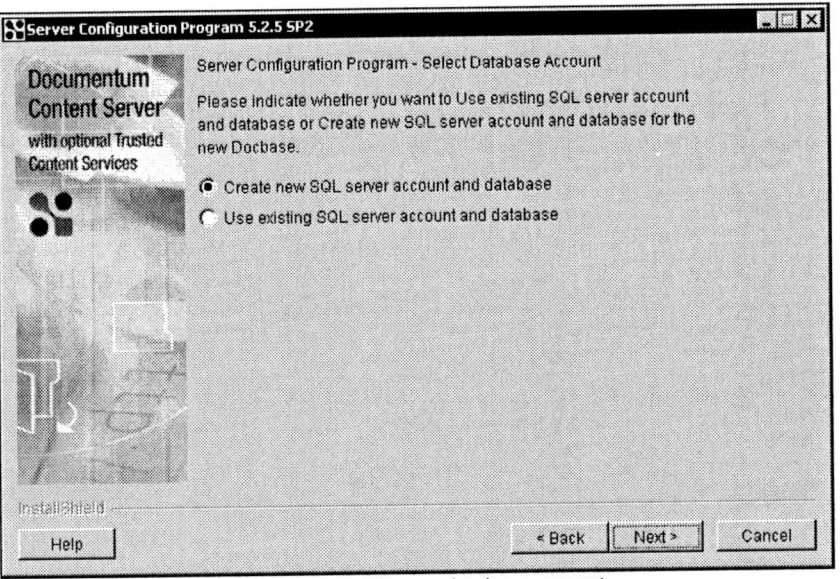

Figure 6.10: Setting up database account

14. Select the DSN for database connectivity (created in the initial few steps).

   In this example, the defaults provided by Documentum for Docbase owner name (the name of the specified Docbase) have been chosen. The default database name is in the following format: DM_<specified Docbase name>_docbase

15. Provide the Docbase owner password and SQL Server DB administrator user name and password.

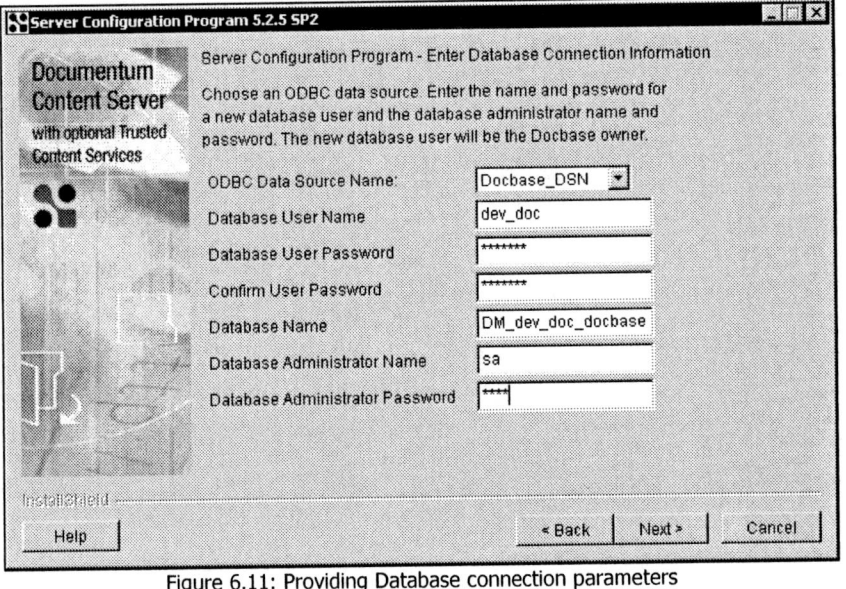

Figure 6.11: Providing Database connection parameters

After the Docbase has been created and if someone has unknowingly changed the password for the Docbase owner (DB owner), then the following error message is seen during Docbase startup:

[DM_SESSION_I_RETRYING_DATABASE_CONNECTION] info: "The following error was encountered trying to get a database connection: STATE=28000, CODE=18456, MSG=[Microsoft][ODBC SQL Server Driver][SQL Server]Login failed for user 'dev_doc'.

16. Provide an SMTP server name or IP address and a valid email address for the Documentum installation owner. Click the Next button.

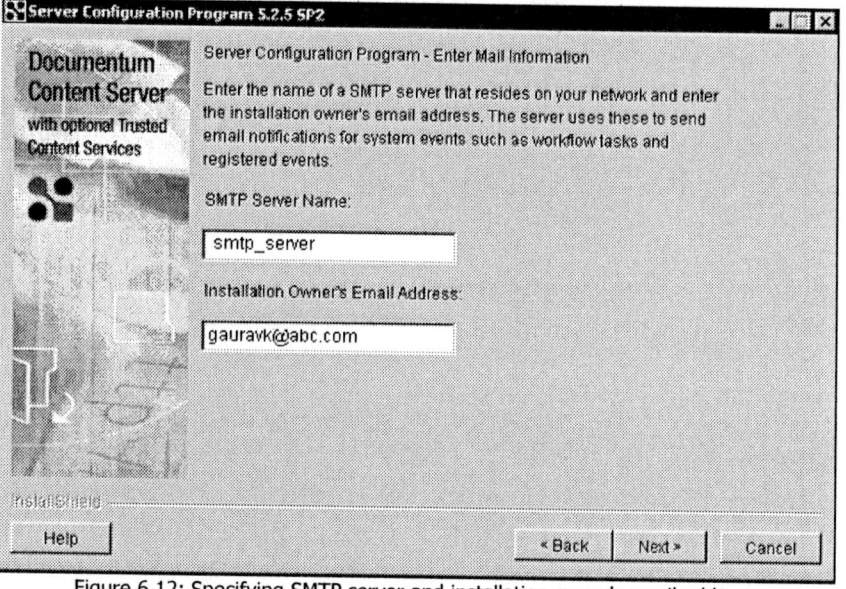

Figure 6.12: Specifying SMTP server and installation owner's email address

17. Choose the WebPublisher DocApp to be installed on the Docbase in case we need to use Web Publisher with the Docbase in question.

18. This completes Docbase creation and the newly created Docbase shows up in the Documentum Server Manager panel under the Docbase tab.

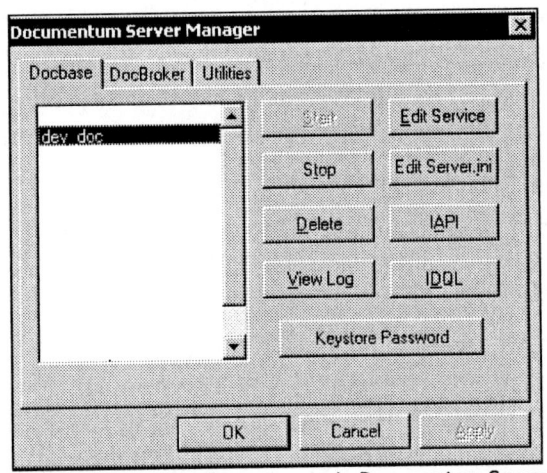

Figure 6.13: Newly created Docbase as seen in Documentum Server Manager

The following error message is seen during Docbase startup if Docbase was configured on a Content Server with case-insensitive SQL Server:

[DM_SESSION_I_INIT_BEGIN]info: "Initialize Crypto Objects."

[DM_SESSION_E_INIT_FAILURE1]error: "Failure to complete Crypto Objects initialization."
[DM_SERVER_I_START_ID]info: "Docbase dev_doc was not successfully opened.

You can create multiple Docbases on the same Content Server with different names to serve the purpose of a development Docbase and a test Docbase (for example). Also, you can create multiple servers for a single Docbase so that request processing is spread across multiple servers to achieve performance gains. However, a detailed discussion regarding such configuration is beyond the scope of this book.

6.2 Installing Web Publisher Server Files and DocApp

Once the Docbase is ready, we can install Web Publisher Server Files on the new Docbase so that Documentum WebPublisher DocApp is installed and available for our use.

Many people confuse 'Web Publisher Server Files' installation with an application server installation. Please note that Web Publisher install contains two components:

- Web Publisher installation

- Web Publisher Server Files installation

Web Publisher installation is typically done on a separate machine hosting the application server. On the other hand, Web Publisher Server Files are installed on the Content Server machine.

Please note that Web Publisher Server Files installation is required since we are going to use Web Publisher web client for entering content and need default Web Publisher objects to work with. The default Web Publisher objects are available from WebPublisher DocApp, which is configured when we install Web Publisher Server Files on the Content Server host.

Documentum recommends installing Web Publisher Server Files and DocApp as the Content Server installation owner. On Windows, the Web Publisher Server Files are installed at the following location on the Content Server:

`%DM_HOME%`, for example: `C:\Documentum\product\<product version>`

6.2.1 What does Web Publisher Server Files Contain?

'Web Publisher Server Files' contains `wcm` and `wcmMethods` JAR files containing some Java methods that are run on the Content Server by Documentum Java method server. These methods call classes that are required to be executed from Web Publisher workflow activities.

6.2.2 What does WebPublisher DocApp Contain?

'WebPublisher DocApp' contains some base Web Publisher objects required by Web Publisher to work with the Docbase in question.

For example:

- Web Publisher jobs and methods
- Web Publisher workflow templates
- Web Publisher lifecycles
- Web Publisher object types
- WebPublisher User Default ACL
- Web Publisher groups: content author, content manager, web developer, and administrator
- Web Publisher roles: `wcm_content_author_role`, `wcm_content_manager_role`, `wcm_web_developer_role`, and `wcm_administrator_role`

6.3 Beginning Installation

First download `web_Publisher_Server_Files_5.2.5_SP2_windows.exe` from the Documentum site.

1. Log in as the installation owner and extract `Web_Publisher_Server_Files_5.2.5_SP2_windows.exe` on the Content Server machine and run `WPServerWinSetup.exe`.
2. Click the Next button.

Figure 6.14: Initial screen for installing Web Publisher server files

3. Accept the license agreements and click the Next button.

4. The path where Web Publisher Server Files will be installed is shown. Click Next. In our case, the default location shown was c:\Documentum\product\5.2\bin.

5. Choose the Docbase where the Web Publisher Server Files/DocApp need to be installed. The example shows that the new Docbase we had just created has been selected.

   Provide the installation owner name and password and click Next.

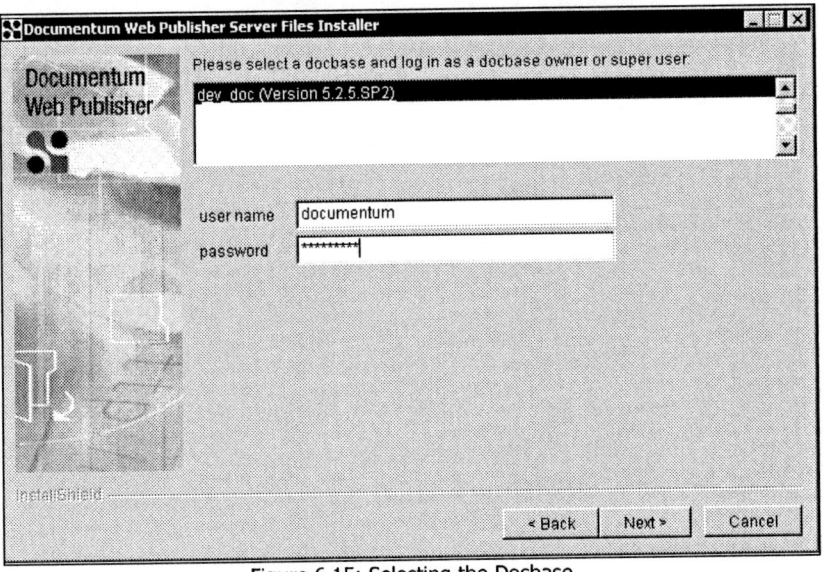

Figure 6.15: Selecting the Docbase

6. Select the checkbox for WebPublisher DocApp and click Next.

   You may additionally choose Accelera DocApp in case you need to work with sample Docbase objects provided by Documentum for its sample website: http://www.Accelera.com.

   Note that if you choose to install Accelera DocApp, you must install the WebPublisher DocApp as well in order for the Accelera application to work properly.

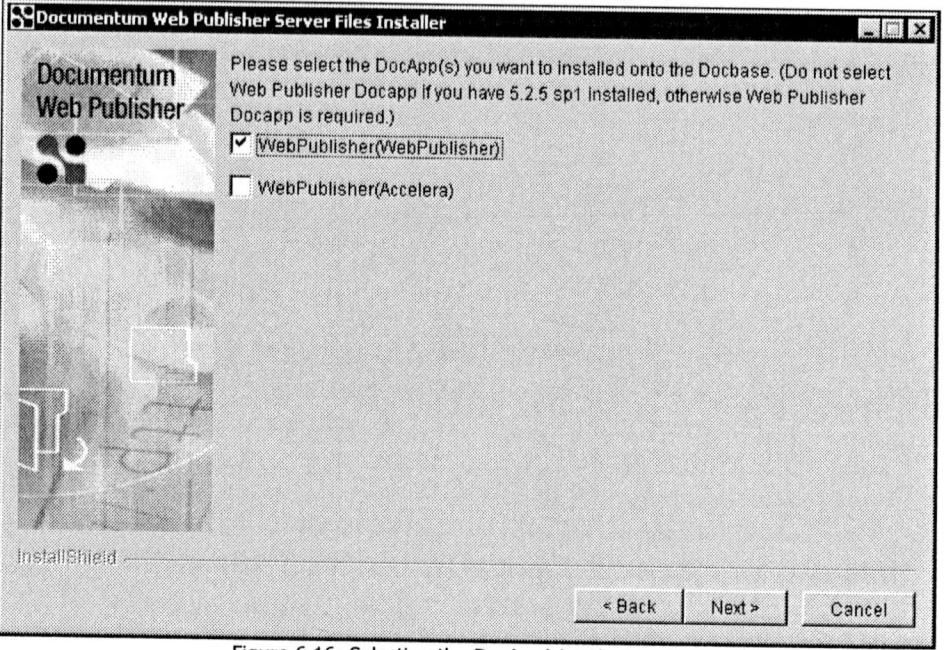

Figure 6.16: Selecting the DocApp(s) to be installed

7. WebPublisher DocApp installation commences on the chosen Docbase (dev_doc in our case).

   A DocApp log file is created by the installer, containing information about the installed objects and mentioning warning and errors, if any.

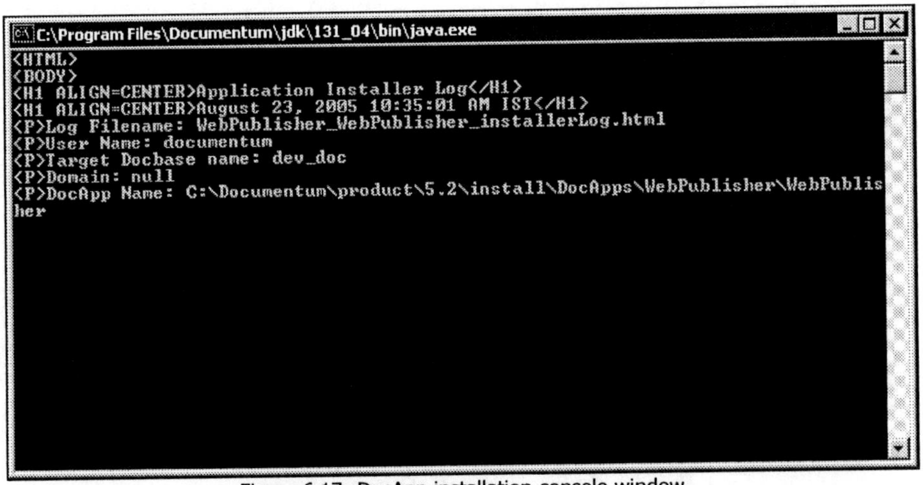

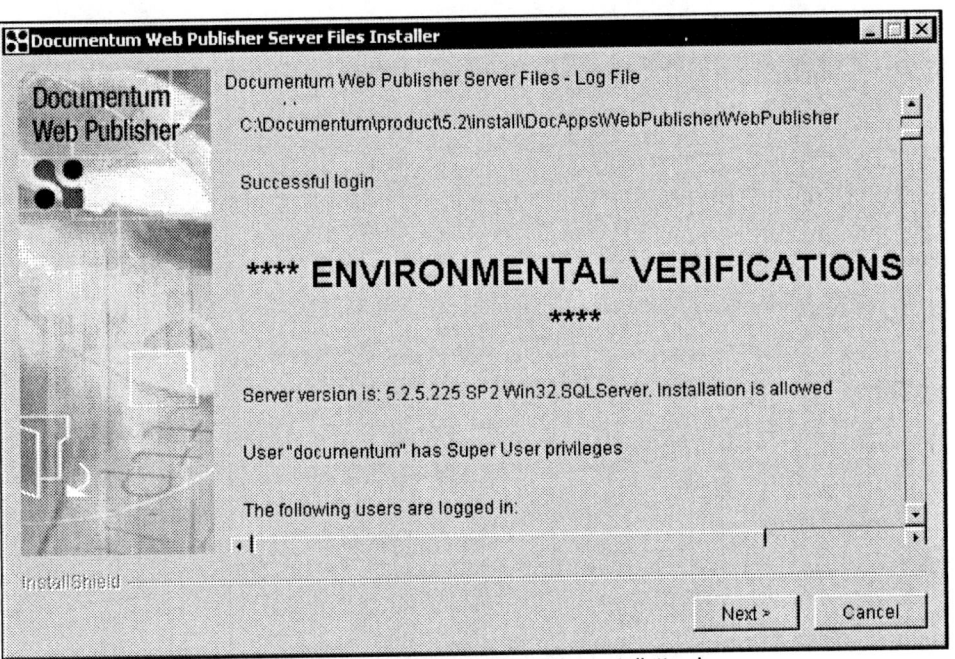

Figure 6.17: DocApp installation console window

8. WebPublisher DocApp installation might take a couple of minutes. Once done, the DocApp installation log is displayed. If there are no errors shown, click Next.

Figure 6.18: Web Publisher Server Files installation log

9. After the installation completes, stop and restart Documentum Java Method Server on the Content Server host.

6.4 Stopping and Starting Docbase and DocBroker

Documentum Server Manager is installed when Content Server has been installed and set up. It is a simple interface that can be used to start and stop DocBrokers and Docbases. In fact, Documentum Server Manager can be used to perform a host of other operations as well, such as:

- Executing DQL and Server API commands
- Viewing Docbase server logs and DocBroker log files
- Modifying server.ini and dmcl.ini files
- Analyzing server performance through performance monitor

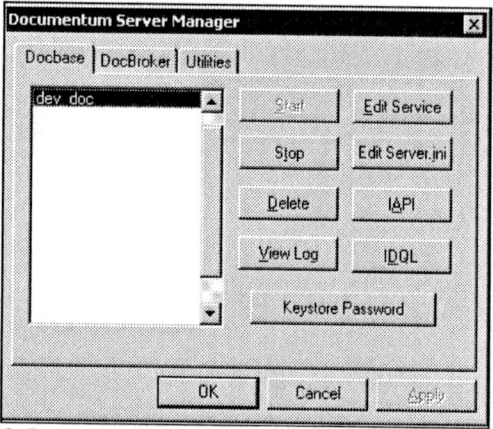

Figure 6.19: Documentum Server Manager displaying existing Docbase(s)

You can stop a running Docbase service by selecting the Docbase in question as shown in figure 6.19 and clicking the Stop button. Alternatively, you can start a stopped Docbase by clicking the Start button.

Similarly, by switching over to the DocBroker tab in Documentum Server Manager, you can start and stop the DocBroker(s) as shown in figure 6.20.

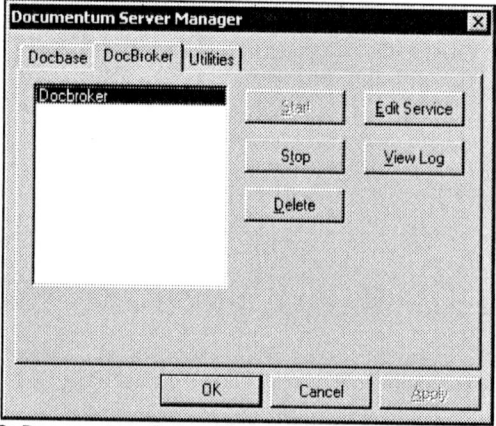

Figure 6.20: Documentum Server Manager displaying existing DocBroker(s)

6.5 dmcl.ini

The dmcl.ini file defines configuration information for client applications and each client needs to have a copy of this file. The location of this file depends on the Documentum client as well as the host machine of the client.

Figure 6.21 lists some of the keys defined in the dmcl.ini file along with their interpretations:

Key	Default value	Explanation
client_caching_enabled	T	This by default allows clients to persistently cache query results and objects.
cache_queries	F	If the key client_caching_enabled is set to False, setting this key to True allows caching of only query results.
client_cache_size	-1	This is used to define the maximum client cache size and its value is interpreted as the number of objects.
connect_pooling_enabled	F	This is used to enable connection pooling.
max_collection_count	10	This controls the maximum number of query collection IDs for a session.
max_session_count	10	This controls the maximum number of sessions allowed for any given client application. Make sure this is in agreement with the concurrent_sessions key in server.ini.
trace_file	Server log	This controls the path and file name of the log of DMCL stack trace when a DMCL exception occurs.
trace_level	3	This sets the tracing level for DMCL traces.

Figure 6.21: Some keys in the dmcl.ini file

6.6 server.ini

As opposed to the dmcl.ini file, which contains configuration information required by clients, the information in the server.ini file is used by the server. The location of server.ini on a Windows Content Server host is:

$DOCUMENTUM\dba\config\<Docbase name>

In our case, the location of server.ini is: C:\Documentum\dba\config\dev_doc.

Figure 6.22 mentions some of the keys defined in `server.ini` along with their interpretations.

Key	Default value	Explanation
client_session_timeout	5 minutes	This defines the duration for which the server waits for a client communication before disconnecting the session.
concurrent_sessions	100	This controls the maximum number of sessions the server can handle at a given time.
database_conn		This contains the database connection string required by Content Server in order to establish connection with the RDBMS server. (Required by Oracle and DB2 and not by Sybase and SQL Server.)
database_name		This identifies the database or tablespace in the RDBMS. (Required by Sybase and SQL Server and not by Oracle and DB2.)
distinct_query_results	F	This can be used to direct the server to return duplicate rows in Query results. Setting to True directs the server to return only distinct rows without any duplicates.
login_ticket_timeout	5 minutes	This determines the duration for which a login ticket remains valid after it has been generated.
mail_notification	T	This controls whether email messages are sent to users when a work item or an event has been queued.

Figure 6.22: Some keys in server.ini file

That's it! We have created our first Docbase and installed WebPublisher DocApp over it, making it ready to be used by Web Publisher. As per the installation roadmap shown in figure 5.1 in Chapter 5, we can now go ahead and install Site Caching Services (SCS) Source and Target, so that the Docbase contents can be published out of the Documentum system.

6.7 Summary

In this chapter we discussed creating a Docbase in Documentum Content Server. We briefly talked about the prerequisites for creating a Documentum Docbase. We then discussed the steps to create a DSN (Data Source Name) for the Docbase to connect to its underlying database.

We later discussed the detailed steps to create a Docbase and then installed Web Publisher Server Files on the newly created Docbase. The server files installation sets up WebPublisher DocApp and objects so that the new Docbase can function well with the Web Publisher application.

We also saw how to start and stop Docbases and DocBrokers via a simple Documentum Server Manager interface and finally discussed some important keys in the `dmcl.ini` and `server.ini` files.

7

Setting Up Publishing

Having set up the Docbases, we can now configure Documentum Site Caching Services (or SCS in short) in order to publish content and attributes from Documentum to our websites. This requires the installation of Documentum SCS software in the form of two components:

- SCS Source component (installed on the Content Server machine that host the Docbase(s)
- SCS Target component (installed on the web servers)

You might want to quickly go through our discussion on publishing via SCS services in Chapter 4 to recall the architecture.

Assuming that you understand the basic flow of publishing from Documentum to websites, we can proceed with our installation. We will first install SCS Source 5.2.5 on the Content Server machine and then upgrade it with the SP2 patch.

Once the SCS Source software has been installed properly, we will install SCS Target 5.2.5 on the web server and then upgrade it with the SP2 patch.

7.1 SCS Source 5.2.5

You can run SCS Source and Target on machines with different operating systems and databases. For example, you could have the SCS Source configured on a Windows machine with SQL Server database and have the SCS Target on a UNIX machine with Oracle database. However, you should ensure that this is a combination certified by Documentum as per the published Release Notes.

7.1.1 Prerequisites

Figure 7.1 lists some of the prerequisites we must take care of before installing SCS Source on Content Server:

Entity	Comments
Content Server	Content Server should be set up properly and available before installing SCS Source.
	Content Servers and Docbases in the server installation should be running.
Database	The database instance used by the Docbase should be accessible
Hardware	80 MB hard disk space, 512 MB RAM, and minimum 400 MHz CPU.
	Post installation, the host should have adequate disk space for storing the published data (export data set)
Others	For supported combinations of Windows OS, RDBMS versions and JRE, please refer to Release Notes from Documentum.

Figure 7.1: Prerequisites for installing SCS Source

To begin, download the following SCS software installers from the Documentum site:

- `Site_Caching_Services_5.2.5_windows_source.exe`
- `Site_Caching_Services_5.2.5_SP2_all.zip`

7.1.2 Installing SCS Source 5.2.5

We will first install SCS Source 5.2.5 on the Content Server host and then upgrade it with the service pack 2 (SP2) patch.

1. Log in to Content Server host as the Documentum installation owner, extract `Site_Caching_Services_5.2.5_windows_source.exe`, and run the following executable: `SCSSourceWinSuiteSetup.exe`.

2. Click the Next button.

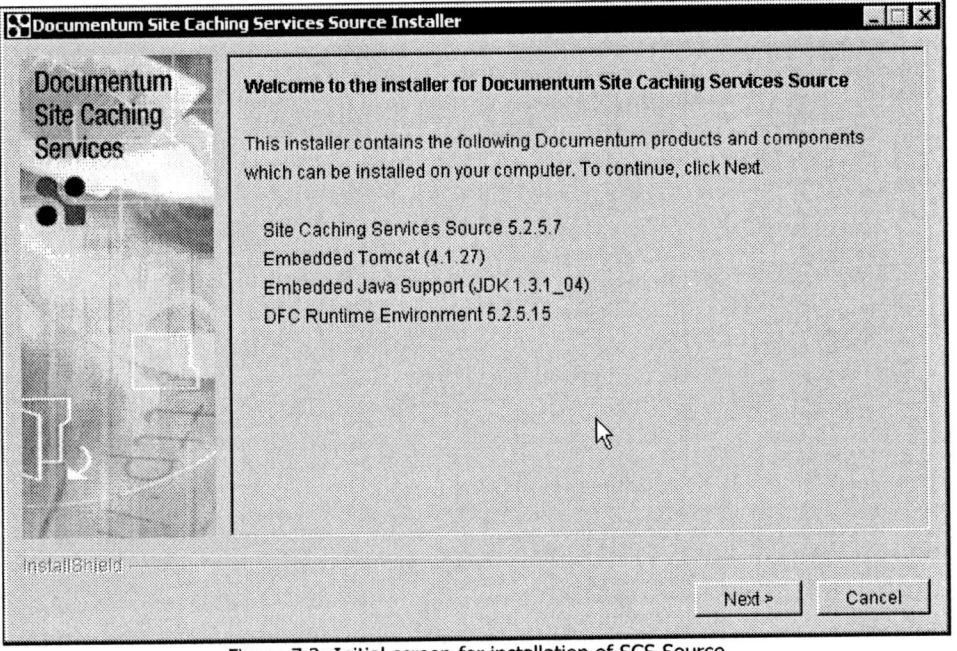

Figure 7.2: Initial screen for installation of SCS Source

3. Accept the license agreements and click the Next button.

4. Optionally choose to install developer documentation and click the Next button.

5. Provide the password for the Content Server installation owner and click the Next button.

6. Provide the primary port numbers for the SCS Source Tomcat instance and administrator instance. We can specify ports that are currently not in use by any other application, or use the defaults provided by the installer. Click the Next button.

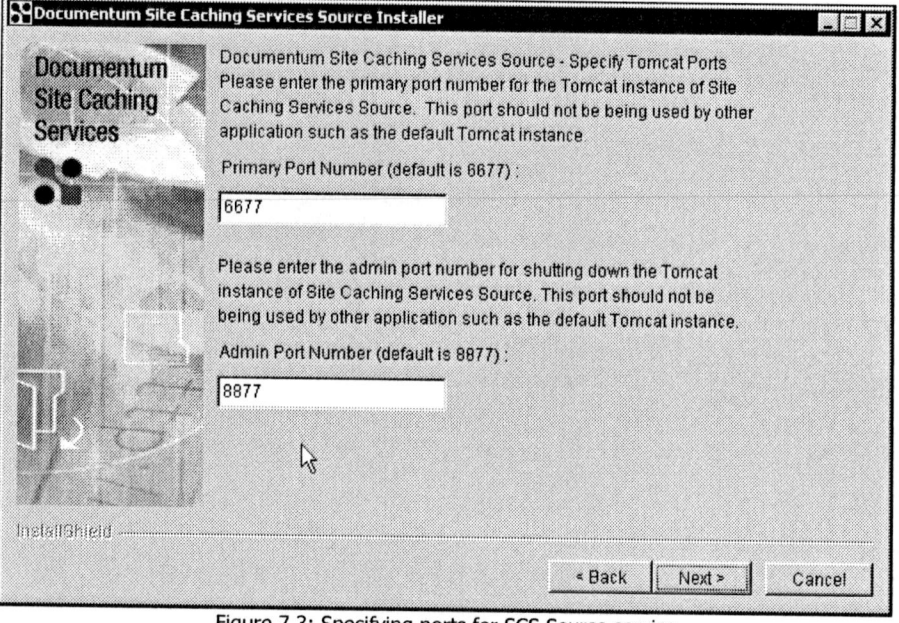

Figure 7.3: Specifying ports for SCS Source service

7.   The components to be installed are shown. Click the Next button.

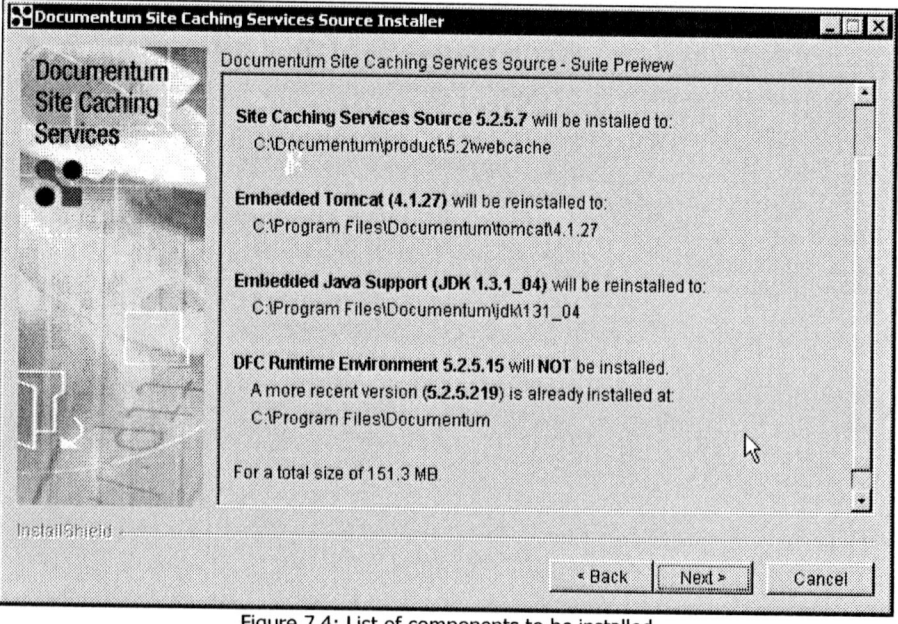

Figure 7.4: List of components to be installed

8. The SCS Source installation program requires configuration of existing Docbases on the Content Server machine. Note that we can always skip this option and later configure the Docbase in question by running the executable config.exe from %DM_HOME%\webcache\install.DM_HOME% on a Windows machine would typically be: C:\Documentum\product\<product version>

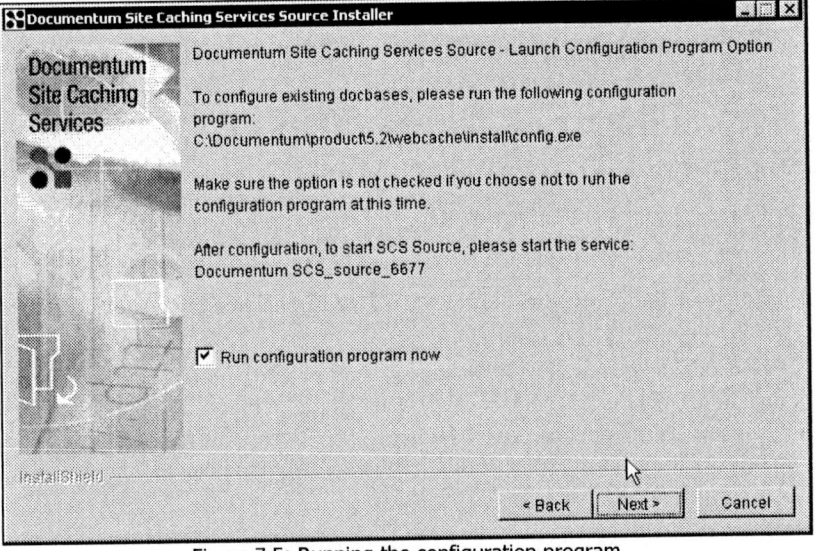

Figure 7.5: Running the configuration program

9. Choose the Docbase on which the SCS configuration program needs to be run and click the Next button.

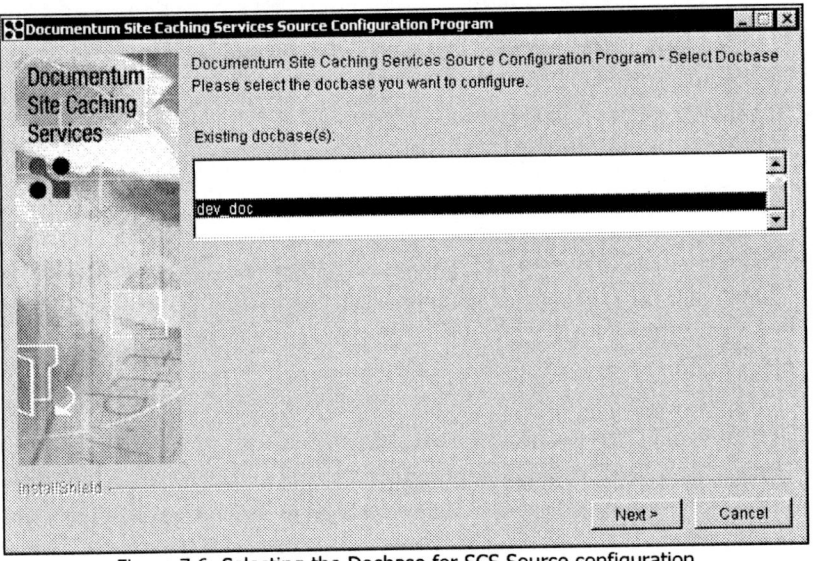

Figure 7.6: Selecting the Docbase for SCS Source configuration

10. The configuration program installs SCSDocApp on the selected Docbase, configuring the Docbase to be used with SCS services. The following objects are installed as part of SCSDocApp:

- dm_webc_config object type
- dm_webc_target object type
- webc_lock object type
- dm_SCSLogPurgeJob job
- dm_SCSLogPurge method
- PostInstall procedure

Click Finish once the DocApp has been installed.

11. Restart the service Documentum SCS_source_<port number> (for example: Documentum SCS_source_6677 if SCS Source is configured on default port 6677).

This completes the installation of SCS Source 5.2.5. We can now safely go ahead and install service pack 2 over this installation.

> Every time a new Docbase has been created, we need to run the SCS Source configuration program (config.exe) from %DM_HOME%\webcache\install on the Content Server host. Failing to do so will result in errors during publishing from the Docbase in question.

7.1.3 Installing SCS Source 5.2.5 SP2

1. Extract Site_Caching_Services_5.2.5_SP2_all.zip on the Content Server host and copy the webcache.jar file to the following location on the Content Server host: %DM_HOME%\webcache\tomcat\webapps\webcache\WEB-INF\lib

   Example: A typical location on Windows could be:

   C:\Documentum\product\5.2\webcache\tomcat\webapps\webcache\WEB-INF\lib

2. Restart the SCS Source service.

That's it! We are done with upgrading SCS Source to SP2 and can now install SCS Target 5.2.5 and then upgrade it with service pack 2.

> You can monitor the state of SCS Source to find out its product version and other information such as total uptime, total incremental publishes, etc by viewing the following URL from your browser: http://<Content Server host>:6677/webcache/state

If the SCS Source service is not running, the following error message is seen when trying to publish using Site Caching Services from a Docbase:

Error occurred while publishing the Site Publishing Configuration
[DM_METHOD_E_HTTP_COMMUNICATION]error: "Failed to obtain socket for host:localhost, at port:6677"

7.2 SCS Target 5.2.5

We will first install SCS Target software on the web server machine and then apply the SP2 pack over it.

7.2.1 Prerequisites

Figure 7.7 lists some of the prerequisites for installing SCS Target on the web server host:

Entity	Comments
SCS Target installation owner	On Windows machines, the user should: • Be a member of Windows 'Administrators' group • Have "act as part of operating system" privilege (Go to Programs | Administrative Tools | Local Security Policy) • Have access to the SCS directories
Transfer user	User name and password for a valid OS user on the SCS Target machine should be known
Web Server	The web server for application servers or web applications should be up and running
Database	If configured with SCS Target software, the database instance should be accessible
	User name and password for Database connectivity should be available
	DB system user name and password should be available for allowing Site Caching Services to create database/tablespaces.
Hardware	250 MB hard disk space, 128 MB RAM, and 133 MHz CPU
	Post installation, the website host should have adequate disk space for storing the published data.
Others	For supported combinations of Windows OS and RDBMS versions, please refer to Release Notes from Documentum.

Figure 7.7: Prerequisites for installing SCS Target

To begin, download the following SCS Target software installation files from the Documentum site:

- Site_Caching_Services_5.2.5_windows_target.exe
- Site_Caching_Services_5.2.5_SP2_all.zip

7.2.2 Installing SCS Target 5.2.5

We will first install SCS Target 5.2.5 on the web server host and then upgrade it with service pack 2 (SP2).

1. Log in to the web server host as the SCS installation owner, extract Site_Caching_Services_5.2.5_windows_target.exe and run the following executable: SCSTargetWinSetup.exe

2. If SCS Target needs to be installed and configured with a database, a DSN needs to be setup before hand so that connectivity can be established to the specified Database.

   Set up a DSN (Data Source Name) on the SCS Target machine, in the way we did when we created our first Docbase. Recall that the DSN can be created on a Windows machine by going to Programs | Administrative Tools | Data Sources (ODBC).

3. On running the SCS Target Installer, the following screen is shown. Click the Next button.

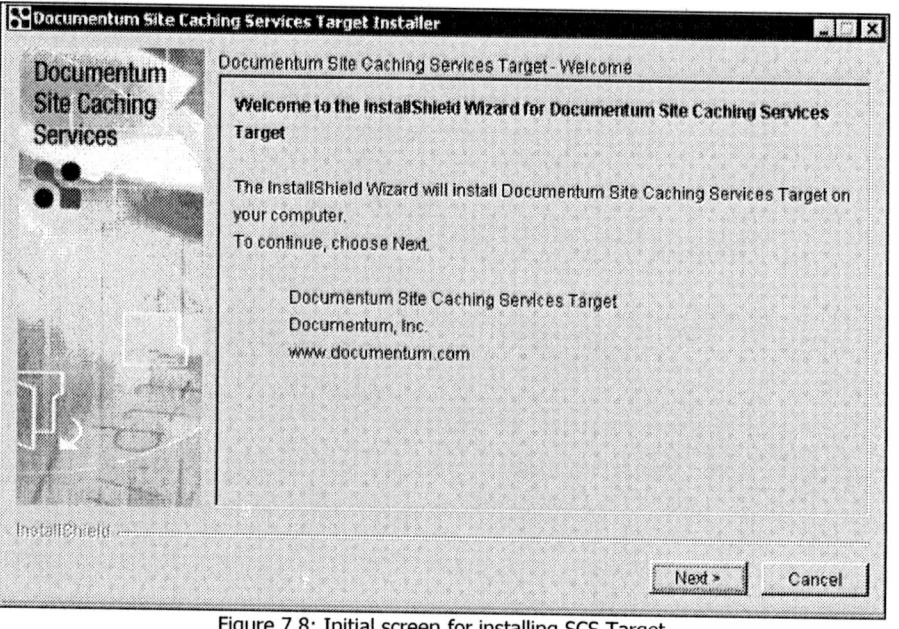

Figure 7.8: Initial screen for installing SCS Target

4. Accept the license agreement and click the Next button.

5. Either choose the default installation directory shown or provide a new path. Click the Next button.

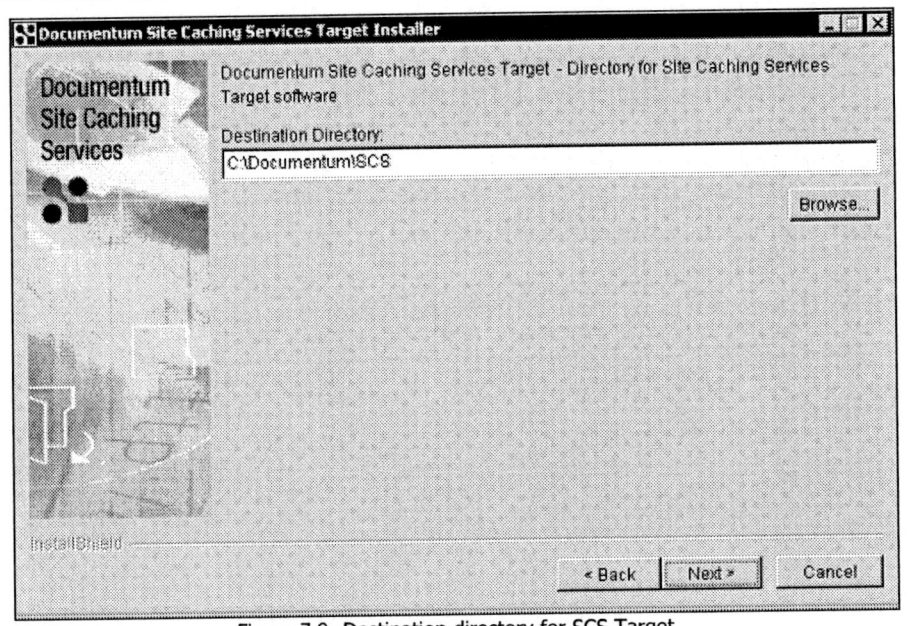

Figure 7.9: Destination directory for SCS Target

6. The Documentum SCS installation directory is shown to user for a preview. Click the Next button.

7. After installation has been completed, run the configuration program to configure the SCS Target software. Click the Next button.

Figure 7.10: Running configuration program for SCS target

8. A confirmation screen is shown for configuring SCS Target. Click the Next button.

9. Select whether you need a secure (HTTPS) or a non-secure (HTTP) connection between the Content Server host machine and the target machine.

Remember that secure (HTTPS) communications can be about 30% slower than non-secure communications. If your network and the traffic between the Content Server host and the target machine is secure, you can select non-secure communication.

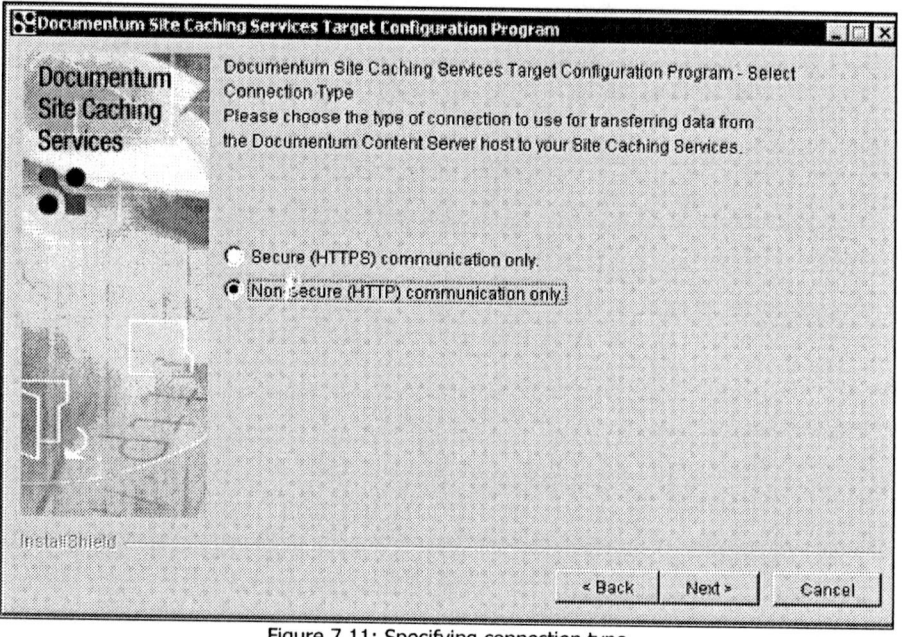

Figure 7.11: Specifying connection type

10. If non-secure communication (HTTP) has been chosen, the default port 2788 can be selected. If secure communication (HTTPS) has been chosen, the default port shown is 2787. We can provide any other port number as well, provided the port is not being used by any other application. Click the Next button.

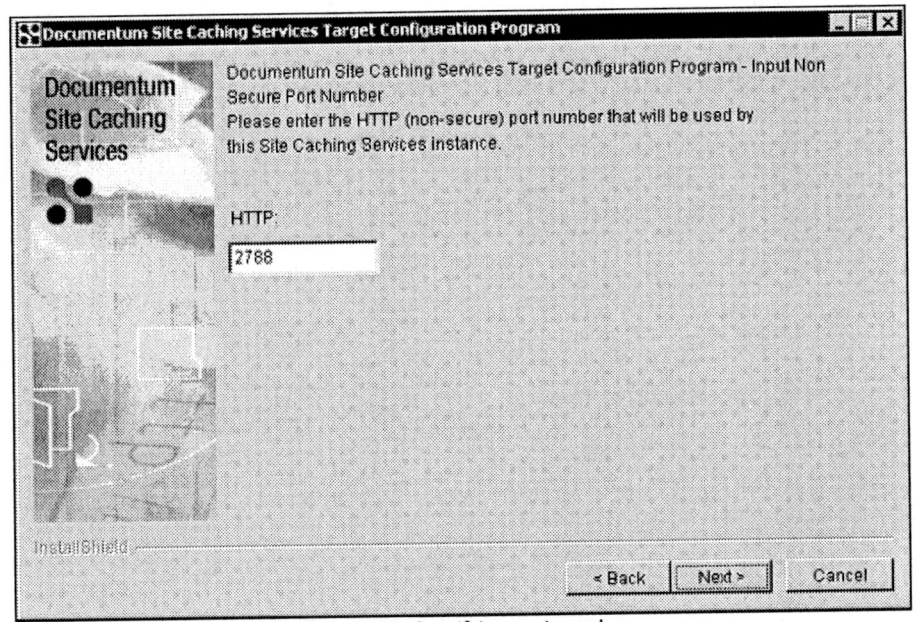

Figure 7.12: Specifying port number

11. Specify the target data transfer directory. We can choose the default shown or provide any other convenient location. Click the Next button.

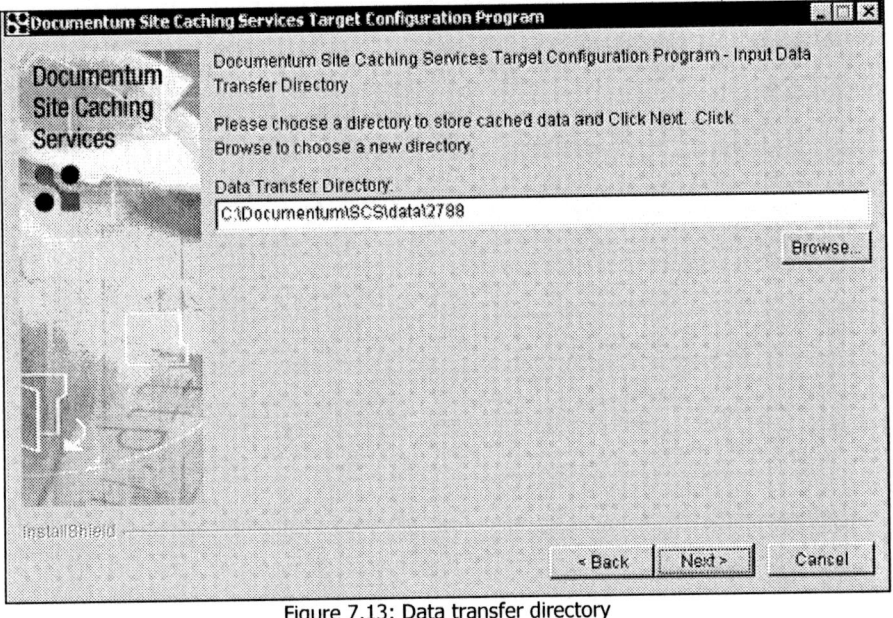

Figure 7.13: Data transfer directory

12. Specify the domain or server against which the transfer user's password is authenticated by SCS software. Click the Next button.

13. We can choose to configure SCS Target software without a database (for storing object attributes/metadata), or choose the database type and click the Next button.

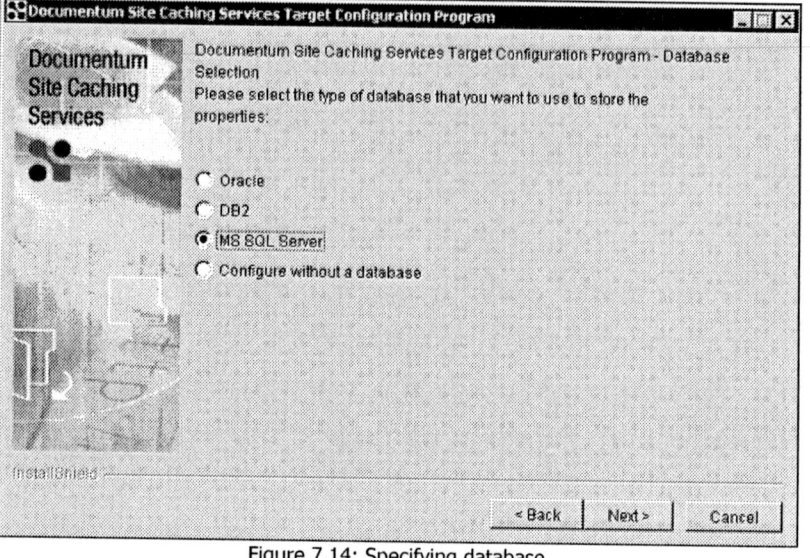

Figure 7.14: Specifying database

14. We can either have an already existing database and account, or create a new one using the installation wizard. Click the Next button.

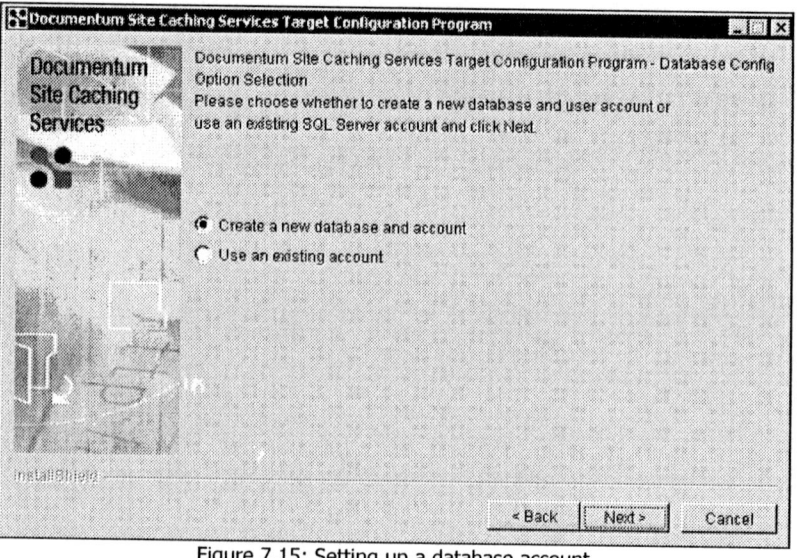

Figure 7.15: Setting up a database account

94

15. Choose the existing ODBC data source from the dropdown and provide the database system user name and password. Click the Next button.

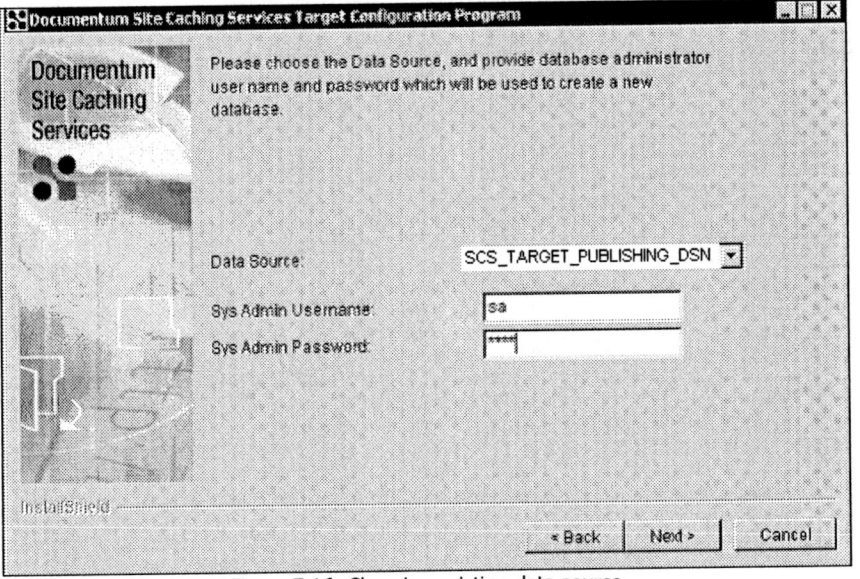

Figure 7.16: Choosing existing data source

16. Either choose the default database name and related information or provide the database parameters (data device file path and log device file path) yourself. Click the Next button.

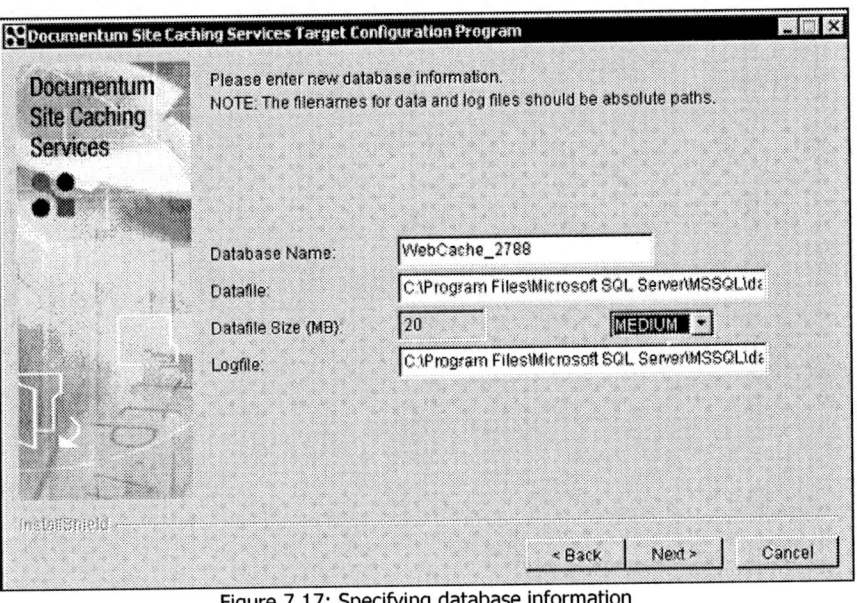

Figure 7.17: Specifying database information

17. Provide the database user's name and password and click the Next button.

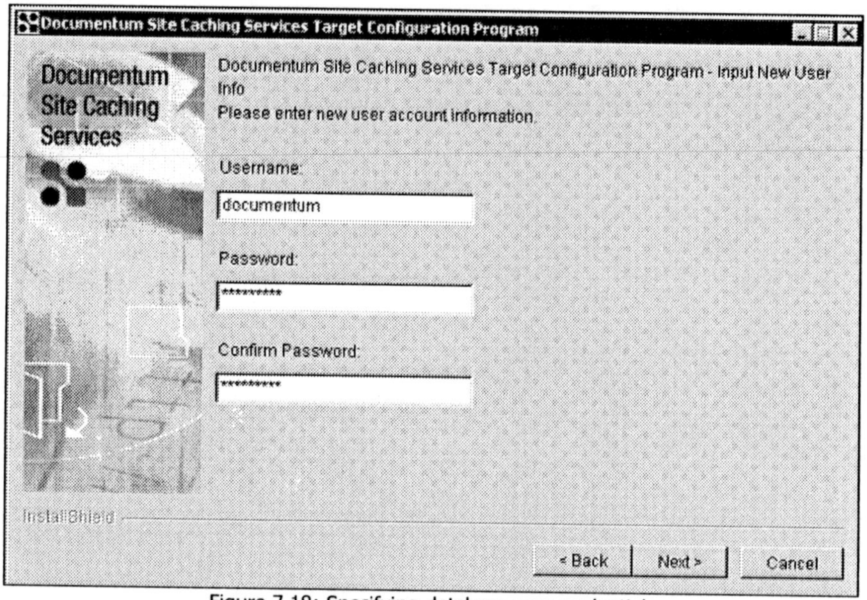

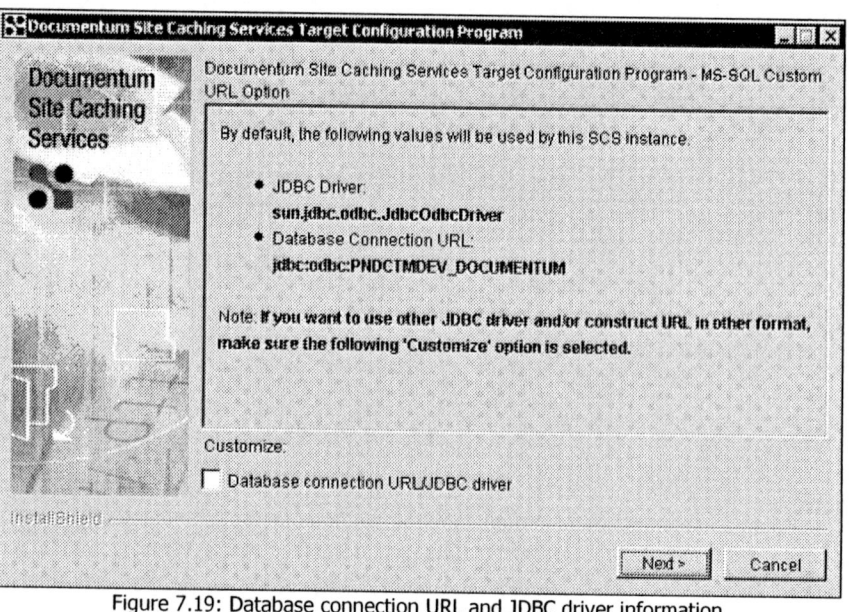

Figure 7.18: Specifying database user credentials

18. The JDBC driver and database connection URL information is shown to the user. We can customize the JDBC driver and/or database connection URL by selecting the Customize checkbox. Click the Next button.

Figure 7.19: Database connection URL and JDBC driver information

19. Choose the option to start the SCS Target service and click the **Next** button.

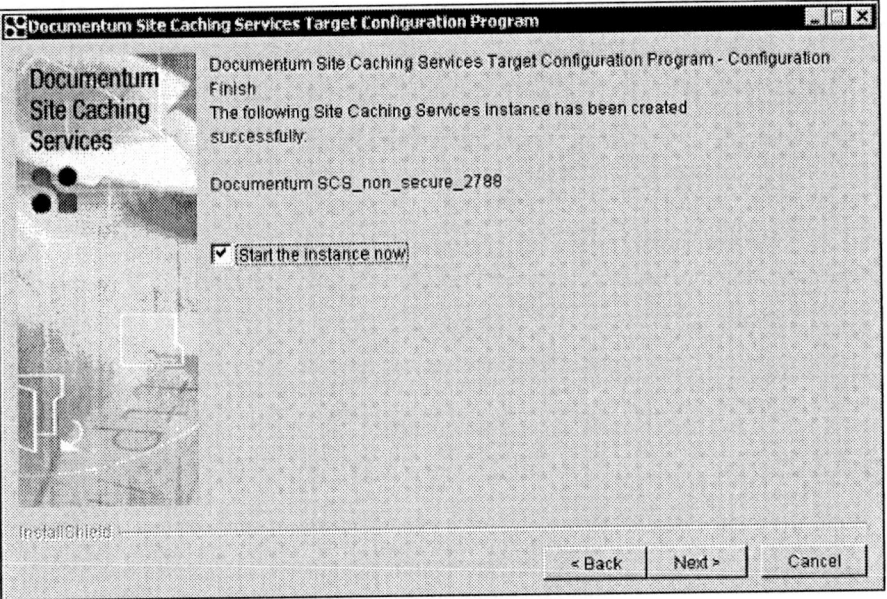

Figure 7.20: Starting SCS Target instance

20. Click on Finish to complete the SCS Target installation and configuration process.

   We are done with installation of SCS Target 5.2.5 on the web server host. The next task is to apply service pack 2 to it. As part of SCS Target configuration, Documentum modifies the agent.ini file on SCS Target host at the following location:

   `<SCS Target Installation Directory>\admin\config\<SCS Target port>`

   On Windows, a typical location would be: `C:\Documentum\SCS\admin\config\2788`

   The following snippet is from the agent.ini file that stores the database information for SCS Target that we just installed above:

   ```
   target_database_connection=jdbc:odbc:SCS_TARGET_PUBLISHING_DSN
   database_user=sa
   database_user_pass=systempass
   JDBC_DRIVER=sun.jdbc.odbc.JdbcOdbcDriver
   database_name=WebCache_2788
   ```

7.2.3 Installing SCS Target 5.2.5 SP2

We will now install SCS Target 5.2.5 SP2 on the web server host.

1. Stop the SCS target service and extract `site_caching_services_5.2.5_SP2_all.zip` on the web server host. This ZIP contains the `webcache.jar` file.

2. Copy the extracted `webcache.jar` file at the following location on the web server host:

    `<SCS Target Installation Directory>\product\jre\win\lib\ext`

    Example: A typical location on Windows could be: `c:\Documentum\SCS\product\jre\win\lib\ext`

3. Restart the SCS Target service.

    If the SP2 upgrade is not done correctly, the following error message is seen during publishing, if there is a mismatch in the versions of `webcache.jar` on the Content Server host and the web server host (for SCS Source and Target):

    ERROR: Failed to login to the target server. Network error retrieving target result com.documentum.webcache.utils.d; Local class not compatible: stream classdescserialVersionUID=1602290069170353386 local class serialVersionUID=4590497449032455007

That's it! We have finished upgrading SCS Target to SP2. We are now ready to publish content and metadata from Documentum.

7.3 Summary

In this chapter, we discussed setting up Site Caching Services (SCS) components for publishing documents created in our new Docbase. We saw that SCS architecture consists of two components:

*   SCS Source, installed on the Content Server host
*   SCS Target component, installed on web server hosts

We discussed some prerequisites for installing SCS Source and SCS Target and then went through the detailed steps for their installation.

8

Setting Up Documentum Application Builder

Documentum Application Builder (earlier known as Documentum Developer Studio) is a tool used to create Documentum application packaging units (called DocApps) which consist of object types, lifecycles, workflow templates, and other Documentum objects.

Recall our discussion about DocApps in Chapter 2. A DocApp can be created using Documentum Application Builder and can be archived and deployed over to other Docbases using Documentum Application Installer.

A DocApp can comprise numerous kinds of Documentum objects, such as:

- Object types
- Lifecycles
- Workflow templates
- Permission Set templates
- Alias Sets
- Jobs
- Methods
- Procedures
- Relation Types
- Data Objects

Using Documentum Application Builder (DAB) we can create these objects via simple graphical wizards. Note that **Workflow Manager** is specifically required for creating Workflow templates. Installing DAB automatically installs Workflow Manager as well. Workflow Manager is seamlessly integrated with DAB and hence it can be opened either from within DAB or as a standalone application.

8.1 Documentum Application Builder

Documentum Application Installer (DAI), used for deploying Documentum DocApps, is also installed along with DAB installer if the user chooses the option correctly. Using a simple user interface, we can create different kinds of Documentum objects in our own custom DocApps, without worrying about details like Docbase connections and sessions.

Note that DAB need not be installed on the Content Server host. It can be installed on a separate desktop as long as the DocBroker connectivity for the Docbase in question is available.

Figure 8.1 shows Web Publisher objects in the WebPublisher DocApp we installed in our custom Docbase.

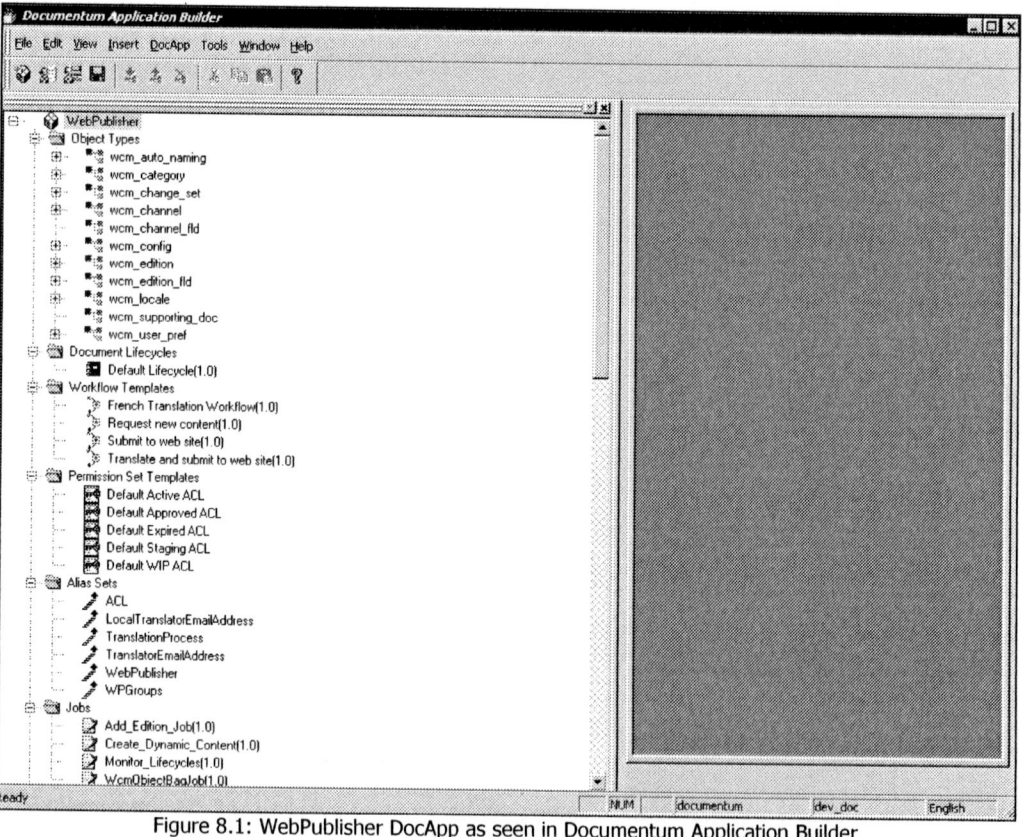

Figure 8.1: WebPublisher DocApp as seen in Documentum Application Builder

8.1.1 Prerequisites

Figure 8.2 specifies some of the prerequisites for installing Documentum Application Builder 5.2.5 SP2 and its associated components:

Entity	Comments
Hardware	90 MB hard disk space, 256 MB RAM, and 450 MHz CPU.
Content Server	Content Server, DocBroker, and Docbase should be set up correctly.
Internet Explorer	Should be available on the desktop in order to view online Help.
Java Runtime Environment	Sun JRE 1.4.1, 1.4.2.
Others	For supported combinations of Windows OS and JRE, please refer to Release Notes from Documentum.

Figure 8.2: Prerequisites for installing Application Builder

8.2 Installing DAB 5.2.5 SP2

Ensure that you have downloaded the installer software
Application_Builder_5.2.5_SP2_windows.exe from the Documentum download site.

1. Extract the executable Application_Builder_5.2.5_SP2_windows.exe on the desktop machine and run setup.exe.

2. Click the Next button.

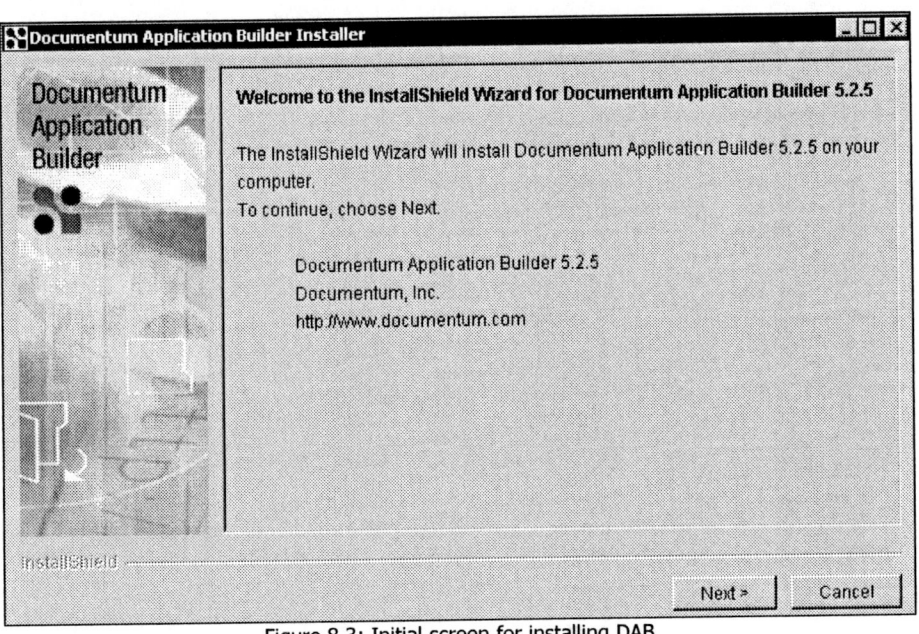

Figure 8.3: Initial screen for installing DAB

3. Select the checkboxes for both Application Builder and Application Installer and click the Next button.

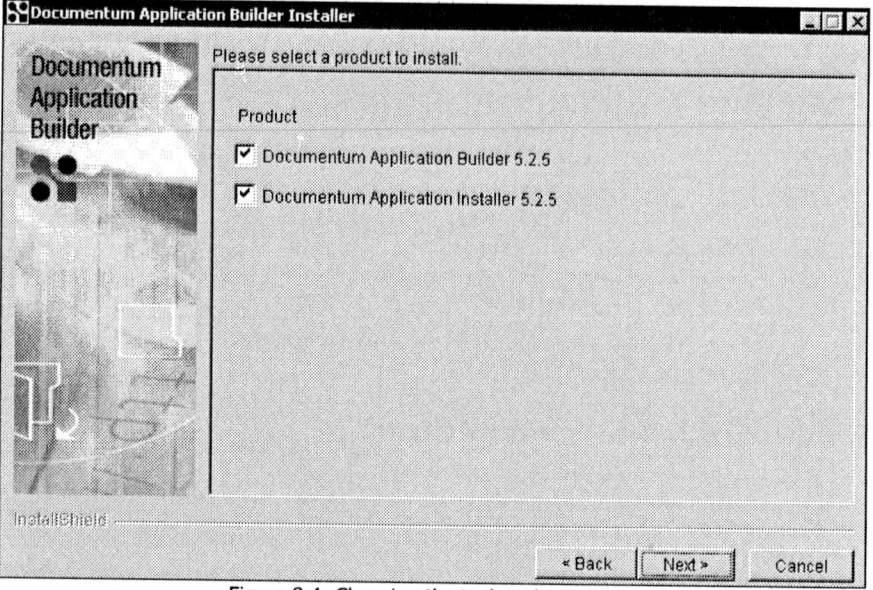

Figure 8.4: Choosing the tools to be installed

4. Optionally choose to install DFC documentation and click the Next button.

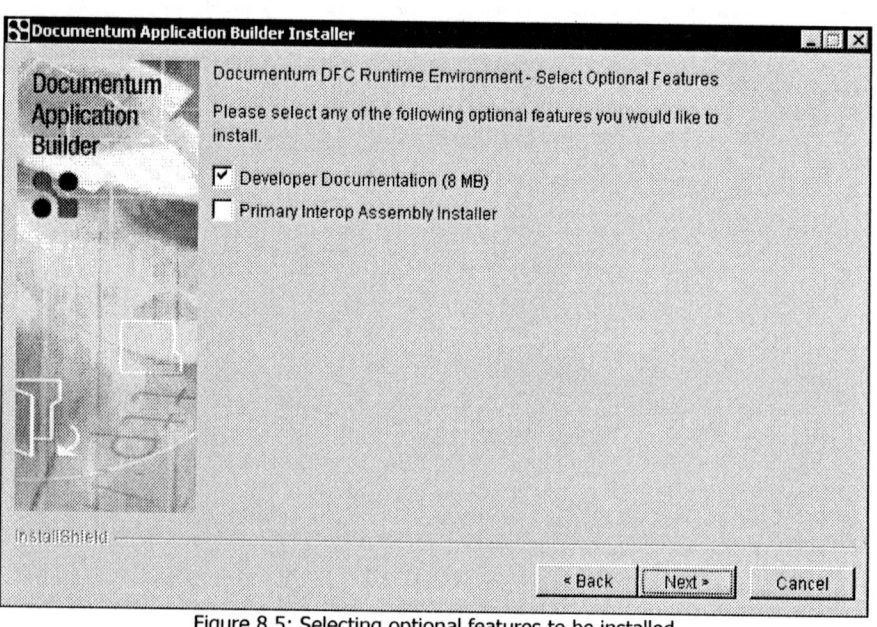

Figure 8.5: Selecting optional features to be installed

5. Specify the primary DocBroker host machine and port number (default shown) so that the Servers projecting to the specified DocBroker can be connected to by DAB.

6. Click the Next button.

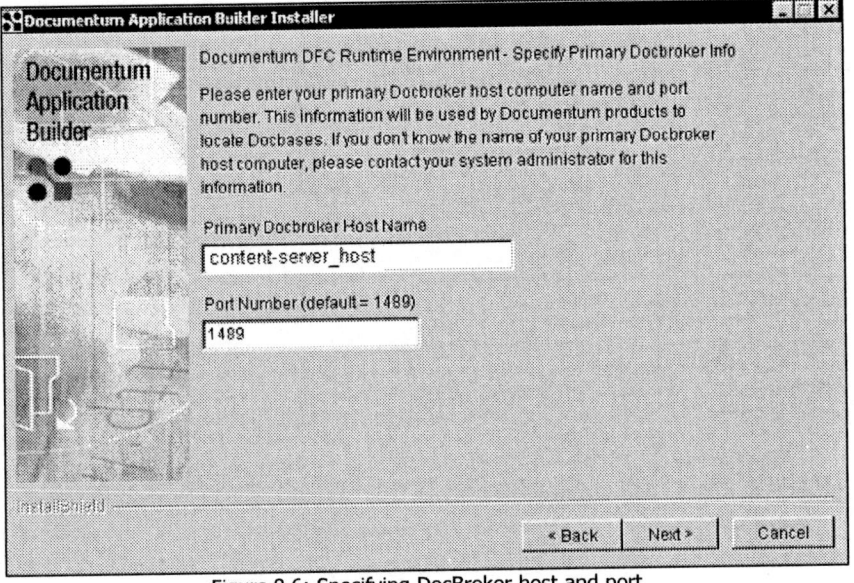

Figure 8.6: Specifying DocBroker host and port

Behind the scenes, Documentum creates the dmcl.ini file under C:\WINNT or C:\WINDOWS (depending on the OS) on the desktop machine and adds the following entries:

```
[DOCBROKER_PRIMARY]
host =content-server_host
port =1489
```

Once DAB has been installed, if someone mistakenly changes the name of the specified DocBroker host to an invalid value (say content-server_host222) in dmcl.ini, then the following error message is seen on opening DAB:

[DM_DOCBROKER_E_HOST_NAME]error: "Unable to find host with name: content-server_host222. Network specific error: Host not found. Network error: invalid host name."

7.   The list of components that will be installed is shown. Click the Next button.

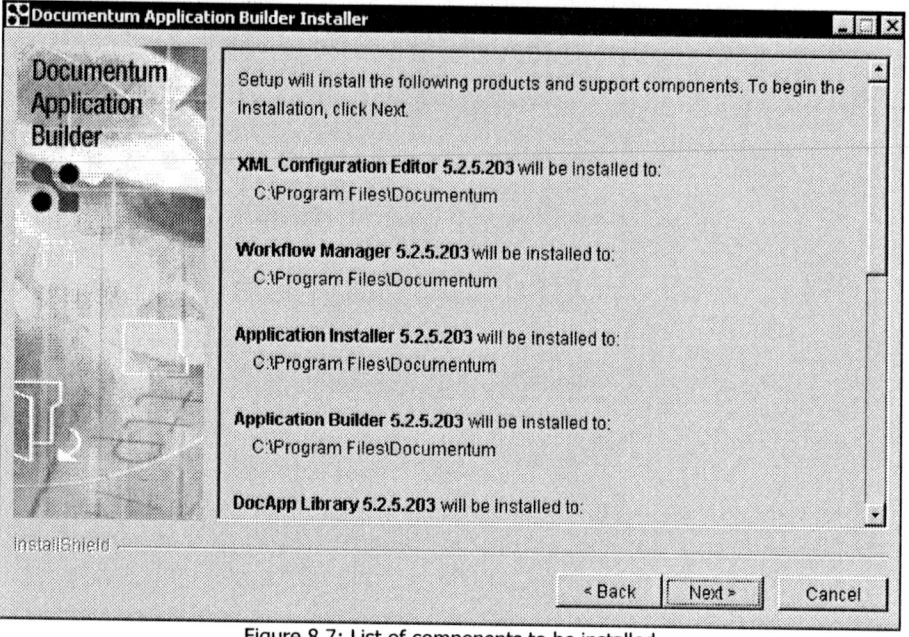

Figure 8.7: List of components to be installed

8.   Restart the system once installation finishes.

After the machine has rebooted, you will see Application Installer, Workflow Manager, and Application Builder icons under Start | Programs | Documentum.

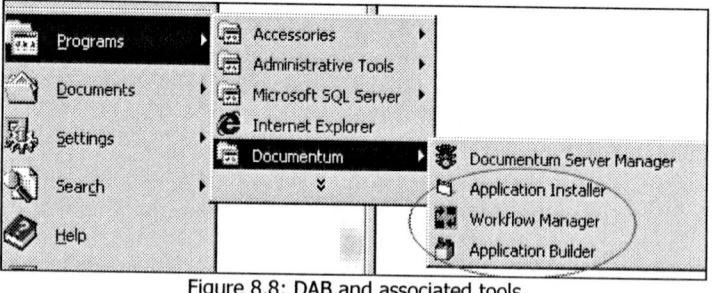

Figure 8.8: DAB and associated tools

DAB sometimes crashes after entering login/password information, if the classpath information for the system and the user environmental variables are different. Make these identical to resolve this issue.

The following error message is seen in such circumstances:

ERROR: "Dab.exe - Application Error"

The instruction at "0x6d393c07" referenced memory at "0x00000000".

Click OK to terminate the program.

Click CANCEL to debug the program

Now that Documentum Application Builder has been installed, you can start playing around with it and create custom objects required for your specific business needs.

8.3 Summary

This chapter introduced Documentum Application Builder as a client tool for creating and managing Documentum DocApps. In our earlier discussion, we talked about DocApps as packaging units for Documentum objects such as Lifecycles, Workflows, Alias Sets, Jobs, and Methods.

We went on to discuss some prerequisites for installing Documentum Application Builder and the detailed instructions for installing it.

9

Setting Up Documentum Administrator and Web Publisher

Documentum Administrator (DA) is a web-based tool that allows administrators to perform system administration and monitoring activities on Documentum Docbases, servers, federations, etc.

To access Documentum Administrator and connect to the respective Docbase and configure/monitor the various Docbase objects, all that a system administrator requires is a web browser. DA is an extremely powerful tool that assists an administrator in performing routine administrative tasks and scores of other activities.

A few of the tasks that can be carried out using Documentum Administrator are:

- System monitoring of Docbase, Docbase sessions, and resources
- Running DQL and Server API commands
- Creation and modification of Docbase objects like Methods, Jobs, Object types, formats, ACLs (permission sets), storage areas, and site publishing configurations (for Site Caching Services)
- Executing Methods and Jobs

It is worth mentioning that Documentum Administrator has been developed using the WDK framework. We will explore Documentum Administrator further in the subsequent chapters of this book. For now, simply understand that it is a browser-based application used for Content Server administrative tasks.

9.1 Documentum Administrator

Documentum Administrator software is installed as a web application on supported application server platforms such as Tomcat, BEA WebLogic, WebSphere, and Oracle AS. In this chapter, we will install Documentum Administrator and Web Publisher on Apache Tomcat.

Please keep the following prerequisites in mind before we proceed with the installation and configuration of Documentum Administrator.

9.1.1 Prerequisites

The table shown in figure 9.1 lists some of the prerequisites for installing Documentum Administrator:

Entity	Comments
Content Server and DocBroker	The Application server machine hosting DA should be able to access the DocBroker host for the Docbase in question.
Installation owner	Documentum recommends using the same installation owner to install application server and DA.
	Limitations for installation owner's user name:
	• Consists of numbers, letters, hyphens (-) and underscores (_)
	• The first character should be a letter
	• All characters must be ASCII
	• User should have 'Write' permission on the content transfer directory
	• Password should consist of numbers, letters, periods (.), hyphens (-), and underscores (_)
Application Server	Before installing DA, the supported Application Server should be installed and configured properly.
Application Server machine	600 MB hard disk space, 1 GB RAM and minimum 800 MHz CPU. (Documentum does not recommend installing DA on the Content Server host due to security reasons)
Browser machine	The Browser Windows machine accessing DA should have 5 MB hard disk space, 128 MB Free RAM, and an 800 MHz CPU.
Others	For supported combinations of Windows OS, Browser versions and JRE, Application Server versions and JDK, please refer to Release Notes from Documentum.

Figure 9.1: Prerequisites for installing DA

To begin, download the following:

- Documentum Administrator 5.2.5 SP2 software installer (Administrator_5.2.5_SP2_windows.exe) from the Documentum site.

- jakarta-tomcat-4.1.30.exe from the Apache Jakarta Tomcat homepage (http://jakarta.apache.org/tomcat/)

9.1.2 Installing Documentum Administrator 5.2.5 SP2

We will now mention the steps involved in installing Documentum Administrator 5.2.5 SP2:

1. Log in to the application server host as the application server installation owner and install Apache Tomcat 4.1.30 Servlet container before installing DA. For details on the installation of Tomcat, please refer to Tomcat documentation available from the Apache Jakarta site.

2. After Tomcat 4.1.30 has been installed on the application server host, the following system environment variables need to be set:

   o JAVA_HOME: This is the Java installation directory, for example, c:\j2sdk1.4.2

   o CATALINA_HOME: This is the Tomcat installation directory, for example, c:\Tomcat 4.1

3. Startup Tomcat 4.1.30 to ensure that it has been installed correctly before proceeding with DA installation.

   Run the batch file startup.bat located under %CATALINA_HOME%\bin.

   Once Tomcat has started up, open the default Tomcat page by invoking the following URL from your web browser: http://<app server host>:<port>/index.jsp.

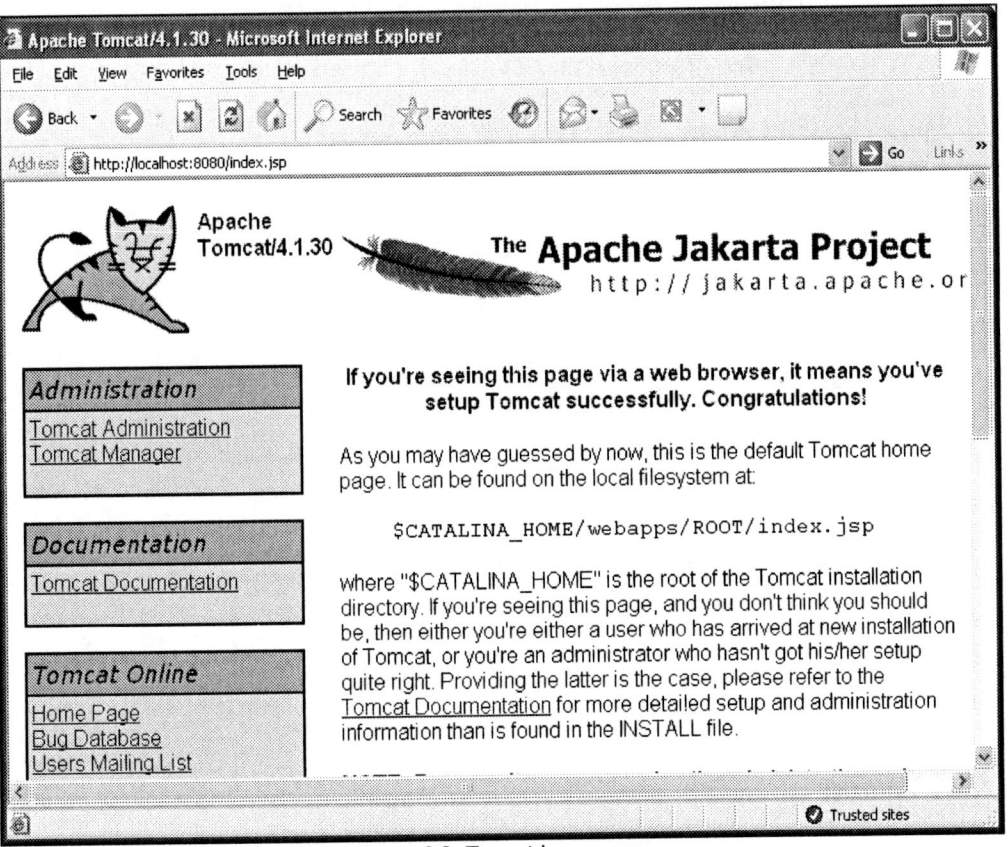

Figure 9.2: Tomcat home page

4. Stop Tomcat server before beginning the installation of Documentum Administrator 5.2.5 SP2. Extract Administrator_5.2.5_SP2_windows.exe on the application server host as the application server installation owner. Run the dawinsetup.exe executable.

5. Click the Next button.

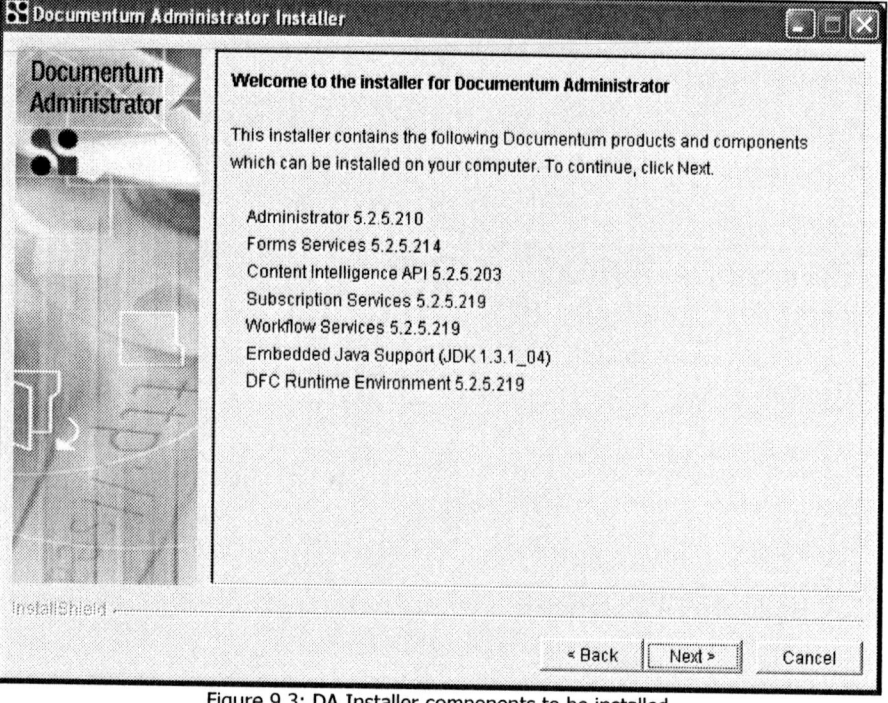

Figure 9.3: DA Installer components to be installed

6. Accept the License agreement terms and conditions and click the Next button.

7. Optionally choose to install Developer Documentation and click the Next button.

8. If Documentum already exists on the machine, the Documentum Destination directory screen will not be shown. If Documentum is being installed for the first time on the application server host, the default destination directory (C:\Program Files\Documentum) is shown. Either choose a different destination directory or continue with the default and click the Next button.

9. If Documentum already exists on the machine, the Documentum user directory screen will not be shown. If Documentum is being installed for the first time on the app server host, the default user directory (c:\Documentum) is shown. Either choose a different user directory or continue with the default and click the Next button.

10. If Documentum already exists on the machine, the primary DocBroker info screen will not be shown. If Documentum is being installed for the first time on the app server host, provide the name of the primary DocBroker host, and the port number (the default port number is 1489), and click the Next button.

11. Select the application server on which DA will be installed. Click the Next button.

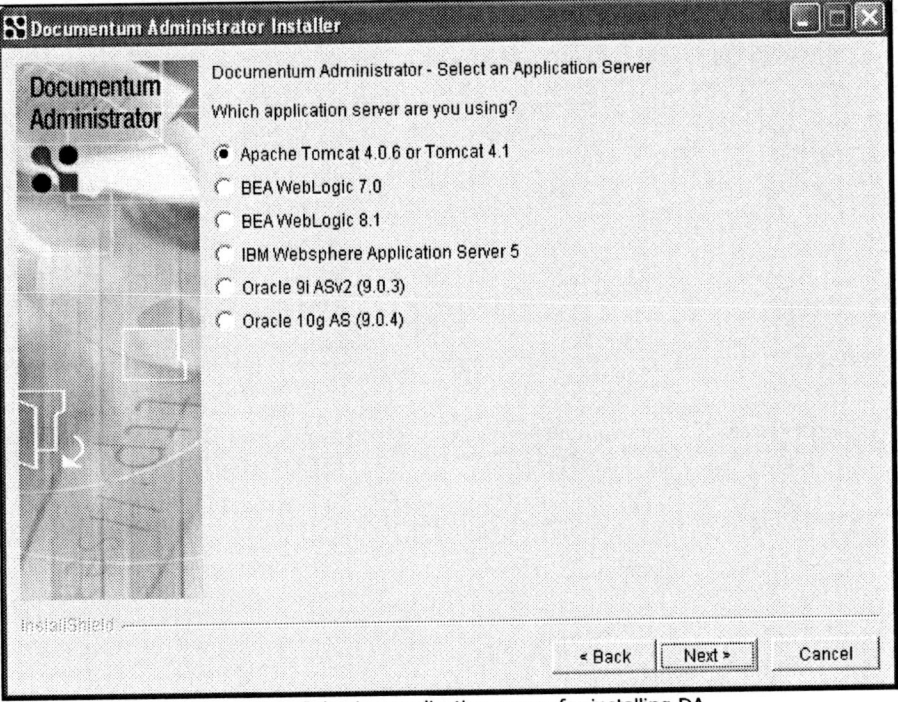

Figure 9.4: Selecting application server for installing DA

12. Ensure that you have stopped Apache Tomcat application server before continuing with the installation setup. Click the Next button.

13. Provide the Tomcat app server home directory and the name of the DA web application (virtual directory). Choose the defaults shown on the screen and click the Next button.

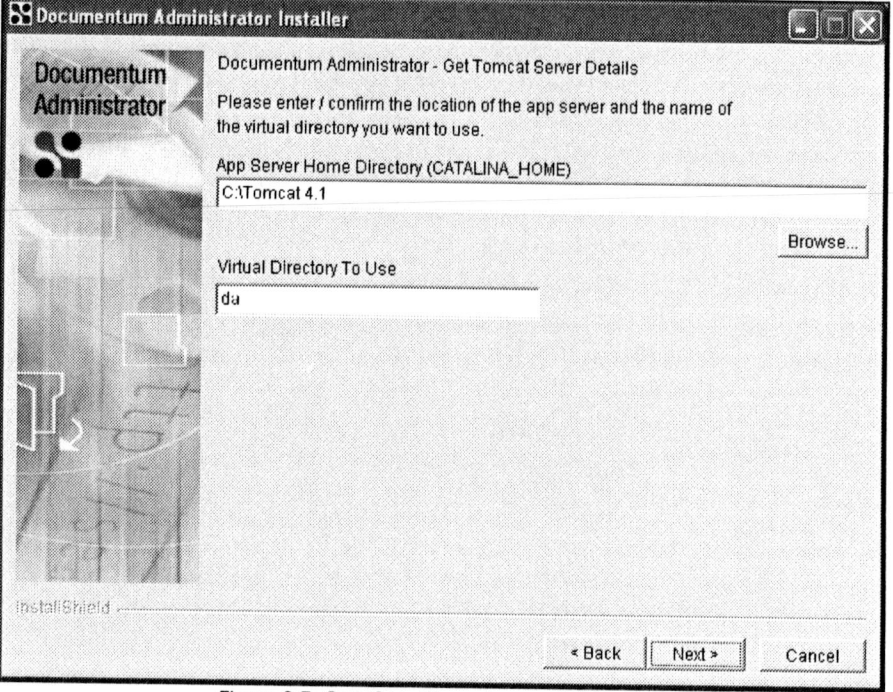

Figure 9.5: Specifying Tomcat server information

14. Choose the default content transfer folder or provide a new one. Click the Next button. The default folder shown on the screen is `C:\Documentum\contentxfer\da`.

15. Do not select the option for installing virtual link support and click the Next button. DA does not require virtual link support to function.

16. The list of products/supported components to be installed with the DA installation will be shown. Click the Next button and finish the installation by pressing the Finish button.

17. Start Tomcat and invoke the following URL from your web browser to ensure that DA has been installed correctly: `http://<app server name>:<port>/da`.

If you have specified a virtual directory other than da, then substitute da in the above URL with the name you have specified.

We have reached the last rung of the ladder as far as Documentum WCM software installation is concerned for our purposes. Having installed Documentum Administrator, we can now go ahead and install Web Publisher 5.2.5 SP2 on the same application server host that is hosting DA.

9.2 Web Publisher

The prerequisites for installing Documentum Administrator hold good for Web Publisher as well. You may want to refer to the prerequisites mentioned for DA in figure 9.1. Additionally, Web Publisher Server files and WebPublisher DocApp must be installed on the Content Server host so that Web Publisher can work properly.

9.2.1 Prerequisites

Before you begin the installation procedure, download:

- Web Publisher 5.2.5 SP2 software installer (Web_Publisher_5.2.5_SP2_windows.exe) from the Documentum site.
- Jakarta-tomcat-4.1.30.exe from the Apache Jakarta Tomcat homepage: http://jakarta.apache.org/tomcat/ (Download this only if Tomcat 4.1.30 has *not* been installed on the application server machine.)

9.2.2 Installing Web Publisher 5.2.5 SP2

We will now mention the steps involved in installing Web Publisher 5.2.5 SP2:

1. Log in to application server host as the application server installation owner and install Apache Tomcat 4.1.30 Servlet container before installing Web Publisher. Note that this step has to be executed *only* if Tomcat does not exist on the application server machine. If you have installed DA, you would have already installed/configured Tomcat and hence this step can be avoided.

   For details surrounding installation of Tomcat, please refer to the Tomcat documentation available from the Apache Jakarta site.

2. Assuming that Tomcat 4.1.30 has been installed correctly, stop Tomcat server and extract Web_Publisher_5.2.5_SP2_windows.exe on the application server host as the application server installation owner. Run wpWinSetup.exe.

3.   Click the Next button.

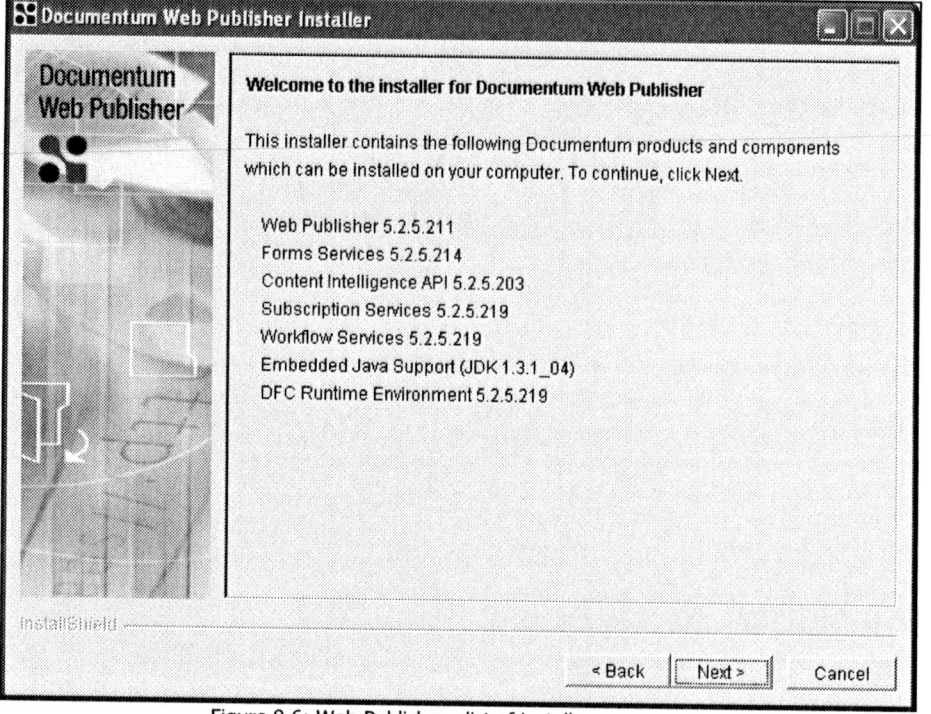

Figure 9.6: Web Publisher—list of installer components

4.   Accept the license terms and agreements and click the Next button.

5.   Optionally choose to install Developer Documentation and click the Next button.

6.   If Documentum already exists on the machine, the Documentum Destination directory screen will not be shown. If Documentum is being installed for the first time on the application server host, the default destination directory (c:\Program Files\ Documentum) is shown. Either choose a different destination directory or continue with the default and click the Next button.

7.   If Documentum already exists on the machine, the Documentum user directory screen will not be shown. If Documentum is being installed for the first time on the application server host, the default user directory (c:\Documentum) is shown. Either choose a different user directory or continue with the default and click the Next button.

8. If Documentum already exists on the machine, the primary DocBroker info screen will not be shown. If Documentum is being installed for the first time on the application server host, provide the name of the primary DocBroker host, and the port number (the default port number is 1489), and click the Next button.

9. Select the application server on which Web Publisher will be installed. Click the Next button.

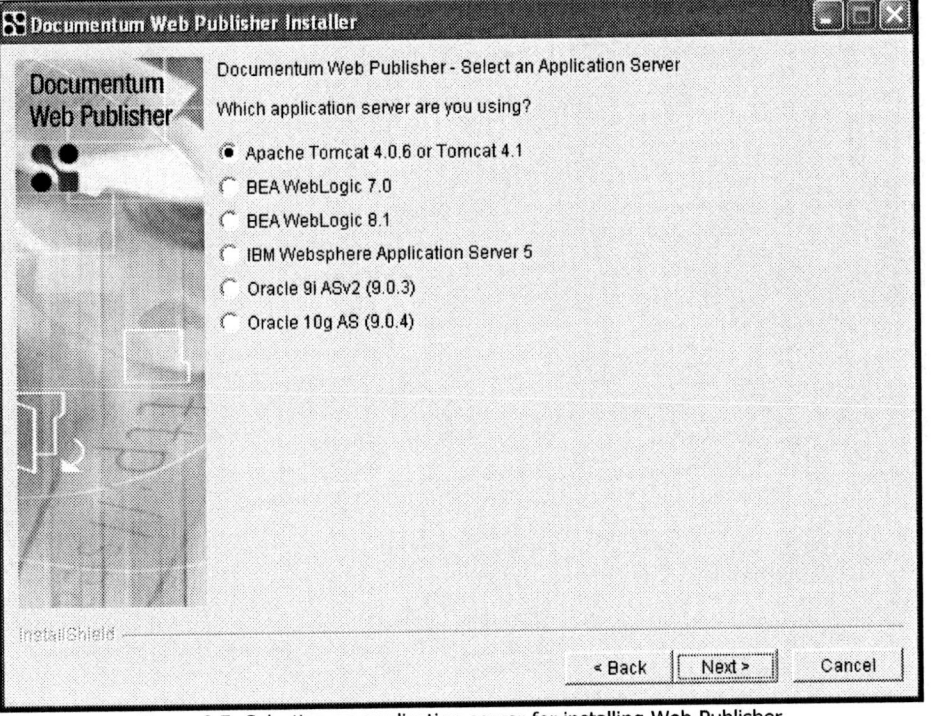

Figure 9.7: Selecting an application server for installing Web Publisher

10. Ensure that you have stopped Apache Tomcat application server before continuing with the installation setup. Click the Next button.

11. Provide the Tomcat application server home directory and the name of Web Publisher web application (virtual directory). Choose the defaults shown on the screen and click the Next button.

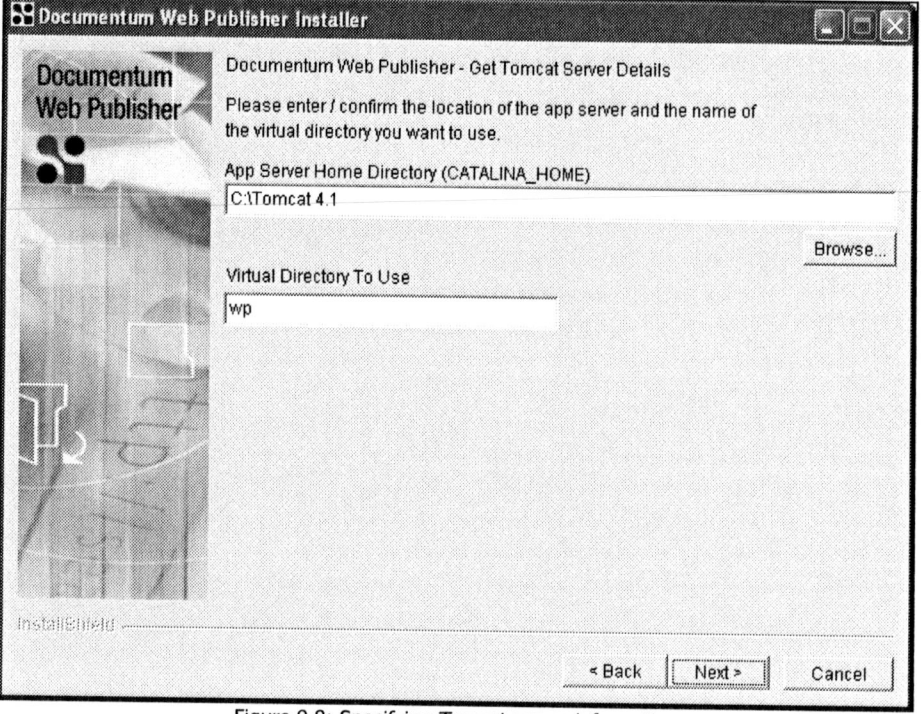

Figure 9.8: Specifying Tomcat server information

12. Choose the default content transfer folder or provide a new one. Click the Next button. The default folder shown on the screen is: c:\Documentum\contentxfer\wp.

13. Select the option for installing virtual link support only if you wish to integrate Ektron eWebEditPro rich-text editor with Web Publisher. Click the Next button.

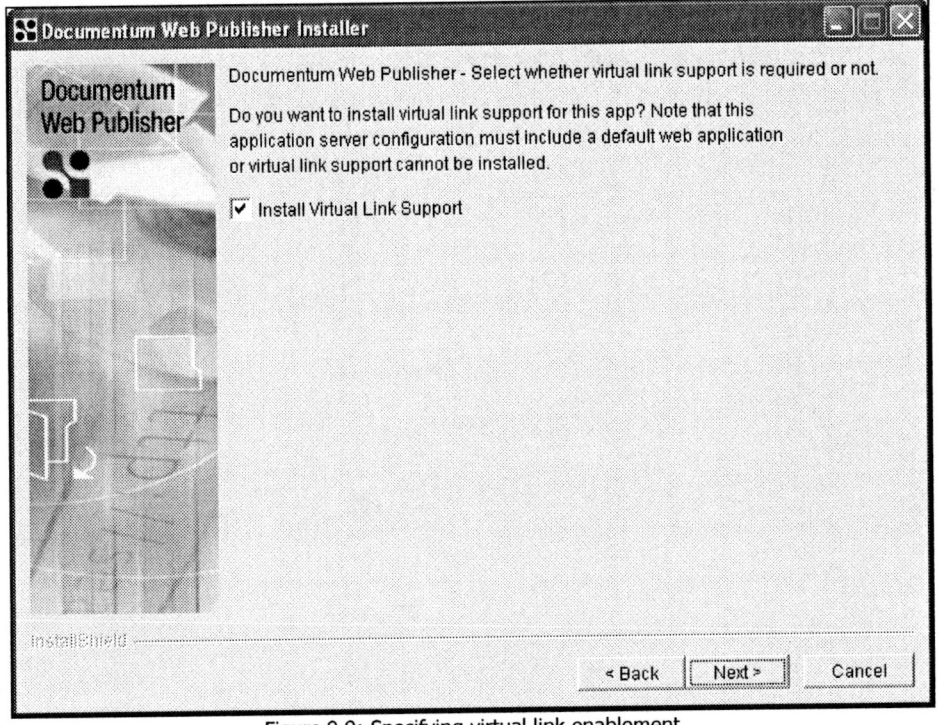

Figure 9.9: Specifying virtual link enablement

14. The list of products and supported components to be installed with the Web Publisher installation will be shown. Click the Next button and finally finish the installation by pressing the Finish button.

15. Start Tomcat and invoke the following URL from your web browser to ensure that Web Publisher has been installed correctly:

    `http://<app server name>:<port>/wp.`

As in the case of DA, if you have provided a different virtual directory for Web Publisher than wp, substitute wp in the above URL with the name you have specified.

That's it! All the necessary Documentum products have been installed and configured for our use. Once the WCM architecture is in place and the necessary product suite has been set up, we can start designing and implementing our applications.

9.3 Summary

We started this chapter with a brief discussion on Documentum Administrator as a tool that comes in handy for performing system administration tasks in the Documentum system.

We then talked about some prerequisites for installing Documentum Administrator. We then installed Apache Tomcat server and then Documentum Administrator as a web application over it.

Similarly, we discussed the prerequisites and detailed steps for installing the Documentum Web Publisher application.

10

Designing Documentum Applications

Slow and steady wins the race—an old adage, but extremely pertinent. Many of you would definitely agree that the key to successful project implementation is a good design. The more robust, flexible, and scalable the design is, the smoother its development turns out to be and further still its maintenance. A good, well-thought design (no matter what technology you may choose) avoids glitches in the later stages of the software development lifecycle.

Documentum is still not a very widely understood technology and thus necessitates building upon a good design. This chapter contains some basic guidelines to be followed and some good design practices that will ensure that a Documentum solution meets acceptable standards and does not cause any known issues during the varied stages of development, deployment, and maintenance/future releases.

Documentum is an exciting technology but needs to be understood and designed well. Look at the following points before starting design and development:

- Analyze the website structure and navigation flow.
- Identify the nature of content on the site and classify it as purely static, frequently updated, purely dynamic, etc.
- Classify the kinds of content, such as images, text documents, banners, tables, and rich media (the list could vary depending upon the nature of your website).
- Run through each and every page on the website and identify the pages that a business user can create/contribute to, and the ones that necessarily require the involvement of the application development team (IT staff).

10.1 Case Study—Simple Newspaper Website

The best way to learn anything is through examples. Let us take up a simple case study of a fictitious newspaper website that chose to publish its online version via Documentum Web Content Management system. Figure 10.1 shows the homepage of the website, displaying its header section, footer section, main body (center pane), and side navigational links.

Most websites have a similar basic kind of layout and differ mostly in the structure and look and feel of the pages. If you study the homepage carefully, you will notice that it can be divided into the following sections:

- Header, displaying the newspaper website name, date, and publication company

- Footer displaying copyright information and other links like Privacy Policy, Contact Us, etc.

- Side navigation links for the various pages in the website

- Center pane displaying the selected news article

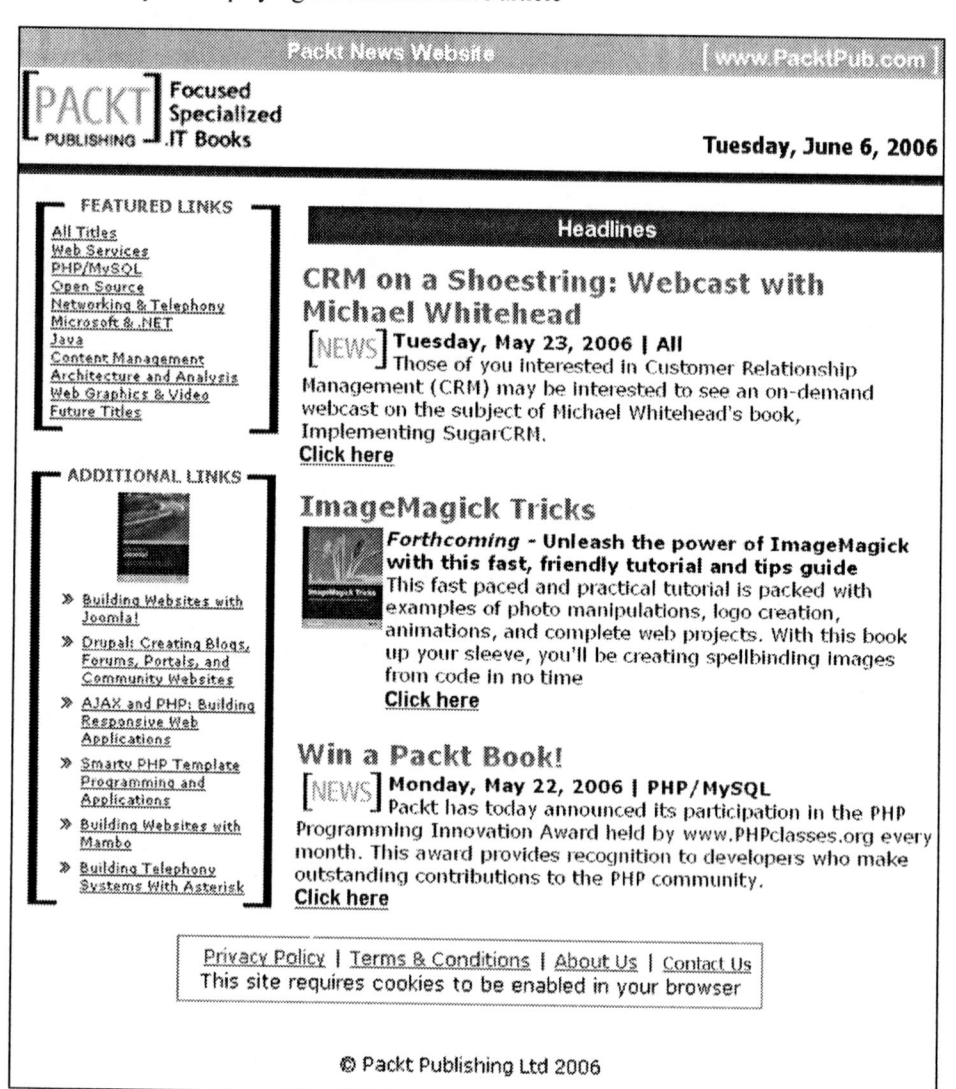

Figure 10.1: Homepage of a fictitious newspaper website

The idea behind using Documentum WCM to manage this site is that irrespective of the website page, the header and footer always remain the same and the structure of the website remains constant, displaying the side navigation links and the center page content.

Every single day, the look and feel of the page remains the same—what changes is the actual news content and the names of the news articles or links.

Imagine the newspaper content contributor staff relying on the IT staff to create and update header date, side navigation links, and articles every day based on the contextual news for the day.

Enter the world of Documentum WCM. We will now discuss, through this simple example, how to define templates and structures of website components using the rich array of features provided by Documentum.

Once the Documentum WCM design is in place, the newspaper business team will simply use the Documentum system to create, update, and publish articles every day to keep the newspaper site up to date and running without involving the technical IT staff!

10.2 Beginning Documentum Design

To *templatize* the contents on the website, let us just take up the center pane news article design and see how we can manage to create and publish it from Documentum.

If you were to analyze the center pane article meticulously, you would notice that it can be sub-divided into the following sections:

- Banner 'Headlines' image
- Date of the news article
- Body text (main news content)
- Full article link (related details)

The idea is to design and create a form in Documentum, using which business users simply need to fill in the relevant details (actual content) and the system then takes care of the look and feel (layout of web page) and publishing to the website host.

In Documentum Web Publisher lingo, such forms are called **Templates**. A template is nothing but an XML file, having XML elements for each of the Template **fields** that the user needs to fill in. The behavior and validation of each of the template fields is controlled via a **Rules file**, which is another XML file. Finally, the layout of the page, based on the template is achieved via a **Presentation file**, which is nothing but an XSL file that styles the content XML file created from the template XML file and generates the necessary HTML output (or any other renditions such as WML, xHTML, etc).

Figure 10.2 illustrates these concepts.

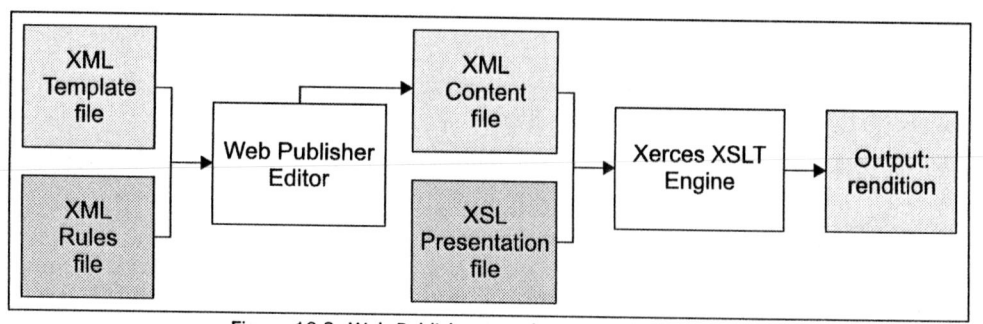

Figure 10.2: Web Publisher template and supporting files

When you create a Web Publisher template, it has to be attached to an object type in Docbase, so that whenever instances or contents are created from the template in question, contents are created as instances of the respective object type.

Say for example, Template `temp.xml` is associated with the object type `my_object`. Whenever content is created using `temp.xml`, it is actually an instance of the object type `my_object`.

Let's first create a custom object type using Documentum Application Builder and then create a template in Web Publisher and associate it with the custom object type.

10.3 Using Documentum Application Builder (DAB)

Launch Documentum Application Builder and choose the Docbase we created earlier. Provide the installation user name and password (and optionally the domain name in the case of Windows NT server) to log in.

Documentum Login	
Docbase: dev_doc	OK
User Name: documentum	Cancel
Password: *********	Help
Domain:	

Figure 10.3: DAB log in dialog box

We will now create our custom DocApp to store and bundle the custom objects for our application. Choose **Create New DocApp** after logging in and provide a name for our custom DocApp.

Provide some friendly name for the DocApp, for example: `TestDocApp`. This DocApp will house the custom objects that we create for our business application.

Once the DocApp has been created, it is stored within a folder having the same name as the DocApp, inside the System cabinet's Applications folder in the Docbase.

So, in our case, the TestDocApp is stored at the following location in dev_doc Docbase: Cabinets/System/Applications/TestDocApp.

Note that the DocApp is in the checked-out state when you initially create it. You need to explicitly check-in the DocApp using the DAB menu options or by right-clicking and choosing Check In DocApp.

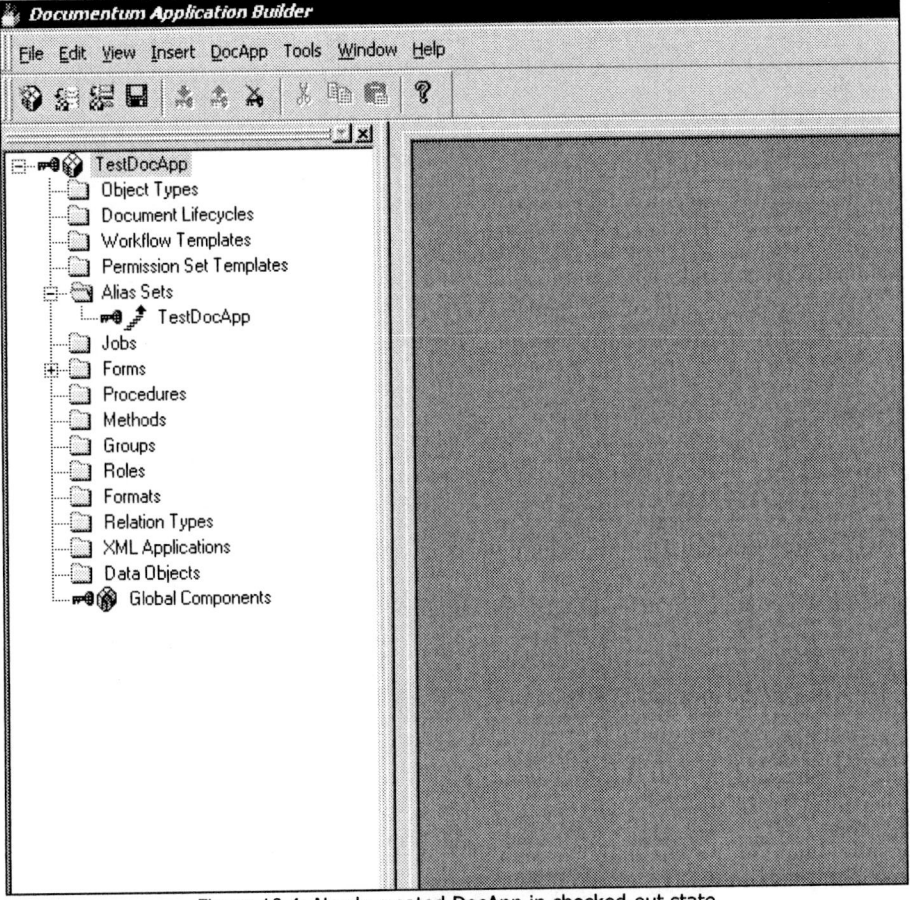

Figure 10.4: Newly created DocApp in checked-out state

10.4 Creating Custom Objects in DocApp

We can now create the objects we require in our custom DocApp. Using DAB we can create various types of Documentum objects like lifecycles, workflows, Permission Sets, object types, Methods, Jobs, and many more. We can do either of the following:

- Choose an existing object from the Docbase and simply include it in the custom DocApp. To do this, choose Insert | Object from Docbase.

- Create a new object from scratch and include it in the DocApp. To do this, choose menu option Insert.

If you make some changes to the objects and are not ready to check-in the DocApp into the Docbase, it is good practice to choose File | Save As and save the changes to a file on the local file system. You can later load these saved changes by choosing File | Open.

Once you save the changes (in the form of a *.dpa file), internally Documentum creates a *.ser file along with it.

In order to remove an object from DocApp, a common mistake committed by most developers is to select the object and choose Edit | Delete Object(s) from Docbase. This should not be done since this destroys the object from the Docbase itself. When you need to simply remove an object from your custom DocApp, select the object and press the *Delete* key.

Documentum application design is not just limited to understanding Application Builder and objects. There is much more to it, and as you progress on your journey in this book, you will discover many other areas where you can put in meticulous thought to implement a content management system tailored to your specific business needs.

In the next chapter, we will design and create object types and attributes for our News article example.

10.5 Summary

In this chapter we briefly discussed the importance of a good design before building an application. We went on to take up a sample case study for a dummy newspaper website, discussing how it could be managed by Documentum using templates.

We then touched upon the Web Publisher template, Rules file, and presentation file architecture.

A Web Publisher template file can be thought of as a simple XML file having pre-defined fields, which content authors can fill in to create contents.

The Rules file is again an XML file that controls the behavior of each of the template field XML elements.

Finally, a presentation file is nothing but an XSL stylesheet that controls the format (layout) of pages created from template files.

At the end of the chapter we discussed how to create a custom DocApp for storing and managing the Docbase objects required for our custom application.

11

Designing and Creating Custom Object Types

We discussed earlier that almost everything in Documentum is treated as an object, and objects are nothing but instances of object types. The key to a successful implementation in Documentum is designing the custom object types well.

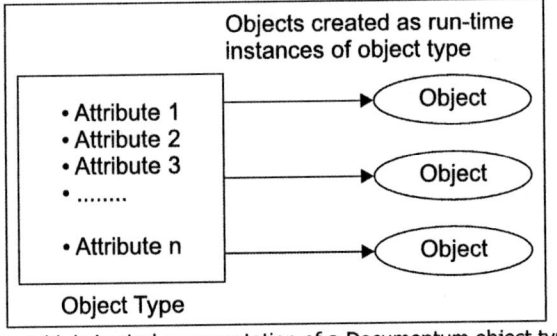

Figure 11.1: Logical representation of a Documentum object type

As discussed in Chapter 2 Documentum object types adhere to a hierarchy protocol. A subtype extends from a supertype and can itself be a supertype for another object type. Figure 11.2 shows a snapshot of the object type hierarchy in Documentum. Note that while SysObject (dm_sysobject) is a subtype of Persistent objects in Documentum, it is the supertype of objects such as Folders, Documents, Jobs, and Methods. Though not depicted in the figure, the Folder object (dm_folder) in turn is a supertype of the Cabinet object (dm_cabinet).

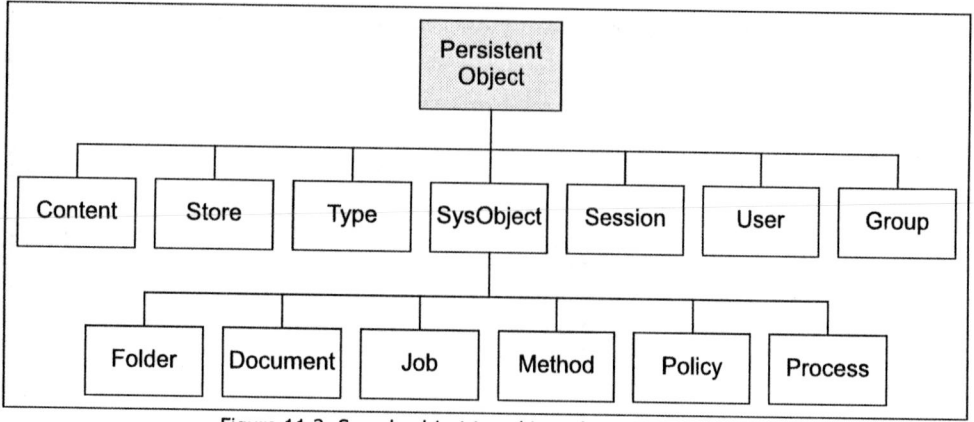

Figure 11.2: Sample object type hierarchy in Documentum

Having understood the basics of Documentum objects, let us continue with our case study of the dummy newspaper site and design/create an object type for the center pane news article.

11.1 Creating Object Types

In this section, we will discuss in detail the steps for creating object types. First you need to identify the object types needed for the application. For the center pane article, we need to have one object type, say cust_newsarticle (short for custom news article) and the News Article template will be associated with this object type. In order to create a new object type, choose Insert | Object Type in the DocApp builder and specify the name cust_newsarticle under Type name as shown in figure 11.3. The new object type shows up in the checked-out mode under the Object Types folder in the left tree pane in Application Builder.

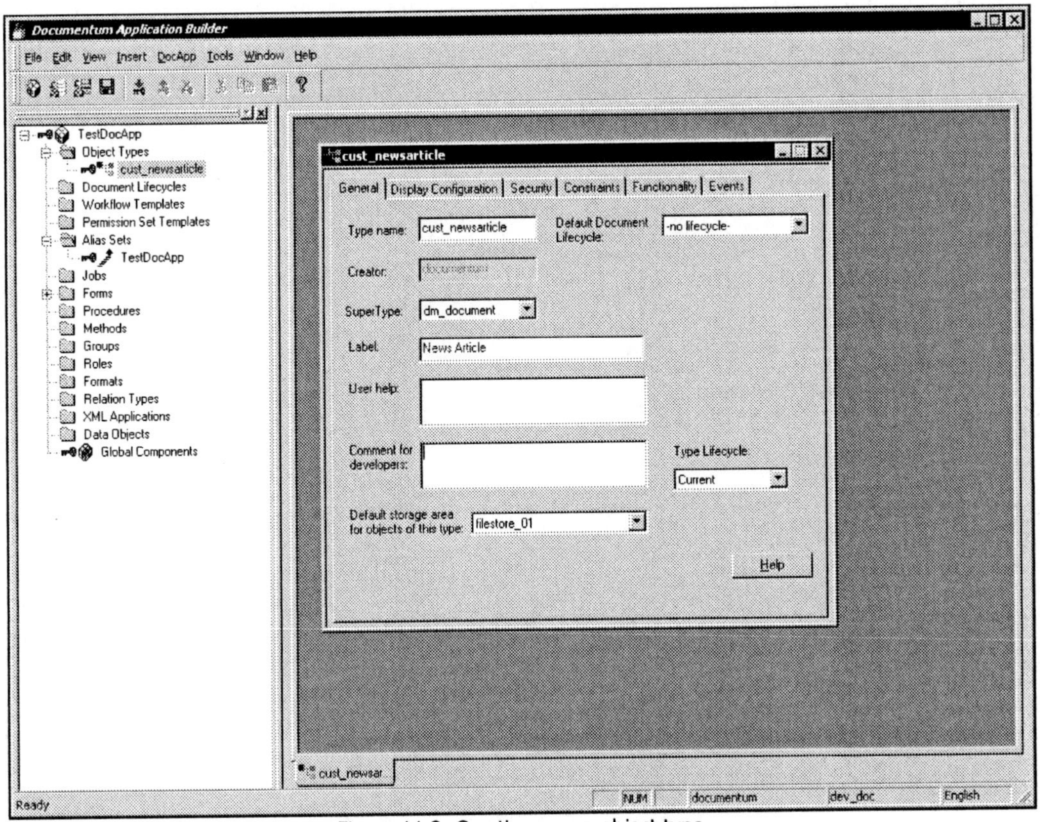

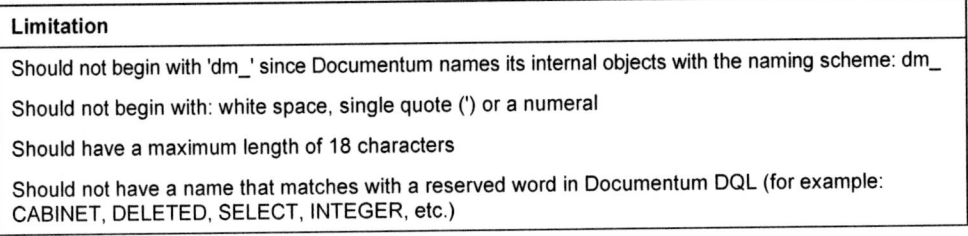

Figure 11.3: Creating a new object type

11.1.1 Type Names

Object type names are unique and globally accessible within the Docbase, so it is critical to adopt an intelligent naming convention for your custom object types to distinguish them from the thousands of existing objects in the Docbase. Additionally, when deploying the object types to other Docbases, a good naming convention avoids any potential naming conflicts in the target Docbase.

11.1.2 Limitations of Object Type Names

Figure 11.4 shows some limitations we need to keep in mind while naming object types.

Limitation
Should not begin with 'dm_' since Documentum names its internal objects with the naming scheme: dm_
Should not begin with: white space, single quote (') or a numeral
Should have a maximum length of 18 characters
Should not have a name that matches with a reserved word in Documentum DQL (for example: CABINET, DELETED, SELECT, INTEGER, etc.)

Figure 11.4: Object type naming convention limitations

The Object Type General tab is shown in figure 11.5:

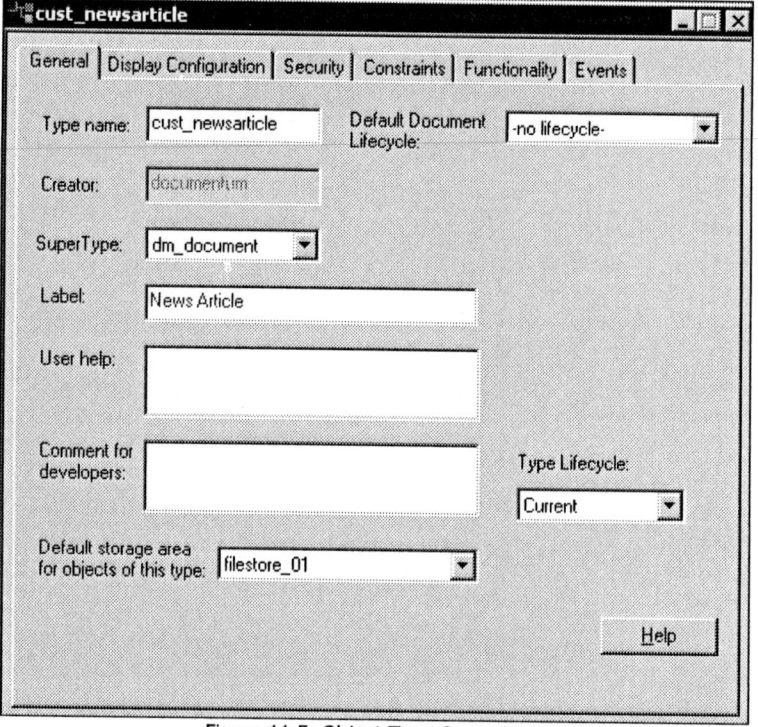

Figure 11.5: Object Type General tab

11.1.3 Supertype

Each object type can either extend from an existing object type in Documentum or have its supertype as NULL.

In our case, News Article is a document object type and so we extended it from dm_document object type. Other object types shown in the Super Type dropdown are: dm_job, dm_folder, dm_user, etc.

Each object type in Docbase is stored within its own database table in the Docbase's underlying RDBMS.

As a rule of thumb, do not extend the object type hierarchy too deep (deeper than three levels) since internally this amounts to as many database joins by Documentum. You could, for example, extend your custom object type cust_newsarticle from dm_document and further extend another custom object type (say cust_newsarticle_sub) from cust_newsarticle, but not deeper than this!

It is better to decide the name and supertype of custom object type well, because after checking in the object type in the Docbase, you cannot change its name or its supertype.

Now follow these steps to finish off with creating object types:

1. Under the Display Configuration tab, the specific attributes to be shown for the specific object type under specific conditions can be configured.

    However, note that this feature is applicable only to WDK 5.2 + applications (such as Webtop, Web Publisher, etc.) and Desktop 5.2 + applications (such as Desktop Client).

    You can see in figure 11.6 that by default three application **scopes** are shown for DcDesktopClient (Desktop), Web Publisher and Webtop (WDK clients).

    For each of these scopes, you can choose which specific attributes (shown in the bottom section of figure 11.6) need to be shown under their respective tabs in the Properties screen.

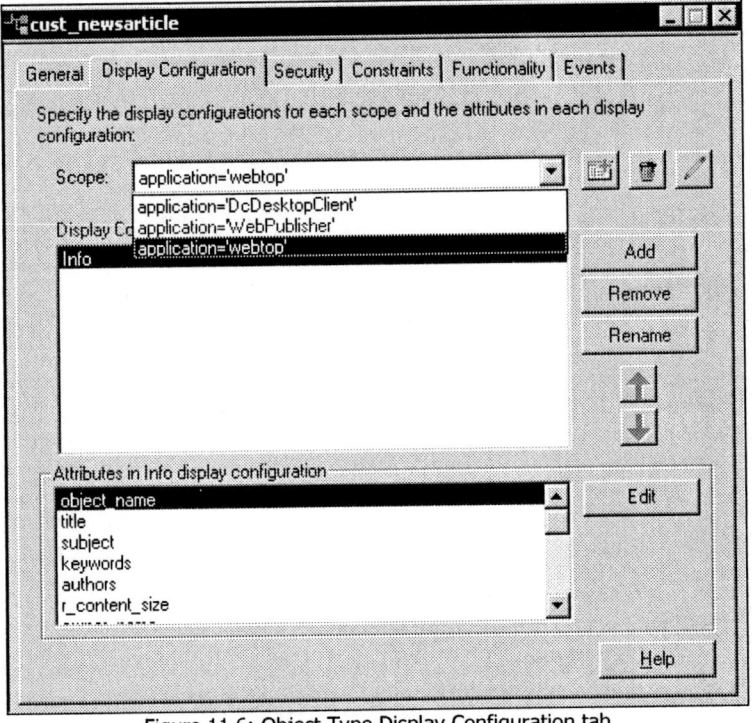

Figure 11.6: Object Type Display Configuration tab

The Properties screen in Web Publisher (refer to figure 11.7) shows the various tabs such as Info, Publishing, History, etc. The attributes shown under each of these tabs can be configured via the Display Configuration section in Object Type.

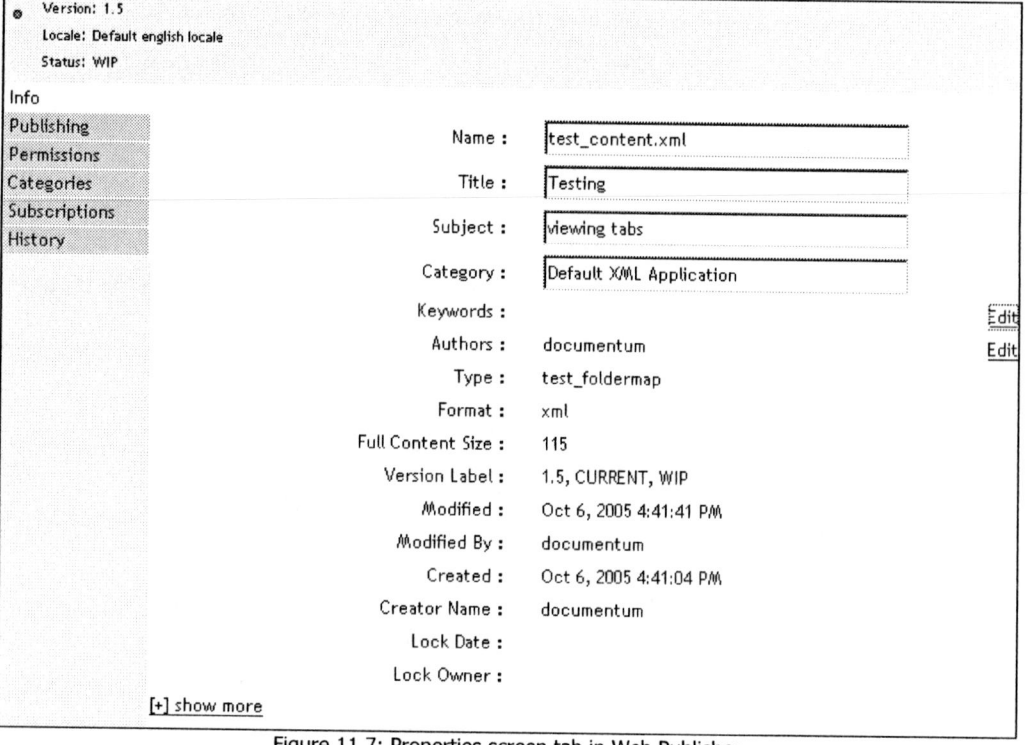

Figure 11.7: Properties screen tab in Web Publisher

Under the Display Configuration List, you can introduce a new tab or rename an existing tab by clicking on the Add or Rename buttons respectively, as shown in figure 11.6. You can even remove a tab altogether via the Remove button.

Under the Attributes in… display configuration section, you can choose the specific attributes to be shown for the selected tab by clicking on the Edit button.

2. Within the Security tab (refer to figure 11.8), there is an option to associate a default Permission Set (Access Control List) with an object type. This ensures that whenever an object is created from this object type, it will be assigned the Permission Set that we have set as default for the object type in question.

    This is a good mechanism for controlling permission levels for accessing or modifying the objects of a specific object type

For specifying the Permission Set, choose from the existing Permission Sets shown in the Name: dropdown. All other fields such as Owner, Description, Permissions, and Your Permission are read-only fields, automatically populated by Documentum once you have chosen a Permission Set from the dropdown.

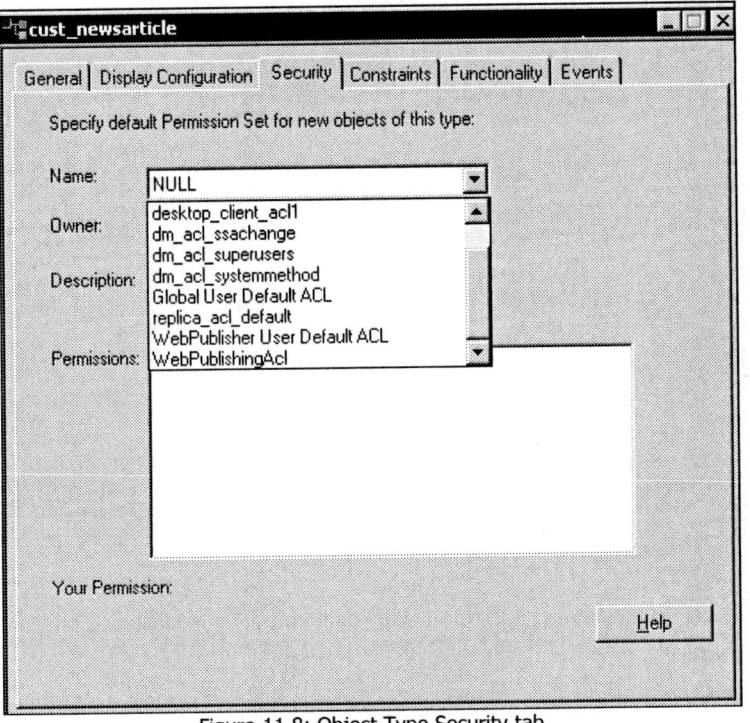

Figure 11.8: Object Type Security tab

3. Within the Constraints tab (refer to figure 11.9), you can specify consistency checks using Docbasic (Documentum's proprietary language) expressions for the object type's attribute values. Under the Constraint expression section, enter a Docbasic expression.

Suppose we need to ensure that whenever a content object is created from the object type cust_newsarticle, its subject property should never be left blank. The Docbasic expression in such a scenario would be:

```
not(subject = "")
```

After entering the Docbasic expression, click on Check Syntax to confirm that the entered Docbasic expression has the correct syntax. You can refer to the Documentum Docbasic reference manual to read about Docbasic and its application usage.

If the attribute constraint is not met, the error message that needs to be shown to the user by the application should be entered in the Error message string... section.

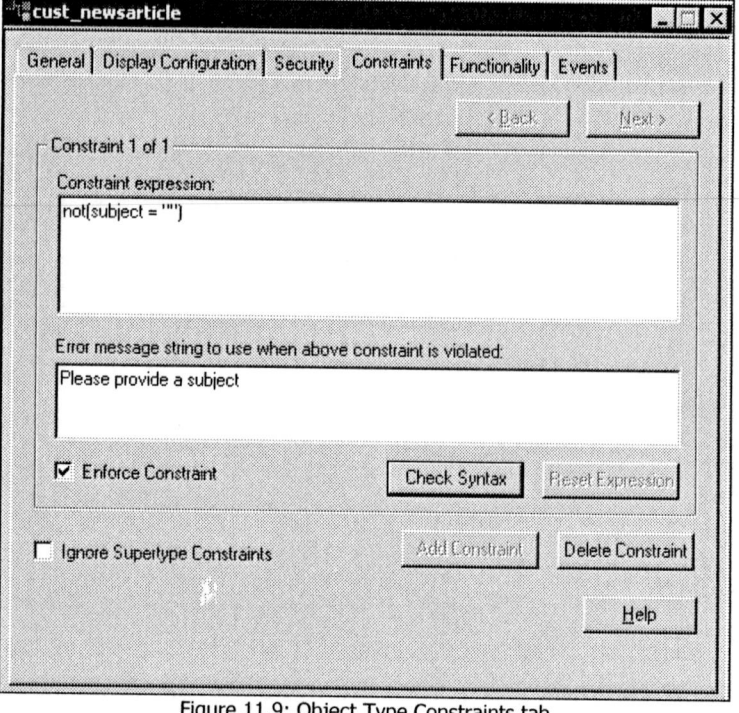

Figure 11.9: Object Type Constraints tab

In our case, if the subject attribute for the content object is left blank, the error message Please provide a subject is shown to the content creator.

You can add multiple constraints, by clicking on the Add Constraint button. On doing so, the Back and Next buttons get enabled, allowing us to move back and forth between the added constraints.

4. An object type inherits most of its functionality from the supertype extended by it. Also, the components of the default DocApp are used to implement most of the functionality inherited from the supertype.

Using Documentum Application Builder, you can perform a variety of operations such as:

- Adding a new functionality class and the component used to implement it.
- Specifying a different component to implement a functionality class inherited from the supertype.
- Disabling an inherited functionality class altogether.

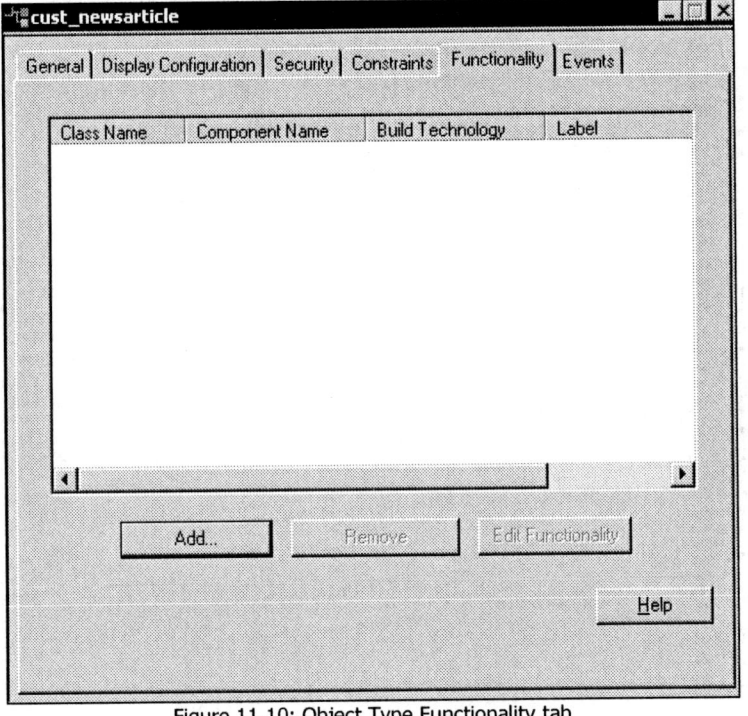

Figure 11.10: Object Type Functionality tab

Figure 11.10 shows the Functionality tab for Object Type in Documentum Application Builder.

5. Under the Events tab (refer to figure 11.11), you are shown the system events (read-only) for the object type.

You can add, modify, and remove application-specific events by clicking on the Add, Remove, and Edit... buttons respectively. These events are used for auditing purposes in the Docbase.

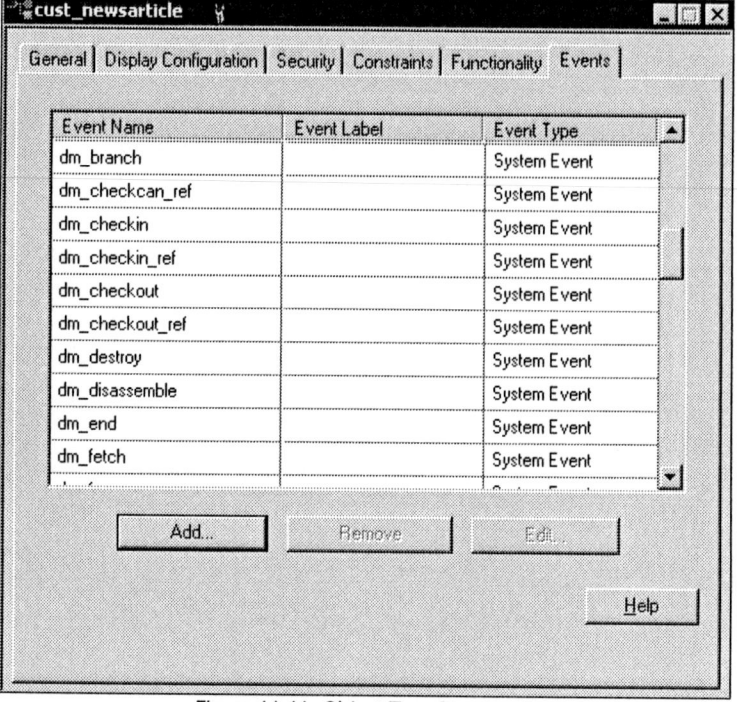

Figure 11.11: Object Type Events tab

6. After you have filled in the relevant data in all the necessary tabs, right-click on the object type cust_newsarticle (in the left tree pane) and choose the option Check in selected object(s) to check-in the object type in Docbase. Doing so makes the newly created object type available in the Docbase for applications.

7. Till now the object type cust_newsarticle was not associated with any lifecycle. Let us now associate it with Documentum's Default Lifecycle, so that whenever content is created from this object type, it is automatically attached to the Default Lifecycle.

    Insert Default Lifecycle into the TestDocApp by choosing Insert | Object from the Docbase | Document Lifecycle menu option.

    Once the Default Lifecycle is included in our DocApp, open it in Edit mode as shown in figure 11.12.

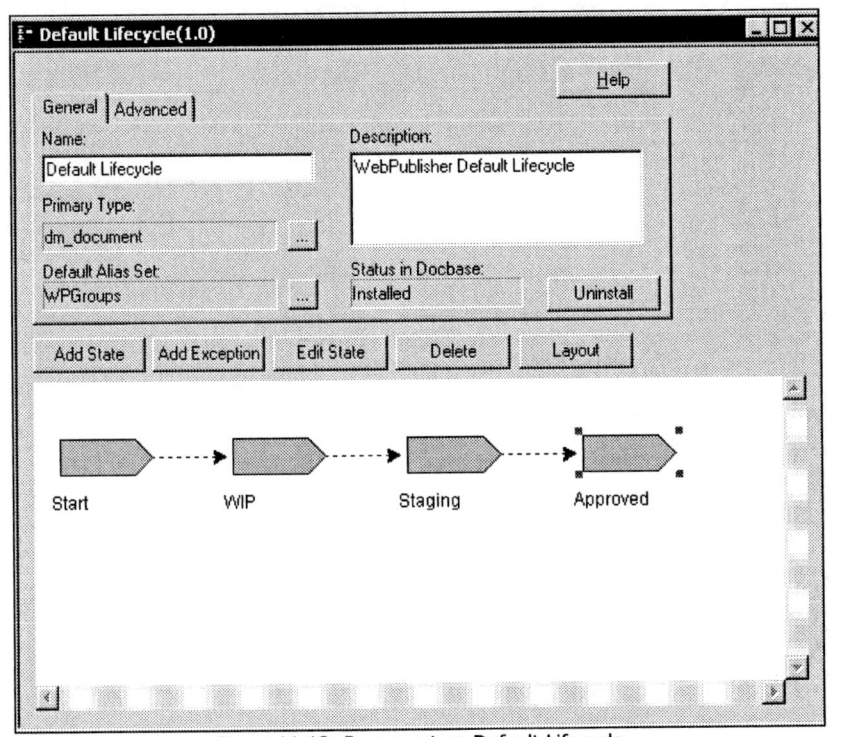

Figure 11.12: Documentum Default Lifecycle

8. Please click on the small box (...) shown against the Primary Type field and in the opened popup (refer to figure 11.13), move the cust_newsarticle object type from Available Subtypes to Acceptable Subtypes section by clicking on the → button. Finally, click on OK.

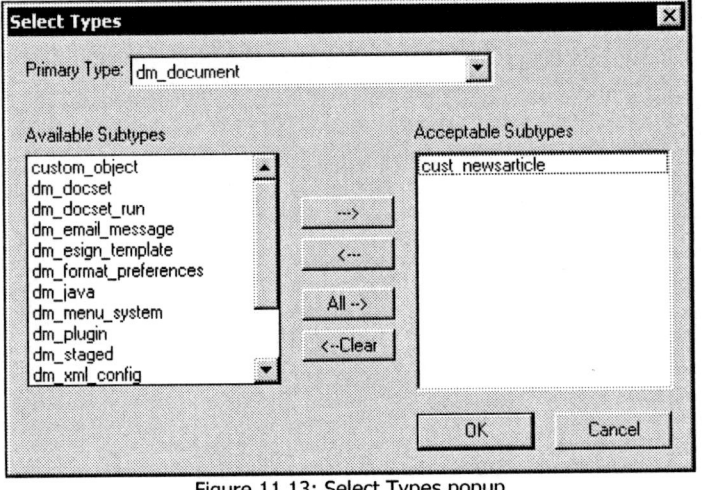

Figure 11.13: Select Types popup

Now check-in the modified lifecycle in the Docbase by right-clicking on the lifecycle object (in the left tree pane) and choose the option Check in selected object(s).

Remember to check-in the lifecycle (refer to figure 11.14) in the Docbase as Same version and not as a Major/Minor version. This will prevent creation of multiple Lifecycle versions in the Docbase and hence avoid possible confusions arising out of numerous versions.

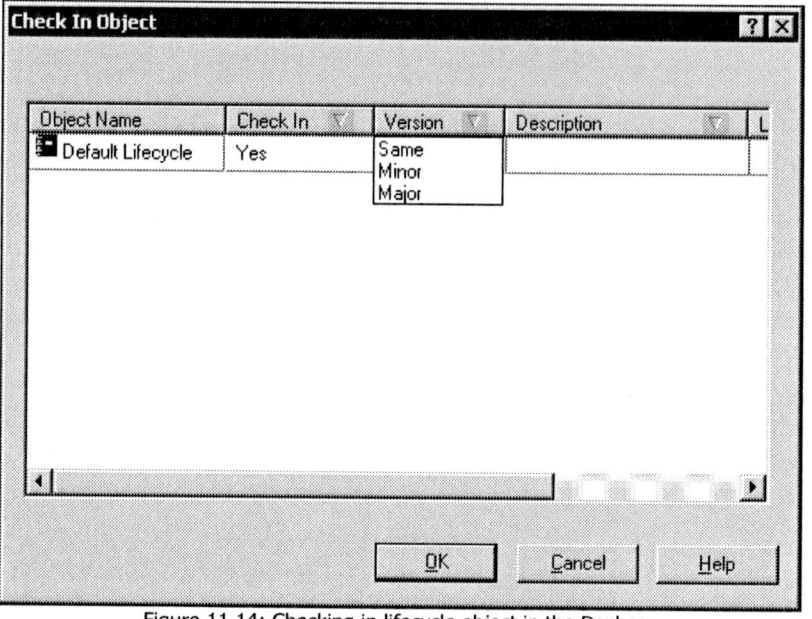

Figure 11.14: Checking in lifecycle object in the Docbase

9. After the Default Lifecycle has been checked in, the system brings it back to Draft state, thus making it unavailable for use by applications. Open the lifecycle in View mode and click on Validate and then Install to install the lifecycle back in the Docbase.

10. Now we need to specify a default lifecycle for the newly created object type. Open the object, type cust_newsarticle in Edit mode and choose Default Lifecycle from the Default Document Lifecycle dropdown as shown in figure 11.15. Checkin the modified object type back into the Docbase.

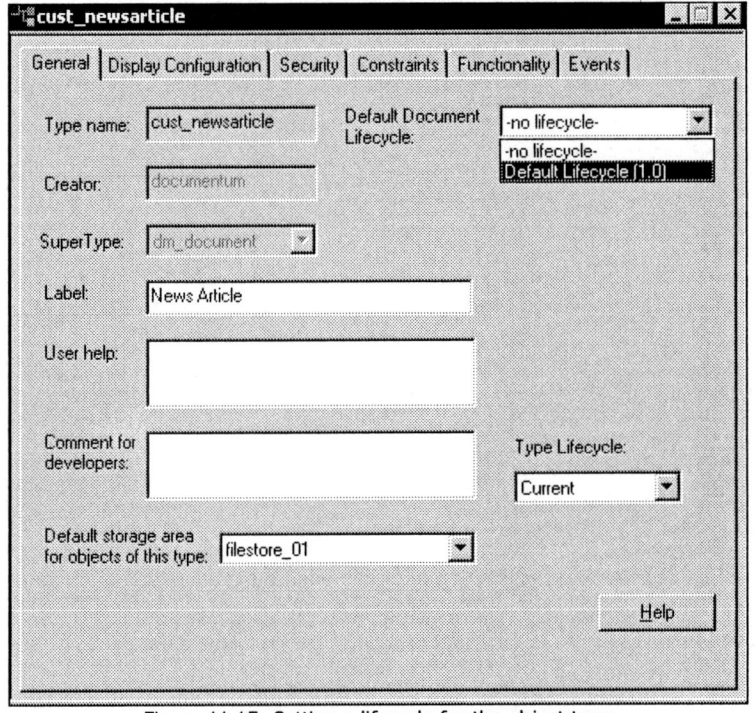

Figure 11.15: Setting a lifecycle for the object type

We will be covering lifecycles in detail in the next chapter; so don't worry if you don't understand the relation between object type and lifecycle well.

11.2 Designing and Creating Custom Attributes of Object Type(s)

Once you have designed your custom object type, it inherits all the attributes (properties) of its supertype object type. You might want to additionally create some custom attributes that are unavailable in its supertype and that are specific only to this object type.

For our cust_newsarticle object type, we might need the following custom attributes (say):

- News article one line summary
- A flag to identify if this news article is a press release or not
- News article priority: Out of all the published news articles, where in the order this article needs to be displayed on the website.
- News article editor(s) and approver(s) names

It is best to prepare a small table to design the attributes for the custom object type and fill in the respective columns of the table as per your business-specific requirements. Let us discuss this in the context of our dummy website (please refer to figure 11.16):

Attribute Name	Attribute Label	Data Type	Length	Single/ Repeating	Mandatory	Values
cust_news_sum mary	News Article Summary	String	200	Single	Yes	None
cust_news_is_ press_rel	Is this for press release?	Boolean	0	Single	No	None
cust_news_ display_order	Display Order	Integer	0	Single	No	Conditional: • 1,3,5,7 if News article is for press release • 0,2,4,6 if News article is not for press release
cust_news_edit_ approvers	Editors/App rovers	String	100	Repeating	No	None

Figure 11.16: Attributes Design table

One should design the attributes very carefully, since after an attribute has been created and checked in to the Docbase, the following cannot be modified:

- Name of the attribute
- Data type of the attribute
- Whether the attribute is single or repeating
- Length of the attribute (can only be increased)

11.3 Adding Attributes to an Object Type

Choose the object type in question within the DocApp and select Insert | Attribute. We will first take an example by creating the attribute cust_news_summary for the object type cust_newsarticle.

Fill in the relevant fields in the new attribute creation screen as shown in the figure 11.17.

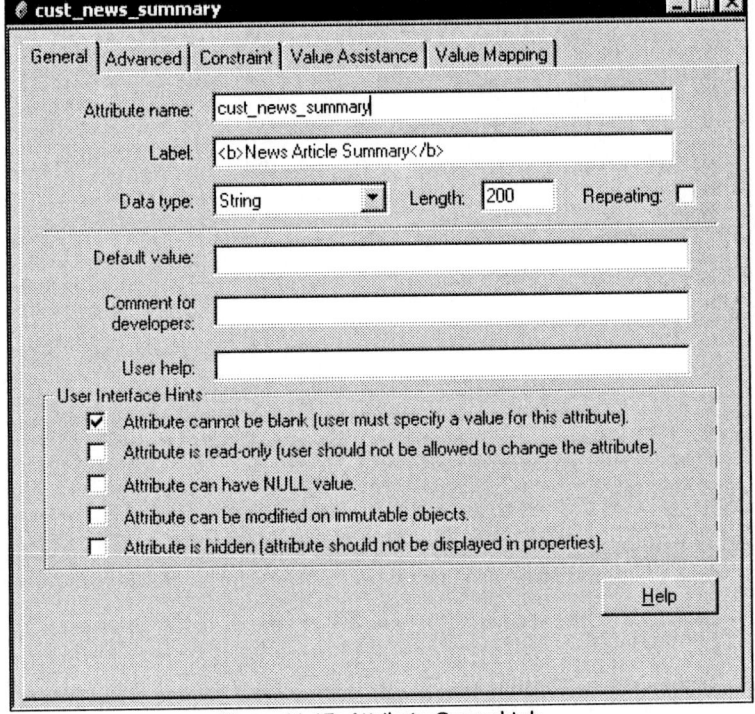

Figure 11.17: Attribute General tab

11.3.1 Attribute Names

Similar to object type names, attribute names have certain restrictions that need to be carefully adhered to. Figure 11.18 lists down some limitations for attribute names.

11.3.2 Limitations of Object Type Attribute Names

Limitations
Should be in lowercase
Should not begin with: white space, single quote (') or a numeral
Should not begin with 'dm_', 'i_', 'r_', and 'a_' since Documentum internally uses these for its object attribute naming scheme
Should not have a name that matches with the following reserved words in Documentum: 'from', 'where' and 'select'

Figure 11.18: Attribute naming convention limitations

11.3.2.1 Label

The Label field will be the actual label shown against this attribute field in the properties page for the object. You can surround the text in HTML markup as well for a visual appeal when displaying the attribute in properties page. We will look more into this in Chapter 24.

11.3.2.2 Data Type

Choose the data type for the attribute from the Data type dropdown. The available data types shown in the dropdown are:

- Boolean
- Integer
- String
- ID
- Time
- Double

11.3.2.3 Length

The Length field is enabled only for attributes of the string data type. Note that using Application Builder, the maximum length that we can specify for a string attribute is 2000.

11.3.2.4 Repeating

In order to specify an attribute as multi-valued, the Repeating checkbox can be selected. If left unchecked, it signifies a single-valued attribute.

Fill in the other attribute fields shown under the General tab as per your specific requirements. In our case we had identified the cust_news_summary attribute to be mandatory (refer to the attribute design in figure 11.16) and hence we checked the checkbox against the field Attribute cannot be blank.

Under the Advanced tab (refer to figure 11.19), you can specify the search parameters used by client applications to search an object in a Docbase, based on its attribute values. By default, every attribute is searchable. You can negate this condition by unchecking the Searchable checkbox shown in the figure.

11.3.2.5 Default Search Value

You can provide some default search value that is always shown when using client applications for searching objects based on this particular attribute.

11.3.2.6 Allowable Search Operators

You can add/remove search operators that client applications will use for searching Docbase objects based on certain conditions for the attribute in question.

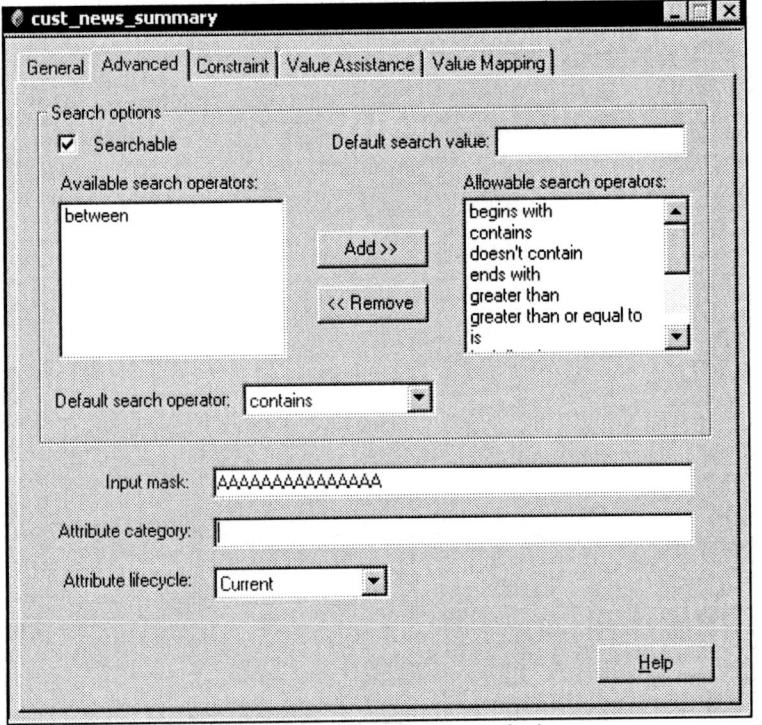

Figure 11.19: Attribute Advanced tab

There are numerous search operators provided by Documentum, such as:

- contains
- ends with
- greater than
- is
- less than

11.3.2.7 Input Mask

This is an important field and if utilized well, can do wonders for you. The input mask field can serve as a useful validation mechanism for the object properties.

Say for example, as per your business needs, you want the content creators to provide an alphanumeric value only 15 characters long for the attribute cust_news_summary. The following input mask in the attribute can achieve the desired condition without any need for scripting/coding of any sort:

AAAAAAAAAAAAAAA

The fifteen A's in a row signify that only 15 characters are allowed of the nature A, i.e. alphanumeric. Please refer to figure 11.20 for all available mask characters and symbols provided by Documentum:

Symbol	Interpretation
A	Only alphanumeric character allowed. i.e. a-z, A-Z, and 0-9
#	Only purely numeric values allowed. i.e. 0-9
?	Only purely alphabetic values allowed. i.e. a-z and A-Z
&	Any ASCII character is allowed
U	Uppercase alphabetic character allowed
L	Lowercase alphabetic characters allowed

Figure 11.20: Masking characters available in Documentum

1. Similar to what we saw in Object Types, within the Constraint tab (refer to figure 11.21), you can specify consistency checks using Docbasic expressions for the object type's attribute values.

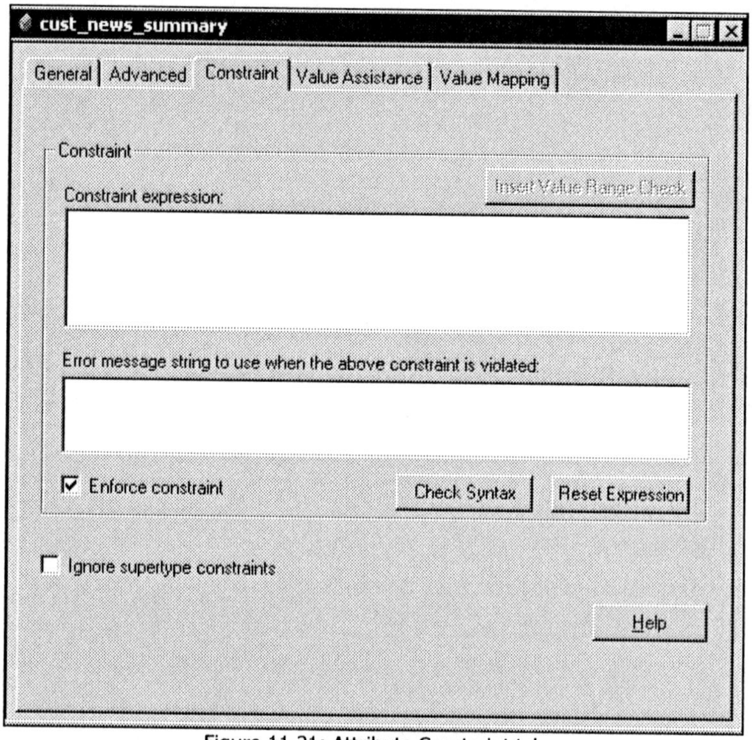

Figure 11.21: Attribute Constraint tab

2. Value Assistance comes in handy when you want the users to choose some pre-defined values for the attribute. Using Value Assistance, you can turn the attribute field into a dropdown (pick-list) in the property screens, from where the user can choose existing values while creating new objects. Click the Add Default button (refer to figure 11.22) to add values for the attribute. The Default Value Assistance popup shows up (figure 11.23).

    It is worth mentioning here that the Value Assistance feature is not available when an attribute is of the data type Boolean. The Add Default button is grayed out in such a scenario.

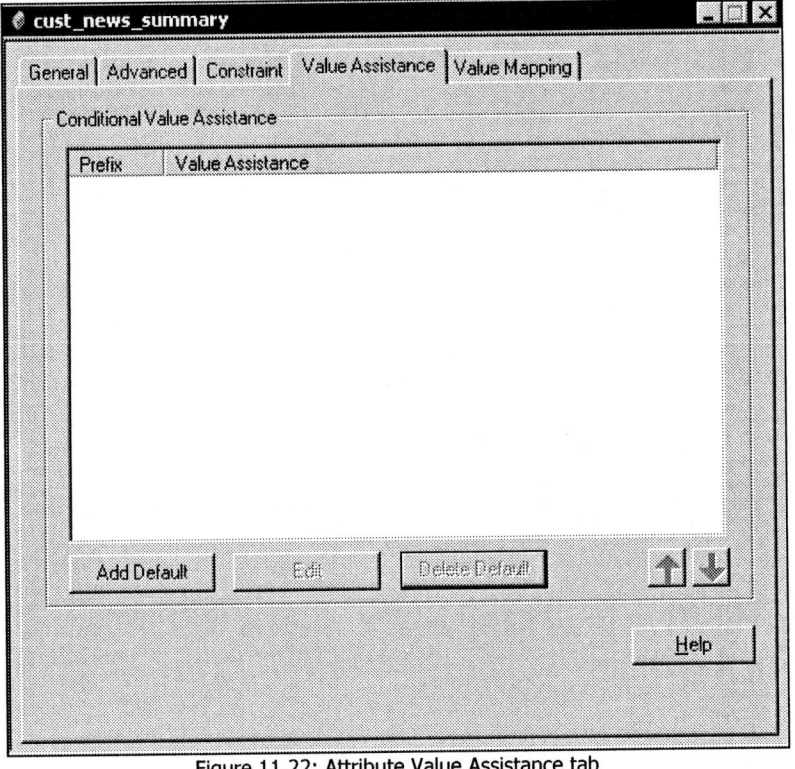

Figure 11.22: Attribute Value Assistance tab

You can provide the individual values, each in a new line (by pressing the *Enter* key), and mark the pick-list as complete by checking the checkbox List is complete…. Please refer to figure 11.23 for details.

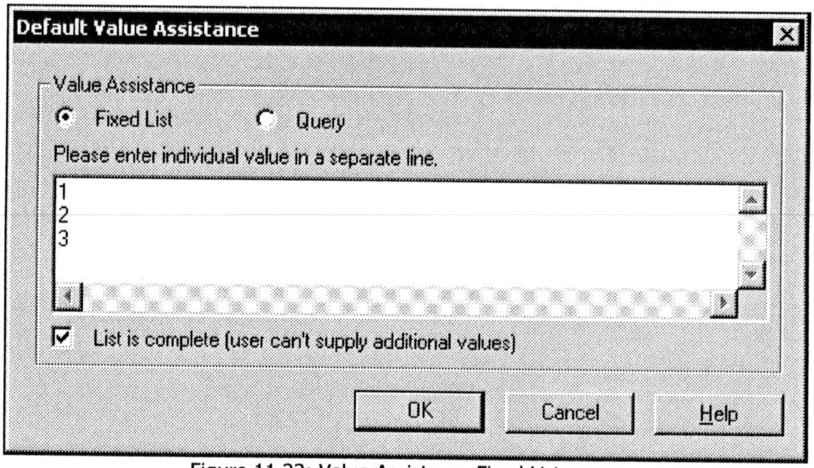

Figure 11.23: Value Assistance Fixed List popup

Alternatively, you could choose the radio button shown against the Query option instead of the Fixed List option (refer to figure 11.24). This will allow you to dynamically populate the dropdown with values queried (via DQL) from an object type or a registered table in Documentum. We will cover this in detail later in this chapter. For now, please do not be bothered about how the Query option is used for querying registered tables. For the cust_news_summary attribute, we do not need to display any pre-defined values in a dropdown. However, for the cust_news_display_ order attribute, we will query a registered table and explain the usage of the Query option in detail.

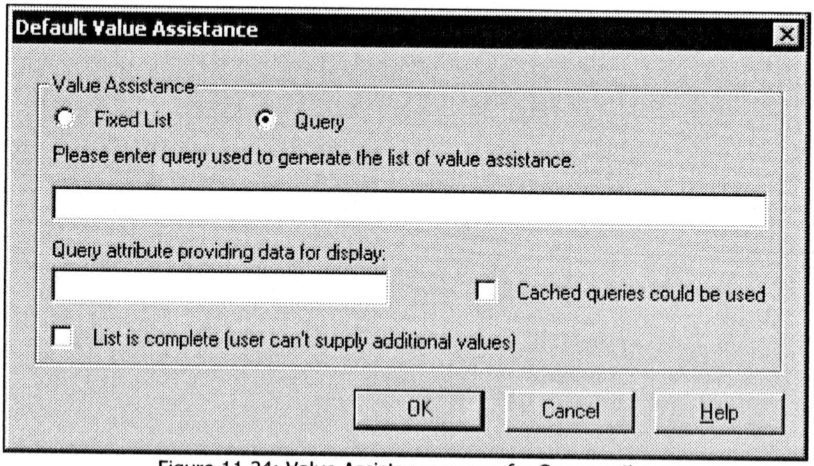

Figure 11.24: Value Assistance popup for Query option

11.3.2.8 Conditional Value Assistance

Documentum improves further on the Value Assistance functionality by allowing developers to configure the dropdown values conditionally, based on certain attribute values. Let us take a quick example to understand how conditional value assistance works in Documentum.

After you have provided a Default Value Assistance for the attribute, the Add Conditional button is enabled, as shown in figure 11.25.

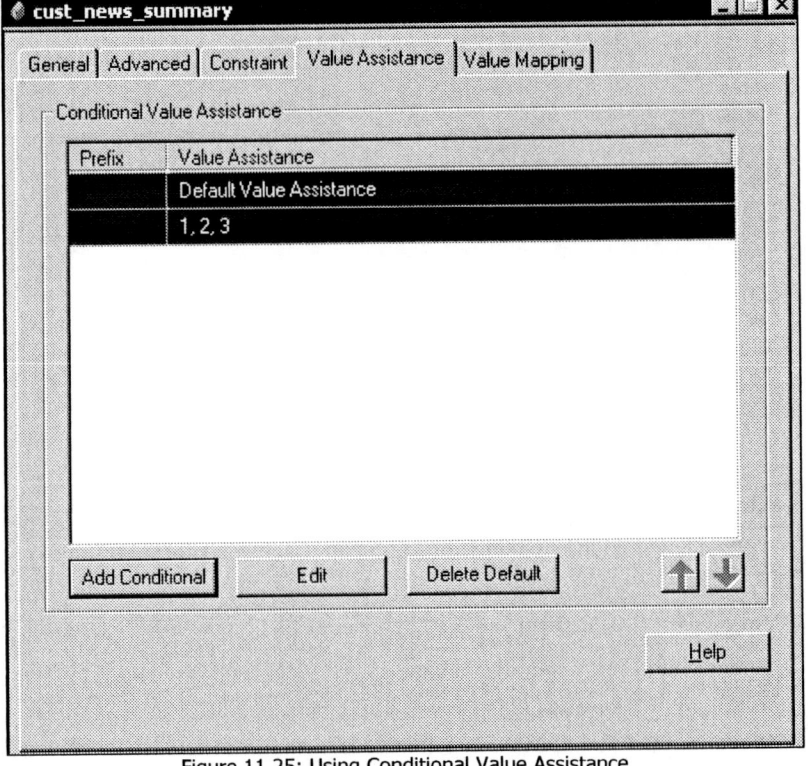

Figure 11.25: Using Conditional Value Assistance

Clicking on the Add Conditional button shows the Value Assistance Clause popup as shown in figure 11.26. The condition can be provided in the form of a Docbasic expression (as we saw earlier in the Constraints tab while creating object types). The entered Docbasic expression can be verified by clicking on the Check Syntax button. Based on the evaluation of the entered Docbasic expression (attribute condition), a dropdown list (under the Value Assistance section in the popup) is provided to the users.

In our case, for example, if the value of the `title` attribute for the object is `alphabets`, the dropdown shown to the users will be A,B,C (refer to figure 11.26).

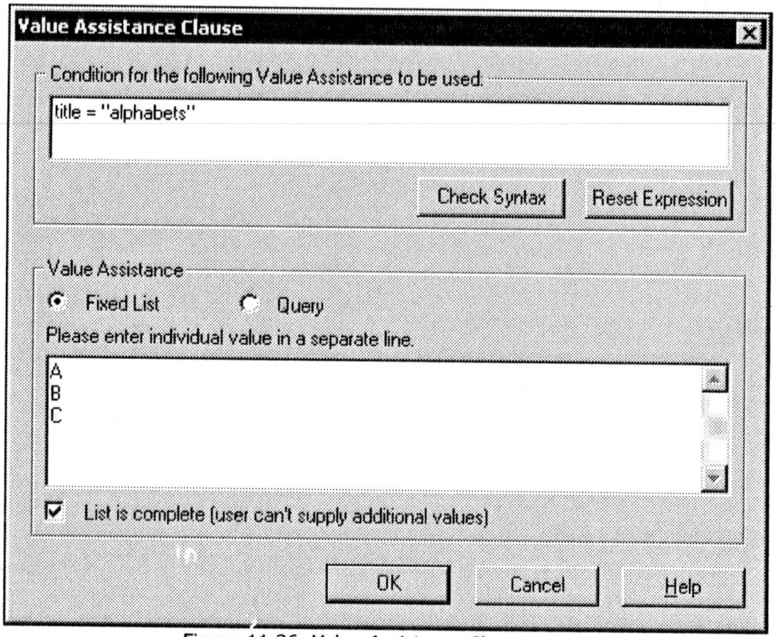

Figure 11.26: Value Assistance Clause popup

You can provide additional conditions and clauses by providing additional Docbasic expressions in the same way you had entered the first conditional clause. All the existing conditions are shown in the form of 'If Then...' clauses as shown in figure 11.27.

It says that if the value of the `title` attribute is `alphabets`, the dropdown will show the values: A, B, C.

If the value of the `title` attribute is `numbers`, the dropdown will show the values: 1, 2, 3, 4, 5.

If none of the conditions are met, the default values shown in the dropdown are: 1, 2, 3.

However, keep in mind that due to Docbasic limitations, you cannot provide more than 35 such conditional values assistance statements in Application Builder.

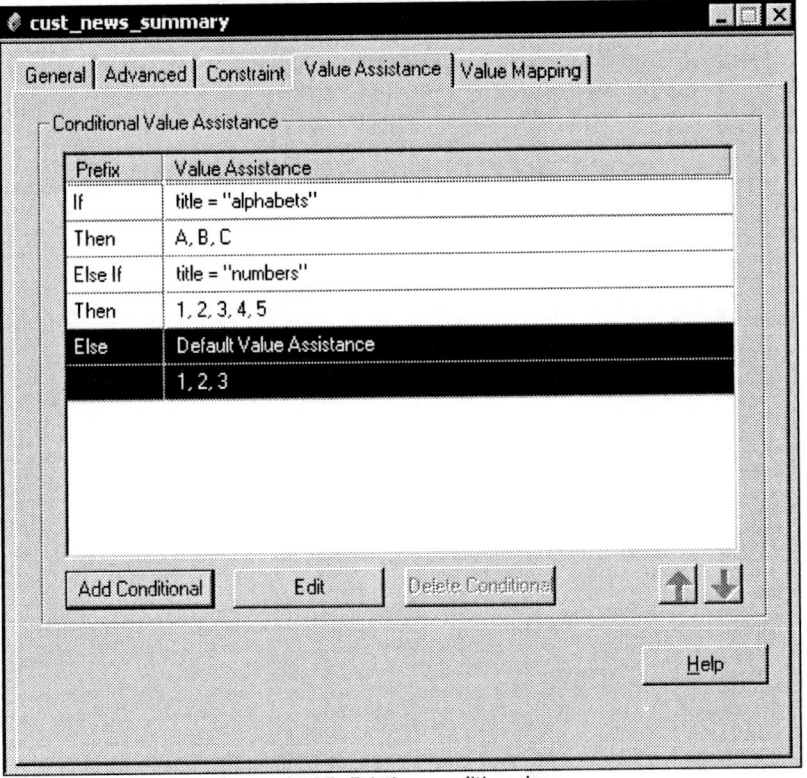

Figure 11.27: Existing condition clauses

One of the frequent requirements is to display some user-friendly text in the dropdown values, along with short codes saved for each of these values for applications to read and understand.

In our example, we might want the users to see the values in the dropdown as 'One, Two, Three', while actually saving them behind the scenes in the Docbase as 1, 2, and 3 respectively.

Under the Value Mapping tab, enter the Docbase value in the Data column and its mapped dropdown display value in the Display String column as shown in figure 11.28.

The values under Display String will only be used for visually display in the dropdown. The values in the Data column would be saved within the Docbase as the value for the attribute.

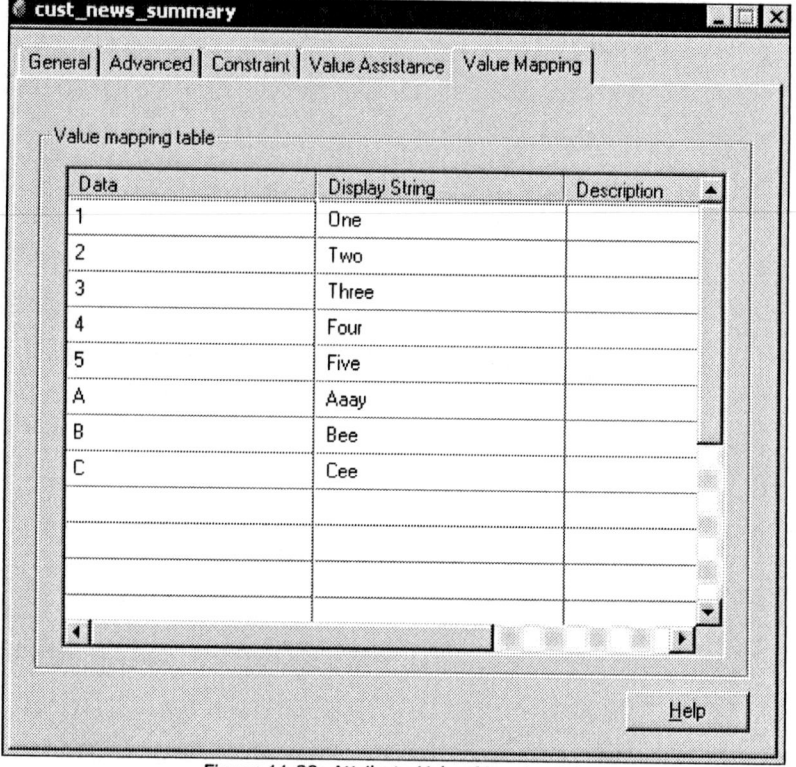

Figure 11.28: Attribute Value Mapping tab

After you have filled in the relevant data in all the necessary tabs, right-click on the object type cust_newsarticle (in the left tree pane) and choose the option Check in selected object(s) to checkin the object type (along with its attributes) in Docbase. Doing so makes the newly created attribute available in the Docbase for applications.

Create the other attributes cust_news_is_press_rel and cust_news_edit_approvers as per the specifications in attribute design table 11.16. We will now take up the example of conditional value assistance using the Query option by creating the attribute cust_news_display_order as follows.

You may want to jump back to Chapter 3 to quickly go through our earlier discussion on registered tables before you continue with the following section.

11.4 Querying Registered Tables using DQL for Value Assistance

Create a new attribute cust_news_display_order and fill in the General tab as shown in figure 11.29.

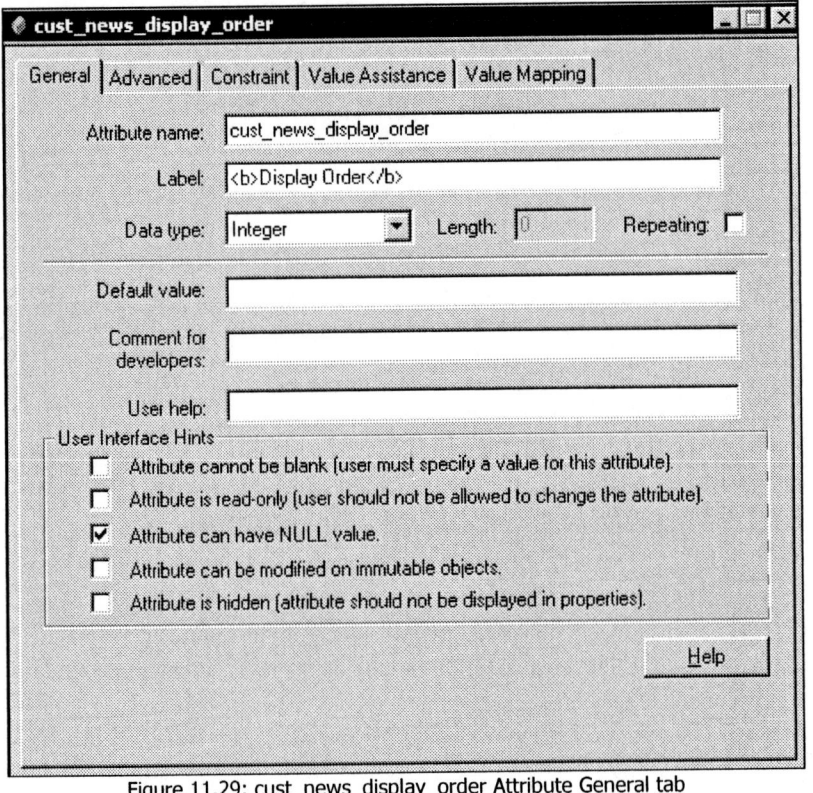

Figure 11.29: cust_news_display_order Attribute General tab

This attribute needs to show the drop-down values: 1, 3, 5, 7 if the value of the attribute cust_news_is_press_rel is true and the values: 0, 2, 4, 6 if the value of the attribute cust_news_is_press_rel is false.

This can be achieved by conditional value assistance and using registered tables as follows:

1. Create a table in the underlying RDBMS as per the following design:
   - **Table name:** cust_values_table
   - **Column 1 (int):** cust_odd_values
   - **Column 2 (int):** cust_even_values

   Insert values for both the columns as shown in figure 11.30:

cust_odd_values	cust_even_values
1	0
3	2
5	4
7	6

   Figure 11.30: cust_values_table database table

2. Log in to Documentum Administrator as an administrator and register the RDBMS table cust_values_table via the following DQL queries:

   ```
   register table dm_dbo.cust_values_table (cust_odd_values
   int,cust_even_values int)
   update dm_registered object set owner_table_permit=15 where
   object_name='cust_values_table'
   update dm_registered object set group_table_permit=15 where
   object_name='cust_values_table'
   update dm_registered object set world_table_permit=15 where
   object_name='cust_values_table'
   ```

   Note that here dm_dbo is an alias for the Docbase owner and permit level 15 is for select, insert, update, and delete rights.

   Now issue the following SELECT query in Documentum Administrator via the DQL query editor to find out if the values in the registered table are returned or not:

   ```
   select cust_odd_values, cust_even_values from dm_dbo.cust_values_table
   ```

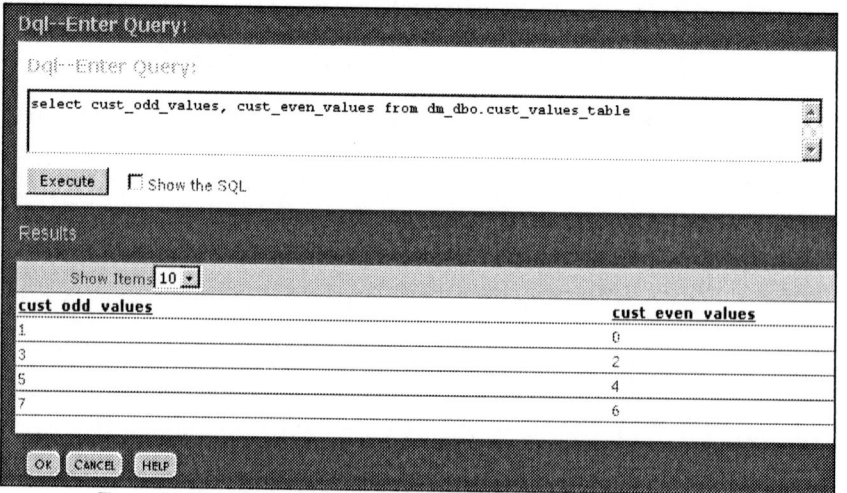

Figure 11.31: Results shown when querying a registered table via DQL

The results shown in figure 11.31 prove that the registered table has been set up correctly and can be accessed through the Query option in Value Assistance Clause within Application Builder.

3. Go to the Value Assistance tab and click the Add Default button to enter the default set of values to be shown for the attribute.

    Select the Query radio button and enter the following DQL query in the textbox Please enter query... (refer to figure 11.32):

    ```
    select cust_odd_values, cust_even_values from dm_dbo.cust_values_table
    ```

    This will evaluate the values available in the registered table at run time and return the result set to the client applications. Note that Documentum internally queries the actual underlying RDBMS table at run time and *not* the registered table object.

    Within the Query attribute... textbox provide the registered table column name that will be used to populate the dropdown. We have set it to cust_odd_values, so that if no conditions/clauses are met, the cust_news_display_order attribute will display the following values in the dropdown: 1, 3, 5, 7.

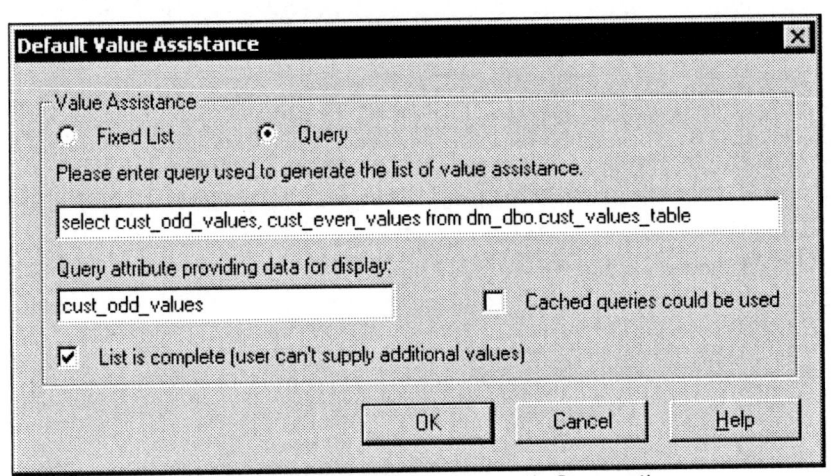

Figure 11.32: Default Value Assistance via Query option

After filling in the Default Value Assistance, click on the Add Conditional button and enter the conditional clauses as shown in figure 11.33. As listed in the Attribute Design table 11.15, the cust_news_display_order attribute will show the dropdown values: 1, 3, 5, 7 if the value of the attribute cust_news_is_press_rel is true and the values: 0, 2, 4, 6 if the value of the attribute cust_news_is_press_rel is false.

- ○ **Condition/Clause**: cust_news_is_press_rel = true
- ○ **Query attribute providing data for display**: cust_odd_values
- ○ **Condition/Clause**: cust_news_is_press_rel = false
- ○ **Query attribute providing data for display**: cust_even_values

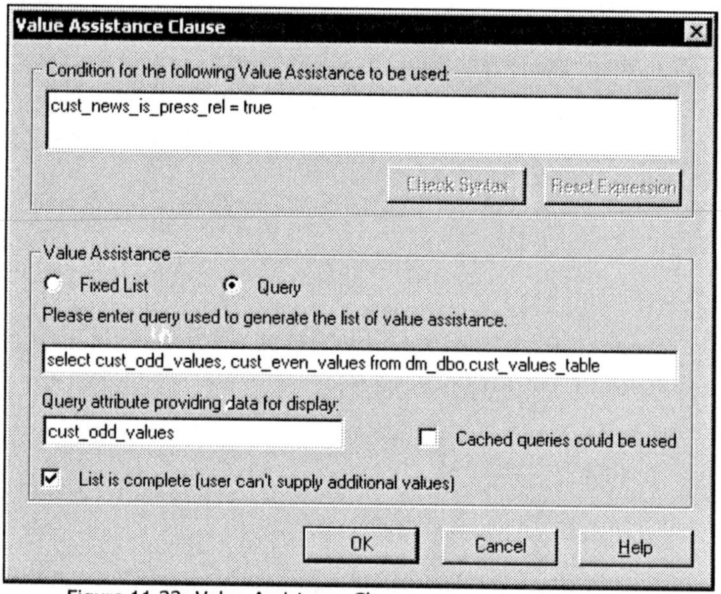

Figure 11.33: Value Assistance Clause popup using Query option

4. After you have filled in the relevant data in all the necessary tabs, right-click on the object type cust_newsarticle (in the left tree pane) and choose the option Check in selected object(s) to check-in the object type (along with its attributes) in Docbase. Doing so makes the newly created attribute cust_news_display_order available in the Docbase for applications.

The newly added attributes cust_news_summary, cust_news_is_press_rel, cust_news_display_order, and cust_news_edit_approvers can be added in the new content properties page by customizing the default new content page. Figure 11.34 shows how the new attributes would look in the actual scenario. The necessary code changes needed to accomplish this customization are beyond the scope of this chapter. We will, however, look into this when we discuss WDK configurations in Chapter 24.

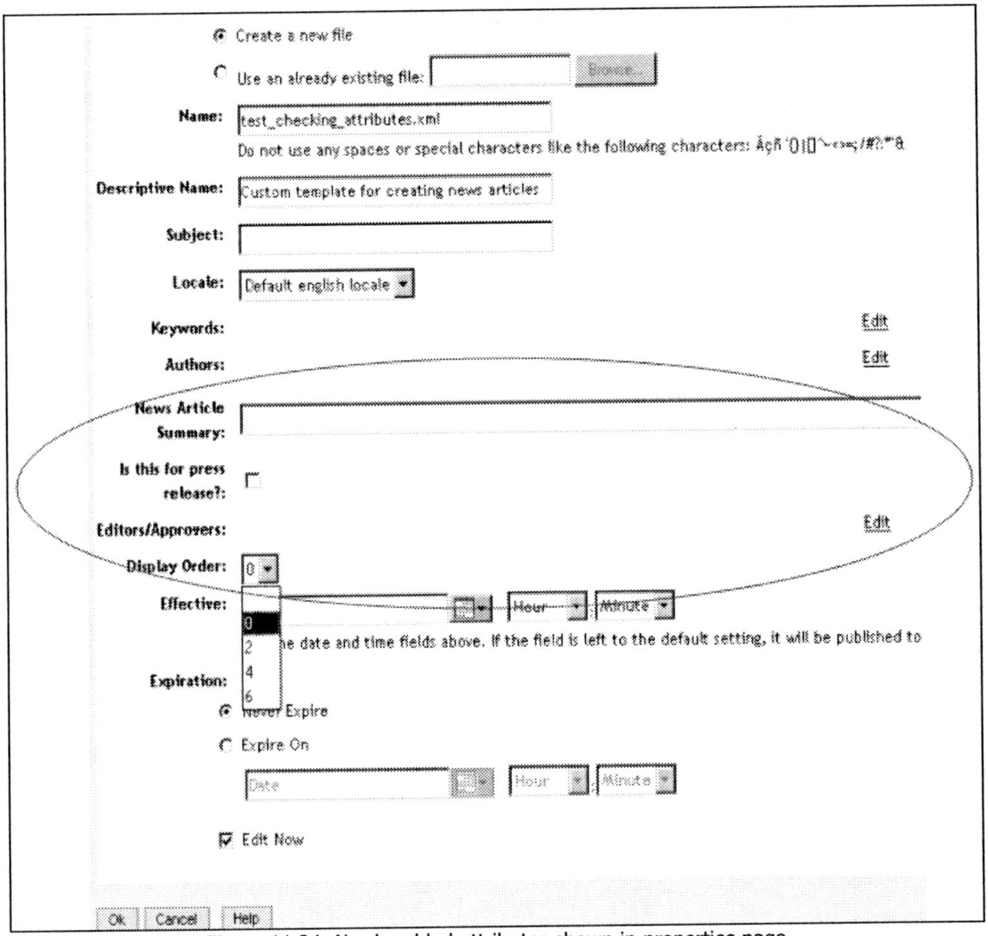

Create a new file

Use an already existing file: [ ] Browse

Name: test_checking_attributes.xml

Do not use any spaces or special characters like the following characters: Àçñ '()[]~<>¡;/#?:*&

Descriptive Name: Custom template for creating news articles

Subject: [ ]

Locale: Default english locale ▼

Keywords: Edit

Authors: Edit

News Article Summary: [ ]

Is this for press release?: [ ]

Editors/Approvers: Edit

Display Order: 0 ▼

Effective: [ ] Hour ▼ Minute ▼

0
2   e date and time fields above. If the field is left to the default setting, it will be published to
4
Expiration: 6

⊙ Never Expire

○ Expire On

Date [ ] Hour ▼ Minute ▼

☑ Edit Now

[Ok] [Cancel] [Help]

Figure 11.34: Newly added attributes shown in properties page

11.5 $value() Keyword

$value() is an important keyword that you should consider while designing conditional value assistance. Let us take a simple example to understand its usage and benefits.

Consider an attribute cust_name, which represents a dropdown of the names of some office employees, for example Tom, Harry, and Chris as shown in figure 11.35.

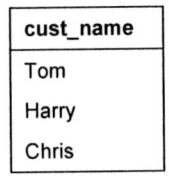

cust_name
Tom
Harry
Chris

Figure 11.35: Employee names table

Another attribute `cust_age` needs to represent a dropdown of ages for each office staff member. Depending on the chosen name in `cust_name`, the value in `cust_age` needs to be populated.

Say for example, the table representing the names and corresponding ages of the office staff is as shown in figure 11.36:

Name	Age
Tom	23
Harry	45
Chris	19

Figure 11.36: Employee name and age table

A conditional value assistance could be established as follows:

```
If cust_name = "Tom"
Then cust_age = 23
Else If cust_name = "Harry"
Then cust_age = 45
Else If cust_name = "Chris"
Then cust_age = 19
Else ...
```

What if the office staff member strength is close to 100 people? Would you define as many conditional statements? Neither is this a good implementation nor does Application Builder support so many conditional values assistance statements.

`$value()` comes to your rescue in such scenarios. Let us see how.

Design a registered table (say `cust_employee_data`) with the columns `emp_name` and `emp_age`. Populate the rows in the underlying table with the actual values of all employees and their ages. Define the value assistance for attribute `cust_age` as follows:

```
select emp_age from dm_dbo.cust_employee_data where emp_name =
'$value(cust_name)'
```

Thanks to `$value()`, at run time Documentum substitutes the value in the attribute `cust_name` in the where clause and hence the query returns the correct employee age without the need for writing multiple conditional statements! Interesting and pretty useful, isn't it?

Now that we have created our custom object type and attributes, we can extend our News Article example and create a News Article Web Publisher template (analogous to a UI 'form') so that during content creation, after filling in the News property page, users can provide the actual News Article content. Before doing that, let us first create a custom lifecycle and attach it to the custom object type we have created in this chapter.

11.6 Summary

This chapter talked about Documentum object types and their attributes (properties). We went through detailed steps to create an object type in Docbase using the Documentum Application Builder tool. We saw some constraints in naming conventions for object types.

We then saw how to create a sample News Article object type and associate it with a Documentum lifecycle.

In the later half of the chapter we designed a few attributes of the sample News Article object type and discussed the detailed steps for creating attributes using Documentum Application Builder tool.

We touched upon usage of Value Assistance for displaying a pre-defined data set for object types' attributes and how to conditionally display different values based on certain conditions.

Value assistance can be used by providing a fixed set of hard-coded data or by querying objects and registered tables at run time.

We discussed how to create registered tables in Documentum and how to query them using value assistance.

We ended this chapter by briefly talking about how the `$value()` keyword helps avoid the need to write multiple conditional statements in value assistance.

12

Creating Lifecycles, Alias Sets, and Permission Sets

In the previous chapter we created a custom object type and some attributes for the News Article object. Let us now design a custom Lifecycle for the News Article object so that when an instance (or content object) is created from News Article object type, it can be moved across the various Lifecycle stages such as Staging (or Review), Approval, etc. before taking the content live. A Lifecycle object in Documentum is associated with some other related objects such as Alias Sets, Permission Sets (ACLs), etc. and it is advisable to quickly go through the introductory chapters to flip through the basics we discussed earlier.

Broadly speaking, while designing Lifecycles, you need to bear in mind three important components:

- Alias Set(s) for the Lifecycle
- Permission Sets (ACLs) for various stages in the Lifecycle flow
- Actual Lifecycle design such as stages, labels, any scripts for pre or post processing, etc.

We will cover each of these in this chapter, by taking very simple examples so that you get a certain level of understanding and comfort that can be further extended and enriched while designing real-time applications in software projects.

12.1 Alias Sets in a Lifecycle

An **Alias Set** in the context of a Lifecycle is a group of Aliases that make a Lifecycle portable across numerous environments. An Alias is nothing but a placeholder or a symbolic name for some actual value in a given context called an **Alias Name**. An **Alias Value** is the actual value for the Alias Name. A pair of Alias Name and Value constitutes an **Alias** and a group of such Aliases constitutes an Alias Set.

Imagine that a content object for a News Article was created by a content author and reviewed by a content manager. In a given department, the content author could be Mr. X and the content manager could be Ms. Y. In another department, the content authors and managers could be different persons and not necessarily Mr. X and Ms. Y.

An Alias Set comes in handy in such circumstances, helping us design an application with symbolic names for content author/manager groups, the actual values for which are resolved by the system at run time as per the current context/environment.

You can specify multiple Alias Sets for a Lifecycle and have one of them designated as the default Alias Set; the others are treated as Additional Alias Sets. This is just the right time to discuss something called the scope of an Alias within Documentum. The **scope** of an Alias is the context in Documentum within which the system resolves the actual value for a given Alias name.

Documentum recognizes the following scopes:

- **Lifecycle scope**: An Alias Set for the Lifecycle. SysObjects in Documentum attached to the particular Lifecycle help the system resolve the values.

- **Workflow scope**: The Alias Set attached to the workflow process template is resolved at run time by finding the actual values of all performers in the workflow, whenever a workflow is started from the given workflow process definition.

- **Session scope**: The Alias Set for the life of a given Docbase session (session config object) helps the system resolve the actual value for an Alias.

- **User scope**: User scope is used to resolve Alias values from the Alias Set that was defined when the given users and groups were created within Documentum.

- **System scope**: This scope is used to resolve the values for Alias names for the Alias Set defined for the server config object for the given Docbase.

Whenever a content object is attached to a Lifecycle in Documentum, the system first evaluates all the Alias values based on the Alias Set attached to the Lifecycle object. This shows the importance of an Alias Set in the context of a Lifecycle. Hence, in this chapter, we will start by first studying how to create Alias Sets for a Lifecycle and then move on to build security in the various Lifecycle stages (using ACLs) and eventually create a full-fledged Lifecycle object.

12.2 Creating an Alias Set

In this section, we will discuss in detail the steps involved in creating an Alias Set.

In our custom DocApp TestDocApp, choose the menu option Insert | Alias Set to create a new Alias Set. Figure 12.1 shows an empty Alias Set screen. Provide a unique name for the custom Alias Set along with a short description to explain its purpose.

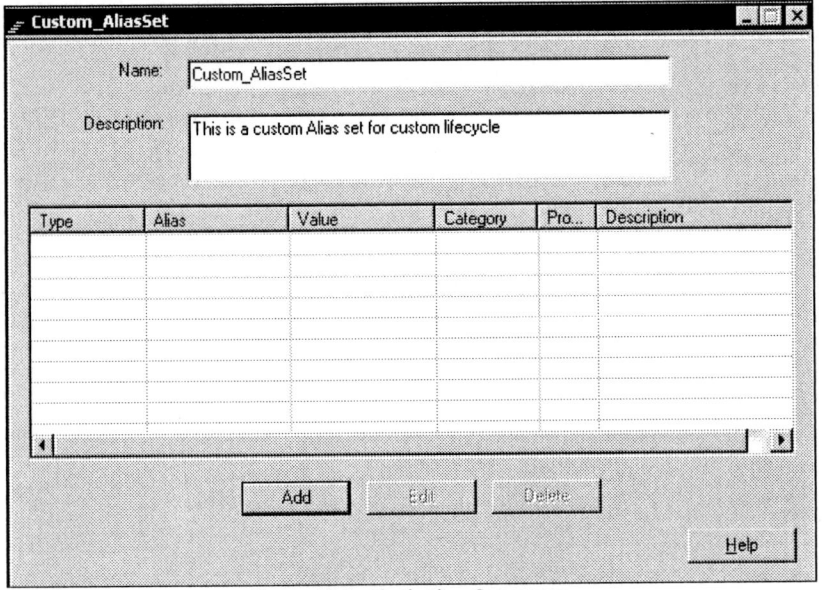
Figure 12.1: Blank Alias Set screen

To add a new Alias in the Alias Set, click on Add. Clicking this button opens up the Alias Object dialog box as shown in the figure 12.2.

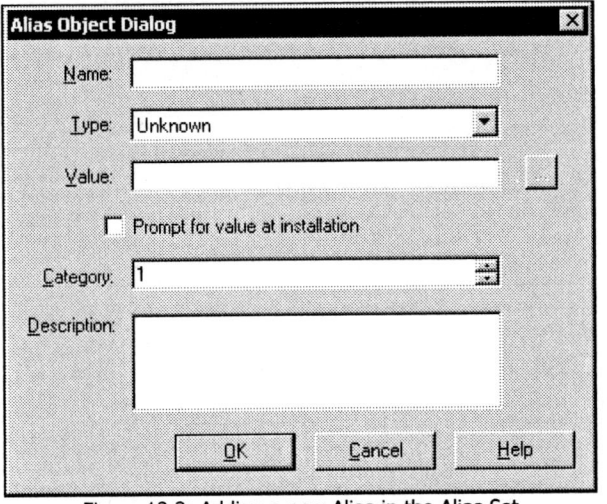
Figure 12.2: Adding a new Alias in the Alias Set

Provide a name for the Alias in the **Name** text box. Choose an Alias Type from the **Type** dropdown. The available Alias Types in the dropdown are:

- Unknown
- User
- Group
- User or Group
- Cabinet Path
- Cabinet or Folder Path
- Permissions Set

Depending upon the chosen Alias Type, the values in **Value** field get populated when you click on the ellipsis button (...).

Choose the **Prompt for value at installation** checkbox if you wish the System to prompt for a value for the Alias while resolving the Alias.

Alias **Category** is not used by the system but can be utilized for categorizing the Alias Sets for your custom application.

A short description can be provided to explain the intent/purpose of the Alias. Click the OK button.

After you have provided Aliases for the Alias Set, the added Aliases are shown as individual rows in the Alias Set screen, as shown in figure 12.3.

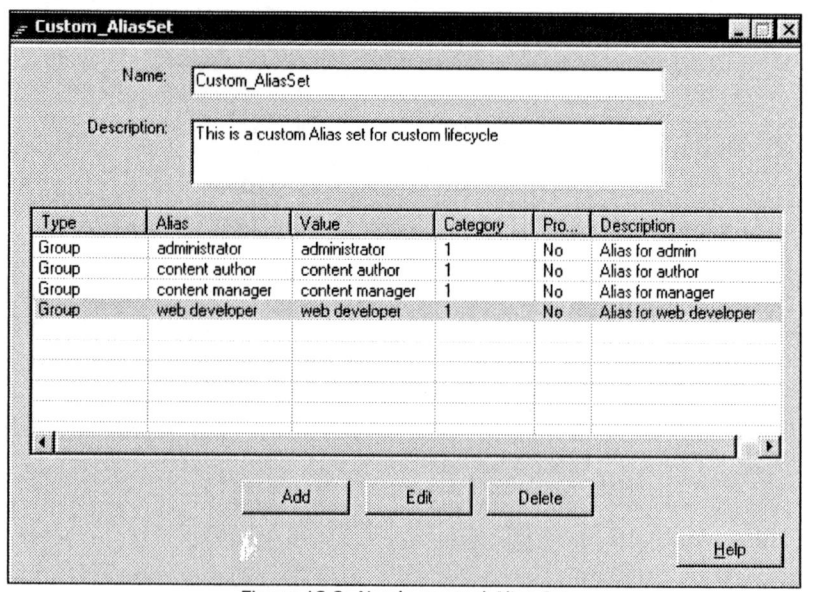

Figure 12.3: Newly created Alias Set

Choose the Custom_AliasSet Alias Set shown in the left window pane of Documentum Application Builder, right-click, and choose Check in selected object(s) to checkin the Alias Set in Docbase.

12.3 Creating Permission Sets

Security measures need to be in place so that during different stages of the Lifecycle, only certain authorized users working on the content objects get specific permissions or rights to work on the content. Say for example, our custom Lifecycle has four stages:

- Start (when content is being created)
- WIP (short for Work in progress)
- Staging (content under review)
- Approved (content finally reviewed and approved and ready to be shown on the live site)

You may design the ACLs (Access Control Lists or Permission Sets) for each of the Lifecycle stages. For example, during the Staging stage of the Lifecycle, the Administrators, Content Managers, Content Authors, and Web Developer users could have VERSION rights while the owner of the content could be given WRITE rights and the rest of the users (termed "world") could be given READ rights.

Please refer to our earlier discussion of ACLs in Chapter 3 to quickly understand the basic and extended permission levels in Documentum and their semantics.

Let us now create a Permission Set template (ACL) for the WIP Lifecycle state of the Lifecycle and accordingly create the ACLs for the other Lifecycle states.

1. In our custom DocApp TestDocApp, choose Insert | Permission Set Template. Provide some unique name (such as Custom WIP ACL) for the custom Permission Set along with some short description to explain its purpose (refer to figure 12.4).

2. Choose the first radio button Show Alias-Sets in Application to choose an Alias Set in our custom DocApp.

   Choose the second radio button Show All Alias-Sets in Docbase to choose an existing Alias Set from the existing Alias Sets in the Docbase.

   Choose the third radio button Show Users and Groups to directly select a group from all the existing groups in Docbase.

   Select an entry from the Alias names (if one out of the first two radio buttons is chosen) or select a group name (if the third radio button is chosen) and provide basic and extended permissions to each of the entities involved.

   Choose one of the seven basic permission levels from the Permissions dropdown and choose the checkboxes against the extended permission levels required (if any). There are in all five extended permission levels in Documentum.

   Accordingly you can click the Add to Set button to include the permissions in the ACL or click the Remove from Set button to remove the added permissions.

   Note that when you start creating a new Permission Set, Documentum automatically includes entries for dm_owner and dm_world aliases. You can obviously amend the specific rights for each of these two aliases.

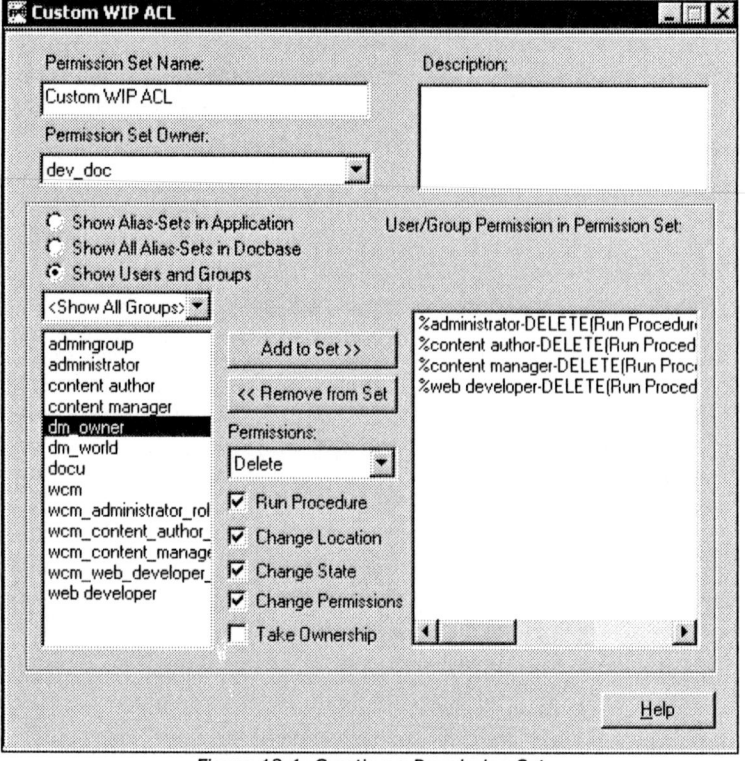

Figure 12.4: Creating a Permission Set

3. After you have provided the necessary permissions, the Permission Set can be selected in the left window pane of Documentum Application Builder, right-clicked, and checked into the Docbase by selecting the Check in selected object(s) option.

Please note that we will not need to create an ACL for the Start stage of the Lifecycle since as soon as you create content in Web Publisher, Documentum automatically pushes it to the WIP Lifecycle state. In effect, the permission sets need to be created for all Lifecycle states beyond the Start state.

Figure 12.5 lays down a design of Permission Sets for each of the WIP, Staging, and Approved Lifecycle states based on Documentum's out-of-the-box ACLs for its Default Lifecycle. Needless to say, you may change the permission levels as per your business requirements.

Lifecycle Stage	Alias	Basic Permission	Run Proc	Change Loc	Change State	Change Perm	Take Ownership
WIP	administrator	DELETE	Y	Y	Y	Y	N
	content author	DELETE	Y	Y	Y	Y	N
	content manager	DELETE	Y	Y	Y	Y	N
	web developer	DELETE	Y	Y	Y	Y	N
	dm_owner	DELETE	Y	Y	Y	Y	N
	dm_world	READ	Y	Y	N	N	N
Staging	administrator	VERSION	Y	Y	Y	Y	N
	content author	VERSION	Y	Y	Y	Y	N
	content manager	VERSION	Y	Y	Y	Y	N
	web developer	VERSION	Y	Y	Y	Y	N
	dm_owner	WRITE	Y	Y	Y	Y	N
	dm_world	READ	Y	Y	N	N	N
Approved	administrator	VERSION	Y	Y	Y	Y	N
	content author	VERSION	Y	Y	Y	Y	N
	content manager	VERSION	Y	Y	Y	Y	N
	web developer	VERSION	Y	Y	Y	Y	N
	dm_owner	WRITE	Y	Y	Y	Y	N
	dm_world	READ	Y	Y	N	N	N

Figure 12.5: Permissions for different Lifecycle states

12.4 Creating a Custom Lifecycle

In this section, we will discuss the detailed steps for creating a custom Lifecycle.

1. In our custom DocApp TestDocApp, choose menu option Insert | Document Lifecycle to create a new Lifecycle. Provide some unique name (such as Custom_Lifecycle) for the custom Lifecycle (refer to figure 12.6) along with some short description to explain its purpose.

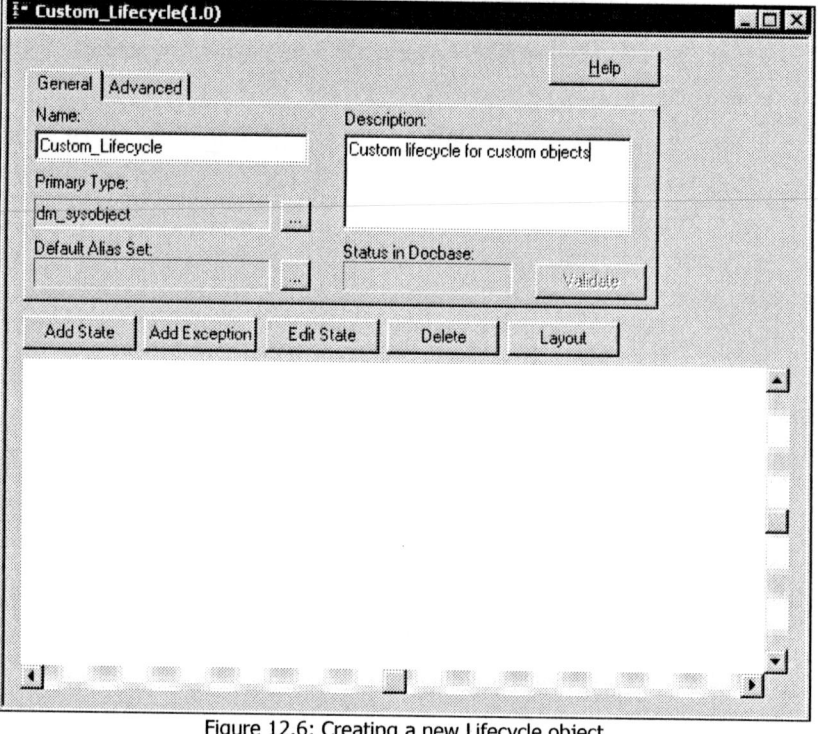

Figure 12.6: Creating a new Lifecycle object

The Lifecycle Editor is used to create a **Lifecycle State Diagram** wherein you create the various states of a Lifecycle along with their specific behavior/attributes.

Note that the Validate button is disabled at this point of time. The Lifecycle is under creation and hence is said to be in the Draft state. When you have completed the creation of the Lifecycle and checked it into the Docbase, the Validate button gets enabled. Clicking on the Validate button amounts to system validation to check if the Lifecycle parameters are consistent or not. If the validation checks pass, the Lifecycle is Validated and the Install button gets enabled. After clicking on the Install button, the Lifecycle gets installed in the Docbase and is finally ready to be used by the appropriate objects.

2. Attach an Alias Set to the Lifecycle by clicking on the ellipsis button corresponding to the option Default Alias Set. The Select Alias Sets dialog box is shown as in figure 12.7.

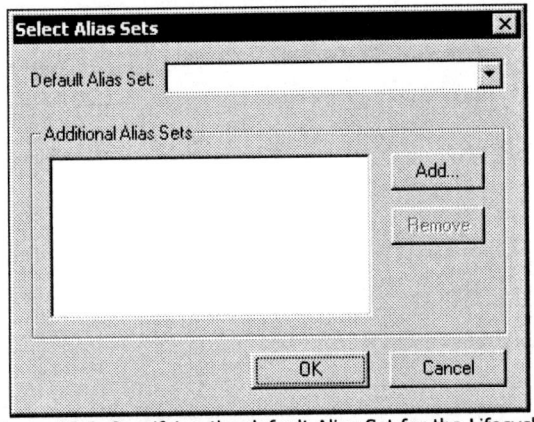

Figure 12.7: Specifying the default Alias Set for the Lifecycle

Choose the Alias Set Custom_AliasSet we created earlier from the dropdown. You can additionally attach some other Alias Sets existing in the Docbase to the Lifecycle, by clicking on the Add... button.

3. Now you need to provide the object types, the object instances of which can be attached to the custom Lifecycle. Say for example, we require our custom Lifecycle to be attached to News Article objects.

Click on the ellipsis button corresponding to Primary Type field and choose dm_document as the Primary Type (refer to figure 12.8). This means that object instances of dm_document object types can be attachable to our custom Lifecycle. Further, the subtypes of the primary object type (dm_document in our case) are shown under the Available Subtypes list. Choose the subtypes of dm_document, the object instances of which can also be attached to the Lifecycle in question. Clicking on the → button will include the dm_document subtype under the Acceptable Subtypes list. Click the OK button.

Note that, as shown in the figure 12.8, we have specified dm_document as the primary object type of our custom Lifecycle and cust_newsarticle object type as the acceptable subtype of dm_document for the Lifecycle.

This ensures that content objects created from the News Article type can be attached to our custom Lifecycle.

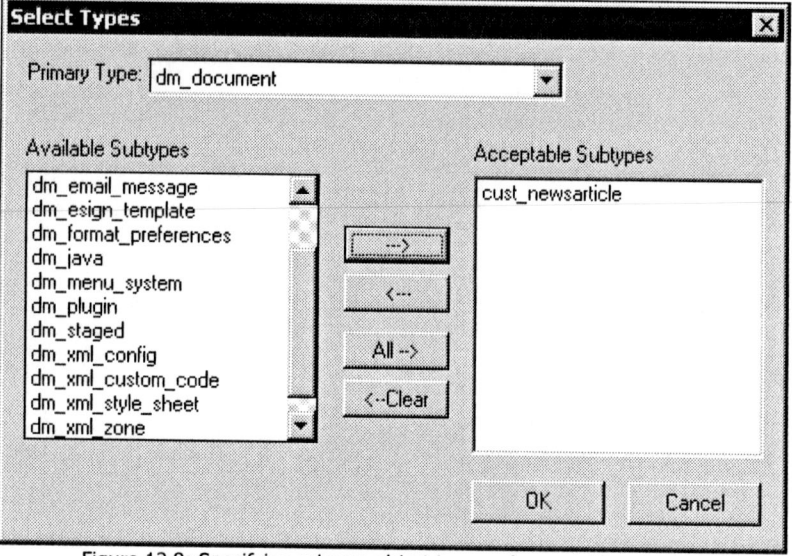

Figure 12.8: Specifying primary object type and acceptable subtypes

We now prepare a Lifecycle State Diagram comprising four normal Lifecycle states:

- Start
- WIP
- Staging
- Approved

Mark the word normal that has been used to describe the Lifecycle states. There could also be exception states in a Lifecycle to represent an abnormal flow or diversions in the otherwise sequential and linear normal flow of the states.

You can introduce states in a Lifecycle by clicking on Add State and providing some unique understandable name for the state. Clicking on Add State adds a pentagon shaped state in the Lifecycle State Diagram as shown in figure 12.9.

The first state is called the **base state** while the end state is termed the **final state**. Our custom Lifecycle has four normal states, including a base state (called start) and a final state (called Approved).

When you attach a document to a Lifecycle, you actually associate the document with the Lifecycle. Doing this allows you to promote the document to the next sequential linear normal state or demote it back to its previous normal state. Let us take a quick example.

We create a Word document abc.doc and associate it with our custom Lifecycle. At this stage, the document is in the WIP state of the Lifecycle. Promoting the document would push it to the next normal state—Staging. At the Staging state, if you demote the document, it will come back to WIP state. Simple, isn't it?

Although we will not be covering exception states in our custom Lifecycle, it is worth mentioning here that similar to promotion and demotion, moving from a normal to an exception state is termed **suspension** while moving back from an exception state to normal state is termed **resumption**.

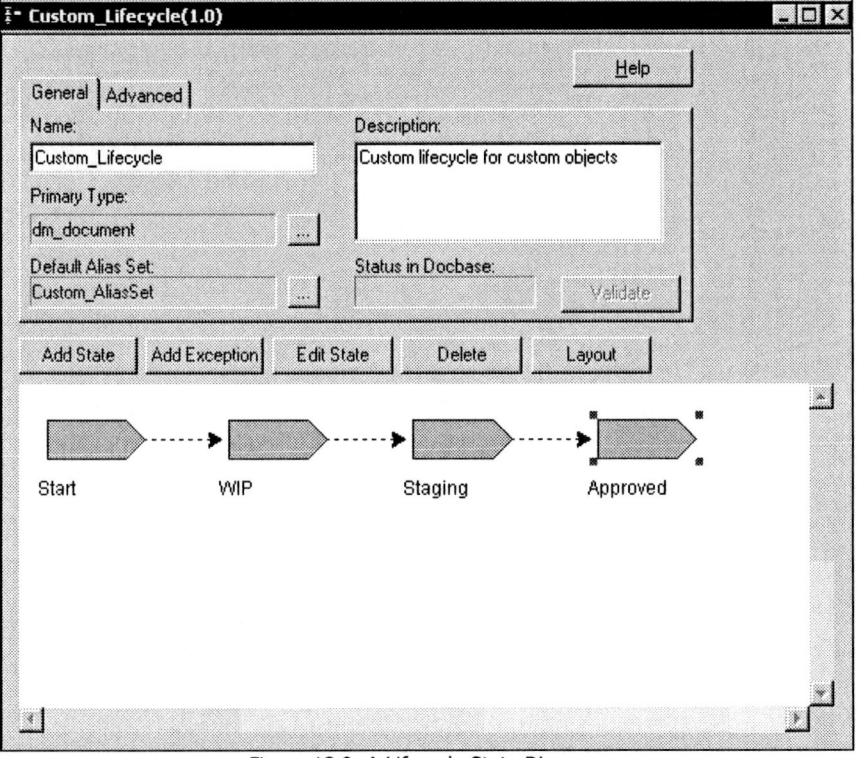

Figure 12.9: A Lifecycle State Diagram

4. Double-click on the added state or select the state and click the Edit State button to open the Lifecycle state editor. We will take an example of creating the WIP state of the Lifecycle. Similarly, other states of the Lifecycle can be created using the Lifecycle editor.

Under the General tab (refer to figure 12.10), you can specify the name and description of the Lifecycle state and provide some state transition (state change) settings as follows:

- o **Allow attachment directly to this state**: If the objects meet the Lifecycle state's entry criteria, this Lifecycle state will be their initial state.
- o **Allow demotion to previous state**: This allows demotion from this state to its previous normal state. For the first state of the Lifecycle, this option is disabled.

o **Allow scheduled transitions from this state**: This allows Lifecycle state changes based on a time schedule without requiring any explicit action initiated by the user.

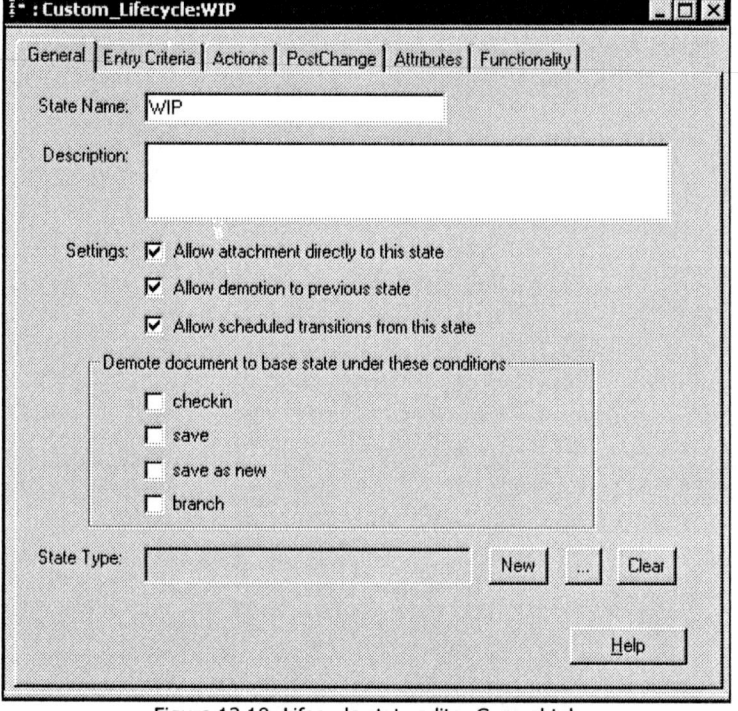

Figure 12.10: Lifecycle state editor General tab

o **Demote document to base state under these conditions**: This option allows demoting documents to the base state in the Lifecycle if the mentioned conditions are met (such as save, check-in, etc.).

5. Under the Entry Criteria tab (refer to figure 12.11), you can specify some conditions or checks that the system performs before a document enters a particular state in the Lifecycle.

Note that during demotion, Documentum does not check the entry criteria for the Lifecycle state.

The entry criteria checks can be performed via attribute values and expression tests. You can specify multiple conditions that are evaluated by Documentum from top to bottom of the list. Additionally, the system ensures that the moment one condition fails, the other conditions are not evaluated, thus saving execution time.

168

Click the Add Value Test button, choose attribute name and relational operator (=, <, >, <>, <=, and >=) and specify a value against which the attribute needs to be evaluated. Click on Add Expression Test…, choose an attribute and click on Validate followed by OK to introduce an expression that the system needs to check while entering this particular Lifecycle state.

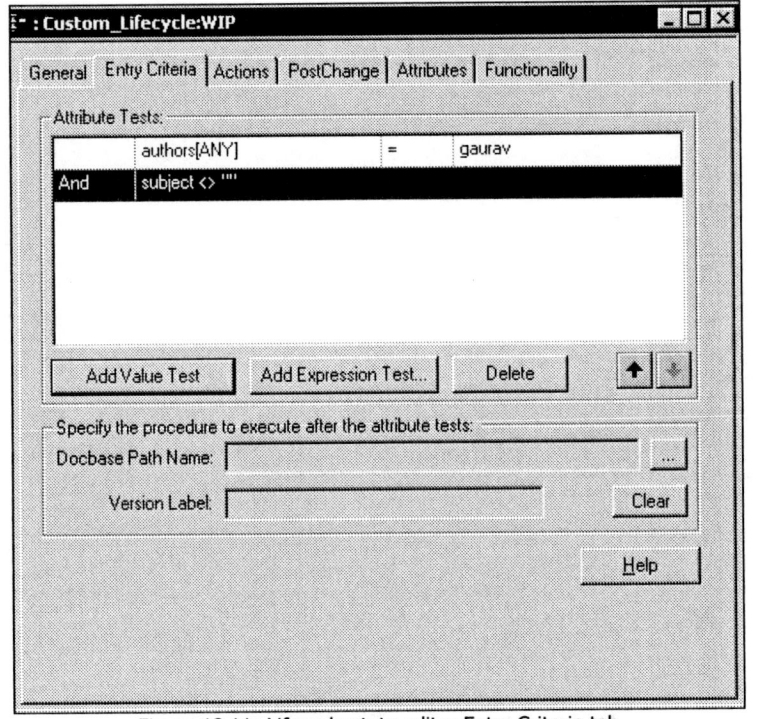

Figure 12.11: Lifecycle state editor Entry Criteria tab

You can even write a custom Docbasic procedure that the system can run after the attribute expressions have been evaluated. The custom procedure can programmatically evaluate certain conditions in the Docbase that must be true before a document enters this particular state in the Lifecycle.

You can optionally specify a Documentum out-of-the-box procedure by clicking on the ellipsis button against Docbase Path Name field and browsing to the procedure under the correct Docbase location.

6. Let's move over to the Actions tab in the Lifecycle state editor now. After the system has evaluated the entry criteria for a Lifecycle state, the set of actions to be performed by the system in the given Lifecycle state are specified within the Actions tab.

The actions are performed by Documentum in the following order of execution:

o   The standard actions are evaluated first
o   The optional Docbasic action procedure is run

169

Clicking on the Add Action... button in the Actions tab shows the Define Action screen (refer figure to 12.12) allowing users to choose one of the numerous action types and define a specific action to be performed by the system. Defining an action is simple via a GUI wizard.

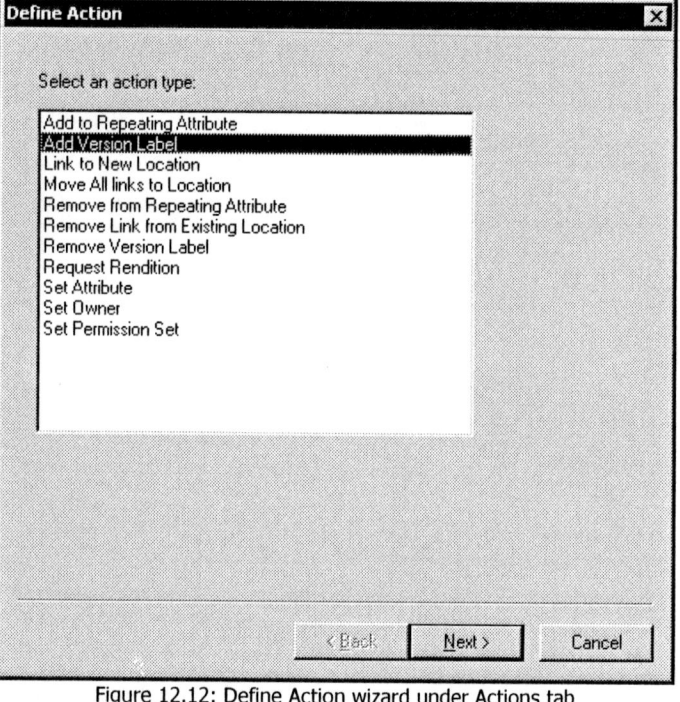

Figure 12.12: Define Action wizard under Actions tab

Using the Define Action wizard, you can specify multiple actions, such as adding a particular version label to or removing a particular version label from a document when it is in the given Lifecycle state.

You could additionally set the document's owner or a particular value for one of its attributes, apart from several other action definitions.

To add a WIP version label to a document when it is in the WIP state of the Lifecycle, choose the Add Version Label option from the Define Action wizard and enter the value WIP in the subsequent screen (refer to figure 12.13).

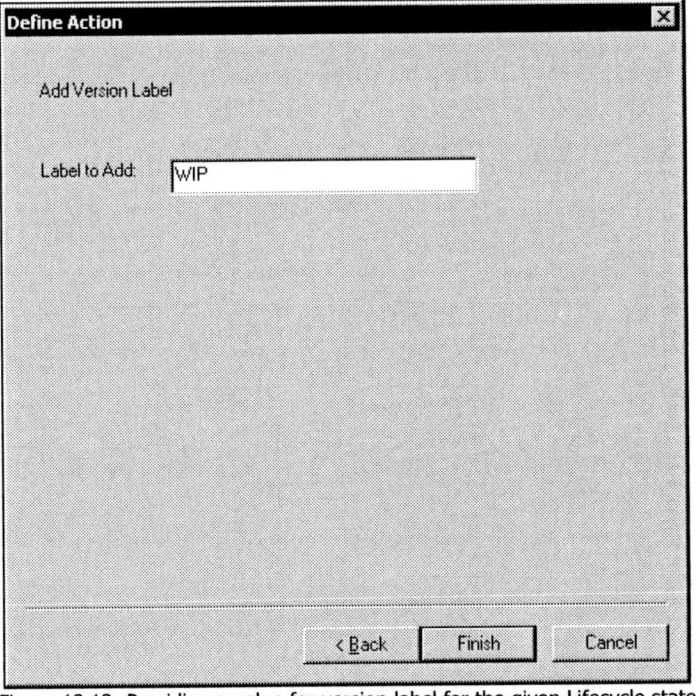

Figure 12.13: Providing a value for version label for the given Lifecycle state

Similarly you can specify that the following version labels need to be removed from the document when it is in the WIP Lifecycle state: Approved, Active, Expired. This can be achieved by choosing the Remove Version Label option from the Define Action wizard.

Also, you can attach the custom Permission Set (Custom WIP ACL) we created earlier to the document when it is in the WIP Lifecycle state by using the same Define Action wizard.

As we saw earlier while setting up the Entry Criteria tab, a Docbasic procedure can be specified for the system to execute after the specified standard actions have been performed.

Figure 12.14 shows all the standard actions added for the WIP Lifecycle state.

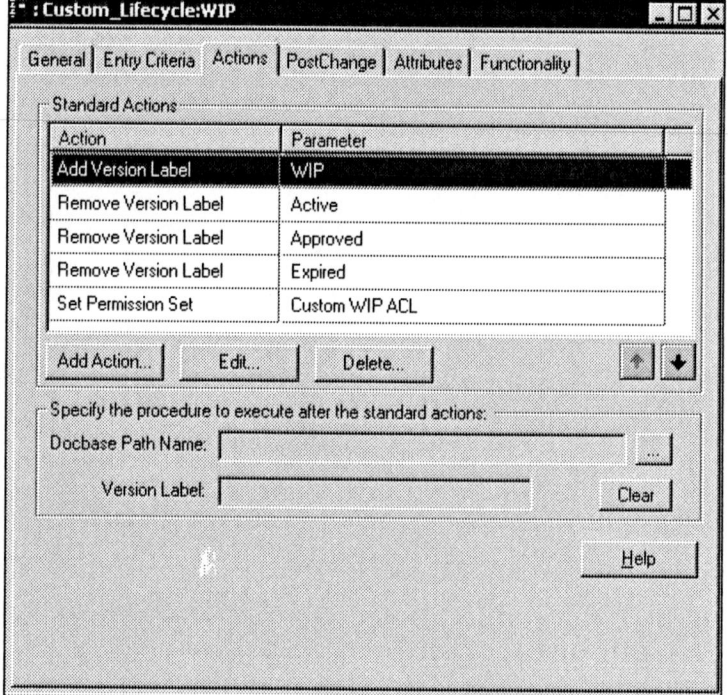

Figure 12.14: Specified actions listed under the Actions tab of Lifecycle state editor

Documentum 5.3 Update

Documentum release 5.3 allows you to specify Java classes as procedures in Lifecycle Entry Criteria, Actions, PostChange, and for validations.

7. Under the PostChange tab (refer to figure 12.15), you can specify a post-change Docbasic procedure that the system can execute after the state transition has been completed.

    Click on the ellipsis button shown against the Docbase Path Name field and browse to the correct Docbase location to specify a Docbasic procedure.

    Note that for the WIP Lifecycle state, we have specified the execution of the out-of-the-box procedure wcmLifecycleScript that is responsible for several standard Lifecycle operations and system checks for documents.

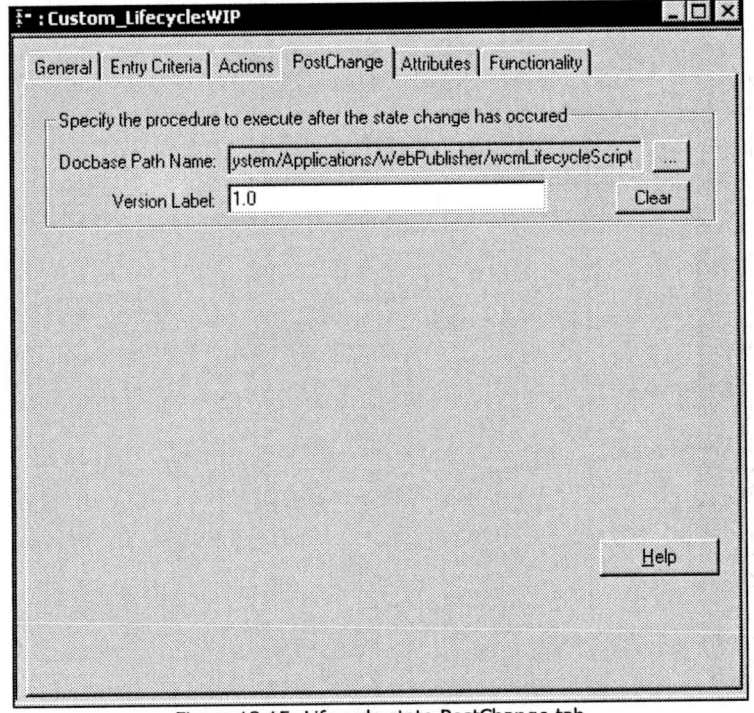

Figure 12.15: Lifecycle state PostChange tab

8. After specifying the PostChange procedure, you can move over to the Attributes tab in the Lifecycle state editor (refer to figure 12.16). This feature allows you to modify certain properties of the selected attribute(s) of the document, whenever the document reaches the particular Lifecycle state.

Select the document attribute whose properties you desire to modify. Let us take an example here by selecting the attribute subject and clicking on Change Properties... button.

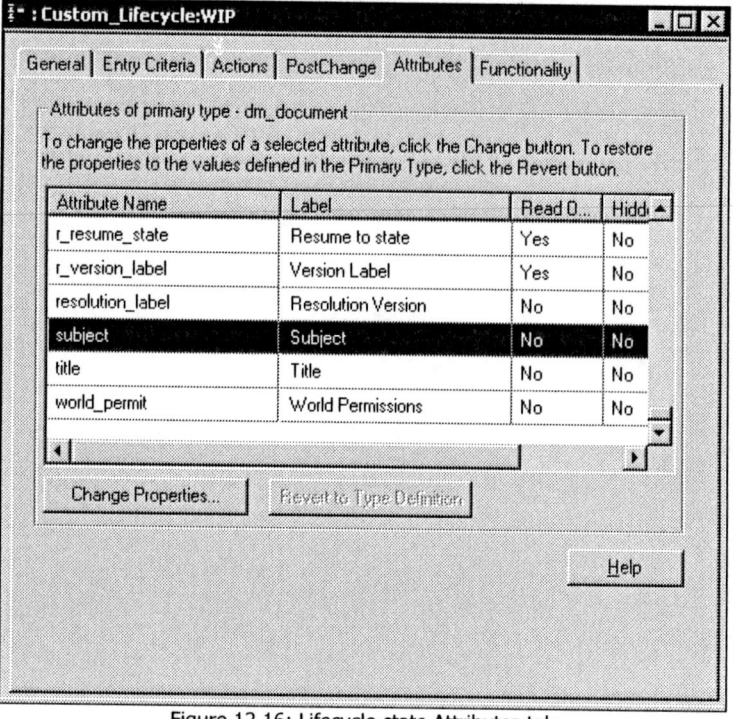

Figure 12.16: Lifecycle state Attributes tab

The Properties window opens (refer to figure 12.17) displaying the selected attribute and allowing users to alter the following in any desired combination:

- **Label Text**: The text (depicting the name of the attribute) shown against the attribute in the client application (e.g. in Web Publisher).
- **Help Text**: Some help text for the attribute in question.
- **Comment**: A short description or comment for the attribute.
- Other properties such as making it read-only, hidden, etc.

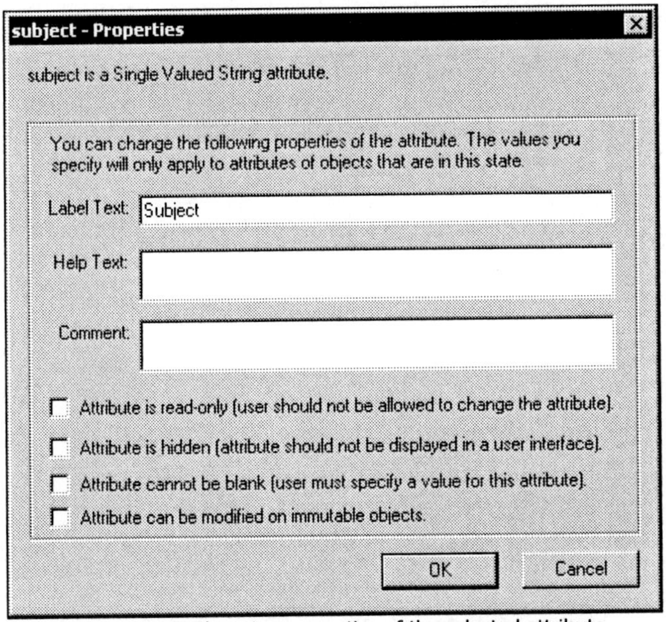

Figure 12.17: Changing properties of the selected attribute

9. Documents in a Lifecycle are manipulated via some client applications such as Desktop Client, Web Publisher, etc. The client programs match the documents' capabilities (for example: checking out, linking it to a location, etc.) with the actual components (functionality classes) that implement these capabilities.

    If you remember our discussion about object types, we saw how an object type definition includes certain functionality classes that implement its capabilities.

    Using Lifecycle state editor, you can modify the associated functionality classes associated with the object type definition, add a new component and its implementation classes, and other such operations.

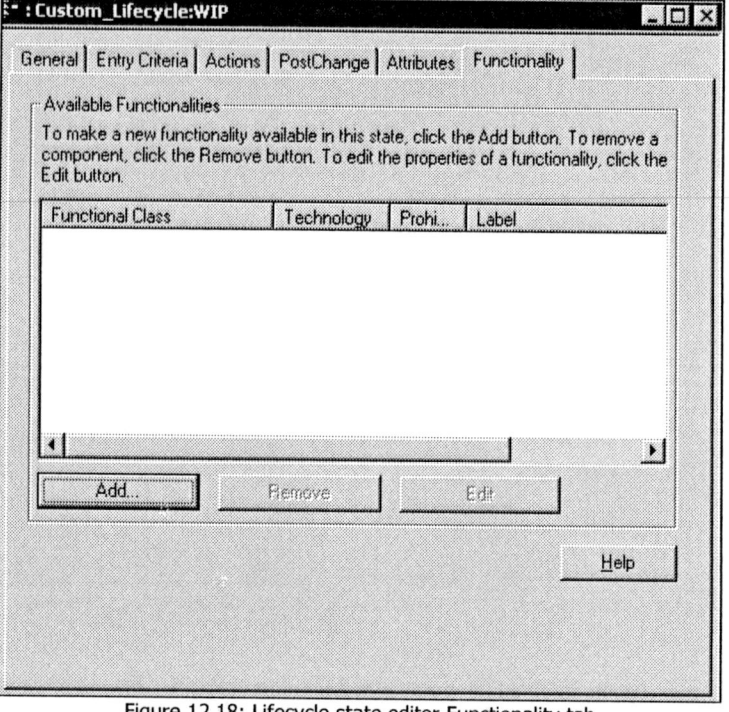

Figure 12.18: Lifecycle state editor Functionality tab

10. Similar to setting up the WIP state, create the Start, Staging, and Approved Lifecycle states as per the definitions shown in figure 12.19. These are based on Documentum's Default Lifecycle and can certainly be altered as per your specific business needs.

After creating all the Lifecycle states, you can check-in the Custom Lifecycle in the Docbase similar to Permission Sets and Alias Sets.

Documentum allows you to version documents as well as Lifecycles. At a given point of time, multiple versions of documents can be attached to multiple versions of the same Lifecycle.

Say, for example, you have a News Article document news_story001.xml created from News Article object type cust_newsarticle and associated with our custom Lifecycle Custom_Lifecycle.

The document is associated with version 1.0 of the Lifecycle at this point of time. A developer modifies the Lifecycle and checks in the modified Lifecycle into the Docbase as version 1.1.

However, this does not mean that the document news_story001.xml now automatically gets associated with version 1.1 of the Lifecycle. It is still linked to version 1.0 of the Lifecycle and this might create confusion in some cases.

Unless absolutely required in your business scenario, do not check-in the Lifecycle in either a minor or a major version into the Docbase. Instead, check-in the Lifecycle as the same version it was prior to modification so that documents do not lose associations.

Figure 12.19 shows Lifecycle State Definitions for our Custom Lifecycle:

Lifecycle State	General	Entry Criteria	Actions	Post Change	Attributes	Functionality
Start	Allow attachment: Yes Allow demotion: No Allow scheduled Transitions: Yes	N/A	N/A	N/A	N/A	N/A
WIP	Allow attachment: Yes Allow demotion: Yes Allow scheduled Transitions: Yes	N/A	Add Version Label: WIP Remove Version Label: Active, Approved, Expired Set Permission Set: Custom WIP ACL	Procedure Docbase Path Name: /System/ Applications/ WebPublisher/ wcmLifecycle Script	N/A	N/A
Staging	Allow attachment: Yes Allow demotion: Yes Allow scheduled Transitions: Yes	N/A	Add Version Label: Staging Remove Version Label: Approved Set Permission Set: Custom Staging ACL	N/A	N/A	N/A
Approved	Allow attachment: Yes Allow demotion: Yes Allow scheduled Transitions: Yes		Add Version Label: Approved Set Permission Set: Custom Approved ACL	Procedure Docbase Path Name: /System/ Applications/ WebPublisher/ wcmLifecycle Script	N/A	N/A

Figure 12.19: Definition for various Lifecycle states

11. After checking in the Lifecycle into the Docbase, install the Lifecycle as we discussed earlier in this chapter so that it is ready to be used by applications.

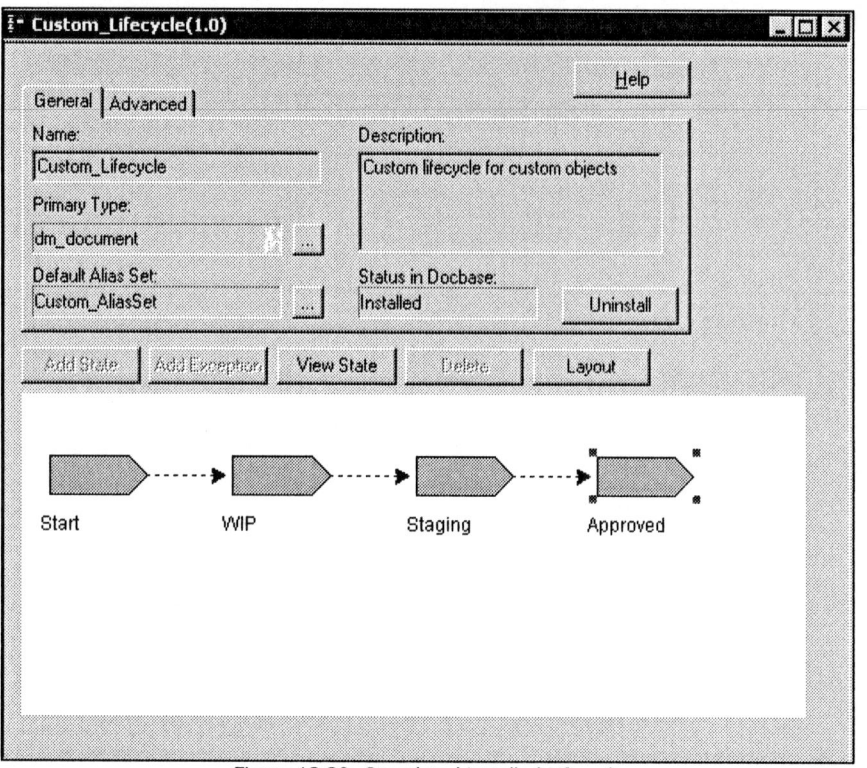

Figure 12.20: Completed installed Lifecycle

12.5 Promoting and Demoting Content through a Lifecycle

Content created and attached to a Lifecycle can be progressed through the various Lifecycle states via one of the following mechanisms:

- Web Publisher Promote and Demote menu options
- Workflows
- Server API commands: promote and demote
- BATCH_PROMOTE administration method

We will create sample content in Web Publisher and see how to promote and demote it through its various Lifecycle states using the above mechanisms.

Create a News Article attached to Custom_Lifecycle in Web Publisher using one of the following methods:

- Using the News Article Web Publisher template that we will cover in Chapter 13
- Importing a content file within a Web Publisher web cabinet through the menu option File | Import and attaching it to custom object type cust_newsarticle and Lifecycle Custom_Lifecycle (refer to figure 12.21)

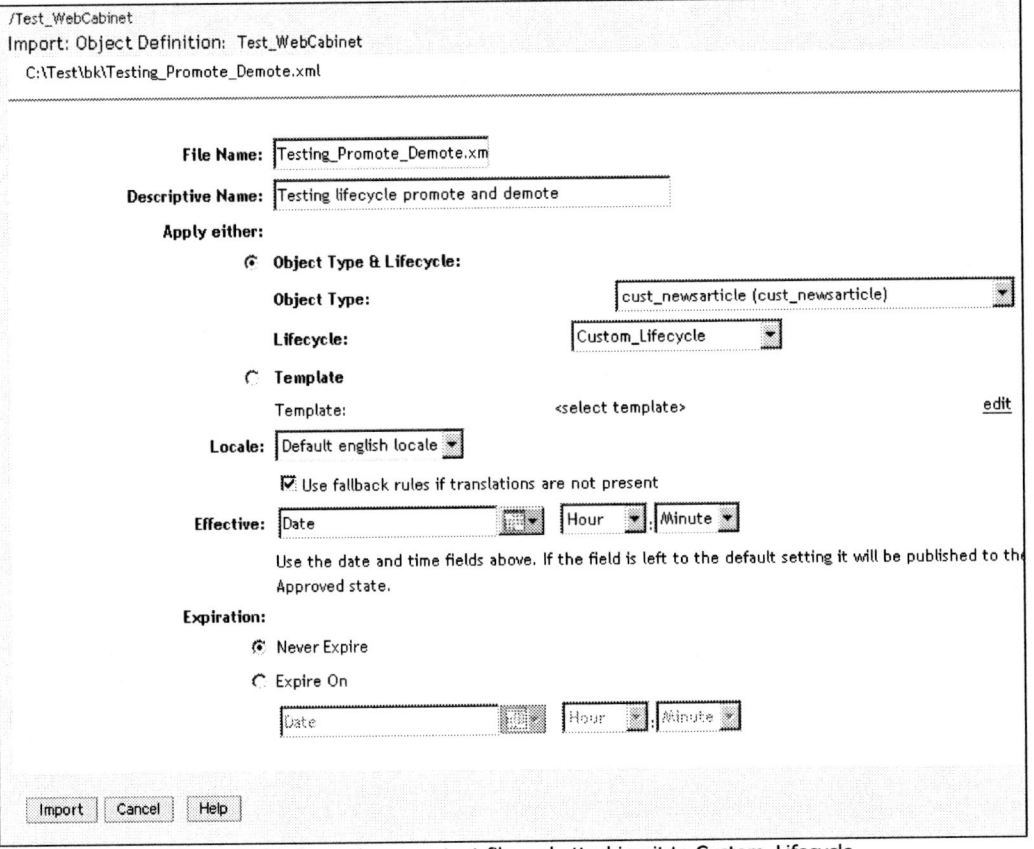

Figure 12.21: Importing a content file and attaching it to Custom_Lifecycle

You can verify from the Status column shown in figure 12.22 that the newly created/ imported content is in the WIP Lifecycle state. Choose the checkbox against the content and select the menu option Document | Lifecycle | Promote.

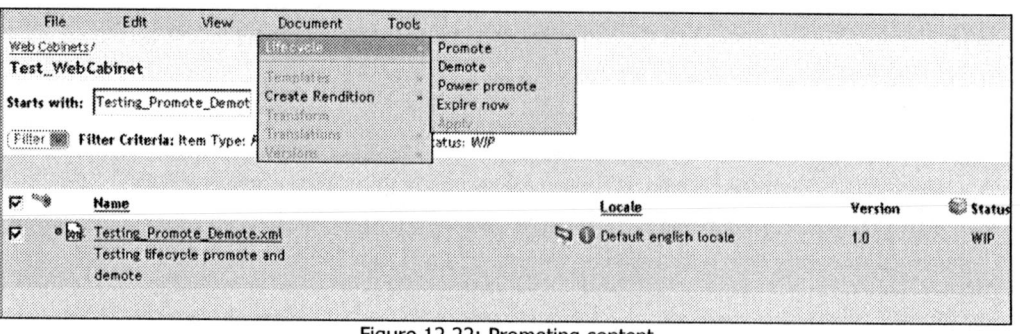

Figure 12.22: Promoting content

The system will take a short while to promote the content to its next normal state in the Lifecycle. You can click on the **Task Status** button to view the status of the Lifecycle promote operation. Once the system has promoted the content, the content can be seen in its next normal Lifecycle state (Staging in the case of custom_Lifecycle) as shown in figure 12.23.

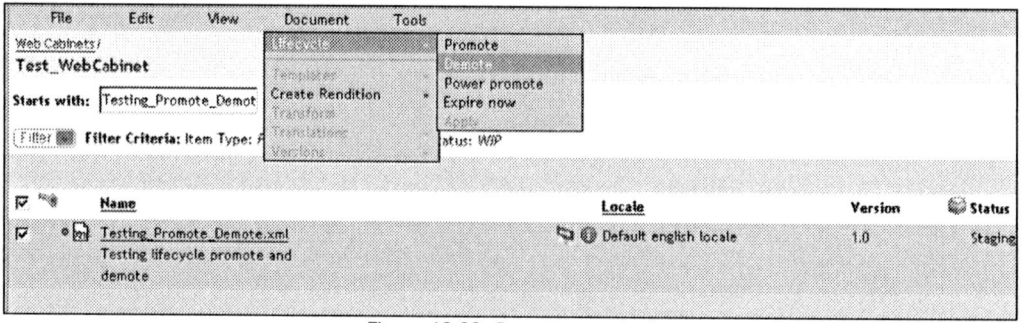

Figure 12.23: Demoting content

In order to demote content from its current normal Lifecycle state, choose the checkbox against the content and select the menu option Document | Lifecycle | Demote (refer to figure 12.23).

In order to power-promote the content, choose the checkbox against the content and select the menu option Document | Lifecycle | Power promote. Power promotion pushes the content directly to its Approved Lifecycle state (i.e. the last state in the Lifecycle). At this point it is critical to discuss the Web Publisher Monitor_Lifecycles Job (refer to figure 12.24).

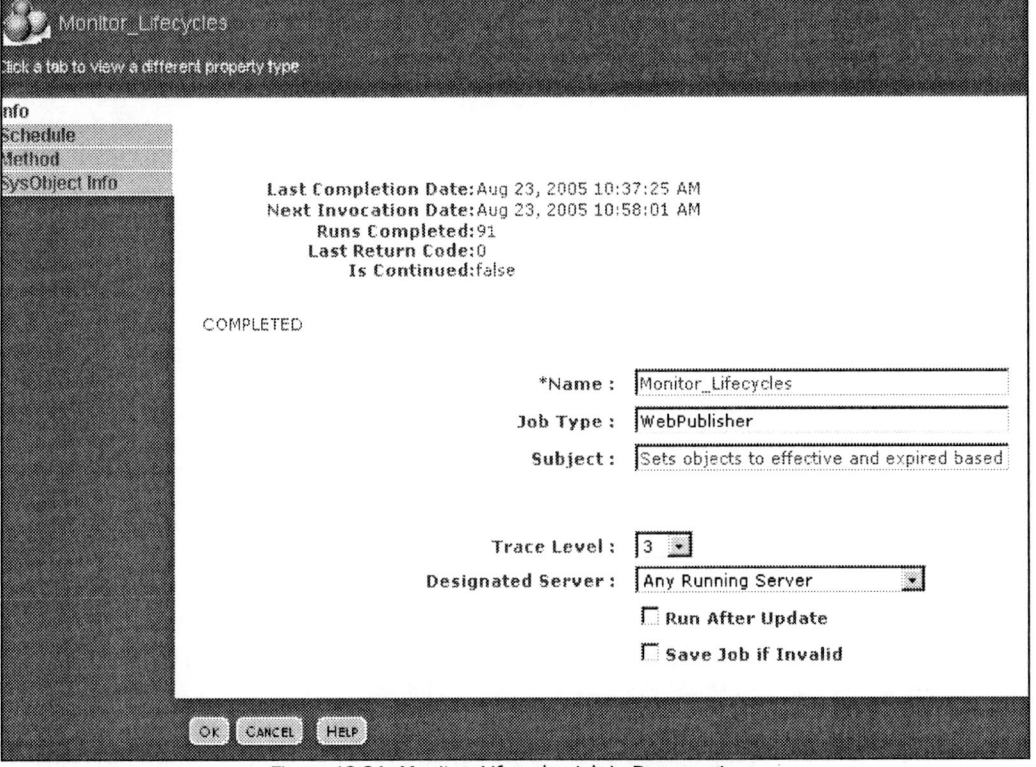

Figure 12.24: Monitor_Lifecycles job in Documentum

The Monitor_Lifecycles job in Documentum runs at pre-defined intervals and performs the following functions:

If an Approved object's effective date (a_effective_date attribute) matches the current system date, the Monitor_Lifecycles job turns the object active, by changing its version label to Active.

If an Active object's expiration date (a_expiration_date attribute) matches the current system date, the Monitor_Lifecycles job expires the object, by changing its version label to Expired.

By default, if the effective date for the content is blank, power promotion immediately turns the file active and the content is published. However, by providing a Web Publisher system setting, you can alter this behavior.

Log in to Web Publisher as an administrator and go to Administration | Web Publisher Admin | Settings under the Lifecycles section.

Delay Publish Active :	☐ Turn on
	If unchecked, an object that has been promoted to Approved and that has a blank (immediate) effective date will immediately be promoted to Active and exported to the appropriate web cache(s); if checked, promotion to Active is handled by the Monitor Lifecycles job configured in Documentum Developer Studio

Figure 12.25: Delay Publish Active setting

As shown in figure 12.25, if you check the Delay Publish Active checkbox, power promotion to the Active state is taken care by the Monitor_Lifecycles Job.

The following API commands (executed via IAPI utility or API Tester in Documentum Administrator) can be used for promoting and demoting content as well. Refer to Chapter 26 to understand Server API commands better.

- **Promoting Content**

  ```
  API>id,c,cust_newsarticle where object_name = Testing_Promote_Demote.xml
  ...
  090015558000bc5b
  ```
  Note that the API command id returns the object ID of the object matching the specified qualification. In our case, 090015558000bc5b is the object ID (r_object_id attribute) of the News Article content with the name Testing_Promote_Demote.xml.

  ```
  API>promote,c,090015558000bc5b
  ...
  OK
  ```
- **Demoting Content**

  ```
  API>demote,c,090015558000bc5b
  ...
  OK
  ```
- **Batch Promoting Content**

  The administrative method BATCH_PROMOTE can be used to promote multiple objects to their next Lifecycle state via a simple API command. The interesting thing about BATCH_PROMOTE is that it can be used on multiple objects existing in different Lifecycle states and attached to different lifecycles. You can promote up to 200 objects in a single execution of BATCH_PROMOTE.

  Let us now promote two content files, Testing_Promote_Demote.xml and Testing_Promote_Demote002.xml, using BATCH_PROMOTE:

  ```
  API>id,c,cust_newsarticle where object_name = Testing_Promote_Demote002.xml
  ...
  090015558000bc71
  ```

  ```
  API>id,c,cust_newsarticle where object_name = Testing_Promote_Demote.xml
  ...
  090015558000bc5b
  ```

  Once you have retrieved the r_object_ids of the two content files, issue the following simple API command for batch promotion.

  ```
  API> apply,c,NULL,BATCH_PROMOTE,ARGUMENTS,S,090015558000bc71,
  090015558000bc5b
  ```

The BATCH_PROMOTE method in turn calls the dm_bp_batch Documentum method and returns a collection with one result object after execution.

12.5 Expiring Content

At times, content appearing on websites needs to be taken off the website when the content is stale or due to any alternations that may be required. Documentum provides some mechanisms to allow you to expire content and pull it off your websites.

Firstly, you need to understand that Documentum provides a SysObject attribute a_expiration_date that content authors can fill in to specify when the content needs to be expired.

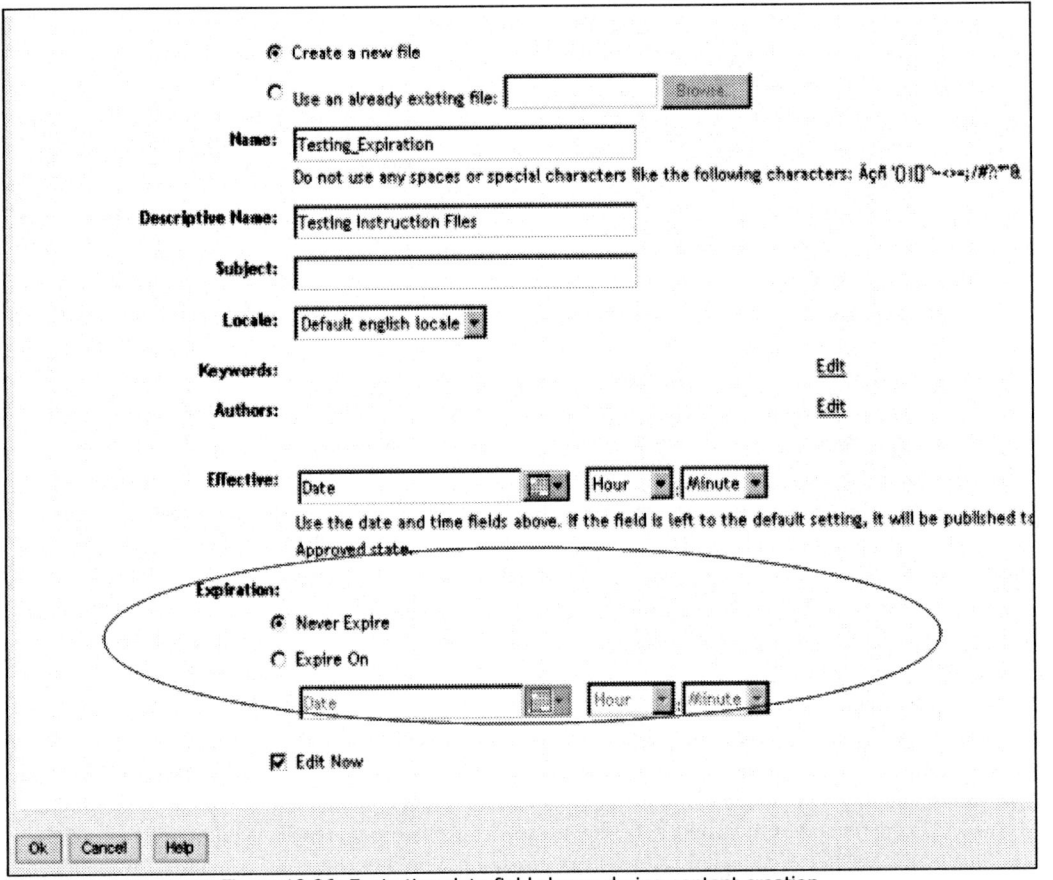

Figure 12.26: Expiration date field shown during content creation

Figure 12.26 shows Expiration date field in the New Content screen while creating new content in Web Publisher. In case you forget to specify the expiration date while creating content, you always have an option to specify it via the Publishing tab in the Properties (info) screen.

Following are some mechanisms to expire content created in Documentum:

- The Monitor_Lifecycles Job for content whose expiration date has been specified
- Web Publisher Expire now menu option

When the expiration date for active content matches the current system date, the Monitor_Lifecycles Job expires the content and pulls it off the website after publishing.

Using the Web Publisher Expire now menu option (Document | Lifecycle | Expire now), you can expire content prior to its specified expiration date, as shown in figure 12.27.

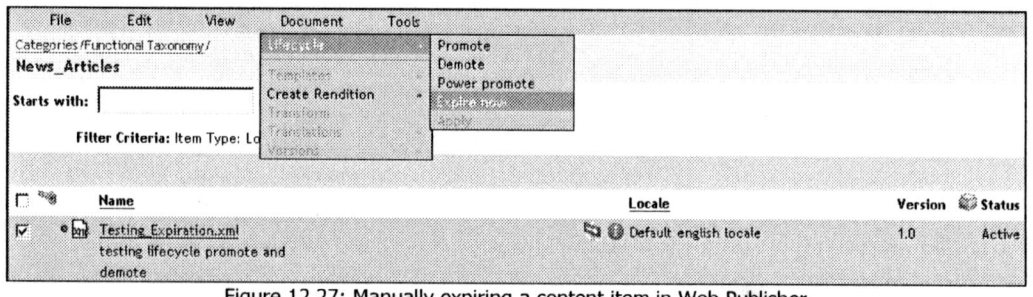

Figure 12.27: Manually expiring a content item in Web Publisher

Note that as shown in figure 12.28, the version label of the content changes to Expired (see Status column). The Expired content still remains in the Docbase, though it is removed from the Active website.

	Name	Locale	Version	Status
	Testing_Expiration.xml testing lifecycle promote and demote	Default english locale	1.0	Expired

Figure 12.28: Expired content as seen in Web Publisher

> In order to make changes in content that is in the Active state, use the Expire now facility to expire the content first and then edit it as required. It is worth noting that content in the following states cannot be demoted: WIP, Approved, Active, and Expired.

That completes our discussion on Lifecycles and their usage in Documentum. You can use a Lifecycle in conjunction with a workflow. While a Lifecycle simply represents the stages in the life of a document such as draft, review, and approved, a workflow actually routes the document through these Lifecycle stages and defines who works on the document, when, and under what conditions. In essence, a Lifecycle and a workflow complement each other. We will discuss workflows in Chapter 19. For now, you are all set to start creating Web Publisher Templates and associating them with custom object types. The content objects created from these can be associated with the custom Lifecycle we created in this chapter.

12.6 Summary

In this chapter we discussed Documentum Alias Sets, Permission Sets (ACL), and Lifecycles in detail. We mentioned the detailed steps for creating an Alias Set for a Lifecycle, Permission Sets for the various states of the Lifecycle, and a custom Lifecycle object.

We also saw how Documentum resolved the alias value for an alias in the Lifecycle scope, Workflow scope, Session scope, User scope, and System scope.

The custom Lifecycle created in this chapter comprised four states: Start, WIP, Staging, and Approved and had dm_document as the primary object type linked to it. We added the News Article object type as an acceptable subtype in the Lifecycle, allowing objects created from News Article object type to be attached to this custom Lifecycle.

Finally we saw the various mechanisms to promote, power-promote, and demote objects in the different states of Lifecycles and some means to expire content from the website.

13

Working with Web Publisher Template Files

Once you have created your custom object type and included it as an acceptable object type in your custom lifecycle, you are all set to go ahead and create a **Template** for the object type. Recall our earlier discussions about templates and object types: object types are the definitions for objects with information such as creator of object, last modified time, title, subject, description, and some custom attributes.

Whenever an object is created from a particular object type, it inherits all its attributes and allows users to assign specific values for each attribute. An object type simply serves as a template for all real-time objects created from it. However, this covers just the metadata or properties for objects. What about the actual content data of such objects (web pages), such as the associated images, the paragraphs/text abstracts, associated hyperlinks and other pieces of information that can be classified as actual content that is seen on the website and not metadata? This is where Web Publisher Templates (or loosely speaking **UI forms**) step in.

Using Web Publisher Templates, you can design and create forms with placeholder fields for the actual data that your business users can fill in for the created objects. The same Template can be used by multiple business users while creating content, to fill in the appropriate values in the template fields as per the specific business scenario.

In a nutshell, if we take up our dummy news website example, we are talking about two types of information:

- **Content**: The HTML content/web page (news article) that shows up on the website displaying actual news information such as headline image, main news content, etc.
- **Properties**: Meta-information/properties of the news article, such as who created the news article, when it was created, whether this is a press release news article, and other related attribute information.

If you are still confused, do not worry but proceed further. We will take up detailed examples in this chapter to understand what Templates are and how they fit in the Documentum architecture. For now, just understand that a Documentum developer simply creates different Templates with placeholder fields for different kinds of web pages on the website. Business users use the appropriate templates for creating the numerous categories of web pages on the website without having to understand any web languages or scripting methodologies such as HTML and JavaScript. The Documentum templates transform the entered data into HTML web pages with the desired look and feel via presentation files (stylesheets).

You may want to refer to Chapter 10 for a quick recap of what Templates are and how they couple with other Web Publisher files in Documentum.

For your convenience, let us discuss the Web Publisher **template-rules-presentation** architecture (refer to figure 13.1) once again to fix up any missing bolts and loose ends.

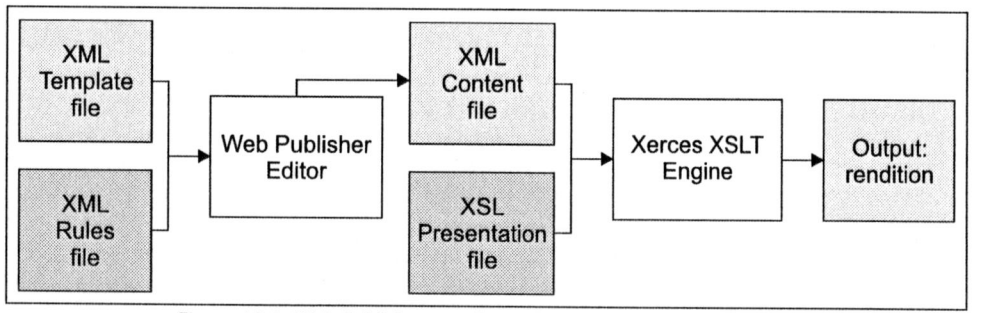

Figure 13.1: Web Publisher template-rules-presentation architecture

Web Publisher Template files can be created in Documentum as XML files with elements corresponding to the various fields in the template.

A **Rules file** is created in Documentum as an XML file with semantics added for the template field elements. Field type (checkbox, text box, etc.), field length, and field validations (mandatory, read-only, etc.), are defined in a Rules file.

Web Publisher internally interprets Template and Rules XML files to create and show the template fields in Web Publisher in a form that users can use to create web pages. The actual values filled in the Web Publisher editor template fields create a content file that is nothing but data assigned to the template XML elements.

Presentation files (XSL stylesheets) style the content XML files using Documentum's Xerces XSL Transformation engine to create web pages in the desired format/rendition (such as HTML, WML, etc.)

If you were to talk about division of responsibilities between the business users (content creators) and the IT development team, then it can be summed up as follows:

The IT development team creates object types, lifecycles, Templates, Rules files, presentation files, and other Documentum configuration items/related objects, while the business users simply use these objects and templates to fill in and create content for their website without the need to understand any programming languages/scripting/configuration settings!

A Web Publisher Template uses the following support files in Documentum:

- **Rules files**: Used for defining template fields for editing in Web Publisher editor.
- **Presentation files**: Used for styling and generating web formats/renditions from content files.
- **Previews**: These are graphical representations (thumbnail images) of templates and let content authors easily identify the templates.

It is worthwhile at this juncture to discuss the relationship between an object type and a template. Figure 13.2 should give you an idea about how these two are related and how they work in tandem during the content creation process.

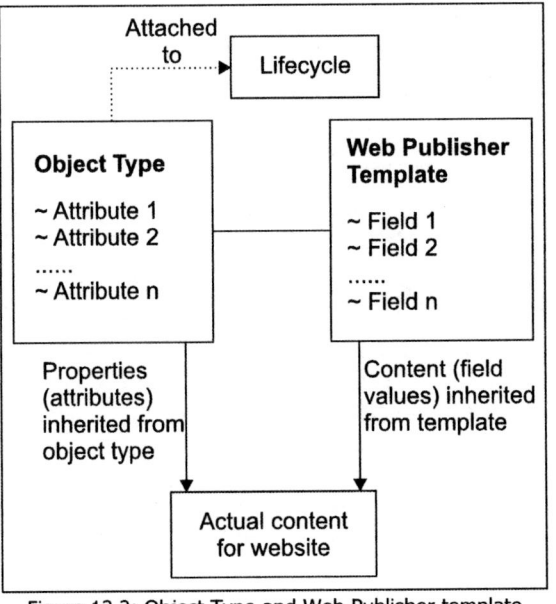

Figure 13.2: Object Type and Web Publisher template

An object type, as we discussed earlier, is associated with a lifecycle (in our example the cust_ newsarticle object type is associated with the custom_Lifecycle lifecycle). A Template in turn is linked to a particular object type in Documentum. Whenever content is created from an object type:

- The newly created content inherits the attributes (or metadata) defined in the object type definition with the actual values specified by content authors.
- The actual web page content is inherited from the values that business users specify while filling template fields.

Having discussed this, let us now begin our tour by creating a Template for our dummy news website example. We will see how simple it is to create Templates and supporting files for use within Documentum.

13.1 Creating a Template File

The first step before creating a Template is to create a category (or taxonomy) in Web Publisher with which the template will be associated.

It is wise to first sort out all the kinds of web pages on the website and then come up with the numerous categories of content. Based on each of the categories, Templates can be created so that content authors know exactly which category to look into in order to find the relevant Templates to create web page content.

1. Log in to Web Publisher as an administrator or a web developer user. Note that Web Publisher Templates reside in the Site Manager | Templates folder within the Docbase. Go to Site Manager | Templates in Web Publisher and click on File | New | Category. The New Category screen is as shown in the figure 13.3.

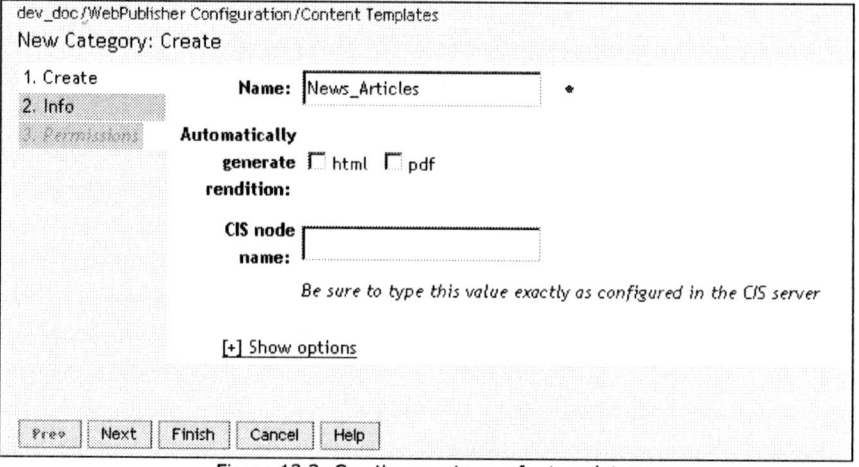

Figure 13.3: Creating a category for templates

Provide an informative and self-explanatory name for the category and click on Finish. If required, set up security settings for the category by going to the Permissions tab as well. Within the Permissions tab, you can assign a Permission Set (ACL) to the category allowing only certain groups to access the category and disallowing/restricting others from accessing the same.

2. The next and unarguably the most important step is to create the Template XML file so that it can be associated with the category created in the previous step.

   A Template file can be created in any of the numerous and varied flavors of XML editors and web authoring applications available in the market such as XML Spy®, Dreamweaver, or even text editors such as WordPad or Notepad.

Even though Web Publisher allows you to create HTML-based Templates as well as XML Templates, it is wiser to use XML Template files. Using XML Templates gives you more flexibility to style and parse the content XML files using XSL stylesheets, which is not the case when using HTML Template files.

Provide some rational name to the Template XML file (say `cust_news_art_templ.xml`) to signify it is a custom Template file for news articles.

Whenever new content is created using this Template file, content creators can provide some valid name to the content file, such as `news_article_oct31_2005.xml`.

There could be scenarios where the name of the content file is not of any consequence to the business team or where they could want some system-generated auto-naming scheme for the content files created from a Template file to avoid the hassles of providing names manually.

Under such circumstances, you could create a Template file with the following name convention, for example `cust_news_art_templ_###.xml`.

Whenever content is created using this Template, at run time Documentum substitutes the hash signs (#) with auto-generated numeric values in sequential order and names the content files as follows:

`cust_news_art_templ_001.xml`

`cust_news_art_templ_002.xml` ... and so on.

This feature is termed **auto-naming** in Web Publisher Templates.

A sample Template XML file created for our news article example is shown below:

```
<?xml version="1.0" encoding="UTF-8"?>
<NEWSART>
   <BANNERIMG></BANNERIMG>
   <IMGALTTEXT></IMGALTTEXT>
   <DATE></DATE>
   <BODYTEXT></BODYTEXT>
   <REPEATBLOCK>
   <NEXTLINKNAME></NEXTLINKNAME>
   <NEXTLINKURL></NEXTLINKURL>
   </REPEATBLOCK>
</NEWSART>
```

Let's discuss the anatomy of a typical XML template file:

```
<?xml version="1.0" encoding="UTF-8"?>
```

This is the standard XML declaration tag with character encoding. Specifying encoding as UTF-8 can support extended characters such as ®, © and not just ASCII characters.

<NEWSART> is the root tag of the XML file. The other XML elements denote individual fields within the template editor. For example, <DATE> denotes a field to enter the date in the template editor while <BANNERIMG> denotes the field for providing the banner image in the template editor.

Use character references and not HTML entity references when using special characters in Web Publisher XML files (Template files, Rules files, Presentation files).

For example, use £ to denote Pound symbol (£) instead of £

This is due to the limitation of the Xerces XML parser, which Documentum internally uses to parse XML files.

3. Copy the template file created in the previous step to some location on your machine's local drive. Go to the newly created category (in step 1 above) and choose menu option File | Import. Click on Add Files (refer to figure 13.4) and browse your machine's local drives till you find the Template file to be imported. Then click on the Next button.

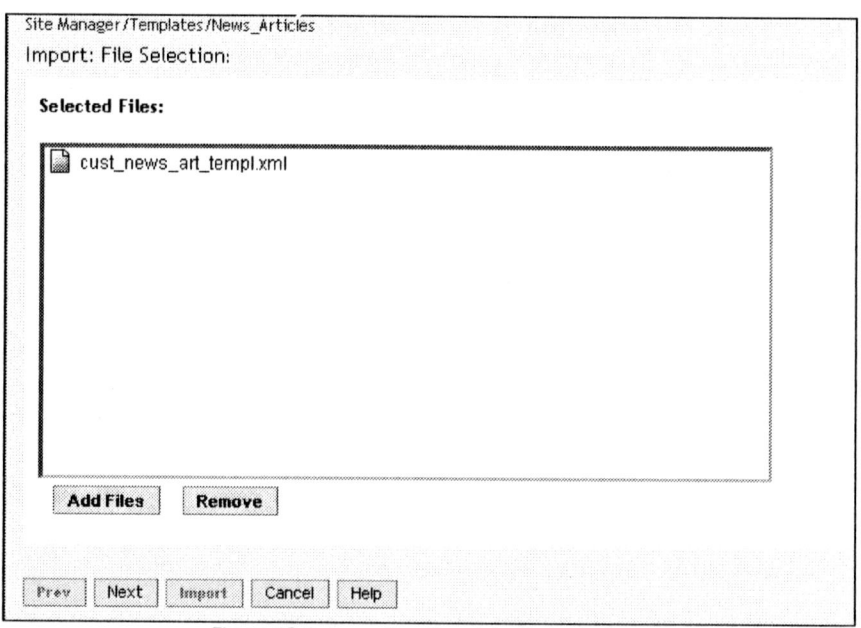

Figure 13.4: Importing Template file in Docbase

4. The Import: Object Definition screen is shown in figure 13.5. Provide some informative descriptive name for the template file in question and choose the object type with which it needs to be associated. Select the cust_newsarticle object type that we created earlier for our news article example.

After you select the object type, the Lifecycle dropdown gets populated with all the existing installed lifecycles in the Docbase that have the chosen object type as their acceptable primary/subtype.

Select Custom_Lifecycle from the Lifecycle dropdown and click the Import button.

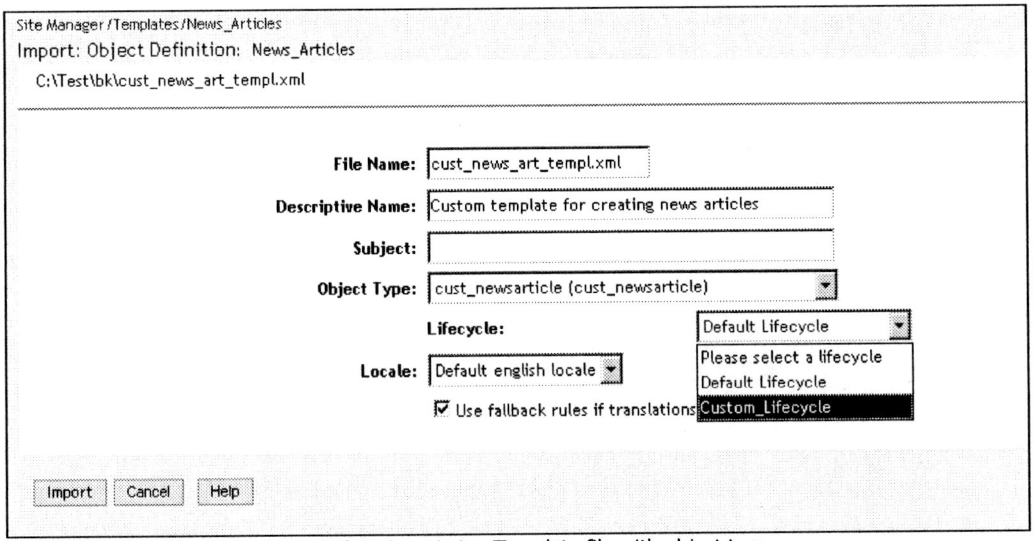

Figure 13.5: Associating Template file with object type

5. The imported Template file is shown in the associated category in an Unavailable state as shown in figure 13.6. This signifies that even though it has been imported into the Docbase, it is not yet ready to be used by content creators.

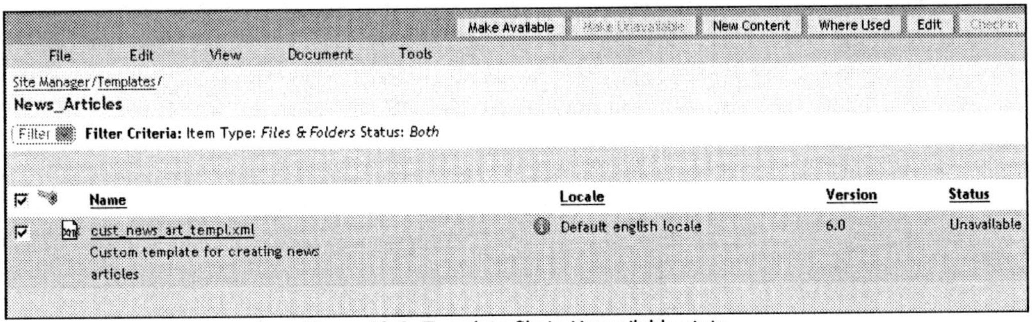

Figure 13.6: Template file in Unavailable state

Run the following DQL query using the IDQL utility or through the DQL editor in Documentum Administrator:

```
DQL> select object_name, a_is_template, r_version_label, r_object_type
     from cust_newsarticle where a_is_template = '1'
```

Note that all content objects created from cust_newsarticle object type will have their a_is_template system attribute set to 0, while only the Template file will have this value set as 1.

Result of the above DQL query:

The r_version_label attribute will have the value CURRENT,1.0.

Now make the Template file available to content authors by choosing it and clicking the Make Available button shown in the tool bar (refer to figure 13.6).

Run the above DQL query again and note that now the r_version_label attribute of the Template file will have the value Approved,WIP,CURRENT,1.0.

6. The Template file is now ready to be used by content authors, but it still needs to be associated with its supporting files such as Rules and Presentation files.

Choose the Template file and select View | Associations to look at the associated supporting files, as shown in figure 13.7.

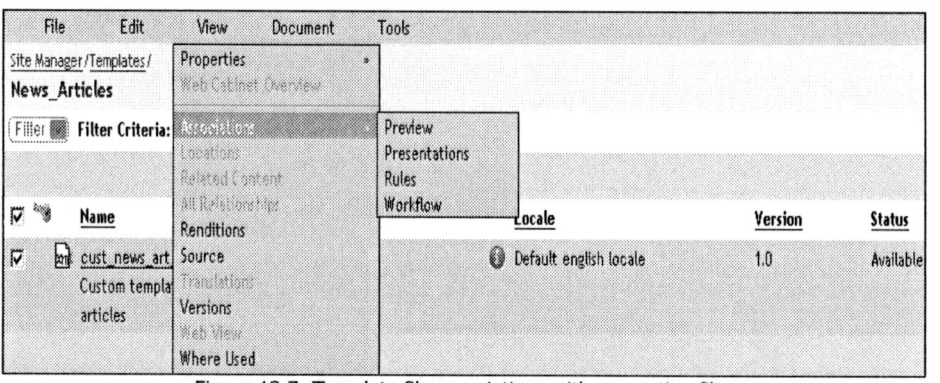

Figure 13.7: Template file associations with supporting files

Congrats! You have successfully created a Template file in Documentum that can be used by content authors for entering content for their websites. Before we proceed any further and start associating the Template file with its supporting files, it is critical to first create the supporting files for the above Template file. Move over to the next chapter in order to learn how to create a Rules file for the Template file we created in this chapter.

13.2 Summary

We talked about two types of information for Documentum objects; the actual content that shows up on websites and the metadata or attributes for the content object.

In Web Publisher, content authors create content using Template files. Internally, Documentum creates content XML files based on the structure of Template XML file used for content creation.

A Template created in Web Publisher is attached to a Docbase object type. Whenever a template is used to create content, the associated objects are created as run-time instances of the linked object type.

As in Chapter 10, we again briefly discussed Web Publisher Rules and Presentation files. Finally, we looked at the detailed steps for creating a sample Template for our News Article example.

14

Creating Rules Files

Having created a Template file for our News Article example in the previous chapter, we are all set to go ahead and design a **Rules file** for the Template. Recall that a Rules file is a simple XML file used to define the various fields in a Template file. Rules files reside in Documentum Web Publisher within the Site Manager | Rules folder in the Docbase. Follow the steps mentioned in the following section to create a Rules file for your Template file. Note that Documentum allows you to associate a particular Rules file with multiple Template files.

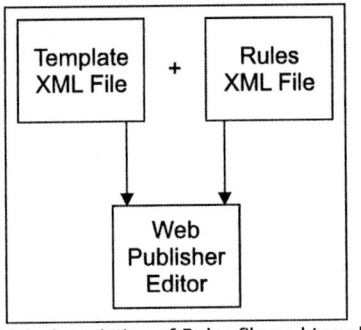

Figure 14.1: Association of Rules file and template file

14.1 Creating a Rules File

In this section, we will discuss the detailed steps for creating a Rules file.

1. Log in to Web Publisher as an administrator or a web developer user and go to the Site Manager | Rules folder. It is a good approach to create a new folder within the Rules folder to identify and separate specific Rules files for your custom application.

Choose the menu option File | New | Folder. The new folder creation screen comes up as shown in figure 14.2.

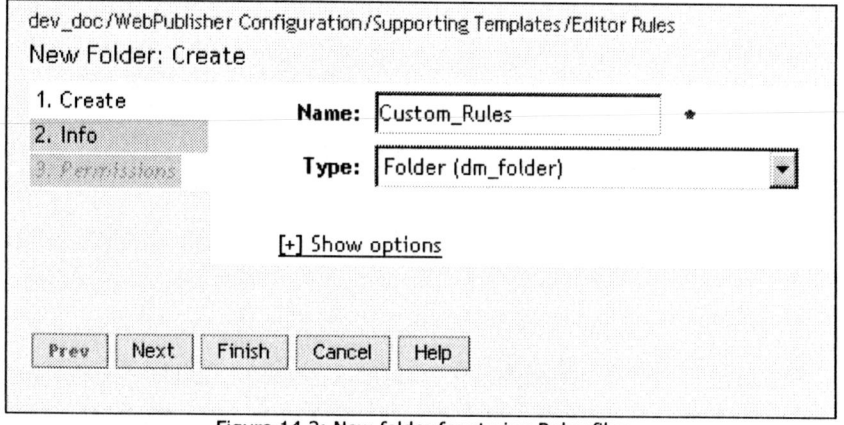

Figure 14.2: New folder for storing Rules files

Provide a valid name for your custom Rules folder (say Custom_Rules) and click on the Finish button. You could also attach some ACL (Permission Set) to the custom Rules folder for security reasons, allowing and disallowing certain groups and users from accessing the same. This can be done by clicking on the Permissions tab shown in figure 14.2.

2. Rules files can be created using any of the available XML/text editors, but that would require you to understand and learn Documentum's Rules file syntax and follow the instructions as provided in Documentum manuals. Instead, Documentum has developed a simple Rules file editor application in Web Publisher that assists you in automatically creating a Rules file based on the parameters you choose/specify through a simple Rules file creation GUI screen.

A simple configuration step needs to be performed before you can start using the Rules file editor application. Click on the Preferences button in Web Publisher and go to the Web Developers tab as shown in figure 14.3.

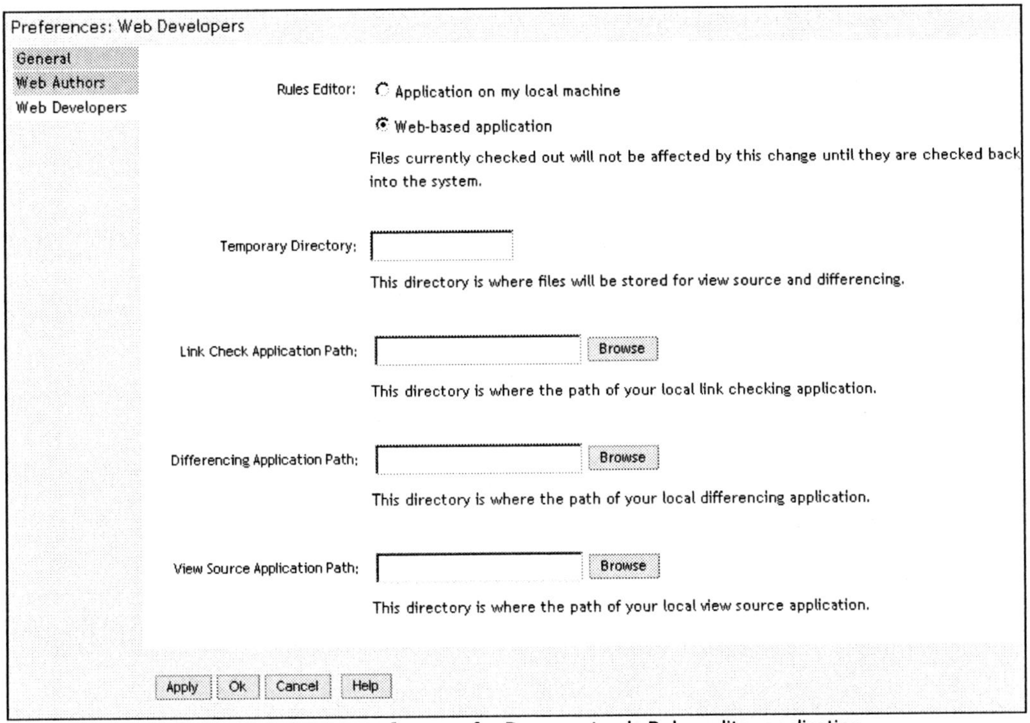

Preferences: Web Developers

General
Web Authors
Web Developers

Rules Editor: ○ Application on my local machine

          ● Web-based application

Files currently checked out will not be affected by this change until they are checked back into the system.

Temporary Directory: [ ]

This directory is where files will be stored for view source and differencing.

Link Check Application Path: [ ] [Browse]

This directory is where the path of your local link checking application.

Differencing Application Path: [ ] [Browse]

This directory is where the path of your local differencing application.

View Source Application Path: [ ] [Browse]

This directory is where the path of your local view source application.

[Apply] [Ok] [Cancel] [Help]

Figure 14.3: Setting preferences for Documentum's Rules editor application

In the Rules Editor section, choose the radio button for Web-based application. Click on Apply and then OK. This ensures that when you create a new Rules file or edit an existing Rules file, Documentum's internal Rules file editor is automatically invoked.

3. Having set the Rules editor preferences, go within the custom Rules folder Custom_Rules and choose menu option File | New | Rule. The new rule creation screen is shown in figure 14.4. Provide some valid name for the rules file (say cust_news_art_rule.xml) and click on OK.

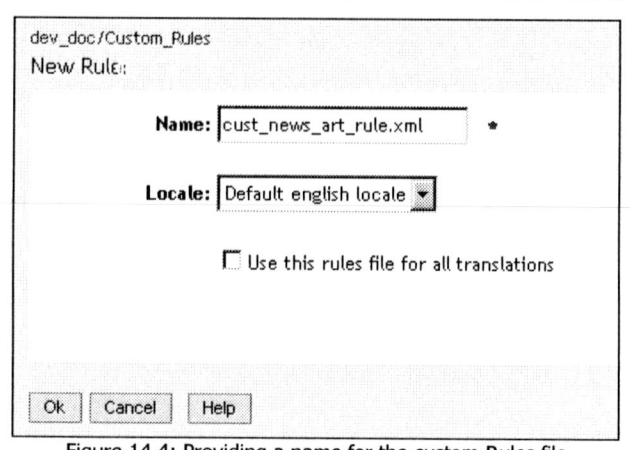

Figure 14.4: Providing a name for the custom Rules file

4. The system asks you to browse through existing categories in the Docbase and choose the Template for which the Rules file needs to be created, as shown in the figure 14.5.

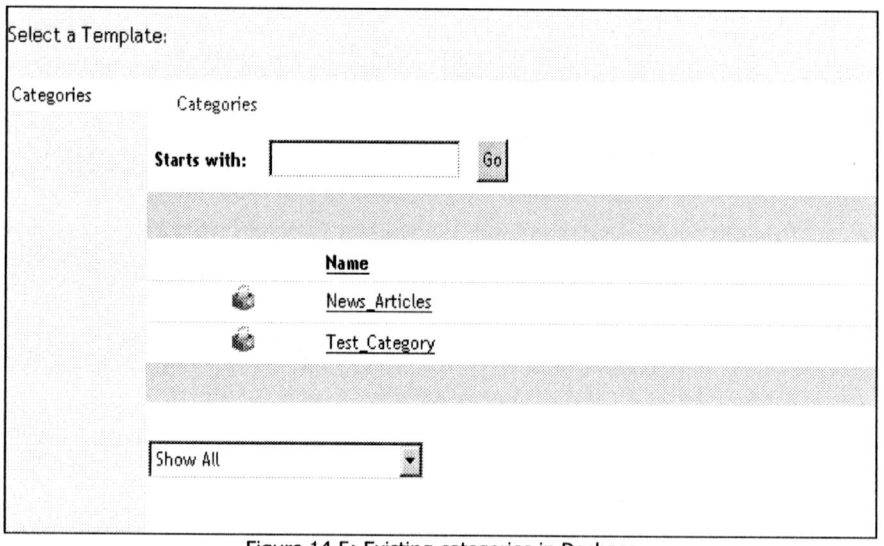

Figure 14.5: Existing categories in Docbase

Refer to figure 14.6; select the category that houses the template we created in the previous chapter (News_Articles) and select the checkbox against the Template file (cust_news_art_ templ.xml in our case). Finally, click on OK.

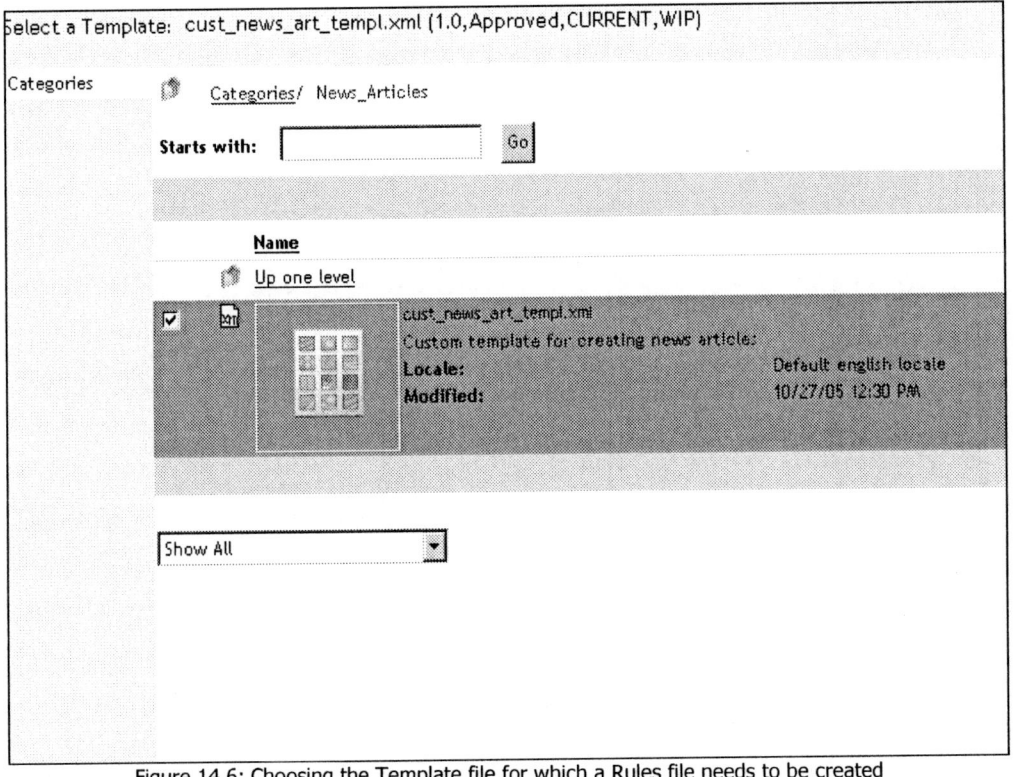

Figure 14.6: Choosing the Template file for which a Rules file needs to be created

Documentum invokes the Rules file editor as shown in figure 14.7. We can now add Rules to the various fields in the Template file.

All the XML elements in the Template file are shown under the Tree View tab of the Rules editor. You simply need to select these XML elements individually and add Rules to them.

Note that within the Tree View tab, the template XML elements are in a read-only mode, preventing you from modifying the Template file structure. However, by switching to Text View tab, you have the flexibility to alter the structure of XML elements in the associated Template file.

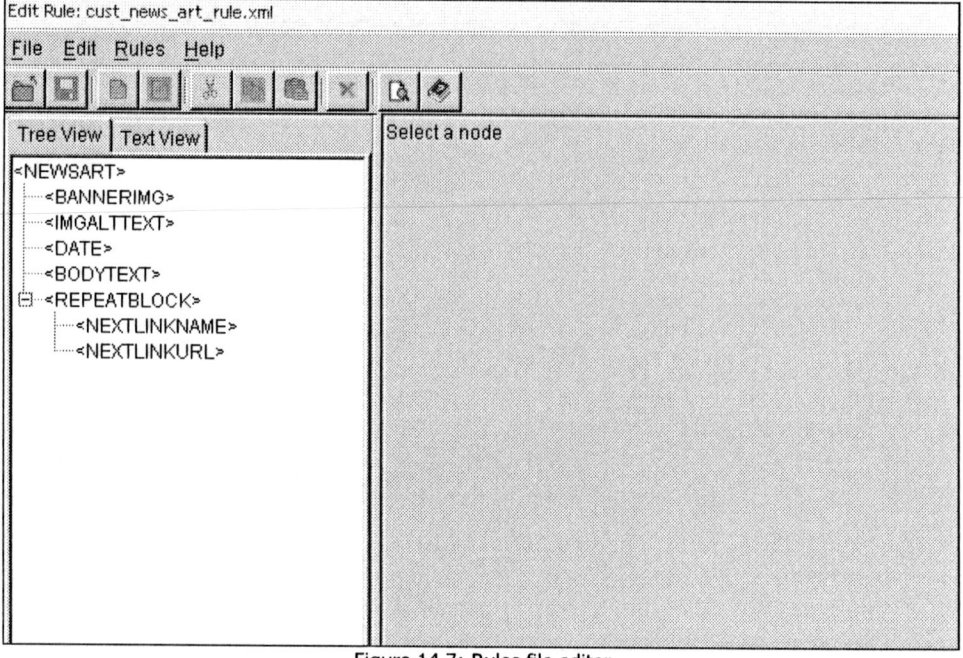

Figure 14.7: Rules file editor

It is recommended to save the Rules file during the creation process by choosing File | Save. At any point of time you can close the Rules editor and exit by choosing the option File | Close.

5. Refer to figure 14.8; select an XML element from the Template file (say <BANNERIMG>) under the Tree View tab and choose menu option Rules | Add Rule.

    The following types of widgets can be created in Web Publisher editor for the template XML elements:

    o   **Textline**: This is a single-line text field widget allowing content authors to type text without any formatting.

    o   **Content**: This is a multi-line text field widget allowing content authors to type text and format the same via available menu options such as: bolding, italicizing, changing fonts, etc.

    o   **Choice**: This is a drop-down selection list allowing content authors to choose a particular value from existing values. Values in the list can be populated from either a hard-coded fixed list or dynamically via a DQL query in Docbase.

    o   **Textselector**: This is a widget allowing content authors to choose some text from a chosen existing file within the Docbase.

    o   **Graphic**: This is a selection list widget allowing content authors to choose an image from the existing images in the Docbase.

- o **Checkbox**: This is a check-box widget allowing content authors to either select or de-select it.
- o **Xselector**: This is a file-selection widget allowing content authors to choose a file from a list of existing files in the Docbase.
- o **Repeating Blocks**: This is a widget that serves as a container for other elements. Designating a set of elements/fields as repeatable allows you to render those elements multiple times in the editor. This allows content authors to duplicate a particular field or specify multiple values for multiple instances of the same field.

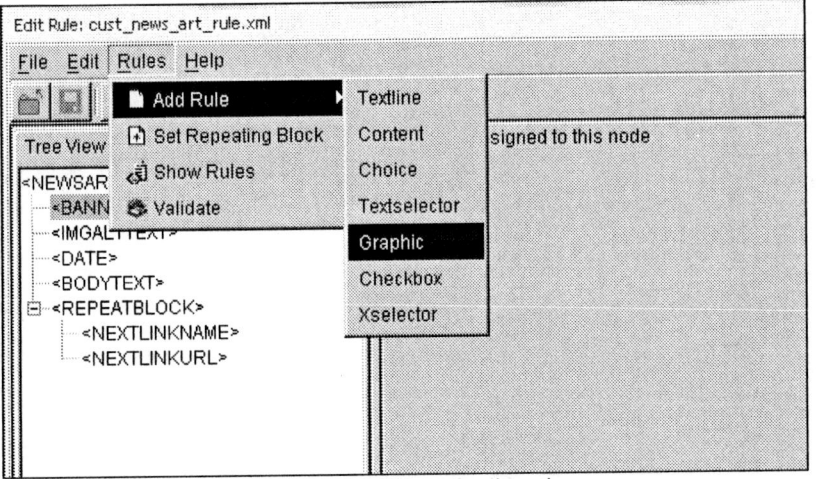

Figure 14.8: Adding a Graphic rule

As shown in figure 14.8, choose the Graphic option to add a rule for the <BANNERIMG> template element.

6. Fill in the fields for the graphic widget as shown in figure 14.9. Provide some label for the field, say Banner Image. Provide some instructional label for the convenience of content authors, say Please choose a banner image. Make the field mandatory by choosing the checkbox against Required.

7. Define the selection list for displaying the existing images in the Docbase from which the content authors can choose. Choose the display option as List control.

Enter a DQL query to populate the selection list:

```
dm_document where folder(/Test_WebCabinet/Custom_Images)
```

Note that you need not provide the keywords select * from.

The assumption here is that there pre-exists a folder Custom_Images in the Docbase within the Test_WebCabinet web cabinet containing image files. If it does not exist, create one and place some images within it.

The attribute name to be used in the select query is to be provided, say object_name. This eventually translates into the following DQL:

```
select object_name from dm_document where
folder(/Test_WebCabinet/Custom_Images)
```

Click on the Test Query button to check if the entered DQL syntax is correct and find out the query results that will be shown in the widget at run time.

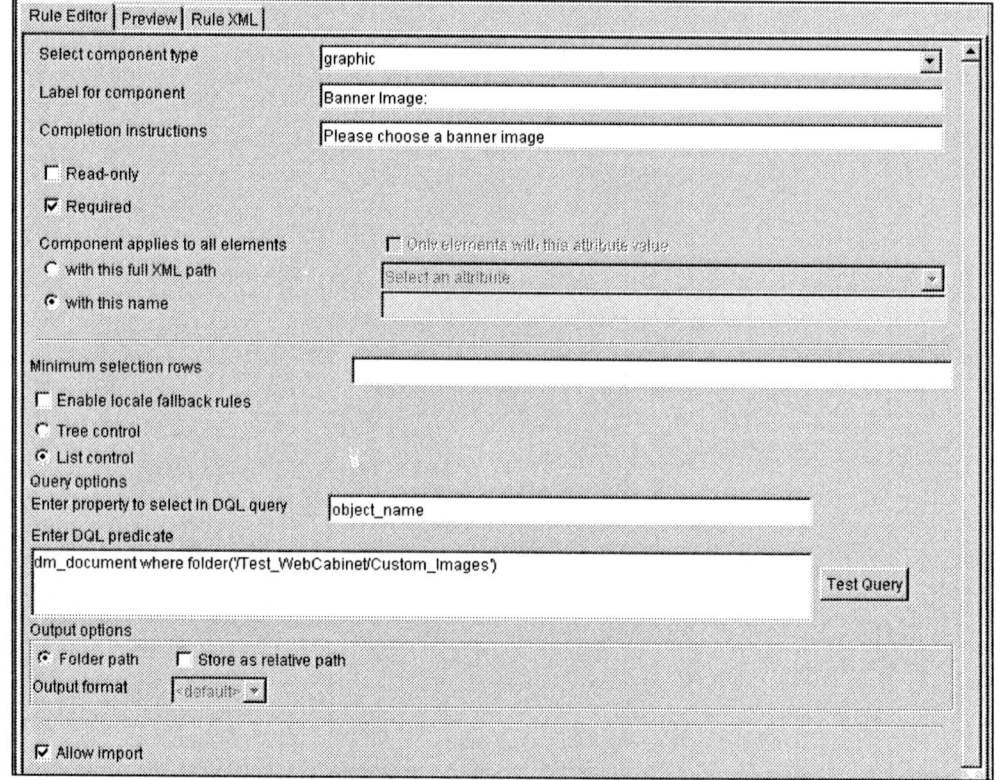

Figure 14.9: Defining Rules for the graphic element

8. You can optionally provide an option for content authors to import images within a specified folder in the Docbase through the graphic widget by selecting the Allow import checkbox.

9. Click on the Browse Docbase button shown in figure 14.10 and select the folder where image files will be imported and saved.

10. Select the object type with which the imported images will be associated by clicking on the Select button next to the Type field.

11. Select the Lifecycle that the imported images will be attached to, by clicking on the Select button next to the Lifecycle field.

12. Select the category that the imported images will be associated with, by clicking on the Select button next to the Category field.

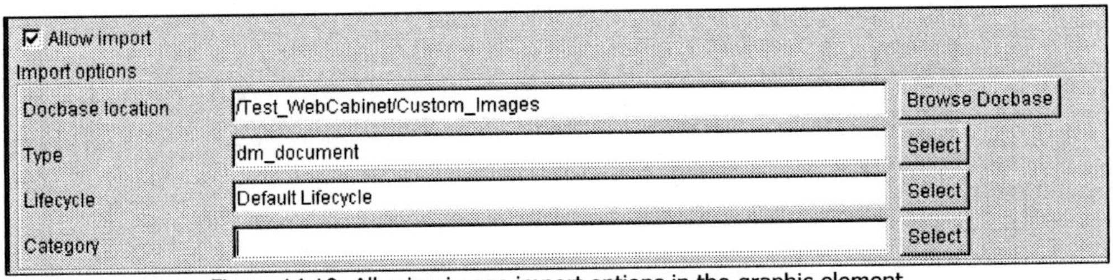

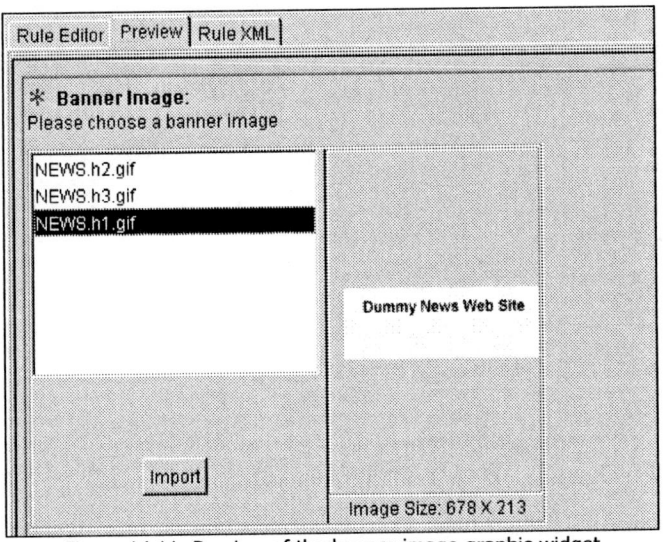

Figure 14.10: Allowing image import options in the graphic element

13. Save the Rules file and click on the Preview tab (refer to figure 14.11) to see how the Banner Image field will appear when the content author creates content using the News Article template.

Figure 14.11: Preview of the banner image graphic widget

Notice that the Import button has also been added allowing you to import image files from your local machine to the specified folder location within the Docbase.

14. In order to view the automatically system-generated Rules file code for the graphic element, click on the Rule XML tab (refer to figure 14.12):

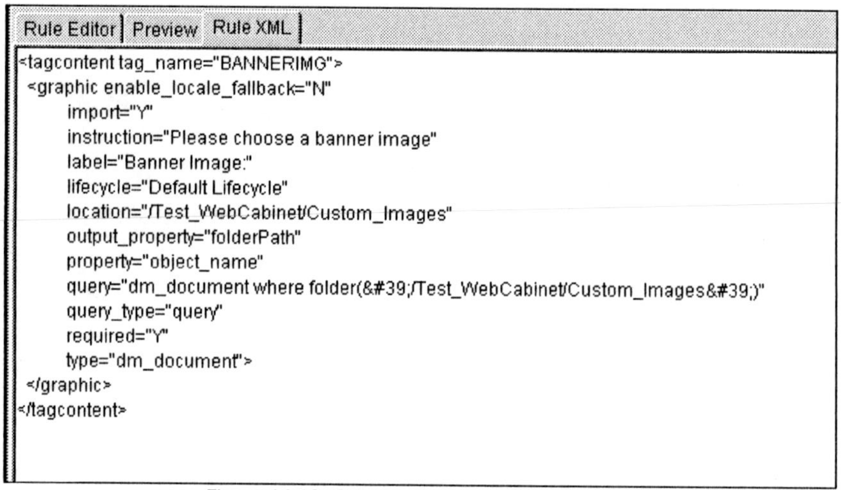

```
Rule Editor | Preview   Rule XML |
<tagcontent tag_name="BANNERIMG">
 <graphic enable_locale_fallback="N"
      import="Y"
      instruction="Please choose a banner image"
      label="Banner Image:"
      lifecycle="Default Lifecycle"
      location="/Test_WebCabinet/Custom_Images"
      output_property="folderPath"
      property="object_name"
      query="dm_document where folder(&#39;/Test_WebCabinet/Custom_Images&#39;)"
      query_type="query"
      required="Y"
      type="dm_document">
 </graphic>
</tagcontent>
```

Figure 14.12: System-generated Rules file code

Similarly, you can create other widgets for the remaining template fields by selecting the Rules editor widget types shown in figure 14.13.

Template XML element	Rules file widget
BANNERIMG	Graphic
IMGALTTEXT	Textline
DATE	Textline
BODYTEXT	Content
REPEATBLOCK	Repeating Block
NEXTLINKNAME	Textline
NEXTLINKURL	Textline

Figure 14.13: Rules file widgets

15. After highlighting the respective template XML elements and adding Rules to them, you can save the Rules file and exit the editor by choosing menu option File | Close.

    Check-in the newly created Rules file (cust_news_art_rule.xml) and make the Template file (cust_news_art_templ.xml) available by clicking the Make Available button as discussed in the previous chapter.

    For your convenience, shown next are some screenshots taken while creating Rules for the remaining template XML elements. You may treat these as guidelines while creating your Rules files:

14.1.1 IMGALTTEXT Element

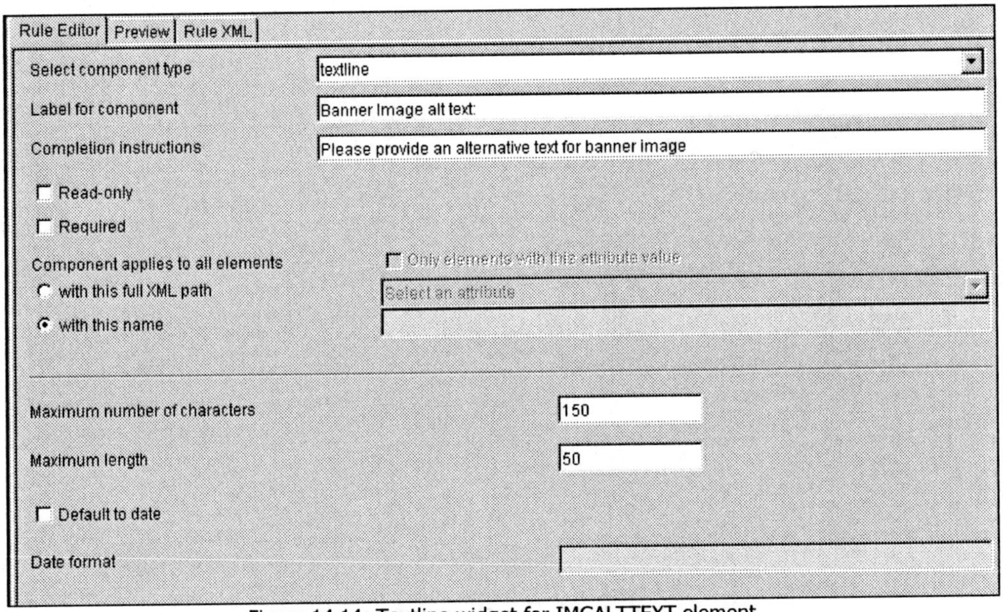

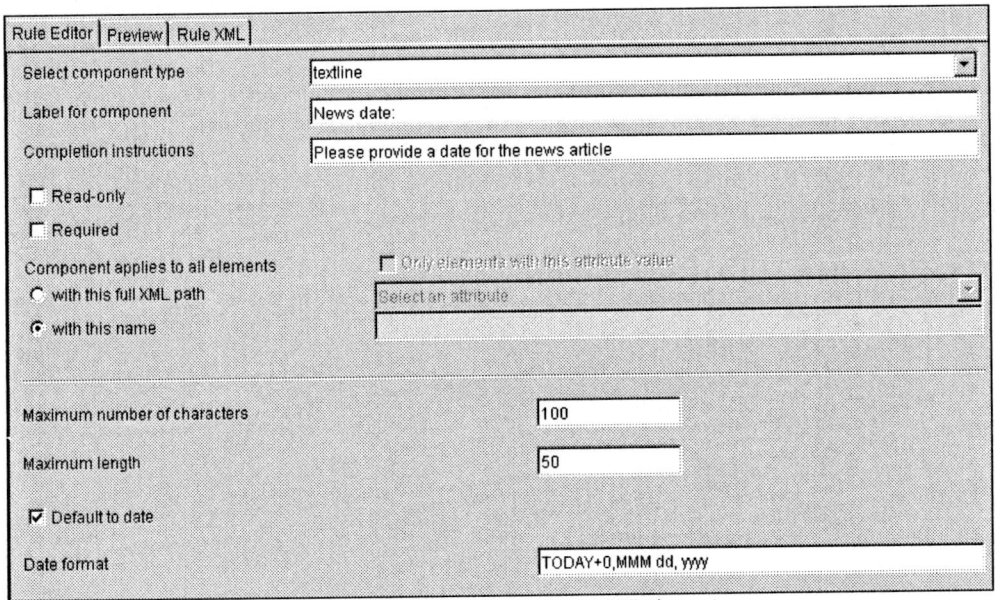

Figure 14.14: Textline widget for IMGALTTEXT element

14.1.2 DATE Element

Figure 14.15: Textline widget for DATE element

Note that the default date format in figure 14.15 has been set as: TODAY+0,MMM dd, yyyy.

Whenever content is created using the News Article template, the News date: field will be pre-populated with that particular day's date in the specified format.

14.1.3 BODYTEXT Element

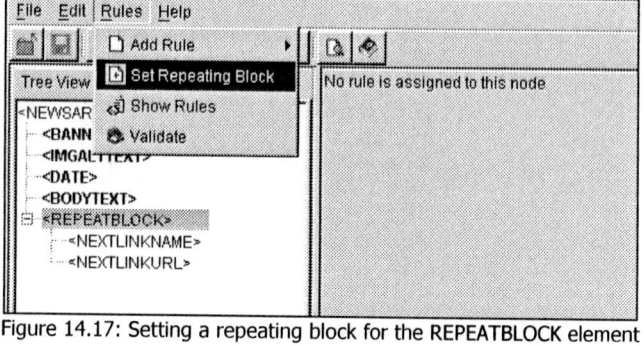

Figure 14.16: Content widget for BODYTEXT element

In figure 14.16, numerous formatting options can be selected for the multi-line text field. Additionally, you can choose the checkbox shown against the Links option to allow content authors to create hyperlinks to existing files in Docbase. Link browser formats allows you to specify the various file formats you wish to be displayed for the content authors to choose from. By default, only html and crtext formats are enabled, allowing files with .htm, .html, and .txt extensions to be shown.

14.1.4 REPEATBLOCK Element

Figure 14.17: Setting a repeating block for the REPEATBLOCK element

The <REPEATBLOCK> template element encloses <NEXTLINKNAME> and <NEXTLINKURL> elements, signifying that content authors can provide multiple article link names and their URLs within this block. In order to make <REPEATBLOCK> a repeating block widget, highlight it and choose menu option Rules | Set Repeating Block, as shown in figure 14.17.

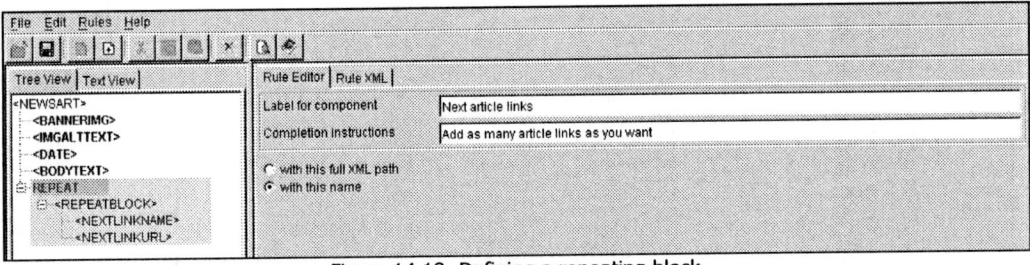

Figure 14.18: Defining a repeating block

Provide a label and instructional text for the convenience of content authors in the repeating block, as shown in figure 14.18.

14.1.5 NEXTLINKNAME Element

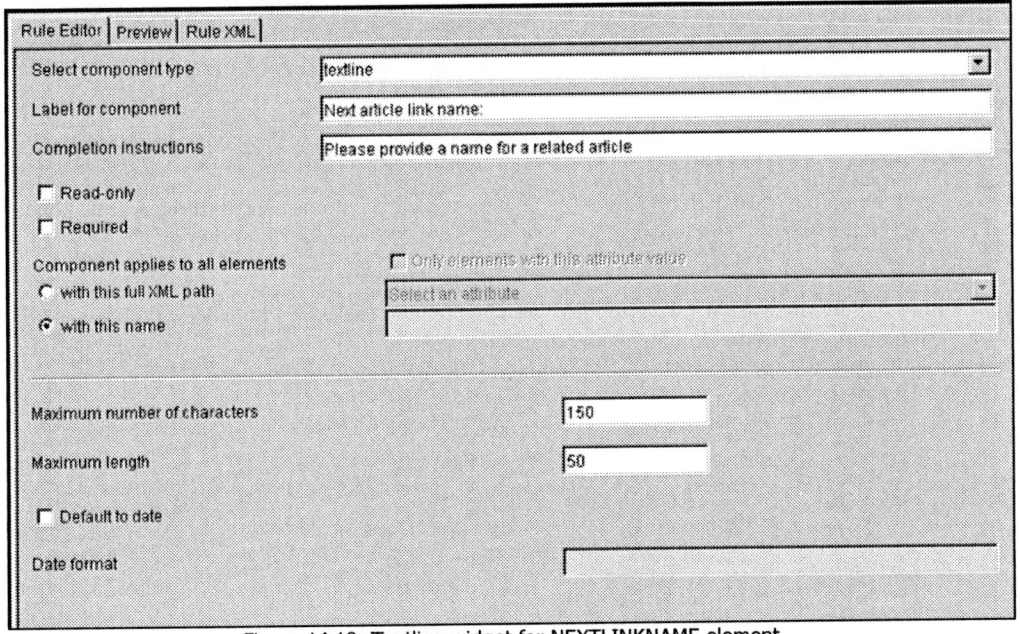

Figure 14.19: Textline widget for NEXTLINKNAME element

14.1.6 NEXTLINKURL Element

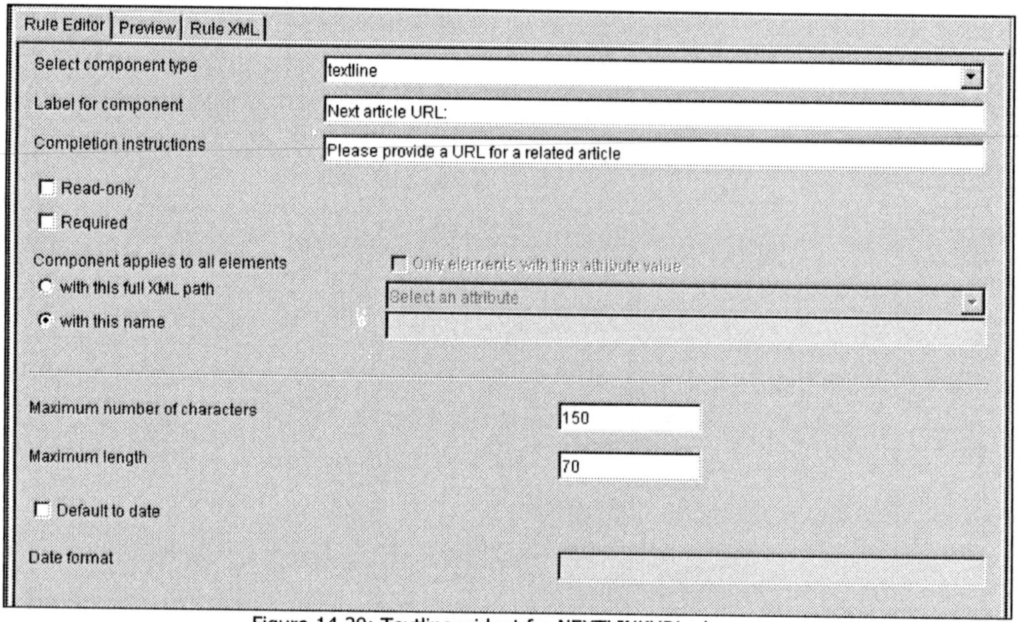

Figure 14.20: Textline widget for NEXTLINKURL element

14.2 Final Template in Web Publisher Editor

Assuming that you have created the Rules file as per the specifications shown in the screenshots and checked-in the same in Docbase, let us create new News Article content by browsing the News_Articles category and choosing menu option File | New | Content.

After filling in the properties information for the new content, the Web Publisher editor opens up, displaying the News Article template as per the Rules defined in the Rules file we created. Figures 14.21 and 14.22 show the News Article template as seen in Web Publisher editor.

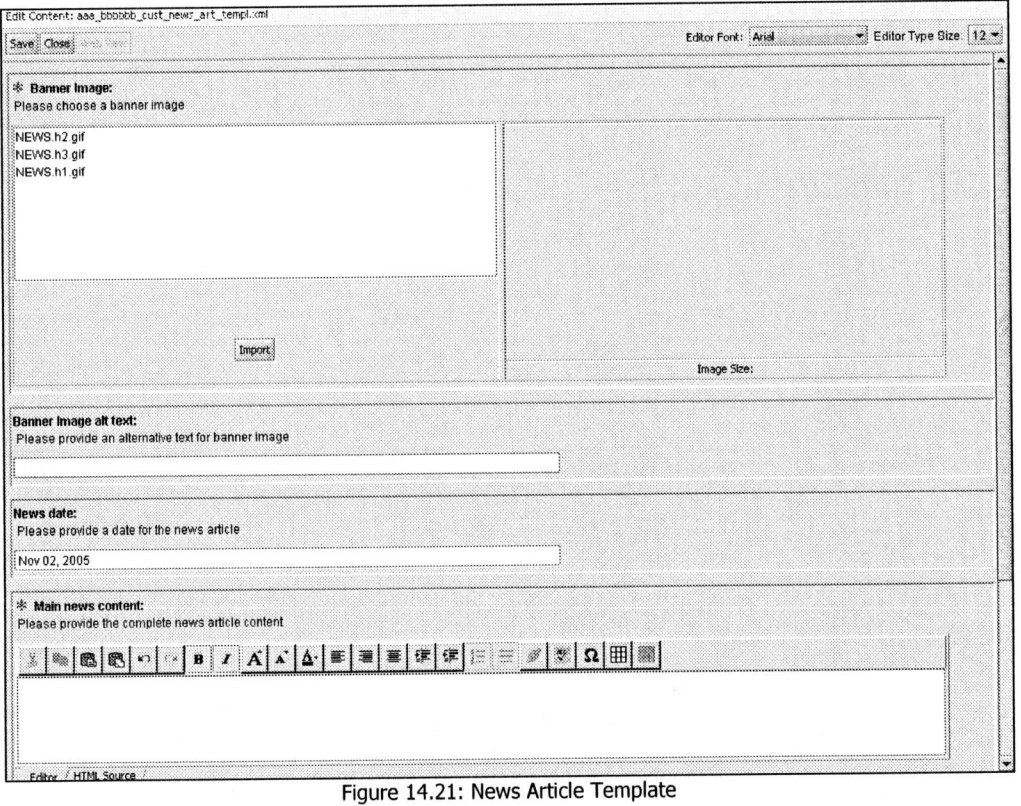

Figure 14.21: News Article Template

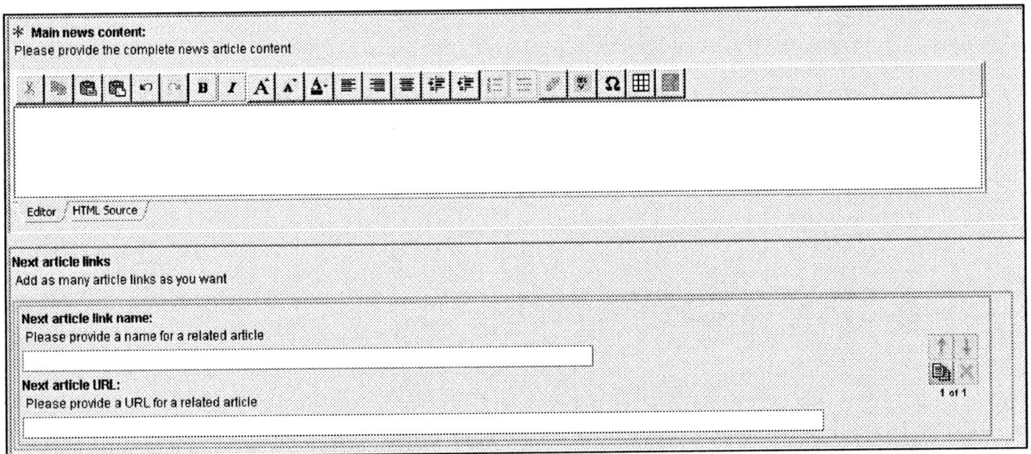

Figure 14.22: News Article Template—continued

Refer to figure 14.22; note the repeating block widget added in the Next article links repeating block. You can duplicate the News article link name/URL fields, re-arrange multiple fields, and even delete newly added fields using the repeating block widget.

14.3 Miscellaneous Rules File Widgets

We have seen some Web Publisher Rules file widgets like textline, content, graphic, and repeating block. Here are some other widgets as they are seen in Web Publisher editor. A visual appeal leaves a lasting impact and will help you design your templates better.

14.3.1 Choice Widget

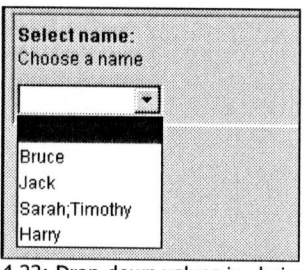

Figure 14.23: Drop-down values in choice widget

> Note that the delimiter in a choice widget is comma (,). This means that the string (Sarah, Timothy) would show up as two values, Sarah and Timothy, in the dropdown. The only workaround to such a scenario is to separate them with a semicolon or some other delimiter instead of a comma. Example: Sarah;Timothy.

14.3.2 Checkbox Widget

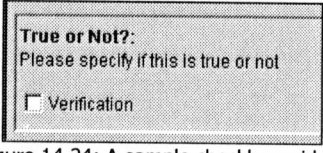

Figure 14.24: A sample checkbox widget

14.3.3 Textselector Widget

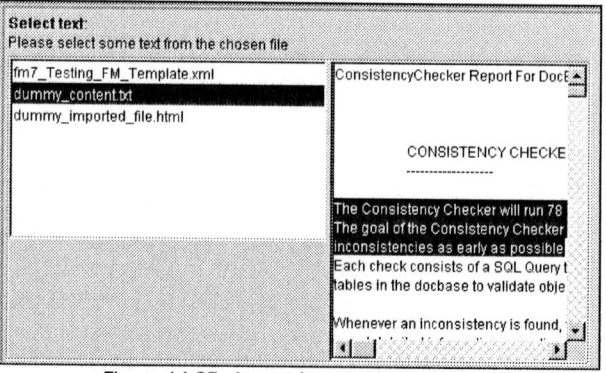

Figure 14.25: A sample textselector widget

14.3.4 Xselector Widget

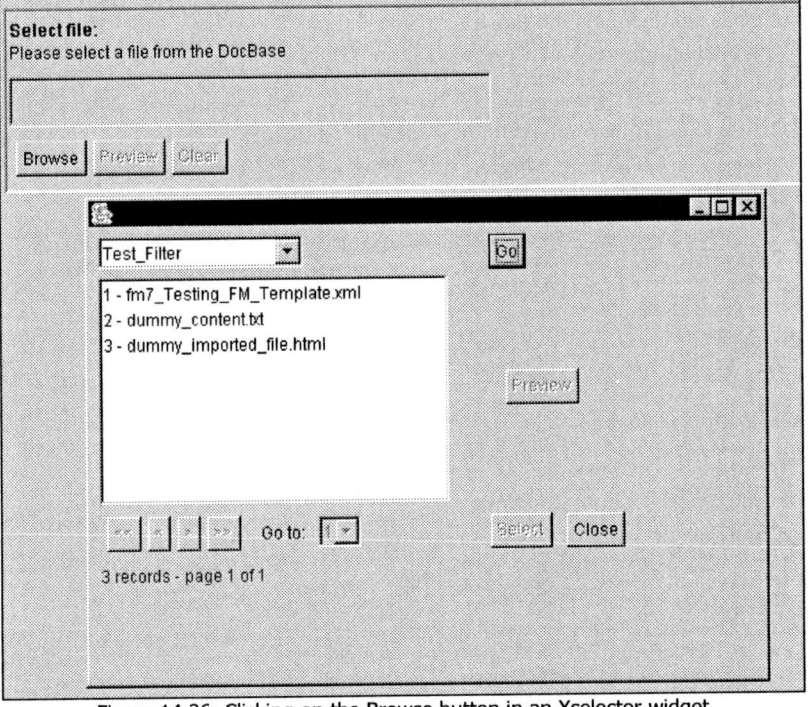

Figure 14.26: Clicking on the Browse button in an Xselector widget

It may be worthwhile to quickly discuss some of the enhancements made to Web Publisher in Documentum release 5.3:

- Enhancements in Web Publisher editor with rich-text editing features and support for link management in content widget

- Browser drag-and-drop support allowing Internet Explorer users to drag items from their desktop to system folders and dragging items within Web Publisher

- Search improvements via a new improved search algorithm

- Support for specifying columns that should appear in folder lists, Inbox, search result pages, etc.

This chapter should have given you a good idea about what Rules file are and how they can be created and associated with template files. You should go through the Documentum Web Publisher administration manuals to learn more about Rules files, different widget types, and their numerous specific attributes in more detail. You can now continue your journey by moving over to the next chapter in order to create a Presentation file for our News Article template.

14.4 Summary

Rules files define the validation and behavior of the various XML elements in Web Publisher Template files. We started our tour by going through a detailed example of creating a Rules file in Web Publisher for our News Article template. We saw how to set preferences for invoking Web Publisher Rules Editor for creating Rules files.

We briefly discussed the following available Rules file widgets:

- Textline
- Content
- Choice
- Textselector
- Graphic
- Checkbox
- Xselector
- Repeating Blocks

Lastly, we saw how some of the Rules file widgets appear when viewed in Web Publisher editor.

15

Creating Presentation Files

We have created a Template file and associated it with a Rules file in the previous chapters. What now remains is the creation of a Presentation file (XSL) to format the data in the content file into a suitable rendition such as HTML, WML, etc. The website pages are nothing but the web renditions of content XML files via Web Publisher presentation files and so the design and creation of Presentation files is crucial in a web content management project.

Additionally, Presentation files separate the structure of content from its layout. While the templates and Rules files simply capture the structure of the content to be entered by content authors, the Presentation files focus on how the entered content is formatted for generating web renditions.

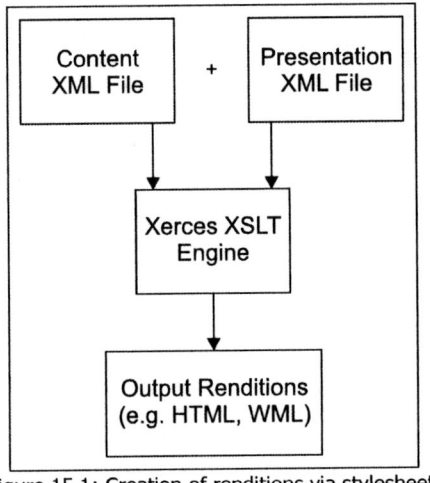

Figure 15.1: Creation of renditions via stylesheets

A rendition is created by Documentum whenever a content file is saved and checked into the Docbase. Behind the scenes, Web Publisher applies the Presentation file (XSL stylesheet) to the content XML file and generates the prescribed rendition. Presentation files in Web Publisher are of two kinds:

- **Editor Presentation files (XSL stylesheets)**: Used for formatting Web Publisher editor XML content and stored in the Docbase at the following location: Site Manager | Presentations | Editor.

- **External Presentation files (HTML wrappers)**: Used for external applications and stored in the Docbase at the following location: Site Manager | Presentations | External. External presentation files provide standard frames and wrappers to the content embedded within the <body></body> elements of HTML content files.

15.1 Creating a Presentation File

Creating Presentation files in Documentum is not a big deal and the following steps explain how they can be easily built and associated with template files.

1. Log in to Web Publisher as an administrator or a web developer user and go to Site Manager | Presentations | Editor. As we saw with Rules files, it is a good approach to create a new folder within the Editor folder to identify and separate specific Presentation files for your custom application.

2. Choose the menu option File | New | Folder. The new folder creation screen comes up as shown in the figure 15.2.

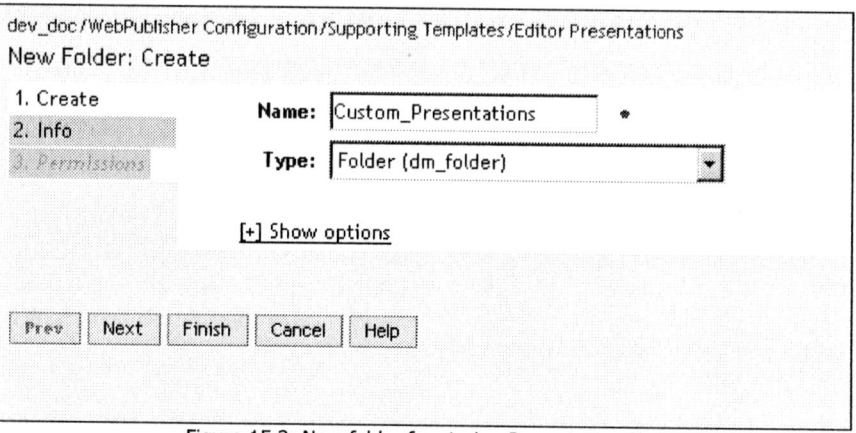

Figure 15.2: New folder for storing Presentation files

3. Provide some valid name for your custom Presentation file folder (say Custom_ Presentations) and click on the Finish button. You could also attach some ACL (Permission Set) to this folder as in the case of Rules files.

4. Create a valid/well-formed industry-standard XSL stylesheet in your favorite editor such as XML Spy®, Notepad, etc. and provide some meaningful name to it (say cust_news_art_pres.xsl for the News Article template). Save the newly created Presentation file within a convenient folder location on your machine's hard drive.

Figures 15.3 and 15.4 show a sample presentation file for the News Article template. Note that you could improve it (and there definitely is enough scope for improvement!) as per your specific business requirements.

```
<?xml version="1.0" encoding="UTF-8" ?>
<!DOCTYPE xsl:stylesheet (View Source for full doctype...)>
- <xsl:stylesheet version="1.0" xmlns:xsl="http://www.w3.org/1999/XSL/Transform" xmlns:fo="http://www.w3.org/1999/XSL/Format"
    xmlns:java="http://xml.apache.org/xslt/java" xmlns:xalan="http://xml.apache.org/xalan" exclude-result-prefixes="xalan java fo">
    <xsl:output method="html" encoding="ISO-8859-1" indent="yes" />
    <xsl:strip-space elements="*" />
- <xsl:template match="*|@*|comment()|processing-instruction()|text()">
  - <xsl:copy>
      <xsl:apply-templates select="*|@*|comment()|processing-instruction()|text()" />
    </xsl:copy>
  </xsl:template>
  <!-- Matching content XML file root element -->
- <xsl:template match="NEWSART">
  - <table border="0">
    - <tr>
        <th>News web site:</th>
      </tr>
    - <tr>
      - <td>
          <br />
        </td>
      </tr>
    - <tr>
        <!-- Capturing location path of inserted banner image -->
      - <xsl:variable name="imagePath">
          <xsl:value-of select="BANNERIMG/Img/@src" />
        </xsl:variable>
        <!-- Capturing alternative text of inserted banner image -->
      - <xsl:variable name="imageAltText">
          <xsl:value-of select="IMGALTTEXT" />
        </xsl:variable>
      - <td>
          <img src="{$imagePath}" alt="{$imageAltText}" />
        </td>
      </tr>
    - <tr>
      - <td>
          <br />
        </td>
      </tr>
    - <tr>
        <!-- Displaying news article date -->
```

Figure 15.3: Sample News Article Presentation file

```
        <!-- Displaying news article date  -->
       - <td>
        - <b>
          - <u>
            <xsl:copy-of select="DATE" />
           </u>
         </b>
        </td>
       </tr>
     - <tr>
       - <td>
          <br />
        </td>
       </tr>
     - <tr>
         <!-- Displaying news article body text  -->
        - <td>
          <xsl:copy-of select="BODYTEXT" />
         </td>
       </tr>
     - <tr>
       - <td>
          <br />
        </td>
       </tr>
         <!-- Iterating through multiple next article links  -->
     - <xsl:for-each select="REPEATBLOCK">
       - <tr>
         - <td>
           - <a href="{NEXTLINKURL}">
             <xsl:copy-of select="NEXTLINKNAME" />
            </a>
          </td>
        </tr>
       </xsl:for-each>
      </table>
    </xsl:template>
   </xsl:stylesheet>
```

Figure 15.4: Sample News Article Presentation file—continued

Note carefully how the various template file XML elements have been formatted in the XSL stylesheet. It may be worthwhile to flip over to Chapter 13 and keep the template XML file beside you while studying the above Presentation file.

5.   Go within the Custom_Presentations folder created in step 1 and choose File | Import. The file import selection screen comes up as shown in figure 15.5. Click on the Add Files button; browse your machine's folder paths to select the newly created presentation file. Once you have selected the presentation file, click on Next.

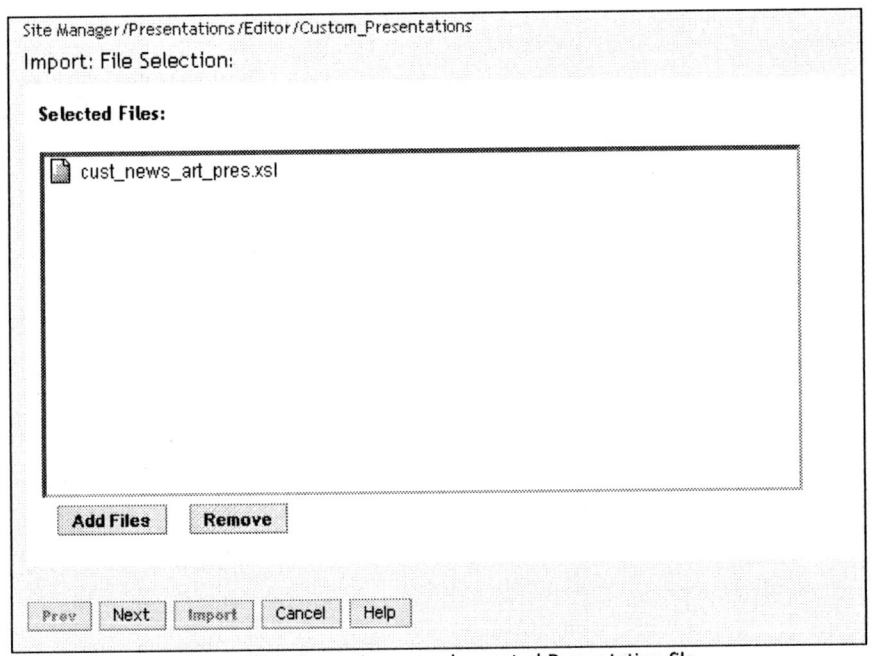

Figure 15.5: Importing a newly created Presentation file

6. The File Name field is shown (refer to figure 15.6) for you to provide some valid name for the selected file. Keep the Presentation file name as it is without altering it and click on Import.

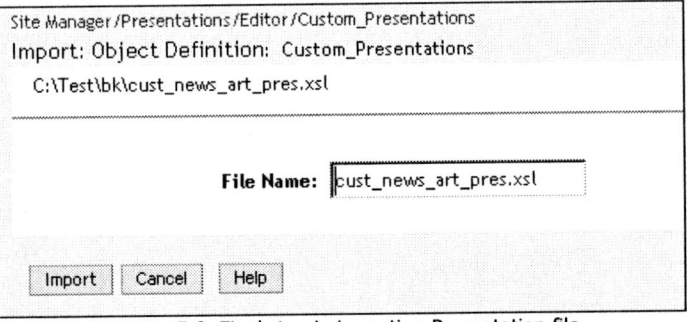

Figure 15.6: Final step in importing Presentation file

7. The Presentation file is imported into the Docbase within the prescribed folder path /Site Manager/Presentations/Editor/Custom_Presentations.

    Now that you have created and imported the Presentation file in Docbase, you need to associate it with the news article Template file we created in chapter 13. However, understand that associating a Presentation file with a Template file requires specifying a rendition format for the output of Web Publisher.

Rendition formats could be default Documentum recognized formats such as html (standard HTML format) or crtext (text format), or custom formats identified for one's business needs. If you require that our Presentation file should style the News Article content file and create a rendition format of the MIME type html but with some custom file extension (say .cshtml), then this is what you need to do:

Log in to Documentum Administrator as an administrator user and go to Administration | Formats.

Choose the menu option File | New | Format and provide the details of the new format as shown in figure 15.7. The details are:

Name: custom_format

Default File Extension: cshtml

Description: Custom format

Mime Type: Text/html

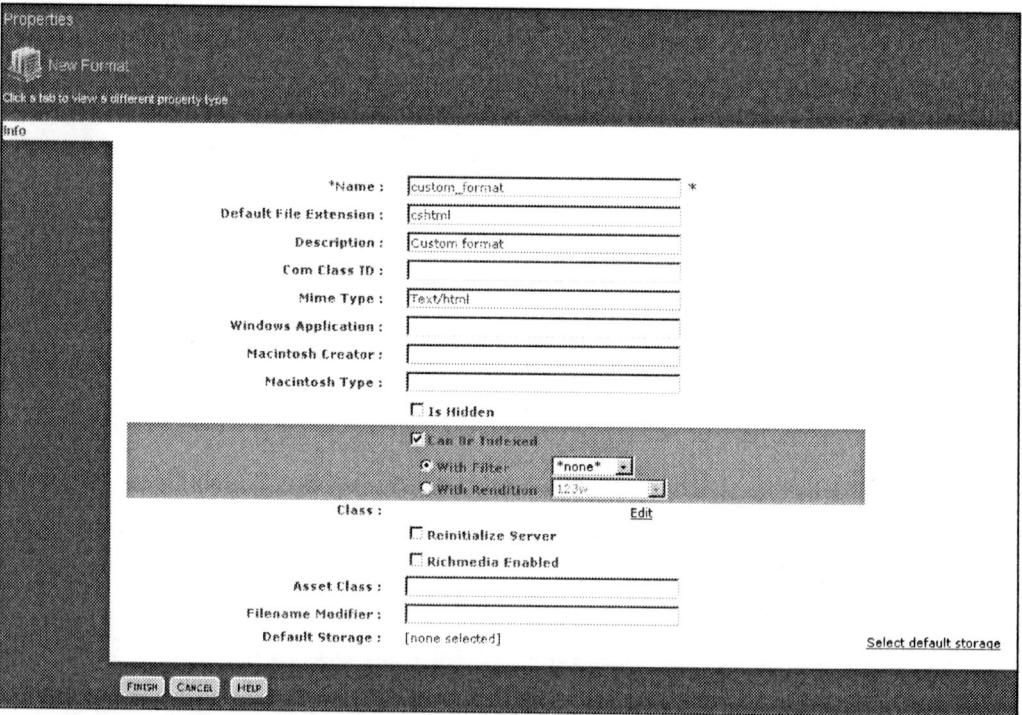

Figure 15.7: Creating a custom format in Docbase

Do not forget to include the custom format within your Site Publishing configuration against the Formats field in the Content Selection Settings section. This ensures that the renditions generated in custom formats are published out from Docbase during publishing operations. More about this in Chapter 21.

8. This step requires associating the Presentation file with the existing News Article Template file. Log in to Web Publisher and go to Site Manager | Templates and select the News_Articles category. Select the checkbox against the cust_news_art_templ.xml template and select the menu option View | Associations | Presentations as shown in figure 15.8.

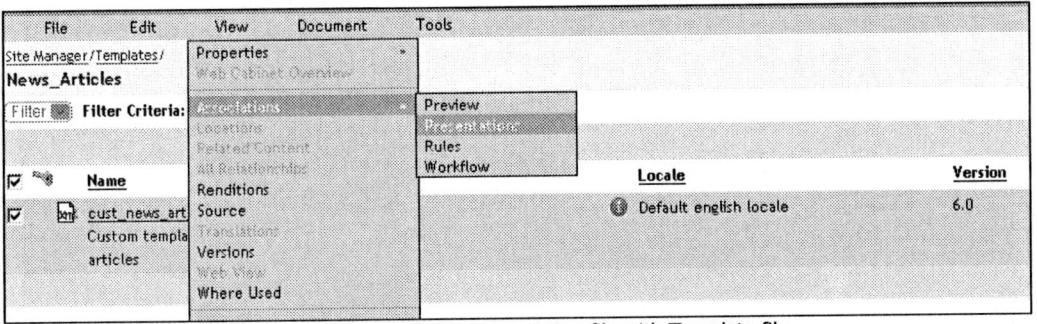

Figure 15.8: Associating Presentation file with Template file

9. The Associations | Presentations screen is shown displaying no associated Presentation files. Note that you can associate a particular Template file with multiple Presentation files, each generating a different rendition format. Click on Add and browse through the custom presentation folder (Custom_Presentations) within the Site Manager | Presentations | Editor folder. Choose the Presentation file cust_news_art_pres.xsl and click on OK.

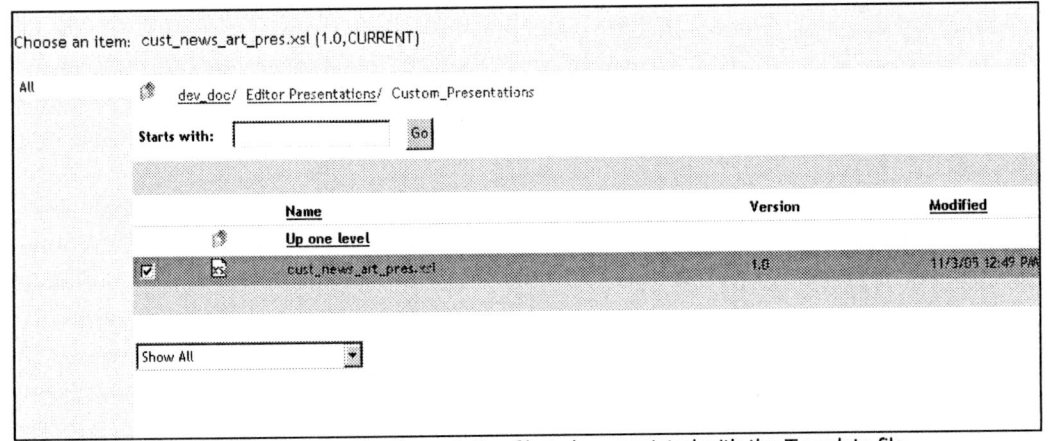

Figure 15.9: Choosing the Presentation file to be associated with the Template file

10. Select a rendition format for transforming the content XML file via the Presentation file, as shown in figure 15.10. In our case, choose custom_format, which we created in step 5. Selecting custom_format from the dropdown automatically populates its description in the field next to the dropdown.

You have an option to specify the chosen rendition format for all content that will be created going forward from the template in question, as well as for content created from the template and already existing in Docbase.

Click on OK and finally Close to complete associating the Presentation file with the Template file.

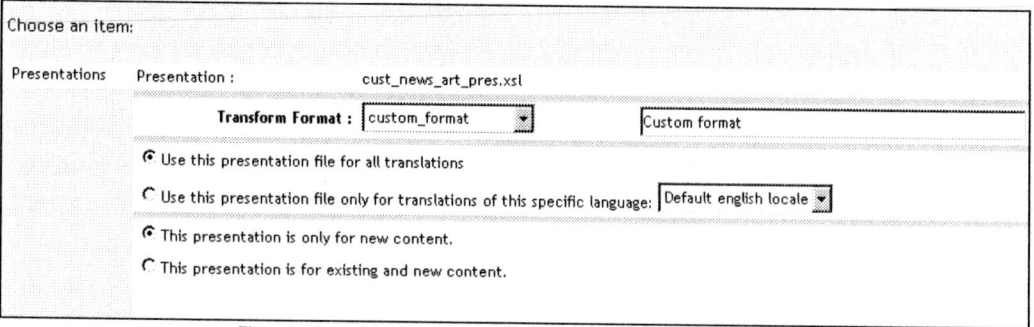

Figure 15.10: Selecting rendition format for Presentation file

15.2 Viewing Content Renditions

Renditions created from content files are stored within the Docbase along with the content files. A convenient way of viewing renditions is by choosing the created content file and selecting View | Renditions as shown in the figure 15.11.

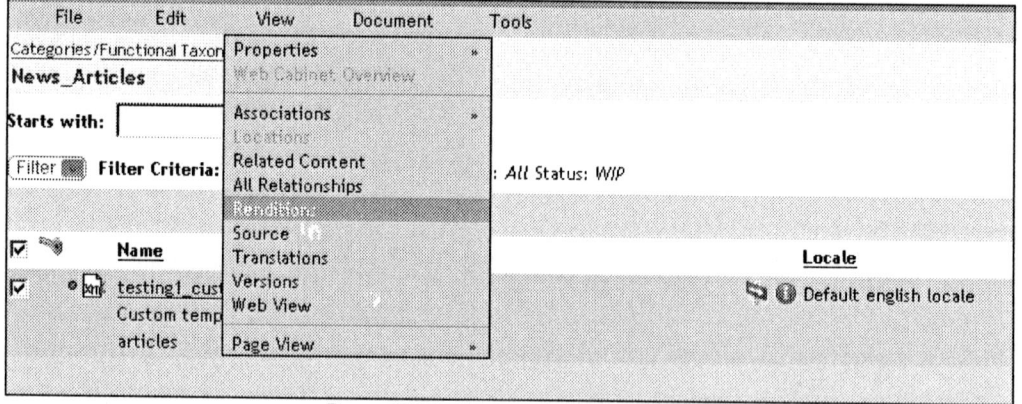

Figure 15.11: Viewing content renditions

Web Publisher displays the main content XML file along with its rendition formats (in our case, just the Custom format rendition) as shown in figure 15.12.

File	Edit	View	Document	Tools		

dev_doc : documentum/Test_WebCabinet/News_Articles_Contents/

Alternate Formats: Renditions

testing1_cust_news_art_templ.xml

Custom template for creating news articles

Version: 4.2

Locale: Default english locale

Status: WIP

		Format	Published Name	Size
□		XML Document	testing1_cust_news_art_templ.xml	1 KB
□		Custom format	testing1_cust_news_art_templ.cshtml	2 KB

Figure 15.12: Renditions associated with content files

15.3 Reapplying Presentation Files

One of the most frequent scenarios in websites is changes required in the layout of web pages. Technically, this would require modifications made at the presentation layer (presentation/XSL files in Documentum) and not within Template files or Rules files. Once the Presentation file has been modified and its altered version is checked into the Docbase, what happens to the content that already exists in the Docbase? Would its rendition be automatically updated as per the modified presentation file? Definitely for new content that is created going forward, correct renditions will be generated by the system. However, in running websites there could be a lot of existing content and it all needs to be updated as per the modified presentation layout.

Do not worry—Documentum provides a feature called as reapply presentation in such cases, allowing you to update renditions of existing content as per modified presentation files.

Following are some easy steps to achieve this:

1. Browse through the existing presentation files in Web Publisher and select the checkbox against the modified presentation file. Click on the Apply Presentation button shown in the tool bar (refer to figure 15.13).

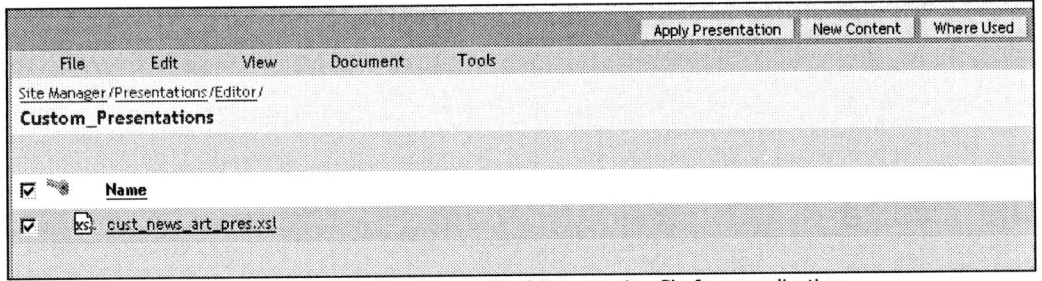

Figure 15.13: Selecting the modified Presentation file for reapplication

2. A list of all existing content files associated with the chosen Presentation file is shown; see figure 15.14. Select the checkboxes against these content files and click on OK.

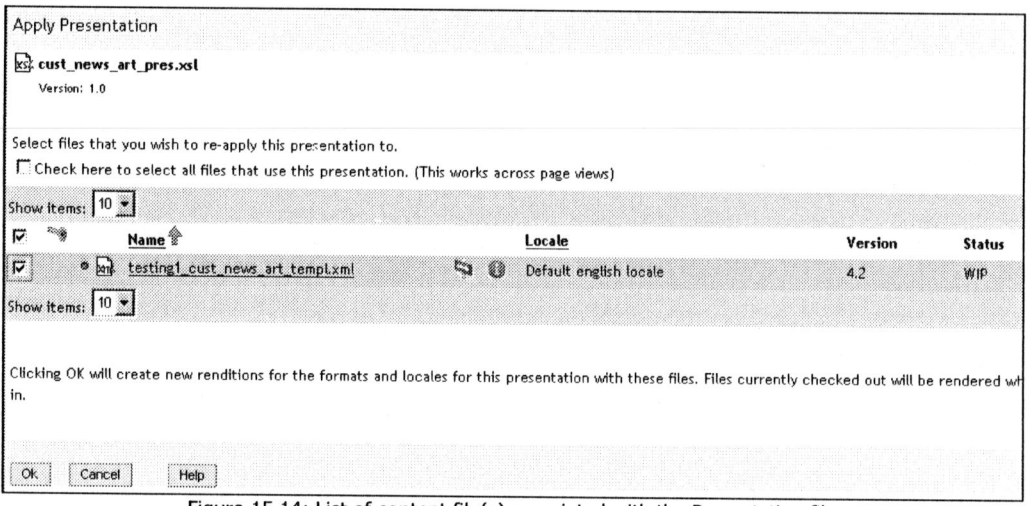

Figure 15.14: List of content file(s) associated with the Presentation file

The system takes some time to reapply the modified presentation layout to the selected content files. You can check the status of the reapply operation by clicking on the Task Status button in Web Publisher browser status bar.

15.4 Using XDQL in Stylesheets

XDQL is short for eXtensible Document Query Language and as the name suggests, is a convenient mechanism to fire DQL queries from within XML and process query results through XML. Presentation files (or XSL stylesheets) can immensely benefit from XDQL.

DQL queries (only selects and not any updates!) can be invoked from within a presentation file using Documentum's XDQL interface: `com.documentum.xml.xdql.IDfxmlQuery`.

The set of methods defined in this interface have been implemented by the class `DfXmlQuery`.

The DQL query results are in the form of XML documents and can be parsed/processed by standard XPath language and other language semantics available in XSL stylesheets.

This leverages the industry-standard and widely used processing powers of XML and XSL via a simple-to-use Documentum interface that serves as an XML wrapper for DQL.

From a performance perspective this is quite reasonable, given the fact that DQL queries are fired within the Docbase and results are processed via XSLT within the Documentum layer. Once dynamic data in the XML content file has been fetched from Docbase via XDQL, it is transformed via XSLT into a web rendition format (web page) and published to the website!

Note that XDQL is typically used in XSL stylesheets whenever you need real-time (dynamic) data from Docbase to be displayed in web pages. In the absence of XDQL, stale data would be presented on the website via static web pages.

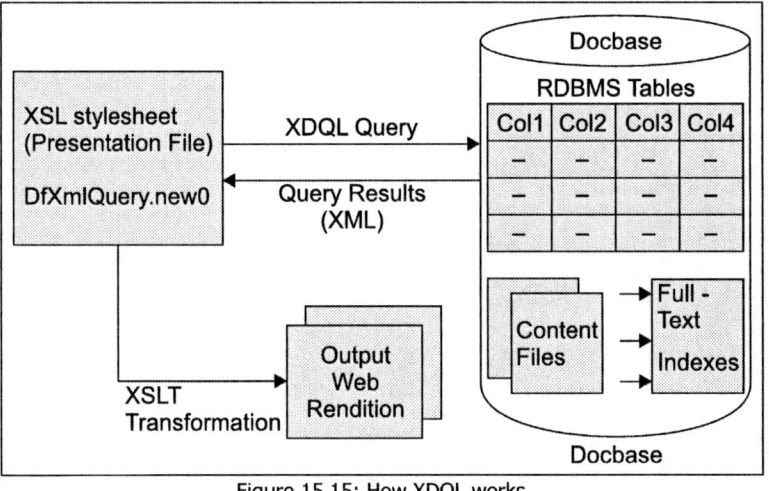

Figure 15.15: How XDQL works

15.5 XDQL Example in XSL Stylesheet

Let us take a simple example to understand how XDQL is used to fetch Docbase data dynamically within Presentation files (XSL stylesheets).

The following sample template file will be transformed via an XSL stylesheet:

```
<?xml version="1.0" encoding="UTF-8"?>
<ROOTTAG>
  <TITLEOFPAGE/>
  <SHORTDESC/>
</ROOTTAG>
```

The XSL stylesheet in this example will be used to create an HTML transformation of the above template XML file. The transformed file (HTML web rendition) will display the name of the content file (`object_name attribute`) that is created using the above template.

Create an XSL file (as shown in figures 15.16 and 15.17) and import it within the Docbase at the following location: `/Site Manager/Presentations/Editor/Custom_Presentations`.

```
<?xml version="1.0" encoding="UTF-8" ?>
<!DOCTYPE xsl:stylesheet (View Source for full doctype...)>
- <xsl:stylesheet version="1.0" xmlns:xsl="http://www.w3.org/1999/XSL/Transform" xmlns:fo="http://www.w3.org/1999/XSL/Format"
    xmlns:java="http://xml.apache.org/xslt/java" xmlns:xalan="http://xml.apache.org/xalan" exclude-result-prefixes="xalan java fo">
    <xsl:output method="html" encoding="ISO-8859-1" indent="yes" />
    <xsl:param name="DMS_SESSION_ID" select="'default value'" />
    <xsl:param name="DMS_INPUT_OBJECT_ID" />
    <xsl:strip-space elements="*" />
  - <xsl:template match="*|@*|comment()|processing-instruction()|text()">
    - <xsl:copy>
        <xsl:apply-templates select="*|@*|comment()|processing-instruction()|text()" />
      </xsl:copy>
    </xsl:template>
    <!-- variable storing the FQL query  -->
  - <xsl:variable name="dqlQuery">
      select r_object_id, object_name from dm_document where r_object_id = '
      <xsl:value-of select="$DMS_INPUT_OBJECT_ID" />
      '
    </xsl:variable>
    <!-- variable storing the DQL query results  -->
  - <xsl:variable name="query_results">
    - <xsl:call-template name="XDQL">
        <xsl:with-param name="dql" select="string($dqlQuery)" />
      </xsl:call-template>
    </xsl:variable>
    <!-- variable storing the 'object_name' attribute from query results  -->
  - <xsl:variable name="ObjectName">
    - <xsl:for-each select="xalan:nodeset($query_results)/xdql/object">
        <xsl:value-of select="object_name" />
      </xsl:for-each>
    </xsl:variable>
    <!-- Matching content XML file root element  -->
  - <xsl:template match="ROOTTAG">
    - <table border="0">
      - <tr>
          <th>File name:</th>
        </tr>
      - <tr>
        - <td>
            <br />
          </td>
        </tr>
      - <tr>
          <!-- Displaying the name of the file ('object name' attribute)  -->
```

Figure 15.16: Sample XSL file using XDQL

224

```xml
        <!-- Displaying the name of the file ('object_name' attribute)    -->
    - <td>
      - <b>
        - <u>
            <xsl:value-of select="$ObjectName" />
          </u>
        </b>
      </td>
    </tr>
  - <tr>
    - <td>
        <br />
      </td>
    </tr>
  - <tr>
      <!-- Displaying short description    -->
    - <td>
        <xsl:copy-of select="SHORTDESC" />
      </td>
    </tr>
  - <tr>
    - <td>
        <br />
      </td>
    </tr>
  </table>
</xsl:template>
<!-- Template code for integrating DQL queries in XSL Starts    -->
- <xsl:template name="XDQL">
    <xsl:param name="dql" />
    <xsl:param name="roottag" select="string('xdql')" />
    <xsl:param name="UpperTags" select="string('false')" />
    <xsl:param name="MaxRows" select="10" />
    <xsl:param name="RowIDAttrName" select="ID" />
    <xsl:param name="RowsetTag" select="Row" />
    <xsl:param name="UseGivenCaseTagNames" select="true" />
    <xsl:param name="UseNullAttrIndicator" select="false" />
    <xsl:variable name="xdql" select="java:com.documentum.xml.xdql.DfXmlQuery.new()" />
    <xsl:variable name="init" select="java:init($xdql)" />
    <xsl:variable name="param" select="java:setDql($xdql,$dql)" />
    <xsl:variable name="param1" select="java:setRootNode($xdql,$roottag)" />
    <xsl:variable name="param3" select="java:includeContent($xdql,false())" />
    <xsl:variable name="setContentEncoding" select="java:setContentEncoding($xdql,string('dom'))" />
    <xsl:variable name="setContentFormat" select="java:setContentFormat($xdql,string('xml'))" />
    <xsl:variable name="execute" select="java:execute($xdql, 'DF_READ_QUERY', $DMS_SESSION_ID)" />
    <xsl:variable name="queryresult" select="java:getXMLDOM($xdql)" />
    <xsl:copy-of select="$queryresult" />
  </xsl:template>
  <!-- Template code for integrating DQL queries in XSL Ends    -->
</xsl:stylesheet>
```

Figure 15.17: Sample XSL file using XDQL—continued

We will now discuss the anatomy of the above XSL stylesheet:

- **Namespaces**: Add the following Java and Xalan namespaces in the `<xsl:stylesheet>` tag of the presentation file. For example:

```
<xsl:stylesheet  version="1.0"
xmlns:xsl="http://www.w3.org/1999/XSL/Transform"
xmlns:fo="http://www.w3.org/1999/XSL/Format"
xmlns:java="http://xml.apache.org/xslt/java"
xmlns:xalan="http://xml.apache.org/xalan" exclude-result-prefixes=
"xalan java fo">
```

- **Parameters**: Declare the parameters that are passed by the system to the stylesheet. For example:

```
<xsl:param name="DMS_SESSION_ID" select="'default value'"/>
<xsl:param name="DMS_INPUT_OBJECT_ID"/>
```

DMS_SESSION_ID is a reference to the current Docbase session and DMS_INPUT_OBJECT_ID is a reference to the current object ID (r_object_id attribute).

- **XDQL classes**: Define an XSL template using the `<xsl:template>` tag to instantiate the DfXmlQuery() class, pass XDQL parameters, and execute DQL queries from within the XSL stylesheet. For example:

```
<xsl:template name="XDQL">
<xsl:param name="dql"/>
<xsl:param name="roottag"  select="string('xdql')"/>
<xsl:param name="UpperTags" select="string('false')"/>
<xsl:param name="MaxRows"  select="10"/>
<xsl:param name="RowIDAttrName" select="ID"/>
<xsl:param name="RowsetTag"  select="Row"/>
<xsl:param name="UseGivenCaseTagNames" select="true"/>
<xsl:param name="UseNullAttrIndicator" select="false"/>
<xsl:variable name="xdql"
select="java:com.documentum.xml.xdql.DfXmlQuery.new()"/>
<xsl:variable name="init"  select="java:init($xdql)"/>
<xsl:variable name="param"  select="java:setDql($xdql,$dql)"/>
<xsl:variable name="param1" select="java:setRootNode($xdql,$roottag)"/>
<xsl:variable name="param3" select="java:includeContent($xdql,false())"/>
<xsl:variable name="setContentEncoding"
select="java:setContentEncoding($xdql,string('dom'))"/>
<xsl:variable name="setContentFormat"
select="java:setContentFormat($xdql,string('xml'))"/>
<xsl:variable name="execute" select="java:execute($xdql, 'DF_READ_QUERY',
$DMS_SESSION_ID)"/>
<xsl:variable name="queryresult" select="java:getXMLDOM($xdql)"/>
<xsl:copy-of select="$queryresult"/>
</xsl:template>
```

It is advisable to go through the DFC Javadocs of the com.documentum.xml.xdql.IDfXmlQuery interface to understand the arguments and return types of the numerous methods used in the `<xsl:template name="XDQL">` shown above.

```
Variables:
Define a variable to store the DQL query to be invoked from within the
stylesheet.
For example:
<xsl:variable name = "dqlQuery">select r_object_id, object_name from
dm_document where r_object_id = '<xsl:value-of
select="$DMS_INPUT_OBJECT_ID"/>'</xsl:variable>
```

This code stores the DQL query string used to fetch the object ID (r_object_id attribute) and the file name (object_name attribute) of the current content file (i.e. whose object ID matches the current object ID: DMS_INPUT_OBJECT_ID).

Also, define a variable to store the results of the above DQL query by calling the pre-defined XDQL template and passing the DQL query string to it. For example:

```
<xsl:variable name = "query_results">
   <xsl:call-template name="XDQL">
   <xsl:with-param name="dql" select="string($dqlQuery)"/>
   </xsl:call-template>
</xsl:variable>
```

Once you have the query results saved in a variable, iterate through it, retrieve the required attribute (object_name in our case) and save it in a variable.

```
For example:
<xsl:variable name="ObjectName">
   <xsl:for-each select="xalan:nodeset($query_results)/xdql/object">
   <xsl:value-of select="object_name"/>
   </xsl:for-each>
</xsl:variable>
```

This is all that needs to be taken care of while using XDQL within XSL stylesheets in Web Publisher. In our example, displaying the content file's name (object_name attribute) is as simple as accessing the value of the objectName variable. For example:

```
<!-- Displaying the name of the file (object_name attribute) -->
<td><b><u><xsl:value-of select="$ObjectName"/></u></b></td>
```

Note that by using $(variableName), the system substitutes the value contained in the variable at run time.

15.6 Create_Dynamic_Content Job

Presentation files using XDQL queries can retrieve the Docbase content and its attributes whenever:

- A new content file is created from a template and saved from within Web Publisher editor
- An existing content file is edited and saved
- The reapply presentation feature is used for existing content

However, what happens to those published active content files that show up on the website but whose underlying data (attribute or content values) has been modified in the Docbase? Do the content authors have to edit/save and republish these content files all over again to ensure that XDQL query is fired again and modified data shows up on the running website? The answer is NO.

The following steps need to be performed under such circumstances to utilize an out-of-the-box feature available from Documentum:

1. Browse to the template XML file in Web Publisher and click on the info icon (i) against the template. Choose the Publishing tab and select the checkbox against Automatically refresh this page when related content is modified (refer to figure 15.18). Click on OK.

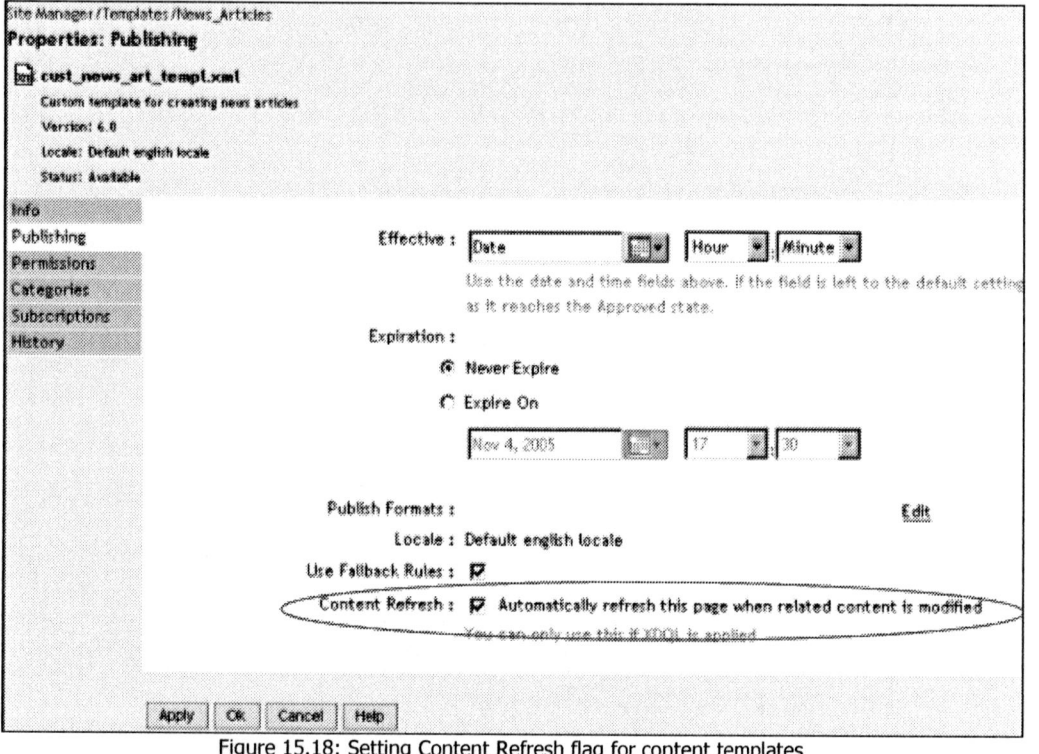

Figure 15.18: Setting Content Refresh flag for content templates

2. Log in to Documentum Administrator as an administrator and go to Job Management | Jobs. Select the Create_Dynamic_Content job as shown in figure 15.19.

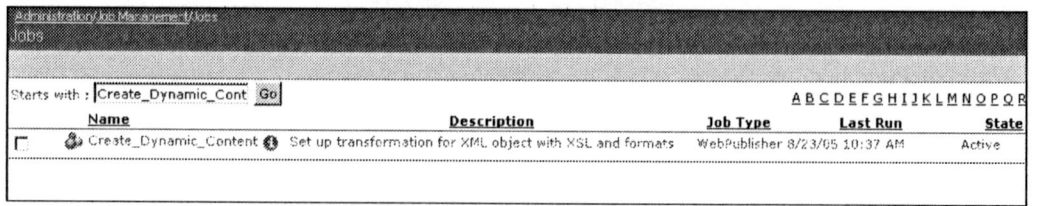

Figure 15.19: Create_Dynamic_Content Job in Documentum Administrator

First make sure that this Job is Active and then set up some convenient schedule for it to run at periodic intervals in the Docbase. This is a Web Publisher Job that can be made to run at periodic intervals to transform content files that are in active state and have their template's Content Refresh flag set as true. This job reapplies Presentation files on the active content files and thus ensures that the correct DQL query results are saved to the transformed output web renditions.

After the Create_Dynamic_Content job transforms existing active objects, you can publish them over to the website (SCS target) via Site Caching Service Site Publishing configuration.

Please note that details of publishing operations will be covered in Chapter 21.

This is all about presentation files, their usage, and features available in Documentum. You can explore stylesheets in general by browsing the Internet. There are scores of websites existing over the Web dedicated to XSLs and their advanced features. For an in-depth knowledge of Web Publisher Presentation files, you should go through Web Publisher administration manuals.

15.7 Summary

Presentation files are stylesheets used for formatting content files in the desired renditions for display purposes on websites. In this chapter, we briefly discussed how Documentum uses Xerces XSL transformation engine to apply Presentation files on the content XML files to create renditions.

We then saw the detailed steps for creating Presentation files and associating them with Template files in Web Publisher. We also saw how to create custom formats in Documentum and output renditions in the custom formats. We then discussed how to reapply updated presentation files to the existing content in Docbase.

Next, we discussed XDQL (eXtensible Document Query Language) and its benefits, and through an example we saw how it is used to fire DQL queries from within XML and process query results through XML.

Lastly, we touched upon a Web Publisher Job, Create_Dynamic_Content, that can be scheduled to run at periodic intervals to automatically reapply Presentation files on active content files, thus creating updated renditions in the Docbase.

16
Folder Mapping

All content contributors face a common problem while creating content for their website. In order to create content, they need to understand the website structure so that they can create the content under the correct folder in Documentum. If they create content under incorrect folders, published content will be incorrectly read by the website application and the content will show up in wrong sections on the website!

Typically, a corporate website folder structure is quite complex and training the users to enter content under the exact mirror folders in Documentum is difficult and involves the possibility of human errors. Let's take a simple example here to elaborate this:

Assume that a hypothetical business manufactures some products categorized as category 1, 2, and 3 depending upon its proprietary business classification. However, the end website displaying product information shows these products under website sections Low end output, Average performance, and High throughput products respectively.

While creating content, business users classify it under category 1, 2, or 3. The Folder Map, behind the scenes, places the content under the appropriate folder structures on the site, without requiring the business users to understand the exact folder structure of the website. If, for some reason, the names of these sections need to be changed on the website, the content creators need not be trained for this. The Folder Map configuration needs to be updated and the content creation process continues seamlessly.

Figure 16.1 shows how business users create content using a simple category and how Documentum uses Folder Map to map them to the actual folder structures as required by the website.

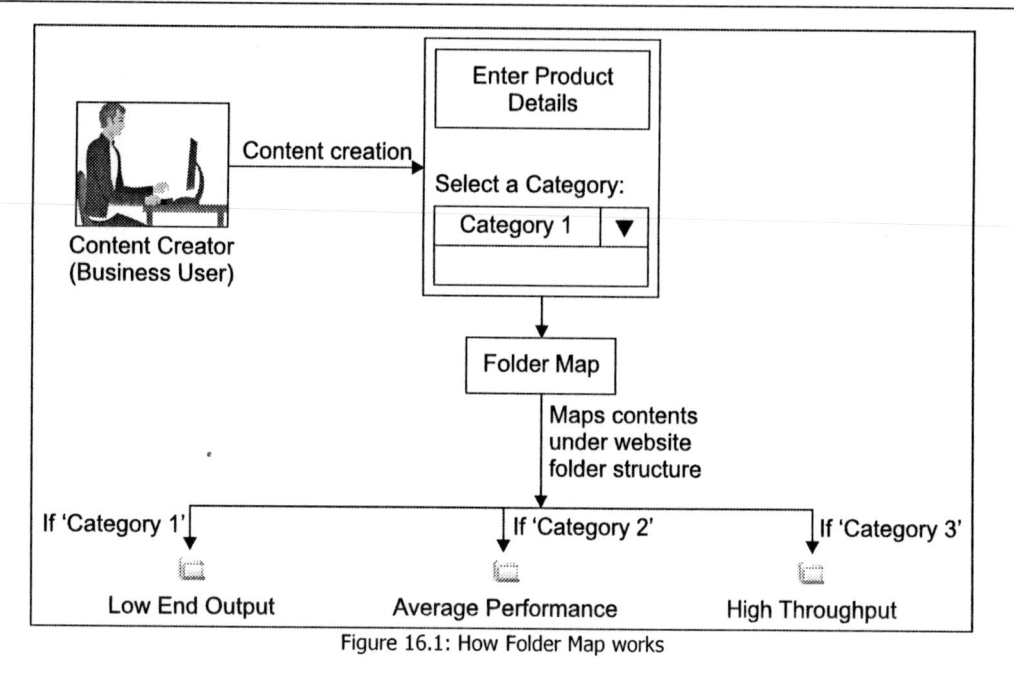

Figure 16.1: How Folder Map works

Web Publisher Folder Map (FolderMap.xml) is a simple XML file that contains rules required to map the created content files under the specified folders in Web Cabinets, depending upon the Docbase properties of the content files.

If Documentum finds that the content file's properties match the property values defined in the Folder Map rules, then Documentum places the content file in the folder location specified in FolderMap.xml.

It is worth mentioning that Documentum Web Publisher reads FolderMap.xml every time new content is created or content properties are updated.

- If you log in as an administrator in Web Publisher, you can view the default FolderMap.xml file under Site Manager | Configurations | Foldermaps folder as shown in figure 16.2.

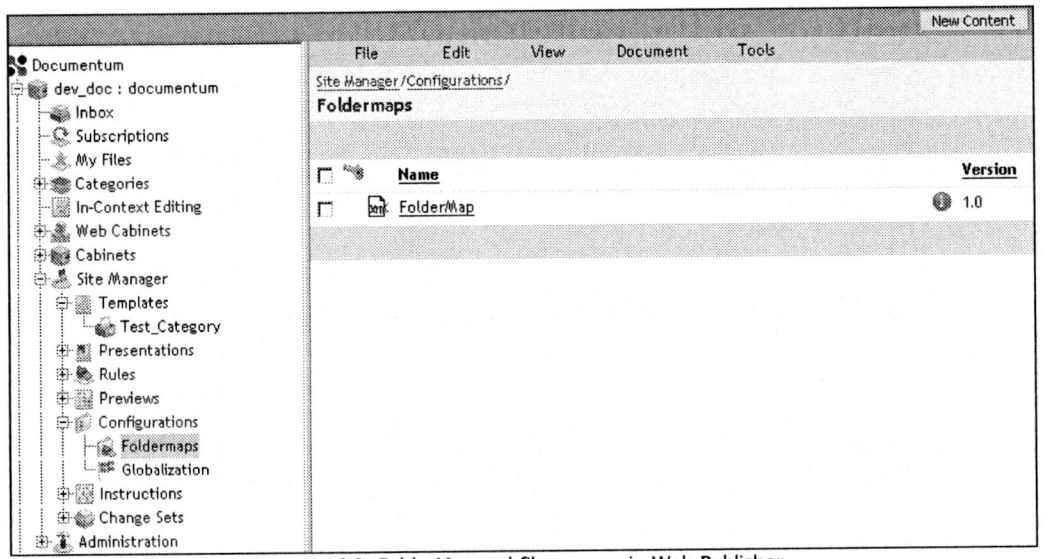

Figure 16.2: FolderMap.xml file as seen in Web Publisher

The structure of an empty FolderMap.xml file is shown below:

```
<folder_map>
  <rule>
    <attr_list>
      <attr>
        <name></name>
        <value></value>
      </attr>
    </attr_list>
    <path_list>
      <path></path>
    </path_list>
  </rule>
  <rule>
    <attr_list>
      <attr>
        <name></name>
        <value></value>
      </attr>
    </attr_list>
    <path_list>
      <path></path>
    </path_list>
  </rule>
</folder_map>
```

16.1 Anatomy of the FolderMap.xml File

Refer to figure 16.3 to understand the various XML elements in `FolderMap.xml`.

Folder Map Element	Function Performed
`<rule>`	Denotes each rule specified in the Folder Map. Each `<rule>` can have 0 or more `<attr_list>` tags and 1 or more `<path_list>` tags.
`<attr_list>`	Denotes a list of attribute rules/criteria. The Folder Map rule applies only when all the property value conditions specified in this tag are met.
`<attr>`	This is a name-value pair and denotes one property name and its value.
`<name>`	Name of the Docbase property, e.g. subject.
`<value>`	The value of the Docbase property.
`<path_list>`	Denotes a set of paths/locations where the content files will be placed if the rules match.
`<path>`	The full path within the Web Publisher Docbase where the content files will be placed.

Figure 16.3: Folder Map XML elements

16.2 Limitations of Folder Map

Like all good systems, Folder Map has its share of limitations that we should be cognizant of while designing mapping rules for content.

Listed below are some of the limitations of Folder Map in Web Publisher. For an exhaustive coverage of Folder Mapping, please go through the Documentum Web Publisher Administrator guide.

- Web Publisher does not allow you to change the name of the Folder Map file (`FolderMap.xml`).

- The permission set (ACL) for `FolderMap.xml` is by default WebPublisher User Default ACL and cannot be changed.

- If the folder structure (specified in `FolderMap.xml`) does not exist in the Docbase, Folder Mapping automatically creates the folders in the Docbase. However, if the specified Web Cabinet does not exist in the Docbase, Folder Mapping does not automatically create it and throws an error instead.

- Folder mapping works from the topmost rule of the `FolderMap.xml` file to the last rule specified in the file. We need to define the specific rules first and then follow up with some generic rules. For those familiar with exception handling best practices in Java, this is analogous to catching the application-specific exceptions before handling generic exceptions.

- As soon as a particular rule is matched, Folder Mapping stops scanning the `FolderMap.xml` file further.

Enough of theory? Let us now understand how Folder Mapping works with the aid of a few practical examples.

16.3 Folder Mapping Examples

This section contains examples explaining how we can practically implement Folder Mapping in Documentum.

16.3.1 Property Matching: Using Wildcard (*)

Let us begin with a simple example, where the Folder Map is configured so that the content file is placed at a specified location in the Web Cabinet if and only if the user provides some non-blank value for its subject property while creating the content.

1. Log in as an administrator in Web Publisher and check-out the `FolderMap.xml` file under Site Manager | Configurations | Foldermaps. Modify the `FolderMap.xml` file as shown below and check it back into the Docbase.

```
<folder_map>
  <rule>
    <attr_list>
      <attr>
        <name>subject</name>
        <value>*</value>
      </attr>
    </attr_list>
    <path_list>
      <path>/Test_WebCabinet/Subject_Content</path>
    </path_list>
  </rule>
  <rule>
    <attr_list>
      <attr>
        <name></name>
        <value></value>
      </attr>
    </attr_list>
    <path_list>
      <path></path>
    </path_list>
  </rule>
</folder_map>
```

Try creating some content using a template and leave the Subject: field blank. The following error is thrown; view it by clicking on the All Messages button in Web Publisher status bar:

The new content cannot be created. This file, based on the folder map, cannot be linked to any Web cabinet. Your file will not be created.

2. Create new content by providing a non-blank value for the Subject: field as shown in figure 16.4.

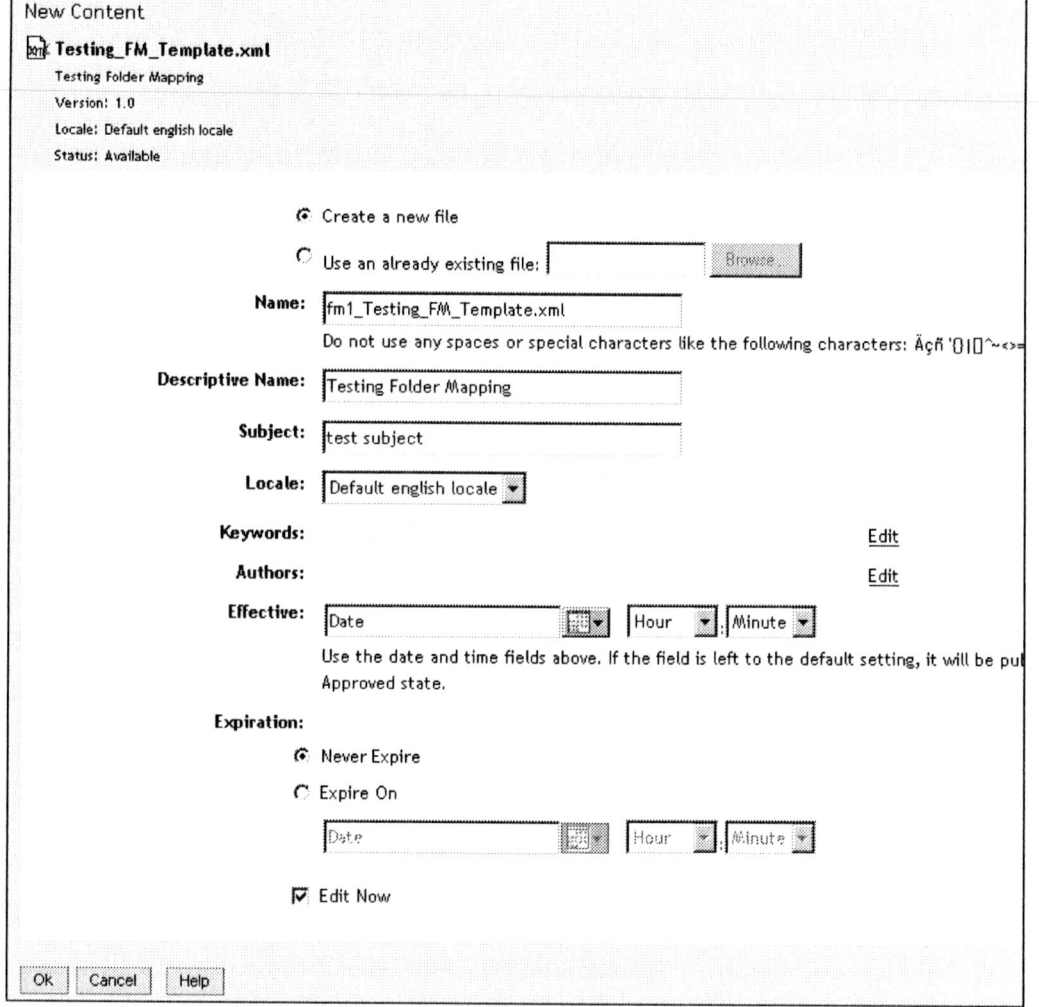

Figure 16.4: Non-blank value provided for Subject property

3. Notice that the new content is created successfully (refer to figure 16.5) under the specified Docbase location in the Web Cabinet at /Test_WebCabinet/Subject_Content.

Ensure that the Web Cabinet Test_WebCabinet already exists in the Docbase. If it does not exist, please create it before you start creating content and trying out Folder Mapping examples.

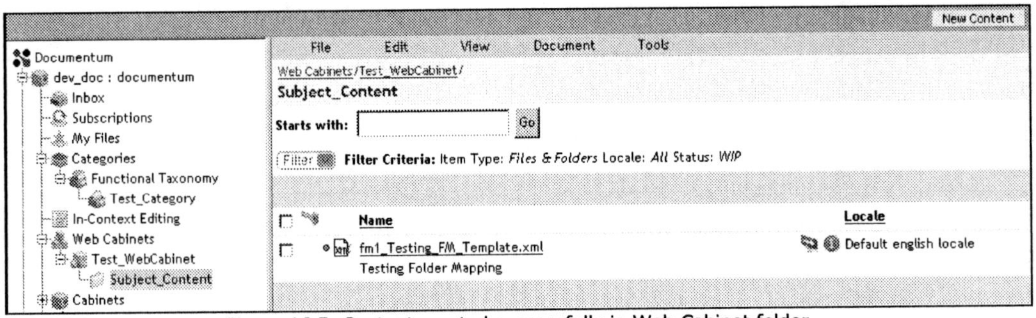

Figure 16.5: Content created successfully in Web Cabinet folder

16.3.2 Property Matching: Using Multiple Properties in <attr_list>

Let us now take an example where the Folder Map is configured so that the content file is placed at a specified location in the Web Cabinet if and only if two property conditions are met for the content as follows:

It should have a non-blank Name: field (object_name property) and its Subject: field (subject property) should have a value office. Until and unless both these conditions are met, the content file is not created.

1. Log in as an administrator in Web Publisher and check-out the FolderMap.xml file under Site Manager | Configurations | Foldermaps. Modify the FolderMap.xml file as shown below and check it back into the Docbase.

```
<folder_map>
  <rule>
    <attr_list>
      <attr>
        <name>object_name</name>
        <value>*</value>
      </attr>
      <attr>
        <name>subject</name>
        <value>office</value>
      </attr>
    </attr_list>
    <path_list>
      <path>/Test_webCabinet/official docs</path>
    </path_list>
  </rule>
  <rule>
    <attr_list>
      <attr>
        <name></name>
        <value></value>
      </attr>
    </attr_list>
    <path_list>
      <path></path>
    </path_list>
  </rule>
</folder_map>
```

Try creating content using a template and do *any one* of the following:

- o Leave the Name: field blank
- o Leave the Subject: field blank
- o Write OFFICE as the value of Subject: field
- o Provide the value of Subject: field as anything other than office, for example JUNK

In all four cases, the following error is thrown (view the All Messages button in Web Publisher status bar) and the new content is not created in Web Publisher:

The new content cannot be created. This file, based on the folder map, cannot be linked to any Web cabinet. Your file will not be created.

2. Let us now provide a valid scenario. Create new content with a valid non-blank name and write office for its Subject: field as shown in figure 16.6:

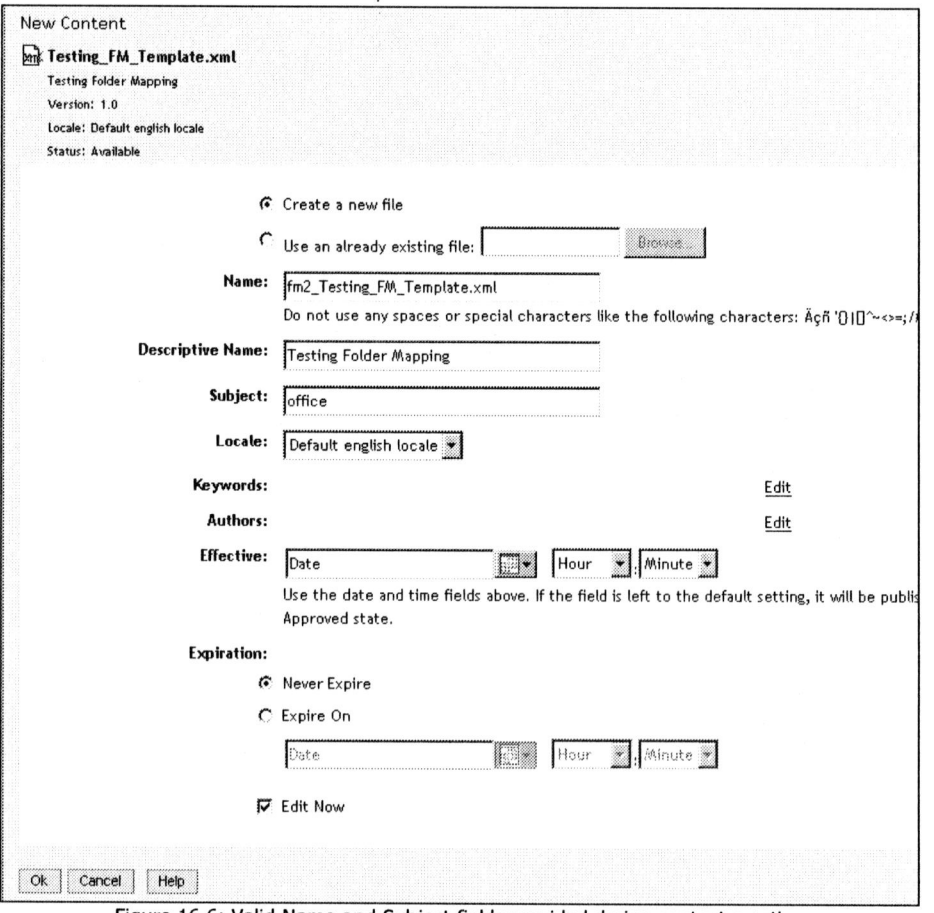

Figure 16.6: Valid Name and Subject fields provided during content creation

3. The new content is created successfully (refer to figure 16.7) under the specified Docbase location in the Web Cabinet: /Test_WebCabinet/Official docs.

As discussed earlier, you must ensure first that the Web Cabinet Test_WebCabinet already exists in the Docbase. If it does not exist, please create it before you start creating content.

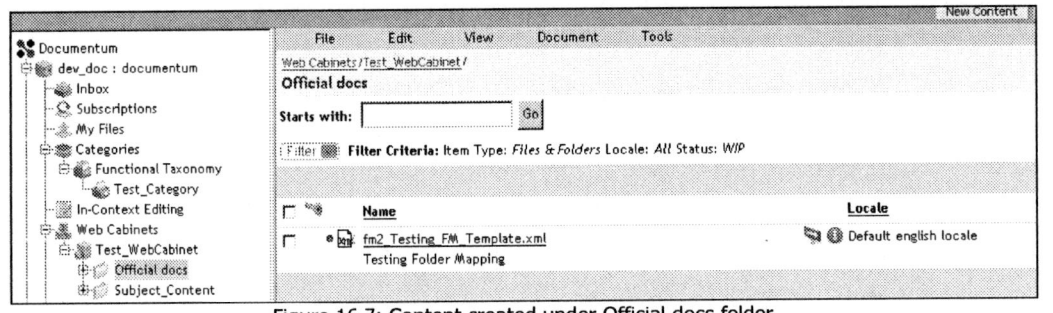

Figure 16.7: Content created under Official docs folder

16.3.3 Placing a Content File in Multiple Locations with <path_list>

Let us now take an example where Folder Map is configured so that the same content file is placed at two different specified locations in the Web Cabinet. An important condition that must be met for the content is that it should have a non-blank file name (object_name property).

If the above condition is met, the same content file is placed under two folders in the Web Cabinet: /Test_WebCabinet/FilePath One and /Test_WebCabinet/FilePath Two.

1. Log in as an administrator in Web Publisher and check-out the FolderMap.xml file under Site Manager | Configurations | Foldermaps. Modify the FolderMap.xml file as shown below and check it back into the Docbase.

```
<folder_map>
  <rule>
    <attr_list>
      <attr>
        <name>object_name</name>
        <value>*</value>
      </attr>
    </attr_list>
    <path_list>
      <path>/Test_WebCabinet/FilePath One</path>
      <path>/Test_WebCabinet/FilePath Two</path>
    </path_list>
  </rule>
  <rule>
    <attr_list>
      <attr>
        <name></name>
        <value></value>
      </attr>
    </attr_list>
    <path_list>
      <path></path>
    </path_list>
  </rule>
</folder_map>
```

Try creating content using a template and provide a non-blank file name (Name: field) as shown in figure 16.8.

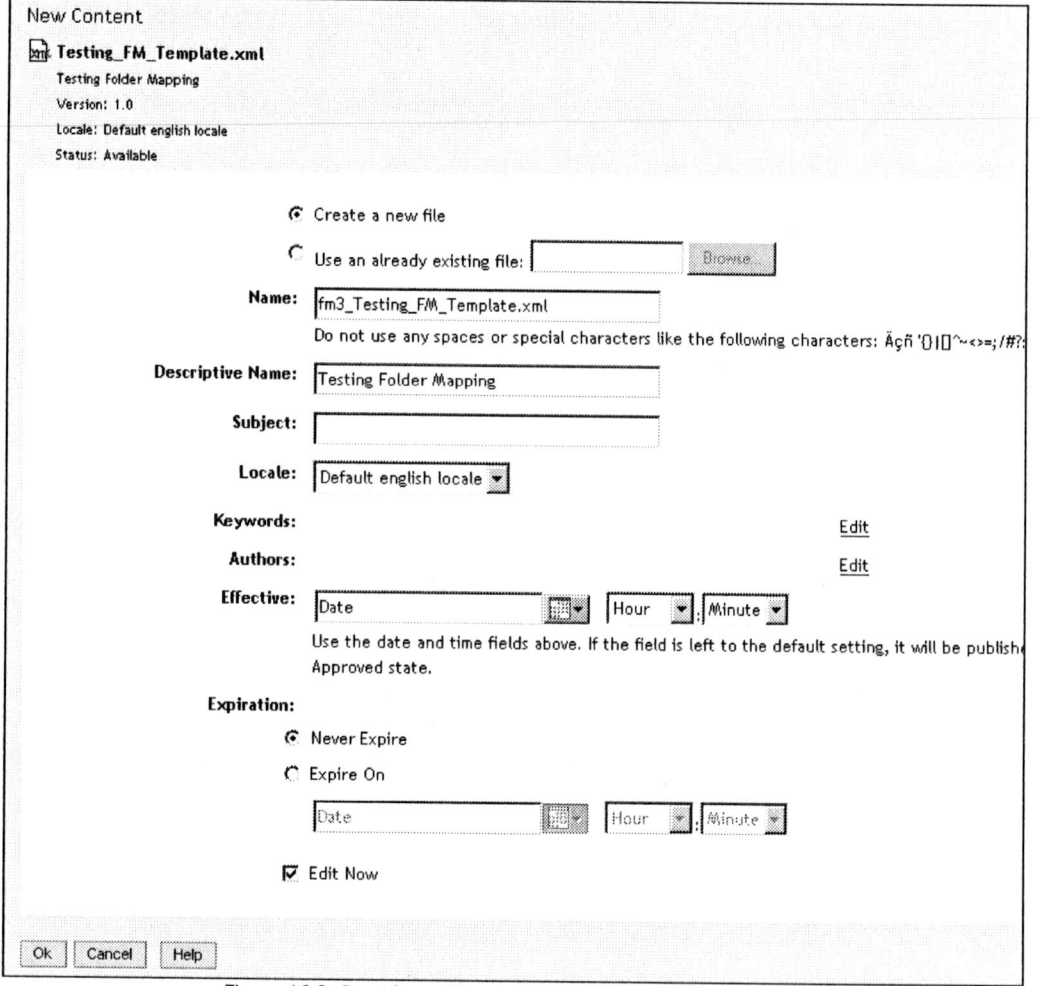

Figure 16.8: Providing a file name while creating a new content

2. You will notice that the new content is created successfully under two specified Docbase locations (refer to figures 16.9 and 16.10) in the Web Cabinet: /Test_WebCabinet/FilePath One and /Test_WebCabinet/FilePath Two.

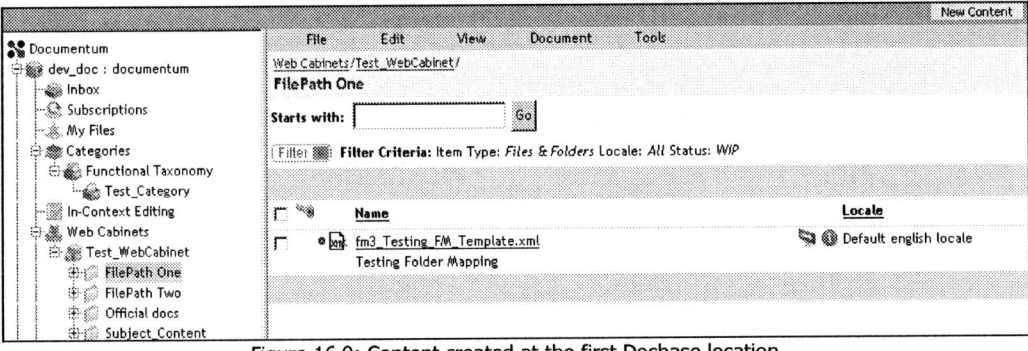

Figure 16.9: Content created at the first Docbase location

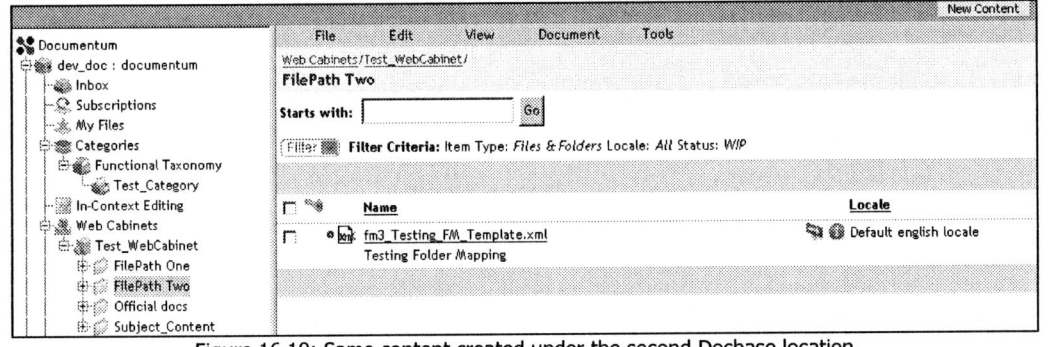

Figure 16.10: Same content created under the second Docbase location

16.3.4 Property Matching: Simple Repeating Attribute

Till now we were dealing with single-valued attributes. Let us now take an example where Folder Map is configured so that the content file is placed at a specified location in the Web Cabinet if a particular *repeating* property condition is met for the content as follows:

> It should have a non-blank keywords property with abc as its first keyword.

If the above condition is met, the content file is placed within the following location in the Web Cabinet: /Test_WebCabinet/Keywords_ABC.

1. Log in as an administrator in Web Publisher and check-out the FolderMap.xml file under Site Manager | Configurations | Foldermaps.

   Modify the FolderMap.xml file as shown below and check it back into the Docbase.

```
<folder_map>
  <rule>
    <attr_list>
      <attr>
        <name>keywords</name>
        <value>abc</value>
      </attr>
    </attr_list>
    <path_list>
      <path>/Test_WebCabinet/Keywords_ABC</path>
    </path_list>
  </rule>
  <rule>
    <attr_list>
      <attr>
        <name></name>
        <value></value>
      </attr>
    </attr_list>
    <path_list>
      <path></path>
    </path_list>
  </rule>
</folder_map>
```

2. Try creating content using a template and do one of the following:

   o   Provide ABC for the Keywords value: keywords[0]='ABC'

   o   Provide xyz for the Keywords value: keywords[0]='xyz'

   o   Provide xyz and abc as Keywords values. Note that here abc is the second keyword and not the first keyword.
       keywords[0]='xyz'
       keywords[1]='abc'

You will notice that the following error is thrown (view by clicking the All Messages button in Web Publisher status bar) and the new content is not created in Web Publisher:

The new content cannot be created.

This file, based on the folder map, cannot be linked to any Web cabinet. Your file will not be created.

3. Create some valid new content and provide abc for its Keywords: field as shown in figure 16.11.

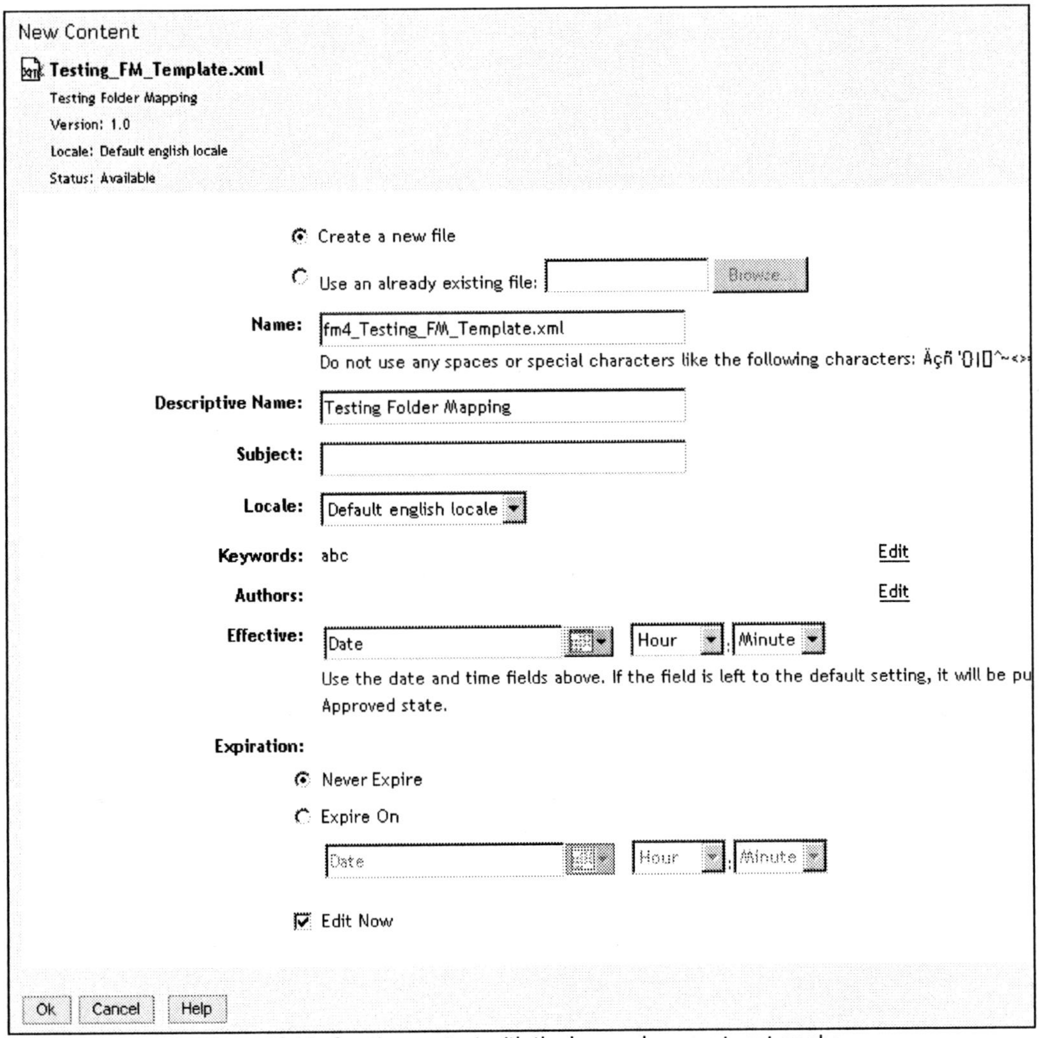

Figure 16.11: Creating content with the keywords property set as abc

4. You will notice that the new content is created successfully (refer to figure 16.12) under the specified Docbase location in the Web Cabinet: /Test_WebCabinet/ Keywords_ABC.

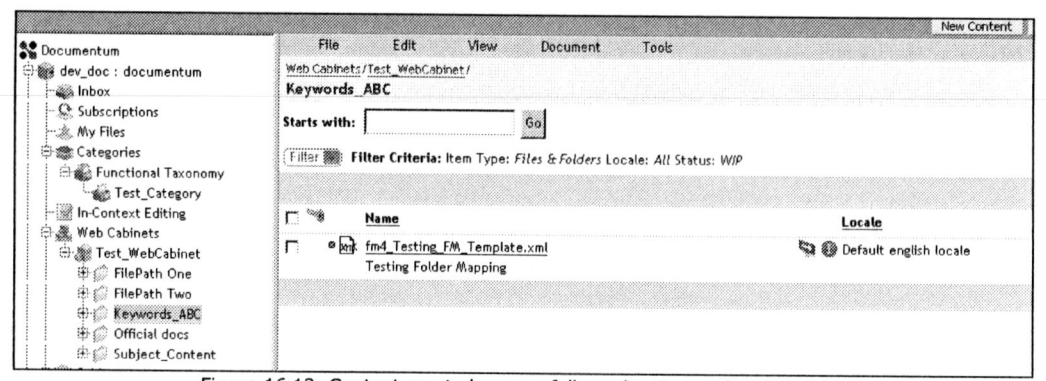

Figure 16.12: Content created successfully under Keywords_ABC folder

16.3.5 Property Matching: Repeating Attribute Index

Let us take an example where Folder Map is configured so that the content file is placed at a specified location in the Web Cabinet. The *repeating* property condition that must be met for the content is that it should have a non-blank keywords property with hello as its second keyword (index position 1).

If the above condition is met, the content file is placed under the following location in the Web Cabinet: /Test_WebCabinet/Keywords_Hello.

1. Log in as an administrator in Web Publisher and check-out the FolderMap.xml file under Site Manager | Configurations | Foldermaps.

   Modify the FolderMap.xml file as shown below and check it back into the Docbase.

```
<folder_map>
  <rule>
    <attr_list>
      <attr>
        <name>keywords[1]</name>
        <value>hello</value>
      </attr>
    </attr_list>
    <path_list>
      <path>/Test_WebCabinet/Keywords_Hello</path>
    </path_list>
  </rule>
  <rule>
    <attr_list>
      <attr>
        <name></name>
        <value></value>
      </attr>
    </attr_list>
    <path_list>
      <path></path>
    </path_list>
  </rule>
</folder_map>
```

2. Try creating some content using a template and:

  ○ Provide `hello` as **Keywords** value: `keywords[0]='hello'`
  Or:

  ○ Provide `xyz` and `HELLO` as **Keywords** values. Note that `HELLO` is in upper case, even though it is the second keyword.
  ```
  keywords[0]='xyz'
  keywords[1]='HELLO'
  ```

You will notice that the following error is thrown (view by clicking the **All Messages** button in Web Publisher status bar) and the new content is not created in Web Publisher:

The new content cannot be created.
This file, based on the folder map, cannot be linked to any Web cabinet. Your file will not be created.

3. Create some valid new content and provide `xyz` and `hello` as values for its **Keywords:** field as shown in figure 16.13.

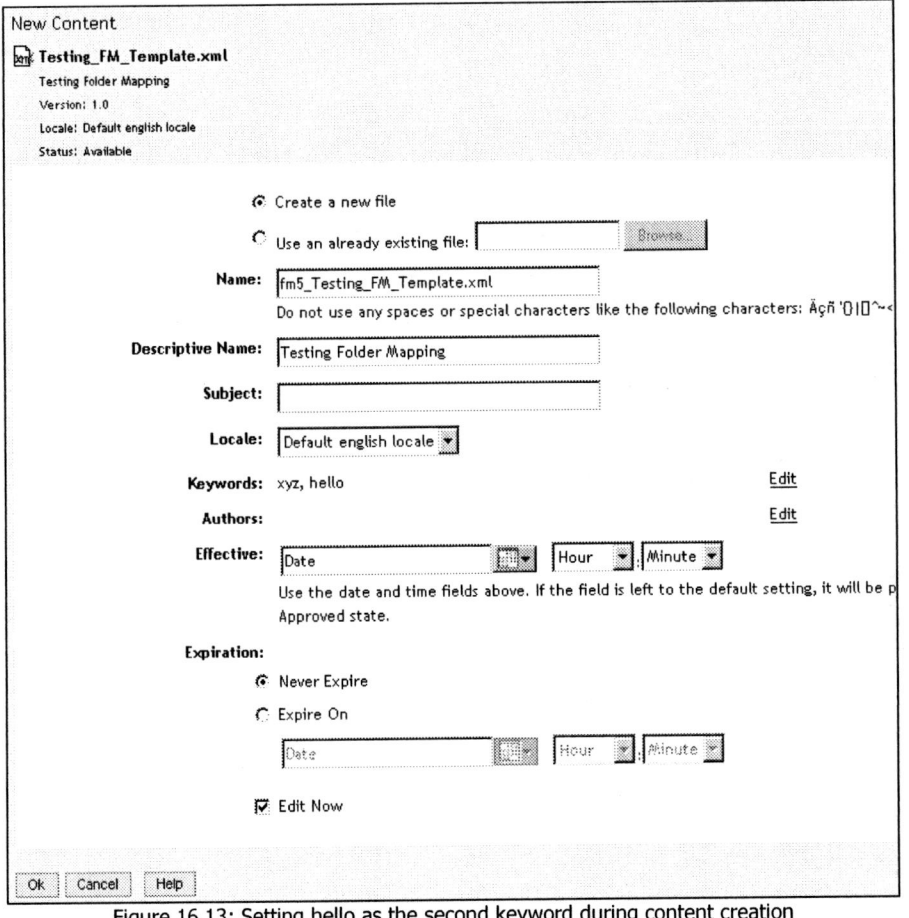

Figure 16.13: Setting hello as the second keyword during content creation

4. You will notice that the new content is created successfully (refer to figure 16.14) under the specified Docbase location in the Web Cabinet: /Test_WebCabinet/ Keywords_Hello.

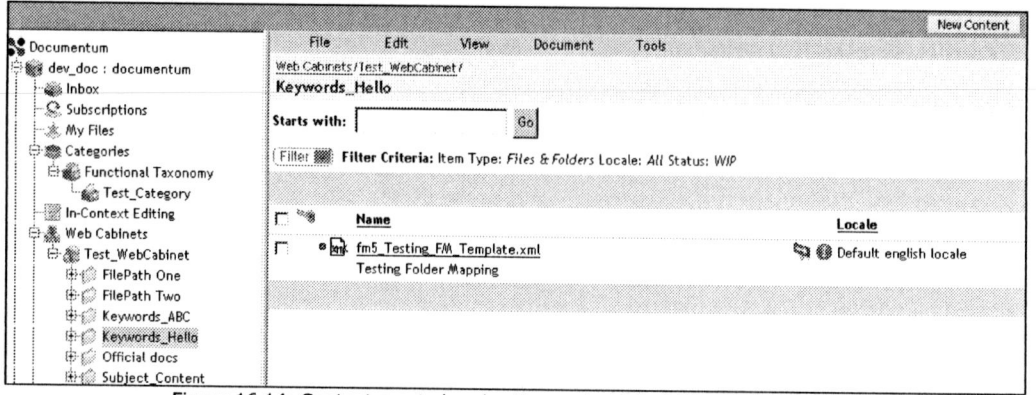

Figure 16.14: Content created under Keywords_Hello folder in Web Cabinet

16.3.6 Dynamic Folder Mapping

Till now, we were considering examples where a fixed location was provided in the FolderMap.xml file based on some property values. Folder Map provides additional features to create the location/paths at run time dynamically based on some attribute/property values.

Let us take an example where Folder Map is configured so that the content file is placed within a dynamically created folder in the Web Cabinet. The property condition that must be met for the content is that it should have a non-blank subject property.

If the above condition is met, the content file is placed under the Test_WebCabinet Web Cabinet within a folder having the same name as the value provided by content creator for the content's subject property.

1. Log in as an administrator in Web Publisher and check-out the FolderMap.xml file under Site Manager | Configurations | Foldermaps.

    Modify the FolderMap.xml file as shown below and check it back into the Docbase.

    ```
    <folder_map>
      <rule>
        <attr_list>
          <attr>
            <name>subject</name>
            <value>*</value>
          </attr>
        </attr_list>
        <path_list>
          <path>/Test_WebCabinet/$(subject)</path>
        </path_list>
      </rule>
      <rule>
        <attr_list>
          <attr>
            <name></name>
    ```

```
        <value></value>
      </attr>
    </attr_list>
    <path_list>
      <path></path>
    </path_list>
  </rule>
</folder_map>
```

At run time Web Publisher substitutes the value of the **subject** property as the name of the folder. Note that $(...) signifies run-time substitution of the specified Docbase property value.

2. Create some new content and provide a non-blank value for its Subject: field (say test subject) as shown in figure 16.15.

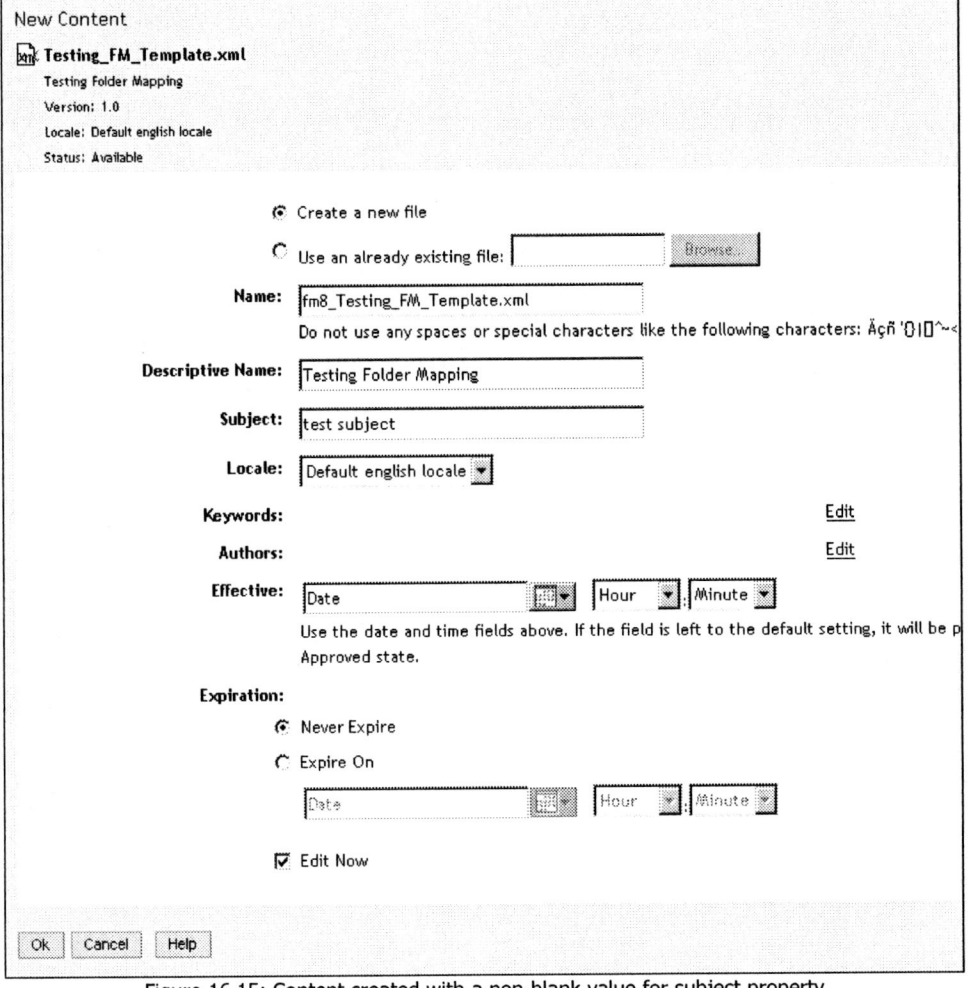

Figure 16.15: Content created with a non-blank value for subject property

3. You will notice that the new content is created successfully (refer to figure 16.16) under the Web Cabinet Test_WebCabinet within the folder test_subject created at run time by Folder Map.

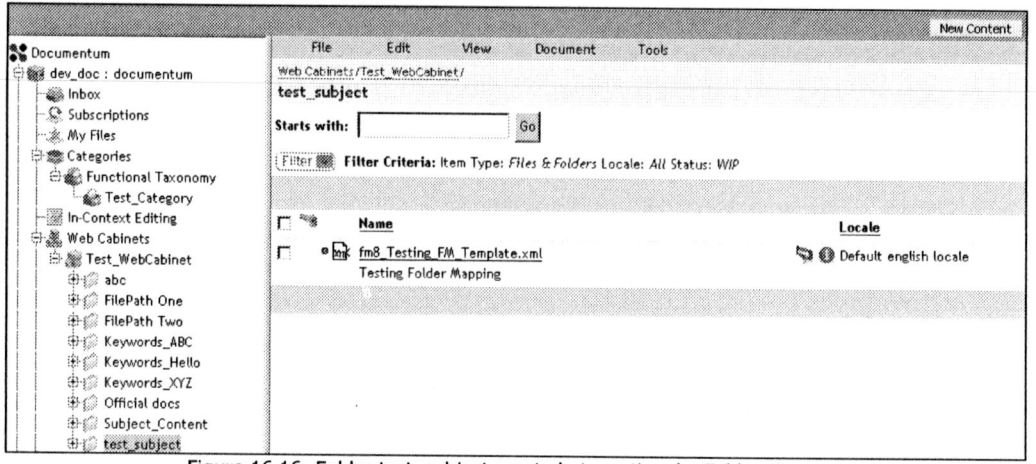

Figure 16.16: Folder test_subject created at run time by Folder Mapping

16.3.7 Dynamic Folder Mapping with Repeating Attribute

Having gone through a simple example of dynamic folder mapping, let's now take an example where Folder Map is configured so that the content file is placed within a dynamically created folder in the Web Cabinet. The *repeating* property condition that must be met for the content is that it should have abc as the second keywords property: keywords[1]='abc'

If the above condition is met, the content file is placed under the Test_WebCabinet Web Cabinet within a folder having the same name as the second value provided by content creator for the content's keywords property (i.e. abc).

1. Log in as an administrator in Web Publisher and check-out the FolderMap.xml file under Site Manager | Configurations | Foldermaps.

   Modify the FolderMap.xml file as shown below and check it back into the Docbase.

```
<folder_map>
  <rule>
    <attr_list>
      <attr>
        <name>keywords[1]</name>
        <value>abc</value>
      </attr>
    </attr_list>
    <path_list>
      <path>/Test_WebCabinet/$(keywords[1])</path>
    </path_list>
  </rule>
  <rule>
    <attr_list>
      <attr>
        <name></name>
```

```
        <value></value>
      </attr>
    </attr_list>
    <path_list>
      <path></path>
    </path_list>
  </rule>
</folder_map>
```

Folder Map will create a folder at run time with the same name as the value of the second keyword (i.e. keywords[1]).

2. Create some new content and write abc as the second entry in the keywords property as shown in figure 16.17.

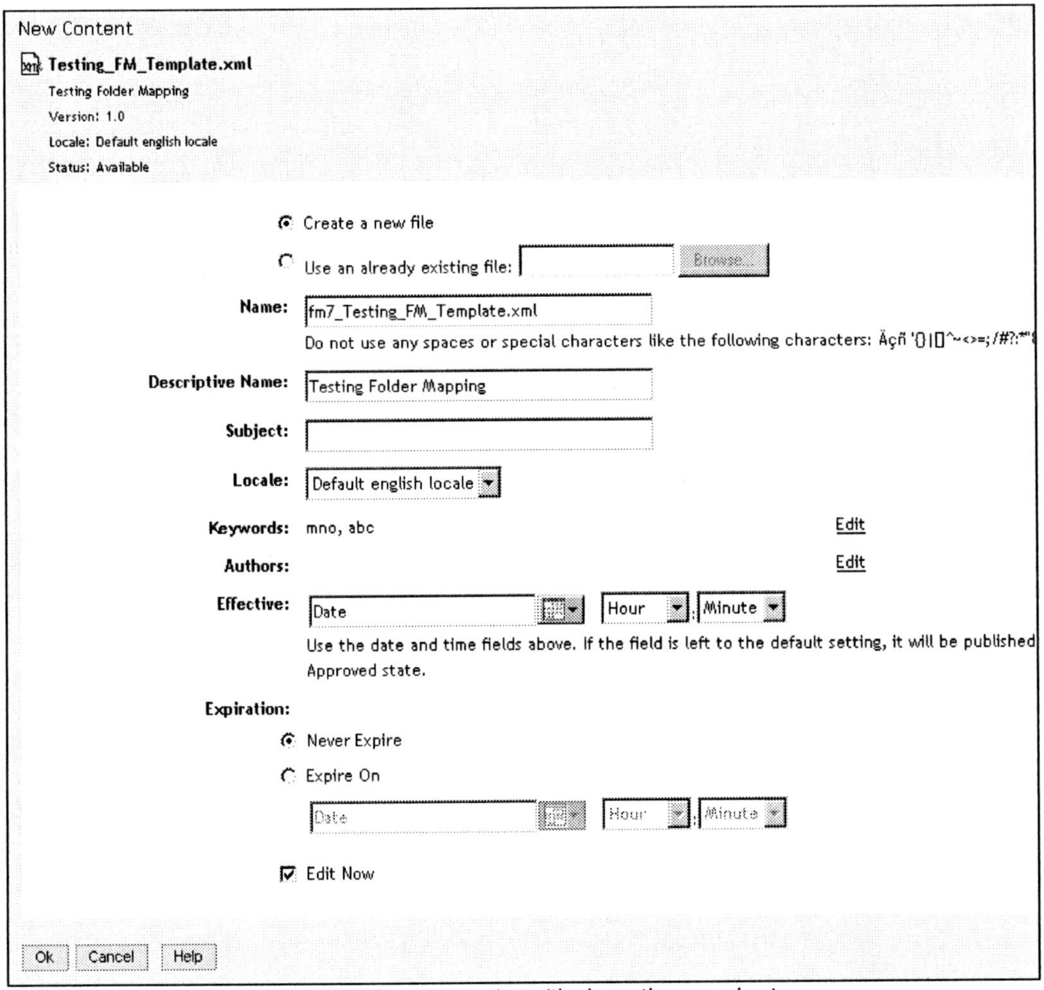

```
New Content

📄 Testing_FM_Template.xml

    Testing Folder Mapping
    Version: 1.0
    Locale: Default english locale
    Status: Available
```

    ◉ Create a new file

    ◯ Use an already existing file: [　　　　　　] [Browse...]

Name: [fm7_Testing_FM_Template.xml　　　]

Do not use any spaces or special characters like the following characters: Äçñ '()|[]^~<>=;/#?:*"(

Descriptive Name: [Testing Folder Mapping　　　]

Subject: [　　　　　　　　　　　]

Locale: [Default english locale ▾]

Keywords: mno, abc   Edit

Authors: Edit

Effective: [Date　　　　　] [▦] [Hour ▾],[Minute ▾]

Use the date and time fields above. If the field is left to the default setting, it will be published Approved state.

Expiration:

    ◉ Never Expire

    ◯ Expire On

    [Date　　　　] [▦] [Hour ▾],[Minute ▾]

    ☑ Edit Now

[Ok] [Cancel] [Help]

Figure 16.17: Content creation with abc as the second entry

3. You will notice that the new content is created successfully (refer to figure 16.18) under the Web Cabinet Test_WebCabinet within the folder abc created at run time by Folder Map.

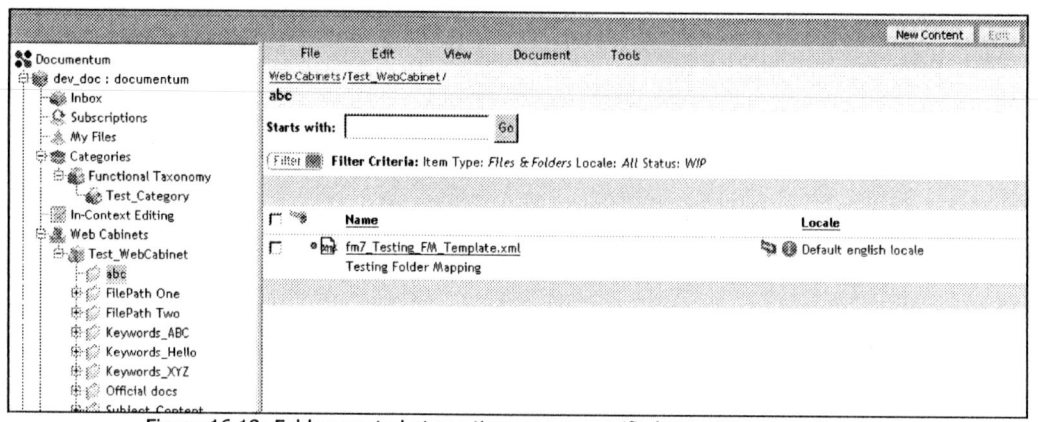

Figure 16.18: Folder created at run time as per specified repeating property value

Documentum 5.3 Update

Documentum Web Publisher release 5.3 provides you the facility to create and configure multiple Folder Maps.

There is much more to Folder Mapping than what we have discussed in this chapter. The Documentum Web Publisher manuals talk about Folder Mapping in detail and you can go through them to get a better understanding of the topic.

16.4 Summary

Web Publisher Folder Map (FolderMap.xml) is an XML file consisting of rules that map the created content files under specified folder locations in Web Cabinets, depending upon the matching Docbase properties of the content files.

In this chapter we initially discussed Folder Maps in the context of a sample product manufacturer firm and how its website is structured. We went ahead and studied the various XML elements in a Folder Map file and some limitations of Folder Maps in Web Publisher.

Finally, we looked at multiple examples for configuring Folder Maps using various property matching mechanisms, single and repeating attributes, and dynamic folder mapping at run time.

17
Using Instruction Files

One of the most frequent problems faced in a running Documentum is changes made to templates. At any given point of time, there is a certain amount of content created from a template file. If, owing to some business needs, the structure of this template file needs to change, what happens to the existing content that has already been made using the older version of the template?

Would the template still function well? Would the new template structure be reflected automatically in the existing content? Would you have to re-create all the existing content all over again so it conforms to the updated template structure?

Extremely pertinent questions—the short answer is: No! Documentum developers anticipated such situations and have included **Instruction Files** in Web Publisher to help you update the structure of existing content as per the updated template file.

Let's consider a small example.

Imagine a template file that content creators use to create a Frequently Asked Questions (FAQ) section for their website. The template has the following fields in the editor:

- A repeating block allowing multiple values to be entered for the template fields
- Question field
- Answer field

Let us assume the content creators create content based on the above template structure, providing values for multiple question-answer sets. However, after a certain time, the business team realizes that they need to tag the questions according to their relevance while creating the content. In short, they want to classify questions as Very important, Important, and Medium while creating content from the same template.

The only two approaches we can take in such a situation are:

- Make a separate template by including all required fields such as Question, Answer, and Relevance Order, and re-create all existing content using this new template.
- Modify the existing template by introducing a third field called Relevance Order and manually edit/update all the existing content.

In general, most business users resort to the second approach because of the following reasons:

- It saves them the overhead of maintaining two versions of the same template.
- It saves them the effort of re-creating content all over again.

Web Publisher Instruction Files helps us achieve this by providing configurable XML elements that update the existing XML content files as per the updated template structure without us having to manually edit/update existing content files.

Instruction Files can perform a wide array of functions on existing XML content files such as those shown in figure 17.1.

Function performed	Instruction File element
Insert new XML element	`<insert-element>`
Delete an existing XML element	`<delete-element>`
Insert an attribute to XML element	`<insert-attribute>`
Delete an attribute from XML element	`<delete-attribute>`
Update the value of an existing XML element	`<update-element-value>`

Figure 17.1: A few XML elements of Instruction Files

The Documentum developer site provides a wizard tool for creating Instruction Files. Please visit the following URL for further details:

`http://customernet.documentum.com/developer/tippage.htm`

You can download this tool and follow the instructions mentioned in the Instruction File Builder PDF to avoid creating the Instruction Files manually.

> Note that the Instruction Files in this book have been created using standard text/XML editors and not the Instruction File Builder tool.

17.1 Limitations of Instruction Files

It is worth mentioning a few limitations of Instruction Files before jumping into the specifics of their usage.

In order to update the value of an existing XML element, the `<update-element-value>` Instruction File element is used. The prerequisite, however, is that the XML element that is being updated should not contain any child element(s).

For example, if `<update-element-value>` is used to update a `<BOOK>` XML element, then the `<BOOK>` element should not have any child elements. The following `<BOOK>` element cannot be updated:

```
<BOOK>
  <AUTHOR></AUTHOR>
</BOOK>
```

On similar lines, `<update-element-value>` works fine if and only if the XML element being updated is not empty. In short, it has some text existing in the element (which might include white spaces). The following `<BOOK>` element cannot be updated:

`<BOOK></BOOK>`

However, the following XML element is a valid candidate for `<update-element-value>`:

`<BOOK>ABC</BOOK>`

For those conversant with XML/XSL, relative path does not work with Instruction Files. The XML Path Language (XPath) // (double slash) expression fails while working with Instruction Files and should not be used as a rule.

An XML file cannot be updated with an Instruction File in the following conditions:

- If the XML file is in the Staging state of its lifecycle
- If the XML file is in a checked-out state
- If the XML file is a part of a Change Set

An Instruction File always versions a file (i.e. provides a new version number to an XML file) even if the instructions do not make any changes to the structure of the XML file in question. Also, the files are placed in the WIP state of their lifecycle.

For example, let's take a scenario where the `<delete-attribute>` instruction is used in an Instruction File to remove the attribute bookname from an XML element `<BOOK>`.

If the `<BOOK>` XML element does not contain any attribute by the name bookname, the instruction `<delete-attribute>` still works on the `<BOOK>` XML element, and when it does not find any attribute by the name bookname, it still saves the XML file as a new version.

17.2 Instruction File Examples

Let us take a few examples to understand how Instruction Files work in Documentum.

17.2.1 Deleting an XML Element from an XML File with `<delete-element>`

Let us walk through a very simple example where content is created from a simple template XML file and later an XML element is removed from the template file. The existing content is updated via a simple Instruction File using the `<delete-element>` instruction.

1. Create a Template file (`Original_Template.xml`) and its associated Rules file (`Original_TemplateRules.xml`) as per the following structure:

   Template File `Original_Template.xml`:

   ```
   <?xml version="1.0" encoding="UTF-8"?>
   <PRODUCTINFO>
     <NAME/>
     <SHORTDESC/>
     <COST/>
     <PRODUCTTYPE/>
   </PRODUCTINFO>
   ```

Rules File `Original_TemplateRules.xml`:

```xml
<?xml version="1.0" encoding="UTF-8"?>
<rules>
 <tagcontent tag_name="NAME">
  <textline instruction="Please enter a name" label="Product name:"
required="Y">
  </textline>
 </tagcontent>

 <tagcontent tag_name="SHORTDESC">
  <content instruction="please provide a short description for product"
label="Product Description:" lines="5">
  </content>
 </tagcontent>

 <tagcontent tag_name="COST">
  <textline instruction="Please enter cost in dollars" label="Cost:">
  </textline>
 </tagcontent>

 <tagcontent tag_name="PRODUCTTYPE">
  <choice instruction="Please choose a type" label="Product Type:"
values="Type A,Type B,Type C">
  </choice>
 </tagcontent>
</rules>
```

2. Create two sets of content using the template file `Original_Template.xml` and provide names to them (refer to figures 17.2 and 17.3). For example: `Testing1_Original_Template.xml` and `Testing2_Original_Template.xml`.

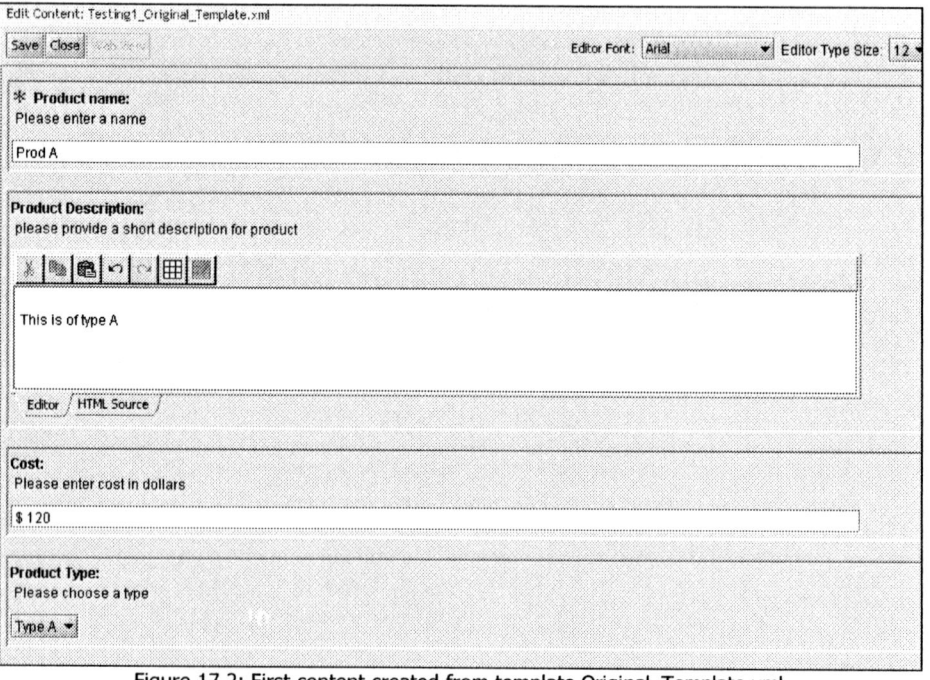

Figure 17.2: First content created from template Original_Template.xml

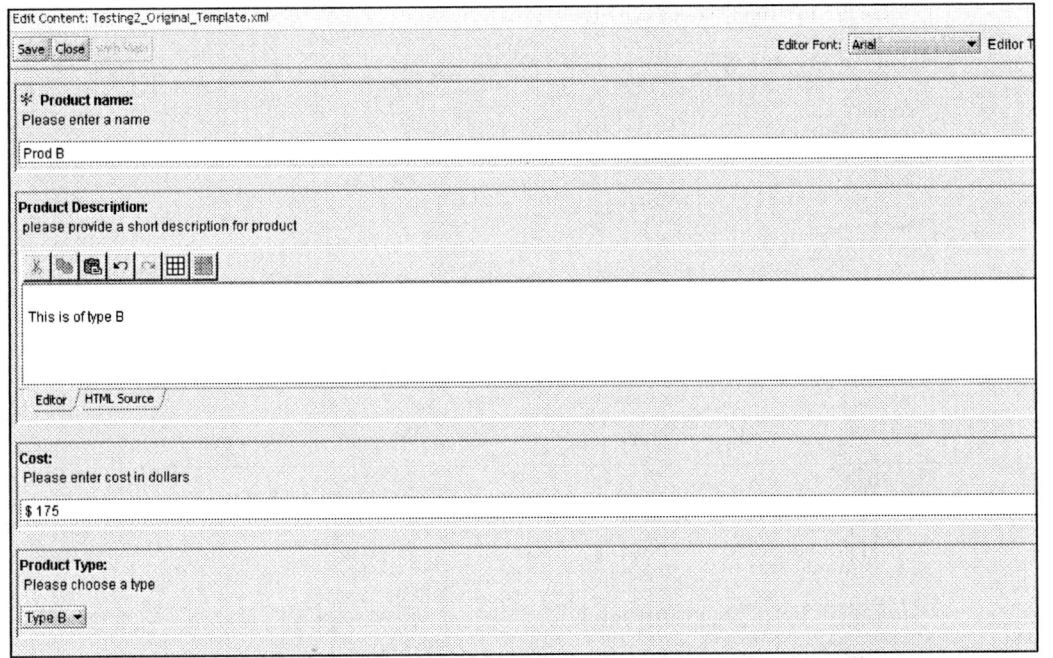

Figure 17.3: Second content created from template Original_Template.xml

You can view the XML structure of the created content from File | Export in Web Publisher, and export the content XML files on the local machine accessing Web Publisher.

Following are the content XML files for the content created above. These have been created from the template file Original_Template.xml version 1.0:

Testing1_Original_Template.xml:

```
<?xml version="1.0" encoding="UTF-8"?>
<PRODUCTINFO>
    <NAME>Prod A</NAME>
    <SHORTDESC>
<p>
This is of type A
</p>
</SHORTDESC>
    <COST>$ 120</COST>
    <PRODUCTTYPE>Type A</PRODUCTTYPE>
</PRODUCTINFO>
```

Testing2_Original_Template.xml:

```
<?xml version="1.0" encoding="UTF-8"?>
<PRODUCTINFO>
    <NAME>Prod B</NAME>
    <SHORTDESC>
<p>
This is of type B
</p>
</SHORTDESC>
    <COST>$ 175</COST>
    <PRODUCTTYPE>Type B</PRODUCTTYPE>
</PRODUCTINFO>
```

3. Modify the original template XML file by removing the `<COST/>` XML element.

   Following is the template file (version 2.0) `original_Template.xml` after modification.

```
<?xml version="1.0" encoding="UTF-8"?>
<PRODUCTINFO>
    <NAME/>
    <SHORTDESC/>
    <PRODUCTTYPE/>
</PRODUCTINFO>
```

4. Using any XML editor, create an Instruction File (`Delete_Element_Instruction.xml`) that updates content XML files by removing their contained `<COST>` XML element.

   The following Instruction File (`Delete_Element_Instruction.xml`) can be used in such a scenario:

```
<?xml version="1.0" encoding="UTF-8"?>
<instructions xmlns ="http://www.documentum.com/wp"
xmlns:xsi="http://www.w3.org/2001/XMLSchema-instance"
xsi:schemaLocation="http://www.documentum.com/wp instructions.xsd">
<delete-element>
<path>/PRODUCTINFO</path>
<nodename>COST</nodename>
<comments>Deleting COST element</comments>
</delete-element>
</instructions>
```

   Anatomy of the above Instruction File:

   ○ `<delete-element>`: Instruction File element to delete an existing XML element

   ○ `<path>`: XPath expression to identify the path where the XML element to be deleted currently exists

   ○ `<nodename>`: Name of the target node (XML element) to be deleted

   ○ `<comments>`: Optional comments stating the purpose of the Instruction File

5. Browse to Site Manager | Instructions from the left tree pane in Web Publisher as an administrator. Create a folder to store the custom Instruction Files. Within the created folder, import the `Delete_Element_Instruction.xml` Instruction File by choosing File | Import as shown in figures 17.4 and 17.5.

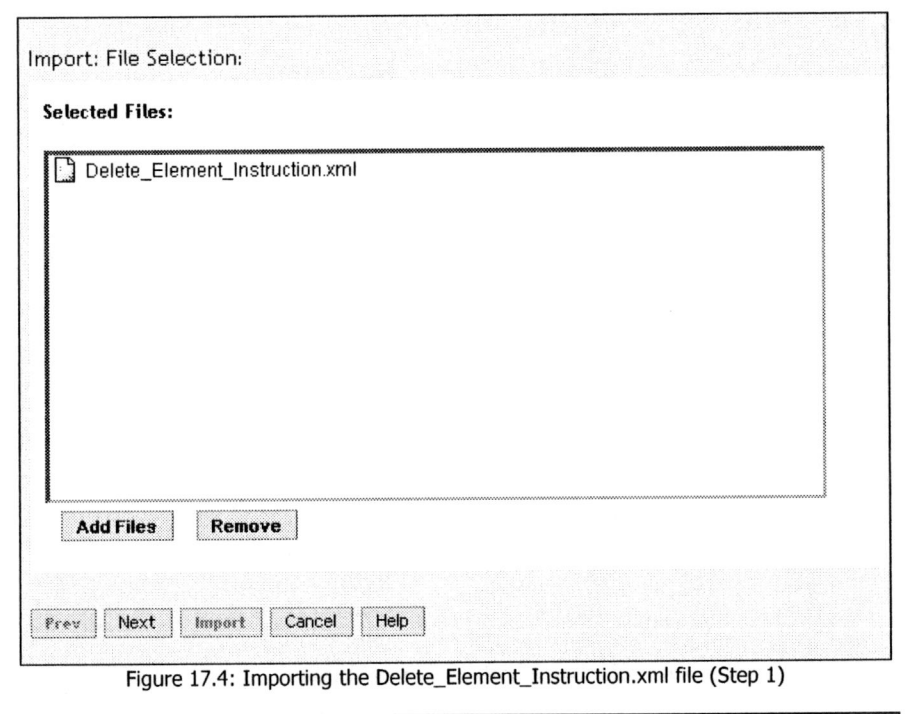

Figure 17.4: Importing the Delete_Element_Instruction.xml file (Step 1)

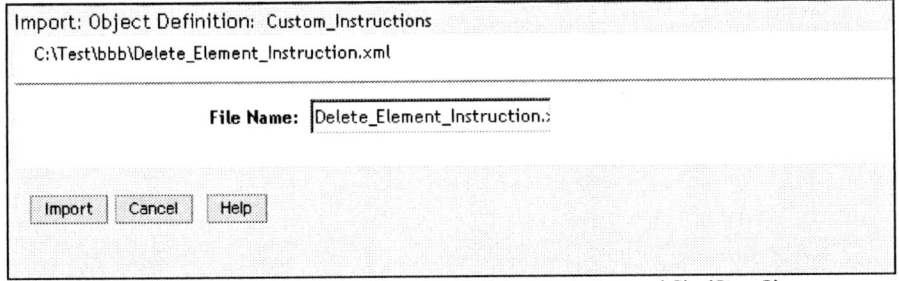

Figure 17.5: Importing the Delete_Element_Instruction.xml file (Step 2)

6. We are all set as far as configurations for Instruction Files are concerned. Now, browse to the respective category for the modified template file `Original_Template.xml` under **Site Manager | Templates**. Choose the modified template file `original_Template.xml` and click on the **View | Versions** option as shown in figure 17.6.

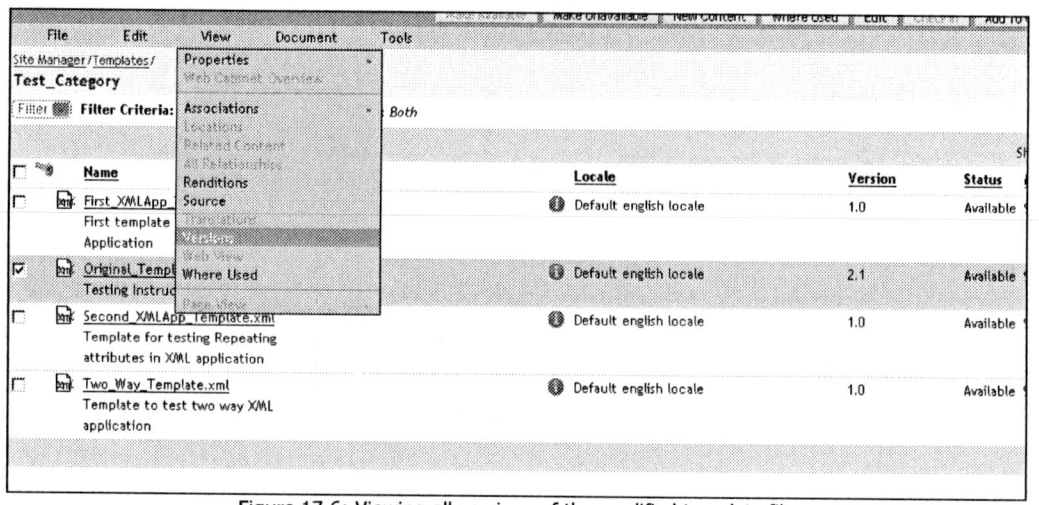

Figure 17.6: Viewing all versions of the modified template file

7. Refer to figure 17.7; from the versions shown, choose version 1.0 of the template file, because the existing content was created from the older version (1.0) of the template and not the modified version 2.0 of the template file.

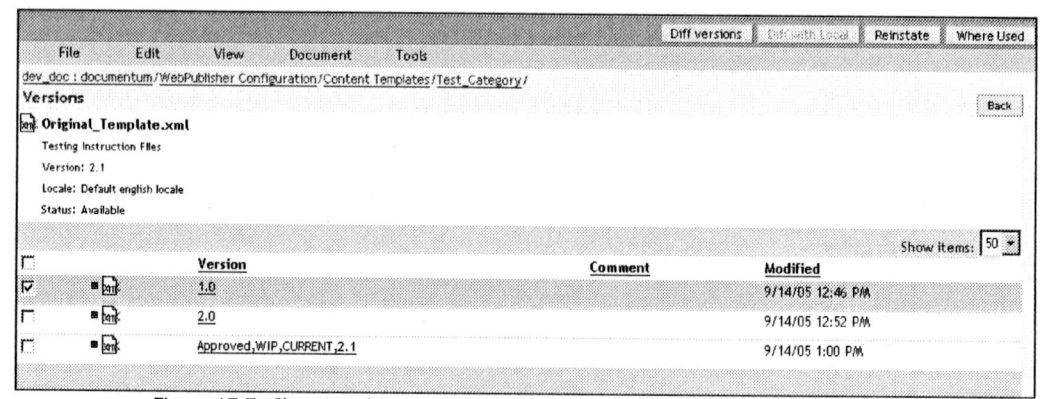

Figure 17.7: Choosing the version of template file with which content was created

After choosing version 1.0, click the **Where Used** button shown at the top right-hand side as shown in figure 17.7. All content files created from the selected version of the template file are shown.

Choose the content file(s) to be updated by the Instruction File and click the **Update Content** button at the top right-hand corner, as shown in figure 17.8.

We have chosen only the Testing1_Original_Template.xml content file.

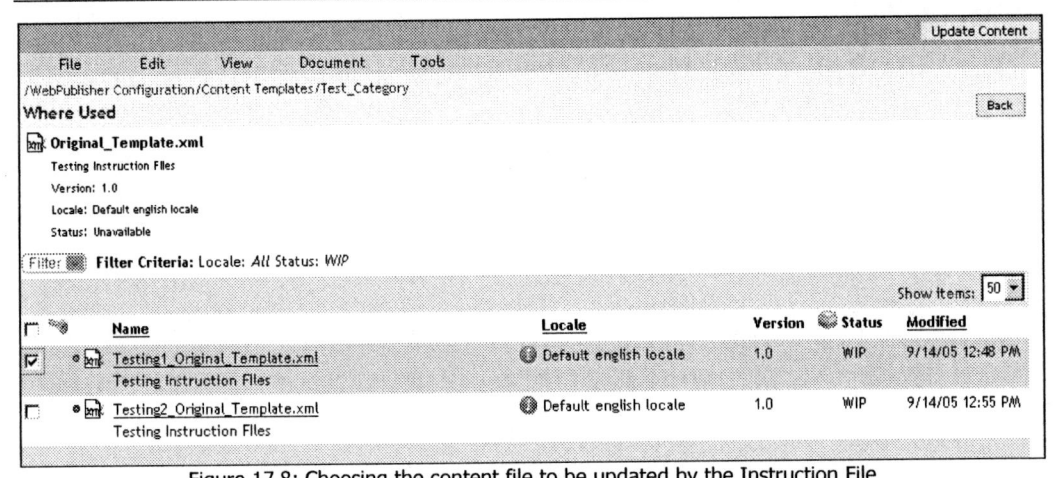

Figure 17.8: Choosing the content file to be updated by the Instruction File

8. Choose the relevant Instruction File by clicking on the **Select Instructions** file link shown in figure 17.9. We have chosen the Instruction File `Delete_Element_Instruction.xml`. Finally click on OK.

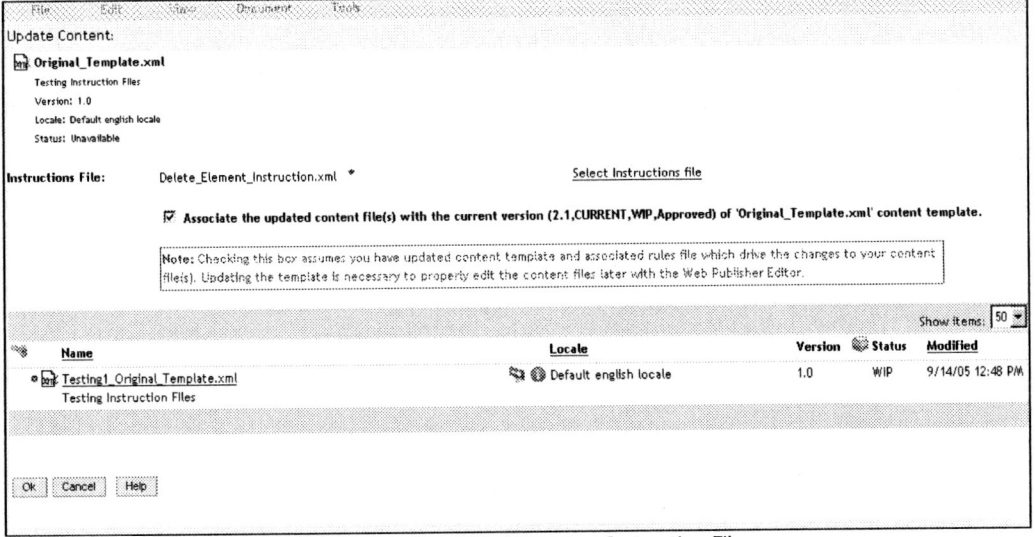

Figure 17.9: Choosing the correct Instruction File

9. The Instruction File processing is triggered and the chosen content files(s) are modified as per the updated template file structure. Clicking on the **Task Status** button in Web Publisher shows the status of the Instruction File processing.

Example: When you update XML Content Task using the `Delete_Element_Instruction.xml` Instructions File, the `UPDATE_XMLCONTENT_1126683079171` log file is created in the `WcmLog` folder.

10. Log in to Documentum Administrator as an administrator and go to Cabinets | WebPublisher Configuration. Click on the WcmLog folder to view the log file generated (refer to figure 17.10) by the above Instruction File processing.

	Name	Size	Format	Modified
	UPDATE_XMLCONTENT_1126678855140	1 KB	Text Document (Windows)	9/14/05 11:53 AM
☑	UPDATE_XMLCONTENT_1126683079171	1 KB	Text Document (Windows)	9/14/05 1:03 PM
	UPDATE_XMLCONTENT_1126683766281	2 KB	Text Document (Windows)	9/14/05 1:14 PM
	UPDATE_XMLCONTENT_1126683916671	2 KB	Text Document (Windows)	9/14/05 1:17 PM
	UPDATE_XMLCONTENT_1126684606234	2 KB	Text Document (Windows)	9/14/05 1:28 PM
	UPDATE_XMLCONTENT_1126684987781	1 KB	Text Document (Windows)	9/14/05 1:35 PM

Figure 17.10: Existing log files due to Instruction File processing

11. Verify the state of the content file Testing1_Original_Template.xml after the Instruction File has been applied as shown in figure 17.11. You can see that the version of the Testing1_Original_Template.xml file is now 1.1 (as opposed to its version 1.0 before the Instruction File was applied). Choose the file and click on File | Export to export the updated content file to your client machine.

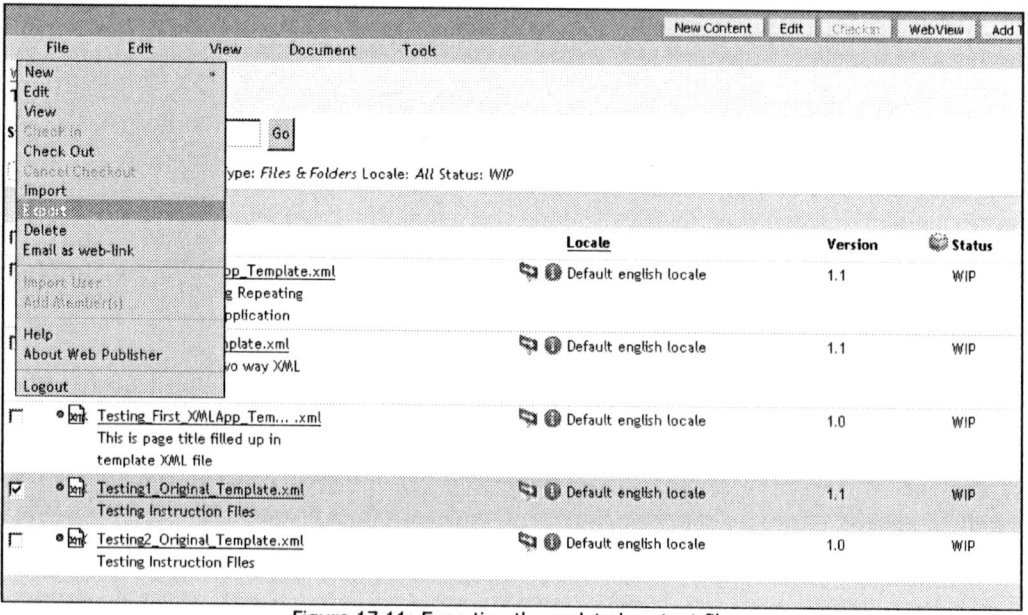

Figure 17.11: Exporting the updated content file

Updated content file `Testing1_Original_Template.xml`:

```
<?xml version="1.0" encoding="UTF-8"?>
<PRODUCTINFO>
    <NAME>Prod A</NAME>
    <SHORTDESC>
<p>
This is of type A
</p>
</SHORTDESC>

    <PRODUCTTYPE>Type A</PRODUCTTYPE>
</PRODUCTINFO>
```

Notice the absence of the <COST> XML element from this content file.

The other content file (`Testing2_Original_Template.xml`) is still in version 1.0 since it was not updated via the Instruction File.

If you edit the content `Testing1_Original_Template.xml` using Web Publisher editor, the Cost: field will not be shown as per the updated template structure. Figure 17.12 shows the updated content file without the Cost field, as seen in Web Publisher editor.

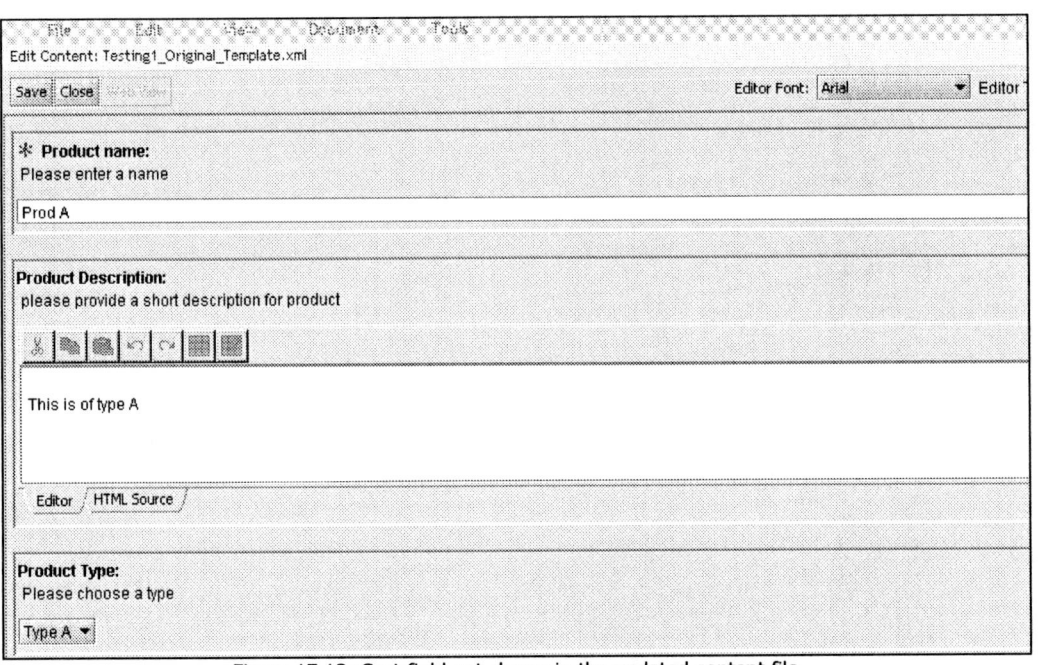

Figure 17.12: Cost field not shown in the updated content file

Opening the other content file `Testing2_Original_Template.xml` in Web Publisher editor will still show the Cost: field as per the older version of template file.

This was a simple example to delete an existing XML element from a content file. Let us now go ahead and take up some more examples so that we can understand the power of Instruction Files in a better fashion.

17.2.2 Adding an XML Element to an XML File with <insert-element>

Let us take an example where content is created from a simple template XML file and then a new XML element is added to the template file. The existing content is updated via an Instruction File using the `<insert-element>` instruction.

1. Update the existing Template file (`Original_Template.xml`) and its associated Rules file (`Original_TemplateRules.xml`) as per the following structure:

   Updated Template file `Original_Template.xml`:

   ```
   <?xml version="1.0" encoding="UTF-8"?>
   <PRODUCTINFO>
        <NAME/>
        <SHORTDESC/>
        <PRODUCTTYPE/>
        <PRICEINFO/>
   </PRODUCTINFO>
   ```

   Note that we have added a new `<PRICEINFO>` XML element to the template file.

   Updated Rules file `Original_TemplateRules.xml`:

   ```
   <?xml version="1.0" encoding="UTF-8"?>
   <rules>
    <tagcontent tag_name="NAME">
     <textline instruction="Please enter a name" label="Product name:"
   required="Y">
     </textline>
    </tagcontent>

    <tagcontent tag_name="SHORTDESC">
     <content instruction="please provide a short description for product"
   label="Product Description:" lines="5">
     </content>
    </tagcontent>

    <tagcontent tag_name="COST">
     <textline instruction="Please enter cost in dollars" label="Cost:">
     </textline>
    </tagcontent>

    <tagcontent tag_name="PRODUCTTYPE">
     <choice instruction="Please choose a type" label="Product Type:"
   values="Type A,Type B,Type C">
     </choice>
    </tagcontent>

    <tagcontent tag_name="PRICEINFO">
     <textline charlength="50" instruction="Please enter a price for the
   product" abel="Enter price:">
     </textline>
    </tagcontent>
   </rules>
   ```

Figure 17.13 shows the Web Publisher template editor screen.

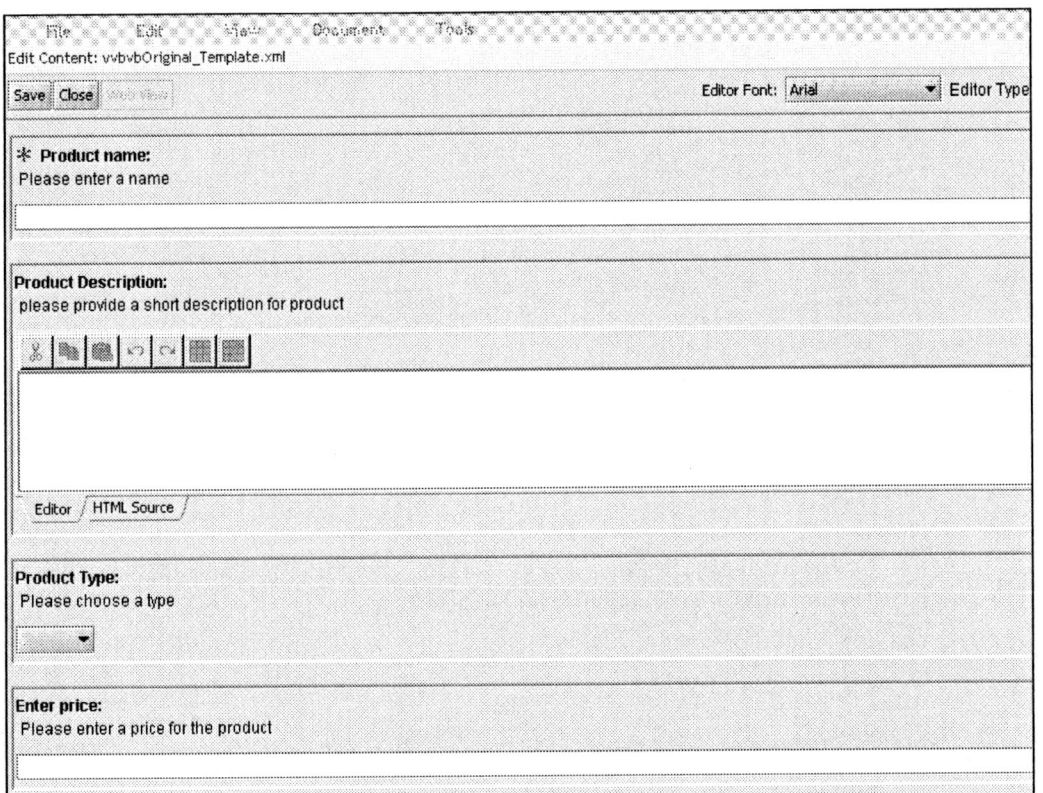

Figure 17.13: Web Publisher editor shown while creating new content

2. Using any XML editor, create an Instruction File (Add_Element_Instruction.xml) that updates content XML files by adding a new <PRICEINFO> XML element.

The following Instruction file (Add_Element_Instruction.xml) can be used in such a scenario:

```
<?xml version="1.0" encoding="UTF-8"?>
<instructions xmlns ="http://www.documentum.com/wp"
xmlns:xsi="http://www.w3.org/2001/XMLSchema-instance"
xsi:schemaLocation="http://www.documentum.com/wp instructions.xsd">
<insert-element>
<path>/PRODUCTINFO</path>
<nodename>PRICEINFO</nodename>
<value>$ 100</value>
<comments>testing insert element PRICEINFO</comments>
</insert-element>
</instructions>
```

Anatomy of the above Instruction File:

- o   <insert-element>: Instruction File element to add an XML element to an XML content file
- o   <path>: XPath expression to identify the path where the XML element to be inserted/added currently exists
- o   <nodename>: Name of the target node (XML element) to be inserted
- o   <value>: Text value of the XML element to be set
- o   <comments>: Optional comments stating the purpose of the Instruction File

3. Browse to Site Manager | Instructions from the left tree pane in Web Publisher as an administrator and import the Add_Element_Instruction.xml Instruction File by choosing the File | Import option. Complete all the steps described in the previous example.

4. Update the content file Testing1_Original_Template.xml with the Instruction File Add_Element_Instruction.xml. You can verify that the version of the Testing1_Original_Template.xml file has been updated.

Choose the file and click on File | Export to export the updated content file on your client machine.

Here is the updated content file Testing1_Original_Template.xml after the Add_Element_Instruction.xml Instruction File has been applied:

```
<?xml version="1.0" encoding="UTF-8"?>
<PRODUCTINFO>
    <NAME>Prod A</NAME>
    <SHORTDESC>
<p>
This is of type A
</p>
</SHORTDESC>

    <PRODUCTTYPE>Type A</PRODUCTTYPE>
<PRICEINFO>$ 100</PRICEINFO>
</PRODUCTINFO>
```

Notice that the <PRICEINFO> XML element has been added in this content file with the value $ 100.

The other content file (Testing2_Original_Template.xml) is still in version 1.0 since it was not updated via the Instruction File.

If you edit the content Testing1_Original_Template.xml using Web Publisher editor, the Enter price: field will be shown as per the updated template structure (refer to figure 17.14).

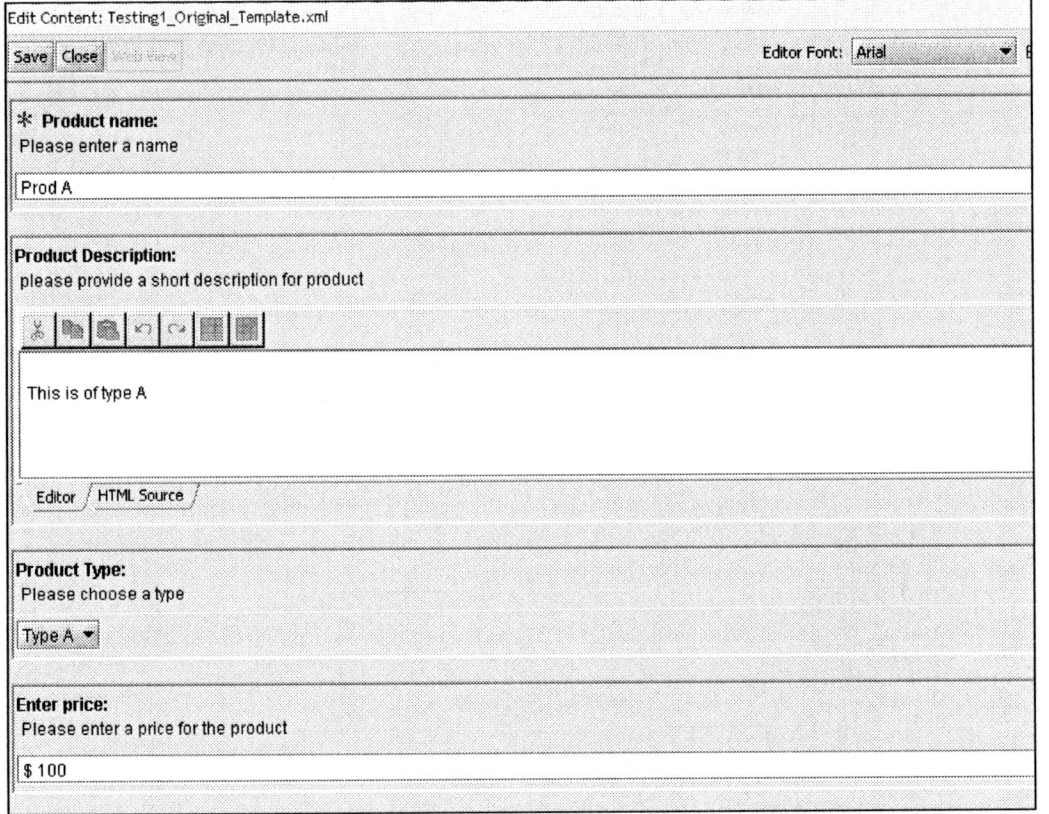

Figure 17.14: Enter price field shown as per updated template file

17.2.3 Updating the Value of an XML Element in an XML File with <update-element-value>

Let us now take an example where content is created from a simple template XML file and then the value of an XML element in content files is to be updated. The existing content is updated via an Instruction File using the <update-element-value> instruction.

1. Using any XML editor, create an Instruction File
   Update_Element_Value_Instruction.xml that updates content XML files by
   updating the value of their <PRICEINFO> XML element.

   The following Instruction File (Update_Element_Value_Instruction.xml) can be used
   in such a scenario:

```
<?xml version="1.0" encoding="UTF-8"?>
<instructions xmlns ="http://www.documentum.com/wp"
xmlns:xsi="http://www.w3.org/2001/XMLSchema-instance"
xsi:schemaLocation="http://www.documentum.com/wp instructions.xsd">
<update-element-value>
<path>/PRODUCTINFO</path>
```

```
<nodename>PRICEINFO</nodename>
<value>Price Not available</value>
<comments>Updating the value of PRICEINFO element</comments>
</update-element-value>
</instructions>
```

Anatomy of this Instruction File:

- o `<update-element-value>`: Instruction File element to set a new text value for the specified XML element in an XML content file
- o `<path>`: XPath expression to identify the path where the XML element to be updated currently exists
- o `<nodename>`: Name of the target node (XML element) whose value needs to be updated
- o `<value>`: The new text value that needs to be set for the XML element in question
- o `<comments>`: Optional comments stating the purpose of the Instruction File

2. Browse to **Site Manager | Instructions** from the left tree pane in Web Publisher as an administrator and import the `Update_Element_Value_Instruction.xml` Instruction File by choosing the **File | Import** option. Complete all the steps as described in the first example.

3. Update the content file `Testing1_Original_Template.xml` with the Instruction File `Update_Element_Value_Instruction.xml`. You can verify that the version of the `Testing1_Original_Template.xml` file has been updated.

4. Choose the file and click on **File | Export** to export the updated content file on your client machine.

   The updated content file `Testing1_Original_Template.xml` after `Update_Element_Value_Instruction.xml` Instruction File has been applied:

```
<?xml version="1.0" encoding="UTF-8"?>
<PRODUCTINFO>
 <NAME>Prod A</NAME>
 <SHORTDESC>
<p>
This is of type A
</p>
</SHORTDESC>

 <PRODUCTTYPE>Type A</PRODUCTTYPE>
<PRICEINFO>
    Price Not available
</PRICEINFO>
</PRODUCTINFO>
```

   Notice that the value of the `<PRICEINFO>` XML element has been updated in this content file with the value `Price Not available`.

   The other content file (`Testing2_Original_Template.xml`) is still in version 1.0 since it was not updated via the Instruction File.

If you edit the content Testing1_Original_Template.xml using Web Publisher editor, the Enter price: field will be shown as per the updated template structure (refer to figure 17.15).

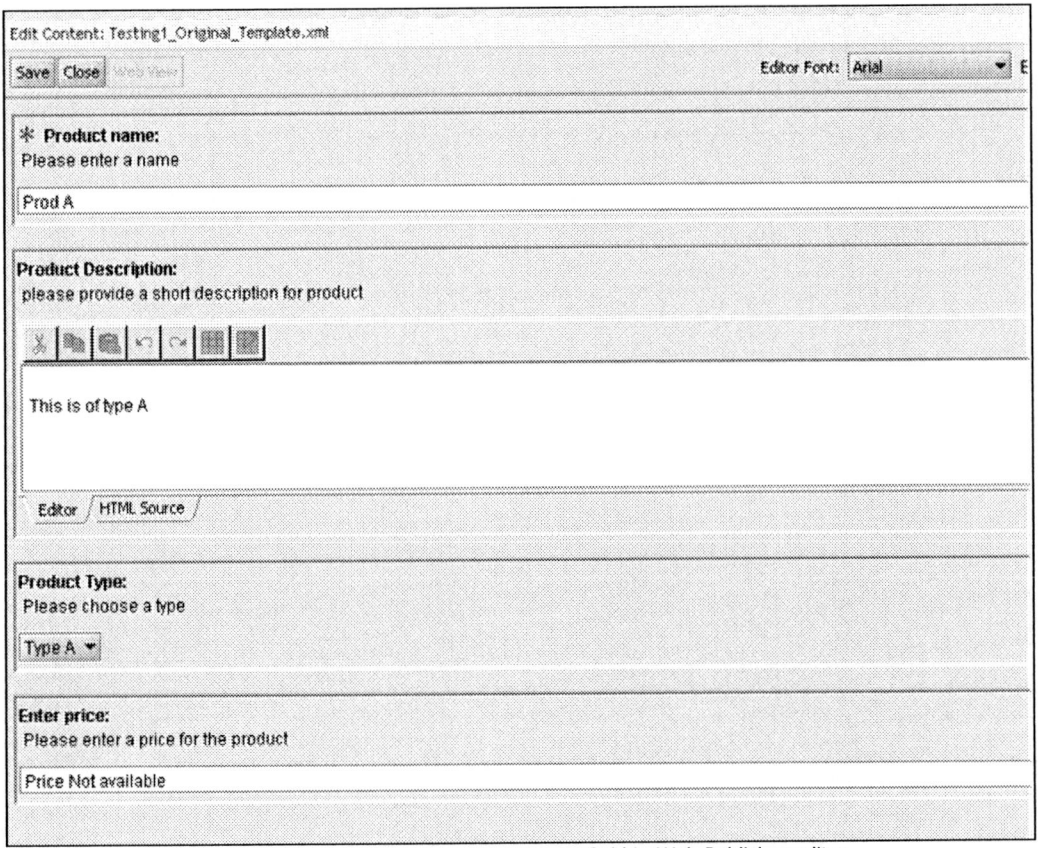

Figure 17.15: Updated value of Enter price field in Web Publisher editor

This should give you all a fairly good understanding of Instruction Files and their usage scenarios. For a comprehensive understanding of Instruction Files, go through the Documentum Web Publisher Administration guide.

17.3 Summary

In this chapter we learned that Web Publisher Instruction Files provide configurable XML elements allowing us to update the structure of existing XML content files as per the updated template structure.

We also looked at some of the XML elements in Instruction Files and discussed the limitations of using Instruction Files in Web Publisher.

With the help of detailed examples, we saw how to use Instruction Files to delete an XML element from a content XML file, add a new XML element, and update the existing value of an XML element.

18

Automatic Property Extraction (APE)

Automatic property extraction (or APE in short) is one of the most powerful and useful features provided by Documentum DFC. One of the most frequent business needs is to automatically set a document's attributes (properties) based on the values set by the content creator in the content template (XML file). Let us understand this through a very simple example.

Imagine a fictitious template that requires users to fill in an Article Title field in the XML template. The requirement is that the value entered by the content creator in this field should be automatically saved in the `title` attribute (property) of the document as well.

Let's say that the content creator provides the following value for Article Title: `Major breakthrough in financial investments`. The value is saved in the `<ARTICLETITLE>` XML element (for example) in the content file created by the user.

Through its Automatic Property Extraction feature (and if configured correctly), Documentum automatically copies the value specified by the user in the `<ARTICLETITLE>` field in to the `title` attribute (property) of the document, whenever the user saves and checks in the document.

Through some other configuration settings, it could even work the other way round. The XML element can also be populated automatically based on the value provided by a user in the attribute for the document.

Property extraction adds value for the business content creators in the following ways:

- It saves the effort of manually entering the same value at two places—the properties page and the content file (template editor).
- It saves the effort (and time) to open Web Publisher editor by allowing them to enter values in the Properties page itself.

Note that Automatic property extraction works with the following Web Publisher widgets only:

- textline
- checkbox
- choice

18.1 How Automatic Property Extraction Works

Internally Documentum uses the following two object types for managing Automatic property extraction for XML elements:

- dm_xml_application (supertype: dm_folder): Used for creating a folder under the \System\Applications folder in Docbase to store the XML configuration objects (dm_xml_config).

- dm_xml_config (supertype: dm_document): Specifies the XML configuration file to be used for the specified XML application.

The property extraction rules need to be specified within the XML configuration file. Once you have created the XML application folder and saved the XML configuration file within it, you need to set the a_category attribute of the content file. DFC queries this attribute and detects the Automatic Property Extraction rules to be applied to the content file based on its XML configuration file. You, however, need to ensure that the dm_xml_application folder and the dm_xml_config application file have exactly the same names, since Documentum Content Server searches for the XML application file based on the exact name that we specify in the content file's a_category attribute.

We are free to not specify any XML Application for the content file. In such cases, the Default XML Application provided by Documentum is used.

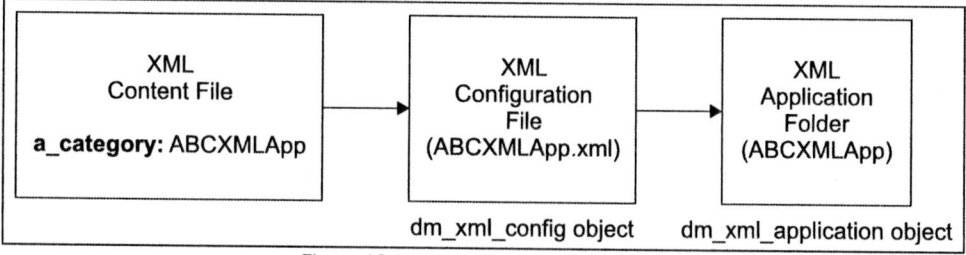

Figure 18.1: How XML Application works

Internally, Documentum uses a SAX parser for XML processing of documents against the associated XML Application and DOM for reading the XML configuration file.

18.2 Simple Example for Automatic Property Extraction

Let us take a simple example to understand how Automatic Property Extraction can be used in Documentum. We will see how an XML Application is created, how it is attached to the content file, and eventually how it works.

1. Refer to figure 18.2; create and import a template in Web Publisher (say First_XMLApp_Template.xml) and attach it to dm_document object type with Default Lifecycle.

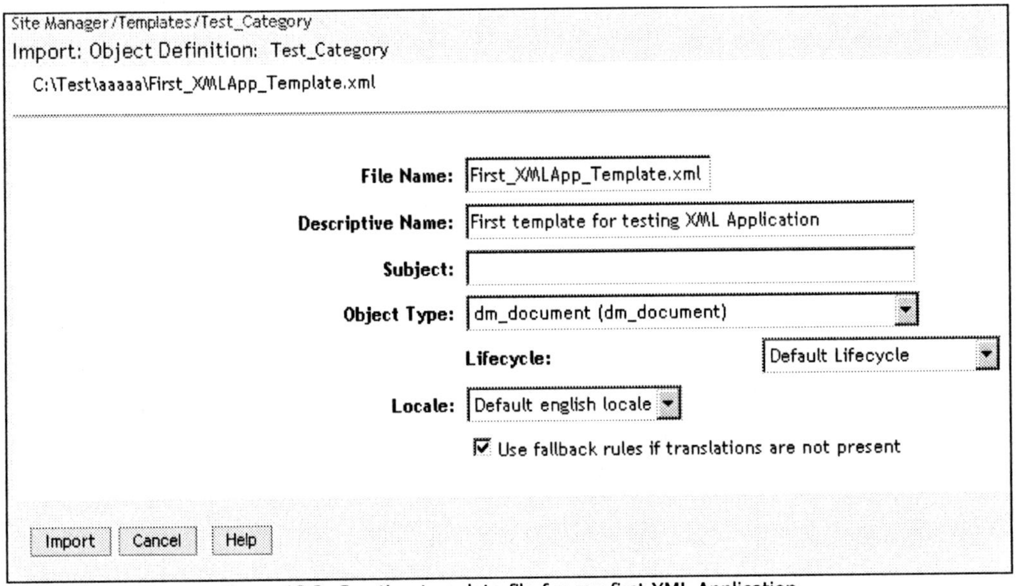

Figure 18.2: Creating template file for our first XML Application

Following is the Template file First_XMLApp_Template.xml:

```xml
<?xml version="1.0" encoding="UTF-8"?>
<ROOTTAG>
  <TITLEOFPAGE/>
  <SHORTDESC/>
</ROOTTAG>
```

2. Create a Rules file (say `First_XMLApp_TemplateRule.xml`) for the template and associate the Template file with this Rules file. Following is the Rules file `First_XMLApp_TemplateRule.xml`:

```xml
<?xml version="1.0" encoding="UTF-8"?>
<rules>
  <tagcontent tag_name="TITLEOFPAGE">
    <textline charlength="200" instruction="Enter Title of the page"
                              label="Page Title" required="Y">
    </textline>
  </tagcontent>

  <tagcontent tag_name="SHORTDESC">
    <textline charlength="200"
      instruction="Enter a small description/subject of the page"
      label="Page subject" required="Y">
    </textline>
  </tagcontent>
</rules>
```

3. Click on the info icon (i) and provide the name of the XML Configuration file in the Category field of the template as shown in figure 18.3. This sets the `a_category` attribute of the template.

4. You could even do this via IAPI as follows:

```
API>id,c,dm_document where object_name = 'First_XMLApp_Template.xml' and
                              a_is_template = '1'
API>set,c,l,a_category
Data: FirstXMLApp

API>save,c,l
```

Note that 'l' shown in the API commands is an alias reference to the object ID returned when you fire a query. More on API commands in Chapter 26.

We will create the XML Application file `FirstXMLApp.xml` in the next few steps.

Please note that while filling in the Category field, you must strip off the `.xml` extension from the name of the XML Configuration file. If this is not done, the XML Application against the template in question will not work.

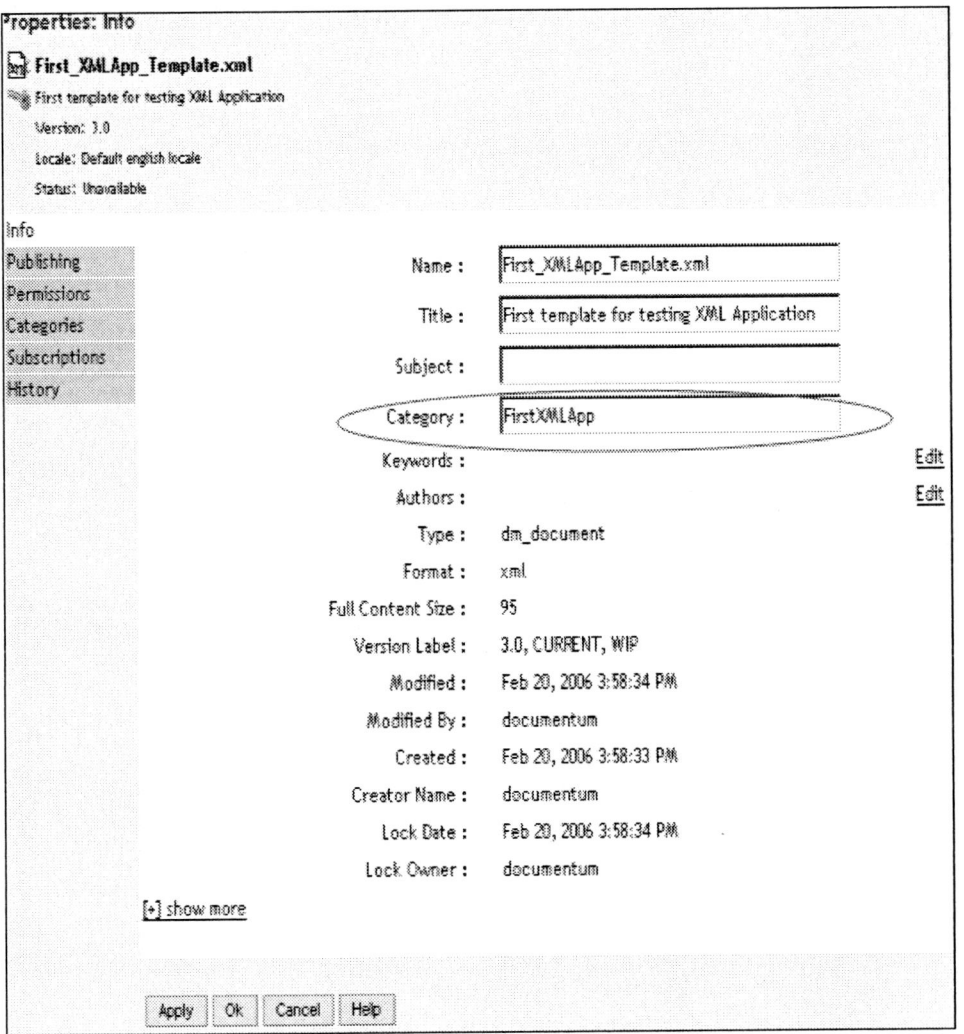

Figure 18.3: Specifying the a_category property for the template

5. Create the XML application configuration file in your favorite XML editor. We will create our first XML Configuration file by the name FirstXMLApp.xml. The purpose of this XML Application will be to map the values in the <TITLEOFPAGE> element and <SHORTDESC> element in the Template XML file to title and subject attributes of the dm_document object respectively. The XML Configuration file FirstXMLApp.xml is shown below:

```
<?xml version="1.0" encoding="UTF-8"?>
<!DOCTYPE application  SYSTEM "config_5.2.dtd">
<application>
  <name>FirstXMLApp</name>
  <app_pattern>
```

```
         <element>ROOTTAG</element>          <!-- Specifying the XML Root element-->
      </app_pattern>

      <map_rules>
        <xml_content_rule>
          <element_selection_pattern>
            <element>ROOTTAG</element>
          </element_selection_pattern>

          <variables> <!-- Defining variables to map values in object
                       attribute-->
          <variable>
            <name>TitleOfPage</name>        <!-- Storing the value of
                                             TITLEOFPAGE template element -->
            <content_of_element>
              <element_selection_pattern>
                <element>TITLEOFPAGE</element>
              </element_selection_pattern>
            </content_of_element>
          </variable>
          <variable>
            <name>ShortDescOfPage</name>     <!-- Storing the value of
                                             SHORTDESC template element -->
            <content_of_element>
              <element_selection_pattern>
                <element>SHORTDESC</element>
              </element_selection_pattern>
            </content_of_element>
          </variable>
          </variables>
          <object_type>dm_document</object_type>   <!-- Specifying the object
                                                    type-->
          <metadata>
            <dctmattr>
              <name>title</name>                 <!-- Saving value in title
                                                  attribute-->
              <template><var name="TitleOfPage"/></template>
          </dctmattr>
          <dctmattr>
            <name>subject</name><!-- Saving value in subject attribute-->
              <template><var name="ShortDescOfPage"/></template>
          </dctmattr>

          </metadata>

          <make_entity/>
        </xml_content_rule>
      </map_rules>

  </application>
```

Let's discuss the anatomy of the above XML configuration file:

```
<!DOCTYPE application  SYSTEM "config_5.2.dtd">
```

This is the XML file prolog. Since the XML configuration is an XML document, the DTD that it will conform to is specified here. The `config_5.2.dtd` file that is referenced in the XML application file can be found at the following location in Web Publisher: Cabinets | System | Applications | Default XML Application.

```
<application>
```

This is the root element of XML configuration file.

```
<name>FirstXMLApp</name>
```

This is the name of the XML Application.

```
<element>ROOTTAG</element>
```

Case-sensitive root element of the Template XML file that has to be processed via the XML Application.

```
<element>ROOTTAG</element>
```

This is the root element name of the Template XML file that has to be processed via the XML Application.

> The scores of XML elements that you see in the XML configuration file are declared in the `config_5.2.dtd` file.

`<variable>` indicates a variable name defined and its value such as XML element name and attribute value. Here two variables have been declared: variable `TitleofPage` stores the value of the `TITLEOFPAGE` XML element and variable `ShortDescofPage` stores the value of the `SHORTDESC` XML element.

```
<object_type>dm_document</object_type>
```

`<object_type>` specifies the Documentum object type whose attributes need to be mapped by the XML elements.

`<dctmattr>`: Sets the value of a single-valued Documentum object property.

Here, we have set the values of the `title` property through the variable `TitleofPage` and the `subject` property through the variable `ShortDescofPage`.

> For repeating-valued Documentum object properties, use the `<dctmattr_repeating>` element in your XML configuration file. We will look at a related example later in this chapter.

6. Now we will perform the necessary configurations required for the XML application to work properly. Log in to Web Publisher as an administrator and go to **Cabinets | System | Applications**.

Choose File | New folder and create a new XML Application folder as shown in figure 18.4.

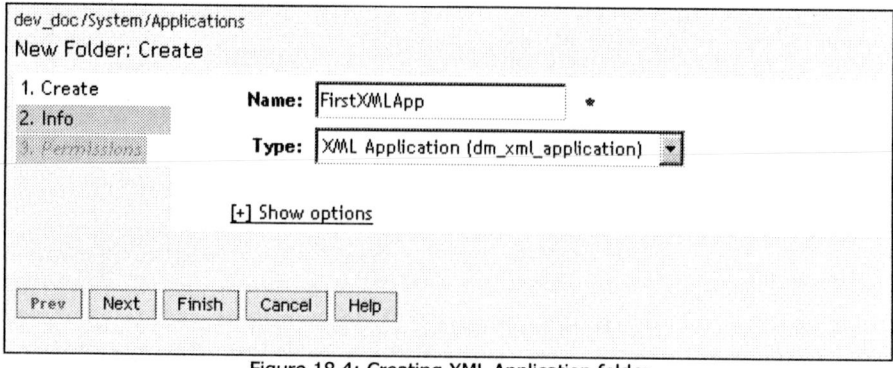

Figure 18.4: Creating XML Application folder

7. After the folder FirstXMLApp has been created, click on it and import the XML configuration file within this folder.

    Before importing the XML configuration file, ensure config_5.2.dtd and the FirstXMLApp.xml file reside at the same location on your machine's local hard drive. Choose File | Import and select the FirstXMLApp.xml file from your local machine as shown in figure 18.5.

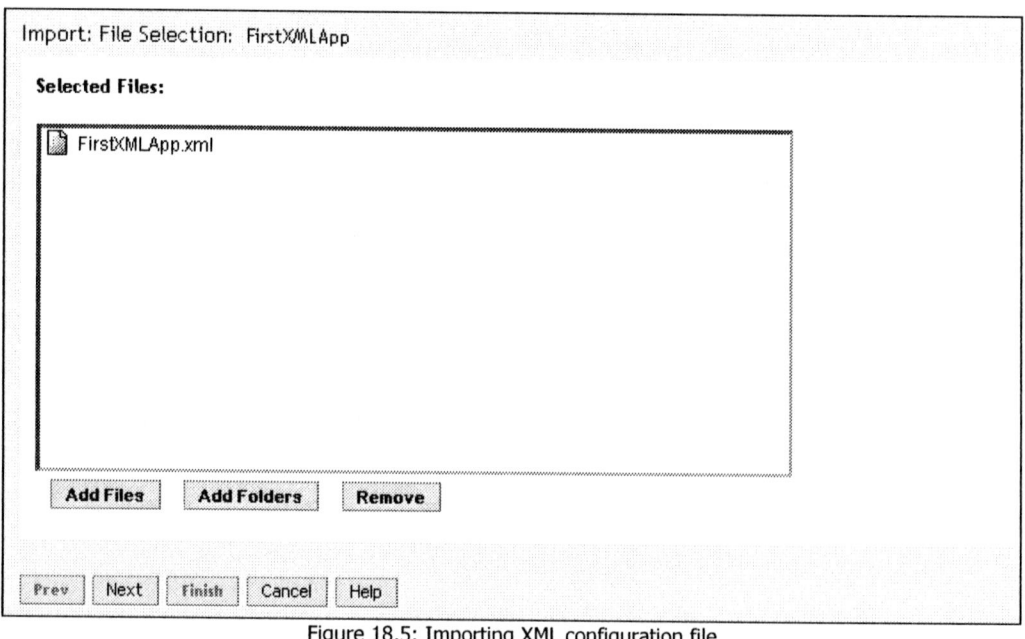

Figure 18.5: Importing XML configuration file

8. While importing the XML configuration file, choose type as `dm_xml_config`, format as XML Document and XML Category as Default XML Application as shown in figure 18.6. Remember to strip off `.xml` from the name while importing this configuration file.

    This completes the steps required for associating the XML Application with a content Template XML file.

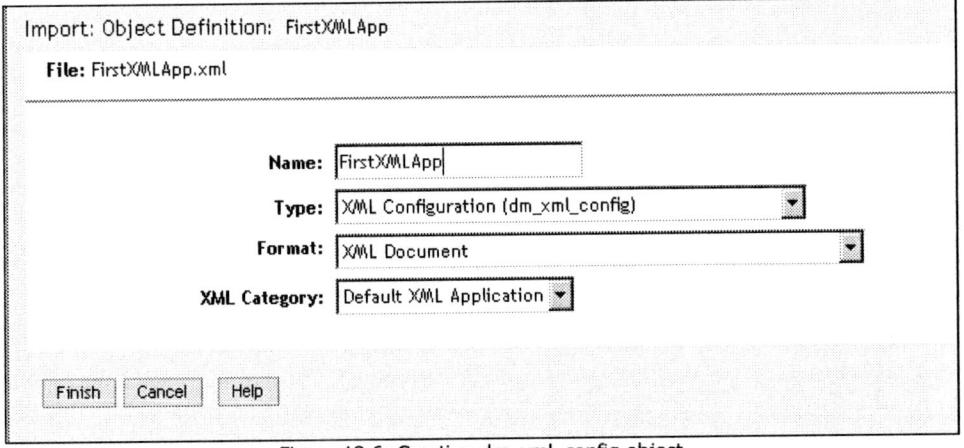

Figure 18.6: Creating dm_xml_config object

18.3 Testing our First XML Application

Let us now create some sample content in Web Publisher and see the XML Application working for us.

Create some new content as shown in figure 18.7 and click on Ok.

After you save the content in template and close the editor, check-in the content using File | Check In.

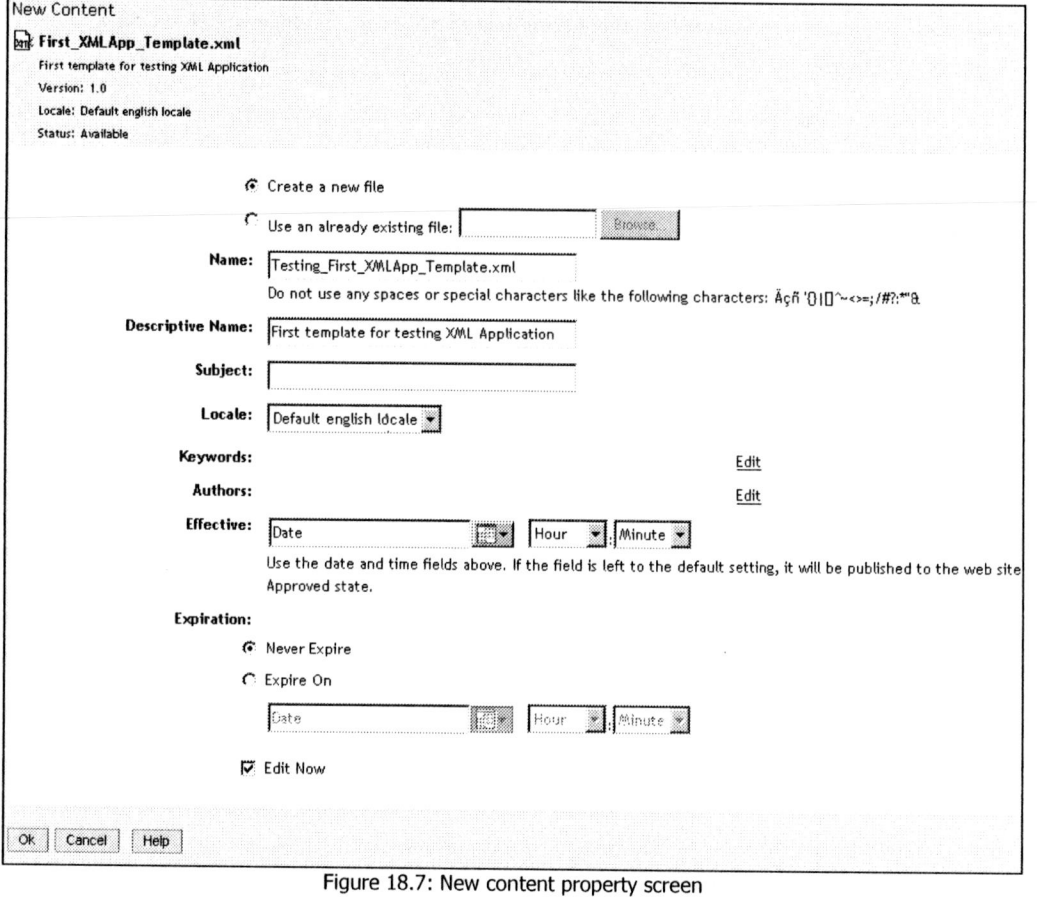

Figure 18.7: New content property screen

Fill out some dummy data (refer to figure 18.8) in the Page Title and Page subject fields in Web Publisher template editor.

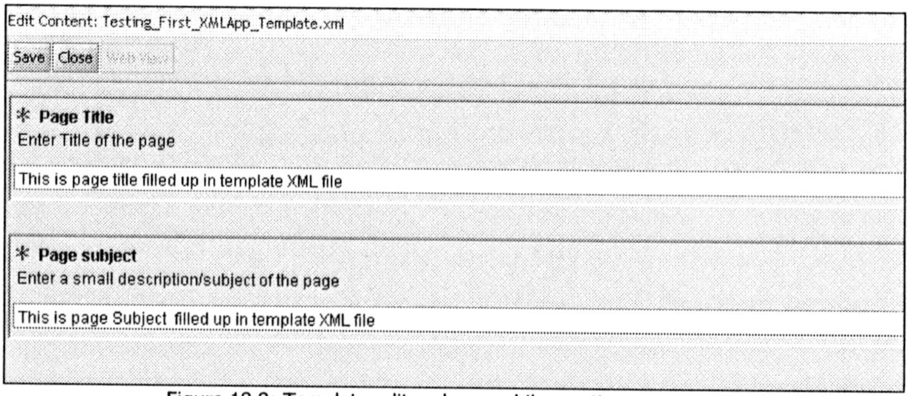

Figure 18.8: Template editor shown while creating new content

You can clearly see (refer to figure 18.9) that the Title and Subject fields have been automatically populated with the values that the user had saved in the Page Title and Page subject fields in the template.

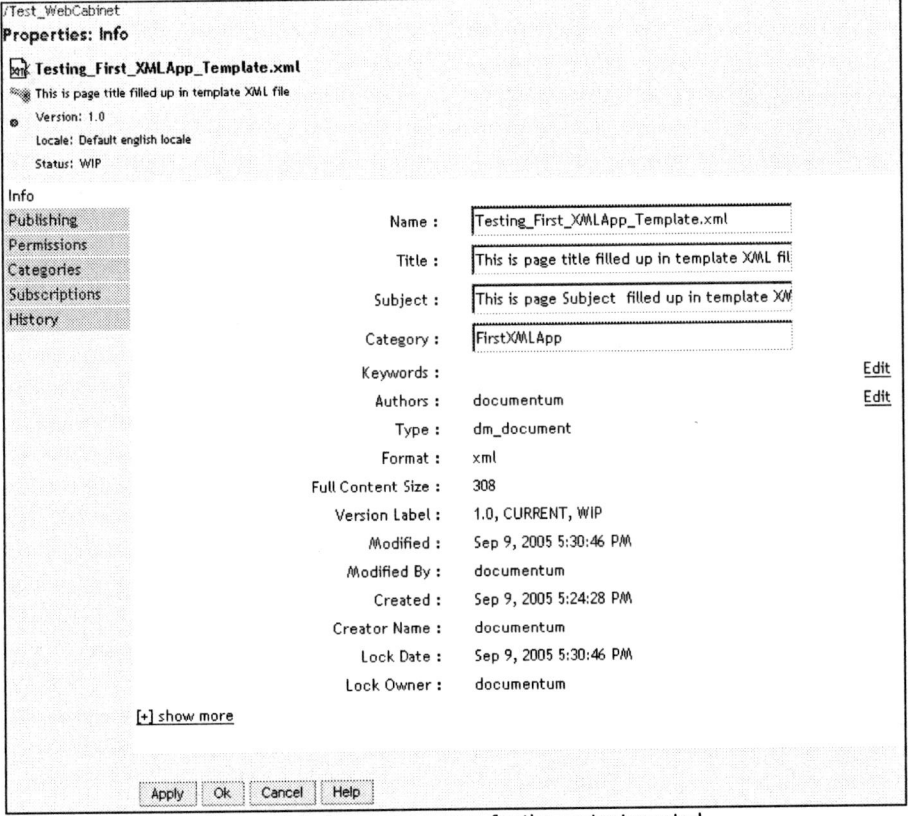

Figure 18.9: Properties screen for the content created

Please note that using Web Publisher template editor's content widget to populate values in object properties throws problems. Say for example, you wish to capture formatted data from a content template field and populate it in an object property. Instead of using content widget in such cases, use a textline widget.

You could enter formatted data within the textline field as follows: `<b>some data</b>`.

This is saved in the attribute through our XML Application. Now that you have seen a very simple working model of an XML Application, let us explore XML Applications further by taking up some complex examples.

18.4 Populating Repeating Attributes using Automatic Property Extraction

Let us create a template file that allows content creators to enter names of multiple books as well as the names of their authors in a repeating block.

We will develop a custom XML Application that will populate the authors multi-valued repeating property of a document with the names of authors entered in the Template file.

1. Create and import a template in Web Publisher (say Second_XMLApp_Template.xml) and attach it to dm_document object type with Default Lifecycle. The Template file Second_XMLApp_Template.xml follows:

```xml
<?xml version="1.0" encoding="UTF-8"?>
<BOOK>
  <REPEATBLOCK>
    <BOOKNAME/>
    <AUTHORNAME/>
  </REPEATBLOCK>
</BOOK>
```

Create a Rules file (say Second_XMLApp_TemplateRule.xml) for the above template and associate the Template file with this Rules file. The Rules file Second_XMLApp_TemplateRule.xml follows:

```xml
<?xml version="1.0" encoding="UTF-8"?>
<rules>
  <tagcontent tag_name="BOOKNAME">
    <textline charlength="100" instruction="Please provide the name of the
    book" label="Book Name">
    </textline>
  </tagcontent>

  <tagcontent tag_name="AUTHORNAME">
    <textline charlength="100" instruction="Please provide the name of the
    author" label="Author Name">
    </textline>
  </tagcontent>

  <repeatdef instruction="Provide as many values as you want"
  label="repeating block for books and authors" tag_list="REPEATBLOCK">
  </repeatdef>
</rules>
```

2. Create an XML configuration file secondXMLApp.xml and provide the name of the XML configuration file (without the .xml) in the Category field of the template Second_XMLApp_Template.xml. This sets the a_category attribute of the template.

The SecondXMLApp.xml file is shown below:

```
<?xml version="1.0" encoding="UTF-8"?>
<!DOCTYPE application  SYSTEM "config_5.2.dtd">
<application>
  <name>SecondXMLApp</name>
  <app_pattern>
    <element>BOOK</element>         <!-- Specifying the XML Root element
                                    BOOK-->
  </app_pattern>

  <map_rules>
    <xml_content_rule>
      <element_selection_pattern>
        <element>BOOK</element>
      </element_selection_pattern>

      <variables>               <!-- Defining variable to map values in object
                                attribute authors-->
        <variable>
          <name>authorName</name>        <!--Getting the value of AUTHORNAME
                                         template element -->
          <content_of_element>
            <element_selection_pattern>
              <element>AUTHORNAME</element>
            </element_selection_pattern>
          </content_of_element>
        </variable>
      </variables>
      <object_type>dm_document</object_type>        <!-- Specifying the object
                                                    type -->
      <metadata>
        <dctmattr_repeating>
          <name>authors</name>    <!-- Saving value in authors repeating
                                  attribute-->
          <template><var name="authorName"/></template>
        </dctmattr_repeating>

      </metadata>

      <make_entity/>
    </xml_content_rule>
  </map_rules>

</application>
```

<dctmattr_repeating>: Sets the value of a multi-valued (repeating) Documentum object property.

Here, we have set the value of the authors multi-valued property through the variable authorName.

The variable authorName captures the multiple values entered by content creators in the AUTHORNAME repeating element in the Template file.

3. Complete all the required steps for configuring this XML Application, exactly the same way that we did for our first XML Application.

18.5 Testing the Second XML Application

Let us again create sample content in Web Publisher using the second_XMLApp_Template.xml template and see the XML Application working for us.

Create some new content as shown in figure 18.10 and click on Ok.

After you save the content in the template and close the editor, check-in the content using File | Check In.

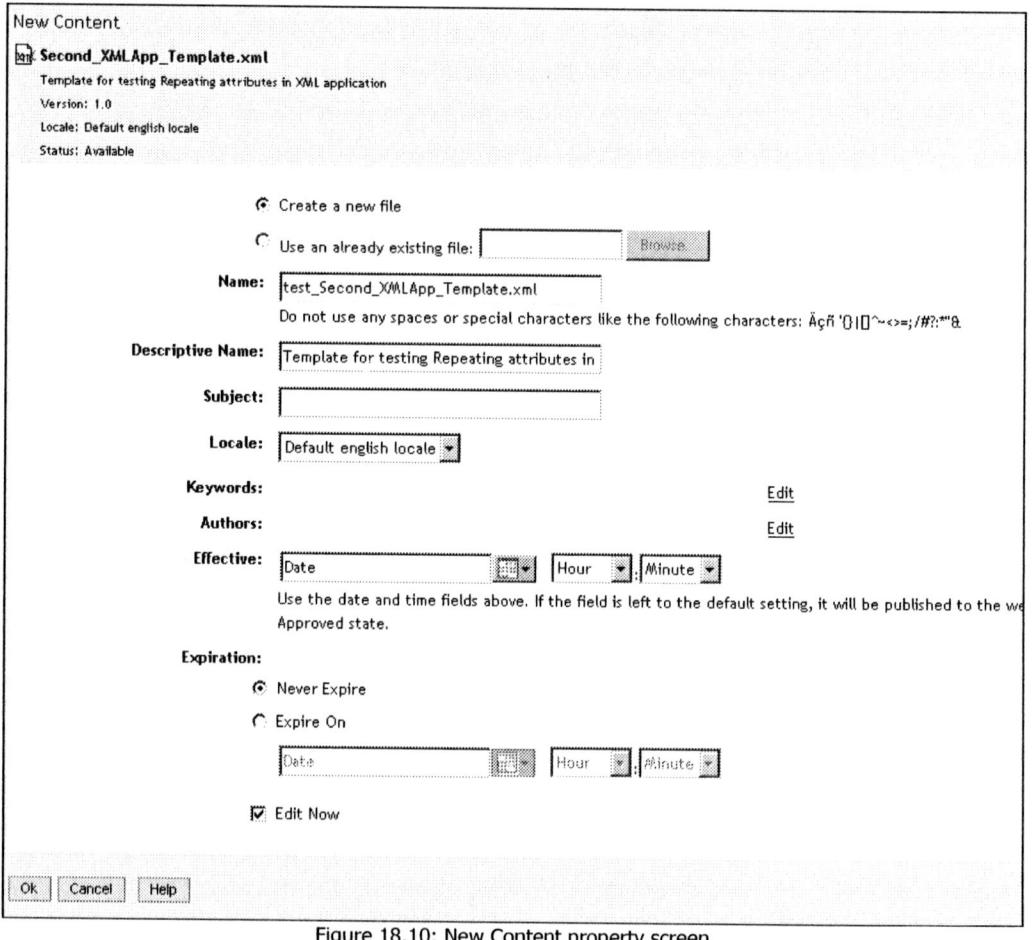

Figure 18.10: New Content property screen

We have filled out two entries (using Template repeating widget) for book name and author name, in Web Publisher template editor. The author names filled out in the template are Mr. Gary Harrow and Ms Jenny Hall, as shown in figure 18.11.

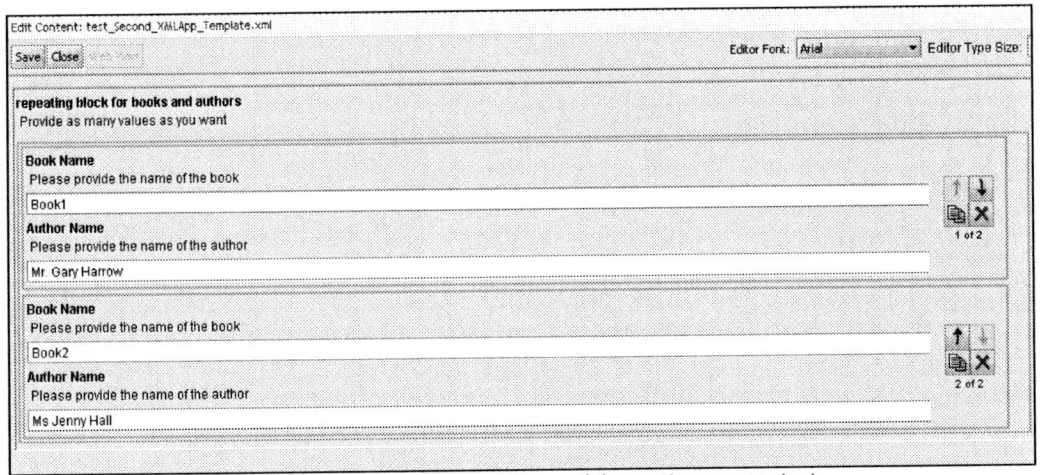

Figure 18.11: Template editor shown while creating new content

You can clearly see that the authors property has been automatically populated with the values that the user had saved in the Author Name fields in the template (refer to figure 18.12). Additionally, by default, Documentum fills out the name of the content creator user in the authors attribute for all content that is created. Since we had created this content as the documentum user, the authors attribute contains this value as well.

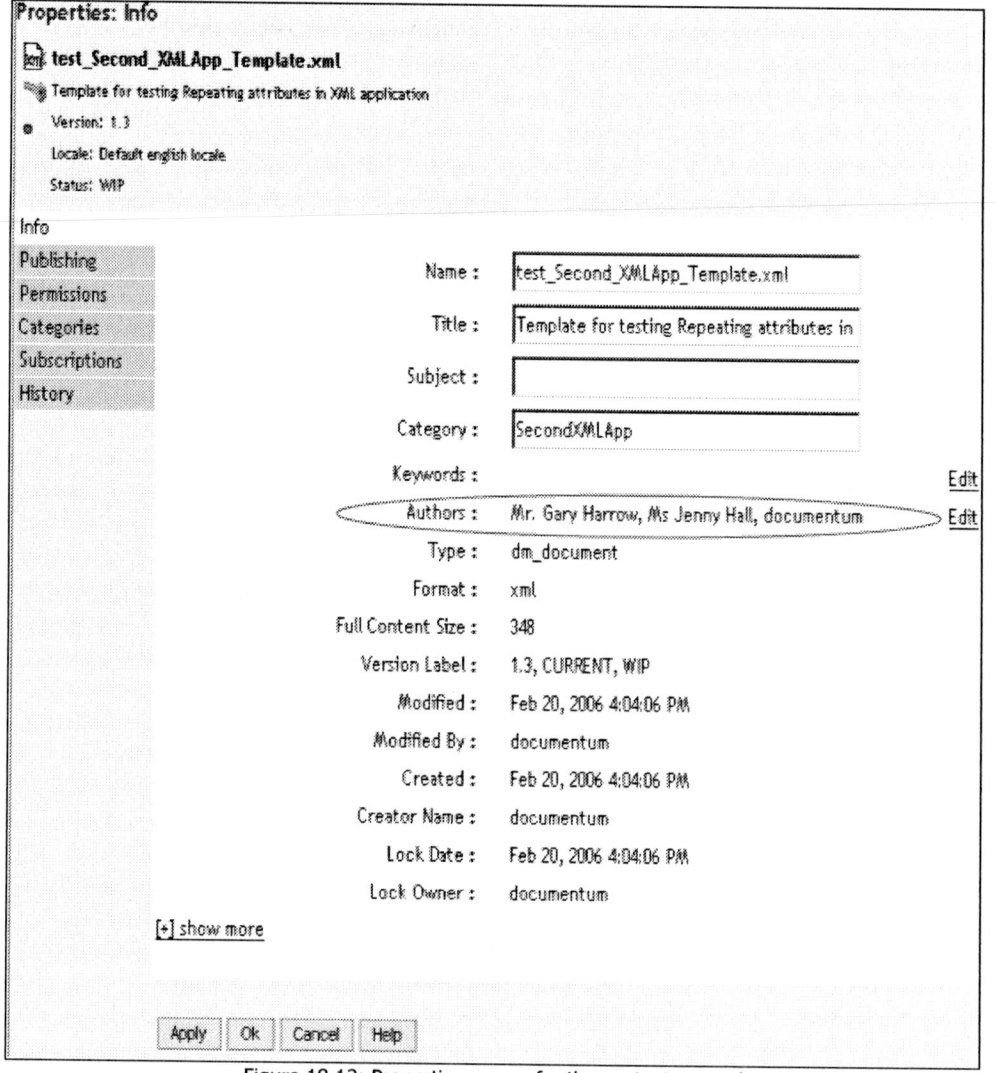

Figure 18.12: Properties screen for the content created

The examples that we have seen till now have one thing in common: The value entered by the content creator in the template field is populated automatically in the object property via the XML Application. What if we need to do it the other way round? A typical business requirement could be that the content creator enters a value in a particular property field (say subject) and the same should be automatically populated in a particular field in Template file.

Documentum provides this feature via the two_way_dctmattr element in XML configuration files, as we will now see.

18.6 Using Two-Way Attribute Extraction

Let us create a Template file that allows content creators to enter the subject property in the document's property screen. We will create a custom XML Application that will populate this value in the SUBJECT element of the Template file.

1. Create and import a template in Web Publisher (say Two_Way_Template.xml) and attach it to dm_document object type with Default Lifecycle. Following is the Template file Two_Way_Template.xml:

```
<?xml version="1.0" encoding="UTF-8"?>
<INFORMATION>
<SUBJECT/>
</INFORMATION>
```

2. Create a Rules file (say Two_Way_TemplateRule.xml) for the above template and associate the Template file with this Rules file. Following is the Rules file Two_Way_TemplateRule.xml:

```
<?xml version="1.0" encoding="UTF-8"?>
<rules>
  <tagcontent tag_name="SUBJECT">
    <textline charlength="150" instruction="Enter a subject here"
                                          label="Subject:">
    </textline>
  </tagcontent>
</rules>
```

3. Create an XML configuration file TwoWayXMLApp.xml and provide the name of the XML configuration file (without the .xml) in the Category field of the template TwoWayXMLApp.xml. This sets the a_category attribute of the template. The TwoWayXMLApp.xml file is shown below:

```
<?xml version="1.0" encoding="UTF-8"?>
<!DOCTYPE application  SYSTEM "config_5.2.dtd">
<application>
  <name>TwoWayXMLApp</name>
  <app_pattern>
    <element>INFORMATION</element>        <!-- Specifying the XML Root element
INFORMATION -->
  </app_pattern>

  <map_rules>
    <xml_content_rule>
      <element_selection_pattern>
        <element>INFORMATION</element>
      </element_selection_pattern>

      <variables>             <!-- Defining variable to map values in object
attribute subject -->
        <variable>
          <name>subjectValue</name>       <!--Getting the value of SUBJECT
template element -->
          <content_of_element>
            <element_selection_pattern>
              <element>SUBJECT</element>
            </element_selection_pattern>
          </content_of_element>
        </variable>
      </variables>
      <object_type>dm_document</object_type>     <!-- Specifying the object type
-->
      <metadata>
        <two_way_dctmattr>
          <name>subject</name>  <!-- Saving value in subject attribute-->
          <var name="subjectValue"/>
        </two_way_dctmattr>

      </metadata>

      <make_entity/>
    </xml_content_rule>
  </map_rules>

</application>
```

In this code, `<two_way_dctmattr>` sets the value of a single Documentum object property and the mapped Template XML file element.

Here we have mapped the value of the subject property through the variable `subjectValue` to the value entered by content creators in the SUBJECT element in the Template file.

In the case of repeating valued Documentum object properties, use the `<two_way_dctmattr_repeating>` element in your XML configuration file.

---

4. Complete all the required steps for configuring this XML Application, exactly the same way as we did for our earlier XML Applications.

18.7 Testing the Two-Way Attribute Extraction XML Application:

Let us create sample content in Web Publisher using the Two_Way_Template.xml template, in order to study how the two-way property extraction works in Documentum.

Create some new content as shown in figure 18.13 and click on Ok.

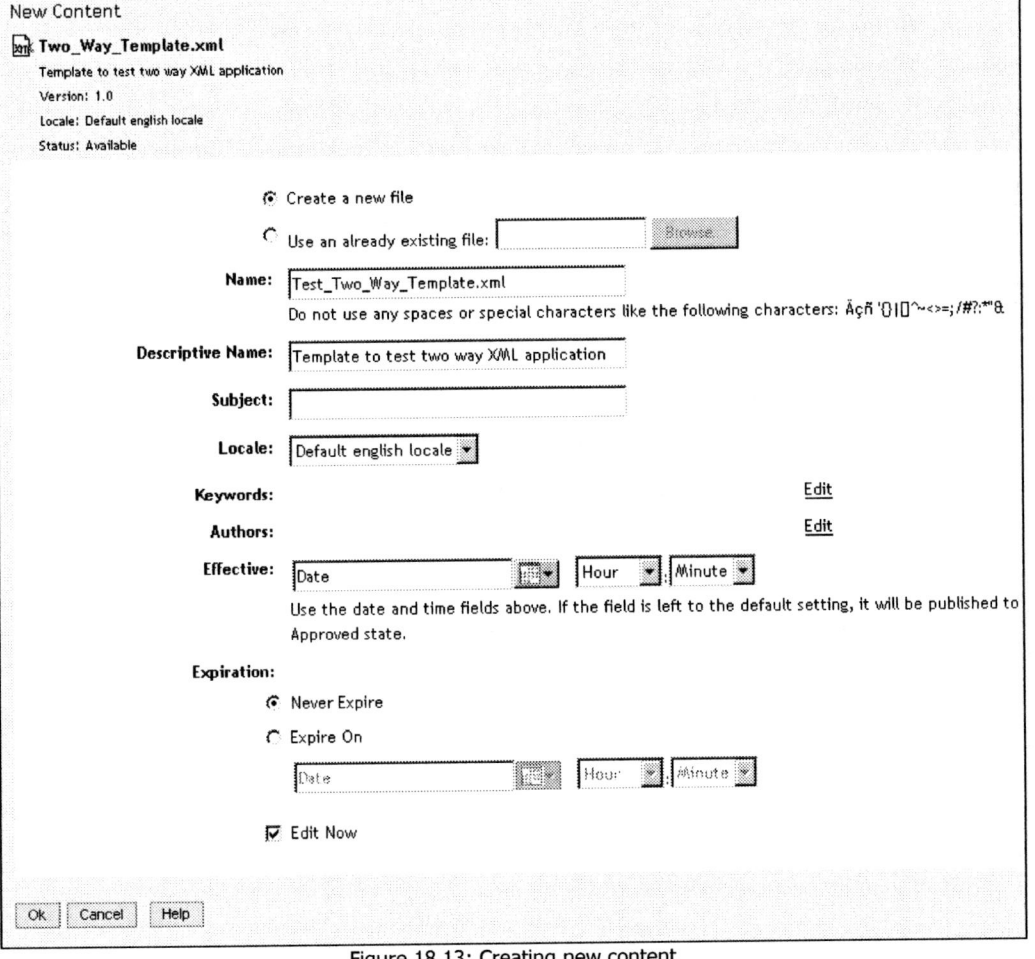

Figure 18.13: Creating new content

Enter some value in the Subject field shown in the template (refer to figure 18.14) and save the data.

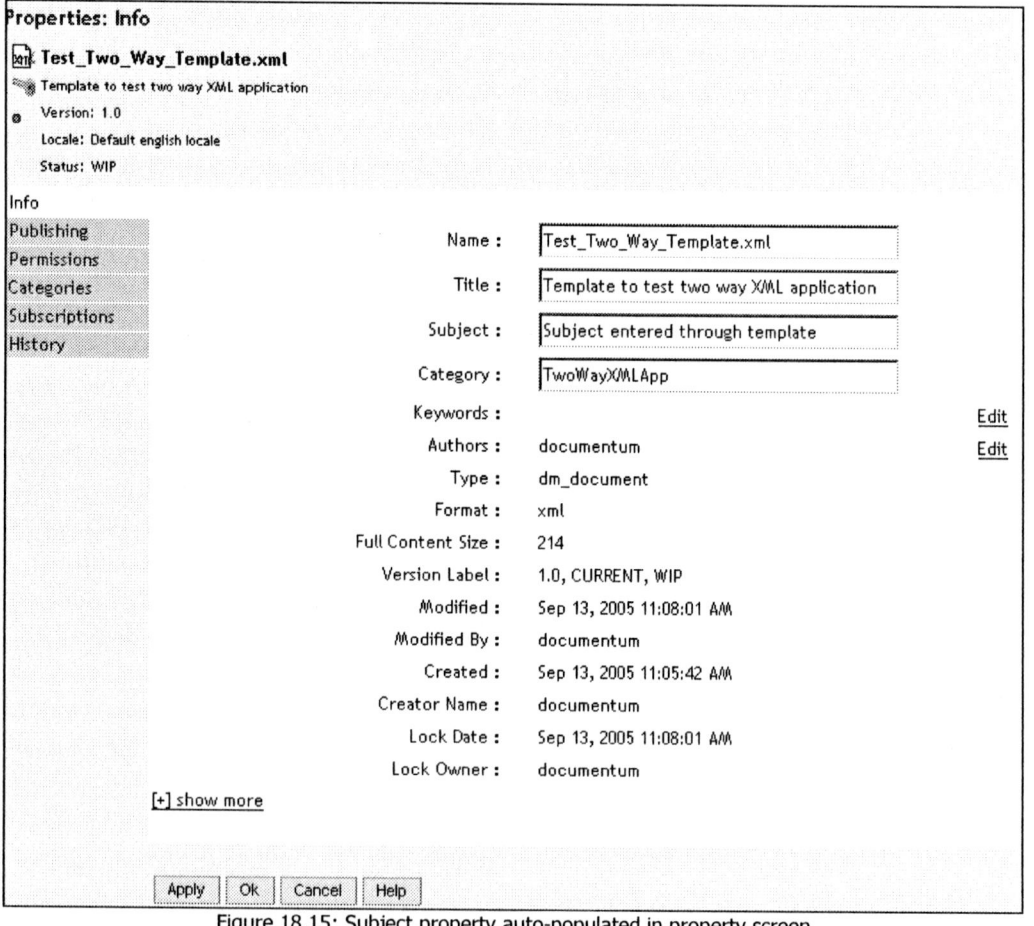

Figure 18.14: Value for Subject entered in the template

After closing the template, click on the info icon (i) against the newly created content. You can see that its Subject property is automatically populated with the value the user had filled out in the template, as shown in figure 18.15.

Figure 18.15: Subject property auto-populated in property screen

Enter a new value in the Subject property (refer to figure 18.16) and click on Ok. Open the Template file for the content again.

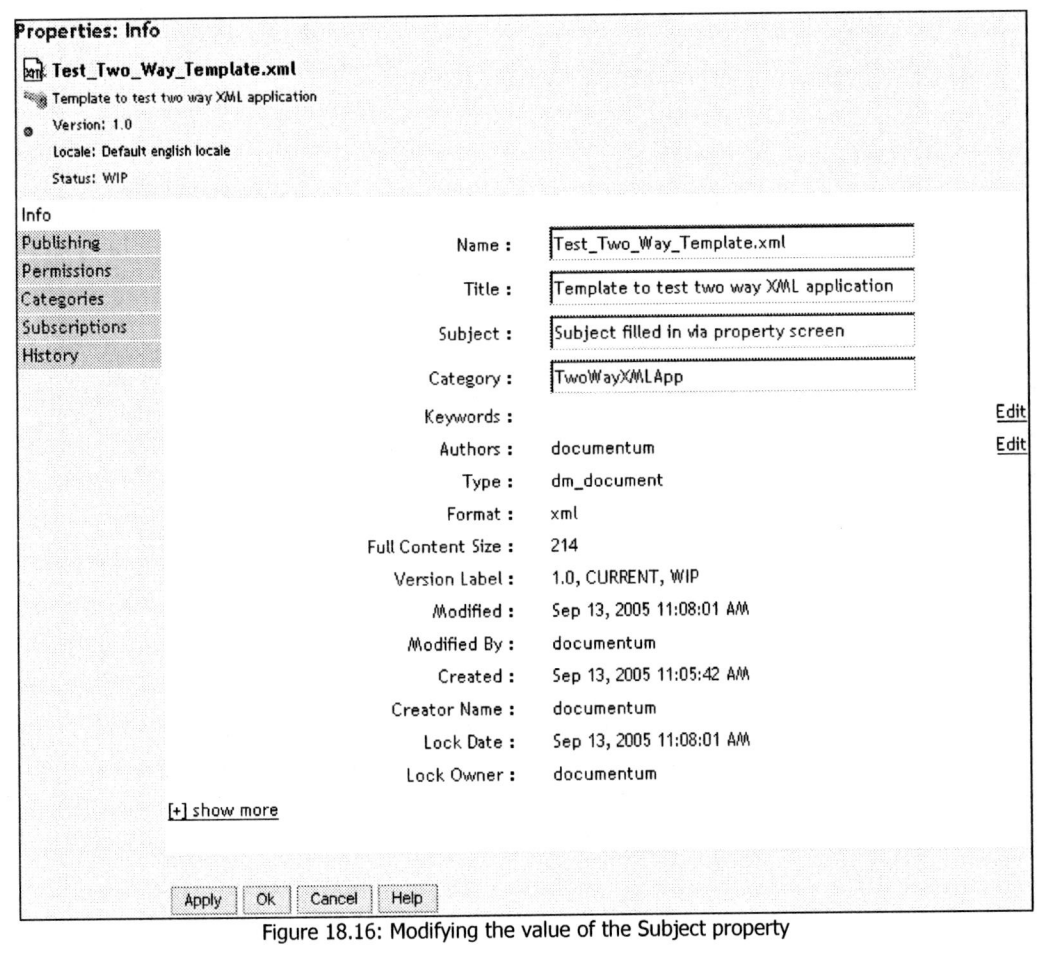

Figure 18.16: Modifying the value of the Subject property

You can verify that the value for the subject property that you provided in the property screen has automatically populated the Subject: field in the template as shown in figure 18.17.

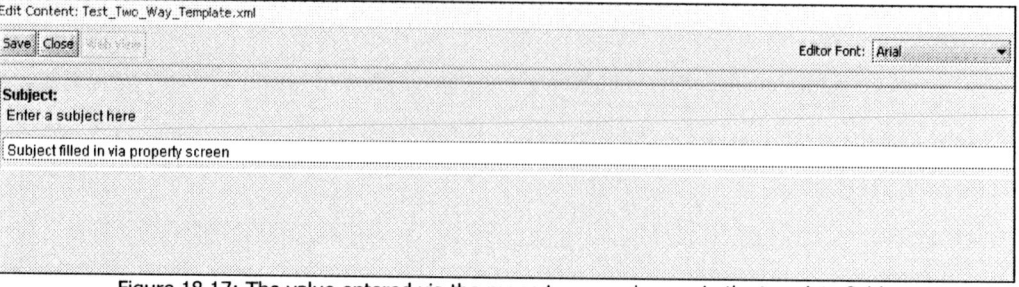

Figure 18.17: The value entered via the property screen is seen in the template field.

There is much more to Automatic Property Extraction than what we have just learned in this chapter. However, to begin with, this chapter will have definitely helped you gauge the rich arena of features available in XML Applications. If need be, read more about XML Applications in the Documentum manuals to get an extensive understanding.

18.8 Summary

Automatic Property Extraction (APE) is a functionality that allows you to automatically assign the value of a specified template XML element to a specified document attribute and vice versa.

During our tour in this chapter, we saw that APE works only with the following Web Publisher widgets: Textline, checkbox, and choice.

We further saw how Documentum uses dm_xml_application and dm_xml_config objects to manage APE.

We then studied a simple example to create an XML application in Documentum and tested it for sample content created in Web Publisher. We also looked at examples using APE to populate repeating attributes and for two-way attribute extraction.

19

Working with Workflows

We have already created a custom lifecycle and associated it with our custom News Article object type in Chapters 11 and 12. This means that content created from the News Article object type (and template) can be routed through the different states of the lifecycle, such as WIP, Staging, and Approved. Have you ever thought about how content automatically progresses through the different lifecycle states? You can certainly select content items and manually promote, demote or power-promote them to move them across various linear lifecycle states. However, in an actual scenario your business users would want an automated process to achieve this. What the business teams typically want is a controlled and automated mechanism whereby content created by a group of users can be sent across electronically to a reviewer group for an initial round of review. The number of sequential/parallel groups of reviewers or approvers could be specific to a particular business. Once the content is finally reviewed and approved, it should be made available on the live website and should be in the terminal lifecycle state (say Approved/Active). At any point of time during the review and approval process, the content should be in the intermediate lifecycle states such as WIP or Staging.

This automated business process required to route content through its numerous lifecycle stages before publishing it to the production website is termed **workflow** in Documentum lingo.

A workflow goes hand in hand with a lifecycle and defines business policies for teams by having the content creators and reviewers adhere to the norms laid down by the organization.

Note that while a lifecycle simply defines the different stages in the life of a content item, a workflow actually defines how content moves through these different stages, who makes it move under various activities, what actions are performed by individual groups and users during the different activities, etc.

In Documentum, a workflow template is used to create various workflow instances (dm_workflow) for routing content in lifecycle stages and exists in the Docbase as a dm_process object. The Documentum Workflow Manager tool used to create and manage workflow templates is available once you install/configure Documentum Application Builder. (Please refer to Chapter 8 for further details.)

You could create a custom workflow as per your specific business needs or use one of the following workflows available out-of-the-box in Web Publisher:

- French Translation Workflow
- Request new content
- Submit to website
- Translate and submit to website

Launch Documentum Application Builder and open the WebPublisher DocApp under /System/ Applications/WebPublisher to view the default Web Publisher workflows as shown in figure 19.1.

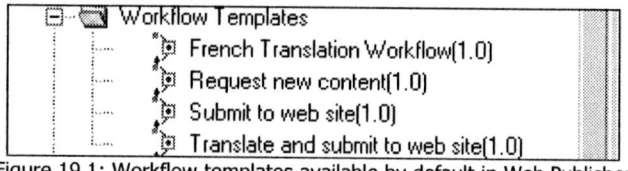

Figure 19.1: Workflow templates available by default in Web Publisher

Double-clicking on the above workflow templates launches the Workflow Manager tool and displays the workflow process definition in the form of a GUI layout.

19.1 Designing Custom Workflows

It is essential to design your workflows well before jumping off to creating them. Understand the need for workflows from your business (end) users. Understand how many levels of review they need and what actions need to be formed on content by which groups/users before publishing the content to a running website.

We will take a simple example in this chapter and create a workflow with the activities/tasks mentioned below. (Make sure that you customize/extend this sample workflow as per your business requirements by removing/altering existing activities or adding some more activities if need be.)

1. Content created by content authors will be submitted to the workflow.
2. The system automatically promotes the content to the Staging lifecycle state at this point.
3. Content (in the form of workflow tasks) reaches the Inboxes of all content manager group users for a round of review.
4. The first content manager user to acquire the workflow task gets to review it.
5. The content manager can review the content and, if it is fine, can submit it.
6. The system automatically promotes the content to the Approved lifecycle state, marking it finally approved and ready to be turned Active based on the specified effective date for the content.

7. If the content manager reviews the content and does not find it satisfactory, he/she can reject it back to the content author group, asking for specific corrections.

8. The system automatically demotes the content to the WIP lifecycle state at this point.

9. Content (in the form of workflow tasks) reaches the Inboxes of all content author group users for correction purposes.

10. The first content author user to acquire the workflow task gets to work on it.

11. The content author can edit and modify the content and submit it again to the content manager group users for review purposes.

12. The system automatically promotes the content to the Staging lifecycle state at this point.

13. The sequence of activities from point 3 is then repeated.

Figure 19.2 depicts the workflow steps mentioned above.

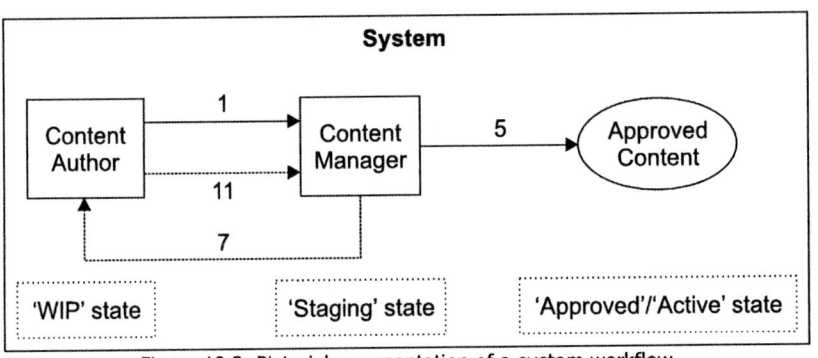

Figure 19.2: Pictorial representation of a custom workflow

19.2 Setting Up a Custom Workflow Template

We will now create the above custom workflow template using the Documentum Workflow Manager tool.

Follow the steps mentioned below to create, save, validate, and install your custom workflow template:

1. Launch Workflow Manager and log in to Docbase as an administrator. Once you have been authenticated, the blank workflow template editor screen is shown to you, as in figure 19.3.

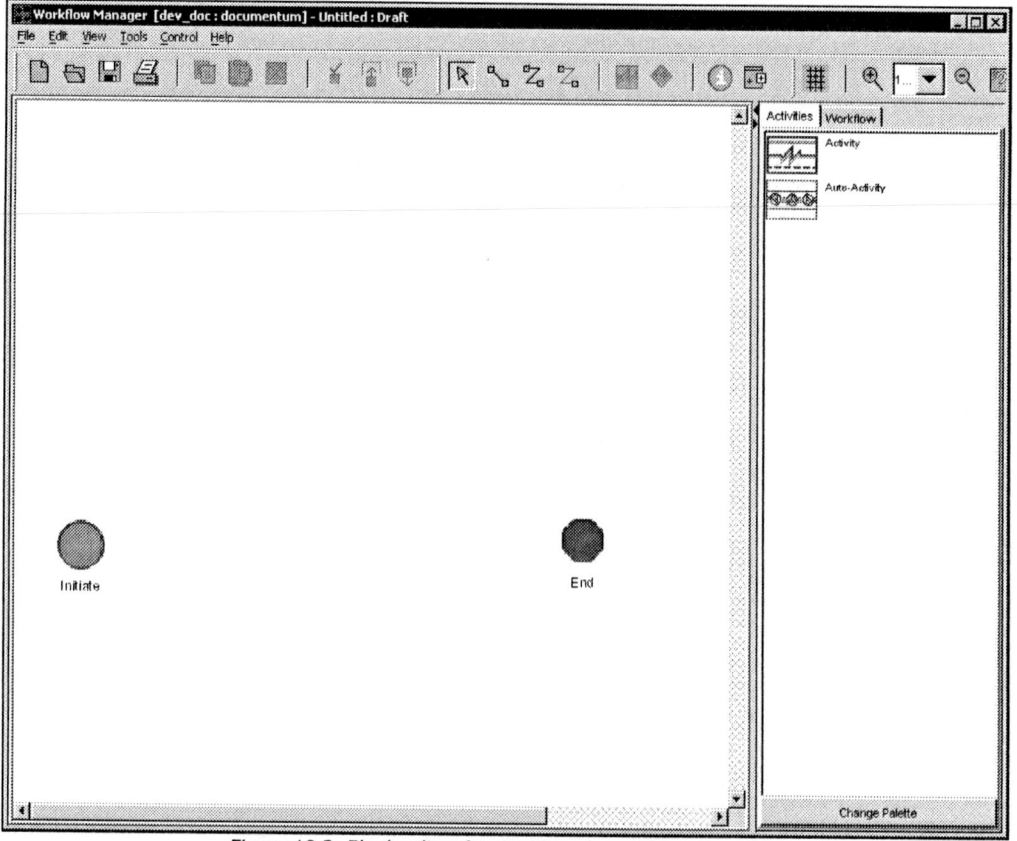

Figure 19.3: Blank editor for creation of a workflow template

Note that the start (Initiate) and End activities are already available in any workflow template that you create using this tool. The system prevents you from removing these two activities from the workflow.

2. A workflow template is created by combining numerous **Activities** (which translate into workflow tasks at run time) and connecting them by **flows**. You then add **packages** to the flows to route the content via workflows. Do not be worried about these terminologies right now. We will cover them in detail as we continue creating the workflow in this chapter.

The Activities tab in the right-hand panel shows two kinds of activities (refer to figure 19.4):

- **Activity**: Performed manually by group(s) or individual user(s)
- **Auto-Activity**: Automatically performed by the system and does not require manual intervention

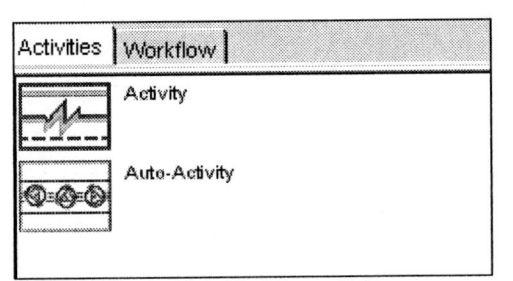

Figure 19.4: Workflow activities

You simply need to drag and drop the activities (manual or automatic) from the Activities palette onto the workflow template creation screen. Include these custom activities between the Initiate and End activities. Now you need to connect these activities with flows.

There are different kinds of flows:

- **Single segment flows**: Shown next to the arrow icon in figure 19.5. Used for connecting two activities with a single straight line in a forward flow.
- **Multi-segment flows**: Connects two activities with a line consisting of multiple segments in a forward flow.
- **Reject flows**: Connects two activities in a backward flow (used when a group/user rejects workflow tasks).

The arrow sign is used to select an object in the workflow template editor pane.

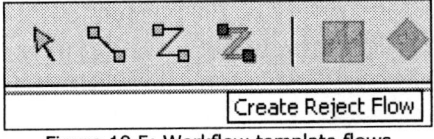

Figure 19.5: Workflow template flows

Double-clicking the activity opens up an Activity Inspector window allowing you to provide configuration details for it. Double-clicking on the connecting flow opens up a Flow Inspector allowing you to add packages to the flow and define other details such as package types and versions.

Figure 19.6 is the final visual representation of our custom workflow as it will be created in the workflow template editor:

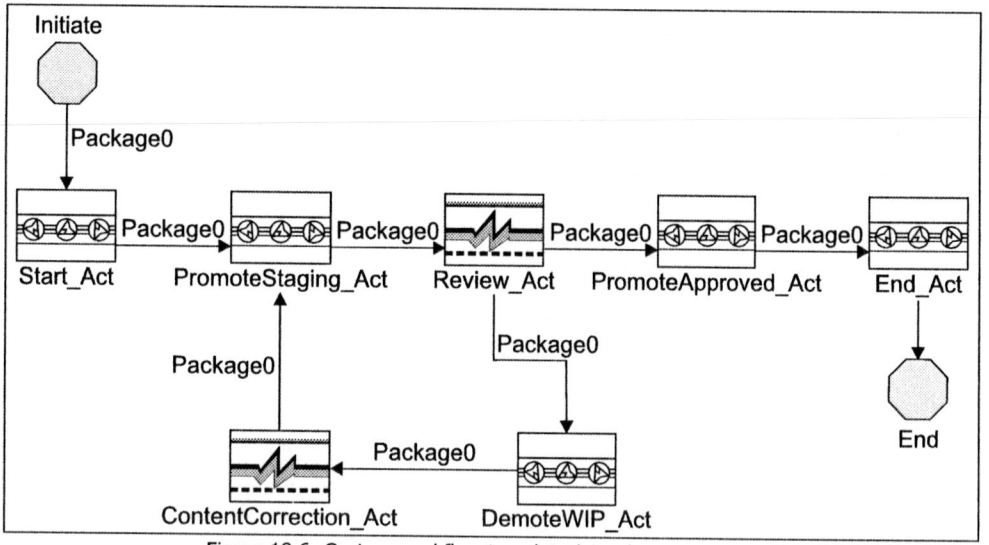

Figure 19.6: Custom workflow template (visual representation)

Note that some activities such as Review_Act and ContentCorrection_Act are manual while others such as Start_Act, PromoteStaging_Act, PromoteApproved_Act, DemoteWIP_Act, and End_Act are automatic. The activities have been connected by flows and are routing content in a package by the name Package0 as shown in figure 19.6.

We will be creating this custom workflow template through the series of steps mentioned subsequently and will define individual activities as you continue reading.

3. Choose menu option File | Template Properties to define some basic information about the custom workflow template in question. Using the workflow template properties screen (refer to figure 19.7), you could specify:

   o Workflow template owner: By default you are the owner of the workflow templates that you create. If you are a superuser, you can change the owner of a workflow template.

   o Description: You could specify a brief description of the workflow template.

   o Default alias set: You could optionally specify an alias set for the workflow template in question.

   o Workflow template instructions: You could provide instructions to activity performers regarding the tasks they are entitled to perform.

   o Template Audit Trail Setting: You could turn on or off the audit trail for workflow instances created from the workflow template.

o   Always show validate and install prompts after save: Choose this checkbox if you want the system to automatically ask you to validate and then install the workflow template whenever you make changes to it and save it.

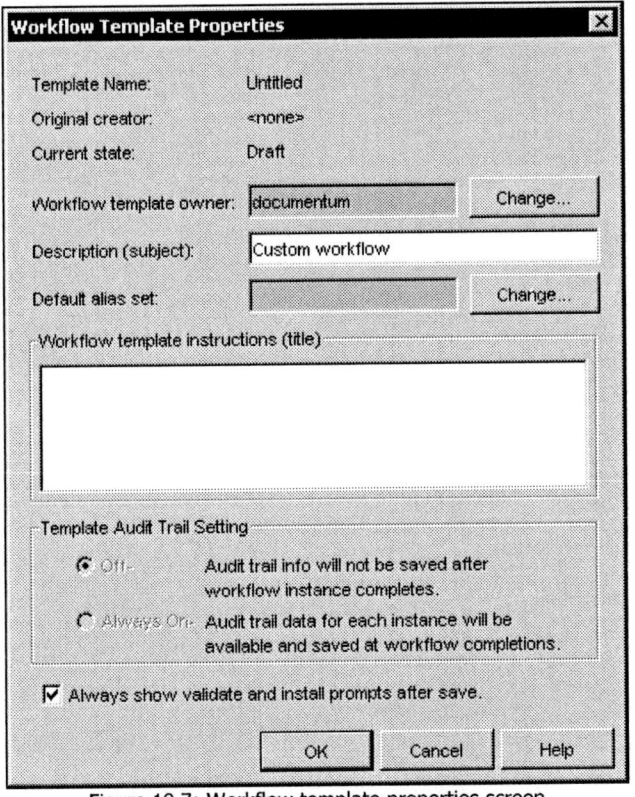

Figure 19.7: Workflow template properties screen

4.   After you have created the workflow template by defining all its activities and flows, choose the menu option File | Save (refer to figure 19.8) to save the workflow template at some convenient location in the Docbase.

Provide a unique name for the workflow template (say Custom_Workflow) and browse through/select the Docbase cabinet path to save it. We have saved it at the following Docbase location: /System/Applications/TestDocApp/Custom_Workflow.

Note that TestDocApp is the name of our custom DocApp in the Docbase.

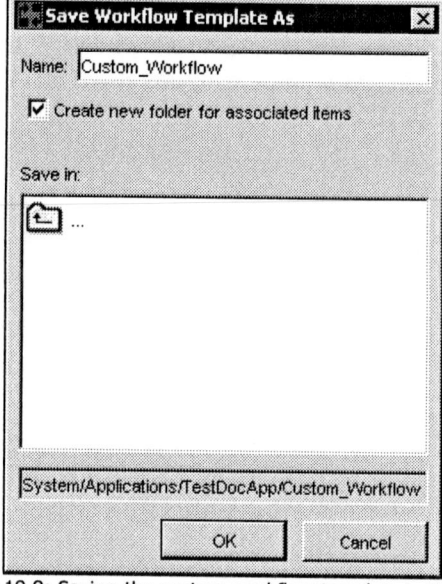

Figure 19.8: Saving the custom workflow template in Docbase

Refer to figure 19.9; after saving the workflow template, the system will prompt you to validate the template and then install it once all validation tests are complete.

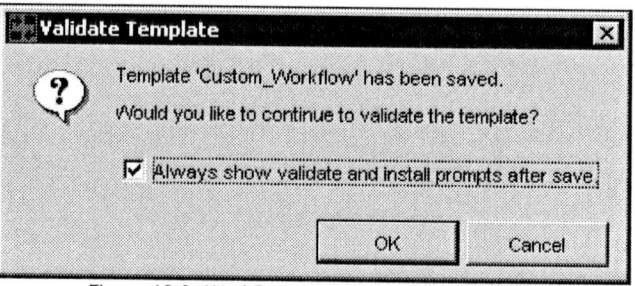

Figure 19.9: Workflow template system validation

Note that it is important to install a workflow template if you want it to be used by Docbase users. An uninstalled workflow can not be used for routing content by users in the different lifecycle states.

5. An installed workflow template further needs to be made Available in Web Publisher so that Web Publisher users can use it to create workflow instances.

    Log in to Web Publisher as an administrator user and go to the section Administration | Web Publisher Admin | Workflow Templates.

    The newly created custom workflow template (Custom_Workflow) in the installed state is shown as not available in Web Publisher (refer to figure 19.10).

Choose the checkbox against the custom workflow template and click on **Make Available** in the tool bar as shown in figure 19.10. This makes the custom workflow template available for use within Web Publisher.

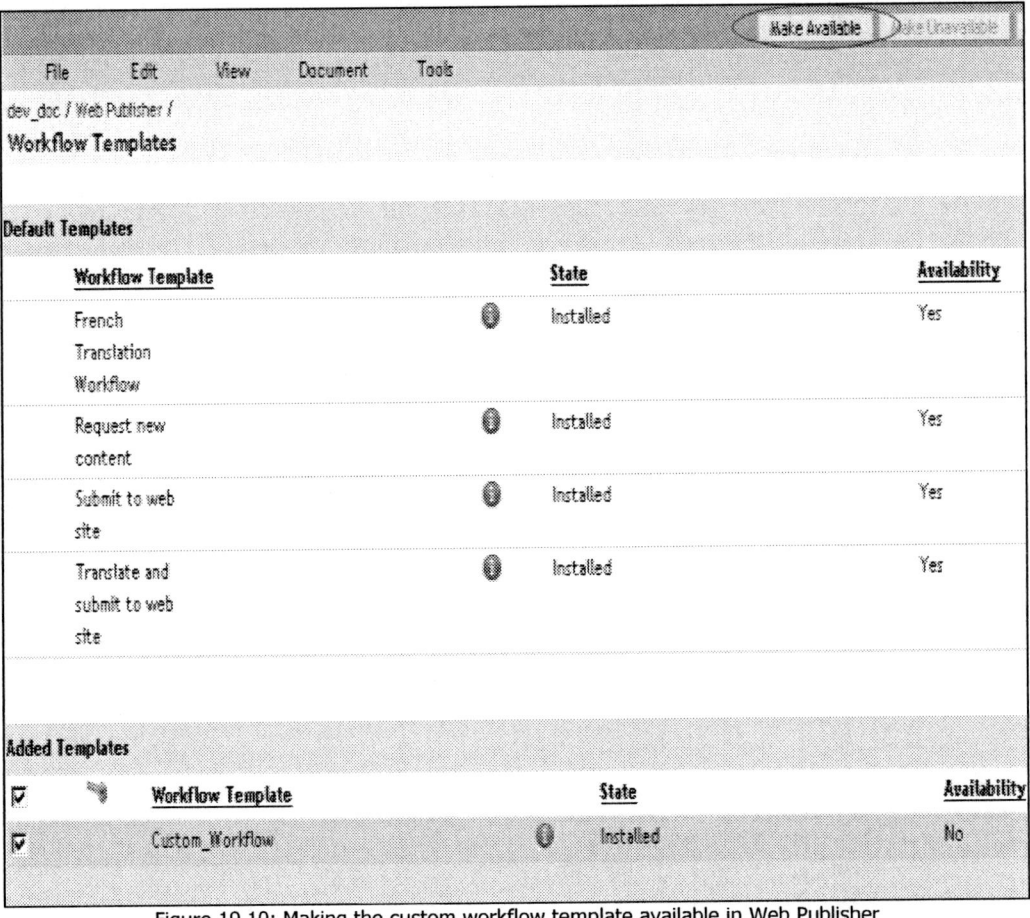

Figure 19.10: Making the custom workflow template available in Web Publisher

6. You need to further set an appropriate Permission Set template (ACL) for the newly created workflow template. The system assigned ACL for the custom workflow template might prevent certain users from submitting content to workflow instances created from this template due to inappropriate permissions. Choose the checkbox against the custom workflow template and select **View | Properties | Permissions**.

Click on the **Select** link shown against the **Active permissions set** field and choose the correct Permission Set to be associated with the workflow template.

We have selected WebPublisher User Default ACL as the permission set for our template, as shown in figure 19.11.

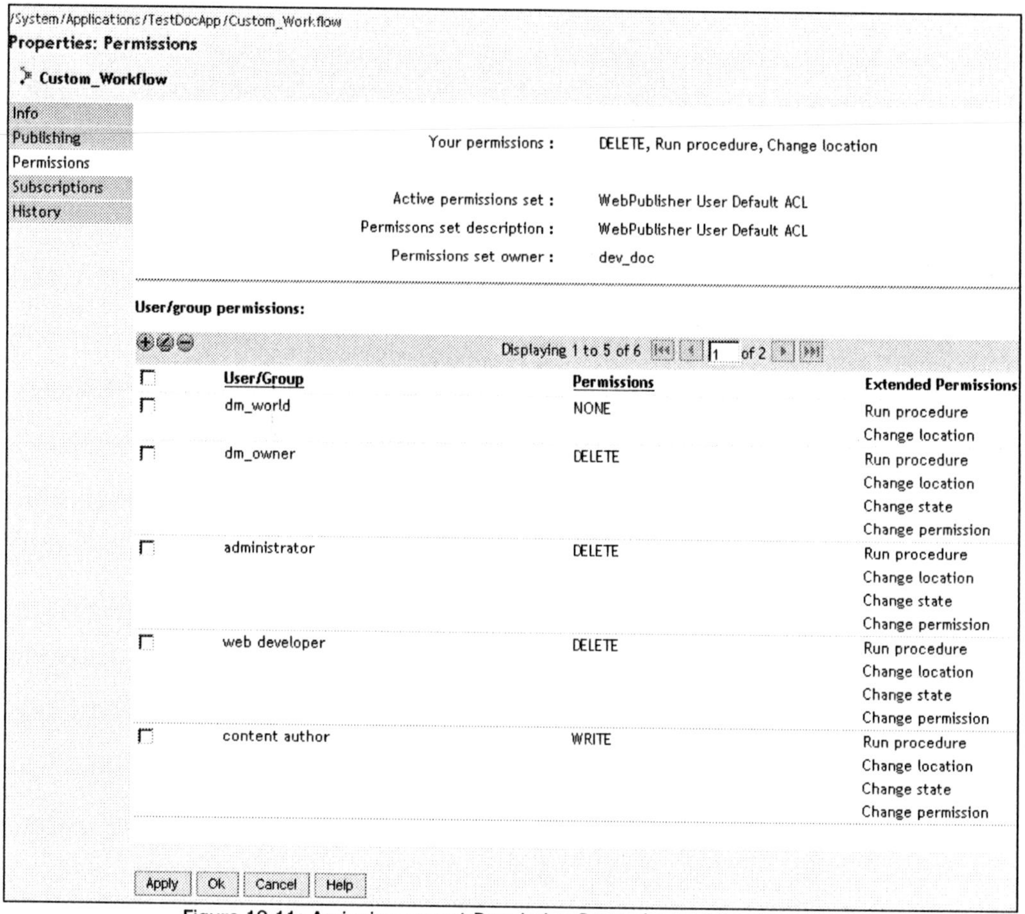

/System/Applications/TestDocApp/Custom_Workflow

Properties: Permissions

⌘ **Custom_Workflow**

Info
Publishing
Permissions
Subscriptions
History

Your permissions : DELETE, Run procedure, Change location

Active permissions set : WebPublisher User Default ACL
Permissons set description : WebPublisher User Default ACL
Permissions set owner : dev_doc

User/group permissions:

Displaying 1 to 5 of 6 ⏮ ◀ 1 of 2 ▶ ⏭

	User/Group	Permissions	Extended Permissions
	dm_world	NONE	Run procedure Change location
	dm_owner	DELETE	Run procedure Change location Change state Change permission
	administrator	DELETE	Run procedure Change location Change state Change permission
	web developer	DELETE	Run procedure Change location Change state Change permission
	content author	WRITE	Run procedure Change location Change state Change permission

Apply   Ok   Cancel   Help

Figure 19.11: Assigning correct Permission Set to the workflow template

Click on Apply and then Ok. Your custom workflow can now be used by Web Publisher users.

19.3 Creating a Custom Workflow Template

Please refer to figure 19.6 and drag-drop the activities from the Activity palette in the workflow template editor. Join the activities with flow arrows as shown in the figure. Note that you need to connect Review_Act and DemoteWIP_Act activities with a reject arrow (and not a multi-segment flow) as shown in the figure. After connecting all activities with flows, double-click on the flows and add a package (default name: Package0) of the type dm_sysobject to all the flows for routing content of the object type dm_sysobject and its subtypes.

1. Let us take an example of creating/configuring the activity definition for the first activity in the workflow template, start_Act.

   The remaining activities can be created in the same manner as we see in this example.

   Drag an Auto-Activity from the activity palette and drop it after the Initiate (the first activity) activity in the workflow template editor.

2. Double-click on the newly added auto-activity to open up the Activity Inspector screen (refer to figure 19.12) for the activity.

   Provide a meaningful name for the activity (say: Start_Act) in the text box shown at the top of the Activity Inspector screen. Each activity requires certain configuration settings that need to be done via the various tabs shown on the Activity Inspector screen.

   The Perfomer tab allows you to select the performers of the activity and the actions that the performers can execute.

   Start_Act in our case is performed automatically by the system when the workflow is started and does not require any manual intervention.

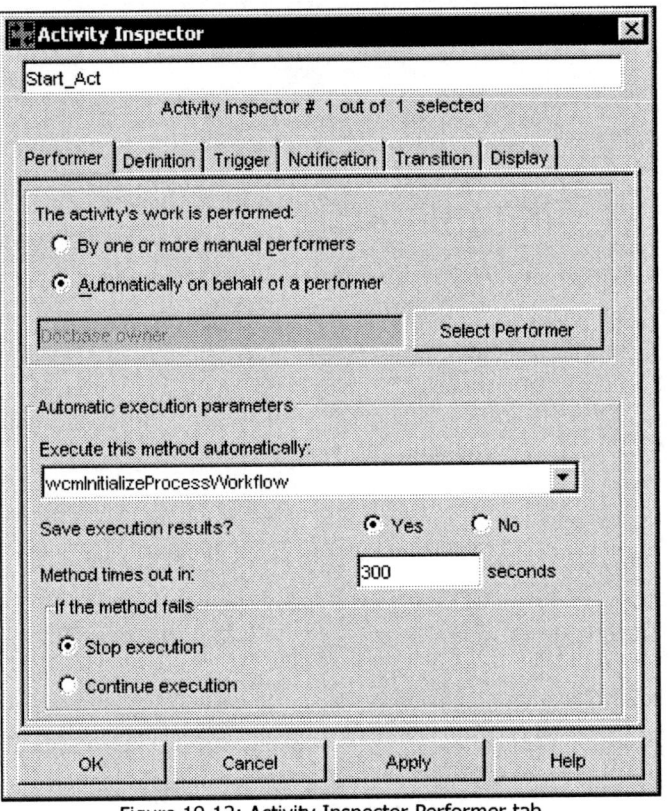

Figure 19.12: Activity Inspector Performer tab

Click on the Select Performer button and choose to perform the activity with the rights of a Docbase owner. You could optionally run this activity as one of the following as well (refer to figure 19.13):

- ○ Workflow supervisor, the default creator of the workflow
- ○ Performer of the previous activity
- ○ Some specific designated user

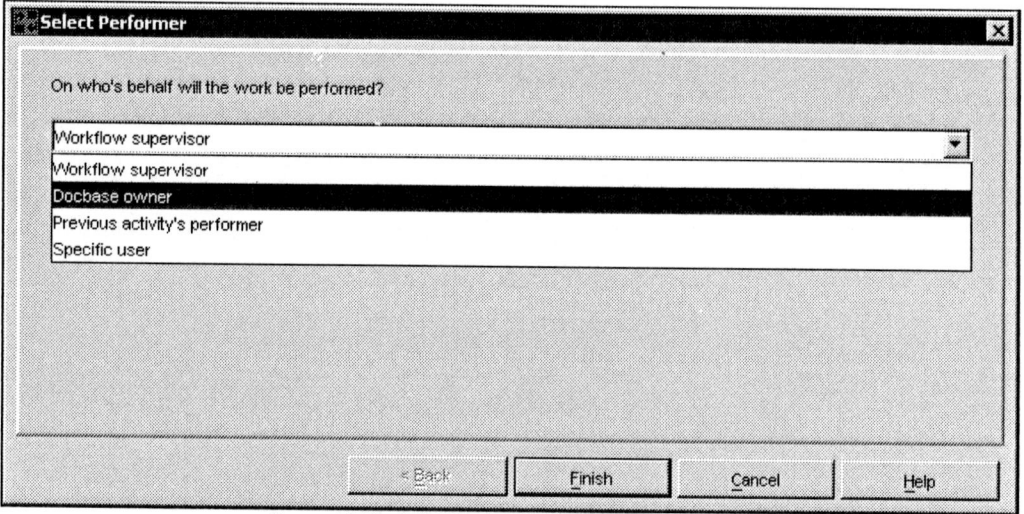

Figure 19.13: Selecting performers in an auto-activity

Select the system method (wcmInitializeProcessWorkflow) to be executed in this activity from the dropdown of existing workflow methods.

It is worthwhile to mention that wcmInitializeProcessWorkflow is a Web Publisher workflow method that must necessarily be called in the start activity of all workflows. This prevents a content file routed in a particular workflow instance from being sent to another workflow instance till the first one has been completed.

> Similarly, there needs to be a clean-up activity in the end to call the Web Publisher wcmTerminateProcessWorkflow method for removing the restrictions imposed by the wcmInitializeProcessWorkflow method.

Choose the appropriate radio button if you need to save the results of method execution in the Docbase.

By default the method execution time-out is 60 seconds for all activities. You could change it to 300 seconds, giving the system additional time to execute the method.

In case the method fails due to some reason, you could prevent the execution of further workflow steps by choosing the radio button Stop execution.

Note that for a manual activity such as Review_Act, which requires a single user from the content manager group to work on the task, the following settings need to be done under the Performer tab:

- ○ Choose the radio button By one or more manual performers and click on the Select Performer button.
- ○ Select the option Single user from group from the dropdown values shown for the performer, as seen in figure 19.14.

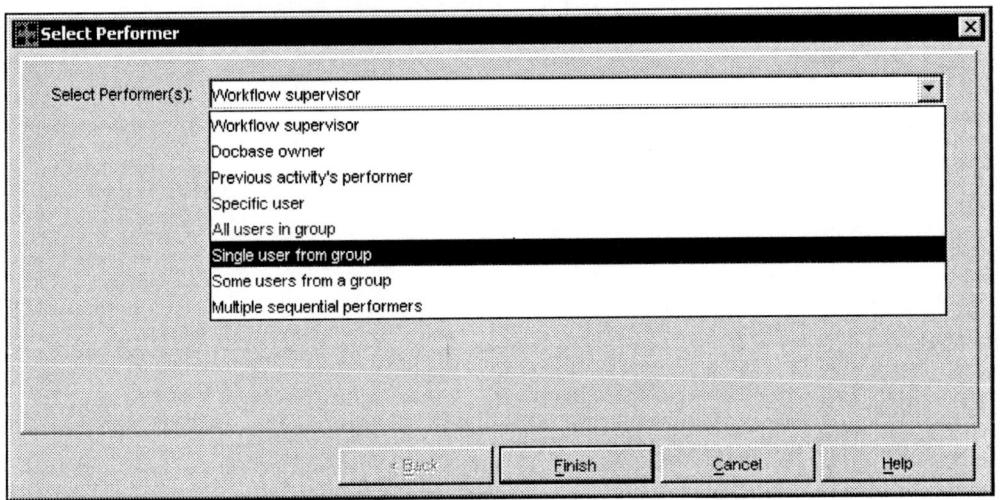

Figure 19.14: Selecting performers for a manual activity

Refer to figure 19.15; choose the radio button against Assign performer(s) now under the Define Performer(s) section and click on Next.

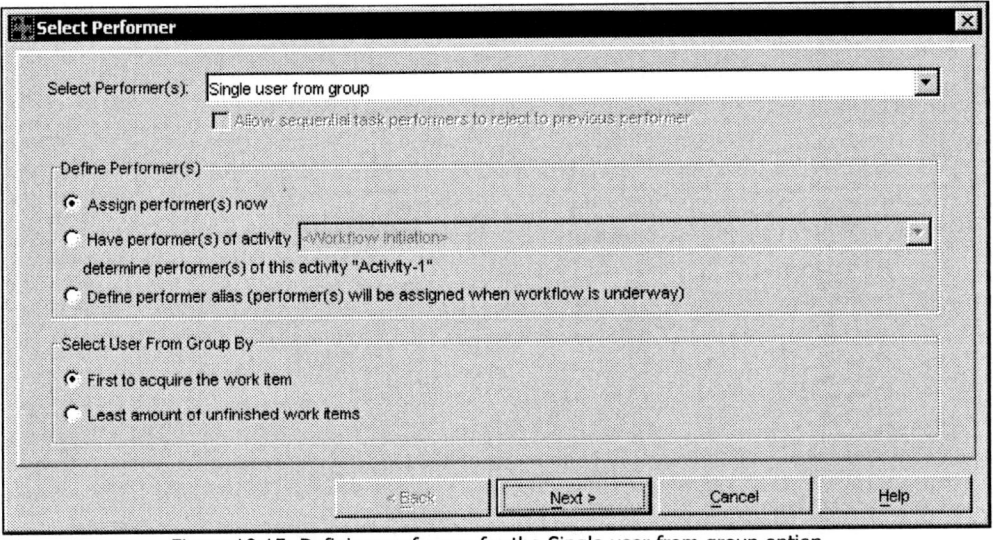

Figure 19.15: Defining performer for the Single user from group option

Choose content manager from the list of Docbase groups shown in figure 19.16.

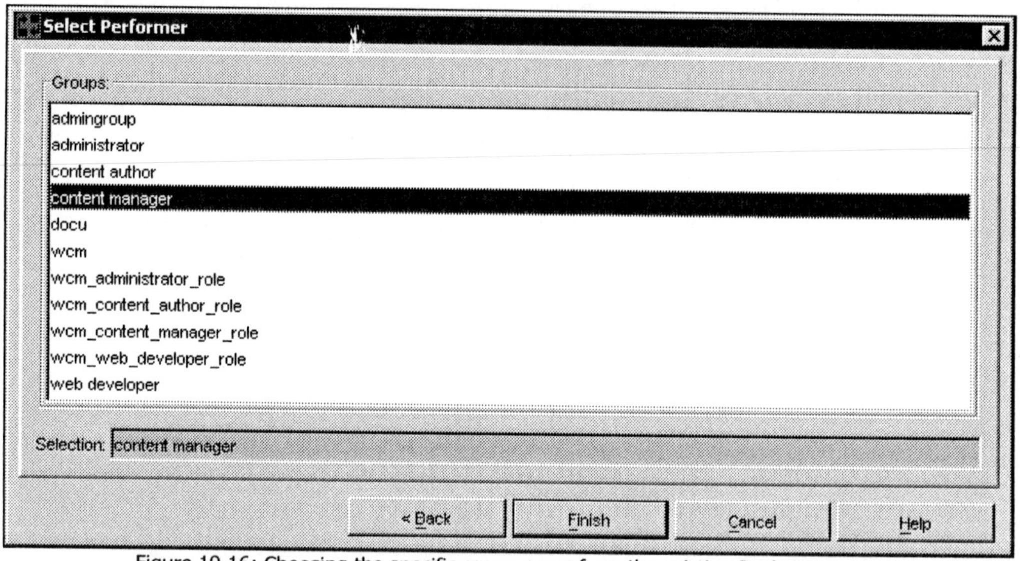

Figure 19.16: Choosing the specific group name from the existing Docbase groups

Click on Finish to complete the settings for the Performer tab of the activity.

3. The Definition tab (refer to figure 19.17) allows you to set the priority of tasks and instructions for manual performers.

Under the Definition tab of the Activity Inspector screen, you can do the following:

- o Assign a priority to the activity: You can flag a task as Low, Medium, or High, directing the Content Server to execute the activity in the specified order relative to the other pending actions in its execution queue. Optionally, you can assign it a priority at run time by choosing Dynamic from the Priority dropdown. This is useful only when you are setting the priority of an activity at run time through some custom-written code for workflows rather than executing workflows via a workflow process template.
- o Provide a short description for the activity.
- o Provide instructions for manual performers of the activity.

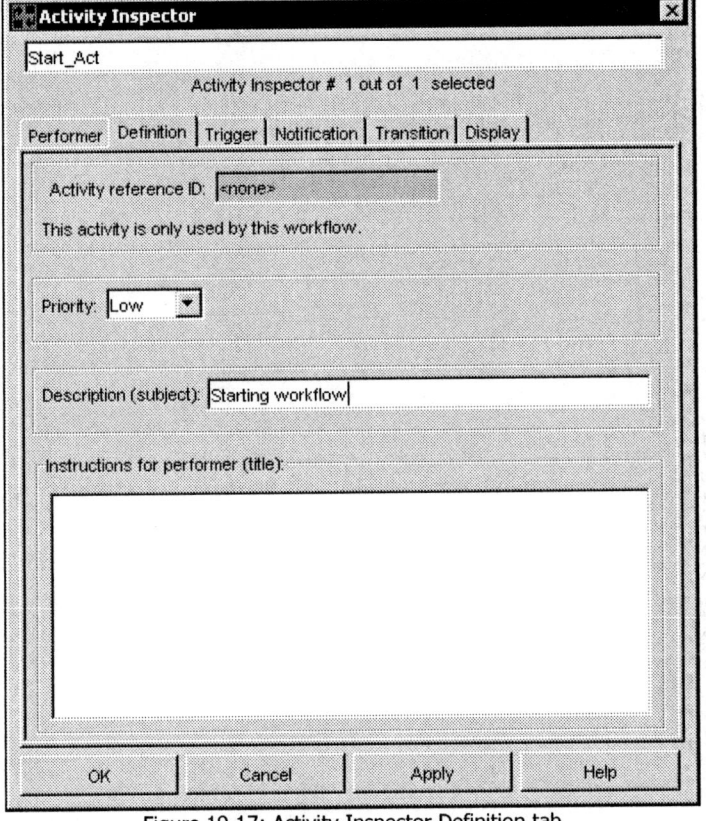

Figure 19.17: Activity Inspector Definition tab

4. The Trigger tab (refer to figure 19.18) allows you to specify the condition when the activity begins and when the task is to be sent to the performer's Inbox. The following activity parameters can be set up under the Definition tab:

   o The activity is triggered when: If the activity has multiple input flows to it and it can be started only once all preceding activities have been completed, choose the first radio button: All input flows are selected. If you require the activity to start even if some of the preceding activities have been completed, choose the second radio button, This number of input flows selected. Note that the total number of input flows is already shown and you need to simply mention the number of flows that must be completed before this activity starts.

   o You can optionally specify a special event to occur before triggering off this activity by providing an event name. You can provide a system event such as: dm_destroy, dm_checkin, dm_checkout, etc. or some custom event. You can flag an activity to be run more than once in a given workflow instance.

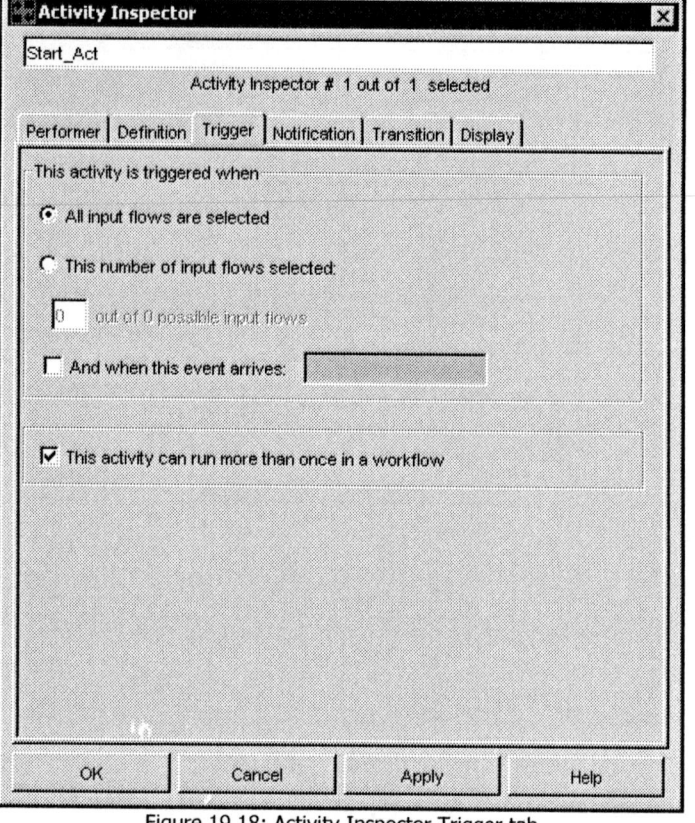

Figure 19.18: Activity Inspector Trigger tab

Note that the activity PromoteStaging_Act (please refer to figure 19.6) has two input flows: one from Start_Act activity and one from ContentCorrection_Act. Figure 19.19 shows the setting that needs to be done in the Trigger tab for such an activity.

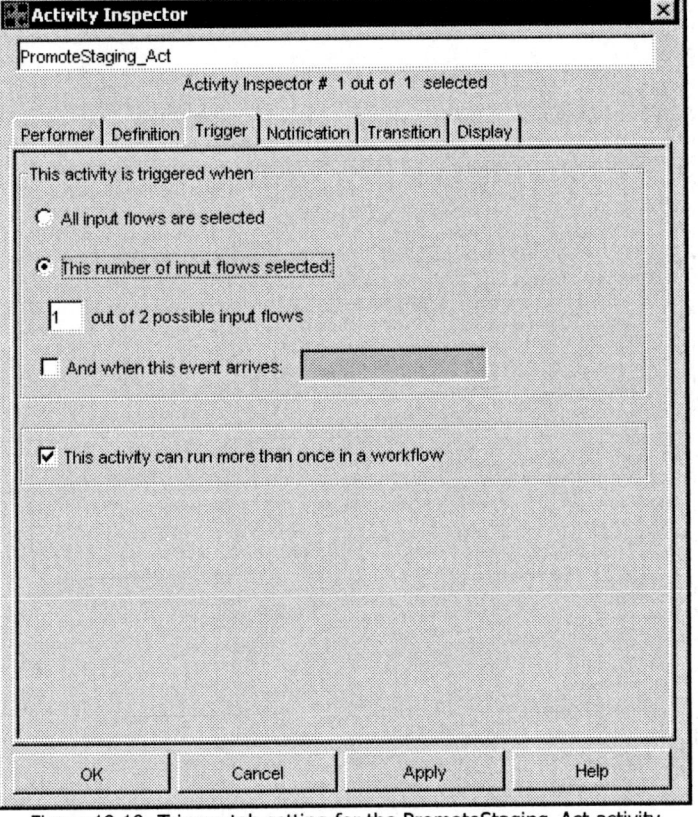

Figure 19.19: Trigger tab setting for the PromoteStaging_Act activity

This setting ensures that the PromoteStaging_Act activity is started when one of the two possible input flows (preceding activities) have been selected.

5. The Notification tab (refer to figure 19.20) allows you to set up warning timers to alert the workflow supervisor in case the activity tasks halt or are left unattended for a specified duration.

    You can have the system notify the workflow supervisor if the particular activity is not triggered within the specified duration (in terms of days and/or hours) after the workflow has started.

    Furthermore, you can have notifications sent across to the workflow supervisor if the particular activity has not completed within the specified duration (in terms of days and/or hours) after the activity has started.

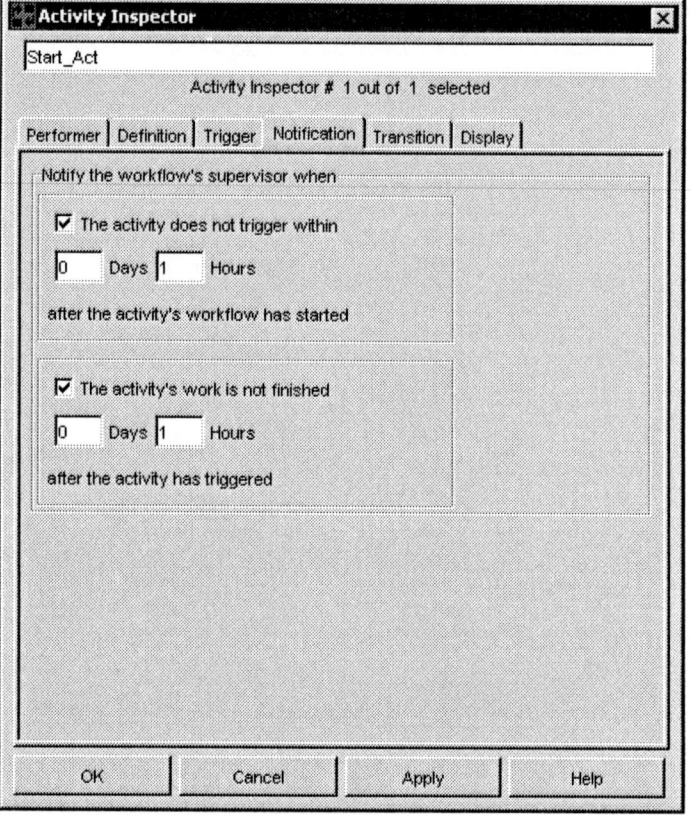

Figure 19.20: Activity Inspector Notification tab

6. The Transition tab (refer to figure 19.21) allows you to specify which activities in the workflow come next to this particular activity. If there are multiple connected activities (output flows) from this activity, you can:

    o   Designate the system to select all connected activities when this activity finishes.
        Let the performer of the activity choose at run time how many next activities can be selected after this activity completes.
        Specify certain conditions based on which the next activities can be selected when this activity finishes.

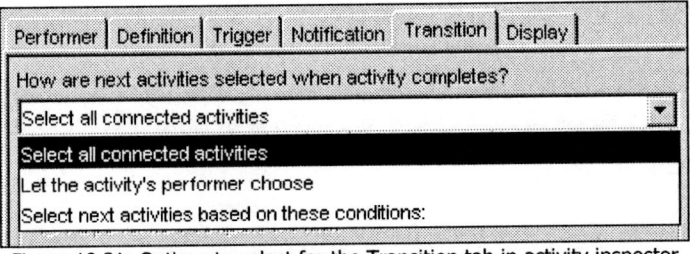

Figure 19.21: Options to select for the Transition tab in activity inspector

Refer to figure 19.22; if there are multiple performers for the activity (based on the settings under the Performer tab), you can specify whether the activity finishes when all the performers complete their task or when a certain number of performers complete their task items.

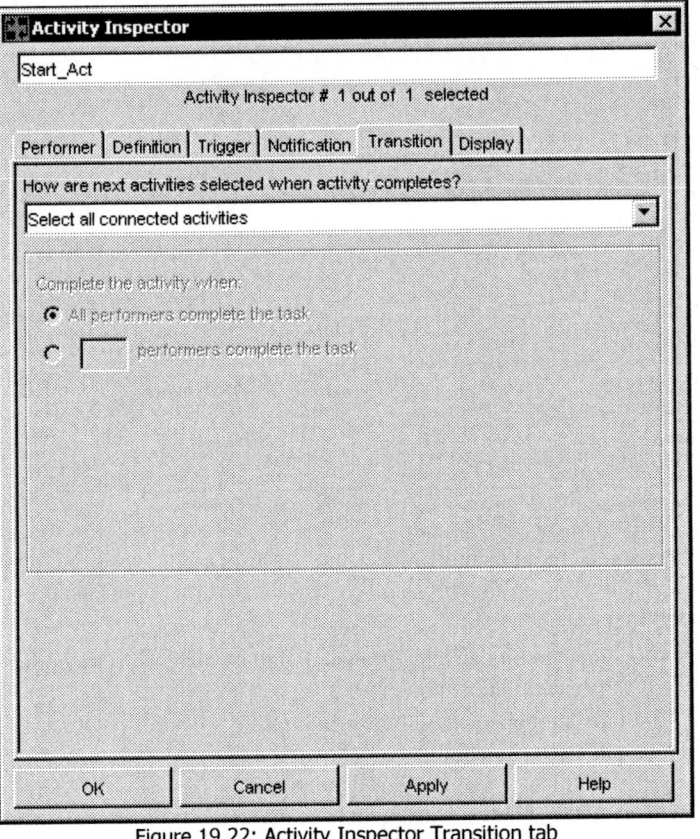

Figure 19.22: Activity Inspector Transition tab

Please refer to figure 19.6 and note that the Review_Act activity has two output flows from it: a forward flow leading it to the PromoteApproved_Act activity and a backward/reject flow leading it to the DemoteWIP_Act activity.

The option **Let the activity's performer choose** is chosen from the dropdown in such a scenario allowing the performer of the activity to select up to two next activities (refer to figure 19.23).

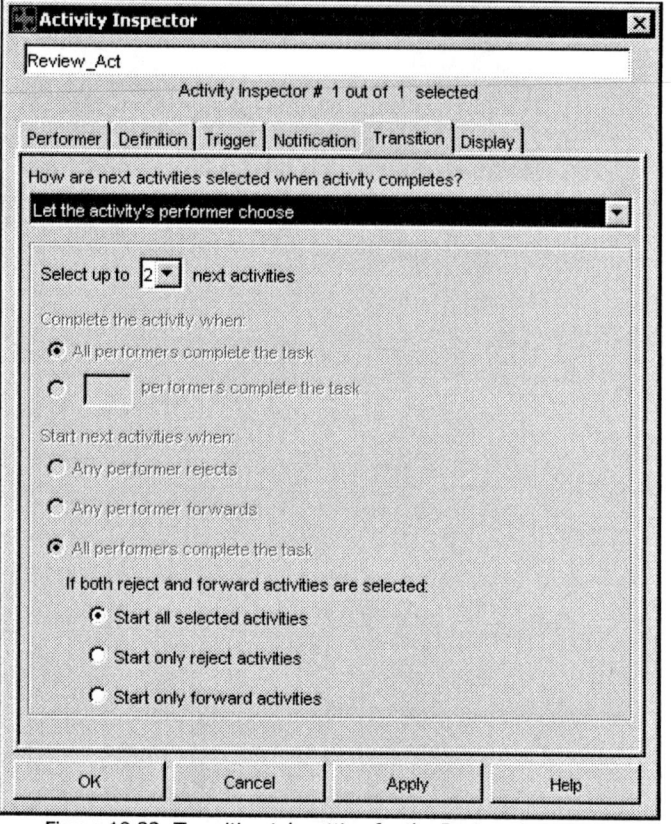

Figure 19.23: Transition tab setting for the Review_Act activity

7. The **Display tab** (refer to figure 19.24) simply allows you to specify how the activities visually appear in the workflow template editor. You can control the following via the **Display tab**:

   o The image and its display size used to display the activity in the workflow template editor.

   o The font, font size, and other formatting features for displaying the labels for activities in the workflow template editor.

   o Whether the activity name or the activity performers should be displayed as labels against activities in the workflow template editor.

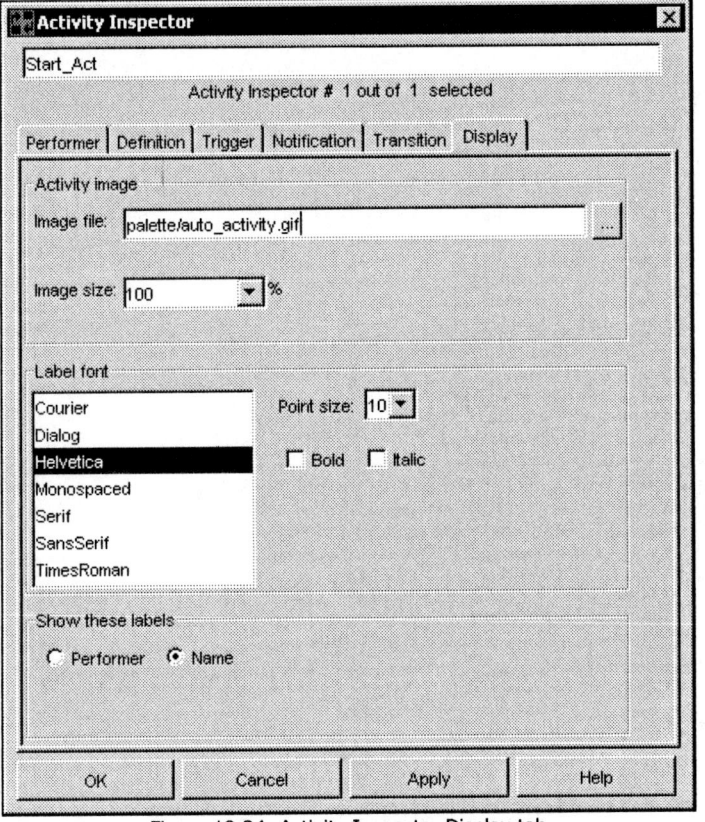

Figure 19.24: Activity Inspector Display tab

Click on Apply and then OK to complete setting up the Start_Act activity. Refer to figure 19.6 and the tables in the following sections to create the other activities for the custom workflow template.

19.3.1 Performer Tab for Activities

Activity name	Manual/ Auto	Performer	Method	Save exec results	Method time out (secs)	If method fails
Start_Act	Auto	Docbase owner	wcmInitializeProcessWorkflow	Yes	300	Stop
Promote Staging_Act	Auto	Docbase owner	wcmPromoteToStaging	Yes	300	Stop
Review_Act	Manual	Single user from group: content manager	N/A	N/A	N/A	N/A
DemoteWIP _Act	Auto	Docbase owner	wcmDemoteToWIP	Yes	300	Stop
Content Correction _Act	Manual	Single user from group: content author	N/A	N/A	N/A	N/A
Promote Approved_Act	Auto	Docbase owner	WcmPromoteTo Approved	Yes	300	Stop
End_Act	Auto	Docbase owner	WcmTerminate ProcessWorkflow	Yes	300	Stop

Figure 19.25: Performer tab settings

19.3.2 Trigger Tab for Activities

Activity name	Activity triggered when	Run more than once?
Start_Act	All input flows selected	Yes
PromoteStaging_Act	1 out of 2 possible input flows	Yes
Review_Act	All input flows selected	Yes
DemoteWIP_Act	All input flows selected	Yes
ContentCorrection_Act	All input flows selected	Yes
PromoteApproved_Act	All input flows selected	Yes
End_Act	All input flows selected	Yes

Figure 19.26: Trigger tab settings

19.3.3 Notification Tab for Activities

Activity name	Activity does not trigger within	Activity work not finished after
Start_Act	1 hour	1 hour
PromoteStaging_Act	1 hour	1 hour
Review_Act	1 hour	1 hour
DemoteWIP_Act	1 hour	1 hour
ContentCorrection_Act	1 hour	1 hour
PromoteApproved_Act	1 hour	1 hour
End_Act	1 hour	1 hour

Figure 19.27: Notification tab settings

19.3.4 Transition Tab for Activities

Activity name	How are next activities selected?	Complete the activity when	If both reject and forward activities selected
Start_Act	Select all connected activities	All performers complete	N/A
PromoteStaging_Act	Select all connected activities	All performers complete	N/A
Review_Act	Let the activity's performer choose (select up to 2 next activities)	All performers complete	Start all selected activities
DemoteWIP_Act	Select all connected activities	All performers complete	N/A
ContentCorrection_Act	Select all connected activities	All performers complete	N/A
PromoteApproved_Act	Select all connected activities	All performers complete	N/A
End_Act	Select all connected activities	All performers complete	N/A

Figure 19.28: Transition tab settings

19.4 Adding a Package to Connection Flows

Double-click the particular connection flow or select the connection flow and choose the menu option Tools | Flow Inspector to open up the Flow Inspector screen as shown in figure 19.29.

Click the Add New Package button and provide details of the routed package such as its name and the object type, as well as the version of routed content.

You could provide some meaningful name to the package or choose the default package naming convention provided by Documentum (Package0, Package1, and so on).

The default version label for the package is CURRENT, which ensures that the package will contain the most recent version of content in the workflow.

You could even specify a symbolic (case-sensitive) label such as WIP or a numeric version label such as 1.0 for the routed content in the package.

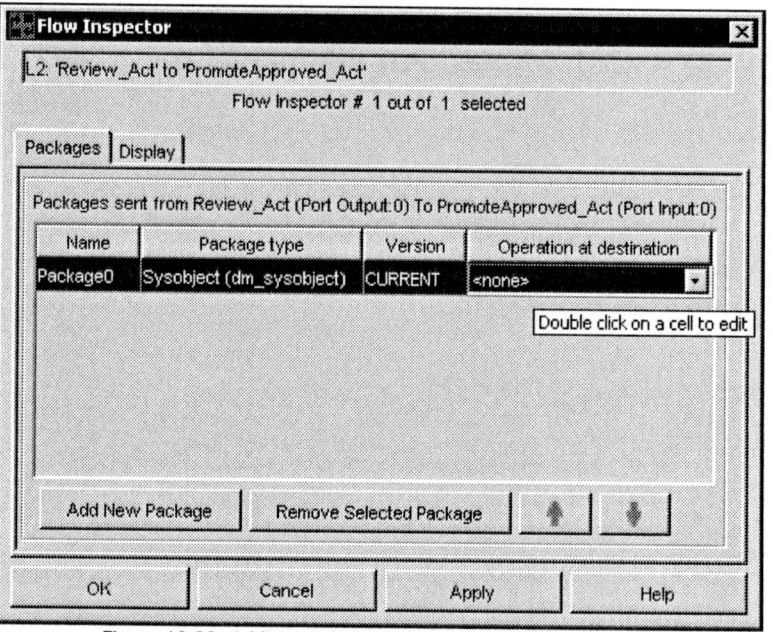

Figure 19.29: Adding packages via the Flow Inspector screen

Remember that you will have to repeat these steps for all the flows connecting the various activities in the workflow template.

Documentum 5.3 Update

Documentum release 5.3 introduces a new feature by providing support for a single Inbox that can contain multiple tasks from multiple Docbase repositories.

Congratulations! You have created your own custom workflow template and are all set to test it out by submitting your content to this custom workflow.

If you are interested in knowing more about workflows and their advanced features, kindly go through the Application Builder user manuals, Web Publisher administration manuals, and Workflow Manager online help. Documentum also provides an advanced workflow management tool with the name Business Process Manager (or BPM in short) extending a lot of the features provided by Workflow Manager. Discussing BPM and its features is beyond the scope of this book though. You may want to download the BPM software from Documentum's download site and go through its administration manuals.

Hop over to the next chapter to test the custom workflow template you have created in this chapter.

19.5 Summary

In this chapter we discussed how a workflow works in tandem with a lifecycle by defining business policies and laying down norms on how content moves through various lifecycle states, under what conditions, and who the participating users and groups are.

We designed a very simple workflow for our application, involving content authors, managers, and approvers as the participating entities.

We saw that a workflow template is created using the Workflow Manager tool. Each time the workflow is started using the workflow template, Documentum creates a new run-time instance for it.

Workflow templates consist of activities that are connected with flows. Packages are added to the flows so they can route content through the workflow.

We briefly discussed that workflow activities are of two kinds—manual and automatic. While manual activities are performed by groups or users, automatic activities are performed by the system.

Finally, through detailed steps we saw how to create the custom workflow template we had designed at the beginning of the chapter.

20
Testing Custom Workflows

Once you have created, validated, installed, and made the custom workflow template available in Web Publisher, you can test it by sending content in a workflow instance created from the custom workflow template.

Figure 20.1 depicts the sequence of activities in the custom workflow we created in the previous chapter. This should serve as a good help while testing the workflow steps.

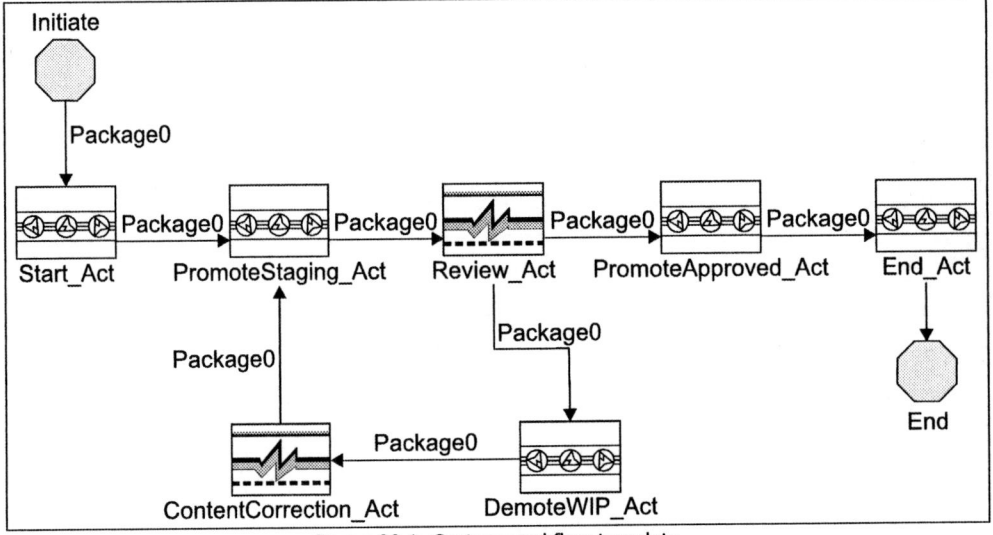

Figure 20.1: Custom workflow template

However, you first need to create the Web Publisher users that will participate in the workflow. In our case, we need to create a content author user and a content manager user in the Docbase before we can start using and testing the workflow.

20.1 Creating Users for Workflow in Documentum

The following steps will explain how to create users in Documentum:

1. Log in to Documentum Administrator as an administrator or superuser and go to User Management | Users.

    Choose menu option File | New | User to open up the New User creation screen.

2. Fill in the details for creating a content author user as shown in figure 20.2.

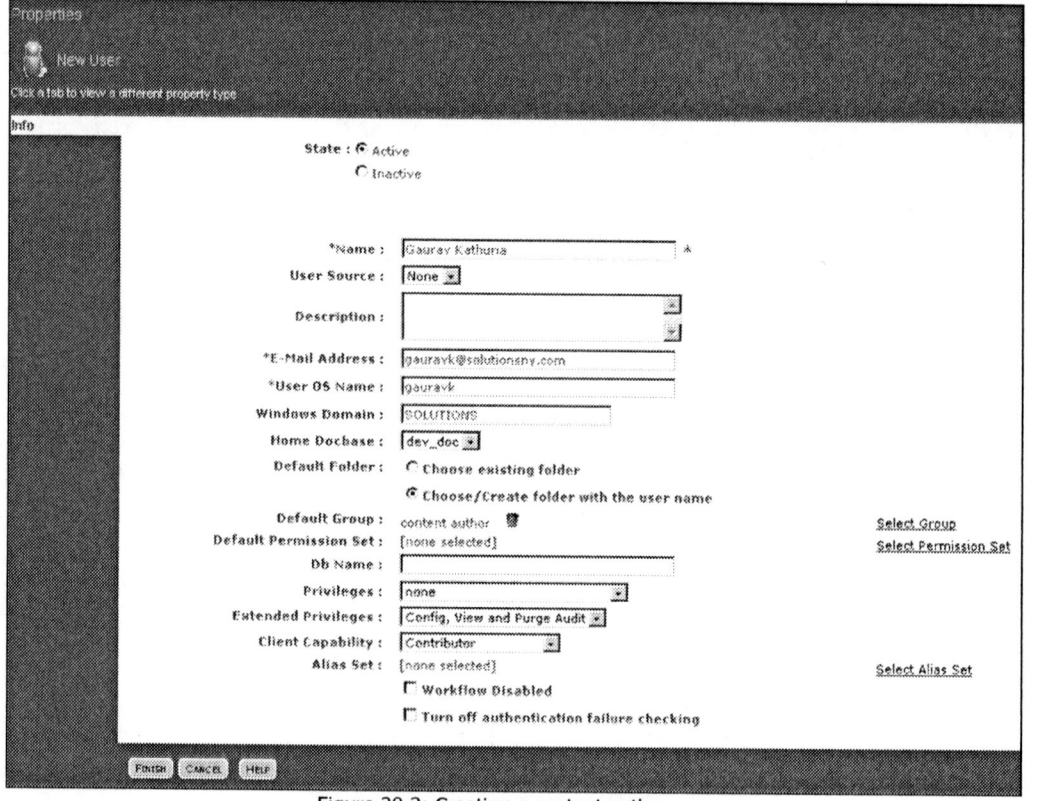

Figure 20.2: Creating a content author user

The User OS name gauravk already exists in the Windows domain and is used by Documentum for OS system authentication purposes. So, you need not provide a password for the NT user in the user creation screen shown in figure 20.2. However, you will have to specify the user settings/parameters as per your own environment.

Similarly create a content manager user as per the details shown in figure 20.3.

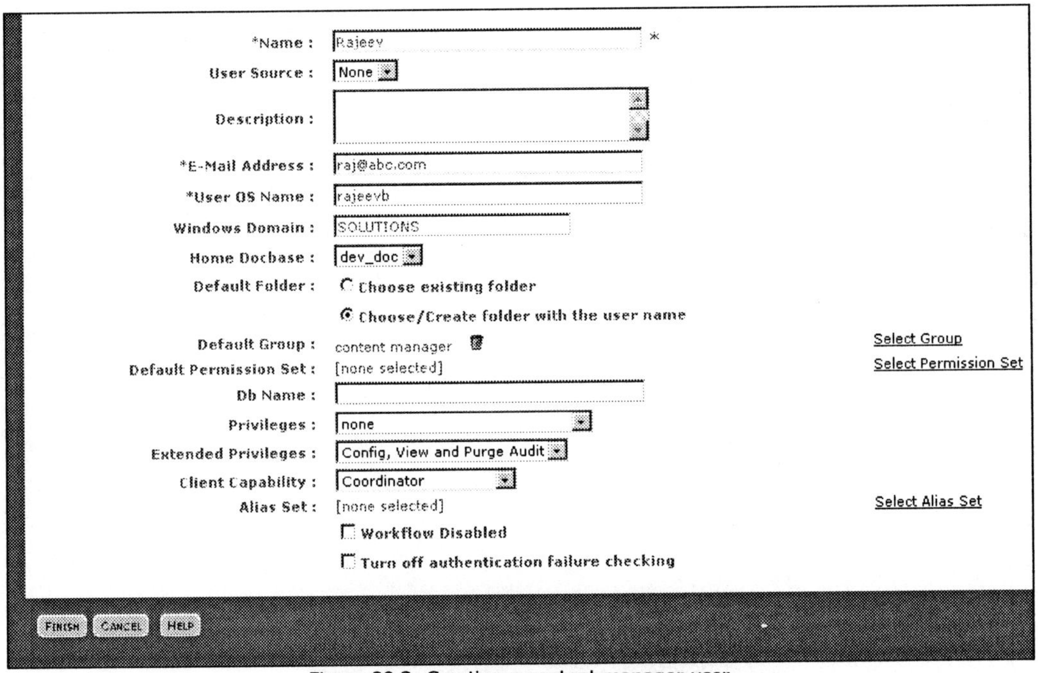

Figure 20.3: Creating a content manager user

For details about users, groups, and their attributes please refer to the Documentum Content Server Fundamentals and Administration manuals.

20.2 Submitting Content to the Custom Workflow

Keep the custom workflow template visual diagram (refer to figure 20.1) in front of you while testing the workflow. This will help you understand which particular activity is currently being executed, who is performing the activity, and what is the next activity in place.

The simple steps mentioned below should be followed to test the custom_workflow we created in the previous chapter.

1. Log in to Web Publisher as a content author user (say: gauravk) and create some News Article content via the News Article template.

    Refer to figure 20.4; choose the checkbox against the newly created content and click on the Start Workflow icon ⬍ (or select the menu option Tools | Workflow | Start) to submit the content to a workflow instance.

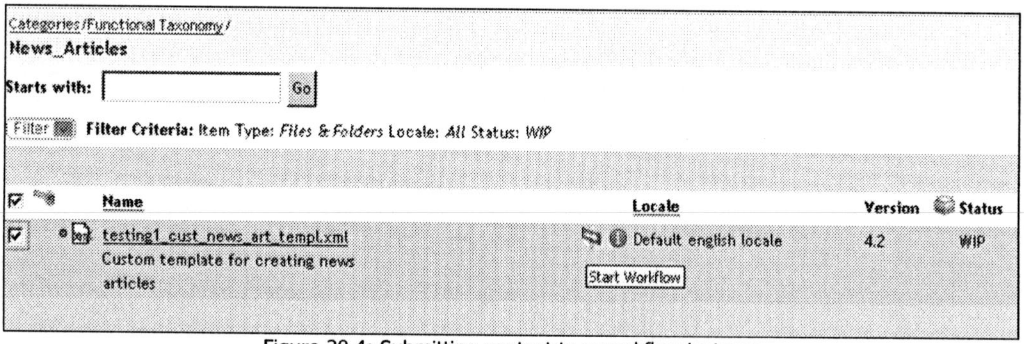

Figure 20.4: Submitting content to a workflow instance

2. Select the Custom_Workflow workflow template from the list of all installed and available workflow templates in the Docbase, as shown in figure 20.5.

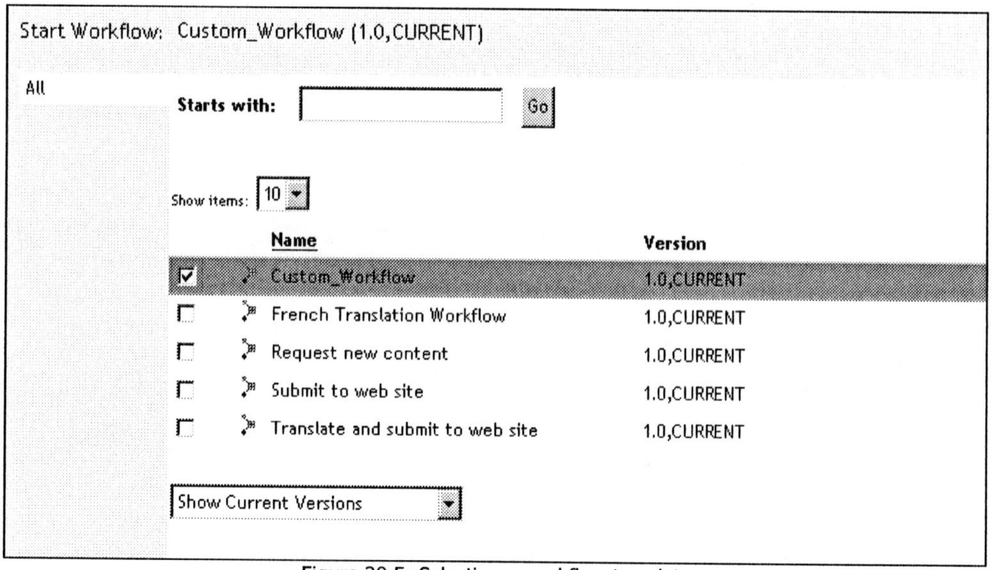

Figure 20.5: Selecting a workflow template

Click on OK.

3. As shown in figure 20.6, provide a brief description for the workflow instance to identify it by its name (say: workflow_Testing).

You could also select a priority for the workflow task and provide an effective date for the routed content (in a change set, as it is termed in Documentum). Note that the effective date of the change set overwrites the existing effective date of the routed content.

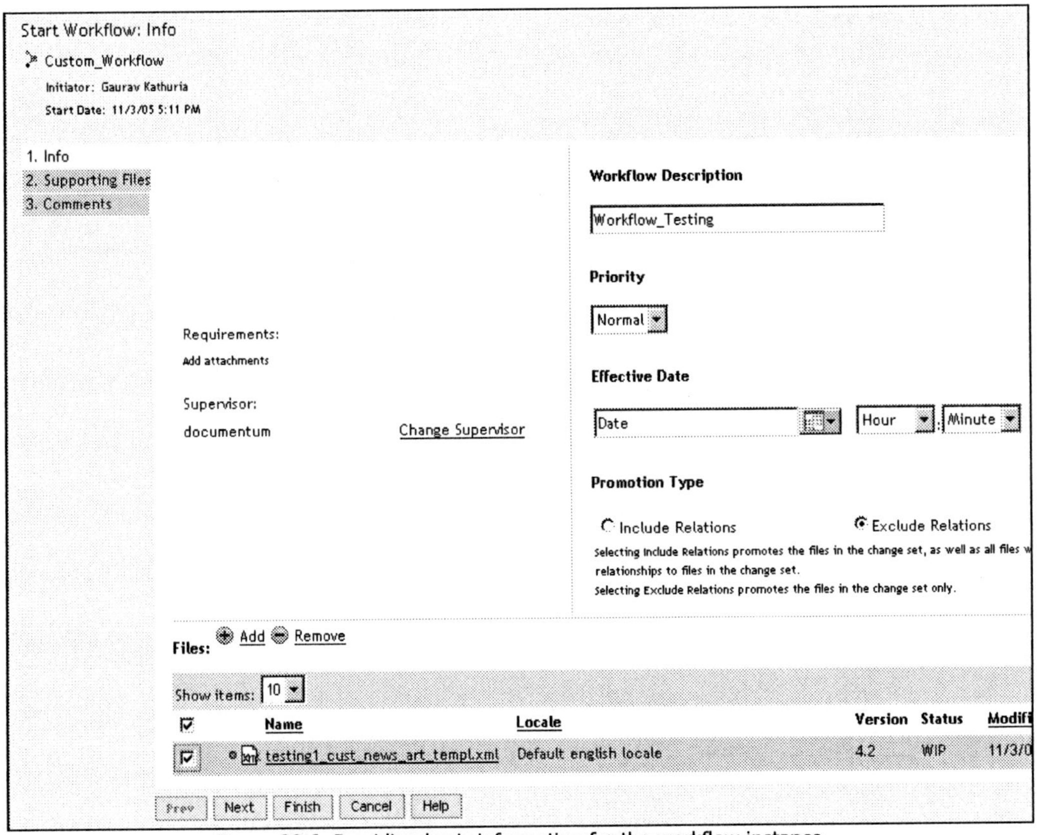

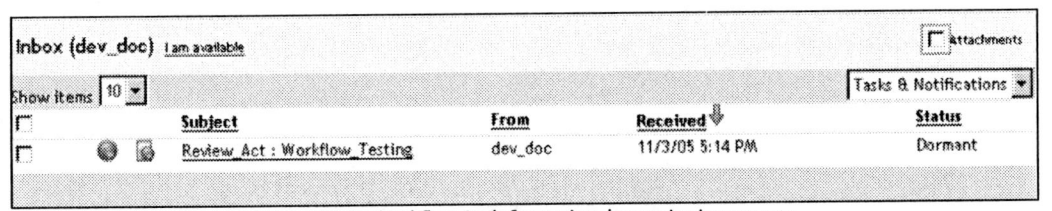

Start Workflow: Info

⟫ Custom_Workflow

   Initiator: Gaurav Kathuria

   Start Date: 11/3/05 5:11 PM

1. Info
2. Supporting Files
3. Comments

Workflow Description

Workflow_Testing

Priority

Normal ▾

Requirements:

Add attachments

Supervisor:

documentum   Change Supervisor

Effective Date

Date   ▦▾   Hour ▾ : Minute ▾

Promotion Type

○ Include Relations   ⦿ Exclude Relations

Selecting Include Relations promotes the files in the change set, as well as all files w
relationships to files in the change set.
Selecting Exclude Relations promotes the files in the change set only.

Files: ⊕ Add ⊖ Remove

Show items: 10 ▾

☑		Name	Locale	Version	Status	Modifi
☑	⊗ ▣	testing1_cust_news_art_templ.xml	Default english locale	4.2	WIP	11/3/0

Prev | Next | Finish | Cancel | Help

Figure 20.6: Providing basic information for the workflow instance

Click on Finish to submit the content to the workflow or click on Next to provide some instructions/comments to the recipients of the next activity/task before finally submitting it to the workflow.

4.   Log in to Web Publisher as a content manager user and go to the Inbox shown in the left-hand panel of Web Publisher.

You will notice the submitted workflow task in the content manager's Inbox (refer to figure 20.7). All content manager users in the Docbase will receive this particular task.

Note that the task is identified by the name of the activity and the name of the workflow (Review_Act : Workflow_Testing in our case).

Inbox (dev_doc) I am available   ☐ attachments

Show items 10 ▾   Tasks & Notifications ▾

☐		Subject	From	Received ⬇	Status
☐	⬤ ▣	Review_Act : Workflow_Testing	dev_doc	11/3/05 5:14 PM	Dormant

Figure 20.7: Workflow task for review by content manager

At this stage the task is in a Dormant state as can be seen in figure 20.7 under the Status column.

Click on the task link Review_Act : Workflow_Testing.

5.   The **Task Manager: Info** screen opens up showing the routed content and instructions for the performer (content manager in this case).

Refer to figure 20.8; note that the content has been promoted to the Staging lifecycle state by the automatic activity PromoteStaging_Act before reaching the content manager's Inbox.

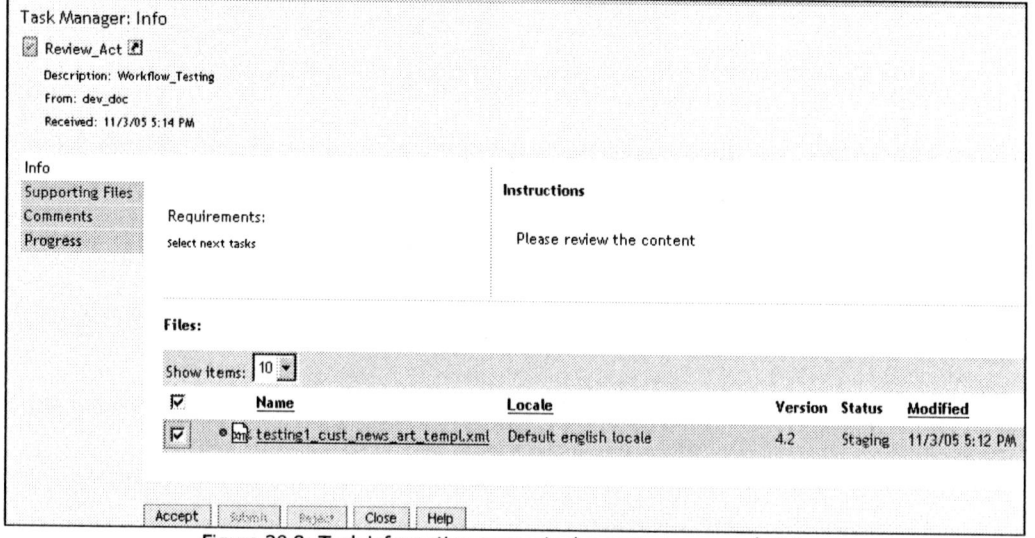

Figure 20.8: Task information screen in the content manager's Inbox

Select the checkbox against the content file and click on Accept to accept this workflow task. This removes this task from the Inboxes of all other content manager users and marks the task as in the Acquired state.

6.   At this point of time, the content is in the Review_Act activity and can either be submitted by content manager in a forward flow to approve it or be rejected in a backward flow to demote it to the WIP state for corrections by the content author.

The two buttons Submit and Reject get enabled for this very purpose, as can be seen in figure 20.9.

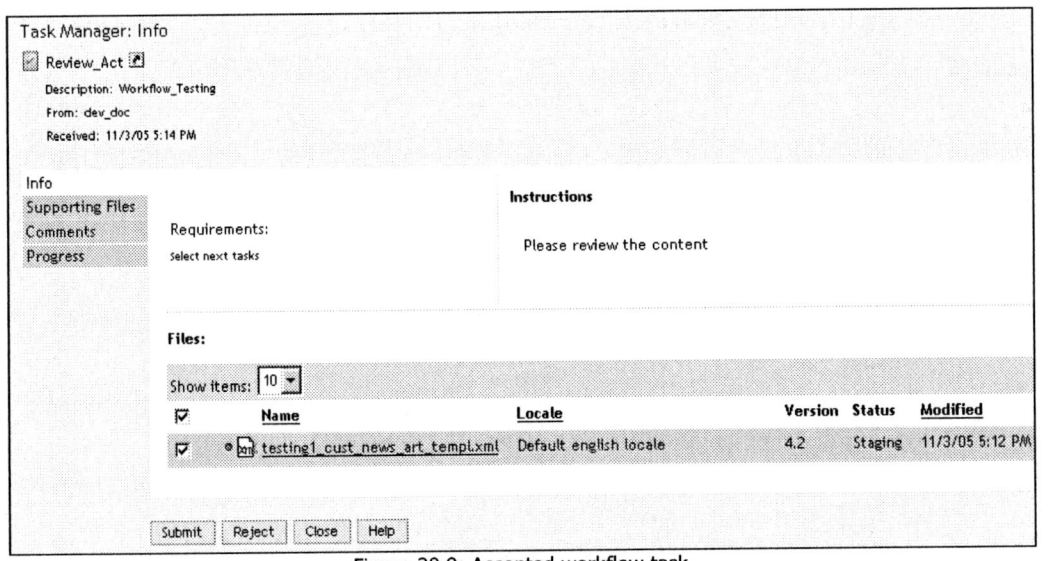

Figure 20.9: Accepted workflow task

The content manager can view the properties of the content by selecting the checkbox against the content file and choosing the menu option View | Properties | Info.

For viewing the actual web content of the content file, the content manager can perform web viewing by choosing the menu option View | Web View.

(Please refer to Chapter 22: *Web Viewing Content Files* for details of Web View and its usage).

7. Let us assume that the content manager is not satisfied by the content and/or its properties and wants to get some corrections done.

    Go to the Comments tab shown in the figure 20.9 and provide comments for the content author. Click on Reject to reject it back to content author users.

    At this point of time, the auto-activity DemoteWIP_Act is called by the system to demote the content back to the WIP lifecycle state.

8. Log in to Web Publisher as a content author user and go to Inbox.

    The rejected task (ContentCorrection_Act : Workflow_Testing) is shown in the Inbox of all content author users, as can be seen in figure 20.10.

File	Edit	View	Document	Tools	

Inbox (dev_doc) I am available   ☐ Attachments

Show items 10 ▼   Tasks & Notifications ▼

☐			Subject	From	Received ⬇	Status
☐	●	🗎	ContentCorrection_Act : Workflow_Testing	dev_doc	11/3/05 5:20 PM	Dormant

Figure 20.10: Rejected task for content authors

Click on the task link to open up the **Task Manager: Info** screen (refer to figure 20.11). Look at the comments provided by the reviewer asking for corrections.

Click on the **Accept** button to accept this workflow task. As we saw earlier, this removes the task from the Inboxes of all other content author users and marks the task as Acquired state.

9. The content author can select the checkbox against the name of the content file and choose the menu option **View | Properties | Info** to make corrections to any content attributes/properties.

Additionally, the content author can choose the menu option **File | Edit** to open up the content in Web Publisher to amend any content fields.

After making the necessary corrections, choose the menu option **File | Check In** to check-in the modified version of content into the Docbase.

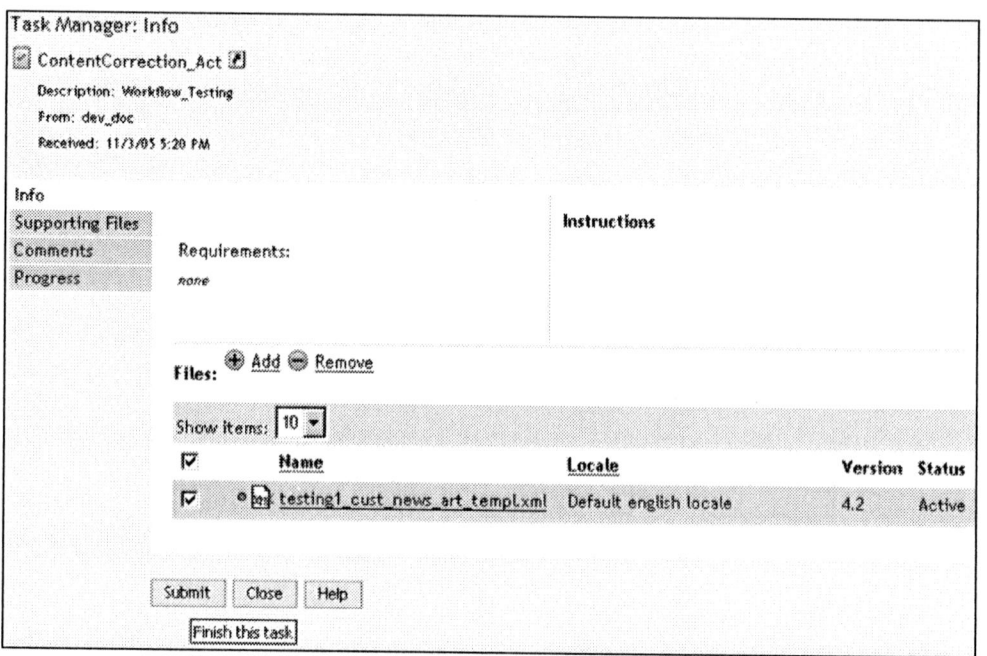

Figure 20.11: Task Manager: Info screen in content author's Inbox

10. Click on Submit to submit the corrected content once again to the reviewer.

    The task Finish screen is shown in figure 20.12. Click on Ok so that the system removes this task from the Inbox of the content author.

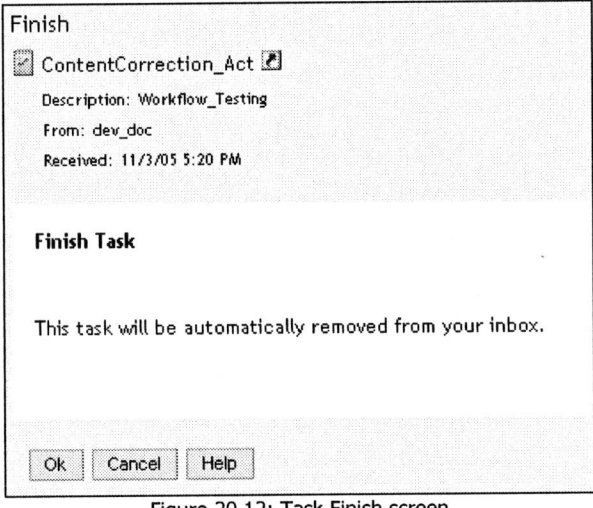

Figure 20.12: Task Finish screen

Note that at this stage, the auto-activity PromoteStaging_Act is called by the system to promote the content to the Staging lifecycle state.

11. Log in to Web Publisher as a content manager user and repeat steps 4 through 6 described above. Once you are satisfied with the corrections made by the content author, choose the content file and click on Submit in the Task Manager: Info screen.

    Submitting the content promotes the content automatically to the Approved state via the PromoteApproved_Act auto-activity.

    Based on the effective date of the content file, the Documentum Monitor_Lifecycles Job turns the content Active. At this stage, the content has finished all workflow steps and is ready to be re-submitted to a new workflow instance!

    This covers the essential steps required to test your custom workflow template. Obviously, the more complex your workflow template is, the more complex is its testing procedure.

    Go ahead and play around with the custom workflow template we created in the previous chapter. Accordingly you can test all possible scenarios in the workflow, such as multiple performers for a particular task, notification timers, and multiple packages routed in the workflow.

20.3 Summary

In the previous chapter, we created a custom workflow template consisting of simple activities. In this chapter, we first created a content author user and a content manager user to act as participating entities in order to test the custom workflow.

Through detailed steps we explained how to test the complete workflow by verifying both the submit (forward flow) and the reject (backward flow) scenarios.

21

Publishing from Docbase Using SCS

Once all the content for the website has been created in Documentum Docbase, a big milestone has been achieved. The next big hurdle to overcome is to make all this content available to the website application (outside the Docbase) so that it can be displayed on the portals/websites. This raises a few questions:

- How difficult or easy is it to export the content (and obviously its associated metadata/properties) from Documentum Docbase to a target server and database repository so that web applications can easily query and display this information on websites?

- Do we need to write some custom code in order to publish/export the huge data set from Documentum Docbase to a file server and database?

- How do we execute this publishing code/utility to run at periodic intervals to ensure that new content entered in the Docbase or existing content that has been updated is seamlessly reflected on the website without much human intervention?

There could be a million other queries in your mind as well. Well, the answer is, you need not write any customized code or application to publish documents and their properties from Documentum Docbases. Documentum Site Caching Services provides an easy-to-configure and definitely extremely easy-to-use interface to set up publishing configurations for your Docbase.

For a quick reference, go through our earlier discussion on Site Caching Services and SCS Architecture in Chapter 4.

Documentum **Site Caching Services** (SCS) allows you to easily configure and publish documents and their properties (such as title, authors, keywords, custom added properties, etc.) from Docbase directly to the website host and database tables. By creating a Site Publishing Configuration in Documentum Administrator, you can specify which types of documents need to be published, from which Web Cabinet folder these documents need to be published, which properties need to be published along with the actual content files, which rendition formats of documents need to be exported, and many other parameters.

A Site Publishing Configuration publishes content from the Docbase if and only if the SCS software (both source and target) is installed correctly and the SCS services are up and running correctly.

21.1 Limitations of SCS

There are some limitations of SCS and Site Publishing Configurations that you need to bear in mind when designing and planning your website. A few of these have been mentioned below:

- Only objects that are subtypes of dm_sysobject can be published from Documentum Docbase.
  Note that objects such as users, groups, etc., which are subtypes of Persistent Object and not SysObject, cannot be published.

- Content needs to be first linked to the publishing folder in Docbase before it can be published.

- The total length of the Docbase path to the object, the object's name (object_name attribute), and the export directory on the SCS Source should not exceed 255 characters. This is a Windows limitation and does not hold good for UNIX servers.

- On Windows servers, documents with the following characters in their file names cannot be published:

  \ / : * ? " < > |

21.2 Publishing Types

SCS publishing operations are of numerous types, based on your requirements:

- **Full refresh**: This deletes the existing published objects and their properties/attributes from the website webroot along with database tables and then republishes the objects.

- **Incremental refresh/publish**: Only objects that are new or have been updated since the last publishing operation are republished.

- **Force refresh**: Forcefully overwrites the existing published objects and their properties/attributes.

- **Single object publish**: Selectively publishes only the selected object.

Assuming that you have already installed SCS Source and SCS Target (the two principal components in SCS architecture) on your Content Server host and website host respectively, let's proceed further. Refer to Chapter 7 for details on installing SCS Source and Target.

21.3 Steps for Setting Up a Site Publishing Configuration

The entry point to a publishing operation is a Site Publishing Configuration, which can easily be created using Documentum Administrator. Follow the steps mentioned next to create a new Site Publishing Configuration as per your specific needs:

1. Log in to Documentum Administrator as an administrator and go to Administration | Site Publishing. Choosing FILE | NEW | SITE PUBLISHING CONFIGURATION brings up the empty Site Publishing Configuration screen as shown in figure 21.1:

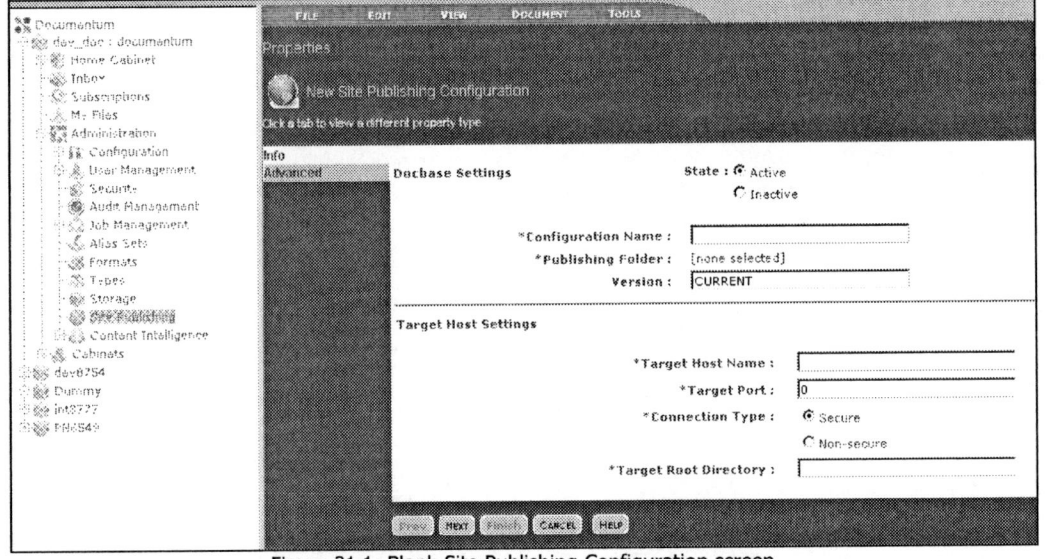

Figure 21.1: Blank Site Publishing Configuration screen

By default, the Site Publishing Configuration is created in an Active state (as shown in figure 21.1). You can deactivate the configuration by choosing the Inactive radio button.

Documentum internally manages Site Publishing Configuration as two objects in the Docbase—dm_webc_config and dm_webc_target. The attribute target_id in the dm_webc_config object stores the object ID of the dm_webc_target object and this is how the two are linked.

When you create a Site Publishing Configuration using Documentum Administrator, the dm_webc_config and dm_webc_target objects are implicitly created and managed for you (refer to figure 21.2).

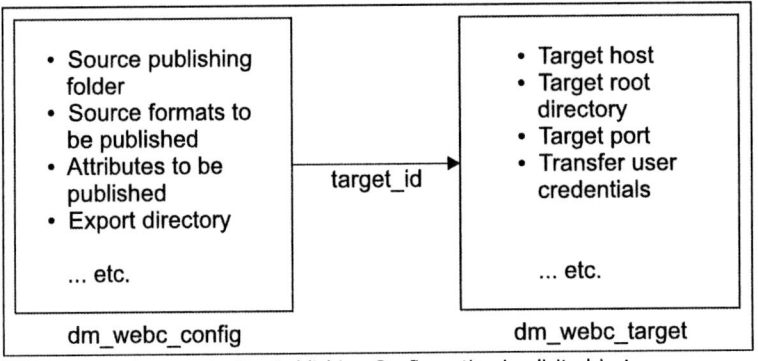

Figure 21.2: Site Publishing Configuration implicit objects

> You can create any number of Site Publishing Configurations for a given Docbase and publish to many websites from the same source Docbase.

2. To create a Site Publishing Configuration, you need to fill in the values under the Info and Advanced tabs. Let us take a look at the Info tab to begin with.

   Fill in the values for the Docbase Settings section as follows (refer to figure 21.3):

   - Configuration Name: A valid name for the Site Publishing Configuration.
   - Publishing Folder: Choose the Web Cabinet (by clicking on Select Source Folder) from which the content needs to be published. In our Docbase, we created the Test_WebCabinet web cabinet. All content created under this Web Cabinet directly or within folders contained under this Web Cabinet will be published.
   - Version: The lifecycle state of the documents at which the publishing should happen. This corresponds to the r_version_label attribute of content.

     In our case, we are publishing all documents that are in the Staging state of their lifecycle. If you do not specify a specific version label, the CURRENT version of content is published by default.

     Fill in the values for Target Host Settings section as follows:

   - Target Host Name: Host name or the IP address of the website host (where SCS Target has been installed).
   - Target Port: The port number on which SCS Target service listens. The default is 2788.
   - Connection Type: Connection to SCS Target. This can be raw (Non-secure) or SSL (Secure)
   - Target Root Directory: This is the webroot on the website host where published files will be placed. If the designated file structure does not exist on the host, Documentum creates it while publishing.

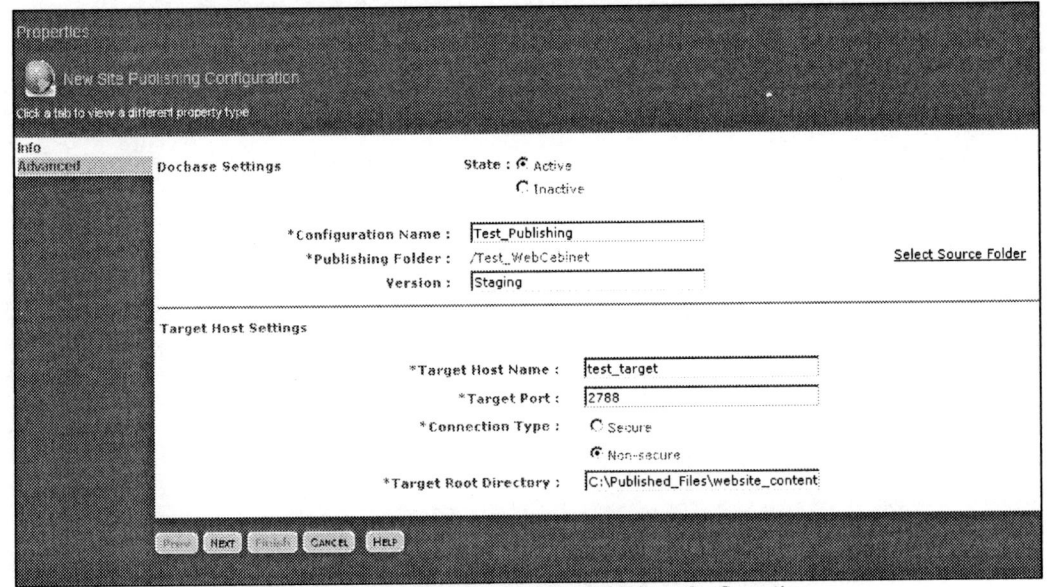

Figure 21.3: Info tab settings in Site Publishing Configuration

Click on the NEXT button and go to the Advanced tab.

3. If you need the document's attributes/properties to be added as HTML metatags, select the checkbox Add properties as HTML Meta Tags (refer to figure 21.4).

    Under such a scenario, published HTML documents contain metatags for the exported attributes under the HTML <HEAD> tag as follows. Note that these metatags are read and indexed by search engine crawlers (such as: Google, Yahoo, Alta Vista, etc.) for web searches.

```
<head>
    <META http-equiv="Content-Type" content="text/html; charset=ISO-8859-1">
    <META name="r_object_type" content="dm_document">
    <META name="keywords" content="product, specifications, medium, tool">
</head>
```

    Note that keywords being a repeating attribute has multiple values separated by commas (,).

    To insert metatags for other published files with non-HTML formats, add the following key in the webcache.ini file:

```
additional_metatag_extensions=jsp, <any other format>
```

    The webcache.ini file is typically found under the following location on the SCS Source, in the case of Windows server:

```
%DOCUMENTUM%\dba\config\<Docbase name>
```

```
For example: C:\Documentum\dba\config\<Docbase name>
```

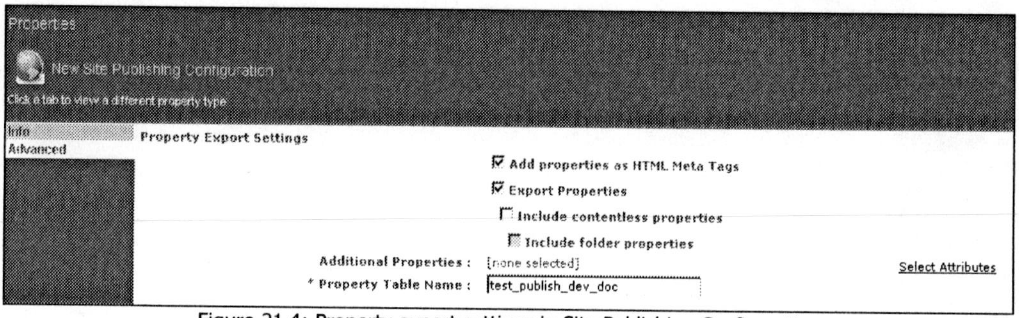

Figure 21.4: Property export settings in Site Publishing Configuration

In order to export/publish the attributes/properties of the documents to the target host, select the Export Properties checkbox.

Documentum SCS exports all the document attributes in the form of a properties.xml file to the target host. SCS Target reads and inserts these values into the specified database tables.

You can select the checkbox Include contentless properties in order to publish objects that do not have any content file associated with them.

Additionally, by choosing the checkbox Include folder properties, you can publish the attributes of folders containing documents as well.

In the Property Table Name field, specify the name of the database table to which the document properties should be published. We have provided a table name test_publish_dev_doc in our Site Publishing Configuration.

The following four tables are created by Documentum when documents are published on the target server's database:

- o test_publish_dev_doc_s: Stores the exported single-valued attributes of documents
- o test_publish_dev_doc_r: Stores the exported repeating-valued attributes of documents
- o test_publish_dev_doc_l: Stores the relations (dm_relation objects) of published documents
- o test_publish_dev_doc_m: Stores information about the state of published documents

The relation objects (dm_relation object type) can be published by setting the following key in the webcache.ini file:

```
export_relations=TRUE
```

By default Documentum exports certain attributes of documents, such as r_object_id, object_name, i_chronicle_id, etc. Additional attributes can be exported by clicking the Select Attributes link as shown in figure 21.4.

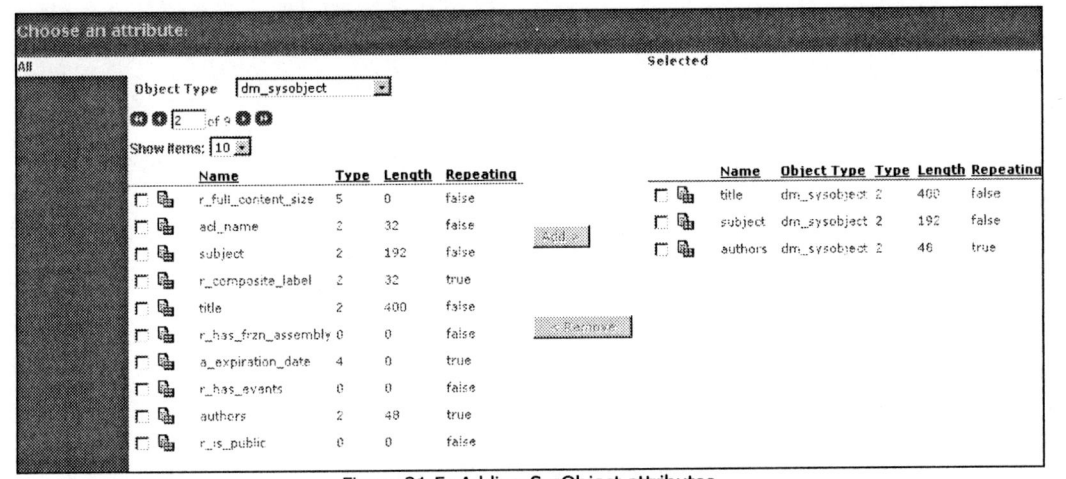

Figure 21.5: Adding SysObject attributes

By default the attributes of the dm_sysobject object type are displayed (refer to figure 21.5). You can select the attributes of dm_sysobject that you want published to the target host. Select the checkboxes against the attribute names and click the Add> button.

In order to include the attributes of custom object types, choose the object type from the Object Type dropdown. This automatically displays the custom (non-inherited) attributes of the selected object type (refer to figure 21.6). As usual, you can choose the checkboxes against the relevant attribute names and click the Add> button.

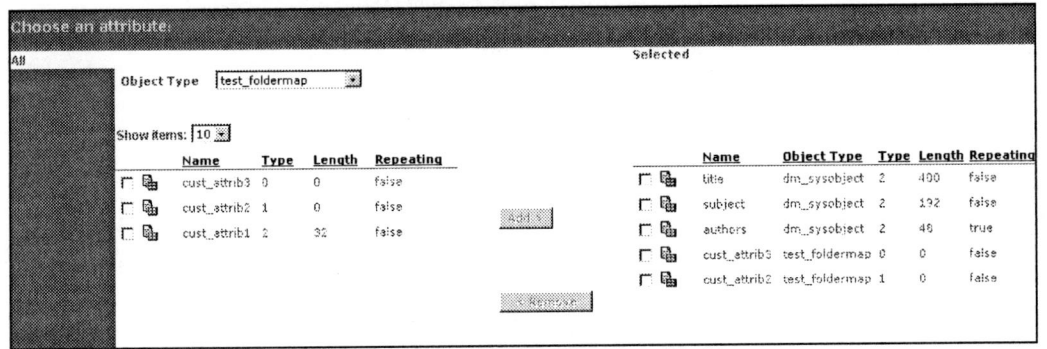

Figure 21.6: Adding attributes of custom object types

If the SCS Target database is SQL Server, a very common error message seen during publishing is:

[Microsoft][ODBC SQL Server Driver][SQL Server]Cannot create a row of size 8140 which is greater than the allowable maximum of 8060.

This is a restriction imposed by SQL Server database, which does not allow more than 8060 bytes per row in a table. To overcome this restriction, add the following key under the WEBC_COMMON section of the webcache.ini file:

```
[WEBC_COMMON]
mssql_store_varchar=TRUE
```

One should be very judicious while adding the publishable attributes while creating the Site Publishing Configuration (in case you have SQL Server as the target database). The greater the size (total length) of all published attributes, the greater are the chances of a publishing error due to the SQL Server row-size limitation.

4. Now you need to fill out the data for the Content Selection Settings section (refer to figure 21.8).

A document in Documentum Docbase can exist in numerous formats. For example, a simple `xyz.xml` file can be styled via XSL to generate multiple renditions such as `xyz.html`, `xyz.wml`, `xyz.shtml`, etc.

In your Site Publishing Configuration, you can specify whether you need to publish just the parent format (`xyz.xml`) or its renditions as well. If you need to publish multiple renditions of the same file, click on the Select Formats link and choose the additional formats that you want published.

Note that in Documentum, formats exist in the form of `dm_format` objects. You could run the following DQL query (via the `IDQL` command-line utility or through Documentum Administrator) in order to look at the various formats within Documentum:

```
DQL > select name,description,dos_extension from dm_format
```

Figure 21.7 lists a few formats in Documentum along with the actual DOS extensions in file names.

Format name	DOS extension
ppt8	ppt
ppt8_slide	ppt
excel8book	xls
mp3	mp3
zip	zip
msw8	doc
rtf	rtf
pdf	pdf
jpeg	jpg
gif	gif
bmp	bmp
html	htm
swf	swf
crtext	txt
mpeg	mpg

Figure 21.7: A few Documentum formats

Please keep in mind that clicking on the Select Formats link displays the existing format names and not the actual DOS extensions.

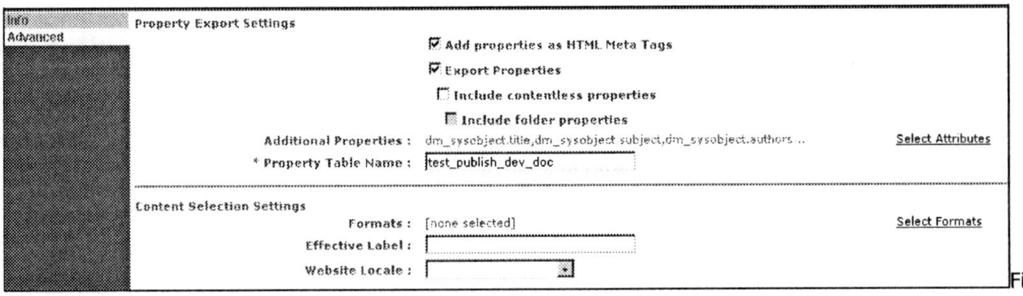

gure 21.8: Content Selection Settings section

Add the formats in the same way you would have added attributes in the Property Export Settings section (refer to figure 21.9). You can even add the custom format custom_format that we created in Chapter 15.

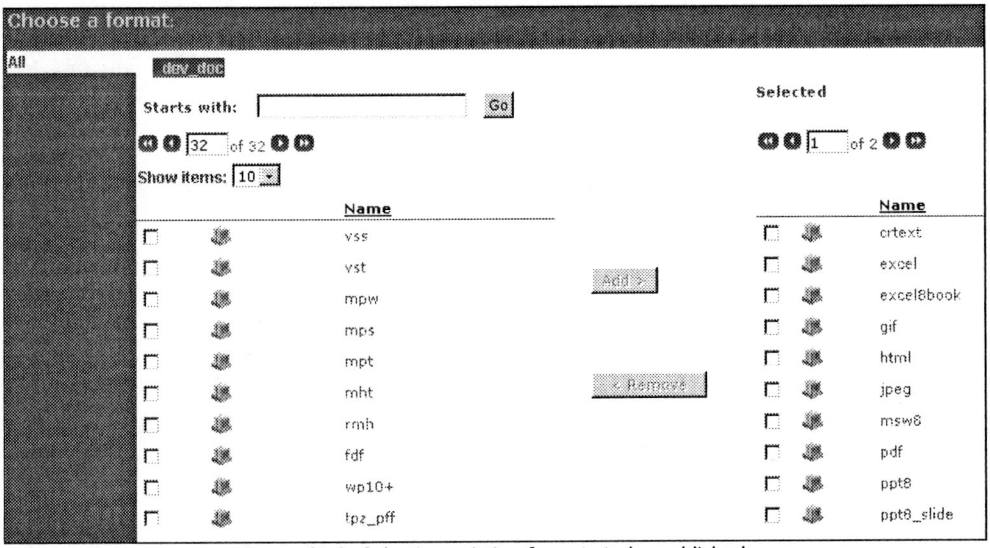

Figure 21.9: Selecting existing formats to be published

Effective Labels assigned in Site Publishing Configuration determine publishing of documents depending upon their effective and expiration dates.

Each document has a_effective_date, a_expiration_date, and a_effective_label attributes by virtue of being a subtype of the dm_sysobject object type.

All the above three attributes are repeating attributes and hence during content creation, users can specify multiple effective and expiration dates for documents corresponding to different effective labels. Based on the specified effective label, the Site Publishing Configuration can publish or expire content based on its specific effective and expiration dates respectively.

For example, content could have the following effective labels and effective expiration dates:

Effective Date: 20/10/2005

Expiration Date: 25/10/2005

Effective Label: UNDER REVIEW

Effective Date: 10/12/2005

Expiration Date: 30/12/2005

Effective Label: FINAL

Appropriately setting up the Site Publishing Configuration could publish the content on 20/10/2005 and withdraw it from the website (expire it) on 25/10/2005 for the UNDER REVIEW effective label of content.

Also, the content with the FINAL effective label would be published on 10/12/2005 and withdrawn from the website on 30/12/2005.

5. Refer to figure 21.10 for filling out the Miscellaneous Settings section in Site Publishing Configuration:

During publishing, Documentum exports the publishable documents along with their attributes to an **export directory** on the Content Server machine in the form of content files and a properties.xml file, which contains attribute information).
This is called an **export data set** and you need to specify the path where export data should be placed. The default location is shown in the screen, but you can change it by clicking the Select Directory link.

Clicking on the Select Directory link shows the existing file/directory structure on the Content Server file system.

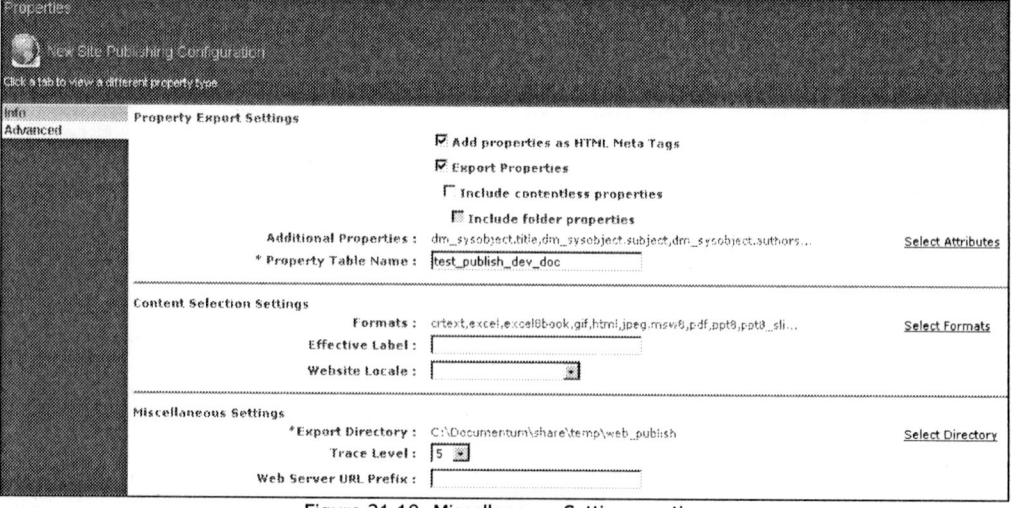

Figure 21.10: Miscellaneous Settings section

You can specify a Trace Level to track the SCS publishing operation traces. These trace levels are used in Trace API methods.

We will discuss the Web Server URL Prefix during our discussion of WebView in Chapter 22.

6. **Online Synchronization Directory** (refer to figure 21.11): Online Synchronization is an important and helpful feature in websites that have bulk publishes happening at periodic intervals, instead of single item publishes.

For a running site, bulk publishes can cause broken sections/links in the site. Using Online Synchronization, you need to specify an Online Synchronization directory on the target host.

The SCS export data set (i.e. published content files + properties) are first placed in the Online Synchronization directory on the target host and then switched to the target root directory (webroot). Actually the webroot directory and Online Synchronization directories are renamed for the synchronization to take place. This causes minimal impact to the running website and reduces inconsistencies to a great extent.

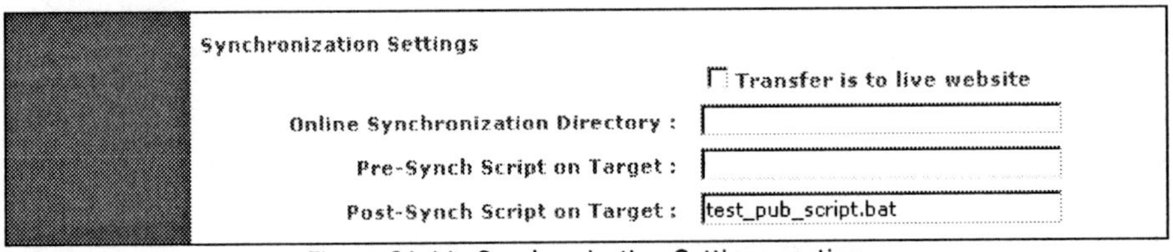

Figure 21.11: Synchronization Settings section

Using the Pre/Post-Synch Script on Target option, you can write custom scripts to perform some tasks specific to your business needs, before or after publishing has updated the website.

The Pre-Synch and Post-Synch scripts execute before and after SCS updates the website respectively.

The execution order (when Online Synchronization is used) is as follows, from left to right: Pre-Synch Script —> Online Synchronization —> Post-Synch Script.

The scripts can be referenced at two locations:

- o **Site Publishing Configuration**: Place the script physically on SCS Target host at the following location: %WEBCACHE%\product\bin
  Example: c:\Documentum\SCS\product\bin

  Or:

- o agent.ini **file on SCS Target host as** pre_sync_script **or** post_sync_script **keys**:
  Place the script physically on the SCS Target host at the following location: %WEBCACHE%\product\bin

Note that agent.ini is found on the SCS Target host at the following location on Windows servers: %WEBCACHE%\admin\config\<SCS Target port number>

Example: `c:\Documentum\SCS\admin\config\2788`

It is worth mentioning that Documentum allows you to pass arguments to scripts as well. For a more detailed understanding, please go through the Documentum Site Caching Services User manual.

In our example, we have specified `test_pub_script.bat` as a Post-Synch script in Site Publishing Configuration.

Content of `test_pub_script.bat`:

```
REM dummy script
echo "Publish done" > C:\Publish_Operation\pub_status.txt
pause
```

After the publishing operation completes, the Publish done message is seen in the file `C:\Publish_Operation\pub_status.txt` on the SCS Target host.

7. Finally, you need to fill in the Transfer Authentication Settings section before completing the details of Site Publishing Configuration (refer to figure 21.12).

   o   **Enable system authentication on target:** Selecting this checkbox requires providing a valid user name and password on the target host for authentication purposes. The data transfer from SCS Source to the SCS target server happens only after user credentials have been authenticated.

   o   Under the **User Name** field, provide a valid user name/account that will be used by the SCS transfer agent to make a connection to the target server.

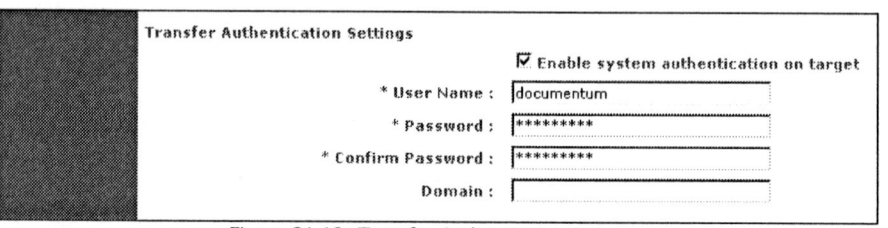

Figure 21.12: Transfer Authentication Settings

After providing all the required Site Publishing Configuration details, click on FINISH to save the newly created Site Publishing Configuration in the Docbase.

The existing Site Publishing Configurations show up under the Administration | Site Publishing section in Documentum Administrator, as can be seen in figure 21.13.

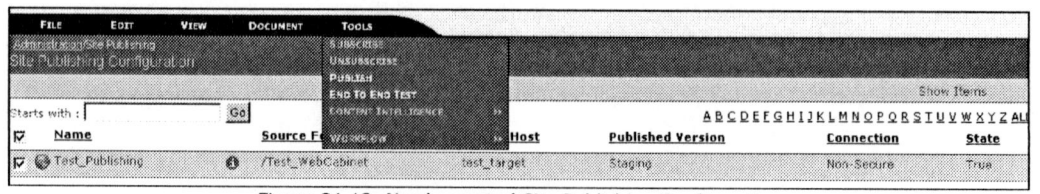

Figure 21.13: Newly created Site Publishing Configuration

21.4 Testing and Publishing Using Site Publishing Configuration

You should always run an End-to-End test (refer to figure 21.14) for the Site Publishing Configuration to ensure that it has been created successfully and is able to publish as per the parameters specified in it. Choose the Site Publishing Configuration and select menu option TOOLS | END TO END TEST.

An End-to-End test performs numerous operations such as making connections to the Docbase, source host, and target host, making test database tables, and inserting records.

The log files generated after an End-to-End test (or for that matter publishing logs) are located under Cabinets | System | Sysadmin | Reports | WebCache in the Docbase.

You need to specify a trace level while running an End-to-End test so that the logs generated have appropriate message/trace levels.

Figure 21.14: Running an End-to-End test

In order to publish from a particular Site Publishing Configuration, select the checkbox against the configuration name and select menu option TOOLS | PUBLISH.

The following Publish screen is shown:

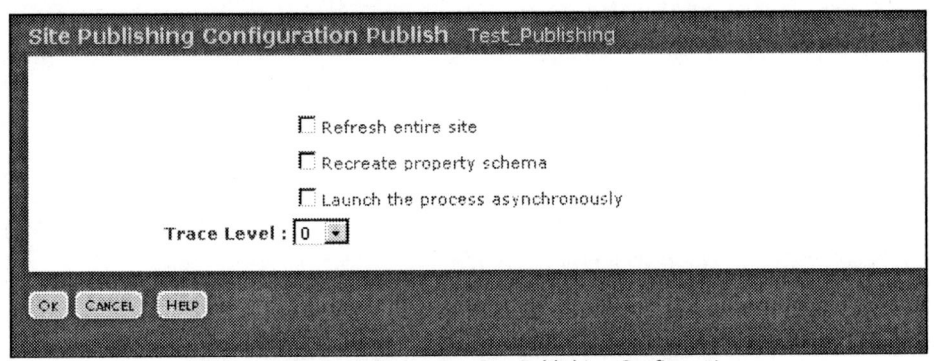

Figure 21.15: Publishing using Site Publishing Configuration

Let's discuss the various options shown in this screen:

- **Refresh entire site:** This performs a full refresh publish, wherein the entire SCS target repository is deleted and the complete source export data set is published.

- **Recreate property schema:** The database tables on the SCS target are dropped and recreated with the latest published data.

- **Launch the process asynchronously:** Check this option in order to refresh the screen before publishing is complete.

- **Trace Level:** Debug tracing level is set from 0 to 10 for the publishing operation.

The SCS publishing logs can be seen by selecting the checkbox against the Site Publishing Configuration in question and clicking on VIEW | LOGS.

Whenever a Site Publishing Configuration is created, Documentum automatically creates a publishing job (in the inactive state) for it so that publishing can proceed at periodic predefined intervals.

Go to **Job Management | Jobs** in Documentum Administrator and select **Web Publishing** from the dropdown shown at the extreme top right hand section of the screen (refer to figure 21.16).

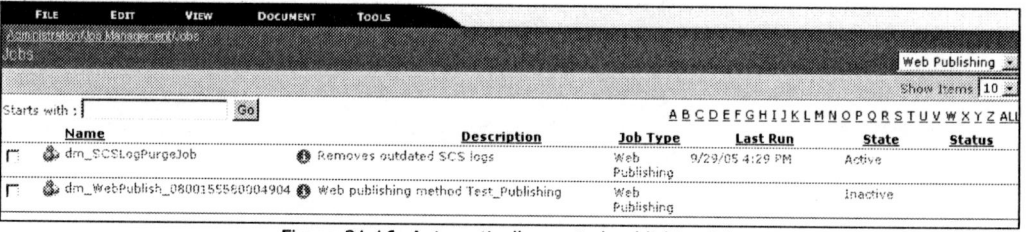

Figure 21.16: Automatically created publishing job

The system generated publishing job can be recognized by its name, which is in the format `dm_WebPublish_< Site Publishing Configuration object ID>`.

Run the following DQL query in Documentum Administrator to find out the object ID of the Site Publishing Configuration in question:

DQL> `select r_object_id,object_name from dm_webc_config`

Results of the DQL query:

r_object_id   object_name

0800155580004904   Test_Publishing

In our case, the publishing job has thus been created with the following name:
dm_WebPublish_0800155580004904

You can always activate the publishing job and schedule it to run at the desired intervals.

21.5 Published Data

Once the publishing operation is complete, you can verify the publish location on the target server and view the published content files. Figure 21.17 shows the published content files on the target host:

Name	Size	Type	Modified
abc		File Folder	10/6/2005 2:11 PM
FilePath One		File Folder	10/6/2005 2:11 PM
FilePath Two		File Folder	10/6/2005 2:11 PM
Hello_&_Hi		File Folder	10/6/2005 2:11 PM
Keywords_ABC		File Folder	10/6/2005 2:11 PM
Keywords_Hello		File Folder	10/6/2005 2:11 PM
Keywords_XYZ		File Folder	10/6/2005 2:11 PM
new_office		File Folder	10/6/2005 2:11 PM
Official docs		File Folder	10/6/2005 2:11 PM
Subject_Content		File Folder	10/6/2005 2:11 PM
test_Second_XMLApp_Template.xml	1 KB	XML Document	10/6/2005 2:11 PM
Test_Two_Way_Template.xml	1 KB	XML Document	10/6/2005 2:11 PM
Testing_First_XMLApp_Template.xml	1 KB	XML Document	10/6/2005 2:11 PM
Testing1_Original_Template.xml	1 KB	XML Document	10/6/2005 2:11 PM
Testing2_Original_Template.xml	1 KB	XML Document	10/6/2005 2:11 PM

Figure 21.17: Published content files on target server

You can see that SCS automatically creates the exact folder structure as present in the Docbase Test_WebCabinet Web Cabinet.

Additionally, you can see the published data in the target host database. Figure 21.18 shows the published database tables (test_publish_dev_doc_s, test_publish_dev_doc_r, and test_publish_dev_doc_m) as seen in SQL Server Enterprise Manager.

sysforeignkeys	dbo	System	8/6/2000 1:29:12 AM
sysfulltextcatalogs	dbo	System	8/6/2000 1:29:12 AM
sysfulltextnotify	dbo	System	8/6/2000 1:29:12 AM
sysindexes	dbo	System	8/6/2000 1:29:12 AM
sysindexkeys	dbo	System	8/6/2000 1:29:12 AM
sysmembers	dbo	System	8/6/2000 1:29:12 AM
sysobjects	dbo	System	8/6/2000 1:29:12 AM
syspermissions	dbo	System	8/6/2000 1:29:12 AM
sysproperties	dbo	System	8/6/2000 1:29:12 AM
sysprotects	dbo	System	8/6/2000 1:29:12 AM
sysreferences	dbo	System	8/6/2000 1:29:12 AM
systypes	dbo	System	8/6/2000 1:29:12 AM
sysusers	dbo	System	8/6/2000 1:29:12 AM
test_publish_dev_doc_m	dbo	User	10/6/2005 10:57:27 AM
test_publish_dev_doc_r	dbo	User	10/6/2005 2:11:50 PM
test_publish_dev_doc_s	dbo	User	10/6/2005 2:11:50 PM

Figure 21.18: Published database tables on target database

Refer to figure 21.19; if you open either the _s or _r table, you can see the records inserted by SCS in the tables with the columns corresponding to the attributes we specified in Site Publishing Configuration under the Additional Properties (attributes) field.

title	subject	cust_attrib3	cust_attrib2	object_name	i_full_format	r_folder_path	a_webc_url	i_chronicle_id
This is page title fill	This is page su	0	<NULL>	Testing_First_XMLApp_Template.xml	xml	/Test_WebCabinet	Testing_First_XMLA	0900155580002296
Template for testin		0	<NULL>	test_Second_XMLApp_Template.xml	xml	/Test_WebCabinet	test_Second_XMLA	0900155580002f9
Template to test tw	Subject filled ii	0	<NULL>	Test_Two_Way_Template.xml	xml	/Test_WebCabinet	Test_Two_Way_Te	0900155580002fa
Testing Instruction		0	<NULL>	Testing1_Original_Template.xml	xml	/Test_WebCabinet	Testing1_Original_	0900155580002fd
Testing Instruction		0	<NULL>	Testing2_Original_Template.xml	xml	/Test_WebCabinet	Testing2_Original_	0900155580002fd
Testing Folder Map	test subject	0	0	fm1_Testing_FM_Template.xml	xml	/Test_WebCabinet	Subject_Content/fr	0900155580000351
Testing Folder Map	new_office	0	0	fm2_Testing_FM_Template.xml	xml	/Test_WebCabinet, new_office/fm2_Te	0900155580000352
Testing Folder Map	new_office	0	0	fm2_Testing_FM_Template.xml	xml	/Test_WebCabinet	Official docs/fm2_T	0900155580000352
Testing Folder Map		0	0	fm3_Testing_FM_Template.xml	xml	/Test_WebCabinet	FilePath Two/fm3_	0900155580000353
Testing Folder Map		0	0	fm3_Testing_FM_Template.xml	xml	/Test_WebCabinet	FilePath One/fm3_	0900155580000353
Testing Folder Map		0	0	fm4_Testing_FM_Template.xml	xml	/Test_WebCabinet	Keywords_ABC/fm	0900155580000354
Testing Folder Map		0	0	fm5_Testing_FM_Template.xml	xml	/Test_WebCabinet	Keywords_Hello/fm	0900155580000355
Testing Folder Map		0	0	fm6_Testing_FM_Template.xml	xml	/Test_WebCabinet	Keywords_XYZ/fm6	0900155580000355
Testing Folder Map		0	0	fm7_Testing_FM_Template.xml	xml	/Test_WebCabinet	abc/fm7_Testing_F	0900155580000357
Testing Folder Map	Hello & Hi	0	0	fm8_Testing_FM_Template.xml	xml	/Test_WebCabinet	Hello_&_Hi/fm8_Te	0900155580000357

Figure 21.19: Published records in the test_publish_dev_doc_s table

You can see that the attributes/properties we included in the Site Publishing Configuration are present as columns in the table—title, subject, cust_attrib3, cust_attrib2, object_name, etc.

The records for repeating valued attributes can be found in the corresponding _r table (i.e. test_publish_dev_doc_r).

21.6 Unlocking Locked Publishing Operations

There are times when the publishing operation gets locked (almost endlessly!). This could be because of some publishing error or some network/hardware failure or because of multiple publishing operations running concurrently.

Under such scenarios, you can unlock the publishing configuration by one of the following means:

1. Stop and start the SCS Source service.

2. Execute the unlockConfig.bat script found under the following location on the SCS Source host:

   %DM_HOME%\webcache\bin

   Example: c:\Documentum\product\5.2\webcache\bin

   Execute the unlockConfig.bat script through the command prompt as follows:

   unlockConfig -u <user> -p <password> [-h <host> | -o <config-id>] <docbase-name>

   o **Unlocking ALL publishing operations on a specific SCS source host for a specific Docbase:**

   unlockConfig -u dummyuser -p userpasswd -h testhost dev_doc

   o **Unlocking a specific publishing operation for a specific Docbase:**

   unlockConfig -u dummyuser -p userpasswd -o 08002232800006d5 dev_doc

In order to find the publishing configuration ID, execute the following DQL:

```
DQL> select r_object_id,object_name from dm_webc_config where object_name
= '<Your Site Publishing Configuration Name>'
```

The returned r_object_id (e.g. 08002232800006d5) is to be used to unlock using the batch file unlockConfig mentioned above.

3. Nullify the holder attribute in the webc_lock object. Whenever SCS Source software is installed, the webc_lock object type is installed in the Docbase. This object is used by Documentum whenever a particular publishing operation is running and the lock gets cleared whenever the operation finishes.

    You could run the following DQL query in Documentum Administrator to find the publishing operation that is holding a lock and then accordingly clear its lock via DQL or API commands as follows:

    ```
    DQL> select r_object_id,holder,object_name from webc_lock
    ```

    This returns the lock status (holder attribute) for all publishing configurations (the object_name attribute is actually the r_object_id of the Site Publishing Configuration).

    Copy the r_object_id value returned from the above DQL query for the case where the holder value is seen to be not null.

    Now execute the following API commands in Documentum Administrator:

    ```
    API>set,c,<object ID copied from above query>,holder
    Data:<Leave this blank>
    API>save,c,<object ID copied from above query>
    ```

    This clears the locked Publishing Configuration by setting the holder attribute as null.

21.7 Monitoring the SCS Source Status

One of the most convenient means of viewing the status of SCS Source publish operations is by accessing the following URL with your browser:

```
http://<SCS Source host name>:<SCS Source port number>/webcache/state
```

Following is a sample XML result set displayed on your browser:

```
<?xml version="1.0" ?>
<state product-version="5.2.5.204 SP2">
  <uptime>
    <hours>26</hours>
    <minutes>59</minutes>
    <seconds>39</seconds>
    <milliseconds>903</milliseconds>
  </uptime>
  <total-publishes>
    <count>1</count>
  </total-publishes>
  <full-refreshes>
    <count>1</count>
    <average-duration>
      <hours>0</hours>
      <minutes>0</minutes>
      <seconds>0</seconds>
      <milliseconds>0</milliseconds>
```

```
        </average-duration>
      </full-refreshes>
      <incrementals>
        <count>0</count>
      </incrementals>
      <asynchronous-publishes>
        <count>0</count>
      </asynchronous-publishes>
      <active-publishes>
        <count>0</count>
      </active-publishes>
    </state>
```

Figure 21.20 explains the valuable information conveyed by the above XML result set.

XML element	Interpretation
`<uptime>`	Total time that the SCS Source service has been up and running.
`<total-publishes>`	Total number of publishes done since the SCS Source service was last restarted.
`<full-refreshes>`, `<incrementals>`, and `<asynchronous-publishes>`	Total number of Full refresh publish, Incremental publish operations, and Asynchronous publish operations done and their total durations.
`<active-publishes>`	Total number of publish operations occurring currently.

Figure 21.20: Interpretation of SCS Source publish state XML

21.8 Summary

We briefly discussed that Site Caching Services (SCS) allows you to easily configure and publish documents and their attributes (such as title, authors, keywords, etc.) from Docbase to the website host and database tables.

We then had a look at some of the limitations of using SCS and discussed the various types of publishing operations: Full refresh, Incremental refresh/publish, Force refresh, and Single object publish.

We then looked at detailed steps to create a Site Publishing Configuration in Documentum Administrator for defining source and target host parameters for publishing using SCS.

After creating a Site Publishing Configuration, we ran an End-to-End test to verify whether it worked correctly.

At times publishing operations hang due to certain publishing errors or due to network/hardware failures as well. We saw various methods to unlock publishing operations under such scenarios.

Finally, we saw a simple mechanism to view the status of SCS Source publishing operations through a URL accessed via a browser.

22

Web Viewing Content Files

Now that we have created a Site Publishing Configuration and studied how publishing works in Documentum, we are all set to take our discussion a step further and learn about Web View.

Web View is one of the areas least explored by most Web Publisher users and if utilized well, is really useful! Web Publisher's Web View feature lets you preview content files on your web servers so that you can QA it and be assured about its look and feel and other aspects such as links to other pages on your website before publishing to the production site.

Just treat Web View as viewing web content on your web server. Web View is available by default in Web Publisher and figure 22.1 shows how web viewing works in Web Publisher:

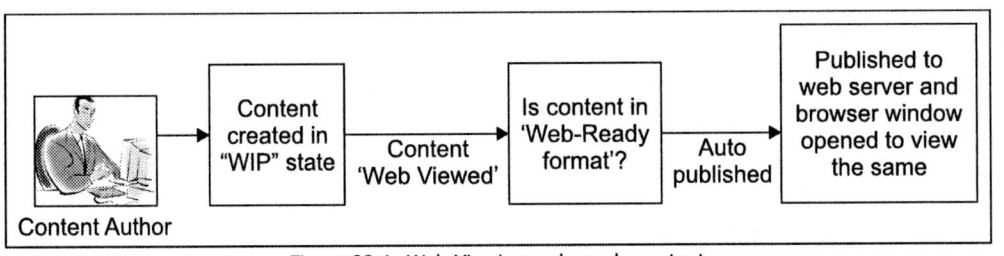

Figure 22.1: Web Viewing web-ready content

The web viewing mechanism is fairly simple and the steps are as follows:

1. Ensure that SCS Target software is installed and configured correctly on the web server.
2. Set up your web server appropriately and point the publish location in Site Publishing Configuration to the home directory of your web server.
3. Decide which lifecycle state of content should be web viewed. If it is WIP, then prepare a Site Publishing Configuration for publishing WIP content using Documentum Administrator. (We will cover the details of this Site Publishing Configuration later in this chapter.)
4. Prepare the presentation files (XSLs) for the content XML files in Web Publisher so that the necessary renditions can be generated for the content files.

5. Before web viewing, ensure that the content to be web viewed is in a web-ready state. This means that it is in a format that can be understood and served by your web server. Normally a green dot next to the content file in Web Publisher denotes that it is web ready. Yellow means it is in the process of getting web-ready while red signifies that no web-ready rendition available.

6. Choose the content to be web viewed and click on the WebView button in Web Publisher.

7. If the content is in web-ready format, Documentum shows the available renditions of the content file.

8. Choose the rendition to be web viewed.

9. Documentum finds the matching Site Publishing Configuration for the lifecycle state of the content (for example: WIP state) and automatically publishes the content to the WIP web server (say).

10. A browser window accessing the published content file from the WIP web server webroot is shown to the user so that the user can preview the look and feel of the page in the context of the website.

If this seems like too much work or too perplexing, do not worry. We will cover all of this via screenshots in this chapter. It is better that you try this out as well to gain some hands-on experience and not just theoretical knowledge.

22.1 Prerequisites

Before you start trying out the steps for web viewing content files, please ensure that the following entities are in place:

- SCS Source software is installed on your Content Server host and the SCS Source service is up and running correctly.

- SCS Target is installed on your web server host and the SCS Target service is up and running correctly.

- The web server (IIS in our example) is set up correctly on your web server host machine.

- The necessary templates and presentation files in Web Publisher have been created and content can be created using the templates and its renditions can be generated by virtue of the associated XSLs (Presentation files).

If all this is set up correctly, you are ready to jump into the next section. Happy Web Viewing!

22.2 Setting Up and Using Web View

In this section, we will cover the detailed steps for setting up and using Web View:

1. Log in your web server host (webview_server machine in our case) and go to Programs | Administrative Tools | Internet Services Manager.

   The Internet Information Services console opens up as shown in figure 22.2. Choose the Default Website, right-click, and choose the Properties option.

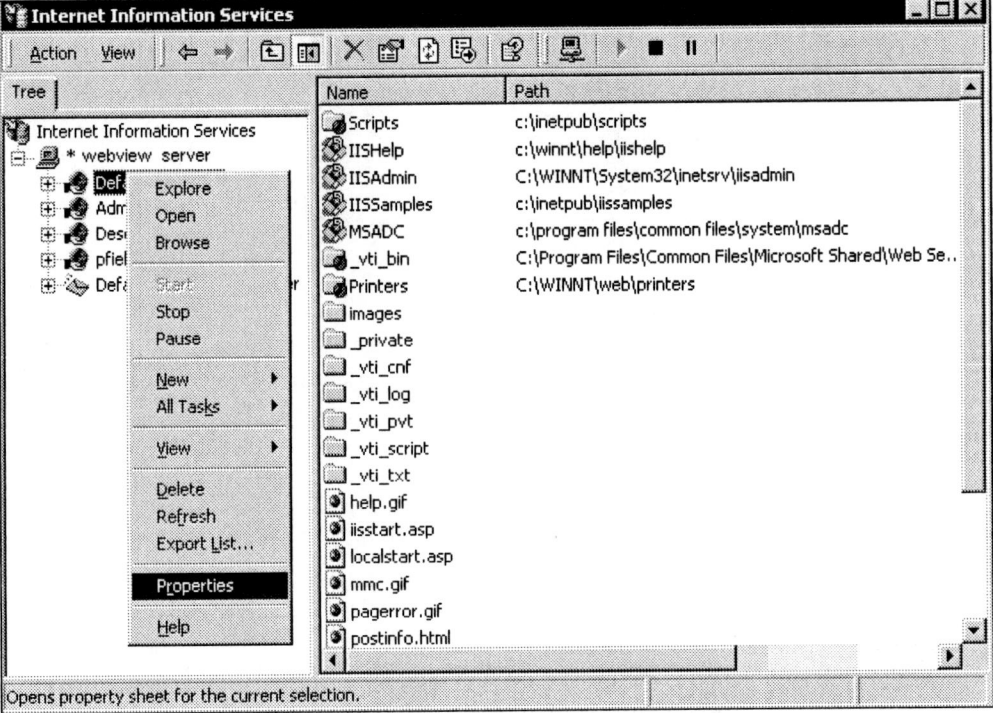

Figure 22.2: Internet Information Services console

2. Go to the Home Directory tab (refer to figure 22.3) in the Default Website Properties window and note down the location mentioned against the Local Path section.

   The default location is: c:\inetpub\wwwroot.

   We will need to specify this under the Target Root Directory field while setting up Web View Site Publishing Configuration.

Close the Default Website Properties window after noting down the local path.

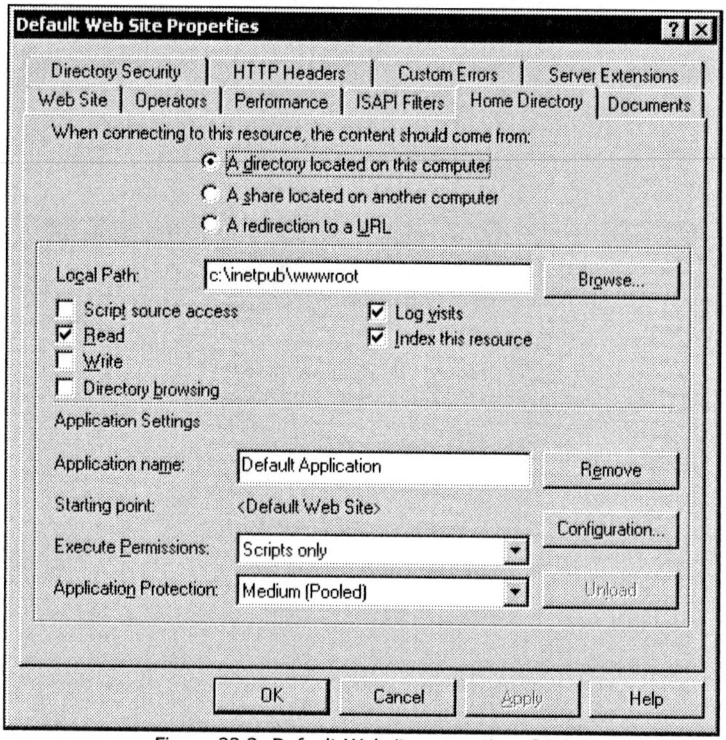

Figure 22.3: Default Website properties of IIS

3. Log in to Documentum Administrator as an administrator and go to Administration | Site Publishing. Choosing FILE | NEW | SITE PUBLISHING CONFIGURATION brings up an empty Site Publishing Configuration screen.

Fill in the information under the Info tab of Site Publishing Configuration as shown in figure 22.4:

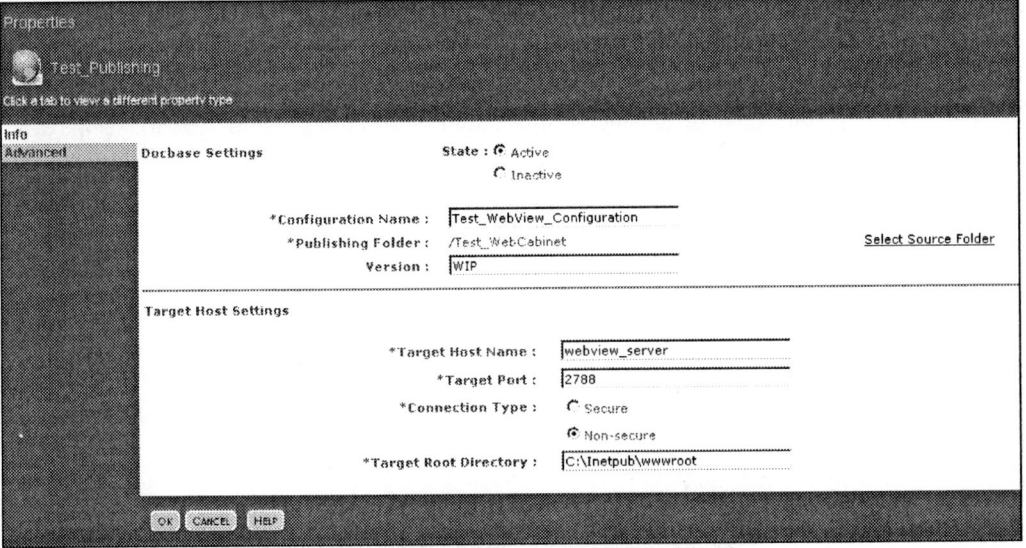

Figure 22.4: Site Publishing Configuration Info tab

Let's discuss the fields shown in this tab in detail:

- o Configuration Name: A valid name for the Site Publishing Configuration, such as Test_WebView_Configuration.
- o Publishing Folder: Choose the Web Cabinet (by clicking on Select Source Folder) from which the content needs to be published. In our Docbase, we created the Test_WebCabinet Web Cabinet. All content created under this Web Cabinet directly or within folders contained under this web cabinet will be published and web viewed.
- o Version: The lifecycle state of the documents for which web viewing should happen. This corresponds to the r_version_label attribute of the content. In our case, we are web viewing all documents that are in the WIP state of their lifecycle.
- o Target Host Name: Host name or the IP address of the web server host (where SCS Target has been installed), in our case webview_server.
- o Target Port: The port number to which SCS Target service listens. The default is 2788.
- o Connection Type: Connection to SCS Target. This can be raw (Non-secure) or SSL (Secure).
- o Target Root Directory: This is the webroot on the website host where published files will be placed. This should be the Local Path we copied from the Home Directory tab in the Default Website Properties window in IIS. Example: c:\Inetpub\wwwroot.

4. After filling in the Info tab, go to the Advanced tab in Site Publishing Configuration.

Fill in the various fields under Property Export Settings and Content Selection Settings sections as shown in figure 22.5.

Under the Miscellaneous Settings section, provide the export directory path and set the trace level. You additionally need to specify the Web Server URL Prefix for Web View to work.

This is the web server name and IIS port number:

`http://webview_server:80/`   (Note that the default port for IIS is 80.)

Whenever a content rendition is web viewed, Documentum publishes the content to the web server under `c:\Inetpub\wwwroot` specified as the target root directory on the web server. While publishing, SCS creates the folder structure existing in Docbase under the published Web Cabinet.

Finally, the Web View browser displays the content file from a concatenated location as follows:

`Web Server URL Prefix + Published folder structure under Target root directory on web server`

Example: A file `webviewedfile.htm` under `web_cabinet_folder` within Docbase is web viewed.

The Web View browser has the following URL:

`http://webview_server:80/web_cabinet_folder/webviewedfile.htm`

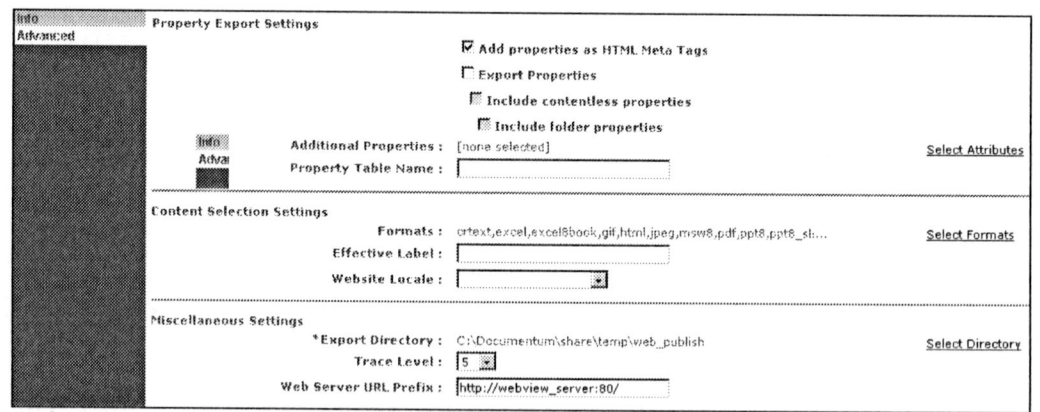

Figure 22.5: Advanced tab in Site Publishing Configuration

Additionally, fill in the Synchronization Settings and Transfer Authentication Settings as appropriate (refer to figure 22.6).

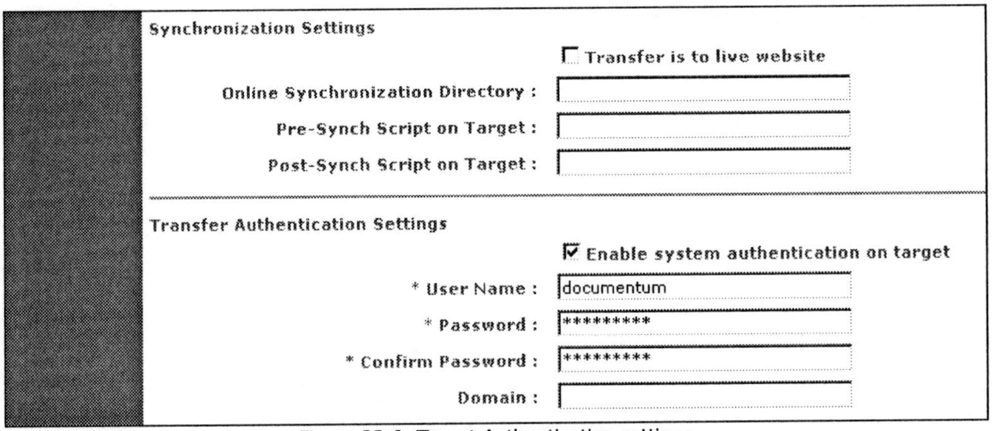

Synchronization Settings

☐ Transfer is to live website

Online Synchronization Directory :

Pre-Synch Script on Target :

Post-Synch Script on Target :

Transfer Authentication Settings

☑ Enable system authentication on target

* User Name : documentum

* Password : ********

* Confirm Password : ********

Domain :

Figure 22.6: Target Authentication settings

5. After providing all the required Site Publishing Configuration details, click on FINISH to save the newly created Site Publishing Configuration in the Docbase.

    The existing Site Publishing Configurations show up under the Administration | Site Publishing section in Documentum Administrator (refer to figure 22.7).

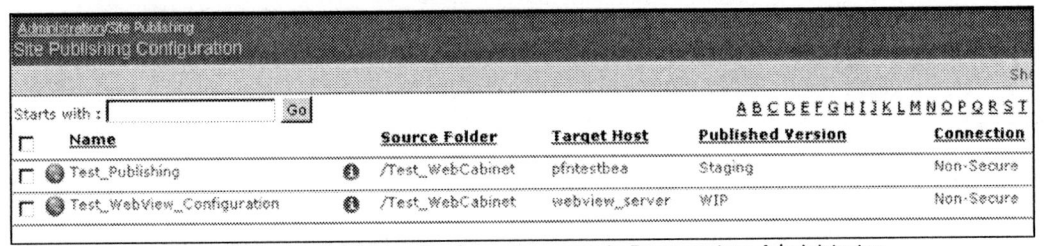

Figure 22.7: Site Publishing Configurations seen in Documentum Administrator

6. You should now run an End-to-End test for the newly created Web View Site Publishing Configuration to ensure that it has been created successfully and is able to publish as per the parameters specified in it. Choose the Site Publishing Configuration and select menu option TOOLS | END TO END TEST.

    The log file generated after an End-to-End test is located under Cabinets | System | Sysadmin | Reports | WebCache in Docbase.

    If the End-to-End test is successful, you are all set to go ahead and test Web View in Web Publisher. Follow some simple steps as mentioned next to Web View a content file.

22.3 Testing Web View

In this section, we will explain in detail how to test the Web View functionality:

1. Log in to Web Publisher and create some content using a template as shown in figure 22.8.

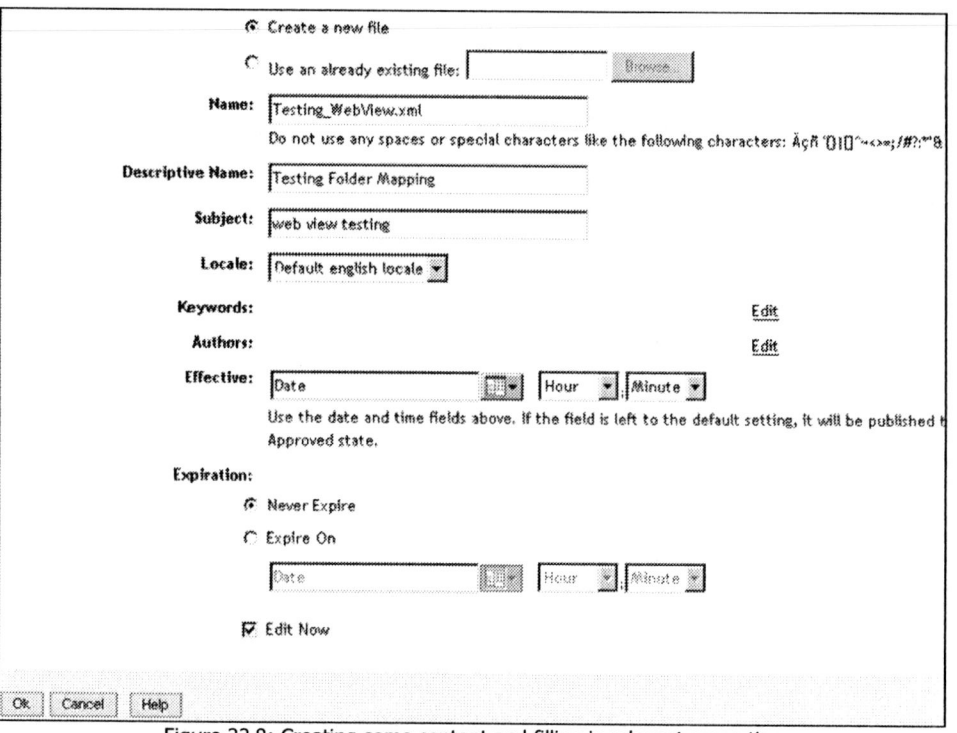

Figure 22.8: Creating some content and filling in relevant properties

Fill in the template fields in Web Publisher template editor as shown in figure 22.9.

Figure 22.9: Filling in template fields for the content

2. Check-in the newly created content. Then select the checkbox against the content and click on the WebView button shown at the top right-hand side of the screen as shown in figure 22.10 (or you could choose the View | Web View menu option instead).

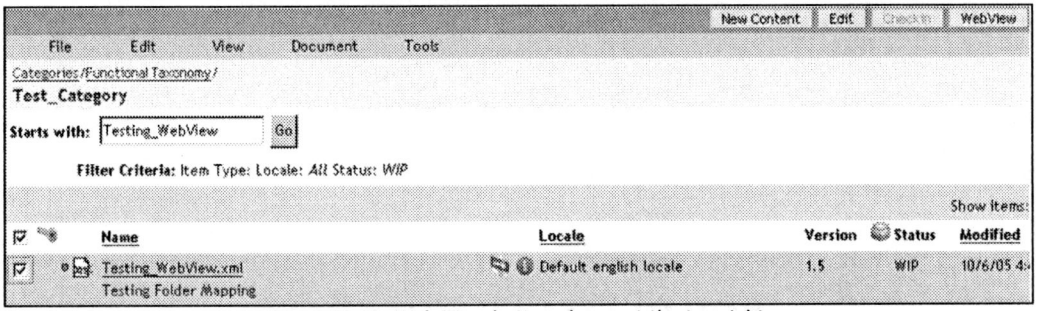

Figure 22.10: Web View button shown at the top right

3. Depending upon the associated Presentation files (XSL), the various rendition formats of the content file are shown. You can choose the required rendition to be web viewed and click on OK.

    In our case the default XML format and the HTML format are shown for the selected content file, as shown in figure 22.11.

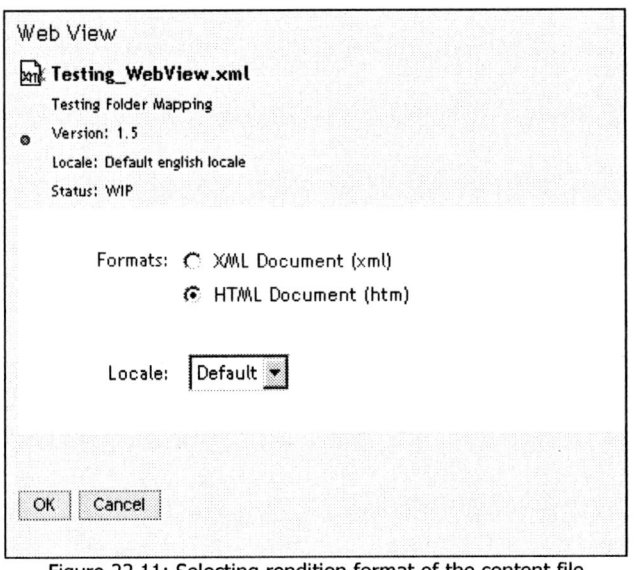

Figure 22.11: Selecting rendition format of the content file

4. Documentum SCS publishes the selected content file to the web server and opens up a browser window pointing to the published file directly from the web server webroot as shown in figure 22.12.

Note that the layout for the content file shown in the figure was specified in the associated XSL (Presentation file) and is not something that Web View automatically does for you.

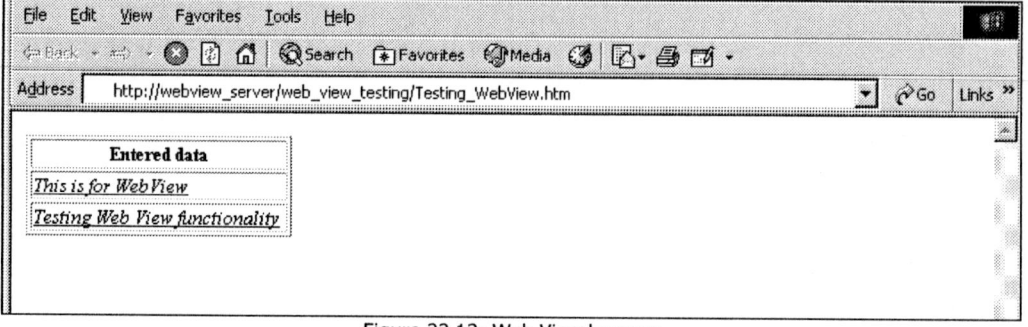

Figure 22.12: Web View browser

This is it. Web View worked! Note that the URL in the browser window (as we discussed earlier) is a concatenation of Web Server URL Prefix and Published folder structure under the Target root directory on the web server.

22.4 Summary

Web Publisher Web View allows you to automatically publish and preview content on web servers so that it can be verified and tested before promoting it to live websites.

In this chapter we saw how Web View works and some prerequisites for it to work properly in Web Publisher.

Through detailed steps, we discussed how to set up WebView in Documentum using Site Publishing Configuration in Documentum Administrator.

Finally, we created some content and web viewed it on our web server to see its HTML rendition.

23
Using DFC

In almost every project that you will execute based on Documentum, you may need to customize and extend basic content management functionalities provided by the Content Server.

You might be required to write some custom lifecycle or workflow methods or perform some business-specific customizations on existing Documentum products such as Desktop or Web Publisher. Would it not be difficult if you had to first understand and learn Documentum native server API calls and a proprietary language such as Docbasic to achieve these goals?

Well, Documentum provides you with a much simpler wrapper interface that shields you from making native calls directly and reduces the learning curve involved in getting familiar with any proprietary language and its syntax. The answer is DFC.

DFC is short for **Documentum Foundation Classes** and is provided as a set of Java interfaces and their implementing classes. However, for those who are working on a Microsoft COM (Component Object Model) environment, DFC comes with a Documentum Java-COM bridge (DJCB) for accessing Java interfaces. Lastly, in a .NET environment, you can utilize DFC PIA (Primary Interop Assembly) to access DFC interfaces. Furthermore, DFC includes a Business Object Framework (BOF) enabling you to wrap your business rules in the form of reusable components, allowing you to extend the functionality provided by DFC implementation classes.

In a nutshell, DFC exists as a Framework exposing the Content Server's content management functionality for you to effectively harness.

> DFC exposes some server API methods such as `apiGet` and `apiSet` to access Content Server functionality by making native server API calls. This has been provided only for backward compatibility with older models that were not based on DFC. You should avoid using such server API methods and instead use alternative methods in DFC that can achieve the same purpose.

For example, consider setting the `object_name` attribute for a SysObject:

- **Incorrect way**: `sysObj.apiSet("set", "object_name", objectNameToBeSet);`
- **Recommended way**: `sysObj.setObjectName(objectNameToBeSet);`

23.1 Introduction to DFC

The best way to get started is by looking at the DFC Javadocs for the API specification. If you have installed DFC (standalone or along with some other Documentum products such as Application Builder or Content Server), browse to the following location on your local machine:

Example: `C:\Program Files\Documentum\help\dfc\api`

Open `index.html` to look at the DFC API and spend some time going through the available packages, interfaces, and classes.

The following naming conventions must be followed in DFC API:

- **Packages begin with** `com.documentum`.

  There are numerous packages available in DFC such as `com.documentum.xml.xdql`, which provides interfaces and classes for using XDQL and `com.documentum.fc.client`, which provides interfaces and classes for creating/managing Docbase sessions and manipulating data in Docbase.

- **Interfaces begin with** `IDf`.

  Two commonly used DFC interfaces are `IDfSessionManager` and `IDfSysObject`.

- **Classes begin with** `Df`.

  Two commonly used classes in DFC are `DfClient` and `DfQuery`.

If you go through the DFC Javadocs, you will notice that the interfaces in DFC follow a hierarchical pattern. This means that each interface inherits all the methods and constants of interfaces above it in the hierarchy chain. For example, in figure 23.1, note that the `IDfPersistentObject` interface inherits `getObjectId()` and other methods from its superinterface `IDfTypedObject` and adds methods such as `destroy()` and `save()` specific to it.

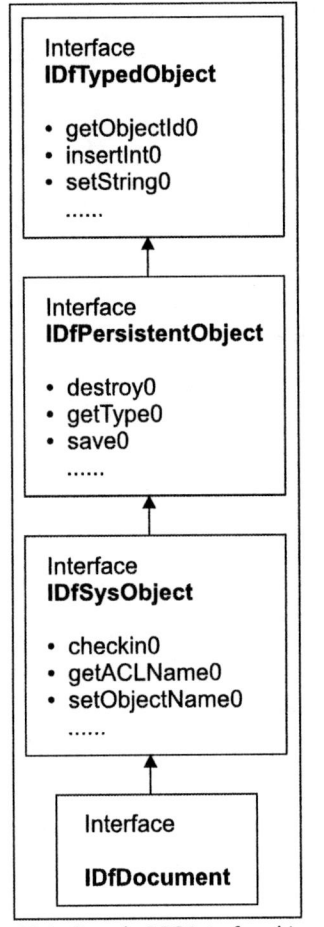

Figure 23.1: Sample DFC interface hierarchy

23.2 Environment Readiness

Once you have DFC available on your machine, you need to ensure that the following entries are present in your system classpath (CLASSPATH environment variable) before you can start programming:

`C:\Documentum\config`

`C:\Program Files\Documentum\dctm.jar`

`C:\Program Files\Documentum\Shared\dfc.jar`

`C:\Program Files\Documentum\Shared\dfcbase.jar`

Assuming that you are working in a Java environment, find out the supported JRE (Java Runtime Environment) for DFC from the published Documentum release notes and install the correct JRE on your machine.

In this book, all DFC examples will be compiled and executed using JDK1.4.2_04.

In order to establish a connection to Docbase via DFC, the dmcl.ini file on your machine should contain correct entries for DocBroker host and port number.

On Windows machines, the dmcl.ini file is usually found under the %SystemRoot% location (such as C:\WINDOWS or C:\WINNT).

23.3 Simple Example Demonstrating DFC Usage

Let us create a simple Java file (save it as FirstDFC.java) as shown below to create and establish a Docbase session via DFC.

```java
import com.documentum.fc.client.*;
import com.documentum.fc.common.*;

import java.io.IOException;

public class FirstDFC{

//Main method
public static void main(String args[]){

    IDfSession session = null;
    IDfSessionManager sMgr = null;

    try
    {
        IDfClient client = new DfClient().getLocalClient();
        sMgr = client.newSessionManager();
        IDfLoginInfo loginInfo = new DfLoginInfo();

        loginInfo.setUser( "documentum" );
        loginInfo.setPassword( "solutions" );
        sMgr.setIdentity( "dev_doc", loginInfo );
        session = sMgr.getSession( "dev_doc" );

        System.out.println("Session created !!");

    }catch(DfException dfe){

        System.out.println("DfException caught in main: " +
                                            dfe.getMessage());
    }
    catch(Exception e){

        System.out.println("Catching generic exception in main: " +
                                            e.getMessage());
    }
    finally {

        sMgr.release( session );

    }

}// end of Main

}// end of class
```

Let's discuss the anatomy of this DFC code:

```
import com.documentum.fc.client.*;
import com.documentum.fc.common.*;
```

The DFC Packages imported are `com.documentum.fc.client` and `com.documentum.fc.common`. Package `com.documentum.fc.client` provides interfaces and classes for establishing Docbase sessions and controlling Docbase data. Package `com.documentum.fc.common` provides some utility functions for manipulating Docbase objects.

```
IDfClient client = new DfClient().getLocalClient();
```

The `IDfClient` interface is used for making connections with Documentum servers. The handle to `IDfClient` interface is obtained by calling the `getLocalClient()` method on class `DfClient`. The `IDfClient` interface is used as a factory for `IDfSessionManager` objects (see line 18), which are used for creating sessions (`IDfSession` objects).

Note that you can use the `IDfClientX` interface for facilitating DFC access through the COM environment.

```
IDfLoginInfo loginInfo = new DfLoginInfo();
```

This references the `IDfLoginInfo` object required for encapsulating login information such as user name and password for a user in the Docbase.

```
sMgr.setIdentity( "dev_doc", loginInfo );
```

The `setIdentity()` method of `IDfSessionManager` sets the identity for user authentication in Docbase. You need to provide two parameters—the Docbase name (`dev_doc`) and the `IDfLoginInfo` set in the steps above.

```
session = sMgr.getSession( "dev_doc" );
```

The `getSession()` method in `IDfSessionManager` is used to obtain Docbase sessions. You need to provide the Docbase name as a parameter to this method.

```
}catch(DfException dfe){
```

`DfException` extends `java.lang.Exception` and is thrown while invoking DFC methods.

```
sMgr.release( session );
```

The `release()` method in `IDfSessionManager` is used to release the session. This makes it available to Session Manager so that the same session can be recycled and made available to anyone who issues a `getSession()` call. This is good practice and should be followed as a rule.

That's it! Compile the code by running `javac FirstDFC.java` and run it by calling `java FirstDFC`. You will see the Session created! message on the console, indicating that a successful Docbase session has been established.

23.4 Creating and Linking a File in a Docbase Cabinet

We saw a very simple example to establish a session with the Docbase. Once the Docbase session has been created, you can perform a host of operations in the Docbase. In this example, we will see how to create a document object in the Docbase, associate it with a text file, and link this object to a cabinet in the Docbase via DFC methods.

Create a simple Java file `LinkingFileDFC.java` as shown below:

```java
import com.documentum.fc.client.*;
import com.documentum.fc.common.*;
import java.io.IOException;

public class LinkingFileDFC{

//Main method
public static void main(String args[]){

    IDfSession session = null;
    IDfSessionManager sMgr = null;

    try
    {
        String strDocbaseName = "dev_doc";

        //Connecting to DocBase
        IDfClient client = new DfClient().getLocalClient();
        sMgr = client.newSessionManager();
        IDfLoginInfo loginInfo = new DfLoginInfo();

        loginInfo.setUser( "documentum" );
        loginInfo.setPassword( "solutions" );
        sMgr.setIdentity(strDocbaseName, loginInfo );
        session = sMgr.getSession(strDocbaseName);

        System.out.println("Connected to DocBase..");

        //Linking a text document to a DocBase cabinet
        IDfDocument document = null;
        document = (IDfDocument)session.newObject( "dm_document" );
        document.setObjectName( "testing_link_file" );
        document.setContentType( "crtext" );
        document.setFile( "C:\\test\\DummyLinkedFile.txt" );
        document.link("/Custom_Cabinet/Custom_Fld");
        document.save();

        System.out.println("Object saved and linked!!");

    }catch(DfException dfe){

        System.out.println("DfException caught in main: " + dfe.getMessage());

    }catch(Exception e){

        System.out.println("main::Exception is " + e.getMessage());
    }
    finally {

        sMgr.release( session );

    }

    }// end of Main

} // end of class
```

The anatomy of the DFC code follows:

```
IDfClient client = new DfClient().getLocalClient();
sMgr = client.newSessionManager();
IDfLoginInfo loginInfo = new DfLoginInfo();

loginInfo.setUser( "documentum" );
loginInfo.setPassword( "solutions" );
sMgr.setIdentity(strDocbaseName, loginInfo );
session = sMgr.getSession(strDocbaseName);
```

A session is established with the Docbase.

```
document = (IDfDocument)session.newObject( "dm_document" );
```

The newObject() method of IDfSession is invoked to create a new persistent object in the Docbase of the type specified as a parameter (dm_document). The returned object is cast to the required interface (IDfDocument).

It is worth mentioning that Documentum does not commit this object to the Docbase until and unless an explicit save() call is made via DFC (see line 36).

```
document.setObjectName( "testing_link_file" );
```

Here we set the name of the document object by passing the name as a parameter to the setObjectName() method of IDfDocument.

```
document.setContentType( "crtext" );
```

Here we set the file format of the document's content by calling the setContentType() method of IDfSysObject object. (Remember that IDfSysObject is a superinterface of IDfDocument.)

Pass the Documentum format name (of the type dm_format) as a parameter to the method. In our case we have passed crtext as the format name to the setContentType() method since we need to link a Windows text file with the document object.

Note that for UNIX, the format name for a text document is text while it is mactext for Mac OS.

```
document.setFile( "C:\\test\\DummyLinkedFile.txt" );
```

This line creates a sample .txt file on your machine by providing the complete path to this file in the setFile() method of the IDfSysObject object.

This method sets the content file for the newly created document object in Docbase.

```
document.link("/Custom_Cabinet/Custom_Fld");
```

The document object is associated with a folder existing in the Docbase by calling the link() method. We have provided the folder path (Custom_Fld folder within Custom_Cabinet cabinet) where the document object needs to be linked in the Docbase.

Note that you can also provide the object ID of the folder instead of its cabinet path in the link() method.

When you compile and execute the LinkingFileDFC.java code, the following messages are printed on your console:

Connected to DocBase. followed by Object saved and linked!!.

You can log in to Web Publisher and browse to the Custom_Fld folder within Custom_Cabinet cabinet in the Docbase. You will notice a text file object with the name testing_link_file created and linked via DFC as shown in figure 23.2.

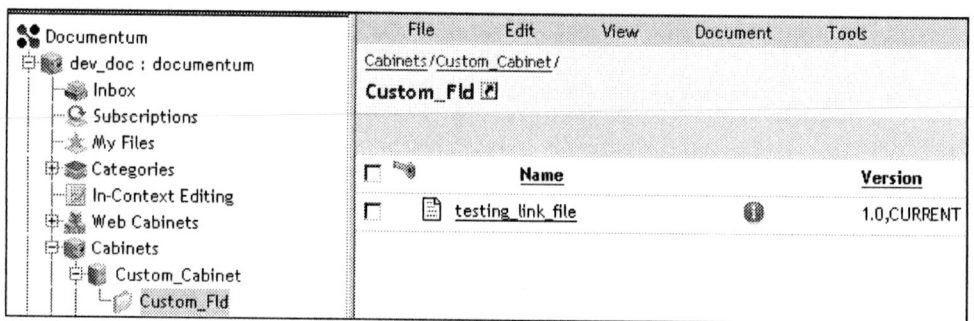

Figure 23.2: Linked text file seen in Docbase cabinet

23.5 Running Docbase Methods via DFC

Docbase methods can be run in a number of ways:

- Scheduling and running via Documentum jobs from Documentum Administrator
- Running methods directly from Documentum Administrator
- Running the DQL command EXECUTE do_method
- Executing the server API call apply

Apart from the above mechanisms, you can also call and run methods by making DFC calls, as we will see in this example.

Create a Java file and save it as RunningMethodThroughDFC.java.

Declare constants, storing the name of the method and its associated job and the method arguments as shown in the code below.

We will be running the Data Dictionary Publisher method via DFC code in this example. This administration tool provided by Documentum publishes the Content Server data dictionary information to client applications. Recall our earlier discussion of the Data Dictionary in Chapter 3.

```java
import com.documentum.fc.client.*;
import com.documentum.fc.common.*;

import java.io.IOException;

public class RunningMethodThroughDFC{

static final String methodName = "dm_DataDictionaryPublisher";
static final String jobName = "dm_DataDictionaryPublisher";
static final String methodArguments =
"-docbase_name dev_doc.dev_doc -user_name documentum -method_trace_level 5";

//Main method
public static void main(String args[]){
```

Note that the method arguments for the Data Dictionary tool shown are docbase_name (dev_doc.dev_doc, i.e. <server>.<Docbase name>), user_name (documentum, i.e. Docbase user used to run the method), and method_trace_level (5, i.e. tracing level for the method execution).

Establish a Docbase session first and then follow the code snippet shown below:

```
IDfQuery q = null;
IDfCollection coll = null;
String methodCmd = null;
String methResult = null;
String methObjectId = null;

// Fetching method reference
q = new DfQuery();
q.setDQL("select r_object_id from dm_method where object_name='" +
                                               methodName + "'");
coll = q.execute(session, DfQuery.DF_READ_QUERY);
while (coll.next()) {
    methObjectId = coll.getId("r_object_id").toString();
}

coll.close();


System.out.println("Object ID of the method:   " + methObjectId );

// Fetching associated job reference
IDfQuery qry = null;
IDfCollection colln = null;
String jobObjectId = null;

qry = new DfQuery();
qry.setDQL("select r_object_id from dm_job where object_name='" +
                                               jobName + "'");
colln = qry.execute(session, DfQuery.DF_READ_QUERY);
while (colln.next()) {
    jobObjectId = colln.getId("r_object_id").toString();
}

colln.close();


methodCmd="DO_METHOD,METHOD,S," + methodName +
                  ",TIME_OUT,I,200,SAVE_RESULTS,B,T,ARGUMENTS,S,"
                       + methodArguments + " -job_id " + jobObjectId;

//Obtaining handle to the method
IDfId sysObjID = new DfId(methObjectId);
IDfSysObject sysObject = (IDfSysObject)session.getObject(sysObjID);
// Executing the method
methResult = sysObject.apiGet("apply", methodCmd);

System.out.println("Result of executing the method: " + methResult );

sysObject.save();

System.out.println("method executed successfully!!");


}catch(Exception e){
     System.out.println("main::Exception is " + e.getMessage());
}
finally {
sMgr.release( session );
```

```
        }
    }
}
```

The anatomy of the DFC code is discussed below:

```
        q = new DfQuery();
```

This gets a reference to an IDfQuery object to run DQL queries against the Docbase.

```
        q.setDQL("select r_object_id from dm_method where object_name='" +
                                        methodName + "'");
```

This calls the setDQL() method of IDfQuery object, passing it the DQL query to be executed as a parameter. Ensure that the DQL query is correct in terms of its syntax.

```
        coll = q.execute(session, DfQuery.DF_READ_QUERY);
```

This calls the execute() method of the IDfQuery object, passing it the Docbase session and the type of query to be executed. In our case, since we need to simply retrieve an object reference from Docbase (in other words a read-only select query), we specify the query type as DfQuery.DF_READ_QUERY.

```
        while (coll.next()) {
```

Executing the DQL query returns a collection result (IDfCollection object).

Iterate through the collection by calling the next() method until it returns false.

It is good practice to close the collection to conserve system resources.

```
        methObjectId = coll.getId("r_object_id").toString();
```

We call the method getId() of IDfTypedObject object to get the object ID (r_object_id) of the retrieved Data Dictionary Publisher method.

```
        IDfQuery qry = null;
        IDfCollection colln = null;
        String jobObjectId = null;

        qry = new DfQuery();
        qry.setDQL("select r_object_id from dm_job where object_name='" +
                                        jobName + "'");
        colln = qry.execute(session, DfQuery.DF_READ_QUERY);
        while (colln.next()) {
            jobObjectId = colln.getId("r_object_id").toString();
        }

        colln.close();
```

In the above lines we obtain the object ID of the associated Data Dictionary Publisher job.

```
        methodCmd="DO_METHOD,METHOD,S," + methodName +
                    ",TIME_OUT,I,200,SAVE_RESULTS,B,T,ARGUMENTS,S,"
                            + methodArguments + " -job_id " + jobObjectId;
```

We define the method execution command arguments as follows:

- DO_METHOD is used to execute Docbase scripts and methods.
- METHOD signifies that a method needs to be executed.
- s indicates that the data type for method name is string.
- TIME_OUT signifies the time-out length in seconds for method execution.
- I indicates that the data type for time out is integer.
- 200 indicates the time-out period in seconds for the method.
- SAVE_RESULTS indicates if you want the execution results to be saved in a document in Docbase.
- B indicates a Boolean data type (true or false) for the SAVE_RESULTS option.
- T stands for option true, asking for the results to be saved in a document.
- ARGUMENTS signifies the command-line arguments for the method execution.
- s indicates that the data type for method arguments is string.
- job_id argument captures the object ID of the associated Data Dictionary Publisher job.

The following statement calls the apiGet() method of IDfPersistentObject object to execute the apply server API call, passing it the arguments we had constructed for methodCmd.

```
methResult = sysObject.apiGet("apply", methodCmd)
```

A result object is returned as the result of executing the method.

When you compile and execute the RunningMethodThroughDFC.java code, the Data Dictionary Publisher method is executed. If you selected the checkbox against Trace Launch field in the method (refer to figure 23.3), you can see the trace for the method execution in the Docbase server logs when the above DFC code is run.

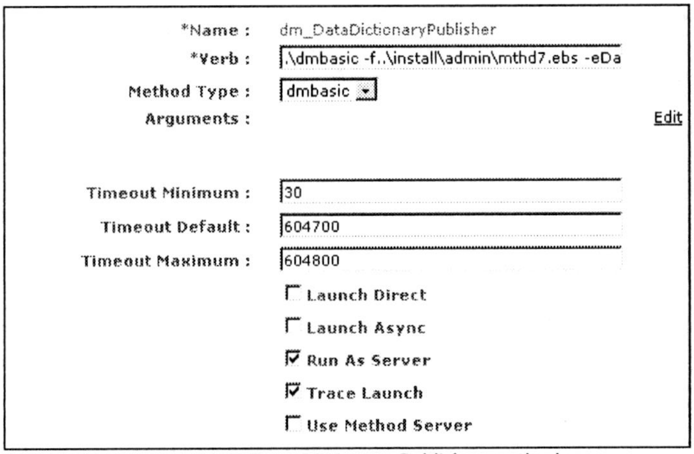

Figure 23.3: Data Dictionary Publisher method

Note that the Data Dictionary Publisher method can be seen in Documentum Administrator by browsing to Administration | Job Management | Methods.

23.6 Creating Users in Docbase with DFC

Users can be created in Docbase via the DFC IDfUser interface and its associated methods.

Create a Java file with the name CreateUsersDFC.java as shown below. Go through the DFC Javadocs to understand the various methods of the IDfUser interface used in this example.

```java
import com.documentum.fc.client.*;
import com.documentum.fc.common.*;
import java.io.IOException;

public class CreateUsersDFC{

//Main method
public static void main(String args[]){

    IDfSession session = null;
    IDfSessionManager sMgr = null;

    try
    {
        IDfClient client = new DfClient().getLocalClient();
        sMgr = client.newSessionManager();
        IDfLoginInfo loginInfo = new DfLoginInfo();
        loginInfo.setUser( "documentum" );
        loginInfo.setPassword( "solutions" );
        sMgr.setIdentity( "dev_doc", loginInfo );
        session = sMgr.getSession( "dev_doc" );

        System.out.println("Session created !!");

        IDfUser userObj = null;
        userObj = (IDfUser)session.newObject( "dm_user" );
        // Seting client capability as 'contributor'
        userObj.setClientCapability(2);
        userObj.setDefaultFolder("/Dummy User",false);
        userObj.setDescription("User created via DFC");
        userObj.setHomeDocbase("dev_doc");
        userObj.setUserAddress("user001@xyz.com");
        // Setting user as member of 'content author' group
        userObj.setUserGroupName("content author");
        userObj.setUserName("Dummy User");
        // Setting user's OS name and Windows domain
        userObj.setUserOSName("user001","sysdomain");
        // Setting extended privileges as 8(config audit) + 16(purge audit) +
32(view audit)
        userObj.setUserXPrivileges(56);
        userObj.save();

        System.out.println("User created in DocBase!!");

    }catch(Exception e){

        System.out.println("Catching generic exception in main: " +
e.getMessage());
    }
    finally {

        sMgr.release( session );

    }
}// end of Main

}// end of class
```

Note that the above DFC code creates a user object in Docbase by the name of Dummy User with OS name user001 and email ID user001@xyz.com.

The user has been made part of the content author group and given extended privileges such as Config, View and Purge Audit.

When you compile and execute the CreateUsersDFC.java code, a user object with the name Dummy User is created in the Docbase! You can verify this by logging in as an administrator in Documentum Administrator and going to the Administration | User Management | Users section.

Searching for a user with name Dummy User shows a valid result. Clicking on the info (i) icon against it shows the user properties as shown in figure 23.4:

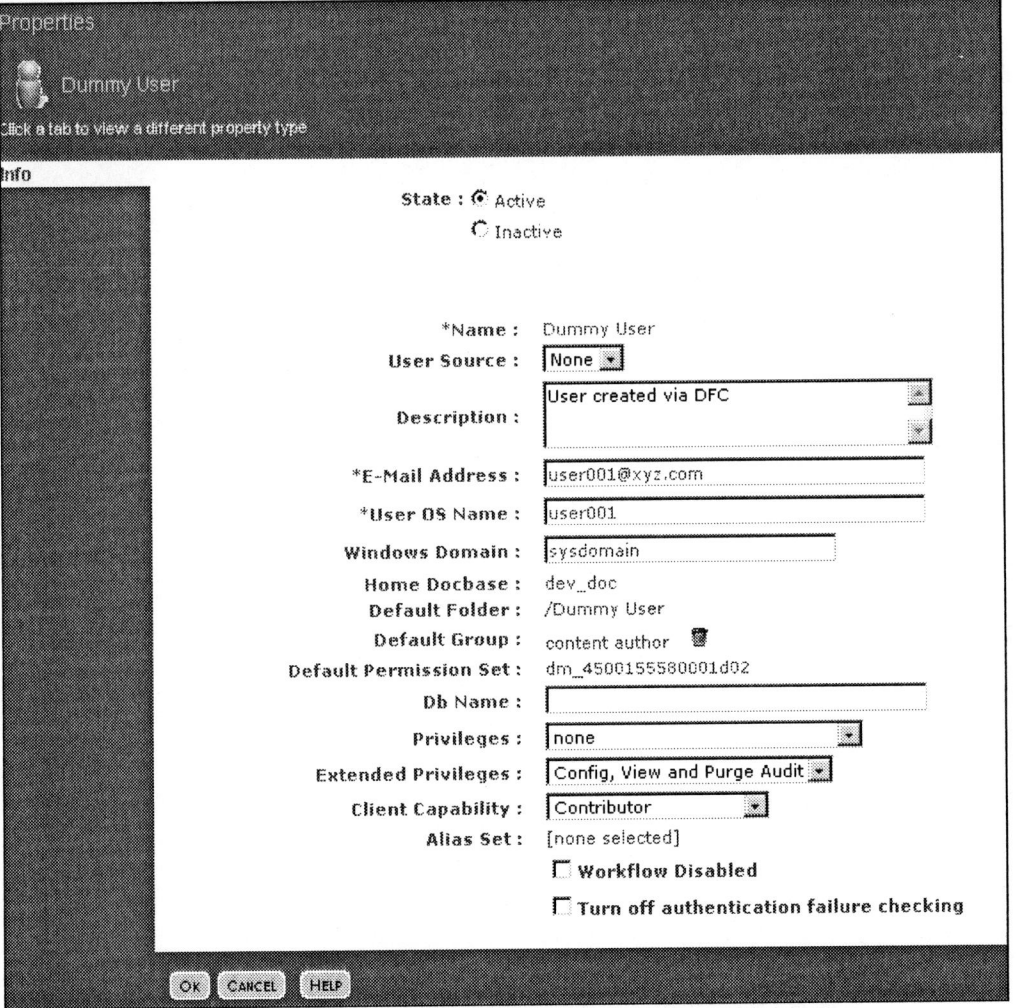

Figure 23.4: User created in Docbase as seen in Documentum Administrator

There are scores of other interesting functions you can perform via DFC. It will be worthwhile to go through the Documentum DFC development guide and Business Objects Framework (BOF) manuals. BOF is not covered in this book, but if you feel comfortable writing DFC code, you can certainly take a step further and start exploring the BOF framework!

23.7 Summary

Documentum Foundation Classes (DFCs) are a set of Java interfaces and implementation classes that expose Documentum content management functionality.

In this chapter we briefly discussed the naming convention in DFC: the interfaces begin with IDf and the classes begin with Df. We further looked at the Documentum JARs that need to be specified in the system classpath for DFC to work correctly. We then covered detailed examples to explain how DFC can be used to programmatically create Docbase sessions, create and link files in Docbase cabinets, and create users in Documentum.

We also saw an example of running the Data Dictionary Publisher method in the Docbase via DFC.

24
Configurations and Customizations Using WDK

Till now we have seen how to create Docbase objects and manage them via the user-friendly interface provided by default Web Publisher screens. We have seen how content files are created through the New Content screen in Web Publisher and how properties of existing objects are modified through the Properties (attributes) screen. In fact all other screens that we have seen in Web Publisher such as the Categories page displaying existing Web Publisher categories, the Inbox screen displaying workflow tasks, and other server notifications, etc. are all default screens provided by the Web Publisher application. Webtop, Digital Asset Manager, and Documentum Administrator are examples of some other web-based applications in Documentum that have their own specific user interfaces.

What if you need to modify the look-and-feel of these default screens or alter some basic functionality associated with these screens? Welcome to the world of Documentum WDK (short for Web Development Kit)!

WDK (as we discussed in Chapter 3) is a framework that Documentum has provided to build and deploy J2EE web applications for connecting with Documentum Content Server. WDK consists of a set of reusable and extensible server-side Java components that interact with Content Server via DFC calls.

Webtop is a reference implementation provided by Documentum using the WDK framework for basic content management functionalities. Web Publisher and the Documentum Administrator tools that we have covered in this book have been built over Webtop. Using WDK, you can alter the user interface of Web Publisher/Documentum Administrator screens and even extend and modify their functionalities via customizations. The WDK framework has been written well and provides flexibility to override default functionality and add your own custom components as well!

Using WDK, you can primarily perform two kinds of tasks:

- **Configuration**: This includes simple operations such as introducing new menu options, modifying labels and texts in screens, altering look-and-feel such as images associated with button controls, and hiding/displaying attributes/fields in various screens. Using XML configuration files and JSPs (Java Server Pages) provided in the WDK, you can achieve simple configurations of web applications.

- **Customization**: This involves comparatively more effort than simple configurations and includes tasks such as adding new actions and components in the WDK framework. Also, this includes extending framework behavior classes to override default functionality and introduce custom logic and functionality. Using behavior Java classes in WDK, you can customize web applications.

Figure 24.1 shows the nature of work (configurations and customizations) that can be performed using the WDK framework.

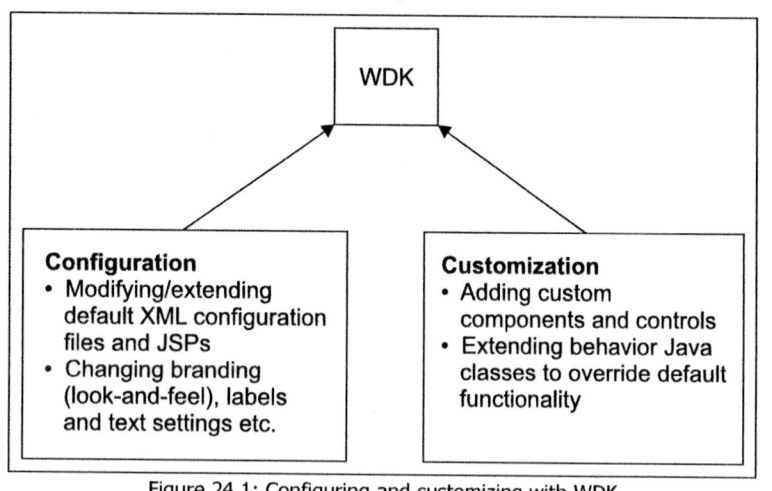

Figure 24.1: Configuring and customizing with WDK

Documentum WDK 5.3 Update:

- Three modes of content transfer supported by WDK: HTTP, Unified Client Facilities (UCF), and Content Transfer Applets

- Support for session failover to other servers running the same WDK-based application in a clustered environment

- Support for multiple Docbase repository searching

24.1 WDK Directory Structure

Before we begin discussing WDK configurations and customizations through examples, let's first go through the WDK directory structure and its contained folders and files. The root of the WDK application has the following directories and files:

- **WDK application configuration file** (config.xml): Starting page for WDK application (index.html/default.html) and unstripped.jar containing the WDK application files with embedded comments for debugging purposes.

- **WEB-INF**: Contains web.xml file (for J2EE web applications), WDK web application Java classes, and classes for other application layers such as wdk, webcomponent, and jars required by the WDK framework and JSP tag libraries.

- **help**: Contains WDK client application help files.
- **plugins**: Contains the JRE plug-in for the WDK client application.
- **Application layer directories** (wdk, webcomponent, webtop, dam, wp, and custom): Application layer directories contain an application's configuration file (app.xml), configuration files for application components, externalized strings, themes, component JSPs, and JavaScript files required by applications.

Do not be intimidated by the number of terminologies we are discussing—WDK, Webcomponent, Webtop, and many more. These are simply the various WDK application layers and each of these extends the layer below it in the hierarchy. Look at figure 24.2 to understand the WDK application layer hierarchy chain.

If you open the application configuration file app.xml for each of the WDK intermediate layers, you will notice that it extends from the layer shown just below it in figure 24.2.

For example, the app.xml for Webtop would extend the app.xml for the webcomponent layer. WDK is the base layer in the hierarchy and does not extend any other layer.

A snippet from the Webtop app.xml file: `<application extends="webcomponent/app.xml">`.

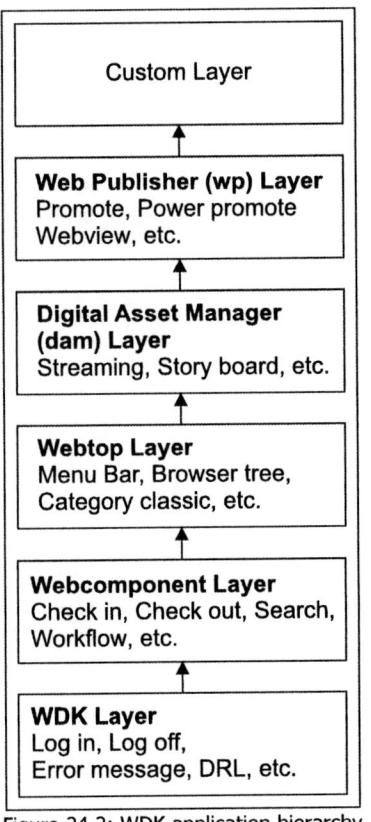

Figure 24.2: WDK application hierarchy

Note that each WDK component has an associated XML configuration file defining it, a behavior Java class, at least one JSP page for defining its layout, and an NLS properties file for externalizing strings.

The **Custom layer** is a very interesting concept and would have definitely caught your attention if you are new to Documentum WDK. The Custom layer sits at the top of the hierarchy chain and is provided by Documentum for you to house all your customizations. It contains any customized configuration XML files, JSP pages, branding themes, and externalized strings. If you place customized component definition configuration and other files in the custom directory, the WDK framework will load it first before it loads the files in the layers below the custom layer.

During WDK application upgrades from one version to another, you need to take a backup of your custom folder before performing the upgrade and later restore it after the upgrade completes. This ensures that your customized files are stored in a centralized location and can be restored easily as required.

24.2 WDK Application Elements

Documentum WDK application framework is vast and comprises of several units such as components, actions, and controls. It is vital to understand each of these and their interrelations before you jump into configurations/customizations and developing your own custom components. Figure 24.3 loosely depicts how the various WDK application elements interact with each other within the confines of the WDK framework.

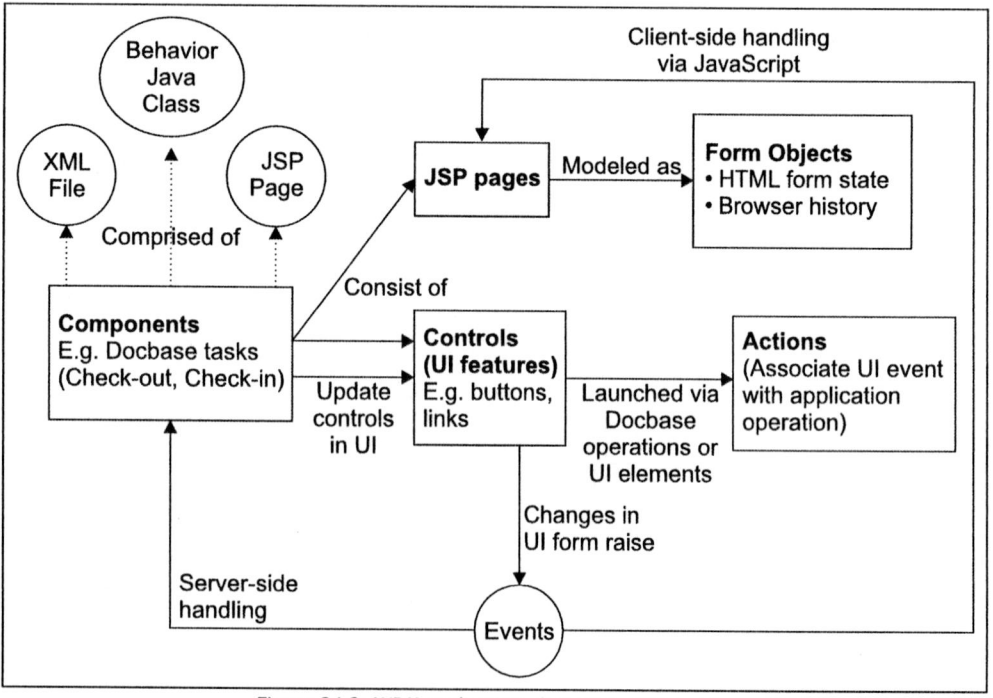

Figure 24.3: WDK application elements' relationships

Let us now discuss figure 24.3 in detail:

- **Components**: These consist of JSP pages and the controls within these JSP pages. Components are reusable units in the WDK framework and perform Docbase operations such as check-out, check-in, export, etc. Each WDK component consists of an XML configuration file, an associated behavior Java class, and at least one JSP page.

- **Controls**: These represent UI features (buttons or links) and provide standard web functionality and operations such as validations, formatting, etc. Controls can be reused in multiple JSP pages and raise events due to changes made to these elements in UI forms.

- **Forms (JSP pages)**: WDK models JSP pages as Form objects on the server to serve two purposes:
  - Maintaining the state of the HTML form
  - Maintaining the browser history

- **Actions**: Actions are launched either by a Docbase operation (such as check-out) or via a UI form element (such as button, menu item, etc.). Actions relate a UI event with an application function.

- **Events**: Events are raised whenever a user action causes changes in the element states in a UI form. Events are either handled client-side via JavaScript in the associated JSP page or on the server, by the associated component.

Some of these terms might not be very clear right now. However, you may go through the Documentum WDK Development guide to get a better understanding. As we proceed with the examples in this chapter, these concepts will definitely become much clearer.

24.3 A Simple WDK Configuration Example

Without spending any more time, let us start off with a very simple example of WDK configuration.

We will override the default New Content (properties) screen in Web Publisher and introduce new attributes for the News Article template.

24.3.1 New Content Screen before Configuration Changes

If you create new content in Web Publisher using a template category, the New Content (properties) screen is shown to you for providing properties (metadata) information for the content such as:

- Name of content (attribute: `object_name`)
- Descriptive name (attribute: `title`)
- Subject (attribute: `subject`)
- Effective date (attribute: `a_effective_date`)
- Expiration date (attribute: `a_expiration_date`)

Figure 24.4 depicts how this default screen appears in Web Publisher.

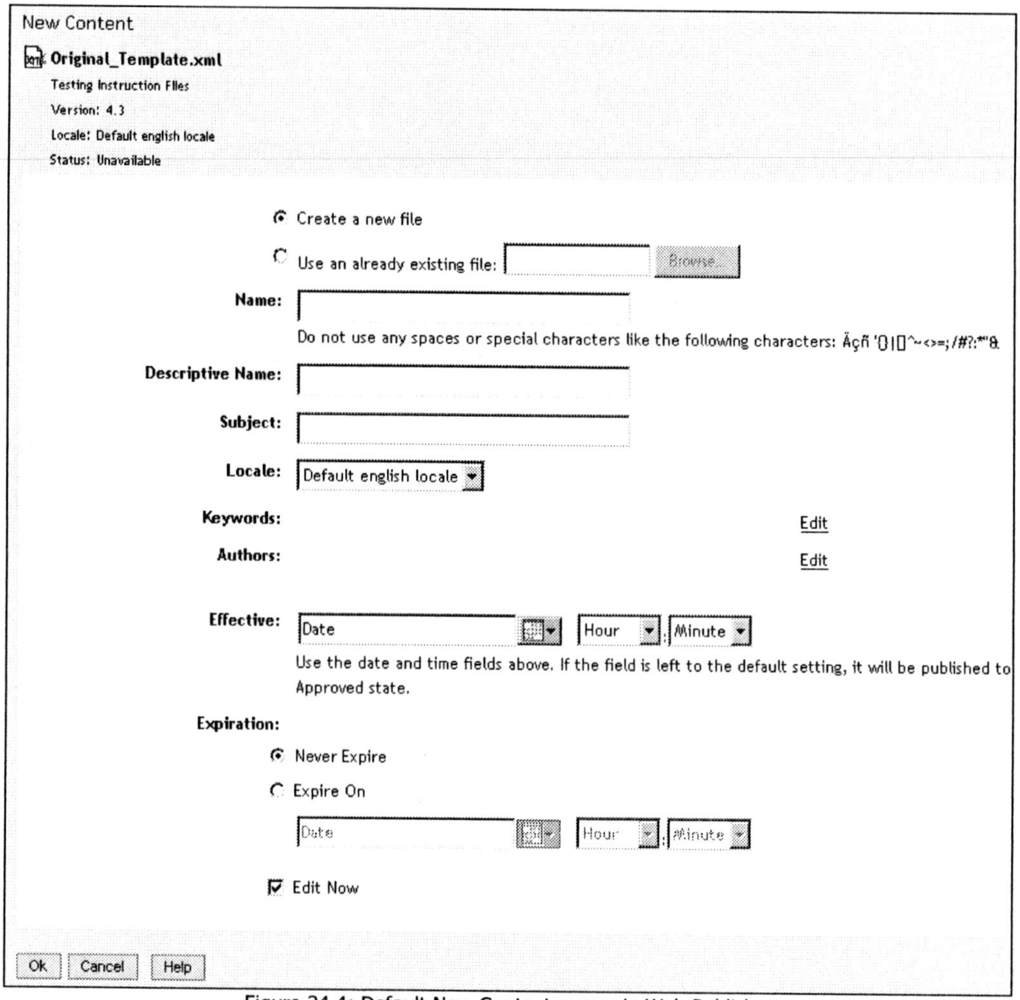

Figure 24.4: Default New Content screen in Web Publisher

24.3.2 Modified New Content Screen after Configuration Changes

Figure 24.5 shows the same New Content screen for the News Article template with the newly added attributes.

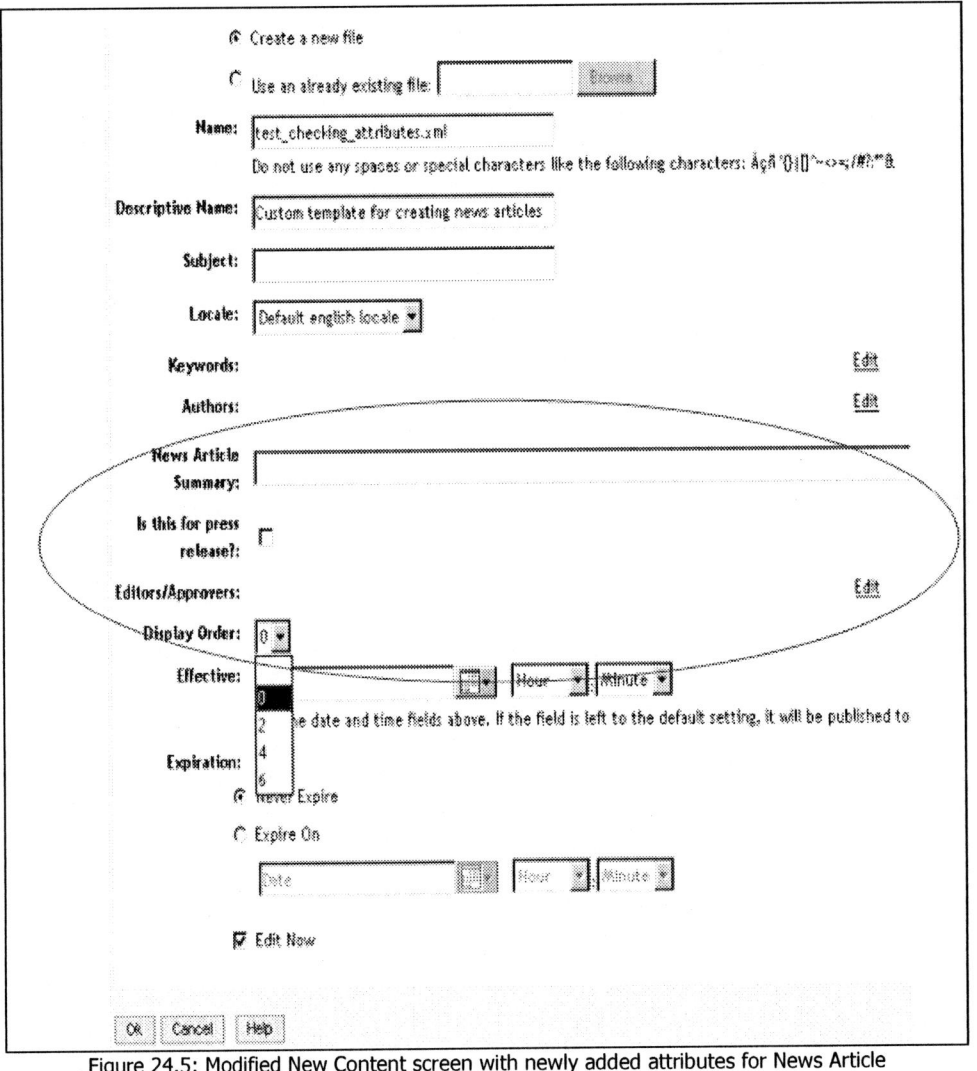

Figure 24.5: Modified New Content screen with newly added attributes for News Article

The following steps will explain how to achieve this simple configuration in Documentum using the WDK framework.

1. Copy the XML configuration file for the New Content component (`newcontent_component.xml`) from the following location in your Web Publisher server:

   `\wp\config\library\newcontent`.

   Note that in all the examples in this chapter, we will assume that the name of the Web Publisher application is `wp`.

   Create the following directories inside the `config` folder within the `custom` folder in Web Publisher server:

   `\library\newcontent`.

   Place the copied `newcontent_component.xml` at the following location:

   `\wp\custom\config\library\newcontent`.

   We will look at the changes to be made in the copied `newcontent_component.xml` file later in the steps below.

2. Copy the New Content JSP file (`newContent.jsp`) from the following location in your Web Publisher server: `\wp\library\newcontent`.

   Create the following directories inside the `custom` folder in Web Publisher server:

   `\library\newcontent`.

   Rename the copied `newContent.jsp` as (say) `custom_newContent.jsp` and place it at the following location:

   `\wp\custom\library\newcontent`.

   We will look at the changes to be made in the `custom_newContent.jsp` file later in the steps below.

3. Modify the `newcontent_component.xml` file under `\wp\custom\config\library\newcontent` as shown below:

```xml
<?xml version="1.0" encoding="UTF-8" standalone="no"?>

<!--******************************************************************-->

<config version='1.0'>

    <scope wpcontext="wpview">

        <!-- the document list component definition -->
        <!--<component id="newcontent">-->
        <component id="newcontent"
        extends="newcontent:wp/config/library/newcontent/
                                        newcontent_component.xml">

            <!-- Component Contract -->
            <params>
                <param name="objectId" required="false"/>
```

376

```
        </params>

        <!-- Component Layout -->
        <pages>
            <!--<start>/wp/library/newcontent/newContent.jsp</start>-->
    <start>/custom/library/newcontent/custom_newContent.jsp</start>
            <return>/wp/library/componentReturn.jsp</return>
        </pages>

        <!-- Component Behavior -->
        <class>com.documentum.wp.library.newcontent.NewContent</class>
        <nlsbundle>com.documentum.wp.library.newcontent.NewContentNlsProp
                                                                </nlsbundle>

        <!-- Component specific Configuration -->

        <!-- Allow the user to import a file from file system.
                                            Default is true. -->
        <allow_import>true</allow_import>

        <enable_full_text_index>true</enable_full_text_index>

        <!-- Component specific Configuration -->
        <helpcontextid>newcontent</helpcontextid>
    </component>

    </scope>
</config>
```

The anatomy of this XML file is given below:

```
<?xml version="1.0" encoding="UTF-8" standalone="no"?>
```

This is the standard XML declaration

```
<config version='1.0'>
```

This is the root element of the XML configuration file.

```
    <scope wpcontext="wpview">
```

This is the scope of the configuration file defines the context within which this configuration definition holds good.

In the tag `<scope wpcontext="wpview">`, `wpcontext` is a qualifier name and `wpview` is a qualifier value. Context matching happens for qualifier values. Qualifiers are specified in the `app.xml` file for the respective WDK application layers.

Following are some of the qualifiers provided by the various WDK application layers such as WDK, Webtop, Web Publisher, etc:

- o   Docbase name
- o   Docbase type
- o   Privilege
- o   Application
- o   Web Publisher context
- o   Web Publisher role

You can even introduce your custom qualifiers in the WDK application if need be. Documentum resolves the scope as per the order in which the qualifiers have been specified in the `app.xml` file for the applications.

```
<component id="newcontent"
```

This is the primary element in the XML configuration file. Apart from `component`, the other valid elements can be `action` (Action components) and `application` (app.xml file). The `id` attribute tags the component/action name with a unique identifier in the application. You can extend other components/actions/applications by using the `extends` attribute in the primary element.

```
<params>
    <param name="objectId" required="false"/>
```

These lines define the parameters that are passed from the configuration to the associated behavior class.

```
<pages>
```

`<pages>` defines the associated JSP page(s) for the layout of component in question. You can see that we have commented out the path for default `newContent.jsp` and instead provided the path for our custom JSP file `custom_newContent.jsp`.

```
<class>com.documentum.wp.library.newcontent.NewContent</class>
```

This line defines the associated behavior Java class for the component. In this particular configuration example, since we are just modifying the xml configuration file and the JSP file for the New Content component, we are not extending the default `NewContent.class`.

```
<nlsbundle>com.documentum.wp.library.newcontent.NewContentNlsProp</nlsbundle>
```

This line defines the associated NLS property file for localizing the strings for the component. Note that in WDK framework, a component extending from another component inherits the strings defined in the NLS property file for the base component.

Other XML elements shown in the code are specific to the `newcontent` component and do not apply generically to all XML configuration files.

4. Modify the `custom_newContent.jsp` file under `\wp\custom\library\newcontent` as shown in the following code snippet.

Note that in the JSP file, we have added lines 137-151 for the following custom attributes of News Article object type (`cust_newsarticle`): `cust_news_summary`, `cust_news_is_press_rel`, `cust_news_edit_approvers`, and `cust_news_display_order`.

These are Docbase attributes and their behavior is handled by default by the WDK framework. We have introduced these new attributes in the JSP similar to the default implementation for attributes such as `keywords` and `authors` shown below (refer to the highlighted line).

```
<dmfx:docbaseattribute object="<%=NewContent.CONTENT_OBJECT%>"
attribute="keywords"
pre="<tr><td align='right' valign='top'><b>"
coll=":</b></td><td> </td><td>"/>
<tr><td colspan='4' height='5'></td></tr>
```

```
<dmfx:docbaseattribute object="<%=NewContent.CONTENT_OBJECT%>"
attribute="authors"
pre="<tr><td align='right' valign='top'><b>"
col1=":</b></td><td> </td><td>"/>
<tr><td colspan='4' height='5'></td></tr>
<%-- To add more attributes, make a copy of the following two
                            lines and enter the attribute name.
Or you can use the data-dictionary.
<dmfx:docbaseattribute object="<%=NewContent.CONTENT_OBJECT%>"
attribute="<attribute name>"
pre="<tr><td align='right' valign='top'><b>"
col1=":</b></td><td> </td><td>"/>
<tr><td colspan='4' height='5'></td></tr>
--%>
<!-- Added by Gaurav for configuration: begins -->
<tr><td colspan='4' height='5'></td></tr>
<dmfx:docbaseattribute object="<%=NewContent.CONTENT_OBJECT%>"
attribute="cust_news_summary"
pre="<tr><td align='right' valign='top'><b>"
col1=":</b></td><td> </td><td>"/>

<tr><td colspan='4' height='5'></td></tr>
<dmfx:docbaseattribute object="<%=NewContent.CONTENT_OBJECT%>"
attribute="cust_news_is_press_rel"
pre="<tr><td align='right' valign='top'><b>"
col1=":</b></td><td> </td><td>"/>

<tr><td colspan='4' height='5'></td></tr>
<dmfx:docbaseattribute object="<%=NewContent.CONTENT_OBJECT%>"
attribute="cust_news_edit_approvers"
pre="<tr><td align='right' valign='top'><b>"
col1=":</b></td><td> </td><td>"/>

<tr><td colspan='4' height='5'></td></tr>
<dmfx:docbaseattribute object="<%=NewContent.CONTENT_OBJECT%>"
attribute="cust_news_display_order"
pre="<tr><td align='right' valign='top'><b>"
col1=":</b></td><td> </td><td>"/>

<!-- Added by Gaurav for configuration: ends -->
<tr>
<td align='right' valign='top'>
<b><dmf:label nlsid="MSG_EFFECTIVE"
cssclass="defaultDocbaseAttributeStyle"/>:</b>
</td>
```

5. You now need to stop and start the Web Publisher application server to see the effect of the newly added custom files. The moment you create some new News Article content in Web Publisher, the modified New Content screen (as shown in figure 24.5) is shown to you.

24.4 A Simple WDK Customization Example

Having seen a very simple configuration example in WDK, we will now take a step further and develop our own custom component in WDK. We will create a new menu option in Web Publisher, clicking on which will take us to a custom screen for creating News Article content.

Figure 24.6 shows a newly added custom menu option Create New News Article under the menu option: File | New.

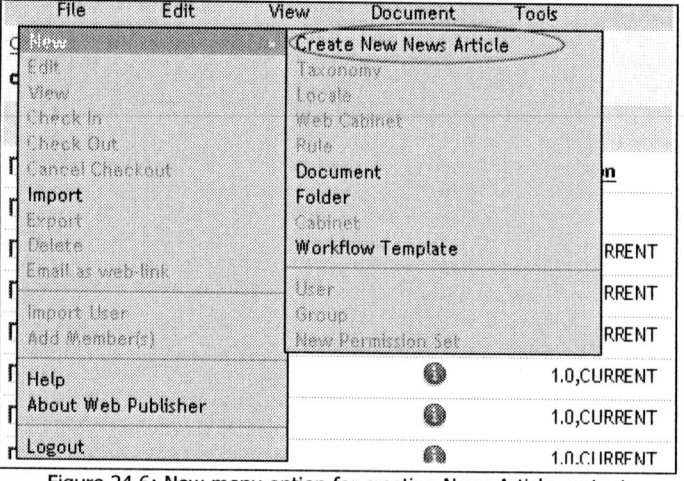

Figure 24.6: New menu option for creating News Article content

When you click on the menu option Create New News Article, a custom screen is shown for creating News Article content as shown in figure 24.7.

Figure 24.7: Custom screen for creating News Article content

Let us now go step by step through this example to understand how to create our own custom components using the WDK framework:

1. Copy `menubar_component.xml` from `\wp\wp\config\app` to the following location on your Web Publisher server: `\wp\custom\config\app`.

   (Needless to say you need to create the appropriate folder structure inside the `custom` folder before copying over the XML file.)

Modify the menubar_component.xml file in the custom folder as shown below:

```
<?xml version="1.0" encoding="UTF-8" standalone="no"?>

<!--**********************************************************************-->
<!--                                                                    -->
<!-- Component xml file for menubar Component                           -->
<!--                                                                    -->
<!--**********************************************************************-->
<!--                                                                    -->
<!-- File           menubar_component.xml                              -->
<!-- Author         Gaurav Kathuria                                    -->
<!-- Description    Extends the menubar component to display the        -->
<!--                the new custom menu option                         -->
<!-- Created on     Nov 28, 2005                                       -->
<!--                                                                    -->
<!--**********************************************************************-->

<config version='1.0'>
   <scope>
      <desc>
      menubar component : Extends the menubar component to display the
                          new custom menu option
      </desc>
     <!-- Component Contract -->
     <!--<component id="menubar"
           extends="menubar:webtop/config/menubar_component.xml">-->
        <component id="menubar"
           extends="menubar:wp/config/app/menubar_component.xml">

     <!-- Component Layout -->
        <pages>
           <start>/custom/app/custom_menubar.jsp</start>
        </pages>

     <!-- NLS properties file -->
        <nlsbundle>com.newsarticle.app.WpMenuBarNlsProp</nlsbundle>
        </component>

   </scope>
</config>
```

Please note that within the <component> XML element we have extended from wp/config/app/menubar_component.xml and as per the highlighted line, pointed to our custom JSP page: custom_menubar.jsp.

Apart from pointing to a custom JSP page, we have created our custom NLS property file for storing the custom strings for the menu option label in the WpMenuBarNlsProp.property file as well.

2. Copy menubar.jsp from \wp\wp\app, rename it as custom_menubar.jsp, and copy it to the following location on your Web Publisher server: \wp\custom\app.

   Modify the custom_menubar.jsp file in the custom folder as shown below:

```
<dmf:menu name='file_menu' nlsid='MSG_FILE' width='50'>
<dmf:menu name='file_new_menu' nlsid='MSG_NEW'>
<dmfx:actionmenuitem dynamic='genericnoselect'
name='file_new_webhtml_template'
nlsid='MSG_NEW_WEBHTML_TEMPLATE' action='createwebhtmltemplate'
showifinvalid='false' showifdisabled='false'/>
<dmfx:actionmenuitem dynamic='generic' name='file_newcontent'
nlsid='MSG_NEW_CONTENT'
```

```
action='newcontent' showifinvalid='false' showifdisabled='true'/>

<!-- Customized to add a new menu option -->
<dmfx:actionmenuitem dynamic='generic' name='custom_new_news'
nlsid='NLS_NEW_NEWS_MENU'
action='newnewsarticlelink' showifinvalid='false' showifdisabled='true'/>

<dmfx:actionmenuitem dynamic='generic' name='create_changeset'
nlsid='MSG_NEW_CHANGESET'
action='newchangeset' showifinvalid='false' showifdisabled='false'/>
```

Note that the first two lines correspond to menu options **File** and **New**. We need to introduce the new menu item **Create New News Article** under this menu option.

```
<dmfx:actionmenuitem dynamic='generic' name='custom_new_news'
nlsid='NLS_NEW_NEWS_MENU'
action='newnewsarticlelink' showifinvalid='false' showifdisabled='true'/>
```

We introduce these lines similar to the way other menu options have been added in the JSP.

The nlsid NLS_NEW_NEWS_MENU is the property string name for the newly introduced menu option. The actual value for this property string will be provided in the WpMenuBarNlsProp.properties file.

The action to be launched when a user chooses this new menu option is specified in the action attribute as newnewsarticlelink. This is the ID of the action configuration launched by the WDK framework. We will create an Action configuration XML file later in this chapter for the ID newnewsarticlelink.

3. Copy WpMenuBarNlsProp.properties from \wp\strings\com\documentum\wp\app and copy it over to the following location on your Web Publisher server: \wp\custom\strings\com\newsarticle\app

    Modify the WpMenuBarNlsProp.properties file in the custom folder as shown below:

```
#*************************************************************************
#
# Author          Gaurav Kathuria
# Description        WebPublisher menu NLS Properties File
# Date            Nov 28th, 2005
#
#*************************************************************************
NLS_INCLUDES=com.documentum.wp.app.WpMenuBarNlsProp

# Generic Action Name


# File menu
NLS_NEW_NEWS_MENU=Create New News Article
#*************************************************************************
#$
#
#*************************************************************************
```

We have used the string NLS_INCLUDES in the modified menu bar NLS property file to include all the key-value pairs from the included NLS property file:

com.documentum.wp.app.WpMenuBarNlsProp

This serves two purposes:

- Maintains consistency in terms of string values throughout the WDK application
- Decreases the individual inclusion of numerous NLS strings in the property file

4. Create a new Action configuration XML file custom_news_article_action.xml at the following location in Web Publisher server: \wp\custom\config\newsarticle.

The details of the newly created Action configuration file are shown below:

```xml
<?xml version="1.0" encoding="UTF-8" standalone="no"?>

<!--****************************************************************-->
<!--                                                                -->
<!-- Action xml file for creating new news article Action           -->
<!--                                                                -->
<!--****************************************************************-->
<!--                                                                -->
<!-- File            custom_news_article_action.xml                 -->
<!-- Author          Gaurav Kathuria                                -->
<!-- Description      This Action launches custom new news          -->
<!--                  article creation screen                       -->
<!--                                                                -->
<!-- Created on       Nov 28, 2005                                  -->
<!--                                                                -->
<!--****************************************************************-->

<config version='1.0'>
    <scope>
  <action id="newnewsarticlelink">
    <desc>
            New news article Action : Check the condition to create
                                the news article Link
        </desc>
    <!-- Component Contract -->
    <params>
        <param name="objectId" required="true"></param>
          <param name="folderPath" required="true"></param>
    </params>

    <!-- Precondition class -->
        <preconditions>
            <precondition
class="com.documentum.web.formext.action.RolePrecondition">
                <role>administrator</role>
            </precondition>
        </preconditions>

    <!-- Component Name -->
        <execution
class="com.documentum.web.formext.action.LaunchComponent">
        <arguments>
            <argument name="component"
value="new_news_article"></argument>
        </arguments>
    <container>dialogcontainer</container>
        </execution>
  </action>
    </scope>
</config>
```

Note that the ID provided to this action configuration newnewsarticlelink is the same as we had provided for the attribute action in the custom_menubar.jsp file.

```
<precondition
class="com.documentum.web.formext.action.RolePrecondition">
```

Here we have designated that only a user with administrator role has access to this particular action. This is termed as a **precondition** in WDK terminology and is implemented by the default com.documentum.web.formext.action.RolePrecondition class.

On clicking the menu option Create New News Article, this action needs to launch a particular component that will correspond to the custom screen we discussed for creating new news articles.

```
<argument name="component" value="new_news_article"></argument>
```

This line designates the component ID of the launched component as new_news_article. The subsequent step will talk about creating this component configuration XML file and associated JSP, Java, and property files.

5. Create a new component configuration XML file custom_news_article_component.xml at the following location in Web Publisher server: \wp\custom\config\newsarticle.

The details of the newly created component configuration file are shown below:

```
<?xml version="1.0" encoding="ISO-8859-1" standalone="no"?>

<!--*********************************************************************-->
<!--                                                                     -->
<!-- Component xml file for New Navigation Link Component                 -->
<!--                                                                     -->
<!--*********************************************************************-->
<!--                                                                     -->
<!-- File          custom_news_article_component.xml                     -->
<!-- Author        Gaurav Kathuria                                       -->
<!-- Description    New News Article Component                           -->
<!--               allows creating new news article                      -->
<!--               and properties file.                                  -->
<!-- Created on     Nov 28, 2005                                         -->
<!--                                                                     -->
<!--*********************************************************************-->

<config version='1.0'>
    <scope>

   <component id="new_news_article">
       <desc>
       New News Article Component: Provides UI for creating new news
                               articles
       </desc>
        <!-- Component Contract -->
      <params>
           <param name="objectId" required="true"></param>
            <param name="folderPath" required="true"></param>
        </params>
```

```
        <!-- Component Layout -->
            <pages>
    <start>/custom/library/newsarticle/custom_newnewsarticle.jsp</start>
            </pages>

        <!-- Component Behaviour -->
            <class>com.newsarticle.content.NewNewsArticle</class>

        <!-- NLS properties file -->

    <nlsbundle>com.newsarticle.content.NewNewsArticleNlsProp</nlsbundle>

        </component>
        </scope>
    </config>
```

We have provided the ID for this component as new_news_article as we discussed in the last step for launching via Action configuration.

```
    start>/custom/library/newsarticle/custom_newnewsarticle.jsp</start>
```

In this line, we have specified the custom JSP for this component as custom_newnewsarticle.jsp, the details of which we will cover later in the chapter.

```
    <class>com.newsarticle.content.NewNewsArticle</class>
    <!-- NLS properties file -->
    <nlsbundle>com.newsarticle.content.NewNewsArticleNlsProp</nlsbundle>
```

Here we specify the component behavior class as com.newsarticle.content.NewNewsArticle and mention the associated NLS property file as com.newsarticle.content.NewNewsArticleNlsProp.property.

We will look into the details of each of these custom files in the subsequent steps.

6. Create a new JSP file custom_newnewsarticle.jsp at the following location in Web Publisher server: \wp\custom\library\newsarticle.

The details of the newly created custom JSP file are shown in two parts below.

```
<%--
    Author : Gaurav Kathuria
    Date : 29-11-2005
    Description : Jsp to Add New News Article.
--%>

<%@ page contentType="text/html; charset=UTF-8" %>
<%@ page errorPage="/wdk/errorhandler.jsp" %>
<%@ taglib uri="/WEB-INF/tlds/dmform_1_0.tld" prefix="dmf" %>
<%@ taglib uri="/WEB-INF/tlds/dmformext_1_0.tld" prefix="dmfx" %>
<%@ page import="com.documentum.web.common.ArgumentList" %>
<%@ page import="com.documentum.web.form.Form" %>
<%@ page import="com.documentum.web.form.control.Link" %>
<%@ page import="com.documentum.web.form.control.databound.Datagrid" %>
<%@ page
import="com.documentum.web.form.control.databound.DataDropDownList"%>
<%@ page import="com.documentum.web.form.control.databound.DataListBox" %>
<%@ page import="com.documentum.web.form.control.validator.
                                        InputMaskValidator" %>
```

```
<html>
  <head>
    <dmf:webform/>
  </head>

  <body class='contentBackground'>
  <dmf:form>
      <table border="0" cellpadding="2" cellspacing="0" width="100%">

    <tr>
      <td>
          <dmf:label name="lbl_news_article_name"
nlsid="MSG_LBL_NEWS_ARTICLE_NAME" />
          </td>
          <td>
      <%--
        Text field where user fill the name of the News Article.
      --%>
              <dmf:text name="txt_news_article_name" />
      <%--
        Documentum provider validator which checks that the News
Article
        name is a mandatory field.
      --%>
      <dmf:requiredfieldvalidator
name="txt_news_article_name_validator"
          controltovalidate="txt_news_article_name"
nlsid='MSG_LBL_NEWS_ARTICLE_NAME_REQUIRED' />
          </td>
        </tr>
```

The anatomy of this code snippet follows:

```
<%@ taglib uri="/WEB-INF/tlds/dmform_1_0.tld" prefix="dmf" %>
<%@ taglib uri="/WEB-INF/tlds/dmformext_1_0.tld" prefix="dmfx" %>
```

In these lines, the necessary tag libraries are specified.

```
<%@ page import="com.documentum.web.common.ArgumentList" %>
<%@ page import="com.documentum.web.form.Form" %>
<%@ page import="com.documentum.web.form.control.Link" %>
<%@ page import="com.documentum.web.form.control.databound.Datagrid" %>
<%@ page import="com.documentum.web.form.control.databound.
                                   DataDropDownList"%>
<%@ page import="com.documentum.web.form.control.databound.DataListBox" %>
<%@ page import="com.documentum.web.form.control.validator.
                                   InputMaskValidator" %>
```

Here the required WDK framework implementation classes are imported in the JSP.

The <dmf:webform/> tag is required for initiating form processing.

The <dmf:form> tag is the HTML form that generates form elements.

The <dmf:label> and <dmf:text> tags are required for generating label and textbox fields in the form. The implementation classes for these are com.documentum.web.form.control.LabelTag and com.documentum.web.form.control.TextTag respectively as can be seen in the dmform_1_0.tld library.

`<dmf:requiredfieldvalidator>` is a WDK validator tag used for performing a mandatory check on the specified field (in the attribute `controltovalidate`). In our case the HTML form field `txt_news_article_name` is being checked by the validator. If the user does not provide a name for the news article, the WDK framework throws a message, the property string for which is specified in the `nlsid` key `MSG_LBL_NEWS_ARTICLE_NAME_REQUIRED`.

The string value for this property string is specified in the associated NLS property file `NewNewsArticleNlsProp.property`. We will discuss this in the subsequent steps.

```
<tr>
  <td>
  <dmf:label name="lbl_news_summary" nlsid="MSG_LBL_NEWS_SUMMARY" />
  </td>
  <td>
    <%-Text field where user fill the value of the News Article
       summary.--%>
    <dmf:text name="txt_news_summary" />
    <%--Documentum provider validator which checks that the News
        Article summary is a mandatory field.--%>
    <dmf:requiredfieldvalidator name="txt_news_summary_validator"
        controltovalidate="txt_news_summary"
        nlsid='MSG_LBL_NEWS_SUMMARY_REQUIRED' />
  </td>
  </tr>
  <tr>
    <td>
    <dmf:label name="lbl_display_order"
        nlsid="MSG_LBL_DISPLAY_ORDER" />
    </td>
    <td>
    <%--DataDropDownList showing display order of news articles.--%>
    <dmf:datadropdownlist name="txt_display_order">
      <dmf:dataoptionlist>
        <dmf:option datafield="DISPLAY_ORDER_ID"
        labeldatafield="DISPLAY_ORDER_VALUE"/>
      </dmf:dataoptionlist>
    </dmf:datadropdownlist>

    </td>
  </tr>
  </table>
 </dmf:form>
 </body>
</html>
```

The `<dmf:datadropdownlist>` tag depicts a `data dropdown` control that translates into a dropdown in the form, showing the designated values in the list.

The <dmf:option> tag specifies that the datafield attribute value will store the actual values in the Docbase property while the labeldatafield will be used to simply display user-friendly labels for the list values to users. For example, we will display the strings One, Two, Three, Four, etc to the users in the dropdown while the actual values for these options persisted in the Docbase attribute will be 1, 2, 3, or 4 respectively.

7. Create a new NLS property file NewNewsArticleNlsProp.properties at the following location in Web Publisher server:

   \wp\custom\strings\com\newsarticle\content.

   The details of the newly created custom NLS property file are shown below.

```
#***************************************************************************
#
# Author       Gaurav Kathuria
# Description   New News Article Component NLS Properties File
# Date         Nov 28, 2005
#
#***************************************************************************
MSG_TITLE=Create new news article
MSG_LBL_NEWS_ARTICLE_NAME=News Article Name
MSG_LBL_NEWS_SUMMARY=News Article Summary
MSG_LBL_DISPLAY_ORDER=Display Order

MSG_OK=Ok
MSG_CANCEL=Cancel
MSG_CLOSE=Cancel

//error messages
MSG_LBL_NEWS_ARTICLE_NAME_REQUIRED=Please enter a name for the news
                                   article
MSG_LBL_NEWS_SUMMARY_REQUIRED=Please enter a summary for the news article
MSG_ERROR_SAVE_OPERATION=Error in saving news article
MSG_ERROR_ORDER_DROPDOWN_POPULATION=Error in populating display order
                                    dropdown
```

The various labels, strings, and messages required for the News Article creation screen have been specified in this NLS property file.

8. Create a new Java file NewNewsArticle.java; compile and place the class file at the following location in Web Publisher server:

   \wp\WEB-INF\classes\com\newsarticle\content.

   The following code snippets show the details of the newly created custom behavior class part by part.

   It is highly advisable to download and browse the Documentum WDK/Webcomponent/Webtop/Web Publisher Javadocs from the Documentum site in order to understand the various methods used in the example that follows.

We have extended our custom New Article class from the WDK base class `Component`. Please refer to figure 24.8 to understand the WDK component hierarchy stack.

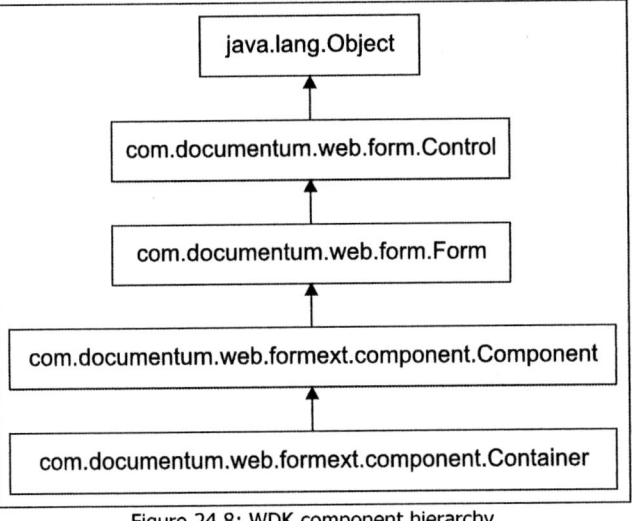

Figure 24.8: WDK component hierarchy

```
package com.newsarticle.content;

import com.documentum.fc.client.*;
import com.documentum.fc.common.DfException;
import com.documentum.fc.common.DfId;
import com.documentum.web.common.ArgumentList;
import com.documentum.web.common.ErrorMessageService;
import com.documentum.web.common.LocaleService;
import com.documentum.web.form.Control;
import com.documentum.web.form.Form;
import com.documentum.web.form.IControlListener;
import com.documentum.web.form.control.*;
import com.documentum.web.form.control.databound.DataDropDownList;
import com.documentum.web.form.control.databound.DataListBox;
import com.documentum.web.form.control.databound.TableResultSet;
import com.documentum.web.form.control.databound.DataOptionList;
import com.documentum.web.formext.component.Component;
import com.documentum.web.formext.control.docbase.DocbaseAttribute;
import com.documentum.web.formext.control.docbase.DocbaseAttributeValue;
import com.documentum.web.formext.control.docbase.DocbaseObject;
import com.documentum.wp.app.WcmHttpAppContext;
import com.documentum.wp.app.WpStatusUtil;
import com.documentum.nls.NlsResourceBundle;

import java.util.*;

/**
 * This class is a behaviour class for News Article component.
 * @author : Gaurav Kathuria
 * @version : 1.0, 29/11/2005
 *
 */
public class NewNewsArticle extends Component
{
```

```
        private String m_strObjectId;
        private String m_strObjectType;

    private Text txt_news_article_name;
    private Text txt_news_summary;
    private DataDropDownList txt_display_order;


// Constructor
    public NewNewsArticle()
    {

        m_strObjectId = null;
    txt_news_article_name = null;
        txt_news_summary = null;
    txt_display_order = null;

    }
```

Let's discuss this code in detail.

```
import com.documentum.fc.client.*;
import com.documentum.fc.common.DfException;
import com.documentum.fc.common.DfId;
import com.documentum.web.common.ArgumentList;
import com.documentum.web.common.ErrorMessageService;
import com.documentum.web.common.LocaleService;
import com.documentum.web.form.Control;
import com.documentum.web.form.Form;
import com.documentum.web.form.IControlListener;
import com.documentum.web.form.control.*;
import com.documentum.web.form.control.databound.DataDropDownList;
import com.documentum.web.form.control.databound.DataListBox;
import com.documentum.web.form.control.databound.TableResultSet;
import com.documentum.web.form.control.databound.DataOptionList;
import com.documentum.web.formext.component.Component;
import com.documentum.web.formext.control.docbase.DocbaseAttribute;
import com.documentum.web.formext.control.docbase.DocbaseAttributeValue;
import com.documentum.web.formext.control.docbase.DocbaseObject;
import com.documentum.wp.app.WcmHttpAppContext;
import com.documentum.wp.app.WpStatusUtil;
import com.documentum.nls.NlsResourceBundle;
```

Here the necessary WDK and DFC classes have been imported.

```
        private String m_strObjectId;
        private String m_strObjectType;

        private Text txt_news_article_name;
        private Text txt_news_summary;
        private DataDropDownList txt_display_order;
```

Here we declare private references to the form controls and object ID of the document that will be created via this screen. Refer to the custom_newnewsarticle.jsp file for understanding the names of the various form controls.

```
/**
     * News Article component initializer method
     *
     * @param argumentlist : ArgumentList
     */
    public void onInit(ArgumentList argumentlist)
    {
```

```
            super.onInit(argumentlist);
            m_strObjectId = argumentlist.get("objectId");
            initControls();

    }


/**
        * Method for initializing controls
        */

    private void initControls()
    {
        txt_news_article_name = (Text) getControl("txt_news_article_name",
            com.documentum.web.form.control.Text.class);
        txt_news_summary = (Text) getControl
            ("txt_news_summary",
                        com.documentum.web.form.control.Text.class);
        txt_display_order = (DataDropDownList) getControl("txt_display_order",
        com.documentum.web.form.control.databound.DataDropDownList.class);
        initializeOrderDropdown();

    }
```

WDK controls pass through definitive lifecycle stages and in each stage of the
lifecycle, they can have varied capabilities and states. Note that there are various
lifecycle methods associated with each of the lifecycle stages that are called by the
form processor.

- o   onInit(): Whenever the component or the JSP page is requested
       for the first time, this method is called.
- o   onRender(): This method is invoked every time a request to the
       form is made via a URL, just before the JSP form processing occurs.
- o   onRefreshData(): This is called when form data is modified.
- o   onRenderEnd(): This is invoked as a clean-up operation after all
       form processing has been done for every request.
- o   onExit(): This is invoked whenever a request is made to another
       form or component.

```
        m_strObjectId = argumentlist.get("objectId");
```

Reference to the object ID of the document is taken through the
com.documentum.web.common.ArgumentList class. This class contains the arguments
that are passed to a form or received by a control's onInit()
event handler.

```
        txt_news_article_name = (Text) getControl("txt_news_article_name",
            com.documentum.web.form.control.Text.class);
```

The getControl() method returns a reference to a named control. Note that we have cast
to the appropriate control depending on whether it is a text field or a data dropdown.

```
    /**
        * Method for initializing display order dropdown
        */
    private void initializeOrderDropdown()
    {
        String strId = "", strLabel = "";
```

```
            IDfCollection idfcollection = null;
            IDfQuery dfquery = new DfQuery();
            IDfSession dfsession = null;

            TableResultSet tableresultset = new TableResultSet
                    (new  String[]{"DISPLAY_ORDER_ID", "DISPLAY_ORDER_VALUE"});

            try
            {
                dfsession = getDfSession();
                dfquery.setDQL("select col1,col2 from dm_dbo.table1");
                idfcollection = dfquery.execute
                                        (dfsession, IDfQuery.DF_READ_QUERY);

                while (idfcollection.next())
                {
                    strId = idfcollection.getString("col1");
                    strLabel = idfcollection.getString("col2");
                    tableresultset.add(new String[]{strId, strLabel});
                }


            }
            catch (DfException dfe)
            {
                ErrorMessageService.getService().setNonFatalError
                        (this, "MSG_ERROR_ORDER_DROPDOWN_POPULATION", dfe);
            System.out.println("Execption caught!!");
              setReturnError("MSG_ERROR_ORDER_DROPDOWN_POPULATION", null, dfe);
                return;
            }
            finally
            {
                try
                {
                    if (idfcollection != null &&
                    idfcollection.getState() != IDfCollection.DF_CLOSED_STATE)
                        idfcollection.close();
                }
                catch (DfException dfexception1)
                {
                    //logMessage.warn(dfexception1.getMessage(),
                                                    dfexception1);
                }
            }

            txt_display_order.getDataProvider().setResultSet
                                            (tableresultset,  null);


    }
```

Let's discuss certain lines in this code snippet in detail:

```
    private void initializeOrderDropdown()
```

We have initialized the values in the Display Order dropdown in the
initializeOrderDropdown method.

```
    TableResultSet tableresultset = new TableResultSet
            (new  String[]{"DISPLAY_ORDER_ID", "DISPLAY_ORDER_VALUE"});
```

We have used the WDK com.documentum.web.form.control.databound.TableResultSet class to store the ID and actual values for the drop-down entities.

> dfquery.setDQL("select col1,col2 from dm_dbo.table1");

A DFC query is fired to select the ID and descriptive labels from the registered table table1 in the Docbase. Please refer to our discussion of the IDfQuery interface in the last chapter for further details.

Figure 24.9 shows the structure/data in the registered table table1 in the Docbase:

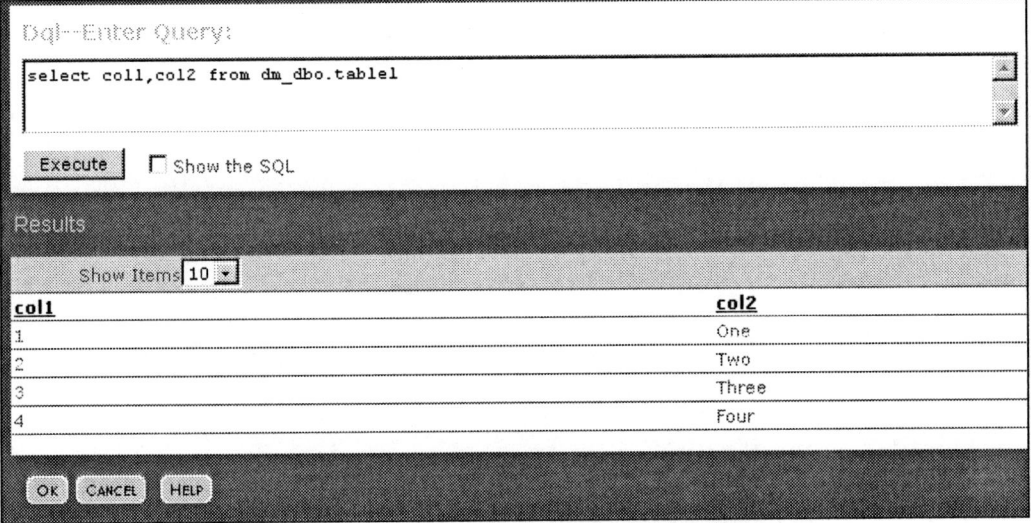

Figure 24.9: Data in Docbase registered table table1.

> tableresultset.add(new String[]{strId, strLabel});

Each row of result returned from the DQL query is added as an individual row to the TableResultSet.

> txt_display_order.getDataProvider().setResultSet
>   (tableresultset, null);

The getDataProvider() method is called on the data dropdown list control to return a handle to the data provider for this control. This returns a reference to the com.documentum.web.form.control.databound.DataProvider class.

The method setResultSet() is invoked on the DataProvider class to bind data to the control.

> ErrorMessageService.getService().setNonFatalError
>   (this, "MSG_ERROR_ORDER_DROPDOWN_POPULATION", dfe);

com.documentum.web.common.ErrorMessageService is a Singleton class whose getService() method looks at the <errormessageservice> XML element in the application's app.xml file to find out the error message service class to be instantiated.

```
/**
 * This Function is executed when user wants want to commit changes by
   clicking on OK button
 */
public boolean onCommitChanges()
{
try
    {
    IDfSession sessionObj = getDfSession();
    IDfSysObject idfsysobject = (IDfSysObject)
                        sessionObj.newObject("cust_newsarticle");

    String newsArticleNameValue = txt_news_article_name.getValue();

     if (newsArticleNameValue != null)
            {
                idfsysobject.setString
                            ("object_name", newsArticleNameValue);
            }

    String newsSummaryValue = txt_news_summary.getValue();

     if (newsSummaryValue != null)
            {
                idfsysobject.setString
                            ("cust_news_summary", newsSummaryValue);
            }

    //Get the the link level from the datadropdown list.
    DataDropDownList displayOrderControl =
                    (DataDropDownList) getControl("txt_display_order",
    DataDropDownList.class);
    String displayOrderID = displayOrderControl.getValue();

     if (displayOrderID != null)
            {
                idfsysobject.setString
                            ("cust_news_display_order", displayOrderID);
            }

    if (idfsysobject.isDirty())  // Checking if object is not updated
    if (idfsysobject.isCheckedOut())  // If object has been checkout
    {
      idfsysobject.saveLock();  // Retains the lock on the object
    }
    else
    {
      idfsysobject.save(); // Saves changes. If object not checked
                           // out.
    }

        return true;
    }
catch (DfException dfe)
    {
        ErrorMessageService.getService().
            setNonFatalError(this, "MSG_ERROR_SAVE_OPERATION", dfe);
        setReturnError("MSG_ERROR_SAVE_OPERATION", null, dfe);
        return false;
    }

    }
```

Let's discuss certain lines of code snippet in detail:

```
public boolean onCommitChanges()
```

Finally, the method onCommitChanges() is called to persist the user-provided data in the form to the Docbase attributes. This method is called when the user clicks on OK in the screen.

```
IDfSysObject idfsysobject = (IDfSysObject)
                sessionObj.newObject("cust_newsarticle");
```

A new object is instantiated for the Docbase object type cust_newsarticle (News Article). Note how the name for the News Article content object (object_name attribute) and its news summary (cust_news_summary attribute) are set in the lines 152 and 159 respectively.

Text, TextArea, Tab, DateInput, DropDownList, etc. are all subclasses of the com.documentum.web.form.control.StringInputControl class. The getValue() method in this class returns the value contained in the control. Examples can be seen in lines 148, 155, and 165.

9. Stop and start the Web Publisher application server to see the changes take effect. The custom menu option will be accessible when you are logged in as administrator and the moment you click on the **Create New News Article** menu option, the **Create New News Article** screen is launched as shown in the figure 24.7.

    Create a new News article by providing a name and summary to it and by choosing a display order value from the dropdown. After you click on OK, the News Article object is created in the Docbase.

    Voilà! We have just created our custom component using WDK framework and tested it as well. However, it is advisable to go through the Documentum WDK manuals and reference guides to get a comprehensive understanding of the rich features that WDK provides.

24.5 Summary

The Web Development Kit (WDK in short) is a framework provided by Documentum, consisting of reusable components to build and deploy J2EE web applications for connecting with Documentum Content Server.

At the beginning of the chapter, we discussed that WDK allows one to perform simple configurations and customizations to WDK framework components.

Configurations involve changes in XML configuration files and JSP pages to alter the labels/texts and to perform some other simple configuration changes.

Customizations on the other hand involve changes in behavior Java classes to override and extend default functionality provided by the WDK framework.

We then briefly looked at the WDK directory structure to understand its contained folders and files.

We also saw the WDK application hierarchy chain, in which each application layer extends from the application layer above it in the hierarchy. The chain is as follows—WDK, Webcomponent, Webtop, Digital Asset Manager, Web Publisher, and Custom layer.

We then saw how various WDK entities such as components, actions, form objects, controls, and events are related to each other in the WDK architecture.

In the later half of the chapter, we discussed a simple WDK configuration and a simple WDK customization example.

In the WDK configuration example, we saw detailed steps to alter the New Content (properties) screen in Web Publisher by adding new attributes for the News Article template.

In the WDK customization example, we discussed exhaustive steps to create a custom component (and screen) for creating News Article content in Web Publisher.

25

Documentum Deployment

In any well-defined software lifecycle, you develop the application on a development environment and get it QA'ed (or system tested) on an altogether separate test environment. By environment we mean a complete hardware and software setup consisting of a suite of servers and programs in place, necessary for the developed application to function properly. Subsequently, the system-tested application is released on staging and then eventually on production servers. While the environments keep on changing from development to system testing to production, what remains constant is a common deployment strategy. This strategy should be well planned, consisting of steps that involve minimal human intervention to ensure they can be performed repetitively for migrating our application across various environments.

In Documentum, a typical application would have the following components or entities that need to be migrated across the various environments:

- Docbase objects such as object types, lifecycles, workflows, alias sets, templates, presentation files, and such other objects that lay the foundation of the application
- Content existing in the Docbase created from templates or imported files, images, etc. in the Docbase
- Web Publisher code and customized files
- Any post-deployment scripts that need to be executed on the target environment (such as scripts for creating Site Publishing Configurations)

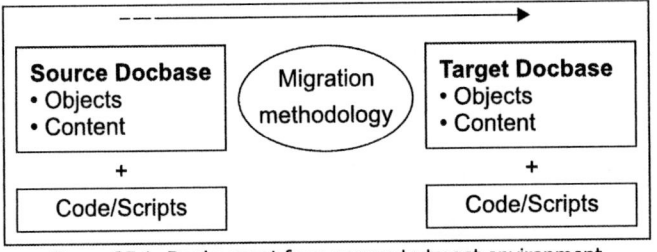

Figure 25.1: Deployment from source to target environment

There are numerous deployment methodologies available that assist us in migrating objects and content from one environment to another. Each of these has its own share of advantages and disadvantages and should be chosen after a proper evaluation of your specific needs.

Figure 25.2 will give you a quick idea about which methodology should be adopted when and under what circumstances. Also, you will understand some of the advantages and disadvantages of each of these methodologies so that you can take a better decision for your custom applications.

Note that this table should not be treated as a comprehensive list. For a detailed evaluation of the multitude of deployment approaches, kindly go through the Documentum manuals and white papers.

Entity to be migrated	Methodology	Advantages	Disadvantages
Docbase objects	DocApp migration	Useful in selectively migrating objects in a Docbase.	Requires setting up installation options meticulously to avoid target Docbase from being corrupted/damaged.
	Dump & Load scripts	Useful in migrating an entire Docbase.	Time-consuming process if the Docbase size is huge.
	Custom-written scripts	Useful if the applications cannot be migrated by the available methodologies.	Requires strong scripting knowledge and understanding of Documentum architecture/objects.
Docbase content	DocApp migration	Useful in selectively migrating contents in a Docbase.	Workflow states/tasks for contents are migrated incorrectly on target Docbase. Also the creation and modification dates of objects in source Docbase are lost on the target Docbase.
	Dump & Load scripts	Useful in migrating an entire Docbase.	Time-consuming process if the Docbase size is huge.
	Custom-written scripts	Useful if the applications cannot be migrated by the available methodologies.	Requires a strong scripting knowledge and understanding of Documentum architecture/objects.
	Documentum FTP Services	Useful for migrating bulk content into a Docbase.	Requires manual drag and drop to import files into Docbase.
Web Publisher code and customizations/ processing scripts	Manual deployment	None.	Error-prone since requires manual intervention and time-consuming as well.
	Automated build scripts using ANT	Systematic means to compile and package code.	Requires good knowledge of ANT scripting.

Figure 25.2: Deployment approaches

In this chapter we will discuss DocApp migration as a methodology to selectively migrate Docbase objects and content, and ANT scripts to migrate Web Publisher code and custom scripts.

25.1 DocApp Migration

Using Documentum Application Builder you can create and package all your objects within a DocApp (refer to Chapter 2). In our case, we created a DocApp with the name TestDocApp to include our custom Documentum objects. Once all the objects have been packaged within a DocApp, you can create a DocApp archive using Documentum Application Builder. A DocApp archive is nothing but a ZIP of the included objects and their related objects in a proprietary format that can read by Documentum Application Installer and released on a target Docbase. However, migration using Application Builder and Application Installer is not as easy as it sounds. There are a couple of things you need to keep in mind to ensure smooth migration. The prerequisites mentioned below list some basic points that you need to take care of if you are using DocApps for migrating Docbase objects and content across environments.

The installation options need to be set correctly for all objects that need to be archived and installed on the target Docbase. We will be covering this in detail later in this chapter.

Be sure to include all objects in your DocApp that need to be migrated onto the target Docbase. Documentum does not automatically include related objects. For example, if you include a Web Publisher Template file in the DocApp, Documentum does not automatically include its associated Rules and Presentation files in the DocApp.

Remove any references to objects that have been deleted in the source Docbase while selecting a DocApp archive. For example, if an Alias Set references a particular group name and this group no longer exists in the source Docbase, then remove its reference from the Alias Set before creating a DocApp archive.

If you have some of the objects already available on the target Docbase and you need to incrementally update them, make sure you do not change their names (object_name property) on the source Docbase while creating a DocApp archive. This is because DocApp archiving and installation looks at the object_name property to locate and identify any existing objects in the target Docbase.

Let us now go through some simple steps to include objects in a DocApp and to set their installation options in the source Docbase. We will then take an archive of this DocApp and install the archive on a target Docbase using Documentum Application Installer.

25.2 Configuring DocApp Objects and Creating/ Installing a DocApp Archive

This section will cover in detail the steps for setting installation options for DocApp objects and explain how to create and install a DocApp archive.

1. Check-out the DocApp and select menu option Insert | Object from Docbase | Object Type (say) to include an object type in your DocApp. Correspondingly, there are options available in Application Builder to insert other objects such as workflow templates, alias sets, etc. as well.

All object types are stored in the system cabinet corresponding to the name of the Docbase (dev_doc in our case). Select the object type to be included in the DocApp and click the Insert button (refer to figure 25.3).

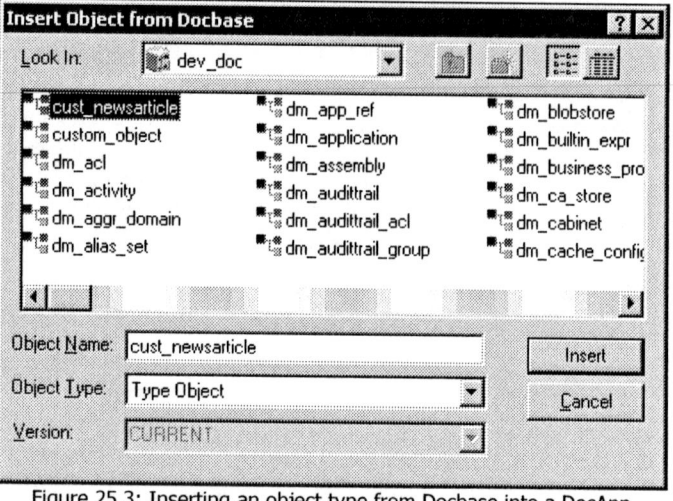

Figure 25.3: Inserting an object type from Docbase into a DocApp

Include all other objects that are to be deployed to the target Docbase via the menu option Insert | Object from the Docbase as depicted in figure 25.4:

Object	Menu option
Object Types	Object Type
Document Lifecycles	Document Lifecycle
Workflow Templates	Workflow Template
Permission Set Templates	Permission Set Template
Alias Sets	Alias Set
Formats	Format
XML Applications	XML Application
Data Objects	
Custom Folder (Custom_Fld)	Folder
Presentation Files folder (Custom_Presentations)	Folder (If Presentation files need to be included selectively, choose menu option Document.)
Rules Files folder (Custom_Rules)	Folder (If Rules files need to be included selectively, choose menu option Document.)
Template Files folder (News_Articles)	Folder (IfTtemplate files need to be included selectively, choose menu option Document.)
Folder Map	Document
Web Cabinet (Test_WebCabinet)	Cabinet

Figure 25.4: Menu options for including objects in DocApp

After you have included all objects that need to be migrated, the left-hand pane of the Application Builder will appear as shown in figure 25.5:

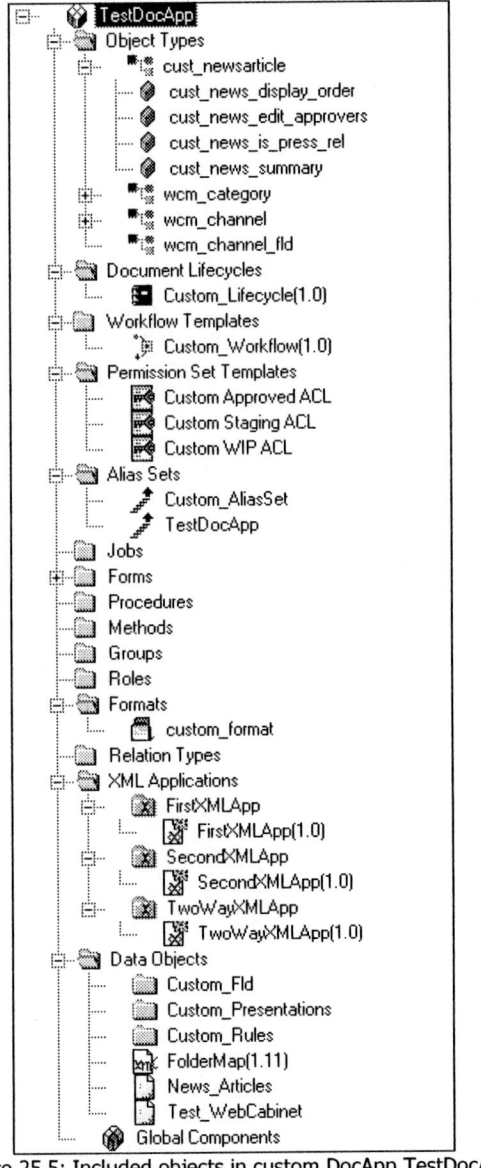

Figure 25.5: Included objects in custom DocApp TestDocApp

Note that we have included default Web Publisher object types such as wcm_category, wcm_channel, and wcm_channel_fld since we need to migrate template categories, content, and web cabinet (channel) folders from the source Docbase to the target Docbase.

Documentum 5.3 Update

Documentum release 5.3 has introduced a new feature called **Modules** in Documentum Application Builder. Modules are nothing but elements of executable code that are represented in the Docbase repository as a `dmc_module` folder object type. For example, Business Objects in Documentum can be treated as a kind of module. This allows you to package your business object classes and supporting files (in the form of JAR files) in a DocApp that can be installed via Documentum Application Installer on a target environment.

2. After you have included the objects in the DocApp, select individual objects in the left-hand pane and choose menu option DocApp | Set Installation Options to set their installation options.

    Setting installation options is extremely important because by doing so you provide a lot of vital instructions to the Application Installer for installing objects in the target Docbase such as:

    - **Upgrade options**: If DocApp Installer finds an object with the same name as in your source Docbase, it can be directed to perform one of the following options:
        - Overwrite the corresponding object in the target Docbase with the version existing in the source Docbase.
        - Update and create a new version of the object in the target Docbase, leaving the original version(s) intact.
        - Do not overwrite the object in the target Docbase.
    - **Data object transfer**: This option is available in the case of XML Applications, Folders, and Cabinets and it directs the installer to include or exclude objects in the manner described as follows:
        - **All content**: Installer will install the specified cabinets, folders, and sub-folders and all objects contained within them.
        - **Top level content**: Installer will install the specified XML Application folder or folder and the objects contained within it.
        - **Hierarchical structure**: Installer will install only the specified cabinets, folders, and sub-folders but no objects.
        - **Object only**: Installer will install only the specified XML Application folder, cabinet, or folder.

    Let us take an example of custom lifecycle object `Custom_Lifecycle` and set its installation options.

3. Select the Custom_Lifecycle object from the left-hand pane and choose menu
    option DocApp | Set Installation Options to set the installation options for the custom
    lifecycle object (refer to figure 25.6).

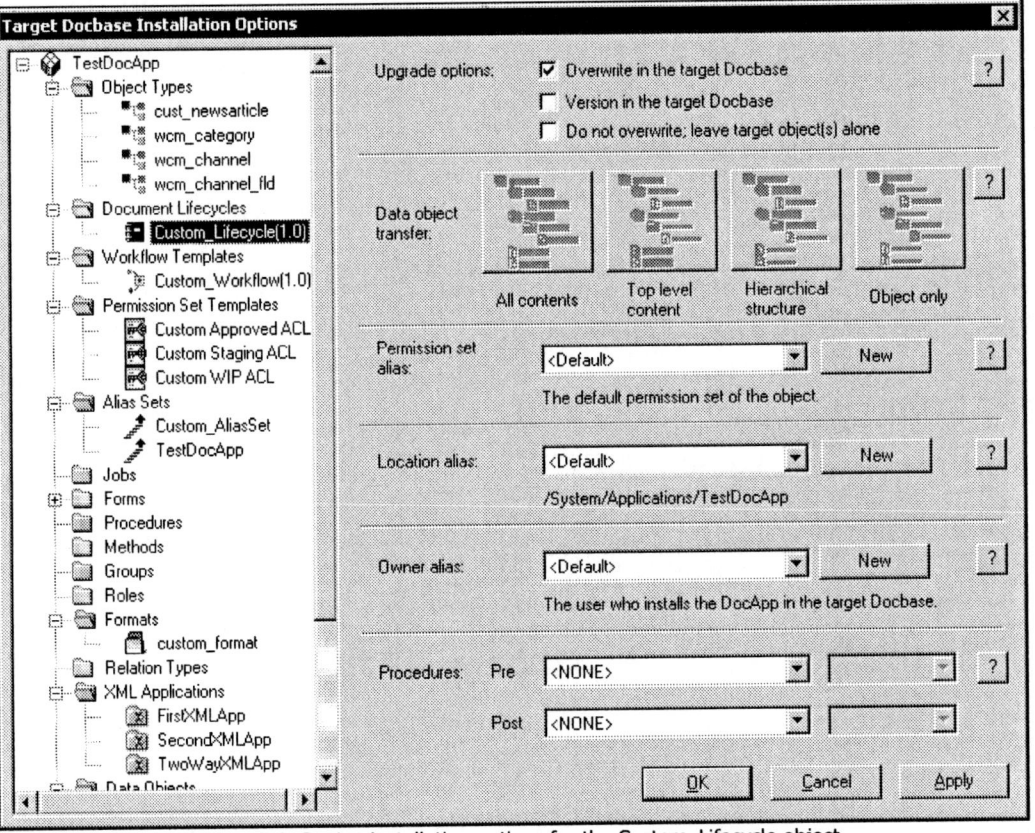

Figure 25.6: Setting installation options for the Custom_Lifecycle object

As shown in figure 25.6, select the Upgrade options checkbox for overwriting the
Custom_Lifecycle object in case it already exists in the target Docbase.

After the lifecycle object is installed in the target Docbase, Documentum assigns a
system-generated ACL (Permission Set of the user who installs the DocApp) to it. You
can, however, direct the system to assign a specific ACL to the lifecycle in the target
Docbase by defining a Permission Set for it.

This can be done by clicking on the New button shown against the Permission set alias
field, which opens up an Alias Object Dialog screen.

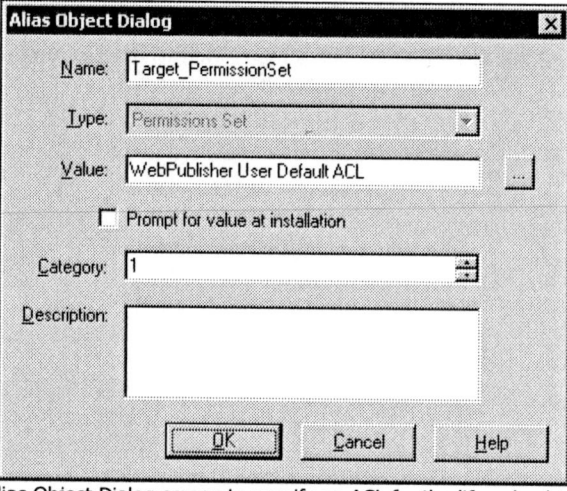

Figure 25.7: Using the Alias Object Dialog screen to specify an ACL for the lifecycle object in the target Docbase

In the Alias Object Dialog screen shown in figure 25.7, fill in the following fields:

- Name: Provide a self-explanatory name to the Permission Set alias.
- Value: Specify the actual ACL that the system needs to assign to the lifecycle object after it has been installed in the target Docbase. We have assigned WebPublisher User Default ACL as shown in figure 25.7.
- Category: This is simply an application-specific flag you can add for categorizing the various aliases in your system. Documentum internally does not use this flag.
- Description: Provide a brief explanatory description for the alias setting.

Figure 25.8 shows the access permissions (rights) available to the various Web Publisher groups within the WebPublisher User Default ACL.

Note that you can even leave the Value field blank and instead select the checkbox so that the system prompts you to specify an ACL at run time when you are installing the DocApp in your target Docbase via the Documentum Application Installer tool.

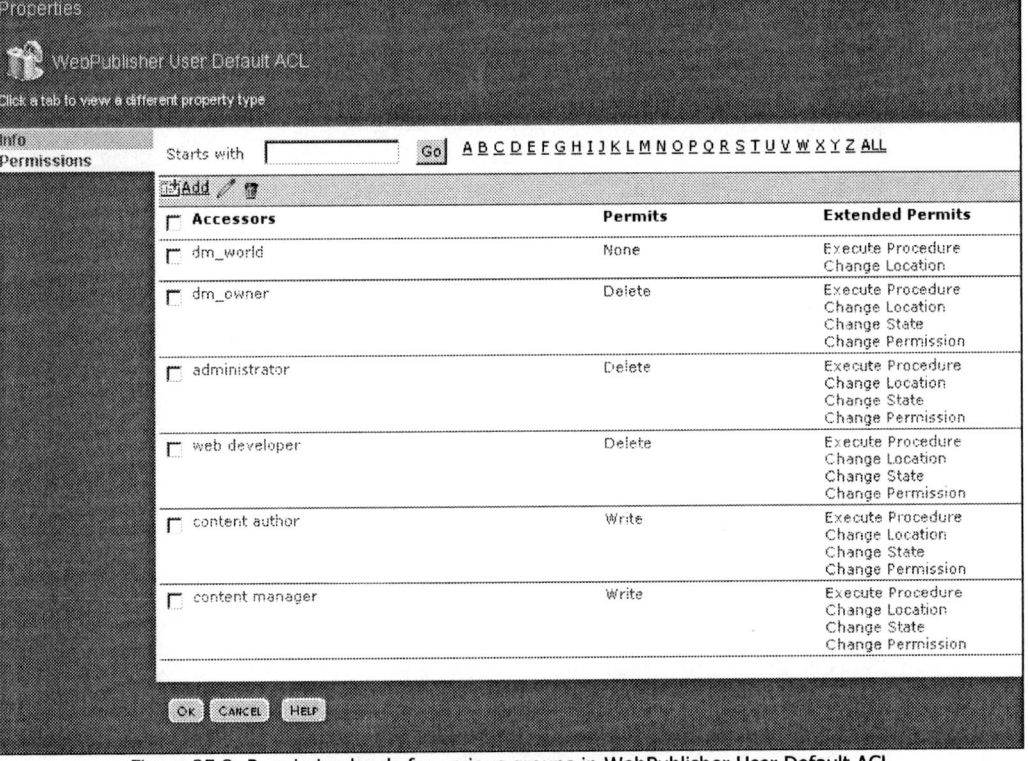

Figure 25.8: Permission levels for various groups in WebPublisher User Default ACL

After filling in the various fields, click on OK.

Similar to the way you have specified a Permission Set for the object in the target Docbase, you can specify the following:

- o **Location alias**: The cabinet/folder path in the target Docbase where the object should be installed
- o **Owner alias**: The user or group in the target Docbase who should be the owner of this object after installation.
- o **Pre- and post-installation procedures**: The procedures that need to be executed by the Application Installer before it starts DocApp installation and after it finishes installing it. You could, for example, write custom procedures (and include them in your DocApp) to create some application-specific groups in the target Docbase and get them executed as pre-installation scripts. This will ensure that the system first creates the specified groups in the target Docbase before installing the other DocApp objects.

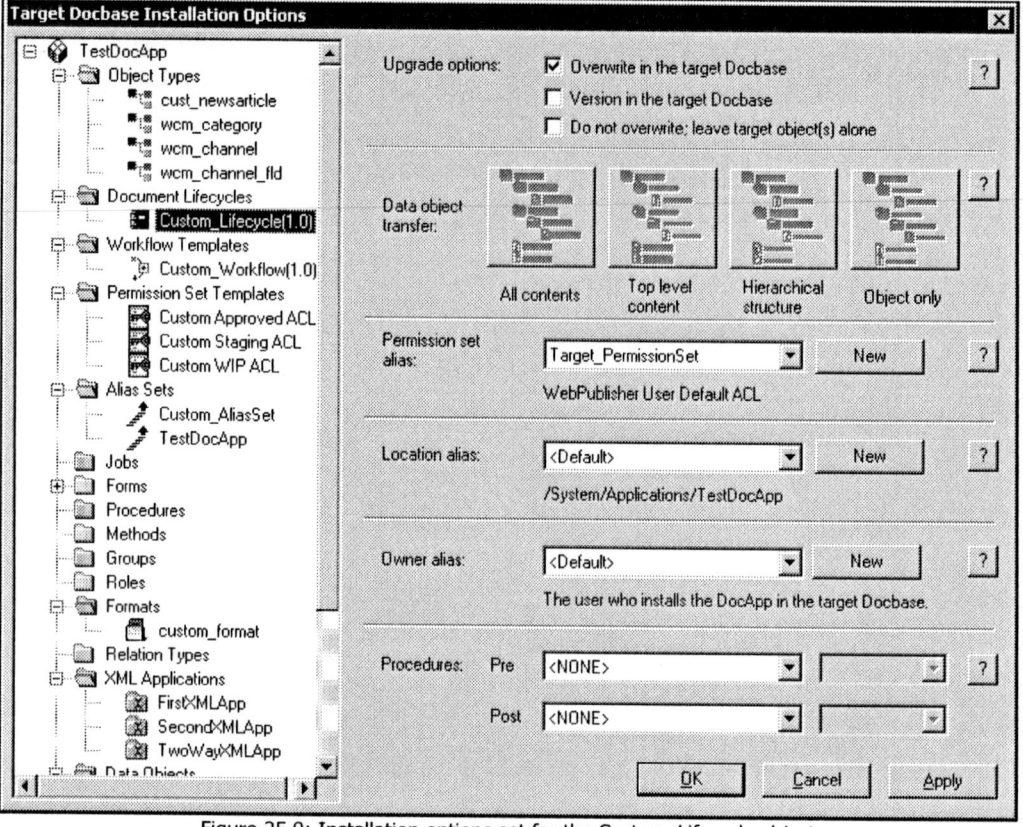

Figure 25.9: Installation options set for the Custom_Lifecycle object

Refer to figure 25.9; after specifying the installation options, click on Apply and OK. Figure 25.10 lists the correct Location Alias installation options for the other objects included in your custom DocApp. You could additionally specify particular Permission set alias and Owner alias values for each of these, if need be.

Do not forget to check-in the DocApp after you have completed setting installation options for all included objects in your custom DocApp.

Object	Location Alias
Object Types	N/A
Document Lifecycles	/System/Applications/TestDocApp
Workflow Templates	/System/Applications/TestDocApp
Permission Set Templates	N/A
Alias Sets	N/A
Formats	N/A
XML Applications	/System/Applications/TestDocApp
Data Objects	
Custom Folder	/Custom_Cabinet
Presentation Files	/WebPublisher Configuration/Supporting Templates/Editor Presentations
Rules Files	/WebPublisher Configuration/Supporting Templates/Editor Rules
Template Files	/WebPublisher Configuration/Content Templates
Folder Map	/WebPublisher Configuration/Common
Web Cabinet	/

Figure 25.10: Location Aliases for DocApp objects

4. Choose menu option DocApp | Create DocApp Archive in order to have a DocApp archive created by the system. The system will prompt you to specify a folder location (refer to figure 25.11) on your local machine drive where the DocApp archive will be created.

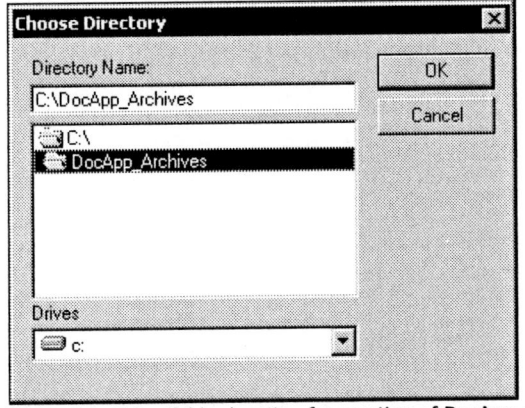

Figure 25.11: Specifying folder location for creation of DocApp archive

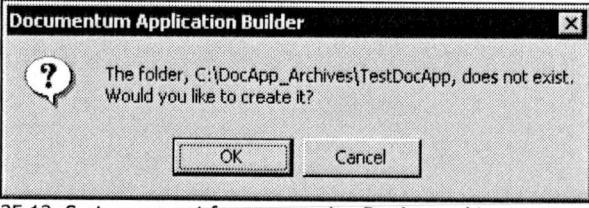

Figure 25.12: System prompt for commencing DocApp archive creation process

Refer to figure 25.12; click on OK, allowing the system to create an archive of your custom DocApp in the specified folder location. Usually the archive creation process takes a few minutes but can vary substantially if the number of objects included in your DocApp is very large. Archiving time can even go up to 5 hours for DocApps containing around 1000 objects.

Once the DocApp archive has been created, browse to the specified location on your machine and open the archive log file (<Your DocApp name>_ArchiveLog.html) to locate any system errors/warnings. It is advisable to look for warnings with the keyword unable to find out any serious failures.

Once you have the DocApp archive of the source Docbase, you can install it on the target Docbase via Documentum Application Installer. Before installing the archive, you may want to clean up the target Docbase and perform any pre-installation steps specific to your application.

It is better to set up Cabinets, Folders, Web Cabinets, Users/Groups, etc. in the target Docbase before you install the DocApp archive. If you want to avoid such manual activities, you can write pre-installation procedures and include them in the DocApp as we saw in step 3 earlier.

5. After the target Docbase is ready, you are all set to install the source Docbase DocApp archive over it. Set up the dmcl.ini file to point to the correct DocBroker host for the target Docbase.

    Launch Documentum Application Installer from your machine and choose the target Docbase name from the Docbase dropdown (PN6549 Docbase in this example).

    Provide Docbase user credentials for login authentication purposes and click on OK (refer to figure 25.13).

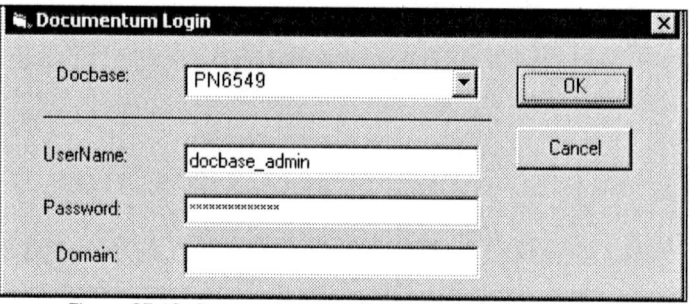

Figure 25.13: Documentum Application Installer login screen

6. In the Select DocApp Archive screen (refer to figure 25.14), click on the Browse...
    button and choose the DocApp archive (created in step 4 above) from your local
    machine. You can optionally provide a path and file name for the log file created
    during the DocApp archive installation process. The default DocApp installation log
    file name and its folder path are shown in figure 25.14.

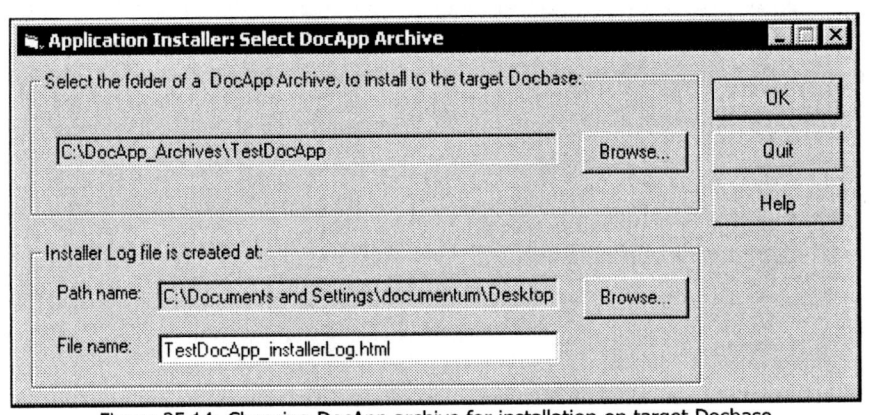

Figure 25.14: Choosing DocApp archive for installation on target Docbase

Click on OK.

7. The target Docbase name, installation user name, and the name and path of the
    DocApp archive are shown as in figure 25.15. Click the Start Installation button to
    commence DocApp installation.

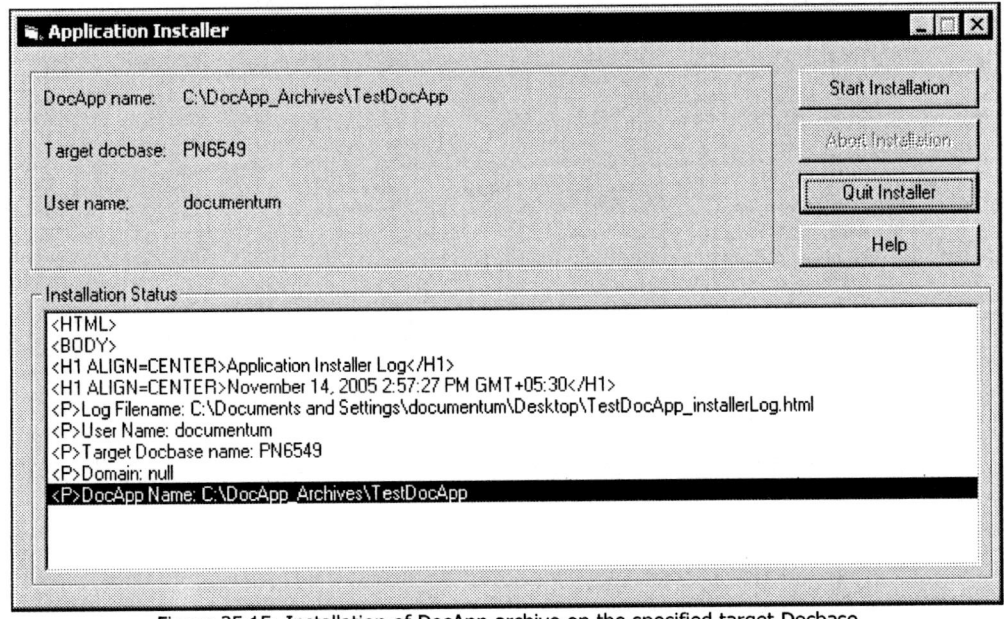

Figure 25.15: Installation of DocApp archive on the specified target Docbase

If there are users connected to the target Docbase, the system will prompt you a message stating this. Click the Yes button to continue with the DocApp installation procedure.

Avoid any activities on the target Docbase while the DocApp installation process is going on. This is just to ensure that there are no inconsistencies while the system is overwriting existing objects or creating new objects in the target Docbase.

---

8. The DocApp installation process takes several minutes as we saw in the case of the DocApp archive creation process. It has been observed that with 1000 objects, the installation process can take more than an hour!

   After the installation has been completed, click the Quit Installer button to exit the DocApp Installer application. Open the installation log file to check for errors or warnings during the installation procedure.

9. That's it! The DocApp has been installed on the target Docbase, which means that the specified objects in source Docbase have been migrated to the target Docbase. You now need to perform Web Publisher-specific tasks for your application to work correctly. For example, you might want to create Site Publishing Configurations in the target Docbase or make migrated workflows Available through the Web Publisher menu option Administration | Web Publisher Admin | Workflow Templates.

25.3 Deployment of Web Publisher Code and Custom Scripts

DocApp installation is just one part of migration. It simply takes care of Docbase objects; what about the WDK/DFC/other custom code you have written for you application or any scripts that you have customized for your business needs? How are these to be migrated?

Typically scripts/code files reside on two Documentum hosts:

- **Content Server:**

  Scripts residing in the `%DM_HOME%\bin` directory

  Example on a Windows machine: `c:\Documentum\product\5.2\bin`

  Or
  Java method code residing in `%DOCUMENTUM%\dba\java_methods`

  Example on a Windows machine: `c:\Documentum\dba\java_methods`

- **Web Publisher host:**

  Customized files residing in the following directories:

  `\wp\custom`

  `\wp\WEB-INF\classes`

  `\wp\WEB-INF\tlds`

Note that wp is the name of the default Web Publisher web application and could be different if you provided a different name during the installation of Web Publisher.

You could either ZIP the customized files and copy them over to the respective directories on the target host or you could automate the process by preparing compiled code via ANT and copying it over to the correct directories.

ANT is a Java-based build tool from Apache (check out `http://ant.apache.org/`) providing an easy-to-write XML-based configuration file for automating build processes.

We will go via the ANT approach and look at a sample ANT script for preparing a build.

1. Download Apache ANT from the following location: `http://ant.apache.org/bindownload.cgi` and install/configure it as per the user manual! (refer to `http://ant.apache.org/manual/index.html`).

    The following example in this chapter has been executed on ANT version 1.6.5.

2. Create a `build.properties` file as shown in the code snippet below. The following name-value pairs have been defined in the properties file:

    - `base_loc`: Location of source code that needs to be compiled

    - `documentum_jar_location`: Location where Documentum JAR files are present in order to compile source code

    - `build_dir`: Location where the compiled classes should be created

    - `compiled_zip_file_name`: Name of the ZIP file containing the created compiled classes

    - `zip_file_loc`: Location where the ZIP file containing compiled classes will be formed

    ```
    # base_loc --> Defines the location where code resides
    base_loc=C:/Documentum_Source/DFC
    documentum_jar_location=C:/Program Files/Documentum/Shared

    build_dir=C:/Documentum_Build
    compiled_zip_file_name=DCTM_code_build.zip
    zip_file_loc=C:/Documentum_Build
    ```

    Create a `build.xml` file as shown below, mentioning the various targets (or task directions) for the ANT build process.

    A detailed discussion of the `build.xml` file and ANT is beyond the scope of this book. You may want to go through the Apache ANT home page (`http://ant.apache.org/`) to know more about ANT, its usage, and its advantages and disadvantages.

    ```
    <!-- Build file Testing Purposes -->
    <project name="BuildDCTMCode" default="all_targets">

        <!-- Machine specific settings -->
        <property file="build.properties"/>

        <!-- Source paths-->
        <property name="base_loc_java" value="${base_loc}/src"/>

        <!-- Destination paths-->
        <property name="build_class" value="${build_dir}/Compiled"/>
    ```

```
<!-- Classpaths-->
<property name="dfcbase_jar"
                value="${documentum_jar_location}\dfcbase.jar"/>
<property name="dfc_jar" value="${documentum_jar_location}\dfc.jar"/>

<path id="totalClassPath">
    <pathelement location="${dfcbase_jar}"/>
<pathelement location="${dfc_jar}"/>
</path>

<target name="all_targets" depends="init, compile_code,
                                    copyFolders, createZip"/>

<target name="init">
<echo message = "Starting init" />
    <mkdir dir="${build_dir}"/>
    <mkdir dir="${build_class}"/>
<echo message = "Finishing init" />
    </target>

<target name="compile_code" depends="init">
<echo message = "Starting to compile code" />
        <javac srcdir="${base_loc_java}" destdir="${build_class}">
            <classpath refid="totalClassPath"/>
        </javac>
<echo message = "Finishing compilation of code" />
</target>

<target name="copyFolders" depends="compile_code">
<echo message = "Starting to copy Folders" />
        <copy todir="${build_dir}/Compiled_Code" overwrite="yes">
            <fileset dir="${build_class}"/>
        </copy>
        <echo message = "Finishing copy Folders" />
</target>

<target name="createZip" depends="compile_code">
    <echo message = "Starting to create Zip" />
        <zip basedir="${build_class}"
destfile="${zip_file_loc}/${compiled_zip_file_name}"/>
    <echo message = "Finishing creatation of Zip" />
    </target>

</project>
```

Copy the source code Java files at the following location:
`C:/Documentum_Source/DFC/src`

Compiled classes will be formed by ANT at the following location:
`C:/Documentum_Build/Compiled`

`dfc.jar` and `dfcbase.jar` files are read by ANT from the following location:
`C:/Program Files/Documentum/Shared`

The following tasks are performed by ANT in the order shown:

- o **Initializing** (`<target name="init">`): Build directory and compiled classes directory is created by ANT.
- o **Compiling Code** (`<target name="compile_code" depends="init">`): Invoke `javac` to compile Java source code from source directory and copy the compiled classes to the `Compiled` directory.

- o **Copying Folders** (`<target name="copyFolders"`
  `depends="compile_code">`): Copy compiled classes .from the
  `Compiled` directory to the following location:
  `C:/Documentum_Build/Compiled_Code`.
- o **Creating ZIP file** (`<target name="createZip"`
  `depends="compile_code">`): Create a ZIP of compiled classes from the
  `Compiled` directory at the following location: `C:/Documentum_Build`.

3. Copy the `build.properties` and `build.xml` files to the same location in a folder on
   your machine. Execute ANT by running the command `ant` from your command
   prompt as shown in figure 25.16.

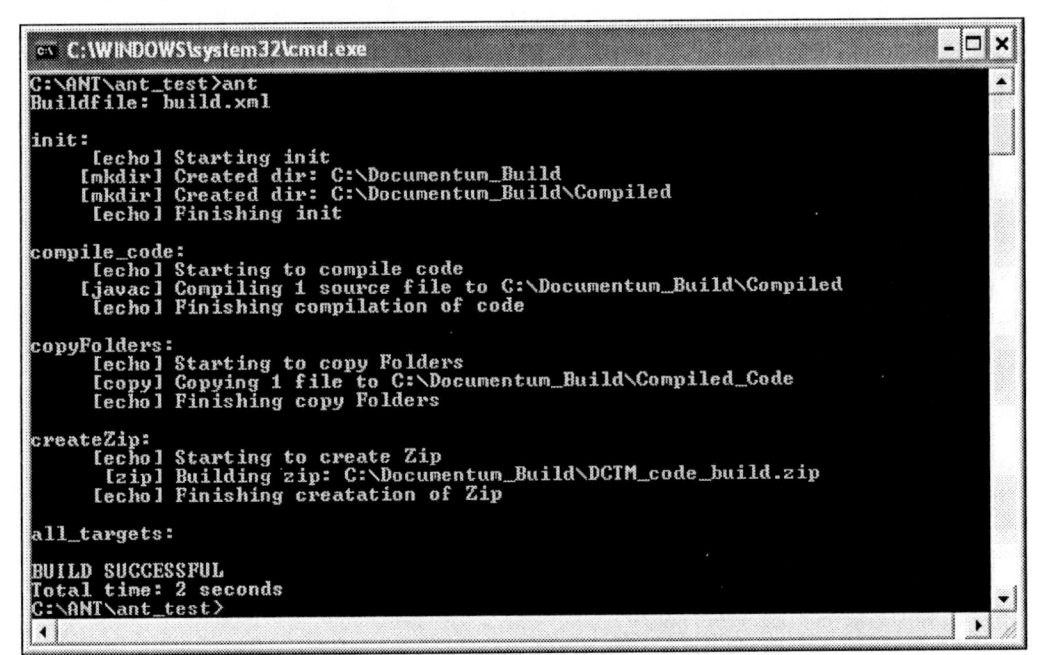

Figure 25.16: Running ANT from the command prompt

Notice the echo messages shown in the console as ANT executes the various tasks mentioned in
the `build.xml` file. These echo messages serve as a good mechanism for debugging ANT scripts.

This concludes our discussion on migration. Documentum provides other mechanisms for migration
as well, such as Dump and Load, Docbase copy, FTP Services (earlier known as `FtpIntegrator`),
etc. Another tool worth mentioning here is **DIXI** (Documentum Import eXport Interface) developed
by Blue Fish Group. This is an XML-based system that helps move content in and out of Documentum
repositories. However, a discussion about each of these is not possible within the boundaries of
this book.

25.4 Summary

Documentum applications, like any other software applications, need to be developed on a development environment, deployed on a separate test environment for system testing purposes, and eventually deployed on to the production environment.

In Documentum, the following entities need to be migrated (deployed) from one environment to the other—Docbase objects in a DocApp, existing content, Web Publisher or any other client application code/customized files, and any deployment scripts for the target environment.

In this chapter we briefly discussed the following existing migration methodologies in Documentum, their benefits and drawbacks—DocApp migration, Dump and Load scripts, Documentum FTP Services, custom-written scripts, manual deployment, and automated mechanisms through ANT scripts.

Using Documentum Application Builder and Documentum Application Installer tools, we discussed in detail how to migrate DocApps from one environment to another by setting correct installation options.

Also, we briefly discussed an example using Apache ANT to automate migration of Web Publisher/DFC/customized code files to a target server.

26

Using DQL and API Commands

Having gone through most of the chapters in this book, you should now have a good understanding of the Documentum system, the Content Server, and the critical bits and pieces in Documentum WCM architecture. As an experienced developer, you ought to have a good understanding of some basic Documentum DQL (Document Query Language) queries and API commands for system troubleshooting and administration/monitoring purposes.

DQL queries and API commands are extremely handy tools when you need to inspect the Documentum system, its contained object types, and their attributes. Both DQL and API ultimately serve the same purpose of querying and making modifications to objects in the Docbase, but they have their own advantages and limitations.

While API commands work on one object at a time, DQL queries can be issued over multiple objects in a run. This chapter will discuss some important API commands and DQL queries that every Documentum professional should be aware of in order to effectively work with the system.

Throughout this chapter, we will execute DQL queries and API commands via the user interface provided by Documentum Administrator.

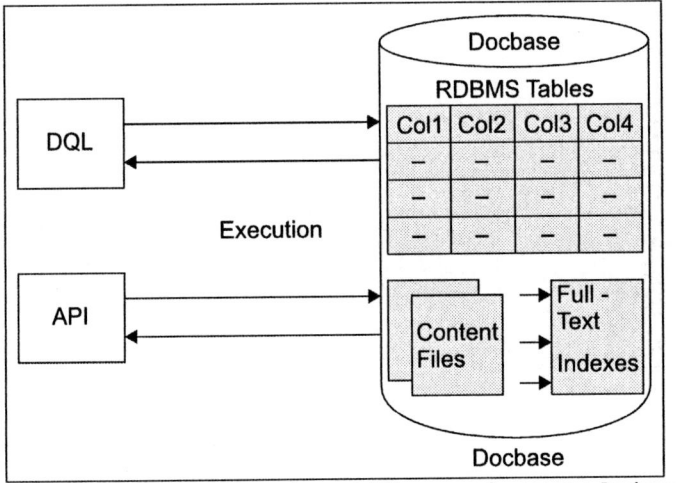

Figure 26.1: Executing DQL queries and API commands against a Docbase

26.1 DQL

For those familiar with SQL (Structured Query Language), DQL is a similar querying language in Documentum.

26.1.1 Uses of DQL

DQL is used for the following purposes:

- Creating new objects in the Docbase
- Retrieving objects from the Docbase
- Updating objects in the Docbase
- Deleting objects from the Docbase
- Accessing registered tables
- Searching content in the Docbase

26.1.2 Command Tools

DQL queries can be executed via the following means:

- The IDQL utility
- Web clients such as Documentum Administrator or Web Publisher

IDQL is an interactive utility for running DQL queries against a Docbase. IDQL is available once you install Content Server and the executable idql32.exe can be found on Windows machines at the following location:

%DM_HOME%\bin, e.g. C:\Documentum\product\5.2\bin

You can invoke the executable directly from the command prompt as shown in figure 26.2 or you can click on the IDQL button shown in the Documentum Server Manager window (refer to figure 26.3). In both scenarios, you will need to provide details such as Docbase name and user/password before you start issuing DQL queries.

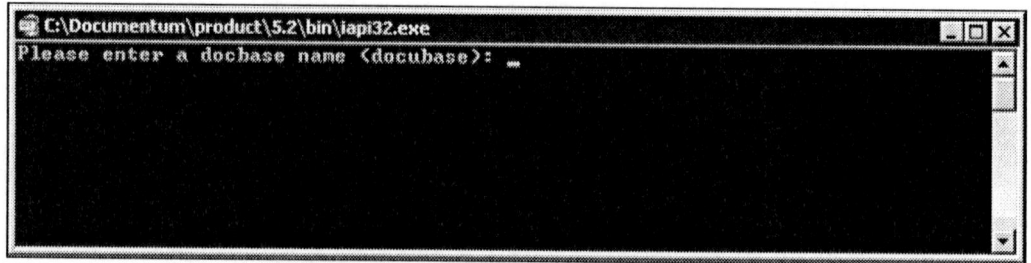

Figure 26.2: IDQL utility invoked from command prompt

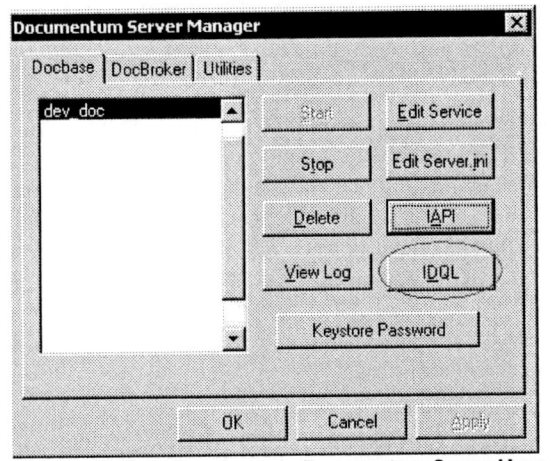
Figure 26.3: IDQL button shown in Documentum Server Manager

DQL queries can also be executed from within Documentum Administrator by clicking on the DQL button shown in the top right-hand side of the toolbar. This opens the Dql--Enter Query screen as shown in figure 26.4.

Figure 26.4: DQL query editor in Documentum Administrator

26.1.3 DQL Examples

Let us take a simple example of creating a document object, setting its attribute values, linking it to a cabinet in the Docbase, and finally saving it. We will then retrieve this document object from the Docbase and delete it. You will come across a number of DQL queries while working on this simple example.

26.1.3.1 Creating a Document Object

Log in to Documentum Administrator as an administrator and open the DQL editor screen.

Refer to figure 26.5; enter the following query in the DQL text box and click on the Execute button:

```
DQL> create dm_document object set object_name = TestDocumentCreated_via_DQL',
     setfile 'C:\Test\testing_dql.xml' with content_format = 'xml'
```

The create ... object DQL query creates an object in the Docbase of the specified object type (dm_document in our example). We have set the object_name attribute of the document object as TestDocumentCreated_via_DQL in the same create ... object query.

Note in particular the setfile keyword used in the above query. This associates a content file with the document object. The prerequisite is that you need to create a valid content file (testing_dql.xml in our example) and place it at a convenient location on the Content Server host before issuing the DQL. The with content_format clause sets a valid format for the content file that is associated with the document object.

Note that the format specified should be understood and recognized by the Content Server.

If the specified format (say xyz) is invalid and not recognized by Content Server, the following error message is seen on executing the query:

Error occurred during query execution :[DM_QUERY_F_UP_SAVE]fatal: "UPDATE: An error has occurred during a save operation." [DM_SYSOBJECT_E_INVALID_FORMAT]error: "The specified format (xyz) is invalid."

The create ... object statement returns the object ID of the newly created object once the DQL runs successfully. In our case running the above DQL query returned the object ID of the document object as 090015558000c972 as shown in figure 26.5.

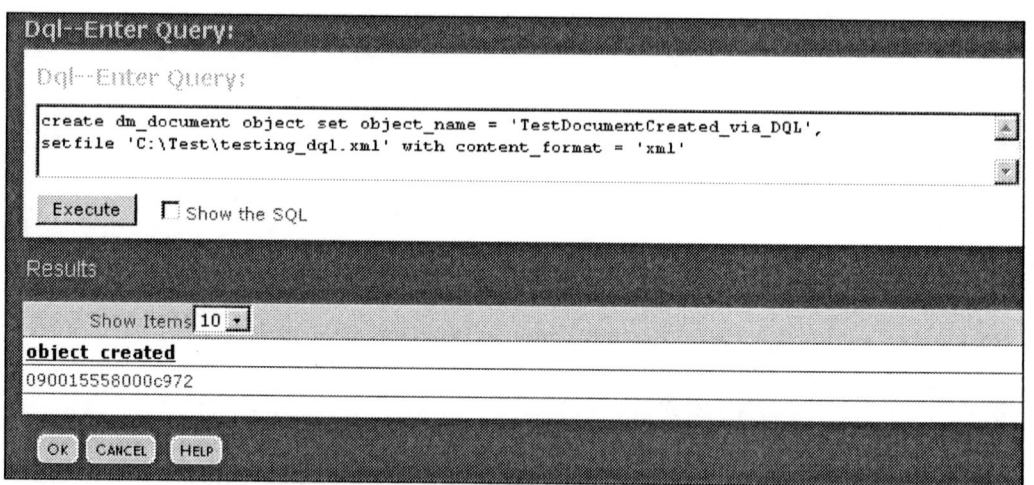

Figure 26.5: Running DQL query to create an object

26.1.3.2 Updating Attributes of a Document Object

An existing object's attributes can be modified by issuing the update ... object DQL query. In this example we will update the newly created document object by setting its title and keywords attributes as follows:

```
DQL> update dm_document object set title = 'File created via DQL' ,
     set keywords = 'first' where object_name = 'TestDocumentCreated_via_DQL'
```

Notice the use of a `where` clause as a qualification criterion to find out the exact document object that needs to be modified. We have used the `object_name` attribute of the document object for qualification purposes.

The server returns the total number of objects updated on running the update ... object DQL query. In our case, since only one document object, `TestDocumentCreated_via_DQL`, existed in the Docbase, the number of object(s) updated by the update query is one.

26.1.3.3 Appending a Value in a Repeating Attribute

The values in a repeating attribute are stored at indexed positions. For example, if the `keywords` repeating attribute has abc and xyz as the first and the second values, then these are stored by Content Server as:

```
keywords[0] = abc
keywords[1] = xyz
```

You can use an append clause in `update` DQL queries to append a particular value to the existing values of a repeating attribute. The following DQL query appends the value second to the existing value(s) in the `keywords` attribute of the document object we created.

```
DQL> update dm_document object append keywords = 'second'
     where object_name = 'TestDocumentCreated_via_DQL'
```

The server adds the specified value at the end of the values of the repeating attribute.

26.1.3.4 Inserting a Value into a Repeating Attribute

Using the `insert` clause in `update` DQL queries, you can insert a particular value at a specific index position in a repeating attribute. The following DQL query inserts the value `middle` at the second position (index '1') in the existing values of the `keywords` repeating attribute of the document object.

```
DQL> update dm_document object insert keywords[1] = 'middle'
     where object_name = 'TestDocumentCreated_via_DQL'
```

Caution

If you do not specify the index position of the repeating attribute while using the `insert` clause, the server inserts the specified value at index position zero.

26.1.3.5 Associating a Document Object with a Cabinet

The document object can be associated with a cabinet or a folder residing within a cabinet in the Docbase. Using the `link` clause in a DQL query and specifying a cabinet or folder path, you can achieve this as follows:

```
DQL> update dm_document object link '/Testing_API_DQL'
     where object_name = 'TestDocumentCreated_via_DQL'
```

This DQL links the document object TestDocumentCreated_via_DQL with a cabinet Testing_API_DQL in the Docbase. However, as a prerequisite create a custom cabinet, say Testing_API_DQL, in Web Publisher before issuing this DQL query.

If you specify an incorrect cabinet/folder path in the link clause or if you specify a cabinet/folder name (say abcdef) that does not exist in the Docbase, the server throws the following error on running the above DQL query:

Error occurred during query execution :[DM_QUERY_E_UP_BAD_FOLDER]error: "You have specified an invalid folder path, /abcdef, in your LINK or MOVE TO clause."

Once you have linked the document object with a cabinet, you can have a look at it by logging in to Web Publisher and browsing to the Testing_API_DQL cabinet. Figure 26.6 shows how the document object appears in Web Publisher.

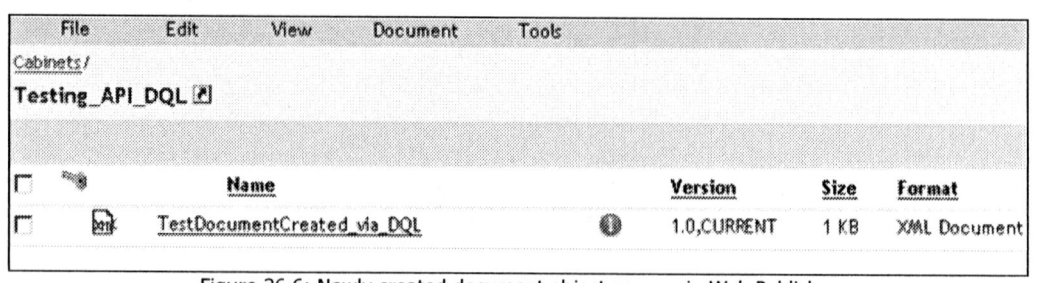

Figure 26.6: Newly created document object as seen in Web Publisher

If you select the checkbox against the document object and choose the menu option File | View, you will be able to view the associated content file testing_dql.xml.

In order to look at the properties of the document object, you can either click on the Info icon ⓘ or select the checkbox against the document object and choose View | Properties | Info. Figure 26.7 shows the various properties for the document object that we had set using DQL queries in this example. Note in particular the Name, Title, and Keywords fields shown in figure 26.7 that we have set using DQL queries.

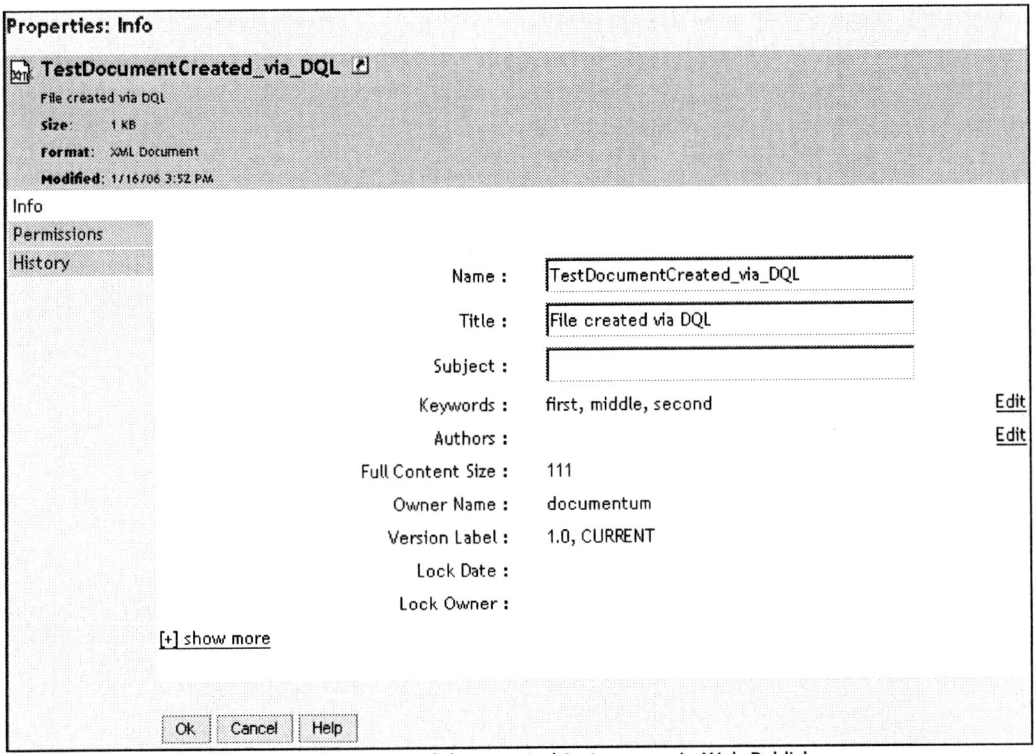

Properties: Info

📄 **TestDocumentCreated_via_DQL** 🔺

File created via DQL

Size: 1 KB

Format: XML Document

Modified: 1/16/06 3:52 PM

Info
Permissions
History

Name :	TestDocumentCreated_via_DQL
Title :	File created via DQL
Subject :	
Keywords :	first, middle, second
Authors :	
Full Content Size :	111
Owner Name :	documentum
Version Label :	1.0, CURRENT
Lock Date :	
Lock Owner :	

Edit (Keywords)
Edit (Authors)

[+] show more

Ok   Cancel   Help

Figure 26.7: Properties of document object as seen in Web Publisher

26.1.3.6 Retrieving a Document Object from the Docbase

DQL can be used for efficiently searching and retrieving objects from the Docbase. Say, for example, you wish to find out the value of the `title` attribute of the document object we created in our example. The following query can be used to accomplish this:

```
DQL> select title from dm_document where object_name =
'TestDocumentCreated_via_DQL'
```

Note that we use a `select` query on the object type `dm_document` to find out the `title` attribute of the object whose name is `TestDocumentCreated_via_DQL`. The `where` clause is used for specifying a qualification criterion.

In order to retrieve values from multiple attributes, separate the attribute names with a comma. For example, run the following DQL query in order to find out the value of the object ID (`r_object_id` attribute), name (`object_name` attribute), and version label (`r_version_label` attribute) of the document object whose name is `TestDocumentCreated_via_DQL`:

```
DQL> select r_object_id, object_name, r_version_label from dm_document
    where object_name = 'TestDocumentCreated_via_DQL'
```

The result shows just one record (the current version of the document) matching the qualification criterion as shown in figure 26.8:

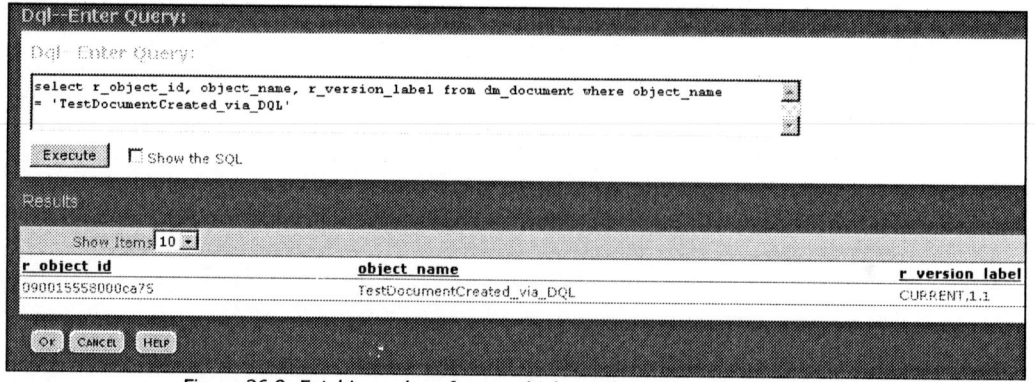

Figure 26.8: Fetching values from multiple attributes using a select query

In order to retrieve all the versions of the document object matching the same qualification, modify the DQL query by including an all keyword as follows:

```
DQL> select r_object_id, object_name, r_version_label from dm_document (all)
     where object_name = 'TestDocumentCreated_via_DQL'
```

As shown in figure 26.9, the results show all the versions of the document object matching the specified criterion.

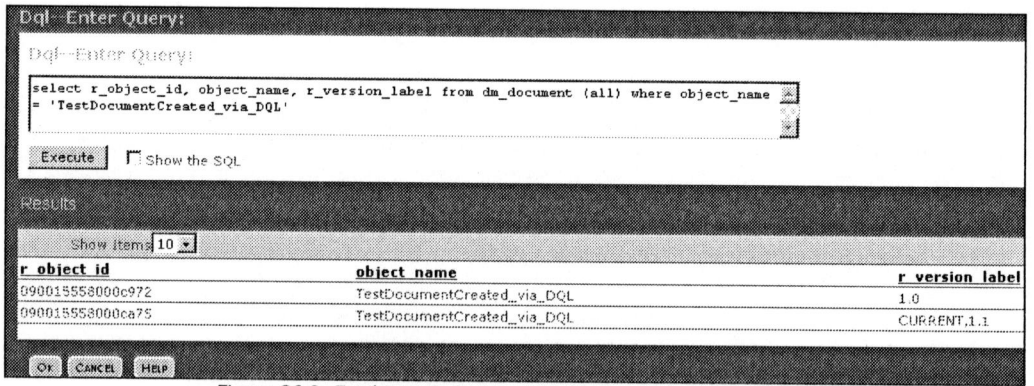

Figure 26.9: Fetching attribute values of all versions of the object

Wildcard searching can also be used along with a where clause to retrieve objects satisfying the specified qualification. The following query is used to retrieve the title attribute of the document objects whose name matches the pattern via:

```
DQL> select object_name,title from dm_document where object_name like '%via%'
```

Note that the like clause is used with percentage sign (%) as a pattern matching character interpreted by Documentum for wild card searches. %via% searches for all objects that contain the string via within their title attribute irrespective of how many characters precede or follow the string via in the attribute value.

422

Similarly, Documentum uses underscore (_) for pattern matching in wild card searches where the underscore strictly matches one character. For example, the following query finds objects whose `title` attribute value has just one character following the string `TestDocumentCreated_via_DQ`:

```
DQL> select object_name, title from dm_document
     where object_name like TestDocumentCreated_via_DQ_
```

You can combine qualification conditions by using the and keyword in the `where` clause of DQL queries. Say for example, the following query is used for retrieving document objects whose name is `TestDocumentCreated_via_DQL` *and* whose `title` is `File created via DQL`:

```
DQL> select object_name, title from dm_document
     where object_name = TestDocumentCreated_via_DQL'
     and title =  'File created via DQL'
```

Similarly you can use the or keyword for retrieving results if *either* specified qualification criterion is met.

For searching repeating attributes, use the any keyword in the `where` clause of DQL queries as follows:

```
DQL> select object_name,title from dm_document where any keywords = middle
```

This DQL query retrieves document objects whose `keywords` repeating attribute contains `middle` as one of its values.

26.1.3.7 Deleting a Document Object from the Docbase

You can remove the document object from the Docbase by running the `delete object` DQL query as follows:

```
DQL> delete dm_document object where object_name = TestDocumentCreated_via_DQL
```

The server returns the total number of objects deleted on running the `delete object` DQL query. In our case, since only one document object `TestDocumentCreated_via_DQL` existed in the Docbase, the number of object(s) deleted by the delete query is one.

It is good practice to first run a `select` query and retrieve objects matching the specified qualification, before issuing a `delete` query. This ensures that you do not end up inadvertently destroying objects that you did not desire to delete from the Docbase.

26.2 API

API commands, also referred to as Server API, are instructions or commands sent by clients to Content Server through DMCL.

26.2.1 Command Tools

API commands can be executed via the following means:

- The IAPI utility
- Web clients such as Documentum Administrator API Tester or Web Publisher

IAPI is short for **Interactive API Utility** and is available once you install Content Server. On the Content Server host you can find the executable iapi32.exe on Windows machines at the following location:

%DM_HOME%\bin, e.g. C:\Documentum\product\5.2\bin (for example)

You can invoke the executable directly from the command prompt as shown in figure 26.10 or you can click on the IAPI button shown in Documentum Server Manager window (refer to figure 26.11). In both scenarios, you will need to provide details such as Docbase name and user/password before you start issuing API commands.

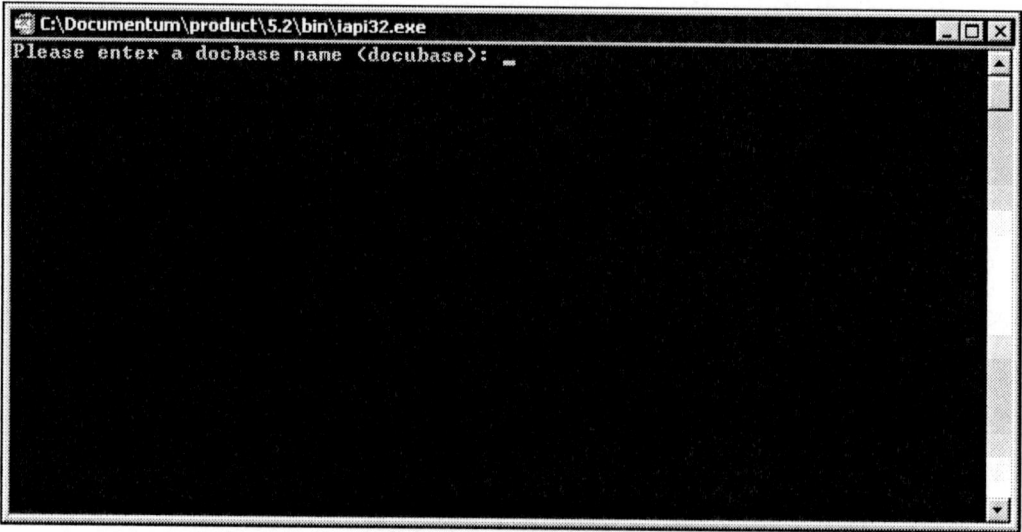

Figure 26.10: IAPI window

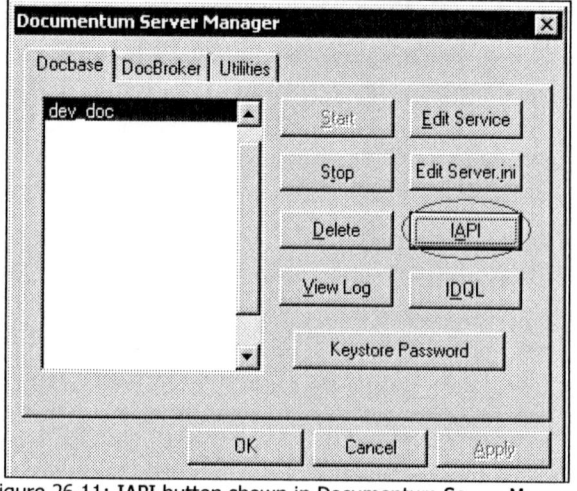

Figure 26.11: IAPI button shown in Documentum Server Manager

424

API commands can be executed from within Documentum Administrator by clicking on the API button shown in the top right-hand side of the toolbar. This opens the Api Tester screen as shown in figure 26.12.

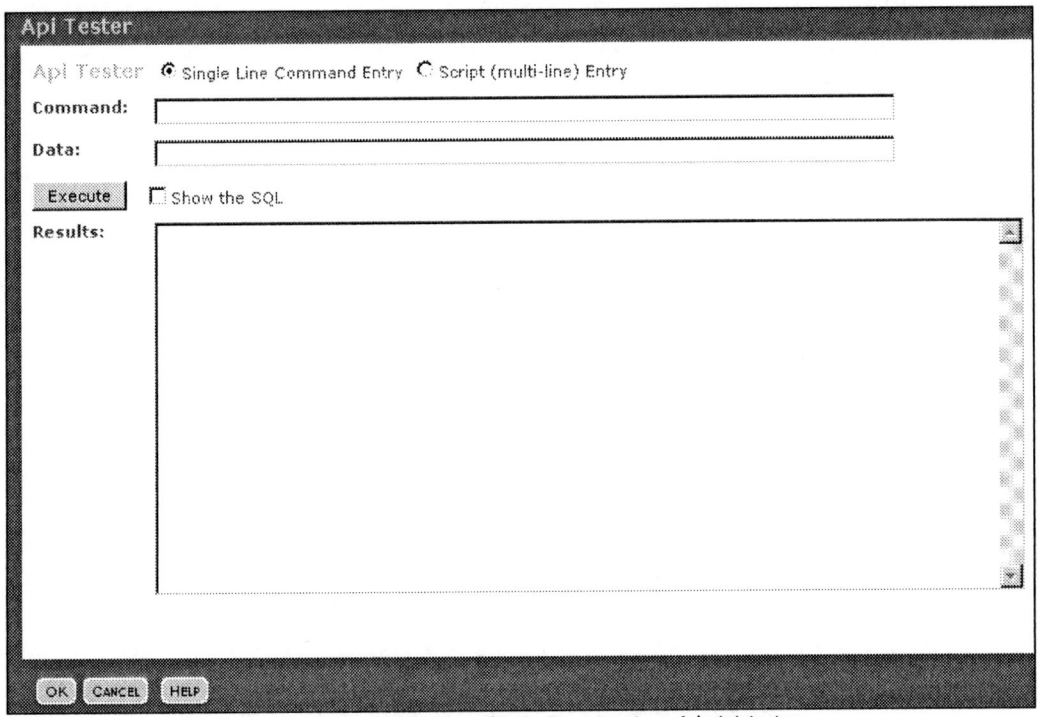

Figure 26.12: Api Tester utility in Documentum Administrator

26.2.2 API Commands

Server API commands follow a defined pattern. You need to type the exact method name followed by arguments as a continuous string with comma as a delimiter, separating the various parts. Here is a sample API command:

`API> create,c,dm_document`

Let us break up this command and explain each term:

- `create`: API method name used to create an object instance of the specified object type.
- `c`: Alias for the current session within which the API command is being executed.
- `dm_document`: The argument of the `create` method. In this case, it is the object type of the object that needs to be created via this API command.

Please keep in mind that the arguments to all the API methods are positional. This means that there are placeholders for all the arguments in an API command even if the argument is optional.

For example, if an API command api_command has four optional arguments first, second, third, and fourth as follows: api_command,c,first,second,third,fourth, then to execute this API command with only one argument, fourth, the command needs to be executed as follows:

```
API>api_command,c,,,,<value of fourth argument>
```

Note how placeholder commas have been put for the arguments first, second, and third, even though we are not specifying any values for these arguments.

26.2.3 Categorizing API Methods

Depending upon their specific nature and purpose, Server API methods can be grouped together into various categories. The table shown in figure 26.13 shows a few methods and categories based on their nature.

Category	API method	Use
Object management	attach	Attaches an object to a lifecycle.
	checkout	Checks out an object from the Docbase and places an explicit lock over it.
	checkin	Removes the lock on a checked out object and saves it in the Docbase as a new version.
	promote	Promotes a SysObject from its current normal lifecycle state to the next normal state.
Server communications	connect	Creates a session with the Docbase.
	disconnect	Disconnects a Docbase session.
	begintran	Begins a database transaction.
	commit	Commits changes made during a database transaction and closes the transaction.
Getting and setting attributes	get	Gets the value of the specified attribute of an object.
	set	Sets the value of the specified attribute of an object.
System administration	apply	Running an administrative function.
	audit	Allows for auditing of the particular event.
	authenticate	User name and password validation.
Docbase search	id	Returns the object ID of the object which satisfies the specified condition
	readquery	Runs a DQL query that does not require database access while processing query results.
Content handling	getfile	Returns the content file in the specified format.
	setfile	Sets a content file to an object.
Lifecycle management	install	Installs a lifecycle that has been validated.
	validate	Determines whether the lifecycle is valid or not.
	uninstall	Uninstalls a lifecycle that is currently installed.
Workflow management	execute	Starts the specified workflow.
	abort	Terminates the specified workflow.
	queue	Posts an event to the specified workflow.

Figure 26.13: Classification of Server API methods

26.2.4 API Method Examples

As we did for DQL, let's take the same example of creating a document object, setting its attribute values, linking it to a cabinet in the Docbase, and finally saving it. We will then retrieve this document object from the Docbase and delete it. You will come across a number of API methods while working on this simple example.

26.2.4.1 Creating a Document Object

Log in to Documentum Administrator as an administrator and open the Api Tester screen.

Refer to figure 26.14; run the create API command by entering the string create,c,dm_document in the Command box as shown in the Api Tester screen and clicking on the Execute button.

Make sure that you do not enter white spaces anywhere in the command string.

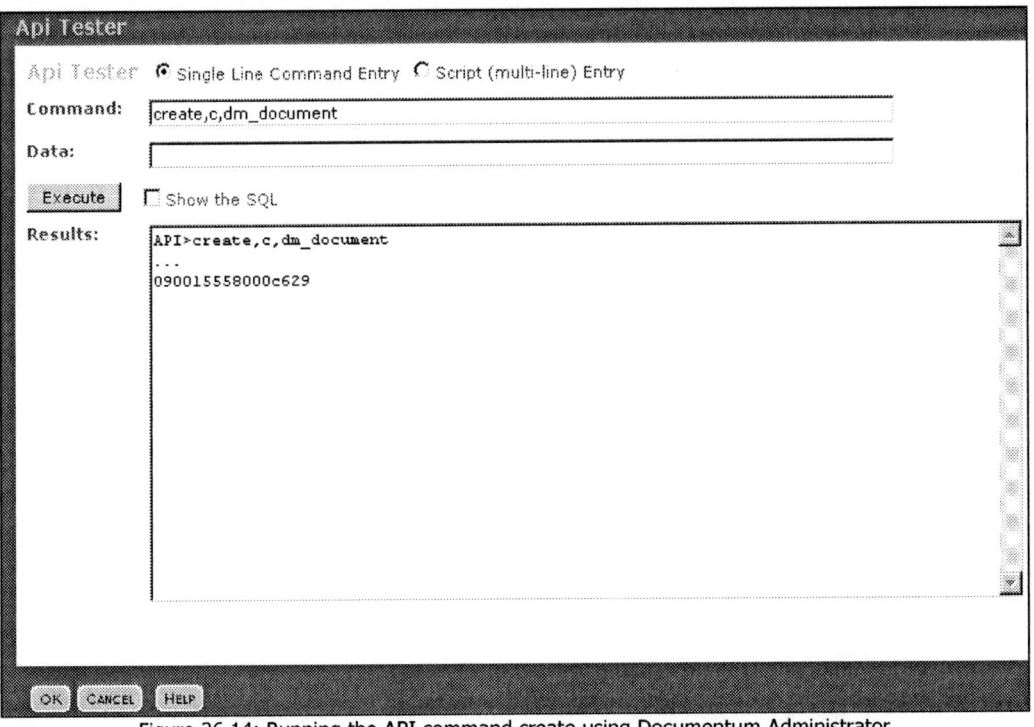

Figure 26.14: Running the API command create using Documentum Administrator

The create API method creates an object of the specified object type (dm_document in our example) and returns the object ID of the newly created object. As shown in the figure 26.14, the object ID of the newly created document object is 090015558000c629.

Note that the newly created object is not committed to the Docbase until you issue an explicit save API command as we will see later in this example.

26.2.4.2 Setting the Attributes of the Object

The set API method can be used to set particular values for single as well as repeating attributes of objects. Set the object_name attribute of the newly created document object as shown in figure 26.15.

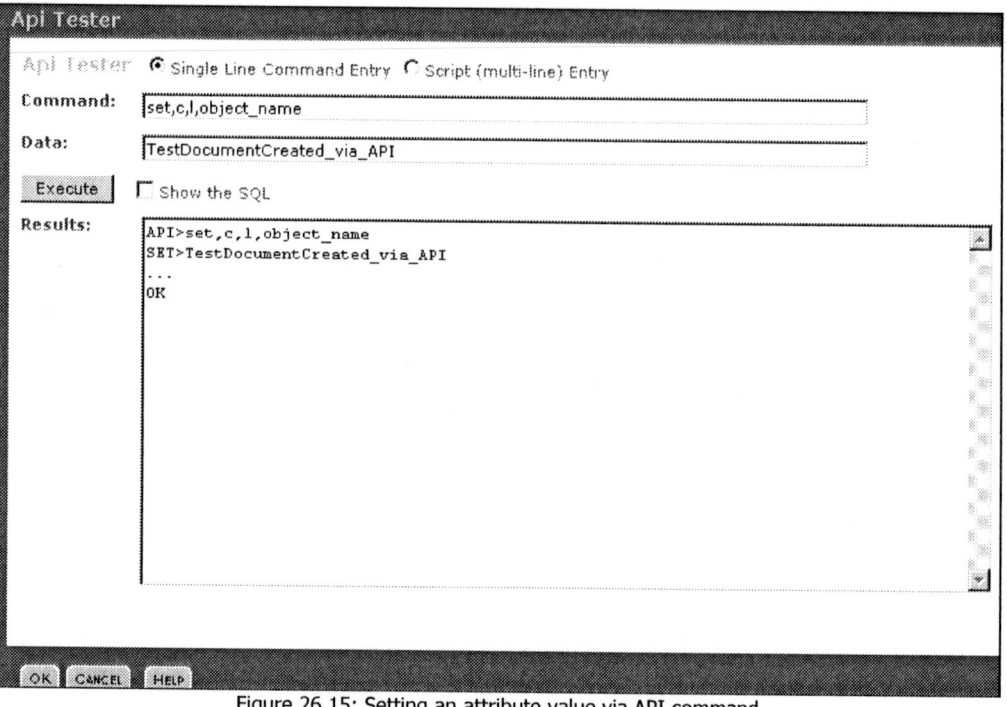

Figure 26.15: Setting an attribute value via API command

Note that the method command and arguments are entered in the Command text box while the value of the argument is specified in the Data box as shown in figure 26.15. You must have noticed the peculiar letter 1 used in the command string: set,c,1,object_name.

This is an alias for the last created, retrieved, checked in/out, or fetched object ID. If you do not want to use the alias 1, you can instead run the command as:

set,c,090015558000c629,object_name

Here 090015558000c629 is the object ID of the newly created document object in our example.

The other attributes, such as title, for the document object can be set accordingly as follows:

```
API>set,c,1,title
Data: File created via API commands
...
OK
```

You can set the repeating attributes (e.g. keywords) as follows:

```
API>set,c,1,keywords[0]
Data: document
...
OK
API>set,c,1,keywords[1]
Data: api
...
OK
```

This sets document and api as the two keywords for the document object at the first and second index positions respectively.

26.2.4.3 Associating a Content File with the Document Object

The setfile API method can be used to associate a content file with an object. The prerequisite is that the content file should be present on the machine (client) from where the setfile command is executed. Note that since in our case we are executing the API commands from the Documentum Administrator host as our client, the content file to be set should be locally present on the machine where Documentum Administrator has been installed.

Create a content XML file (say testing_api.xml) and place it at a convenient location on the. Documentum Administrator host, for example: c:\Test.

Issue the following setfile command:

```
API>setfile,c,1,C:\Test\testing_api.xml,xml
...
OK
```

Notice the additional argument (xml) specified in the setfile command following the complete path to the content file. This is the name of a valid format for the content file and should be recognized by the Content Server.

Most people place the content file locally on the machine through which they access Documentum Administrator URL via a browser, rather than placing it on the Documentum Administrator machine. Under such scenarios, the following error is thrown by Content Server when you issue the setfile API command:

"[DM_SYSOBJECT_E_CANT_ACCESS_FILE]error: "Cannot access file C:\Test\testing_api.xml due to Operating System error: The system cannot find the file specified.

"; ERRORCODE: 100; NEXT: null"

26.2.4.4 Associating a Document Object with a Cabinet

Once you have created a document object and set its attributes and content file, the next step is to associate it with either a cabinet or a folder residing within a cabinet. We will use the link API command in our example to associate the newly created document object with a custom cabinet.

As a prerequisite, create a custom cabinet `Testing_API_DQL` in Web Publisher and then issue the following `link` command:

```
API>link,c,1,'/Testing_API_DQL'
...
OK
```

You can either link an object with a cabinet or folder using the folder path as we saw in our example, or by referring to the object ID of the cabinet or the folder. For example, if the object ID of `Testing_API_DQL` cabinet is `0c0015558000c62a`, you can link the document object to this cabinet as follows: `API>link,c,1,0c0015558000c62a`

26.2.4.5 Saving the Document Object in the Docbase

Until and unless you explicitly issue the `save` API command, the newly created document object is not saved in the Docbase. Following is an example displaying how to use the save API:

```
API>save,c,1
...
OK
```

Once you have saved the document object, you can have a look at it by logging in to Web Publisher and browsing to the `Testing_API_DQL` cabinet. Figure 26.16 shows how the document object appears in Web Publisher.

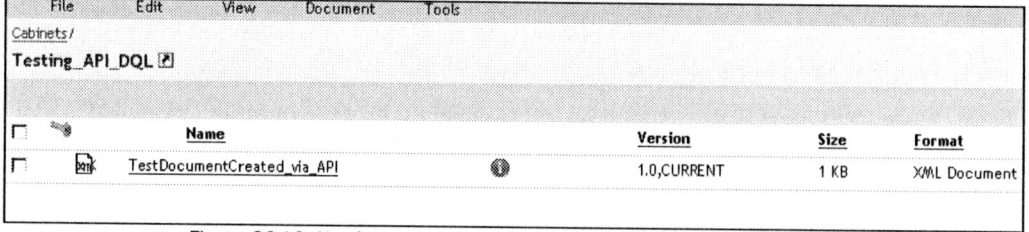

Figure 26.16: Newly created document object as seen in Web Publisher

If you select the checkbox against the document object and choose the menu option File | View, you will be able to view the associated content file `testing_api.xml`.

In order to look at the properties of the document object, you can either click on the Info icon ⊚ or select the checkbox against the document object and choose the menu option View | Properties | Info. Figure 26.17 shows the various properties for the document object that we set using API commands in this example. Note in particular the Name, Title, and Keywords fields shown in figure 26.17 that we set using the API command `set`.

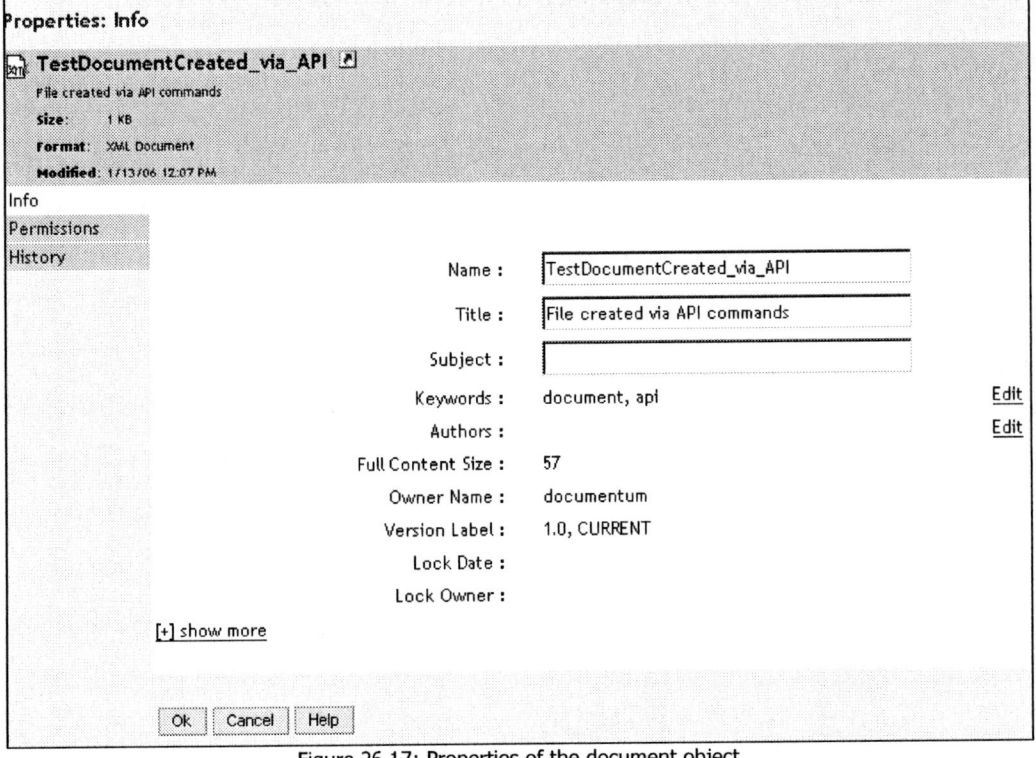

Figure 26.17: Properties of the document object

26.2.4.6 Obtaining a Reference to the Document Object in Docbase

You can issue the id API command to obtain the object ID of an object that satisfies a particular qualification. Say for example we issue the id API command with a qualification statement "dm_document object whose name is TestDocumentCreated_via_API" as follows:

API>id,c,dm_document where object_name = 'TestDocumentCreated_via_API'

**...
090015558000c629**

The server returns the object ID 090015558000c629 for the document object TestDocumentCreated_via_API.

Note that you need not enter the complete search qualification starting from select and specifying the from clause. Instead you simply need to enter the clause starting after the from keyword.

26.2.4.7 Setting Specific Attribute Information

Once you have obtained the object ID of the document object, getting the values of its various attributes is very simple. All you need to do is issue a get API command specifying the attribute whose value needs to be found out.

For example, in order to find out the value of the second keywords attribute for the retrieved document object, run the get API command as follows:

```
API>get,c,1,keywords[1]
...
api
```

The server returns the value api as the value contained at the second position in the keywords attribute. We have used an index position [1] in this case because keywords is a repeating attribute that stores values starting at index position 0 onwards. In the case of a single-valued attribute, you need not use any square brackets. For example, to find out the value of the title attribute, run the command as follows:

```
API>get,c,1,title
```

26.2.4.8 Viewing all Attributes and Values for an Object

In order to look at all the attributes and their values for a particular object in the Docbase, use the dump API command. Run the dump API command as follows:

```
API>dump,c,090015558000c629
...
```

We have specified the object ID of the document object (090015558000c629) as an argument in the dump API command. Figure 26.18 shows a snapshot listing a dump of the various attributes values of the document object we had created.

```
API>dump,c,l
...
USER ATTRIBUTES

  object_name                 : TestDocumentCreated_via_A
  title                       : File created via API comm
  subject                     :
  authors                  []: <none>
  keywords                 [0]: document
                           [1]: api
  resolution_label            :
  owner_name                  : documentum
  owner_permit                : 7
  group_name                  : docu
  group_permit                : 5
  world_permit                : 3
  log_entry                   :
  acl_domain                  : documentum
  acl_name                    : dm_4500155580000102
  language_code               :

SYSTEM ATTRIBUTES

  r_object_id                 : 090015558000c629
  r_object_type               : dm_document
  r_creation_date             : 1/13/2006 12:02:33
  r_modify_date               : 1/13/2006 12:07:48
  r_modifier                  : documentum
  r_access_date               : 1/13/2006 12:03:34
  r_composite_id           []: <none>
  r_composite_label        []: <none>
  r_component_label        []: <none>
  r_order_no               []: <none>
  r_link_cnt                  : 0
  r_link_high_cnt             : 0
  r_assembled_from_id         : 0000000000000000
  r_frzn_assembly_cnt         : 0
  r_has_frzn_assembly         : F
  r_is_virtual_doc            : 0
  r_page_cnt                  : 1
  r_content_size              : 57
  r_lock_owner                :
  r_lock_date                 : nulldate
  r_lock_machine              :
  r_version_label          [0]: 1.0
                           [1]: CURRENT
  r_immutable_flag            : F
  r_frozen_flag               : F
  r_has_events                : F
  r_creator_name              : documentum
  r_is_public                 : T
  r_policy_id                 : 0000000000000000
  r_resume_state              : 0
  r_current_state             : 0
  r_alias_set_id              : 0000000000000000
  r_full_content_size         : 57

APPLICATION ATTRIBUTES

  a_application_type          :
  a_status                    :
  a_is_hidden                 : F
  a_retention_date            : nulldate
  a_archive                   : F
  a_compound_architecture     :
  a_link_resolved             : F
  a_content_type              : xml
  a_full_text                 : T
  a_storage_type              : filestore_01
  a_special_app               :
  a_effective_date         []: <none>
  a_expiration_date        []: <none>
  a_publish_formats        []: <none>
  a_effective_label        []: <none>
  a_effective_flag         []: <none>
  a_category                  :
  a_is_template               : F
  a_controlling_app           :
  a_extended_properties    []: <none>
  a_is_signed                 : F
  a_last_review_date          : nulldate

INTERNAL ATTRIBUTES

  i_is_deleted                : F
```

Figure 26.18: Snapshot of a document object dump

Note that the server returns the object attributes organized into various categories such as USER ATTRIBUTES, SYSTEM ATTRIBUTES, APPLICATION ATTRIBUTES, and INTERNAL ATTRIBUTES.

26.2.4.9 Deleting an Object from the Docbase

You need to issue the `destroy` API command in order to remove a particular object from the Docbase. Run the following API command in order to delete the document object we created in our example:

```
API>destroy,c,090015558000c629
...
OK
```

If the object is checked-out (and thus locked), running the `destroy` API command throws the following error:

Error processing command:DfException:: THREAD: http8080-Processor8; MSG: [DM_SYSOBJECT_E_CANT_DELETE_LOCKED]error: "Cannot delete sysobject TestDocumentCreated_via_API since its locked by user documentum."; ERRORCODE: 100;

In order to remove the lock on the object either check-in the object by running the API command: `checkin,c,090015558000c629` or unlock the. object as follows: `unlock,c,090015558000c629`.

We have covered several examples in this chapter, demonstrating the power of DQL queries and Server API commands in Documentum. For a complete and exhaustive coverage of DQL and API, it is advisable to go through the Content Server DQL and API reference manuals respectively.

26.3 Summary

In this chapter we introduced DQL (Document Query Language) queries and Server API commands as extremely handy tools for inspecting the Documentum Docbase. DQL queries and API commands can be issued from IDQL and IAPI utilities respectively or from within web clients such as Documentum Administrator and Web Publisher.

Using DQL queries and API commands, we saw examples of creating a document object, setting its attributes, associating a content file with it, linking it to a cabinet, and finally retrieving it and deleting it from the Docbase.

While API commands are issued one by one and can work on one object at a time, DQL queries can affect multiple objects in a single execution.

Frequently Asked Questions and Answers

The following set of questions and answers are based on the sections covered within this book and can serve as a good refresher once you have gone through the various chapters. Moreover, Documentum developers (both amateurs and specialists) are often confronted with such questions either during interviews or during the routine course of work.

What serves as the heart of the Documentum system providing basic services such as managing and versioning objects?

Content Server.

What are the logical entities that constitute a Docbase repository?

A Docbase can be thought of as a centralized repository in Documentum consisting of content, its associated properties (or metadata), and full-text indexes.

What purpose does a DocBroker serve in Documentum system architecture?

A DocBroker acts as an intermediary when client applications need to establish a connection with the Content Server.

Is it necessary for every object type to extend from an existing supertype in Documentum?

No. There can be object types having no supertypes.

What are the names of object types for lifecycle definitions and workflow templates in Documentum?

Lifecycle: `dm_policy`

Workflow template (process definition): `dm_process`

What are the attributes of Documentum's internal persistent object type?

`r_object_id`, `i_is_replica`, and `i_vstamp`

How do you infer the object type of an object from its object ID?

The first two characters of the 16-character object ID string are termed **type identifiers** and denote the object type of the object. For example, an object with object ID 0b0004578000c8b1 is a folder object because the first two characters 0b denote a type identifier for a folder in Documentum. Hence the object type for such an object is folder (dm_folder).

What are computed attributes?

Unlike the attributes of persistent objects in Documentum, computed attributes are not stored in the Docbase. They are generated by the Content Server at run time. Examples are _alias_set and _policy_name.

What is an FTDQL query introduced in Documentum release 5.3?

An FTDQL query differs from a SELECT query in the following way: while a SELECT query is executed against a Docbase repository, an FTDQL query is run against the full-text index, causing a considerable gain in performance.

What is IAPI?

IAPI is an Interactive utility available with Content Server that helps you to execute Server API commands against a Docbase.

Is dm_cabinet a supertype of dm_folder object type in Documentum?

No. It is the other way round; dm_cabinet is a subtype of dm_folder object type.

What are the two kinds of version labels managed by the Content Server?

Numeric (or Implicit) and Symbolic labels. Numeric labels are generated by the server, for example: 1.0, 2.1, 3.0, etc. Symbolic labels can be either system or user defined. For example: WIP, CURRENT, Staging, etc.

What is the relationship between an object ID (r_object_id) and a chronicle ID (i_chronicle_id) of a SysObject?

The various versions of a particular SysObject have different object IDs (r_object_id) assigned to them by the Content Server. However, these different versions share the same chronicle ID (i_chronicle_id). Chronicle ID stores the value of the object ID of the root (original) version of the object.

What is the difference between a lifecycle and a workflow?

A lifecycle defines the various stages in the life of an object, such as creation, authoring, review, and approval. A workflow on the other hand works along with a lifecycle and routes the object in the various lifecycle states. It defines how the object passes through various states, who the participating users and groups are, and what activities need to be performed during this flow.

What is the relationship between DMCL and DFC?

DFC is short for Documentum Foundation Classes and is a set of Java interfaces and classes provided to access and extend the capabilities of Content Server. DMCL is Documentum Client Library, consisting of a C library of APIs and serves as a communication layer between clients and Content Server.

436

DFC can be treated as a wrapper written over DMCL with additional features such as data validation.

Explain the two types of Business Objects available in Documentum Business Object Framework (BOF).

Type-based business objects (or TBOs in short) and Service-based business objects (or SBOs in short).

TBOs are tied to a particular object type and extend/override its capabilities while SBOs are independent of object types and provide generic services in the system. In release 5.3, TBOs are tied to both object type and Docbase repository.

Mention a few services provided by the Documentum WDK framework.

The WDK framework provides a number of essential services such as error handling, messaging, content transfer, and history management.

With reference to ACLs, mention all the extended permissions available in Documentum.

The extended permissions available in Documentum are: Change State, Change Permission, Change Ownership, Change Location, and Execute Procedure. In release 5.3, Documentum has provided an additional extended permission for deleting an object.

This new extended permission is different from the basic Delete permission since it does not provide the hierarchical Browse, Read, Relate, Version, or Write access.

For which types or entities can an alias be defined in an Alias Set?

An alias can be defined in an Alias Set for the following entities: user, group, user or group, cabinet path, folder path, permission set, and unknown (for cases where no entity fits).

What are the three mandatory attributes required to create a user (dm_user object) in Documentum?

In order to create a user in Documentum, you need to provide its user name (user_name), user OS name (user_os_name), and email address (user_address).

What is the difference between a public and a private group?

A public group is a group that has been created by either a sysadmin or a superuser in Documentum, while a private group is one that has been created by any user that has Create group privileges.

What purpose do Registered Tables serve in Documentum?

Registered Tables (dm_registered objects) are RDBMS tables external to a Documentum system and not a part of Content Server, but that need to be accessed within the Documentum system.

Name the execution agents that can execute Documentum methods.

Content Server (default execution agent), Method Server, and Java Method Server.

Which Documentum process executes jobs?

Documentum agent exec process in Content Server executes jobs.

How is Web Publisher able to make a connection to the Docbases hosted in Content Server?

The `dmcl.ini` file in the Web Publisher host has an entry for the DocBroker name and port number. The Content Server broadcasts its connection information to this DocBroker and then a connection can be established.

Mention a few system administration tasks that can be performed using Documentum Administrator.

Documentum Administrator can be used to create and maintain users and groups, object types and attributes, manage audit trails, set up jobs and methods, and execute DQL queries and Server API commands.

Which Documentum tool can be used for creation of renditions (alternative formats) of documents in a Docbase?

Content Rendition Services (CRS). Note that in Documentum release 5.3, Content Rendition Services has been split into two products: Document Transformation Services (DTS) and Advanced Document Transformation Services (ADTS).

Subtypes of which object type can alone be published via Site Caching Services (SCS) from Docbase?

Only subtypes of `dm_sysobject` object type can be published by SCS from a Docbase.

What are the two major components in Site Caching Services?

Site Caching Services (SCS) has two major components: SCS Source and SCS Target.

Why is Site Deployment Services (SDS) typically used?

SDS is typically used to deploy and synchronize website content from SCS target server to multiple local or remote servers.

Can two Content Servers be installed on a single Windows host?

No. This is possible only in case of UNIX and Linux environments.

What is the difference between an installation owner and a Docbase owner?

An installation owner is one whose login account has been used for installing Content Server. On the other hand, a Docbase owner is a database user account who has access to the underlying RDBMS tables in the Docbase.

Mention some limitations that need to be kept in mind while providing a Docbase ID for a Docbase.

The Docbase ID should be unique if multiple Docbases exist on a particular Content Server, it should not start with zero (0), and should be a number in the range 1 to 16777215.

Is Web Publisher Server Files installed on Content Server host rather than on Web Publisher application server host?

Yes. Web Publisher Server Files contains some Java method JARs that are run on the Content Server by Documentum Java Method Server. Hence, these need to be installed on the Content Server host and not on the Web Publisher application server host.

Which key in the dmcl.ini file is used for enabling connection pooling?

connect_pooling_enabled. This is false by default.

Which file stores server information required by Content Server?

server.ini file located on a (Windows) Content Server host at:
$DOCUMENTUM\dba\config\<Docbase name>

Which tool is used to deploy DocApps created in Documentum Application Builder?

Documentum Application Installer (DAI).

What are Web Publisher Template, Rules, and Presentation files?

Web Publisher Template is a flat XML file having XML elements for fields that need to be filled in by content authors.

A Rules file is another XML file that controls the behavior and validation of each of the template fields.

A Presentation file is an XSL stylesheet that styles the template content file and generates outputs in the specified formats.

What is a DocApp?

A DocApp is a packaging unit of a Docbase used to house various Docbase objects such as object types, lifecycles, workflow templates, permission sets, alias sets, etc. The objects in a DocApp can be migrated/deployed to other Docbases using Documentum Application Installer (DAI).

Mention a few subtypes of sysobject (dm_sysobject object type).

A few subtypes of sysobject are: job (dm_job), method (dm_method), document (dm_document), policy (dm_policy), process (dm_process), etc.

Can a custom object type be named SELECT or DELETED?

No. These are reserved keywords in DQL (Document Query Language) and should not be used as names of object types.

What are the data types available in Documentum for attributes of an object type?

The available data types for attributes are: Boolean, double, id, integer, string, and time.

What does the input mask character # for attributes signify?

A hash masking character (#) allows only numeric values (0 through 9) for the attribute in question.

What is meant by Value Assistance?

Value Assistance is used for displaying a pre-defined list of values for a specific attribute. Users can choose from the set of values displayed in Value Assistance for the attribute. Note that this feature is not available for attributes of Boolean data type.

With reference to Registered Tables, what is the alias used for referring to the Docbase owner of the RDBMS table?

dm_dbo is the alias used for referring to the Docbase owner.

What are the various scopes that Documentum uses for resolving an alias?

The various scopes used by Documentum for resolving an alias are: lifecycle scope, workflow scope, session scope, user scope, and system scope.

In the context of permission sets, what is the reserved alias that Documentum uses for referring to the current owner of the object and all the users present in Docbase?

dm_owner is an alias for the current owner of the object and dm_world is an alias for all Docbase users.

What are the different states of a lifecycle policy object before it can be used by the applications?

The various states of a lifecycle policy object are: Draft (when the lifecycle has been created or modified but not validated), Validated (when the lifecycle has passed all system validation tests), Uninstalled, and Installed (when it has been validated and is ready to be used by applications).

What are the two types of states that can be created in a Lifecycle State Diagram?

Normal and Exception states. Normal states are for the normal linear flow of object, while Exception states represent an abnormal flow or diversions in the linear flow.

Mention a few standard Actions that can be performed by the system in a lifecycle state.

A few standard Actions that can be performed by the system in a lifecycle state are: adding or removing version label, setting owner, setting permission set, requesting rendition, etc.

Can one specify Java classes as procedures in lifecycle Entry Criteria, Actions, PostChange, and for validations?

Yes, this is possible in Documentum release 5.3.

Mention a few mechanisms to promote an object through the various states of a lifecycle.

A few mechanisms to promote objects through lifecycle states are: Web Publisher Promote menu option, workflows, promote server API command, and the BATCH_PROMOTE administration method.

What is the role of the Monitor_Lifecycles job in the Documentum system?

`Monitor_Lifecycles` job in Documentum runs at periodic intervals and turns Approved objects Active if their effective date matches current system date and also expires Active objects if their expiration date matches the current system date.

Which system attribute helps differentiate a template file from a content file?

`a_is_template` attribute: The value of this attribute is 1 for a template file and 0 for content files that have been created using this template.

What are the various widget types available in Web Publisher editor?

The various widgets available in Web Publisher editor are: `textline`, `content`, `choice`, `textselector`, `graphic`, `checkbox`, `xselector`, and `repeating blocks`.

What is a Repeating Block widget in Web Publisher editor?

A Repeating Block widget in Web Publisher editor allows content authors to create and subsequently work with multiple instances of enclosed widgets (say, `textline`, `content`, etc.) at run time in Web Publisher editor.

Can you associate multiple Rules files with a single Web Publisher Template file?

Yes, the system allows you to associate multiple Rules files with a single Web Publisher Template file

What purpose does a Textselector widget serve in Web Publisher editor?

A `textselector` widget in Web Publisher editor allows selecting a section of text from a file that has been uploaded in the Docbase.

What are the two types of Presentation files in Web Publisher?

The two types of Presentation files in Web Publisher are: Editor Presentation files (XSL stylesheets) and External Presentation files (HTML wrappers).

Editor Presentation files are used to format/style Web Publisher editor XML content files and are stored in Web Publisher under the Site Manager | Presentations | Editor folder.

On the other hand, External Presentation files provide standard frames and wrappers to the content embedded within <body></body> tags of HTML content files. They are stored under Site Manager | Presentations | External folder.

What benefit does the Reapply presentation feature in Web Publisher provide?

The Reapply presentation feature in Web Publisher allows you to update the renditions of existing content in the Docbase as per the modified Presentation files.

What is XDQL?

XDQL is short for eXtensible Document Query language and is a mechanism in Documentum that allows you to execute DQL queries from within XML and process the query results through XML.

What is the use of Web Publisher Create_Dynamic_Content job?

Web Publisher `Create_Dynamic_Content` job can be made to run at periodic intervals to transform content files that are in Active state and which have their template's Content Refresh flag set as true. This job reapplies Presentation files on the Active content files and thus ensures that the correct XDQL query results are saved to the transformed output web renditions.

What is a Web Publisher Folder Map?

A Web Publisher Folder Map is a flat XML file containing rules defining property matching conditions for Docbase properties (attributes), based on which the contents can be created under specified folder locations in Web Cabinets.

For example, a Folder Map could define a rule that states that all contents whose `title` attribute is not blank, should be created under a Web Cabinet channel folder `TitledContents_Fld` (say).

Can a Folder Map be configured so that the same content is created under two different folder locations based on a specified matching property condition?

Yes. You can specify two folder locations for a given attribute matching condition in the `<path>` tags.

What happens if you specify folder locations or Web Cabinet names in Folder Map that do not exist in the Docbase?

If the specified Web Cabinet does not exist in the Docbase, Folder Map throws an error. However, if the specified folders (within an existing Web Cabinet) do not exist, then Folder Map creates them automatically.

What is meant by dynamic folder mapping?

Folder Map can be used to automatically create folders at run time with names based on specified property values using the `$(...)` notation. For example, you can configure Folder Map so that content is created within a newly created folder at run time with a name that has been provided for the title attribute of the content.

E.g.: Value specified for title attribute: `Dummy Title`

Folder path specified in Folder Map: `/<Web Cabinet name>/$(title)`

At run time, the system creates a folder named Dummy Title under the specified Web Cabinet.

What is the use of Instruction Files in Web Publisher?

Instruction Files created in Web Publisher are flat XML files that can be used for automatically creating or updating the structure of existing content XML files as per the updated structure of Template files, without the need for manually updating existing contents.

Mention a few XML operations that can be performed by Instruction Files in Web Publisher.

Instruction Files in Web Publisher can manipulate XML content files by inserting new XML elements, deleting existing XML elements, inserting an attribute to an XML element, deleting an attribute from an XML element, and many other such operations as well.

Does relative path (the XML Path Language (XPath) // (double slash)) work in the case of Instruction Files?

No, this does not work and is a known limitation with Instruction Files.

What is meant by the Automatic Property Extraction (APE) feature in Web Publisher?

Automatic Property Extraction (APE) in Web Publisher is a feature that allows you to automatically set the values of specified XML elements in content XML files based on values provided for content attributes and vice versa.

Which particular widgets does Automatic Property Extraction work with in Web Publisher?

The following widgets are supported by Automatic Property Extraction (APE) in Web Publisher: Textline, Checkbox, and Choice.

Which object types does Documentum use for managing Automatic Property Extraction (APE)?

Documentum uses the following object types for managing Automatic Property Extraction (APE) in Web Publisher: dm_xml_application (subtype of dm_folder), and dm_xml_config (subtype of dm_document).

What is the difference between a Workflow process template and a Workflow in Documentum?

A Workflow process template (dm_process object) contains the definition for the workflow process, containing specifications regarding the various activities and their performers, actions performed in the workflow process, and so on and so forth.

On the other hand, Workflows (dm_workflow objects) are run-time instances created from the Workflow process template for routing content.

What are flows in Documentum Workflows?

Flows connect the various activities in a workflow template and could either take routed objects in a forward direction (in case of approvals) or a backward direction (in case of rejects).

Mention the two types of Workflow activities.

The two types of activities in Workflows are: Manual and Automatic.

While Manual activities are performed manually by a specified set of groups or users, Automatic activities are automatically performed by the server.

What are packages with reference to Workflows?

Packages are added to flows connecting various activities in a workflow template. These in turn route the objects in a workflow.

Mention the different types of publishing operations in Site Caching Services (SCS).

The different types of publishing operations in Site Caching Services (SCS) are: full refresh, incremental refresh, force refresh, and single object publish.

Where do you specify the various publishing parameters for SCS such as: objects to be published, source publishing folder, export directory, target host, etc.?

The various publishing parameters for SCS are specified in a Site Publishing Configuration, which can easily be created using Documentum Administrator.

Which objects does Documentum use for internally managing a Site Publishing Configuration created in Documentum Administrator?

In order to internally manage a Site Publishing Configuration created in Documentum Administrator, Documentum uses the following objects: dm_webc_config (for Source parameters) and dm_webc_target (for Target parameters).

Can you add HTML metatags for object attributes in published documents using Site Publishing Configuration?

Yes. You can add HTML metatags for object attributes in published documents, by choosing the checkbox Add properties as HTML metatags in the Advanced tab of Site Publishing Configuration.

What tables are created by SCS when data is published to a target database?

SCS creates the following tables on the target database as part of the publishing operation:

_s table (for storing single-valued attributes), _r table (for storing multi-valued attributes), _l table (for storing information about relation objects if specified), and _m table (for storing information about the state of published documents).

What is an Export Directory specified in a Site Publishing Configuration for SCS?

An Export Directory specified in a Site Publishing Configuration is a directory on the Content Server host where Documentum SCS exports the publishable documents along with their attributes in the form of content files and properties.xml file (containing attribute information) respectively.

With reference to SCS publishing operations, what is meant by Online Synchronization?

Online Synchronization is useful in the case of websites that have bulk publishes happening at periodic intervals, instead of single item publishes.

For a running site, bulk publishes can cause broken sections/links in the site.

Using Online Synchronization, you need to specify an Online Synchronization directory on the target host in a Site Publishing Configuration.

The SCS export data set (i.e. published content files + properties) is first placed in the online synchronization directory on the target host and then switched to the target root directory (webroot). Actually the webroot directory and online synchronization directories are renamed for the synchronization to take place. This causes minimal impact to the running website and reduces inconsistencies to a great extent.

What are pre- and post-synch scripts specified in Site Publishing Configuration?

Pre- and post-synch scripts can be written and specified in Site Publishing Configuration to perform custom tasks before or after SCS publishing has updated the website. Note that these scripts execute before and after SCS updates the website respectively.

444

What is the Transfer User specified in a Site Publishing Configuration?

The Transfer User specified in a Site Publishing Configuration is the user account that SCS uses in order to connect to the target server (web server machine).

What are the various available mechanisms for unlocking locked SCS publishing operations?

The following methods can be used in order to unlock locked SCS publishing operations: Stopping and starting SCS Source service, executing the `unlockConfig.bat` script found on SCS Source host, or nullifying the holder attribute in `webc_lock` object.

What is the simplest means to monitor the status of SCS Source publish operations, such as the total number of publish operations, break-down in terms of full refreshes and incremental publish operations, etc.?

The easiest means to monitor the status of SCS Source publish operations is by invoking the following URL from your browser:

http://<SCS Source host name>:<SCS Source port number>/webcache/state

This will return a flat XML file displaying the various publishing operation details you require.

What is the Web View feature available in Web Publisher?

The Web View feature allows you to preview the content files on your web servers for testing purposes before finally publishing over to the production website.

How can you access DFC Java interfaces if you are working on a Microsoft COM (Component Object Model) environment?

DFC includes a Documentum Java-COM bridge (DJCB) for accessing DFC Java interfaces in case you are working in a Microsoft COM (Component Object Model) environment.

What is the inheritance hierarchy of the IDfDocument interface in DFC?

In DFC, `IDfDocument` interface extends from `IDfSysObject` interface, which extends from `IDfPersistentObject` interface, which in turn extends from `IDfTypedObject` interface.

What is the use of the com.documentum.fc.client package in DFC?

The `com.documentum.fc.client` package in DFC contains classes and interfaces used for creating/managing Docbase sessions and for common data manipulation in Docbase.

What purpose does the IDfClient interface serve in DFC?

The `IDfClient` interface in DFC serves as a factory for `IDfSessionManager` objects, which help in creating sessions for establishing connection with servers.

Mention a few methods available in the IDfSysObject interface in DFC.

A few of the methods available in the `IDfSysObject` interface in DFC are: `checkout()` for checking-out and placing a lock on an object, `getACL()` for fetching the ACL associated with an object, `getTitle()` for retrieving the `title` attribute of an object, and `setObjectName()` for setting the `object_name` attribute of an object.

What are WDK configuration and customization?

Documentum WDK configuration involves simple configuration changes such as introducing new menu options, modifying labels and texts in screens, altering look-and-feel such as images associated with button controls, and hiding/displaying attributes/fields in various screens. This is achieved by modifying XML configuration files and JSP pages. WDK customization on the other hand requires modifications to Java behavior classes in order to add new actions or components or extend framework behavior and introduce custom logic and functionality.

What are the three modes of content transfer supported in Documentum WDK release 5.3?

The three modes of content transfer supported in Documentum WDK release 5.3 are: HTTP, Unified Client Facilities (UCF), and Content Transfer Applets.

Specify the extension hierarchy of WDK applications layers.

The extension hierarchy of WDK applications layers is as follows (from the lowest layer to the topmost layer): WDK, Webcomponent, Webtop, Digital Asset Manager, Web Publisher, and Custom Layer.

What are WDK controls?

WDK controls are UI features (buttons, links, and menus) that raise events in response to any changes made to these elements in a UI form. These events in turn are then handled either on the client side or on the server side.

What is meant by WDK Actions?

WDK Actions relate a UI event with an application function and are launched either by a Docbase operation (such as check-out, check-in, etc.) or via a UI form element (such as a button, a link, or a menu item).

Mention a few types of scopes defined in XML configuration files.

A few types of scopes defined in XML configuration files are: Docbase type, Application, Docbase name, etc.

How do you include all the strings defined in a particular NLS property file within another NLS property file that needs to use these?

This can be achieved by defining the full path of the included NLS property file in the parent NLS property file by using the string NLS_INCLUDES.

Describe the lifecycle stages of WDK controls.

The various lifecycle stages of WDK controls are:

onInit(): For example, a control is in a pre-created state by virtue of its name and a reference to it in a form or a components onInit() method. Whenever the component or the JSP page is requested for the first time, this method is called.

onRender(): This method is invoked every time a request to the form is made via a URL, just before the JSP form processing occurs.

onRefreshData(): This is called when the form data is modified.

`onRenderEnd()`: This is invoked as a clean-up operation after all form processing has been done for every request.

`onExit()`: This is invoked whenever a request is made to another form or component.

Which migration methodology comes in most handy when it comes to migrating selective objects from one Docbase to another?

DocApp migration via Documentum Application installer can be used for migrating selective objects from one Docbase to another.

What is the need for setting installation options in Documentum Application Builder before migrating DocApps to another Docbase?

It is critical to set installation options in Documentum Application Builder before migrating DocApps to another Docbase, so that the Documentum Application Installer (DAI) gets appropriate directions for installing objects on the target Docbase. By virtue of the installation options, DAI knows vital information such as: whether to overwrite objects or create new versions in the target Docbase or not, whether to install all objects contained within a folder or not, etc.

Mention one striking difference between the mode of execution of DQL queries and Server API commands.

A DQL query, once executed can work on multiple objects in a run, while Server API commands affect only one object in a single execution.

What are some of the uses of running DQL queries against a Docbase?

DQL queries can be useful for creating, updating, retrieving, and deleting objects and searching through content in a Docbase and for accessing registered tables.

Write a DQL query for inserting a value at the third index position of a document object's authors repeating attribute.

The update DQL query in this case will be:

```
update dm_document object insert authors[2] = '<specified value>'
```

What does the link clause in DQL queries do?

The `link` clause in DQL queries associates the object with a cabinet or a folder in the Docbase.

What is the use of the any keyword in DQL queries?

The any keyword is used in DQL queries to search for a specific value in a repeating attribute.

What is IAPI?

IAPI is the Interactive API utility that is available once you install Content Server. It can be used to issue Server API commands against a Docbase.

What exactly does the symbol c represent while executing Server API commands?

The symbol c is an alias for the current session in which Server API commands are being executed.

Mention two examples of Server API methods used for lifecycle management in a Docbase.

Two examples of Server API methods used for lifecycle management in a Docbase are: `install` and `uninstall`.

What does the get API method do?

The `get` API method retrieves the value of the specified attribute of an object.

Write a Server API command for linking an object to a folder abc residing within a cabinet xyz in a Docbase.

The Server API command in this case would be: `link,c,<object ID>,'/xyz/abc'`

Which Server API command shows all the contained attributes in an object along with their respective values?

The Server API command dump shows all attributes and their respective values for the object in question. Usage: `dump,c,<object ID>`

Can the destroy Server API method be used for deleting an object that is currently checked-out (and hence locked) in the Docbase?

No. In the case of locked objects in Docbase, running the `destroy` API method throws an error.

B

New Features and Enhancements in Release 5.3

Most of the features added or enhanced by Documentum in its 5.3 release have been clearly mentioned under the appropriate sections of this book.

Additionally, this chapter categorizes and consolidates these features under one umbrella for a quick reference. The various changes made by Documentum in its WCM architecture, participating entities, and product suite as part of release 5.3 are mentioned in this chapter. However, please note that a detailed explanation of each of these enhancements is not within the scope of this book.

B.1 Content Server Changes

A few of the changes/enhancements made to Content Server in release 5.3 are:

- Documentum has replaced Verity with Fast Search & Transfer™ (FAST™) as its new search infrastructure.

- A separate index agent and an index server are required in 5.3 for handling full-text indexing. While an index agent exports and prepares the documents in a Docbase repository for full-text indexing, the index server creates and maintains the full-text indexes and provides responses to Content Server full-text queries.

- Each repository requires its own index agent and index server.

- In the new full-text indexing environment, all attributes of SysObjects and their custom subtypes are indexed. The content files associated with all the SysObjects are indexed as well and case-sensitive searching is not supported by Documentum in 5.3.

- In order to improve query performance, Documentum has introduced a new querying ability: FTDQL SELECT with syntax that is a subset that of a SELECT statement. Using an FTDQL SELECT statement ensures that the query is executed against the full-text index rather than Docbase repository to achieve performance gains.

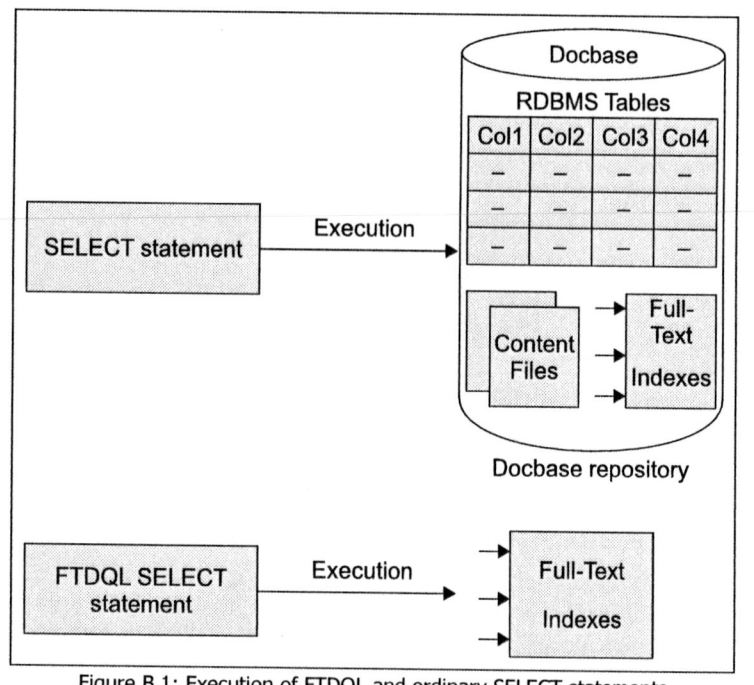

Figure B.1: Execution of FTDQL and ordinary SELECT statements

- A Trusted Content Services license is not required in order to control SSL communication between Content Server and client libraries. This feature is available in the standard Content Server package.

- Enhancements have been made to ACLs (Access Control Lists) to provide better object-level permissions.

- Apart from the five extended permissions shown in the table in figure 3.4 of Chapter 3, Documentum has provided an additional extended permission for deleting an object.

- This new extended permission is different from the basic Delete permission in that it does not provide hierarchical Browse, Read, Relate, Version, or Write access.

Apart from specifying the access permissions for basic and extended permissions, Documentum provides an ability to restrict these permissions as well in 5.3. There are two Access Restriction entries: AccessRestriction for restricting certain basic permissions and ExtendedRestriction for restricting certain extended permissions.

The following example of an ACL on a document belonging to the HR department in an organization explains the utility of this feature:

HR_ACL

Group name: HR_Department

> Permit Type: AccessPermit

> Permission Level: Delete

Group name: HR_Department_subgroup

> Permit Type: AccessRestriction

> Permission Level: Write

This ACL generically provides Delete access to the HR department group, but does not allow a particular subgroup within this HR department to update or delete the document. By using AccessRestriction, the system allows this sub-group to only browse, read, relate (annotate), and version the document.

- **Flexibility to create groups as Dynamic Groups**: A Dynamic Group allows your application to find out whether the users specified in the group's membership list are considered members of this group or not by default when they establish a connection with the Docbase repository.

  Say for example you assign a group abc as a Dynamic Group, setting its default membership behavior to treat its users as not members of this group. In the event of a user accessing the Docbase repository from a secure application, your application could add this user to the group but if the access is from a non-secure application, this user is not added to the group. Thus, using Dynamic Groups can assist you in setting up a group (or a role-based) security.

- Java programs have been supported in lifecycle Entry Criteria, Actions, Post Change, and for validation purposes.

- Improvements in workflows, such as support for work queues and a workflow timer for automatically resuming the suspended activities.

- Support for Global Login Tickets.

- Login Tickets are ASCII-encoded strings used by applications in place of a user's password while establishing a connection with the Docbase repository. A Global Login Ticket is an extension to this; it is a Login Ticket that can be accepted by any server of a trusted Docbase repository.

- The verity_locale key in server.ini file has become obsolete and the verity_location attribute in dm_server_config object type has been deprecated in the 5.3 release.

- Introduction of Privileged Groups in the system: Members of these system groups have special privileges for performing specific operations that they do not individually have.

Example: Members of the `dm_browse_all` group have the privilege to browse all the objects in the Docbase repository.

B.2 Object Types Changes

A few of the newly introduced object types in release 5.3 are:

- `dmc_jar`: This is a subtype of `dm_sysobject` object type and represents a JAR file that is stored in the Docbase repository.

- `dm_job_sequence`: This is a subtype of `dm_sysobject` object type and stores details about a job that belongs to a set of jobs that have been scheduled to run in a specified sequence.

- `dmc_module`: This object type represents a business module. Modules are covered later in the appendix.

- The `permanent_link` attribute in the `dm_relation` object type has been deprecated and instead the new `permanent_link` and `copy_child` attributes of the `dm_relation_type` object type should be used.

B.3 API and DQL Changes

A few of the enhanced Server API methods in release 5.3 are:

- `connect` and `getlogin`: Support Global login Tickets.

- `grant` and `revoke`: Support the enhancements made to Access Control Lists (ACLs).

- `queue`: Allows queuing of an event to a work item.

A few of the changes made to DQL in release 5.3 are:

- The `SEARCH TOPIC` clause has been deprecated and the `FT_OPTIMIZER` clause has been removed from the `SELECT` statement syntax.

- A new DQL hint: `UNCOMMITTED_READ` has been added for MS SQL Server, DB2, and Sybase databases, for read-only queries for retrieving query results fast even if the tables in question are locked by another database session.

- Introduction of the `FTDQL SELECT` statement described earlier in the appendix.

B.4 DFC Changes

A few of the changes made to DFC in release 5.3 are:

- Deeper integration with .NET.

- Support for accessing Documentum Business Objects using Web Services.

- Support for lightweight Unified Client Facilities (UCF), providing content transfer functionality to clients based on the WDK framework, thus removing any impositions of having DFC available on the clients. It provides support for some of the basic content library services such as check-in/check-out, view/edit and import/export.

- The existing BOF deployment model using DBOR (Documentum business object registry) on each client machine has been deprecated.

- Introduction of a ClassCastException that is thrown if one tries to cast a persistent object to a concrete class rather than its corresponding interface.

- For example, casting to DfDocument (instead of IDfDocument) will throw a ClassCastException.

B.5 BOF Changes

Following are a few of the changes made to BOF in release 5.3:

- TBOs (Type-based business objects) are associated with not just a type but also a Docbase repository. Thus, this does not necessitate having the same implementation of a TBO for all Docbase repositories.

- Support for dynamic deployment of an SBO (Service-based business object) from a central repository to multiple clients.

- In order to implement TBOs in pre-5.3 releases, one needed to override multiple methods to perform the same task, such as: overriding save(), saveLock(), checkinEx(), etc. to customize check-in behavior.

- In release 5.3, Documentum instead provides a set of supported *do* methods of DfSysObject such as doSave(), doCheckin(), etc. to achieve overriding. Additionally, Documentum provides a set of supported *do* methods in the DfPersistentObject and DfTypedObject classes for overriding purposes as well.

B.6 Application Builder and Application Installer Changes

A few of the enhancements made to Application Builder in release 5.3 are:

- Support for creating and managing Modules. Modules are units of executable code in a Docbase repository. An example could be Documentum business objects.

- Support for procedures written as Java classes in the various lifecycle states.

- Support for inserting user profiles and doc profiles, as well as work queues.

A few of the enhancements made to Application Installer in release 5.3 are:

- Support for installation of Modules.

- Support for installation of lifecycles having procedures written as Java classes in the various lifecycle states.

- Support for installation of user profiles and doc profiles, as well as work queues.

B.7 WDK Changes

Following are a few of the changes made to WDK in release 5.3:

- Support for three mechanisms of content transfer: HTTP, UCF (Unified Client Facilities), and Content transfer Applets.

- Support for session failover to other servers that are running the same WDK application, in the case of a clustered environment. This is achieved by persisting the session data available for a user and sending the last HTTP request.

- Support for integrating features such as notes, threads, discussions, rooms, etc. in applications based on the WDK framework.

- Support for a unified Inbox feature for users in a federated environment.

- Support for multi-repository search. Some of the other enhancements made on the search front are: support for searching external sources (such as Google), support for saving search preferences in the case of multi-repository search, and support for searching within specified folders in the Docbase repository.

- Support for making Docbase repositories available within authoring applications such as Microsoft Excel, Word, and PowerPoint with the help of application connectors (AppConnectors).

- Support for allowing user-selected Docbase repositories to appear in the UI (user interface) and selected columns to appear in features such as Inbox, My Files, folder listings, etc.

- Support for drag and drop from individual desktops to system folders when using Internet Explorer.

- Support for saving user login credentials.

B.8 Documentum Administrator Changes

A few of the enhancements made to Documentum Administrator in release 5.3 are:

- **Support for Job sequencing**: A series of jobs are designated to run at specified intervals in the prescribed manner. These jobs can be in any number of Docbase 5.3 repositories and should have at least one job that is designated to run first, without having any predecessor.

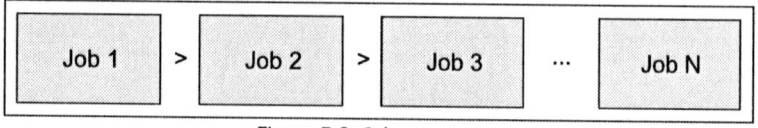

Figure B.2: Job sequencing

- Support for restricting users from accessing certain folders in the repository.
- Support for Global Login Tickets.
- Support for additional entries in permission sets.

B.9 Web Publisher Changes

Following are a few of the changes made to Web Publisher in release 5.3:

- Enhancements made in Web Publisher editor as regards the rich-text editing features and query capabilities.
- Support for deep folder import.
- Support for Link Management in the Web Publisher <content> element.
- Support for drag and drop from individual desktops to system folders and items within Web Publisher, when using Internet Explorer.
- Support for multiple Folder Maps.
- Integration with Business Process Services (BPS), allowing users outside Docbase repositories to review content using external workflows.
- Support for multi-repository search using advanced search functionality.
- Support for a single Inbox containing tasks from multiple Docbase repositories.
- Enhancements in search functionality by virtue of a new searching algorithm, resulting in a faster search.
- Support for Discussion threads.
- Improvements in user interface (UI) such as visible Docbase repositories, user-selected columns, layout enhancements, etc.
- The following methods have been updated to execute as Java methods: wcmObjectBagMethod, wcmCreateTransformation, and wcmLifecycleMonitor.
- Newly introduced methods wcmVersionInfo and wcmAddEdition and newly introduced job Add_Edition_Job.

The features introduced or enhanced in Documentum release 5.3 are not just limited to those that have been listed under various headings in this chapter. There are several other features improved and introduced by Documentum in its massive product suite. Even though we have discussed several changes introduced by Documentum in its 5.3 release, a detailed explanation of each of these features can be obtained by going through the Documentum 5.3 System Migration Guide.

Index

$

$value keyword, conditional value assitance, 153, 154

A

Accelera DocApp. See DocApp
access control list. See ACL
Access Control List. See ACL
access levels, Documentum, 33
ACL
    about, 33
    access levels, 33
    aliases, reserved, 34
    creating for lifecyles stages, 161
    lifecyles stages, 161
    permission set, 33
    template, creating, 161
alias, 34
    adding to alias set, 159
    alias types, 160
    custom, 160
    scope, 158
alias set
    about, 34, 35
    alias, adding, 159
    attaching to lifecycle, 165
    creating, 158
    sample, 35
ANT approach for building Web Publisher code, 411-413
APE, automatic property extraction
    about, 269
    attributes, populating, 280-283, 285
    attributes, two-way extraction, 285-287, 289, 290
    example, 271-277
    repeating attributes, populating, 280
    rules file, creating for a template, 280
    working, 270
    XML Application, creating, 271
    XML Application, testing, 277-279

API commands. See also DQL
    about, 22, 425
    attributes, setting for object, 428, 429
    commands, executing from Documentum Administrator, 425
    content, demoting, 182
    content, promoting, 182
    DQL queries, differences, 22
    file, associating with object, 429
    IAPI utility, 22, 424
    methods, categorizing, 426
    methods, examples, 427
    object attributes, viewing, 432, 434
    object ID, obtaining, 431
    object, associating with cabinet, 430
    object, associating with content file, 429
    object, creating, 427
    object, deleting from Docbase, 434
    object, saving in Docbase, 430
    release 5.3, enhancements, 452
    structure, 425
    syntax, 425
    tools, 423
    understanding, 22
attributes. See also objects, Documentum concept, See objects, Documentum concept
    adding to object type, 138
    condition value assistance, 145
    constraints, adding, 132
    creating, 137
    data type, 140
    input mask, 141
    label, 140
    multi-valued attributes, 140
    naming, 139
    populating using automatic property extraction, 280
    repeating attributes, populating, 280
    search operators, 140
    updating in objects, 418
    value assistance, 143
    value checks, 169
    value, appending to repeating attribute, 419

value, inserting into repeating attribute, 419
value, viewing for an object, 432
**automatic property extraction. See APE,
automatic property extraction**
AutoRender Pro, 50

B

BOF. See Business Objects
about, 30
release 5.3, enhancements, 453
Business Objects
about, 30
types, 31
**Business Objects Framework.
See Business Objects**

C

cabinet object type
about, 23
files, linking, 359
object, associating with cabinet, 419
CMS
advantages, 7, 8
content management, about, 6
content management, methodology, 6
Documentum, 10
qualities, 9
conditional value assistance, 145
$value keyword, 153
**content. See also folder mapping, See also Web
Publisher, See also WCM**
authoring, 46
content file, placing in multiple locations, 239
content file, specifying location in
web cabinet, 235
content rendition, viewing, 220
demoting through a lifecycle, 178
deploying, 55
dynamic content, creating, 228
expiring outdated content, 183, 184
folder mapping for structuring content, 231
instruction files, 251
lifecycle, 178
modification, handling, 251
outdated content, 183
page, refreshing on content modification, 228
placing in multiple locations, 239
promoting through a lifecycle, 178

published content, querying, 54
querying, 54
rendition, 50
rendition, viewing, 220, 221
storing, 47
updates, handling, 251
WCM, 43
WCM system, when to not use, 44
WCM system, when to use, 43
WCM, case study, 119
web content management, 43
Web Publisher, 46
workflow, submitting content to
workflow, 319-325
content management. See CMS
Content Rendition Services, 50
**Content Server. See also objects,
Documentum concept**
about, 13, 47
API commands, 22
Content Server 5.2.5 SP2, installing, 64
Content Server 5.2.5, installing, 60
Content Server 5.3, enhancements, 449-451
installing version 5.2.5, 60-64
installing version 5.2.5 SP2, 64-66
object ID, 19
prerequisites, 59, 60
versioning, 24
CRS, 50

D

**DAB, Documentum Application Builder. See
also DocApp**
about, 99
ACL, 162
DocApp custom store, creating, 122, 123
installing, 101-105
permission set, 162
prerequisites, 101
DD, Data Dictionary, 38
DFC
about, 29, 356
code structure, 364
directory, choosing, 61
Docbase methods, running, 362-365
environment, preparing, 357, 358
file, linking in Docbase cabinet, 359, 361, 362
naming conventions, 356
release 5.3, enhancements, 452, 453

458

users, creating in Docbase, 366-368
using, 358, 359
DMCL
about, 29
dmcl.ini file, Documentum client
configuration, 81
DocApp. See also DAB, Documentum
Application Builder, See also Docbase
about, 16
Accelera DocApp, 78
ACL template, 161
alias set, creating, 158
archive files, 16
archive, creating, 407
content, 76
creating, 122
DAI, Documentum Application Installer, 100
DocApp migration, methodology, 398
Docbase objects, migrating, 398
Documentum Application Builder, 100, 122
installing, 75-79
lifecycles, associating with an object
type, 134, 136
objects, creating in a custom DocApp, 123
objects, including in a DocApp, 399-401
permission set template, 161
SCSDocApp, 88
workflows, 292
Docbase. See also DocApp
about, 13-15
administering with Documentum
Administrator, 48
alias set, 35
cabinets, 23
content, placing in multiple Docbase
locations, 239
creating, 67, 71, 72, 74, 75
creation prerequisites, 68, 69
data dictionary, 38
Docbase ID, 14
DQL, 21
file, linking in cabinet, 359
folders, 23
IDQL utility, 21
methods, running via DFC, 362
object, deleting from Docbase, 423, 434
object, migrating, 398
object, retrieving from Docbase, 421-423
object, saving in Docbase, 430
objects, oraganizing, 23
owner, creating, 72

presentation file, importing, 217
registered tables, 38
rules file, choosing template, 198
SCS, using to publish from Docbase, 327
template, importing into Docbase, 192
user objects, 36
users, creating with DFC, 366-368
Docbasic, 131
DocBroker
about, 15
host, choosing, 62
port number, choosing, 62
Document Query Language. See DQL
document rendition, 37
Documentum
5.3, content server enhancements, 449
about, 10
access levels, 33
application components, 397
as a platform, 10
content management architecture, 45
Content Server, 13
deployment, 397
Documentum Application Builder, 100
entities, 397
features, 11-13
installing, 57
objects, 16
permission levels, 33
site, designing, 119
system administration, 48
templates, 187
versioning, 24
website, designing, 119
workflow, 26
Documentum Administrator, administration tool
about, 48, 49
API commands, executing, 425
content, dynamic, 228
Docbase operations, 48
DQL Editor, 49
DQL queries, executing, 417
installing, 108, 110-113
prerequisites, 108
presentation file, associating with
template file, 218
RDBMS table, registering, 150
release 5.3, enhancements, 454, 455
Site Publishing Configuration, setting up, 328
Tomcat, installing, 108, 110
users, creating, 318, 319

Documentum Application Builder. See DAB,
Documentum Application Builder
Documentum Client Library. See DMCL
Documentum Content Server. See
Content Server
Documentum deployment
    DocApp archive, creating, 407
    DocApp objects
    installation options, 399
    entities, 397
    methodologies, 398
    migration, 399
    migration entities, 397
    scripts, deploying, 410
    Web Publisher code, deploying, 410
Documentum Foundation Classes. See DFC
Documentum JDBC Services, 54, 55
Documentum jobs. See jobs,
Documentum objects
Documentum methods. See methods,
Docbase programs
Documentum Server manager
    operations, 80
DQI
    release 5.3, enhancements, 452
DQL. See also API commands
    about, 21, 22
    API commands, differences, 22
    attributes, updating, 418
    document object, creating, 417
    DQL Editor, Documentum Administrator, 49
    IDQL utility, 21, 416
    object attributes, updating, 418
    object, creating, 417
    object, deleting from Docbase, 423
    object, retrieving from Docbase, 421
    object,associating with cabinet, 419
    queries, executing from Documentum
    Administrator, 417
    registered tables, querying, 149
    tools, 416
    uses, 416
    XDQL, example, 223, 224
    XDQL, using in stylesheets, 222
    XDQL, using to retrieve Docbase content, 227
    XDQL, working, 223
dynamic folder mapping. See folder mapping

E

extensible document query language. See DQL

F

file widgets, in rules files, 210, See also rules files
    choosing for rules file, 200
folder mapping. See also content
    <attr_list>, 237
    <path_list>, 239
    about, 231
    content, placing in multiple locations, 239-241
    content, specifying location in web
    cabinet file, 235
    dynamic folder mapping, 246-248
    dynamic folder mapping with repeating
    attribute, 248-250
    folder map XML elements, 234
    FolderMap.xml, 232
    FolderMap.xml, functions performed, 234
    FolderMap.xml, structure, 233
    limitations, 234
    property matching using multiple properties in
    <attr_list>, 237-239
    property matching using wildcards, 235-237
    property matching, repeating attribute index, 244
    property matching, with simple repeating
    attribute, 241-244
    repeating attribute, using for property
    matching, 241
    role in website structure, 231
    wildcards, using for property matching, 235-237
    XML elements, 234
folder object type, 23

G

groups
    as objects, 36
    types, 37

I

i_chronicle_id attribute, 24
IAPI utility, 22

IDQL utility, 21, 416
**input mask, object-property validation
mechanism**, 141-143
instruction files
    about, 251
    content update, 251
    limitations, 252, 253
    role in content update, 251
    working, 253
    XML element, adding to XML file, 262-265
    XML element, deleting from XML file, 253-261
    XML element, updating element value in
    XML file, 265-267

J

jobs, Documentum objects, 39
    creating, 40
    example, 41
    job sequences, 41
    method objects, executing, 39

L

lifecycle creation
    ACL, attaching, 171
    ACL, creating, 161
    alias set, attaching, 165
    alias set, creating, 158
    entry criteria checks, 168
    lifecycle state editor, 173-175
    lifecycle, creating, 163
    lifecycle, 164
    Lifecyle State Definitions, 177
    Lifecyle State Diagram, preparing, 166
    object types, 165
    permission set, attaching, 171
    permission set, creating, 161
    state editor, 174, 175
    state, creating, 166
    state, describing, 167, 168
    state, introducing, 166
    versioning, WIP, 170
lifecycles
    about, 25
    content, demoting, 180, 182
    content, promoting, 179
    creating, 163
    draft state, 164
    installing, 164
    lifecycle object, installation options, 403

Lifecyle State Diagram, 164
object types, associating with a
lifecycle, 134-136
    stages, 161
    state editor, 173
    states, 166

M

methods, Docbase programs
    about, 39
    creating, 39
    method object, 39

O

objects, XE, 430
**objects, Documentum concept. See also
    attributes**
    about, 16
    attributes, 18, 20
    attributes, adding to object type, 138
    attributes, setting, 428, 432
    attributes, types, 19, 20
    attributes, updating, 418
    attributes, viewing for an object, 432
    cabinet, associating with Documentum
    object, 419, 429, 430
    constraint, adding, 133
    constraints, adding, 132
    creating, 417, 427
    creating in a custom DocApp, 123
    deleting from Docbase, 423, 434
    lifecycle, 25
    object ID, 19
    object ID, obtaining, 431
    object type, 17, 18
    object type heirarchy, 17
    object type names, 127
    object type, adding attribute, 138
    object type, associating with template, 193
    object type, creating, 126, 128
    object type, enahcements in release 5.3, 452
    object type, logical representation, 125
    object type, security, 130
    object types, providing to lifecycle, 165
    organizing, 23
    retrieving from Docbase, 421-423
    template, associating with object type, 193
    type identifiers, 19

P

permission set. See ACL
permission set alias, 403
presentation files, 188
    associating with template files, 217-220
    creating, 214
    example, 215
    importing, 216, 217
    structure, 215, 216
    template file, associating with
    presentation file, 217-220

R

r_version_label attribute, 24
registered tables, 38
    querying using DQL, 149
    value assistance, 149-151
rendition, 37, 50
repositories. See Docbase
rules file, 188
    about, 195
    checkbox widget, 210
    choice widget, 210
    creating, 195, 196
    graphic rule, adding, 201-204
    repeated blocks widget, 201
    Rules file editor, preferences, 196, 197
    template, choosing, 198
    textline widget, 200
    textselector widget, 210
    Web Publisher, configuring before using
    Rules file editor, 196, 197
    widget, types, 200
    widgets, 205, 210, 211
    XML elements, altering structure in a
    template, 199, 205-208
    Xselector widget, 211

S

scope, 158
SCS, Site Caching Services
    about, 52
    architecture, 53
    limitations, 328
    publishing operations, 328
    publishing operations, unlocking, 342, 343
    SCS publishing process, 53, 54
    SCS Source 5.2.5, installing, 84-88

SCS Source 5.2.5, prerequisites, 84
SCS Source 5.2.5, upgrading to SP2, 88
SCS Target 5.2.5 SP2, installing, 97
SCS Target 5.2.5 SP2, prerequisites, 89
SCS Target 5.2.5, installing, 89-97
Site Publishing Configuration, property
export, 332
Site Publishing Configuration, publishing, 340
Site Publishing Configuration, setting
up, 328-338
Site Publishing Configuration, settings, 348-350
Site Publishing Configuration, testing, 339, 340
Site Publishing Configuration, web viewing, 350
source status, monitoring, 343, 344
Web View functionality, 350
SCSDocApp, 88, See also DocApp
SDS, Site Deployment Services, 55
Server API. See API commands,
See API commands
server.ini file, Documentum server
configuration, 81
Site Caching Services, 52
Site Deployment Services, 55
Site Publishing Configuration. See SCS, Site
Caching Services
super type, object type, 128

T

templates, 121
    choosing for rules file, 198
    content update, 251
    creating, 190
    importing into Docbase, 192
    instruction files, role in template updates, 251
    modification, handling, 251
    object type, associating with a template, 193
    rules file, 195
    sample XML file, 191
    structure, 191
    updates, handling, 251
    Web Publisher, 190
type identifiers, for Documentum object types, 19
type names, 127

U

users
    as objects, 36
    attributes, 36
    privileges, 36

V

value assistance, 143-147
Verity search engine, Content Server, 14
versioning
   about, 24
   i_chronicle_id attribute, 24
   version labels, 24
   version labels, types, 24
   version tree, 24

W

WCM. See content
WDK
   about, 31, 369
   application heirarchy, 371, 372
   application-element interaction, 372, 373
   architecture, 32
   components, creating, 380-391
   components, heirarchy, 389
   configuration example, 373-379
   custom components, 380-391
   customization example, 379, 380,
   382-393, 395
   directory structure, 370, 371
   features, 31
   JSP configuration, 376, 385
   precondition, 384
   release 5.3, enhancements, 454
   XML configuration, altering content, 376, 377
Web Content Management. See content
Web Development Kit. See WDK
Web Publisher. See also web viewing, See also
   content
   about, 46
   ANT, 411
   code, deploying, 410-413
   configuring for Rules file editor, 196
   content, submitting to workflow, 319-325
   features, 46, 47
   folder mapping, 235
   GUI options, 46
   installing, 113-117
   instruction files, 251
   prerequisites, 113
   presentation file, creating, 214
   release 5.3, enhancements, 455
   roles, 47
   rules file, creating, 195

SCS, integrating with, 52
templates, 122, 187-189, 208
templates, creating, 190
Tomcat, 113
users, 47
virtual directory, specifying, 115
Web Publisher code, preparing via
ANT, 411-413
Web View, 345
widgets, 210
workflows, 291, 292
XML Application, creating, 271
Web Publisher Folder Map. See
folder mapping
Web Publisher Instruction Files. See
instruction files
Web Publisher Server Files, 75, 76
Web Publisher web application, 32
web viewing
   about, 345
   browser settings, 350
   prerequisites, 346
   Web View browser, 350, 351
   Web View functionality, testing, 352-354
   working, 345, 346
WebPublisher DocApp. See DocApp
website. See also content
   alias sets, 157
   application scopes, 129
   attributes, adding, 138
   attributes, creating for object types, 137, 138
   example, 119
   file widgets, 210
   folder mapping for structuring content, 231
   instruction files, 251
   layout, 120
   lifecycle, designing, 157
   object types, creating, 126
   permission sets, 161
   planning, 121, 122
   presentation files, 213
   rules file, 195
   templates, 187
   templates, creating, 190
   templatizing, 121
   widgets, 210
Webtop Documentum reference, 32
widgets, in rules files, See also rules files
   about, 210
   choosing for rules file, 201
   types, 200

workflow
 about, 26, 27, 291
 content, submitting, 319
 content, submitting to workflow, 319-325
 designing, 292, 293
 flow inspector, 314
 package, adding to connection flows, 314, 315
 setting up, 293-300
 template, creating, 300-313
 testing, 317

types, 295
users, creating, 318, 319

X

XDQL. See DQL
XSL stylesheet
 structure, 226, 227
 XML elements, template file, 21

Thank you for buying Web Content Management with Documentum

About Packt Publishing

Packt, pronounced 'packed', published its first book "*Mastering phpMyAdmin for Effective MySQL Management*" in April 2004 and subsequently continued to specialize in publishing highly focused books on specific technologies and solutions.

Our books and publications share the experiences of your fellow IT professionals in adapting and customizing today's systems, applications, and frameworks. Our solution-based books give you the knowledge and power to customize the software and technologies you're using to get the job done. Packt books are more specific and less general than the IT books you have seen in the past. Our unique business model allows us to bring you more focused information, giving you more of what you need to know, and less of what you don't.

Packt is a modern, yet unique publishing company, which focuses on producing quality, cutting-edge books for communities of developers, administrators, and newbies alike. For more information, please visit our website: www.packtpub.com.

Writing for Packt

We welcome all inquiries from people who are interested in authoring. Book proposals should be sent to authors@packtpub.com. If your book idea is still at an early stage and you would like to discuss it first before writing a formal book proposal, contact us; one of our commissioning editors will get in touch with you.

We're not just looking for published authors; if you have strong technical skills but no writing experience, our experienced editors can help you develop a writing career, or simply get some additional reward for your expertise.

Building Websites with
Microsoft Content Management Server

A fast-paced and practical tutorial guide for C# developers
starting out with MCMS 2002

Lim Mei Ying   Joel Ward   Stefan Goßner   PACKT

Building Websites with Microsoft Content Management Server

ISBN: 1904811167   Paperback, 638 pages

A fast-paced and practical tutorial guide for C#
developers starting out with MCMS 2002

1. Learn directly from recognized
   community experts

2. Rapid developer-level tutorials built logically
   throughout the book

3. Develops a feature-rich custom site
   incrementally

4. Tips and Tricks from developer newsgroups
   and online communities

Business Process Execution Language
for Web Services
Second Edition

An architect and developer's guide to orchestrating web
services using BPEL4WS

PACKT

Business Process Execution Language for Web Services 2nd Edition

ISBN: 1904811817   Paperback, 350 pages

An Architect's and Developer's Guide to BPEL and
BPEL4WS

1. Architecture, syntax, development, and
   composition of Business Processes and
   Services using BPEL

2. Advanced BPEL features such as
   compensation, concurrency, links, scopes,
   events, dynamic partner links, and correlations

3. Oracle BPEL Process Manager and BPEL
   Designer Microsoft BizTalk Server as a
   BPEL server

Please check **www.PacktPub.com** for information on our titles

Printed in the United Kingdom
by Lightning Source UK Ltd.
111747UKS00002B/91-108